ISSUES IN
ADOLESCENT PSYCHOLOGY

Edited by

Dorothy Rogers

State University College at Oswego

ISSUES IN
ADOLESCENT PSYCHOLOGY

APPLETON-CENTURY-CROFTS

EDUCATIONAL DIVISION

NEW YORK **MEREDITH CORPORATION**

To My Students

Preface

This volume deals with twenty-one issues, or topics involving issues, arranged under six general headings. The introduction to each issue analyzes its significance and present status, and introduces the selections that follow. Students may explore topics in greater depth by using the annotated bibliographies and the footnote references which accompany selections.

Various criteria governed the choice of topics; for example, their relevance to the student's own special concerns. Students are particularly interested in such subjects as dating, sex role, and youth culture, but they should also become acquainted with those issues which have attracted special attention from researchers, for example, the relative importance of early or late maturing. Certain issues (such as the meaning of adolescence and the adolescent image) have been considered noteworthy for a long time; other topics (such as sex role and youth culture) have won attention more recently. Some of the topics (significance of puberty, storm-and-stress hypothesis) represent specific issues; others (biological-sex role, social-sex role) are not issues as such but embrace areas which involve unresolved questions. Cultural variations in adolescent development are included to show that issues affecting teen-agers vary within the same culture and around the world. Generally, students' concepts of adolescence have been limited to their own experience and subculture, and their perspective is consequently provincial. Moreover, most textbooks on adolescence relate largely to the middle-class American adolescent, because available data on the topic predominantly concern middle-class American subjects.

Other criteria guided the specific choice of readings; for example, when distinctly different points of view exist, selections were chosen to represent these varied positions. In complex topics, where problems are relatively undifferentiated and involved, selections have been used which help sort out the jigsaw of points. Selections may also have been chosen because they were especially well-written, lucid, or provocative. In general, the authors are authorities in the areas concerned, and collectively provide a wide range of writing styles, philosophies, and points of view. For the most part, current or recent articles have been used because the rapid proliferation of research constantly yields new insights and evidence. Certain older selections have been included, however, because of special significance or merit. In most cases, articles have been written by psychologists, but in a few cases by authorities in related disciplines. Students should come to appreciate that walls do not exist between disciplines and that different areas of knowledge may effectively contribute to each other.

Many articles, often equally excellent, have been excluded because of space limitations. For the same reason, a few readings presented here have been abridged, although care has been taken to preserve the author's main thesis and ideas. Where selections from books are chosen, the student will be rewarded if he browses through the entire volume.

Books of readings in general, and readings about issues in particular, have certain merits. They afford a range of subject matter, written by experts in the field. While textbooks may provide excellent summaries of research, space limitations preclude source materials except for brief quotations. Granted, it is better for students to seek out source materials for themselves, and books of reading cannot compensate for this sort of experience. However, libraries often lack particular periodicals and books in which important selections appear. Even large libraries lack the multiple copies of source materials which permit an entire class to study the same articles within a limited period of time, thus permitting group discussion of the same material.

A book of readings about issues possesses additional merits of its own. When the student reads articles by several authorities about the same topic, he comes to realize that several valid, though differing, points of view may relate to the topic. In a scientific age, especially, students should overcome the dogmatic belief that one authority represents all to be said on a matter. Moreover, in a fast-moving age, full of ever-emerging problems, students need experience in appraising problems not yet resolved. As a result, the student learns to look at topics critically, to perceive problems as dynamic, not static, and to take a permanently tentative position. One hopes he will learn to read and think critically, and be able to revise his views when new evidence dictates. Meantime, he learns to seek source materials for information, and to use such materials effectively.

The issues approach permits certain interesting variations in course organization and instruction. Several students may investigate each topic, and then, as a panel, discuss it before the class; or students may select specific issues as subjects for term papers. Often they may supplement library research with original studies of their own. For instance, on the subject of adolescent image, a student may interview different age groups concerning their views of the adolescent. Sometimes two or more instructors within the department may discuss a topic informally before combined sections of their students. Tapes of such discussions may be used in future classes when it is not feasible for the instructors to get together in person. In any case, the investigation of issues excites student interest more readily than does a conventional survey of subject matter.

I wish to express my appreciation for the invaluable assistance of the staff of the Penfield Library at Oswego. I am grateful to Ann Hoefer and Cherie Blanchard for their competent clerical assistance, and to Marjorie Kalins and Madeline Haynes for their assistance in the editing and production of this book. Finally, I am indebted to Betty Moody for general advice and help in completing this project.

D. R.

Contributors

Joseph Adelson
University of Michigan

Gordon Allport
Late of Harvard University

David Ausubel
The Ontario Institute for Studies
in Education

Albert Bandura
Stanford University

Robert Bealer
The Pennsylvania State University

Joseph Brenner
Massachusetts Institute of Technology

Daniel G. Brown
USPHS, Mental Health
Atlanta, Georgia

Judith K. Brown
Radcliffe College

Roger V. Burton
National Institute of Mental Health
Bethesda, Maryland

James Coleman
Johns Hopkins University

Robert Coles
Harvard University

Elizabeth Douvan
University of Michigan

Leon Eisenberg
Massachusetts General Hospital

S. N. Eisenstadt
Hebrew University
Jerusalem, Israel

David Epperson
University of Illinois

Erik H. Erikson
Harvard University

Margaret Siler Faust
Scripps College

Jacob R. Fishman
Howard University

Edgar Z. Friedenberg
State University of New York
at Buffalo

M. Frisk
Folkholson Teen-Age Clinic
Helsinki, Finland

J. C. Gustin
Late editor of *Psychoanalysis*

Robert J. Havighurst
University of Chicago

Joseph S. Himes
North Carolina College at Durham

H. Hortling
Folkholson Teen-Age Clinic
Helsinki, Finland

Philip E. Jacob
University of Pennsylvania

Jerome Kagan
Harvard University

ix

Herbert Klausmeier
University of Wisconsin

Irving Krauss
University of Hawaii

Eleanor B. Luckey
University of Connecticut, Storrs

David B. Lynn
University of California, Davis

Peter Maida
The Pennsylvania State University

Esther Matthews
University of Oregon

David Matza
University of California, Berkeley

Howard A. Moss
National Institute of Mental Health
Bethesda, Maryland

Robert P. O'Hara
Harvard University

Herbert A. Otto
University of Utah

Sarah T. Otto
Community Action Program
Salt Lake City, Utah

Gerald J. Pine
State College, Salem

Albert J. Rabin
Michigan State University

Bernard Rosen
Cornell University

Susanne M. Shafer
Arizona State University

George Sherman
Newspaper correspondent and
journalist

Ernest A. Smith
Hunter College

Eldon E. Snyder
Bowling Green State University

Fredric Solomon
Howard University

J. M. Tanner
University of London
London, England

T. Tenhunen
Folkholson Teen-Age Clinic
Helsinki, Finland

David V. Tiedeman
Harvard University

E. Paul Torrance
University of Georgia

Read D. Tuddenham
University of California, Berkeley

J. W. M. Whiting
Harvard University

O. Widholm
Folkholson Teen-Age Clinic
Helsinki, Finland

Fern K. Willets
The Pennsylvania State University

Contents

Two   STAGE THEORY VERSUS ADOLESCENCE

Three   ISSUES IN SELF-ACTUALIZATION

Contents

One

General Issues Concerning Adolescence

I. The Nature and Meaning of Adolescence

Books and articles about adolescence, both popular and professional, reveal broad discrepancies as to what adolescence means. The topic is variously treated as a specific span of years, a stage in development, a subculture, a state of mind, or some combination of these. Thus, any teenager may be called "an adolescent." We may say an adult's behavior seems "adolescent," meaning he is behaving in a silly, irresponsible way. Or we may say a child is "preadolescent," but exactly when a child arrives at adolescence proper is uncertain. The result has been confusion as to what adolescence signifies. We may ask: is it possible, or even desirable, to attempt a more precise definition? Do we need different ways of viewing adolescence; and should we simply make clear within any context the frame of reference employed?

Let us take a closer look at various definitions of adolescence. The term itself is derived from the Latin word, *adolescere,* which means to grow to maturity. In this sense, adolescence is a process rather than a period, a process of evolving from child to adult. More precisely, adolescence is often defined as a stage in physical development. This approach requires an acquaintance with several terms.[1]

Pubescence, or preadolescence, generally refers to the period of about two years preceding puberty and to the physical changes that take place during that time. It is marked by a spurt in physical growth, by changes in body proportions, and by the maturation of primary and secondary sex characteristics. The climax of pubescence is called puberty which is distinguished by certain signals of sexual maturity: in girls by the menarche, or first menstruation; and in boys by several signs, probably the most valid being the presence of live spermatozoa, or male reproductive cells, in the urine. Early adolescence, in the biological sense, dates from the onset of the pubescent growth spurt until about a year after puberty when the new biological functions have been pretty well established. Late adolescence is even less definite, and lasts until physical growth is relatively complete and early adulthood begins.

In the selection that follows, Tanner interprets adolescence in the biological sense. He describes the changes characteristic of the adolescent

---

[1] Dorothy Rogers, *The Psychology of Adolescence* (New York, Appleton-Century-Crofts, 1962), p. 6.

period, and the dynamics of growth. He indicates how pervasive pubertal changes are, and how such changes vary according to individual, age-stage, and sex.

Adolescence may also be defined chronologically—for instance, Hurlock designates preadolescence as the age period, 10 through 12; early adolescence, 13 through 16; and late adolescence, 17 through 21.[2] Such designations are distorting, in that neither psychological nor biological maturity proceeds at the same rate in all individuals. Nor do all aspects of biological or psychological maturity develop at the same rate in the same individual. A boy who, because of glandular malfunction, has experienced premature puberty may remain a child in every other sense. However, specific age designations may be defended on certain grounds; for instance, legal ones. What sort of criterion, other than the chronological one, could logically be used to determine when an individual may be licensed to drive, or to obtain a marriage license?

A third approach to adolescence is sociological. While physical adolescence is inevitable among animals and humans, social adolescence is largely a creation of the Western world. Thus viewed, the adolescent has outgrown the social status of the child but ·has not yet been accorded the mature privileges of the adult. In the sociological sense, the status of adolescents varies with certain conditions. The lower-class boy who leaves school at 18 to help support the family may be judged a man. However, the girl of 20 who has no job and lives at home is looked upon and treated as an adolescent.

Related to the sociological frame of reference is the cross-cultural one. In this approach, adolescence would be viewed in terms of the way of life accorded youth down through the years and around the world. Certain constants may be identified which have characterized adolescent development regardless of culture. Such information makes it easier to detect variations in the over-all pattern within specific cultures.

The study of adolescence may also be approached through a theoretical frame of reference. The phenomenologist emphasizes the adolescent's perception of himself and his environment. The field theorist is concerned with how elements within the adolescent's experience fit together into meaningful patterns. The psychoanalytic approach, which is built on Freudian theory, provides a prototype for children's development. Whether this prototype may be considered as valid or not has been widely disputed, but no psychologist questions the impact of psychoanalytic theory on the psychology of adolescence. The psychoanalyst portrays early life stages as highly significant, and each stage as important for all that follows. The prototype of the child at each stage involves certain libidinal and aggressive energies as well as frustrations, defenses, and anxieties.

[2] Elizabeth Hurlock, *Child Development,* 3rd ed. (New York, McGraw-Hill, 1956), pp. 27–28.

Still another approach to adolescence is developmental—that is, it is treated in relation to other stages of development, and in terms of the psychological dynamics involved. Eisenberg considers in particular the special role that adolescence plays in total development, in helping the individual to establish an identity.

It is unlikely that psychologists will ultimately agree on the best way to define adolescence. Perhaps, as scientific data and dialogue proliferate, concepts of adolescence, within the various frames of reference, will become better defined. Meantime, we shall have to muddle along, adapting to hazy and constantly shifting concepts of the term.

1

J. M. Tanner

THE COURSE OF CHILDREN'S GROWTH

Tanner treats adolescence from the physical frame of reference. He analyzes the nature of the adolescent growth spurt, the changes in body shape, size and athletic ability, the development of the reproductive system, and the order in which parts of the body develop.

THE GROWTH CURVE OF HEIGHT

In Fig. 1–1 is shown the growth curve in height of a single boy, measured every six months from birth to 18 years. Above is plotted the height attained at successive ages; below, the increments in height from one age to the next. If we think of growth as a form of motion, and the passage of a child along his growth curve as similar to the passage of a train between stations, then the upper curve is one of distance achieved, and the lower curve one of velocity. The velocity, or rate of growth, naturally reflects the child's situation at any given time better than does the distance achieved, which depends largely on how much the child has grown in all the preceding years. Accordingly it is usually more important to concentrate on the velocity rather than on the distance curve. In some circumstances the acceleration may reflect physiological events even better than the velocity; thus at adolescence it seems likely that the great increase in secretions from the endocrine glands is manifested most clearly in an acceleration of growth. In general, however, nothing more complex than velocity curves will be considered here.

The record of Fig. 1–2 is the oldest published study of the growth of a child; it was made during the years 1759 to 1777 by Count Philibert de Montbeillard upon his son, and published by Buffon in a supplement to the *Histoire Naturelle*. It shows as well as any more modern data that in general the velocity of growth in height decreases from birth (and actually from as early as the fourth intrauterine month) onwards, but that this decrease is interrupted shortly before the end of the growth period. At this time, from 13 to 15 in this particular boy, there is a marked acceleration of growth, called the *adolescent growth spurt*. From birth up to 4 or 5 the

From J. M. Tanner, *Education and Physical Growth* (London, University of London Press, Limited, 1961), pp. 14–19, 522–34. Reprinted by permission.

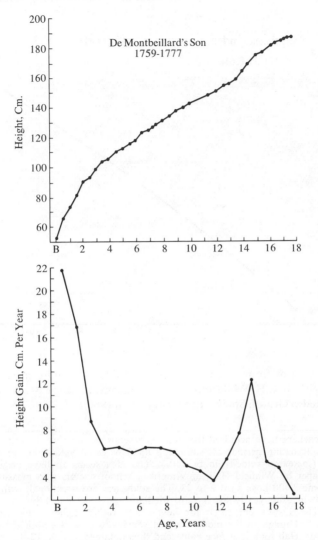

Fig. 1–1. Growth in height of de Montbeillard's son from birth to 18 years, 1759–77. Above, distance curve, height attained at each age; below, velocity curve, increments in height from year to year. Data from Scammon, 1927, *Amer. J. phys. Anthrop.* (From Tanner, *Growth at Adolescence*, Blackwell Sci. Publ.: Oxford.)

rate of growth declines rapidly, but the decline, or deceleration, gets gradually less, so that in some children the velocity is practically constant from 5 or 6 up to the beginning of the adolescent spurt.[1]

[1] A slight increase in velocity of height growth from about 6 to 8 years, providing a second wave on the general velocity curve, has been sometimes thought to occur and has been called the juvenile or mid-growth spurt. I can find no satisfactory evidence of its presence in the individual records covering the period 3 to 13 that are known to me.

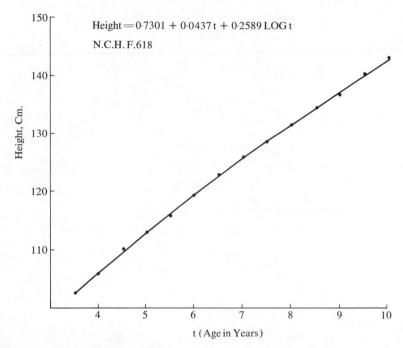

Fig. 1–2. Curve of form $y = a + bt + c \log t$ fitted to stature measurements taken on a girl by R. H. Whitehouse every six months from age 3½ to 10. Data from Harpenden Growth Study. (From Israelsohn, 1960.)

Some teachers have acquired the quite erroneous notion that growth occurs in a series of alternating periods of 'stretching up' (increased velocity in height) and 'filling out' (increased velocity in breadth). The idea seems to have originated in 1896 in a paper by Winfield Hall, an American school doctor, who measured, very carefully, some 2,400 boys aged 9 to 23. The study was cross-sectional, with between 100 and 300 in each yearly age group. Medians were calculated but no standard deviations. The 13-year-old value for height was rather higher than might have been expected. Though to the modern eye its deviation is well within the limits of sampling error, Hall took it at face value and thus obtained a large 12–13 increment, small 13–14 increment and large 14–15 increment, this last being the adolescent spurt proper. In circumferences of the joints this did not occur, the curves being fairly regular. Hence, when the values were expressed as percentages of the 9-year-old value, the distance curves for height and for circumferences crossed at 12–13, 13–14 and 14–15. Hall thereupon formulated (in italics) a Law of Growth: 'When the vertical dimension of the human body is undergoing an acceleration in its rate of growth the horizontal dimensions undergo a retardation and vice versa.' The idea was taken up and generalized to the whole period of growth by the German anthropologist C. H. Stratz, who in many articles wrote of a first *Streckung* at 5 to 7 and a second at 8 to 10. The data on which these opinions were based were quite insufficient to support them, but somehow they got into textbooks, where in some instances they have remained safely cocooned till the present day, despite the severest attempts to dislodge them by people such as Schiotz (1923) whose measurements of children were adequate in number, taken longitudinally (see below), and interpreted with statistical sense.

As the points of Fig. 1–3 show, growth is an exceedingly regular process. Contrary to opinions still sometimes met, it does *not* proceed in fits and starts. The more carefully the measurements are taken, with, for

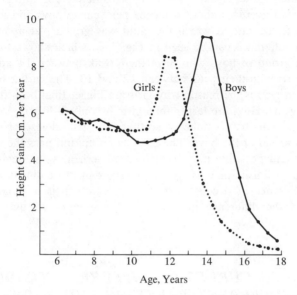

Fig. 1–3. Adolescent spurt in height growth for girls and boys. The curves are from subjects who have their peak velocities during the modal years 12–13 for girls, and 14–15 for boys. Actual mean increments, each plotted at center of its half-year period. Data from Shuttleworth, 1939, Tables 23 and 32. (From Tanner, *Growth at Adolescence,* Blackwell Sci. Publ.: Oxford.)

example, precautions to minimize the decrease in height that occurs during the working day for postural reasons, the more regular does the succession of points on the graph become. In a series of children each measured for seven years or more by the same measurer, my colleagues and I have found that at least over the age range 3 to 10 the deviations of the actual points from a very simple mathematical curve

$$\text{Height} = a + bt + c \log t, \qquad (\text{where } t \text{ is age})$$

were seldom more than 6 mm., or ¼ in., and were on average equally above and below the curve at all ages (see Fig. 1–2). There is no evidence for 'stages' in height growth except for the spurt associated with adolescence. Perhaps the increments of growth at the cellular level are discontinuous, and proceed by starts and stops; but at the level of bodily measurements, even of single bones measured by X-rays, one can only discern complete continuity, with a velocity that gradually varies from one age to another.

The adolescent spurt is a constant phenomenon, and occurs in all children, though it varies in intensity and duration from one child to another. In boys it takes place, on the average, from 12½ to 15, and in girls about two years earlier, from 10½ to approximately 13. The peak height velocity reached averages about 4 inches per year in boys and a little less in girls; this is the rate at which the child was growing at about 2 years old. The sex difference can be seen in Fig. 1–3, which shows the velocity curves for a group of boys who have their peak between 14 and 15 and a group of girls with their peak between 12 and 13. The earlier occurrence of the spurt in girls is the reason why girls are bigger than boys from about 10½ to 13 years. Boys are larger than girls by only 1–3 per cent. in most body measurements before puberty, so that the girls' adolescent spurt soon carries them ahead of the boys. The boys catch up and pass the girls when their greater and probably more sustained adolescent spurt begins to take effect, and they finish some 10 per cent larger in most dimensions. Thus the adult difference in size between men and women is to a large extent the result of the difference in timing and magnitude of the adolescent spurt. . . .

GROWTH CURVES OF DIFFERENT TISSUES AND DIFFERENT PARTS OF THE BODY

Most measurements of the body show a generally similar growth curve to the curve of height given in Fig. 1–1. The great majority of skeletal and muscular dimensions, whether of length or breadth, grow in this manner. But some exceptions exist, most notably the brain and skull, the reproductive organs, the lymphoid tissue of the tonsils, adenoids and intestines, and the subcutaneous fat. Fig. 1–4 shows these differences in diagram form, using size attained, or distance curves. Height follows the 'general' curve. The reproductive organs, internal and external, follow a curve which is not, perhaps, very different in principle, but strikingly so in effect. Their prepubescent growth is very slow, and their growth at adolescence very rapid; they are less sensitive than the skeleton to one set of hormones and more sensitive to another.

The brain and skull, together with the eyes and ears, develop earlier than any other part of the body and have thus a characteristic postnatal curve. Brain growth and development is discussed in detail in [. . .]; suffice it here to say that by 1 year old the brain has attained about 60 per cent of its adult weight, and by 5 years about 90 per cent. Probably it has no adolescent spurt, although a slight spurt does occur in the measurements of head length and breadth due to thickening of the skull bones. The face, unlike the portion of the skull encasing the brain, follows a path

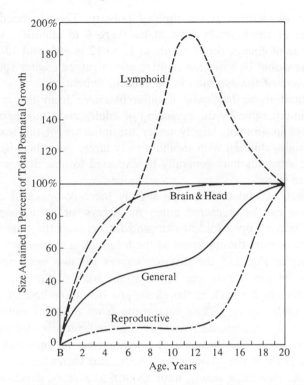

Fig. 1–4. Growth curves of different parts and tissues of the body, showing the four chief types. All the curves are of size attained (in per cent of the total gain from birth to maturity) and plotted so that size at age 20 is 100 on the vertical scale. Redrawn from Scammon, 1930, *The Measurement of Man*, Univ. Minn. Press. (From Tanner, *Growth at Adolescence*, Blackwell Sci. Publ.: Oxford.)

Lymphoid type: thymus, lymph nodes, intestinal lymph masses.

Brain and head type: brain and its parts, dura, spinal cord, optic apparatus, head dimensions.

General type: body as a whole, external dimensions (except head), respiratory and digestive organs, kidneys, aortic and pulmonary trunks, musculature, blood volume.

Reproductive type: testis, ovary, epididymis, prostate, seminal vesicles, Fallopian tubes.

closer to the general skeletal curve, with a considerable adolescent spurt in most measurements. The jawbone, for example, has only completed 75 per cent of its growth in length before adolescence in boys.

The eye seems probably to have a slight adolescent acceleration in growth, though no data are accurate enough to make the matter certain. Very likely it is this that is responsible for the increase in frequency of short-sightedness in children at the time of puberty. Though the degree of myopia increases continuously from at least age 6 to maturity, a particularly rapid rate of change occurs at about 11 to 12 in girls and 13 to 14 in boys, and this would be expected if there was a rather greater spurt in the axial dimension of the eye than in its vertical dimension.

The lymphoid tissue has quite a different curve from the rest: it reaches its maximum value by the beginning of adolescence and thereafter actually decreases in amount, largely under the influence of the sex hormones. Accordingly, children with troublesomely large, but otherwise normal, tonsils and adenoids may generally be expected to lose their snuffles when adolescence starts.

The subcutaneous fat undergoes a slightly more complicated evolution. Its thickness can be measured either by X-rays, or more simply at certain sites by picking up a fold of skin and fat between the thumb and forefinger and measuring the thickness of the fold with a special, constant-pressure, caliper. In Fig. 1–5 the distance curves for two measurements of subcutaneous fat are shown, one taken at the back of the upper arm (triceps), the other at the back of the chest, just below the bottom of the shoulder blade (subscapular). The data come from different sources at each of the three age ranges, and this has been indicated by leaving the three sections separate. The thickness of subcutaneous fat increases from birth to reach a peak at nine months or a year, and thereafter decreases, rapidly at first and then more slowly, until about 6 to 8 years, depending on the individual child. At that time the width of fat begins to increase again. In the trunk fat (subscapular measurement) this increase continues up to maturity in both boys and girls. The limb fat (triceps measurement) follows this same pattern in girls, but in boys it thins out at the time of the adolescent spurt in height.

The curves for muscle and bone widths follow the general height curve. Because weight represents a mixture of these various components of the body its curve of growth is somewhat different from those discussed above, and often less informative. Though to some extent useful in following the health of a child, weight has severe limitations; an increase may be due to bone or muscle or merely to fat. A boy may cease growth in height and muscle and put on fat instead (as happens in certain clinical circumstances when large doses of cortisone are given) and his weight curve may continue to look perfectly normal. Even failure to gain weight or actual loss of weight in an older child may signify little except a better attention to diet and exercise, whereas failure to gain height or muscle would call for immediate investigation. For these reasons regular measurements of height and weight in the schools should be supplemented by measurements of subcutaneous fat by skinfolds, and muscular dimensions by circumference of upper arm and calf corrected for the covering subcutaneous fat.

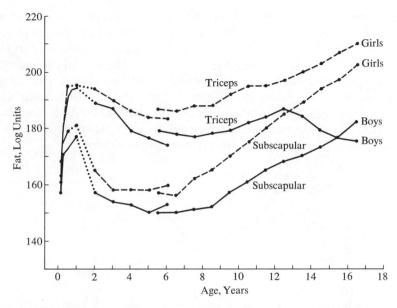

Fig. 1–5. Amount of subcutaneous fat on the back of the arm (triceps) and on the chest (subscapular) from birth to age 16. Distance curves; measurements by skin-fold calipers, reported as logs of readings less 1.8 mm. (From Tanner, *Growth at Adolescence,* Blackwell Sci. Publ.: Oxford.)

GROWTH AND DEVELOPMENT AT ADOLESCENCE

Practically all skeletal and muscular dimensions take part in the adolescent spurt. There is a fairly regular order in which the dimensions accelerate; leg length as a rule reaches its peak first, followed a few months later by the body breadths and a year later by trunk length. Most of the spurt in height is due to trunk growth rather than growth of the legs. The muscles appear to have their spurt a little after the last skeletal peak.

At adolescence a marked increase in athletic ability occurs, particularly in boys. The heart, just like any other muscle, grows more rapidly, as can be seen from Fig. 1–6. The strength of the muscles also increases sharply, especially in boys. The results of two strength tests given to a group of girls and boys every six months throughout adolescence are plotted (as distance curves) in Fig. 1–7. Arm pull refers to the movement of pulling apart clasped hands held up in front of the chest, the hands each grasping a dynamometer handle; arm thrust refers to the reverse movement, of pushing the hands together. Each individual test represents the best of three trials made in competition against a classmate of similar ability, and against the individual's own figure of six months before. Only with such precautions can reliable maximal values be obtained. There is a considerable adolescent spurt visible in all four of the boys' curves from about age 13 to 16 (the curves turn more sharply upwards), and a less definite spurt from about 12 to 13½ in the girls' hand-grip curves. There is no sex difference before puberty in strength of arm thrust and little in arm pull (the same is true of calf and thigh muscle strengths). The boys' later superiority arises partly from their greater adolescent growth in muscular bulk, and partly because the male sex hormone secreted then for the first time acts on muscle to produce more strength per cross-sectional area.

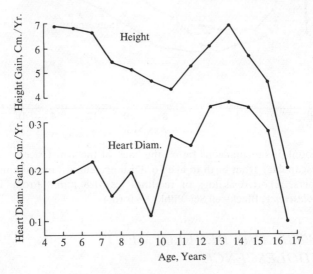

Fig. 1–6. Velocity curves of transverse diameter of the heart, measured by X-ray, for 71 boys. Mixed longitudinal data, reported cross-sectionally. Height curves of same boys given above for comparison. Data from Maresh, 1948. (From Tanner, *Growth at Adolescence*, Blackwell Sci. Publ.: Oxford.)

   In hand-grip a more considerable sex difference appears to be present as early as age 11. This is a reflection of the greater development, even before puberty, of the male forearm. It is often forgotten that a number of sex differences, besides those of the reproductive organs, antedate puberty, and are not the result of the endocrine gland secretions of adolescence. At birth boys have longer and thicker forearms, relative to upper arms, legs and other parts of the body, and the sex difference increases steadily throughout the whole growing period. (This is not peculiar to man, but occurs in several species of apes and monkeys as well.) Another difference which is already present at birth is the relatively greater length of the second finger in comparison to the fourth in girls. Whether any similar sex differences occur in the brain is not known, but the possibility of them clearly exists. . . .

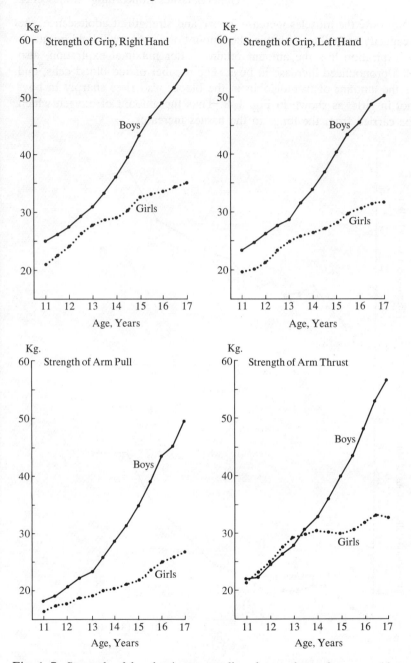

Fig. 1–7. Strength of hand grip, arm pull and arm thrust from age 11 to 17. Mixed longitudinal data, 65–93 boys and 66–93 girls in each age group. Data from Jones, 1949, Tables 15–22. (From Tanner, *Growth at Adolescence*, Blackwell Sci. Publ.: Oxford.)

Not only the muscles increase in size and strength at adolescence; the vital capacity of the lungs, that is, the amount of air they will hold on maximum inspiration less the amount retained after maximal expiration, also shows a pronounced increase in boys. The number of red blood cells, and hence the amount of hæmoglobin in the blood, also rises sharply in boys but not in girls, as shown in Fig. 1–8. Thus the amount of oxygen which can be carried from the lungs to the tissues increases.

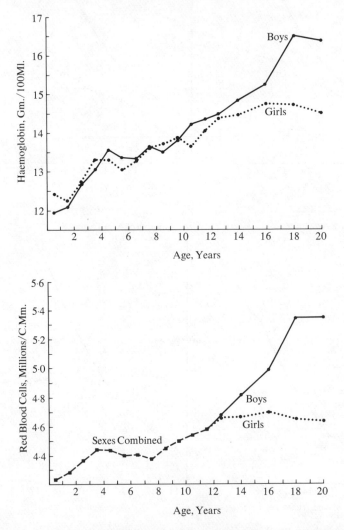

Fig. 1–8. Change in blood haemoglobin and number of circulating red blood cells during childhood, showing the development of the sex difference at adolescence. Distance curves. Mixed longitudinal data reported cross-sectionally. Redrawn from Mugrage and Andresen, 1936, 1938, *Amer. J. Dis. Child.* (From Tanner, *Growth at Adolescence*, Blackwell Sci. Publ.: Oxford.)

It is as a direct result of these anatomical and physiological changes that athletic ability increases so much in boys at adolescence. The popular notion of a boy 'outgrowing his strength' at this time has little scientific support. It is true that the peak velocity of strength increase occurs a year or so after the peak velocity of most of the skeletal measurements, so that a short period exists when the adolescent, having completed his skeletal, and probably also muscular, growth, still does not have the strength of a young adult of the same body size and shape. But this is a temporary phase; considered absolutely, power, athletic skill and physical endurance all increase progressively and rapidly throughout adolescence. It is certainly not true that the changes accompanying adolescence even temporarily enfeeble, through any mechanism except a psychological one.

Though the main change at puberty is in body size, there is also a considerable change in body shape. The shape change differs in the two sexes, so that boys acquire the wide shoulders and muscular neck of the man, and girls the relatively wide hips of the woman. Before puberty it is usually impossible to distinguish whether a particular child is a boy or girl from its body proportions or amounts of bone, muscle and fat alone (despite the few small but perhaps important differences mentioned above). After puberty it is easy to do so in the great majority of cases.

ENDOCRINOLOGY OF GROWTH

Thus at adolescence there is a great and sudden increase in body size and strength and a change in many physiological functions beside the reproductive ones. These changes all take place in a co-ordinated manner and a child who is early in respect of one feature is early in respect of all. The changes are mostly more marked in boys than girls, and take place approximately two years later in boys than in girls.

The immediate cause of all these changes is the secretion into the blood stream (and hence the contact with all tissues) of hormones from the ovaries, testes and adrenal glands. However, ovaries, testes and the particular functional part of the adrenal which secretes androgenic (i.e. male-determining) hormones have first to be stimulated to grow and function by other hormones. These come from the pituitary gland, which lies just underneath the base of the brain in approximately the geometrical centre of the head. The pituitary itself, however, awaits the receipt of a chemical stimulus before manufacturing and releasing these trophic hormones, and this stimulus comes from a particular small area in the basal part of the brain known as the hypothalamus. What causes the hypothalamus to initiate all these events we do not know; it seems to be normally under some form of restraint emanating from its anterior portion. There is a hereditary disorder, manifested only in boys, in which this restraint is partially lacking and a precocious puberty occurs any time from 4 years onwards. When this happens all the events of puberty take place normally, including the production of sperm. In girls a similar, though not hereditary, condition occurs occasionally and the youngest known mother, who had a child by Cæsarian section at age 5, was an example of this. In these cases no other untoward effects take place; the children otherwise are quite healthy. In certain progressive diseases of the brain, however, the restraint on the hypothalamus may be destroyed and precocious puberty may also occur then.

Evidently certain maturational changes have to take place in the restraining anterior hypothalamus before it releases its grip and lets the mechanism begin; but we are totally ignorant of their nature. Starvation retards puberty, which simply waits for the body to reach its usual prepubertal size, irrespective of the passage of time. Maturation of the hypothalamus occurs at a certain sequence in a chain of events and not, fundamentally, at a certain chronological age. We shall return to this very important point again.

The factors controlling growth before adolescence are imperfectly understood, but it is clear that another pituitary hormone, called growth hormone, controls to a great extent the speed of growth. Its absence causes the type of dwarf who has approximately normal body proportions. Thus the pre-adolescent phase of growth has been called the growth-hormone phase, and the adolescent the steroid-hormone phase (since the hormones concerned then belong to a class of compounds called by this name). Several other hormones, notably that secreted by the thyroid gland, have to be maintained within normal limits for growth to occur normally; but they do not act directly to regulate growth rate. Presumably because of the different hormonal control there is a considerable degree of independence between growth before, and growth at, adolescence.

DEVELOPMENT OF THE REPRODUCTIVE SYSTEM

The adolescent spurt in skeletal and muscular dimensions is closely related to the great development of the reproductive system which takes place at that time. The sequence of events for the average boy and girl is shown diagrammatically in Figs. 1–9 and 1–10. This sequence is not exactly the same for every boy and girl, but it varies much less than the time at which the events occur.

The first sign of impending puberty in boys is usually an acceleration of the growth of testes and scrotum (beginning of bar marked 'testis' in Fig. 1–9). Slight growth of the pubic hair may begin at about the same time, but proceeds slowly until the advent of the general spurt. The accelerations in height and in penis growth begin about a year after the

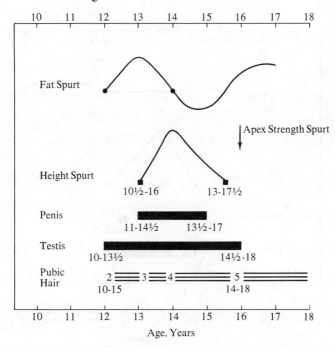

Fat Spurt

Apex Strength Spurt

Height Spurt

10½-16   13-17½

Penis
11-14½   13½-17

Testis
10-13½   14½-18

Pubic
Hair   2 ≡≡≡ 3 ≡≡ 4 ≡≡≡≡≡ 5 ≡≡≡≡
            10-15   14-18

Age, Years

Fig. 1–9. Diagram of sequence of events at adolescence in boys. An average boy is represented: the range of ages within which each event charted may begin and end is given by the figure (appropriate to 1955) placed directly below its start and finish. (From Tanner, *Growth at Adolescence*, Blackwell Sci. Publ.: Oxford.)

testicular acceleration, when the cells of the testis have grown and begun to secrete male sex hormone. Axillary hair usually first appears about two years after the beginning of pubic hair growth, though the relationship is sufficiently variable so that a very few children's axillary hair actually appears first. Facial hair in boys begins to grow at about the same time as axillary hair. There is first an increase in length and pigmentation of hairs at the corners of the upper lip, then a spread of this to complete the moustache, then the appearance of hair on the upper part of the cheeks and just below the lower lip, and finally along the sides and border of the chin. This last development seldom occurs until genital and pubic hair development is far advanced. The enlargement of the larynx occurs a little after the spurt in height and the voice begins to deepen perceptibly during the period when the development of the penis is approaching completion. A few boys undergo a slight breast enlargement at puberty, which in the majority is temporary, and soon disappears; only a minority need medical treatment.

In girls the beginning of growth of the breast is usually the first sign of puberty, though the appearance of pubic hair sometimes precedes it. Men-

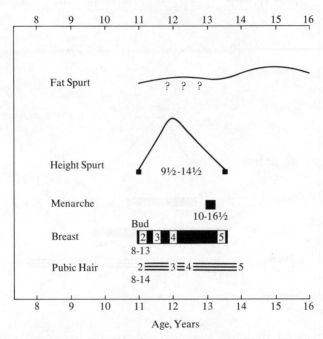

Fig. 1–10. Diagram of sequence of events at adolescence in girls. An average girl is represented: the range of ages within which some of the events may occur is given by the figures (appropriate to 1955) placed directly below them. (From Tanner, *Growth at Adolescence*, Blackwell Sci. Publ.: Oxford.)

arche, the first menstrual period and a landmark much used by students of growth, almost invariably occurs after the peak of the height spurt is passed. It occurs currently in Great Britain at an average age of 13.1 years, with a normal range of 10 to 16. Though its occurrence marks a definitive and probably mature stage of uterine growth, it does not usually signify the attainment of full reproductive function. A period of infertility of a year or eighteen months follows in most, though not all, cases; and maximum fertility is probably not reached till the early or middle twenties.

In Figs. 1–9 and 1–10 the average age of occurrence of each event is given by the scale of age at the bottom on the diagram (e.g. menarche a little after 13 years, the figures being for 1955). The *range* of ages within which some of the events may normally occur is given by the figures placed directly below the event (e.g. for menarche 10–16½). A glance will suffice to show how very large these ranges are. One boy, for example, may complete his penis growth at 13½, while another has not even started at 14½. An early-maturing boy may have finished his entire adolescence before a late-maturing boy *of the same chronological age* has even begun his first enlargement of the testes. . . .

2

Leon Eisenberg

A DEVELOPMENTAL APPROACH TO ADOLESCENCE

Eisenberg, a professor of child psychiatry, interprets the nature of adolescence and its place in human development. He emphasizes conceptualization at the abstract level, establishment of a sense of identity, and acquisition of role-appropriate behaviors.

Adolescence may be defined as a critical period of human development manifested at the biological, psychological, and social levels of integration, of variable onset and duration but marking the end of childhood and setting the foundation for maturity. Biologically, its onset is signaled by the acceleration of physiological growth and the beginnings of secondary sexual development, its termination by the fusion of the epiphyses of the bones and the completion of sexual maturation. Psychologically, it is marked by an acceleration of cognitive growth and of personality formation, both of which continue to be subject to further evolution, though at a less marked rate, in subsequent stages of adulthood. Socially, it is a period of intensified preparation for the assumption of an adult role, and its termination is signaled when the individual is accorded full adult prerogatives, the timing and nature of which vary widely from society to society.

Adolescence is a "critical period" in development in being both a time of rapid and profound change in the organism and a time providing the necessary—but not sufficient—conditions for full maturation in adulthood. Optimal development in adolescence depends on successful accomplishment of the developmental tasks in infancy and childhood. Thus, clinical experience has indicated that adolescence is likely to be particularly stormy, prolonged, and sometimes poorly resolved if it follows a childhood marked by severe deficits.

Whether or not appropriate "experiential supplements" during adolescence can lead to successful negotiation of this period despite pathology in earlier life is not known. The heuristic hypothesis is to assume that re-

From Leon Eisenberg, "A Developmental Approach to Adolescence," *Children,* Vol. 12, No. 4 (July–August 1965), pp. 131–135. (Reprinted by permission of the author and CHILDREN, U.S. Department of Health, Education, and Welfare, Welfare Administration, Children's Bureau.)

pair can occur and that the task of the physician is to search for ways of encouraging optimal growth during the adolescence of a previously damaged child.

Although a rich, fulfilling adolescence provides the best groundwork for a successful adulthood, such an outcome is not automatic; it depends, in turn, on the provision of opportunities during adulthood for the creative exercise of the abilities achieved in adolescence.

The structural groundwork for adolescent development is laid by physical maturation. This developmental sequence is not preformed or automatic but depends upon an interaction between biological capacity and environmental stimulation. Just as growth requires adequate nutrition —being subject to delay or even cessation in the presence of starvation and to acceleration in the presence of optimal intake—so psychological maturation is dependent upon "psychological nutrition," that is, sequential opportunities for cognitive and social stimulation so timed that they promote further mental development.

INTERDEPENDENT DEVELOPMENTS

Thus, adolescence is simultaneously a biological, a social, and a psychological phenomenon. Development at each of these levels of integration proceeds not independently but with significant interaction, with events at any one level able to impede or to accelerate developments at each of the others.

For example, although the time at which the hypothalamic-pituitary axis initiates the biological sequence of adolescent growth is a function of individual heredity, it may, in a given individual, be delayed or advanced by environmental factors. Thus, the ultimate height attained by adolescents in economically developing countries has shown striking gains as nutrition has improved. Similarly, the time of menarche has shown a trend toward acceleration in countries in which increasingly better health of the children has been achieved. These physiological trends are the result of industrial and social organization.

Or again, biological maturation provides the increasing muscular strength and dexterity which permit the adolescent to participate successfully in the activities of his social group, thus acquiring a psychological sense of adequacy. At the same time, positive psychological motivation is a prerequisite for task perseverance and the search for variety of experience, which provide the conditions necessary for full muscular development through exercise.

Developments at the biological and psychological levels occur in a social framework, which may promote or retard them. Thus, unscientific notions about diet prevalent in a specific culture may lead to inadequate nutritional intake, and social prejudices against minority group members may deprive them of experiences necessary for full development.

The importance of such reciprocal influences is underscored by the fact that each society is dependent upon its adolescents as its future adults. Failure to provide them with the conditions necessary for optimal development will severely handicap the growth potential of that society.

Biological adolescence has fairly precise signs of its onset and termination, such as growth acceleration, sexual development, and epiphyseal fusion, but there is remarkable variation in the timing of their appearance in different individuals. Onset in normal children may occur as early as age 7 or 8 or as late as 17 or 18; termination as early as 15 or 16 or as late as 24 or 25. The timing seems to be a function both of internal factors, such as sex and inheritance, and external factors, such as nutrition or illness. In other words, the biological factors set wide limits for the onset, termination, and achievements of adolescence, the potential limits being subject to modification by environmental influences, among which both psychological and social factors play a role.

SOCIAL PREPARATION

Adolescence as a social phenomenon, though restricted in range by biological considerations, is a function of cultural norms. In general, the more sophisticated the society is in its technology, the more prolonged is adolescence, since the complexity of the preparation required for the assumption of adult roles depends upon the demands the society sets. In the United States, for example, the long period of study required for specialized occupational roles delays the age of self-support, the opportunity for marriage, and the age of creative contribution to society—all attributes of the adult role.

In many cultures, the onset of adolescence is clearly signaled by puberty rites, usually in the form of tests of strength and courage, the completion of which entitles the individual to recognition as a young adult. In technologically advanced societies, such clear signification of the end of childhood is absent and the requirements for adulthood less clearly defined: the individual must, therefore, undergo a more prolonged and, at times, confused struggle to attain adult status.

Each culture provides experience specifically designated as part of the training of the adolescent, such as schooling and apprenticeship; other experiences, such as dating and courtship, which are for the most part limited to adolescence but are not formally organized; and other non-age-related opportunities for personal development which may be particularly meaningful for the adolescent, such as opportunities to participate in cultural and political life.

Deliberate social planning based on a scientific analysis of adolescents' needs has been relatively neglected, the forms and structures society provides having evolved empirically. Only within school systems has such planning been explicit, but even there with little careful research. Yet careful assessment of the needs of adolescents at all levels of developmental integration could lead to the design and provision of external conditions that would greatly accelerate the rate, and markedly increase the ultimate level, of the development of the human adolescent's full potentialities.

THE IDEALISM OF ADOLESCENCE

At a psychological level, the most striking attainment during adolescence is the ability to conceptualize at an abstract level. The further evolution of what Piaget calls the "concrete operations" of childhood [1] through interaction with increasingly more demanding intellectual tasks, provided both by formal schooling and informal social experience, leads to the ability to "think about thinking" and to analyze problems at a high level of generalization. It is here that the *Anlage* of scientific thought and creativity is to be found. This evolution of intellectual function requires appropriate environmental stimulation.

The adolescent's capacity for abstract thought accounts for his increasing concern with, on the one hand, national and international problems and, on the other, with the basic meanings and values of human existence. This "idealism" of adolescence is, of course, shaped by the cultural envelope which surrounds the individual, but its very existence leads to questioning, to examination of basic premises, and to dissatisfaction with the imperfections in the world adults have created. Its cultivation may be regarded as one of the most important tasks of society.

Fostering and strengthening this "suprapersonal" psychological trait in adolescents will lead to the creation of adults who will in turn enhance the society that bred them. The lack of adequate opportunity for its positive expression will warp the adolescent's normal development and lead to a generation of self-preoccupied adults who will fail to meet the challenge of history.

PERSONAL IDENTITY

A second and related psychological theme of adolescence is the search for a sense of personal identity, to employ the terminology of Erikson.[2]

[1] Flavell, J. H.: The developmental psychology of Jean Piaget. Van Nostrand, New York. 1963.

[2] Erikson, E. H.: Identity and the life cycle. *In* Psychological issues, monograph 1. International Universities Press, New York. 1959.

No longer a child and not yet an adult, the adolescent is busily engaged in determining who he is and what he is to become.

In this effort, he examines his parents from a more critical perspective and leans more to peer groups for his sense of belonging. If his relations with his parents have been soundly constructed during earlier years, and if they meet his doubts and criticisms with sympathetic understanding, this temporary unsettling of his prior role as a child leads to a resynthesis of his relations with them on a firm and lasting basis, one marked by reciprocal respect and by personal independence without abandonment of filial loyalty. Where the parent-child relationship has been one of excessive dependence or excessive hostility, the turmoil of adolescence may be prolonged and lead either to failure of emancipation or to rejection of family ties and a lasting sense of isolation.

SEXUAL ROLE

A third key developmental task consists of the further evolution of sexual identity and role-appropriate behavior. Learning the social role of one's sex is firmly rooted in childhood—in culturally differentiated role assignments, in emulation of the like-sexed parent, and in peer interactions. These experiences provide a constant feedback, both by comparison of the self with others and by praise or blame from them, which informs the child as to what sex he is and what kind of behavior expectations this entails. These preliminary psychological structures are challenged by the adolescent's consciousness of his development of adult sexual characteristics and his experience of a bewildering array of new physical sensations, both of which lead to an upsurge of interest in physical sex and a psychological sensitization to a new aspect of interpersonal relationships. The forces in the social field then determine the further steps in his sexual development.

Comparative studies indicate that, as the evolutionary scale is ascended, sexual behavior is less dependent upon hormones and more upon learning. In man, the role of hormones is limited to priming the organism for biological sexual maturation and to influencing—but not solely determining—the level of libido; the direction, nature, and adequacy of sexual performance are controlled by psychosocial factors. Thus, the many investigations of the biology of sex deviants have failed to identify chromosomal, hormonal, or gonadal aberrations; and conversely, individuals with such biological incongruencies usually exhibit a sex-role identity conforming to sex-role assignment.

The remarkable variation in sexual behavior between societies as well as between social classes within a single society emphasizes the cultural determination of sexual behavior, given adequate biological maturation.

The ambivalence of Western society toward sexuality—manifested by the conflicts between official attitudes and private behavior, and the pervasive emphasis on sex side by side with sanctions against its expression —accounts for the difficulty, so common in adolescence, of attaining the basis for a sense of competence, freedom, and pleasure as a sexually functioning adult. Persons concerned with the development of adolescents have an important obligation to give them a clear and full explanation of biological function with emphasis on its *ethical significance* based upon a mutually meaningful relationship between human beings. Adolescents need a comprehensive knowledge of the physical and physiological differences between the sexes, of the development of sexuality, and of the appropriate stages of sexual experience en route to full maturity.

Commonly expressed fears that giving adolescents such information will lead to premature experimentation run contrary to clinical experience which indicates that ignorance and impoverishment of human relationships account for most sexual misadventures. A sense of inadequacy in sexuality not only impairs sexual function but also leads to disabilities in other adult roles and is an important source of psychological malfunction.

ORIGINS OF DELINQUENCY

The search for identity is markedly influenced by peer groups. If these are constructive social groups which provide creative outlets for adolescent energy, the result is a sense of meaningful membership in the community and identification with its larger goals. If the peer group is a delinquent gang, with values antagonistic to those of the larger society, the result is likely to be antisocial personality organization—especially if the adolescent is a victim of discrimination for religious, ethnic, political, or economic reasons.

The experience of growing up as a member of a disadvantaged minority group, with attendant humiliation and denial of opportunity, makes it difficult for the adolescent to identify with the values of the society at large and favors, instead, hostility toward its norms and a disposition to anarchistic individualism. However, even under these circumstances, leadership and social forms which permit the disadvantaged adolescent to employ his energy in efforts to change unjust social patterns can foster his emergence into creative adulthood. If such opportunities for constructive social action are denied, the distortion of development leads to a frustrating and progressively more embittering "individual war against society" characterized by criminal activities.

Some theorists focus upon family pathology in explaining the evolution of delinquent behavior. Their thesis is based upon the finding that family psychopathology is frequent in the history of delinquents. The family is indeed an important agent in transmitting the behavior pattern and values expected of the adolescent by society. Consequently, distortions in family structure, whether idiosyncratic or socially induced, will inevitably have profound effects upon individual development. However, the family-centered viewpoint fails to recognize that family psychopathology is closely related to social structure and that the adolescent is also molded by social experiences outside the family.

The social consequences of economic disadvantage—poor health and reduced longevity, poor education, extralegal marital arrangements, inability to plan for future contingencies, necessity for exploiting children economically—themselves erode family structure and are likely to cause the victims of these social circumstances, the genesis of which they do not understand, to turn on each other in destructive ways. The unemployed, drifting father and the unmarried, deserted mother not only fail to provide their children with adequate nurture but also serve as poor identification models.

However, even though family structure be distorted, the adolescent may attain a degree of normal development *if* provided adequate education and constructive peer group experience. Unfortunately, the aggregation of disadvantaged families in decaying neighborhoods is all too likely to reinforce family psychopathology and, by exposing the adolescent to delinquent gangs and ineffective schooling, heighten his growing sense of bitterness.

HAZARDS AND SYMPTOMS

The sensitivity of the adolescent to the good opinion of his peers and the dependence of his sense of identity upon the attainment of competence in an adult role render him psychologically vulnerable to variation in physiological development, such as precocious or delayed growth, facial acne, obesity, enlarged mammary glands in the male, or inadequate or overabundant breast development in the female. These deviations from the expected pattern of maturation, though of no great medical significance, may, nonetheless, lead to major psychological trauma if not offset by sensitive guidance.

The adolescent with limited intellectual or physical capacity can develop a persisting and even irremedial feeling of inferiority if he is forced to compete in situations in which he experiences continual failure. The individualization of educational and vocational training for adolescents is essential, both to permit the talented individual to exploit his abilities, as well as to direct the youngster with specific limitations to activities which will develop what abilities he has.

Characteristic of adolescence is fluidity of psychological structure in the struggle to attain a new and more meaningful sense of identity. In consequence, the formation of transient symptoms, resembling many of the psychopathological syndromes of adulthood, is not uncommon during this period. The clinician must exercise great caution lest he attribute too great a significance to the turbulent but temporary maladaptive patterns manifested by the adolescent. Incorrect diagnostic formulations may lead to social consequences—for example, withdrawal from school or institutionalization—that will freeze into permanence an otherwise readily correctable deviation in the growth pattern.

It is, of course, important to recognize that schizophrenia often first appears in adolescence, as does manic-depressive psychosis. However, these are uncommon disorders and may be simulated by panic reactions in the youngster who is confronted by overwhelming internal and external stimulation. If the recent trend toward a specialty of adolescent psychiatry has any justification, it lies in the opportunity for psychiatrists to acquire particular competence in the differential diagnosis and special management of adolescents' adjustment reactions. Experience with the psychiatric problems of adolescents leads to respect for their extraordinary range of individual variability and their remarkable restorative capacity under corrective and supportive experience.

The psychological basis for a sense of individual worth as an adult rests upon the acquisition of competence in a work role during adolescence. A sense of competence is not acquired on the basis of "reassurance," but rather upon the actual experience of succeeding in a socially important task. The challenge to the educator, therefore, is to stimulate abilities to the utmost without setting standards so high that they lead to an enduring sense of defeat.

The educational accomplishment must be matched by an opportunity for the individual to exercise his competence as a worker in the economic world. The sustained motivation necessary for mastering a difficult work role is only possible when there is a real likelihood of fulfilling that role in adult life and having it respected by others. The task of providing full employment in a world in which automation is revolutionizing traditional work roles provides a challenge to the abilities of leading thinkers in all societies.

THE WORLD'S HOPE

No society can hope to survive that does not succeed in harnessing the constructive, searching suprapersonal and supranational drives of the adolescent. In recent world history, adolescents in underdeveloped countries have participated heroically in overthrowing the dead hand of the past and attaining the beginnings of a meaningful nationhood. The picture in the relatively developed countries is less clear and less heartening. As affluence is attained, societies tend to become frozen into traditional molds, with resultant trends toward self-preoccupation and egocentric goals that afford less challenge to adolescents. There are, fortunately, notable and inspiring exceptions to this self-preoccupation, as youngsters dedicate their energies to improving the lot of disadvantaged fellow citizens and to social betterment in underdeveloped countries far from their shores.

The capacity for engagement in meaningful social activity is clearly present in young people in every country of the world. The challenge to the behavioral scientist is to help his own country develop the forms and means to enable the adolescent to take a leading role in the struggle for the attainment of a world in which peace, freedom, and economic opportunity are omnipresent. No task is more suited to the adolescent. No task has greater potentiality for permitting the full flowering of his capacities.

Thus, the provision of an optimal framework for adolescent development is inseparable from the struggle to create a better world by helping to mold the citizens who will build it.

ADDITIONAL READINGS

Blum, Gerald S. Prepuberty and adolescence. *Psychoanalytic theories of personality*. New York: McGraw-Hill, 1953. Pp. 136–155. Blum reviews orthodox and neo-orthodox psychoanalytic concepts as they relate to adolescence, and interprets these points of view in terms of adolescent development.

Freud, Anna. Clinical applications to problems of adolescence. From "Adolescence." *The psychoanalytic study of the child.* Vol. 13. New York: International Universities Press, Inc., 1958. Pp. 264–277. In this excerpt from an article that first reviews the origins of psychoanalytic theory as related to adolescence, this distinguished writer relates how insights acquired with difficulty may be applied to the adolescent's most pressing problems. Specifically, she considers whether adolescent upset is inevitable, and also predictable; specific pathologies of adolescence; and the concept of adolescent normality. She suggests that disharmony in psychic structure is normal for adolescents.

Grinder, Robert E. & Strickland, Charles E. G. Stanley Hall and the social significance of adolescence. In Robert E. Grinder (ed.), *Studies in Adolescence*. New York: Macmillan, 1963. Pp. 3–16. The authors indicate how Hall's 19th-century Darwinism and his concepts of social reform resulted in an unusual interpretation of adolescence. Hall was the father of the child study movement in the United States and the author of a classic two-volume treatise on the psychology of adolescence.

Kiell, Norman. *The universal experience of adolescence.* New York: International University Press, 1964. The author's main thesis is that the internal turmoil and external disorder of adolescence are universal and only moderately affected by cultural determinants. Using a psychoanalytic frame of reference, the author cites references about various cultures to test his point of view. He concludes that in the more literate, achieving societies, adolescent turmoil is common.

Mann, J. W. Adolescent marginality. *Journal of Genetic Psychology,* 1965, **106,** 221–235. The adolescent is often portrayed as occupying a marginal status, neither child nor man, with no clear-cut status of his own. However, data obtained in a study of college students in the Union of South Africa failed to confirm this theory. The marginal theory might better describe the adolescent's situation than his personality.

Muuss, Rolf E. Theories of adolescent development—their philosophical and historical roots. *Adolescence,* Spring 1966, **1** (1), 22–44. The writer traces theories and philosophies of human development from the early Greeks to the early twentieth century, discussing in particular the contributions of the early Greeks, the medieval Christians, Comenius, Locke, Rousseau, and Charles Darwin.

Shapiro, Roger L. Adolescence and the psychology of the ego. *Psychiatry,* 1963, **26,** 77–87. Shapiro reviews the development of the psychoanalytic theory of adolescence and examines implications of the study of adolescence for psychoanalytic ego psychology.

II. The Adolescent Image

Indictments of youth have a venerable history. Over two thousand years ago, Socrates described youth as disrespectful of their elders, and as tyrants—not servants—of their households. "They are also mannerless," said Socrates, "and fail to rise when their elders enter the room. They chatter before company, gobble up dainties at the table, cross their legs, and tyrannize over their teachers." Such indictments have continued down the ages.

A present-day psychiatrist, Robert Nixon, sees the majority of youth as maladjusted—including the conformists, the abnormals, and the rebels. The normal youth, who compose a minority, he describes as somewhere between the ages of 16 and 21; introspective, not schizophrenic; self-concerned; self-critical; self-appraising. The fact that psychologically normal youth exist makes it possible to identify the unhealthy majority. Nixon agrees with a New York cabbie who remarked, "I get sick of all this well-adjusted psychology jazz. If you're well-adjusted to a sick world, you're sick, aren't you? Who needs it?" [1]

Hurlock's view of adolescents is no more positive than Nixon's. She describes today's adolescents as a new species, with several dominant traits. They are conformists, she says, and follow the herd, whether for good or bad. They are preoccupied with status symbols, and anxious to be identified with the leading crowd. They are irresponsible and follow the philosophy, "Let John do it." They are also anti-intellectual, and their eagerness for higher education merely reflects a desire for better jobs and for meeting the right people. They lack respect for the older generation, and for rules and laws. Today's teen-agers, she concludes, are unhappy, and turning into second-rate students and citizens. [2]

At the other extreme are those whose picture of teen-agers drips with sentiment. The teen-ager, says Davidson, is a scapegoat, whose "basic crime is merely that he is over 12 and under 20." In fact, teen-agers are "stronger, smarter, more self-sufficient, and more constructive than any other generation in history." [3] Other writers are more analytical than

[1] Robert E. Nixon, "Psychological Normality in the Years of Youth," *Teachers College Record*, Vol. 66, No. 1 (October 1964), pp. 71–79.
[2] Elizabeth B. Hurlock, "American Adolescents of Today—A New Species," *Adolescence*, Vol. 1, No. 1 (Spring 1966), pp. 7–21.
[3] Bill Davidson, "18,000,000 Teenagers Can't Be Wrong," *Colliers* (January 4, 1957), p. 13.

judgmental in describing adolescents. Throughout Friedenberg's *The Vanishing Adolescent,* we stumble on passages which collectively represent his concept of youth. Sometimes he simply refers to the teen-ager; at other times he distinguishes between boys and girls. In one passage, he calls adolescents "cliquish and clannish, but not usually smug or parochial." Adolescents are generally "sound and stable" in judgment, and mistakes made are due to factors beyond their experience. Boys, he says, are vain; their vanity is very personal. They are more concerned over their appearance than girls; and a well-built, sun-bronzed boy will fight like a tiger to keep his mother from getting him out of his torn T-shirt. Boys bask in physical regard like "alligators on a log," while girls find satisfaction in attractiveness because it produces interesting relationships.

Paulston, like Friedenberg, takes a benign view of youth's eccentricities. She describes them as mildly and temporarily insane, to the extent that diverted psychic energy obstructs their being the "whole" individuals they really are." [4]

Other writers warn against unwarranted over-generalizations. Even in a society devoted to publicity, notes Denny, youth have a great capacity for concealment. This masquerade, the range of youth, and the pace of change make it hard to categorize. The variations strengthen and illuminate the broad contours of the universal phenomenon.[5] Similarly, Sorenson speaks of society's "confused image of youth." Society cannot even make up its mind how to designate him. Is he a "youth," a "teen-ager" or a "young person?" In any case, he is generally seen as an individual in transition. In no other stage of the life cycle, Sorenson quotes Erikson as saying, are the promise of finding oneself and the threat of losing oneself so closely allied.[6]

The matter of teen image is important for various reasons. For one thing, an individual's self-image is importantly affected by the way others view him. In turn, the way he views himself—as worthwhile or stupid, as responsible or trustworthy, as stable or flighty—will affect how he deals with his environment. If he views himself as competent and successful he will persist longer against difficulty than if he sees himself as mediocre in attainment.[7] A healthy self-concept is also important for mental health. Adolescents who have stable, realistic self-concepts make a better adjustment.[8] Moreover, adults' views of teen-agers will affect adolescents' rela-

[4] Christina Bratt Paulston, "On Creativity and Teaching," *Teachers College Record,* Vol. 69, No. 4 (January 1968), p. 374.

[5] Reuel Denney, "American Youth Today: A Bigger Cast, A Wider Screen," *Daedalus,* Vol. 91 (1962), pp. 124–145.

[6] Roy Sorenson, "Youth's Need for Challenge and Place in Society," *Children,* Vol. 9, No. 4 (July–August 1962), pp. 131–138.

[7] Elizabeth Douvan and Joseph Adelson, "The Psychodynamics of Social Mobility in Adolescent Boys," *Journal of Abnormal Psychology,* Vol. 56 (1958), pp. 31–44.

[8] S. S. Spivack, "A Study of a Method of Self-Acceptance and Self-Rejection," *Journal of Genetic Psychology,* Vol. 88 (1956), pp. 183–202.

tions to the adult world. Adults who look on teen-agers as responsible are more likely to elicit their cooperation. Youth can hardly relate to, and profitably be guided by, adults who regard them with disrespect.

In 1959, Hess and Goldblatt reported that adolescents, as a group, believed themselves subject to condemnation, criticism, and general devaluation by adults. Adolescents claimed they were perceived as sloppy, irresponsible, unreliable, and inclined toward destructive and antisocial behavior. These same adolescents credited themselves with an acceptable degree of achievement, though acknowledging a subordinate status to adults. They were also generous in their views of adults, and tended to idealize adulthood. What is the effect of these conflicting images? Perhaps a moderate overestimation of adults may help motivate the adolescent to attain maturity. However, adolescents who simultaneously over-idealize adults and believe themselves disparaged by adults may encounter difficulties in ego development.[9]

It becomes obvious that the adolescent has several images of himself. It varies with time, and place, and circumstance, and above all, with the viewer. The adolescent is looked upon differently by the small child, who, by his standards, is very big and wise; and by the older person to whom he is still wet behind the ears. This kaleidoscopic image is reflected in the diversity of views that follow. In the first selection, Friedenberg portrays youth as thwarted by an environment which inhibits them and fails to permit them to be all they are capable of becoming. He laments society's image of the teen-ager as unwholesome and unfair. In the next article, Adelson says society holds several images of youth—no one picture can embrace all of them. Like Friedenberg, he believes societal images unwholesome, although he defines them differently. The third selection, by Otto and Otto, counterbalances these less fortunate portrayals with a new image that emphasizes youth's strengths and gives them something worthwhile to live up to. In conclusion, perhaps the only *valid* image is a *confused* image, reflecting youth's uncertain position in the world today, and the particular ways that other groups experience him.

[9] Robert D. Hess and Irene Goldblatt, "The Status of Adolescents in American Society: A Problem in Social Identity," *Child Development,* Vol. 28 (1957) pp. 459–468.

3

Edgar Z. Friedenberg

THE IMAGE OF THE ADOLESCENT MINORITY

In America, says Friedenberg, adolescent boys are perceived as a "hot-blooded minority," and "cut down." Girls, by contrast, are simply wasted, and the wastage continues all their lives. Each sex suffers from the special type of discrimination accorded it. The boy's quality of experience is "starved and repressed," while the girl simply fails to develop at all.

In our society there are two kinds of minority status. One of these I will call the "hot-blooded" minorities, whose archetypical image is that of the Negro or Latin. *In the United States, "Teen-agers" are treated as a "hot-blooded" minority.* Then, there are the "long-suffering minorities," whose archetype is the Jew, but which also, I should say, includes women. Try, for a second, to picture a Jewish "teen-ager," and you may sense a tendency for the image to grate. "Teen-agers" err on the hot side; they talk jive, drive hot-rods and become juvenile delinquents. Young Jews talk volubly, play the violin, and go to medical school, though never on Saturday.

The minority group is a special American institution, created by the interaction between a history and an ideology which are not to be duplicated elsewhere. Minority status has little to do with size or proportion. In a democracy, a dominant social group is called a majority and part of its dominance consists in the power to arrange appropriate manifestations of public support; while a subordinate group is, by the logic of political morality, a minority. The minority stereotype, though affected by the actual characteristics of the minority group, develops to fit the purposes and expresses the anxieties of the dominant social group. It serves as a slimy coating over the sharp realities of cultural difference, protecting the social organism until the irritant can be absorbed.

Now, when one is dealing with a group that actually is genetically or culturally different from the dominant social group, this is perhaps to

From Edgar Z. Friedenberg, "The Image of the Adolescent Minority," *Dignity of Youth and Other Atavisms* (Boston, Beacon Press, 1965), pp. 66–78. Reprinted by permission of the Beacon Press, copyright © 1965 by Edgar Z. Friedenberg.

be expected. It is neither desirable nor inevitable, for xenophobia is neither desirable nor inevitable; but it is not surprising.

What is surprising is that the sons and daughters of the *dominant* adult group should be treated as a minority group merely because of their age. Their papers are in order and they speak the language adequately. In any society, to be sure, the young occupy a subordinate or probationary status while under tutelage for adult life. But a minority group is not merely subordinate; it is not under tutelage. It is in the process of being denatured; of becoming, under social stress, something more acceptable to the dominant society, but essentially different from what its own growth and experience would lead to. Most beasts recognize their own kind. Primitive peoples may initiate their youth; we insist that ours be naturalized, though it is what is most natural about them that disturbs adults most.

The court of naturalization is the public school. A high school diploma is a certificate of legitimacy, not of competence. A youth needs one today in order to hold a job that will permit even minimal participation in the dominant society. Yet our laws governing school attendance do not deal with education. They are not *licensing* laws, requiring attendance until a certain defined minimum competence, presumed essential for adult life, has been demonstrated. They are not *contractual;* they offer no remedy for failure of the school to provide services of a minimum quality. A juvenile may not legally withdraw from school even if he can establish that it is substandard or that he is being ill-treated there. If he does, as many do, for just these reasons, he becomes *prima facie* an offender; for, in cold fact, the compulsory attendance law guarantees him nothing, not even the services of qualified teachers. It merely defines, in terms of age alone, a particular group as subject to legal restrictions not applicable to other persons.

SECOND-CLASS CITIZEN

Legally, the adolescent comes pretty close to having no basic rights at all. The state generally retains the final right even to strip him of his minority status. He has no right to *demand* the particular protection of *either* due process or the juvenile administrative procedure—the state decides. We have had several cases in the past few years of boys eighteen and under being sentenced to death by the full apparatus of formal criminal law, who would not have been permitted to claim its protection had they been accused of theft or disorderly conduct. Each of these executions has so far been forestalled by various legal procedures,[1] but none in such a way as to establish the right of a juvenile to be tried as a juvenile; though he long ago lost his claim to be treated as an adult.

[1] Two were finally hanged this past June, five years later.

In the most formal sense, then, the adolescent is one of our second-class citizens. But the informal aspects of minority status are also imputed to him. The "teen-ager," like the Latin or Negro, is seen as joyous, playful, lazy, and irresponsible, with brutality lurking just below the surface and ready to break out into violence.[2] All these groups are seen as childish and excitable, imprudent and improvident, sexually aggressive, and dangerous, but possessed of supurb and sustained power to satisfy sexual demands. *West Side Story* is not much like *Romeo and Juliet;* but it is a great deal like *Porgy and Bess.*

The fantasy underlying this stereotype, then, is erotic; and its subject is male. The "hot-blooded" minorities are always represented by a masculine stereotype; nobody asks "Would you want your *son* to marry a Negro?" In each case, also, little counter-stereotypes, repulsively pallid in contrast to the alluring violence and conflict of the central scene, are held out enticingly by the dominant culture; the conscientious "teen-ager" sold by Pat Boone to soothe adults while the kids themselves buy *Mad* and *Catcher;* the boy whose Italian immigrant mother sees to it that he wears a clean shirt to school every day on his way to the Governor's mansion; *Uncle Tom.* In the rectilinear planning of Jonesville these are set aside conspicuously as Public Squares, but at dusk they are little frequented.

One need hardly labor the point that what the dominant society seeks to control by imposing "hot-blooded" minority status is not the actual aggressiveness and sexuality of the Negro, the Latin, or the JD, but its own wish for what the British working classes used to call "a nice game of slap-and-tickle," on the unimpeachable assumption that a little of what you fancy does you good. This, the well-lighted Public Squares cannot afford; the community is proud of them, but they are such stuff as only the driest dreams are made of. These are not the dreams that are wanted. In my experience, it is just not possible to discuss adolescence with a group of American adults without being forced into the topic of juvenile delinquency. Partly this is an expression of legitimate concern, but partly it is because only the JD has any emotional vividness for them.

I would ascribe the success of *West Side Story* to the functional equivalence in the minds of adults between adolescence, delinquency, and ag-

---

[2] A very bad—indeed, vicious—but remarkably ambivalent reenactment of the entire fantasy on which the minority-status of the teen-ager is based can be seen in the recent movie *13 West St.* Here, the legal impotence of the "teen-ager" is taken absolutely for granted, and sadistic hostility of adults against him, though deplored, is condoned and accepted as natural. Occasional efforts are made to counterbalance the, in my judgment, pornographic picture of a brutal teen-age gang by presenting "good" teen-agers unjustly suspected, and decent police trying to resist sadistic pressure from the gang's victim, who drives one of its members to suicide. But despite this, the picture ends with a scene of the gang's victim—a virile-type rocket scientist —beating the leader of the gang with his cane and attempting to drown the boy in a swimming pool—which the police dismiss as excusable under the circumstances. A Honolulu paper, at least, described this scene of attempted murder as "an old-fashioned caning that had the audience cheering in its seats."

gressive sexuality. Many who saw the show must have wondered, as I did, why there were no Negroes in it—one of the best things about Juvenile Delinquency is that, at least, it is integrated. Hollywood, doubtless, was as usual reluctant to show a member of an enfranchised minority group in an unfavorable light. But there was also a rather sound artistic reason. Putting a real Negro boy in *West Side Story* would have been like scoring the second movement of the *Pastorale* for an eagle rather than flute. The provocative, surly, sexy dancing kids who come to a bad end are not meant realistically. Efforts to use real streets-adolescents in *West Side Story* had to be abandoned; they didn't know how to act. What was depicted here was neither Negro nor white nor really delinquent, but a comfortably vulgar middle-class dream of a "hot-blooded" minority. In dreams a single symbolic boy can represent them all; let the symbol turn real and the dreamer wakes up screaming.

Adolescents are treated as a "hot-blooded" minority, then, because they seem so good at slap-and-tickle. But a number of interesting implications flow from this. Slap-and-tickle implies sexual vigor and attractiveness, warmth and aggression, salted with enough conventional perversity to lend spice to a long dull existence. Such perversity is a kind of exuberant overflow from the mainstream of sexuality, not a diversion of it. It is joyous excess and bounty; extravagant foreplay in the well-worn marriage-bed; the generosity of impulse that leads the champion lover of the high school to prance around the shower room snapping a towel on the buttocks of his team-mates three hours before a hot date, just to remind them that life can be beautiful.

EXPERIENCE REPRESSED

When a society sees impulsiveness and sexual exuberance as minority characteristics which unsuit the individual for membership until he is successfully naturalized, it is in pretty bad shape. Adolescents, loved, respected, taught to accept, enjoy, and discipline their feelings, grow up. "Teen-agers" don't; they pass. Then, in middle-age, they have the same trouble with their former self that many ethnics do. They hate and fear the kinds of spontaneity that remind them of what they have abandoned, and they hate themselves for having joined forces with and having come to resemble their oppressors.[3] This is the vicious spiral by which "hot-blooded" minority status maintains itself. I am convinced that it is also the source of the specific hostility—and sometimes sentimentality—that adolescents arouse in adults. The processes involved have been dealt with

[3] Cf. Abraham Kardiner and Lionel Ovesey's classic, *The Mark of Oppression* (New York: Norton, 1951), for a fascinating study of these dynamics among American Negroes.

in detail by Daniel Boorstin, Leslie Fiedler, Paul Goodman, and especially Ernest Schachtel.[4] Their effect is to starve out, through silence and mis-representation, the capacity to have genuine and strongly felt experience, and to replace it by the conventional symbols that serve as the common currency of daily life.

Experience repressed in adolescence does not, of course, result in amnesia, as does the repression of childhood experience; it leaves no tem-poral gaps in the memory. This makes it more dangerous, because the adult is then quite unaware that his memory is incomplete, that the most significant components of feeling have been lost or driven out. We at least know that we no longer know what we felt as children. But an adolescent boy who asks his father how he felt on the first night he spent in barracks or with a woman will be told what the father now thinks he felt because he ought to have; and this is very dangerous nonsense indeed.

Whether in childhood or in adolescence, the same quality of experi-ence is starved out or repressed. It is still the spontaneous, vivid and im-mediate that is most feared, and feared the more because so much desired. But there is a difference in focus and emphasis because in ado-lescence spontaneity can lead to much more serious consequences.

This, perhaps, is the crux of the matter, since it begins to explain why our kind of society should be so easily plunged into conflict by "hot-blooded" minorities in general and adolescent boys in particular. We are consequence-oriented and future-oriented. Among us, to prefer present delights is a sign of either low or high status, and both are feared. Schachtel makes it clear how we go about building this kind of character in the child—by making it difficult for him to notice his delights when he has them, and obliterating the language in which he might recall them joyfully later. This prepares the ground against the subsequent assault of adolescence. But it is a strong assault, and if adolescence wins, the future hangs in the balance.

THE ADOLESCENT GIRL

In this assault, adolescent boys play a very different role from ado-lescent girls and are dealt with unconsciously by totally different dynamics. Adolescent girls are not seen as members of a "hot-blooded" minority, and

[4] Daniel Boorstin, *The Image,* New York: Atheneum, 1962; Leslie Fiedler, "The Fear of the Impulsive Life." *WFMT Perspective,* October, 1961, pp. 4–9; Paul Good-man, *Growing Up Absurd.* New York: Random House, 1960, p. 38; Ernest Schachtel, "On Memory and Childhood Amnesia." Widely anthologized, cf. the author's *Meta-morphosis.* New York: Basic Books, 1959, pp. 279–322. A more systematic and pro-found treatment, I have since learned, is to be found in Norman Brown, *Life Against Death* (Middletown, Wesleyan University Press, 1959).

to this fact may be traced some interesting paradoxes in our perception of the total phenomenon of adolescence.

Many critics of the current literature on adolescence—Bruno Bettelheim [5] perhaps most cogently—have pointed out that most contemporary writing about adolescents ignores the adolescent girl almost completely. Bettelheim specifically mentions Goodman and myself; the best novels about adolescents of the past decade or so have been, I think there would be fair agreement, Salinger's *The Catcher in the Rye,* John Knowles' *A Separate Peace,* and Colin MacInnes' less well known but superb *Absolute Beginners.* All these have adolescent boys as heroes. Yet, as Bettelheim points out, the adolescent girl is as important as the adolescent boy, and her actual plight in society is just as severe; her opportunities are even more limited and her growth into a mature woman as effectively discouraged. Why has she not aroused more interest?

There are demonstrable reasons for the prominence of the adolescent boy in our culture. Conventionally, it is he who threatens the virtue of our daughters and the integrity of our automobiles. There are so many more ways to get hung up on a boy. "Teen-agers," too, may be all right; but would you want your daughter to marry one? When she doesn't know anything about him except how she feels—and what does that matter when they are both too young to know what they are doing; when he may never have the makings of an executive, or she of an executive's wife?

For this last consideration, paradoxically, also makes the *boy,* rather than the girl, the focus of anxiety. He alone bears the terrible burden of parental aspirations; it is his capacity for spontaneous commitment that endangers the opportunity of adults to live vicariously the life they never manage to live personally.

Holden, Finny, and the unnamed narrator of *Absolute Beginners,* are adolescent boys who do not pass; who retain their minority status, their spontaneous feelings, their power to act out and act up. They go prancing to their destinies. But what destiny can we imagine for them? We leave Holden in a mental hospital, being adjusted to reality; and Finny dead of the horror of learning that his best friend, Gene, had unconsciously contrived the accident that broke up his beautifully articulated body. The Absolute Beginner, a happier boy in a less tense society, fares better; he has had more real contact with other human beings, including a very satisfactory father, and by his time there is such a thing as a "teen-ager," little as it is, for him to be. On this basis, the Beginner can identify himself; the marvelous book ends as he rushes out onto the tarmac at London Airport, bursting through the customs barrier, to stand at the foot of the gangway and greet a planeload of astonished immigrants by crying, "Here I am! Meet your first teen-ager."

[5] In "Adolescence and the Conflict of Generations," *Daedalus,* Winter, 1962, p. 68.

POLITICAL DISINTEREST

There are still enough Finnys and Holdens running around free to give me much joy and some hope, and they are flexible enough to come to their own terms with reality. But the system is against them, and they know it well. Why then, do they not try to change it? Why are none of these novels of adolescence political novels? Why have their heroes no political interests at all? In this respect, fiction is true to American life; American adolescents are notably free from political interests. I must maintain this despite the recent advances of SANE kids and Freedom Riders; for, though I love and honor them for their courage and devotion, the causes they fight for are not what I call political. No controversy over basic policy is involved, because nobody advocates atomic disaster or racial persecution. The kids' opponents are merely in favor of the kind of American society that these evils flourish in, and the youngsters do not challenge the system itself, though they are appalled by its consequences.

Yet could they, as adolescents, be political? I don't think so; and I don't know that I would be pleased if they were. American politics is a cold-blooded business indeed. Personal clarity and commitment are not wanted in it and not furthered by it. I do not think this is necessarily true of all politics; but it becomes true when the basic economic and social assumptions are as irrational as ours.

Political effectiveness in our time requires just the kind of caginess, pseudo-realism, and stereotyping of thought and feeling; the same submergence of spontaneity to the exigencies of collective action, that mark the ruin of adolescence. Adolescents are, inherently, anti-mass; they take things personally. Sexuality, itself, has this power to resolve relationships into the immediate and interpersonal. As a symbol the cocky adolescent boy stands, a little like Luther, an obstacle to compromise and accommodation. Such symbols stick in the mind, though the reality can usually be handled. With occasional spectacular failures we do manage to assimilate the "teen-age" minority; the kids learn not to get fresh; they get smart, they dry up. We are left then, like the Macbeths, with the memory of an earlier fidelity. But Lady Macbeth was less resourceful than ourselves; she knew next to nothing about industrial solvents. Where she had only perfume we have oil.

THE GIRL AS WOMAN

This is how we use the boy, but what about the girl? I have already asserted that, since she is not perceived as a member of the "hot-blooded" minority she cannot take his place in the unconscious, which is apt to turn very nasty if it is fobbed off with the wrong sex. Is she then simply not much involved by our psychodynamics, or is she actively repressed? Is she omitted from our fantasies or excluded from them?

It may seem very strange that I should find her so inconspicuous. Her image gets so much publicity. Drum-majorettes and cheerleaders are ubiquitous; *Playboy* provides businessmen with a new *playmate* each month. Nymphets are a public institution.

Exactly, and they serve a useful public function. American males are certainly anxious to project a heterosexual public image, and even more anxious to believe in it themselves. None of us, surely, wishes to feel obligated to hang himself out of respect for the United States Senate; it is, as Yum-Yum remarked to Nanki-Poo, such a stuffy death. I am not questioning our sincerity; the essence of my point is that in what we call maturity we feel what we are supposed to feel, and nothing else. But I am questioning the depth and significance of our interest in the cover or pin-up girl. Her patrons are concerned to experience their own masculinity; they are not much interested in her: I reject the celebration of "babes" in song and story as evidence that we have adolescent girls much on our minds; if we did we wouldn't think of them as "babes." I think, indeed, that in contrast to the boy, of whom we are hyperaware, we repress our awareness of the girl. She is not just omitted, she is excluded.

The adolescent heroine in current fiction is not interpreted in the same way as the adolescent hero, even when the parallel is quite close. Her adolescence is treated as less crucial; she is off-handedly accepted as a woman already. This is true even when the author struggles against it. *Lolita,* for example, is every bit as much a tragic heroine of adolescence as Holden is a hero—she isn't as nice a girl as he is a boy, but they are both victims of the same kind of corruption in adult society and the same absence of any real opportunity to grow up to be themselves. Lolita's failure is the classic failure of identity in adolescence; and Humbert knows this and accepts responsibility for it; this is the crime he expiates. But this is not the way Lolita—the character, not the book—is generally received. Unlike Holden, she has no cult and is not vouchsafed any dignity. It is thought to be comical that, at fourteen, she is already a whore.

A parallel example is to be found in Rumer Godden's *The Greengage Summer.* Here the story is explicitly about Joss's growing up. The author's emphasis is on the way her angry betrayal of her lover marks the end of her childhood; her feelings are now too strong and confused, and too serious in their consequences, to be handled with childish irresponsibility; she can no longer claim the exemptions of childhood. But what the movie presented, it seemed to me, was almost entirely an account of her rise to sexual power; Joss had become a Babe at last.

One reason that we do not take adolescent growth seriously in girls is that we do not much care what happens to people unless it has economic consequences: what would Holden ever be, since he never even graduates from high school; who would hire him? He has a problem; Lolita could always be a waitress or something; what more could she expect? Since we define adulthood almost exclusively in economic terms, we obviously cannot concern ourselves as much about the growth of those members of society who are subject from birth to restricted economic opportunity. But so, of course, are the members of the "hot-blooded" minorities; though we find their hot-bloodedness so exciting that we remain aware of them anyway.

But girls, like Jews, are not supposed to fight back, we expect them, instead, to insinuate themselves coyly into the roles available. In our society, there are such lovely things for them to be. They can take care of other people and clean up after them. Women can become wives and mothers; Jews can become kindly old Rabbis and philosophers and even psychoanalysts and lovable comic essayists. They can become powers behind the power; a fine old law firm runs on the brains of its anonymous young Jews just as a husband's best asset is his loyal and unobtrusive wife. A Jewish girl can become a Jewish Mother, and this is a role which even Plato would have called essential.

EFFECTS OF DISCRIMINATION

Clearly, this kind of discrimination is quite different from that experienced by the "hot-blooded" minorities and must be based on a very different image in the minds of those who practice it and must have a different impact upon them. Particularly, in the case of the adolescent, the effect on the adult of practicing these two kinds of discrimination will be different. The adolescent boy must be altered to fit middle-class adult roles, and when he has been he becomes a much less vital creature. But the girl is merely squandered, and this wastage will continue all her life. Since adolescence is, for boy and girl alike, the time of life in which the self must be established, the girl suffers as much from being wasted as the boy does from being cut down; there has recently been, for example, a number of tragic suicides reported among adolescent girls, though suicide generally is far less common among females. But from the point of view of the dominant society nothing special is done to the female in adolescence— the same squeeze continues throughout life, even though this is when it hurts most.

The guilts we retain for our treatments of "hot-blooded" and "long-suffering" minorities therefore affect us in contrasting ways. For the boy we suffer angry, paranoid remorse, as if he were Billy the Kid, or Budd. We had to do our duty, but how can we ever forget him? But we do not attack the girl; we only neglect her and leave her to wither gradually through an unfulfilled life; and the best defense against this sort of guilt is selective inattention. We just don't see her; instead, we see a caricature, not brutalized as in the case of the boy, to justify our own brutality, but sentimentalized, roseate, to reassure us that we have done her no harm, and that she is well contented. Look: she even has her own telephone, with what is left of the boy dangling from the other end of the line.

A LONELY RIDE

This is the fantasy; the reality is very different, but it is bad enough to be a "Teen-ager." The adolescent is now the only totally disfranchised minority group in the country. In America, no minority has ever gotten any respect or consistently decent treatment until it began to acquire political power. The vote comes before anything else. This is obviously true of the Negro at the present time; his recent advances have all been made under—sometimes reluctant—Federal auspices because, nationally, Negroes vote, and Northern Negroes are able to cast a ballot on which their buffeted Southern rural fellows may be pulled to firmer political ground. This is what makes it impossible to stop Freedom Rides; just as the comparative militance of the Catholic Church in proceeding toward integration in Louisiana may have less to do with Louisiana than Nigeria, which is in grave danger of falling into the hands of Black Muslims. People generally sympathetic with adolescents sometimes say, "Well, it really isn't fair; if they're old enough to be drafted, they're old enough to vote," which is about as naive as it is possible to get.

Can the status of the "teen-ager" be improved? Only, presumably, through increased political effectiveness. Yet, it is precisely here that a crucial dilemma arises. For the aspirations of the adolescent minority are completely different from those of other minorities. All the others are struggling to obtain what the adolescent is struggling to avoid. They seek and welcome the conventional American middle-class status that has been partially or totally barred to them. But this is what the adolescent is left with if he gives in and goes along.

In the recent and very moving CORE film, *Freedom Ride,* one of the heroic group who suffered beatings and imprisonment for their efforts to end segregation says, as nearly as I can recall, "If the road to freedom leads through the jails of the South, then that's the road I'll take." It may be the road to freedom; but it is the road to suburbia too. You can't tell which the people are headed for until they are nearly there; but all our past ethnic groups have settled for suburbia, and the people who live there bear witness that freedom is somewhere else.

I am not sure there *is* a road to freedom in America. Not enough people want to go there; the last I can recall was H. D. Thoreau, and he went on foot, through the woods, alone. This still may be the only way to get there. For those with plenty of guts, compassion, and dedication to social justice, who nevertheless dislike walking alone through the woods, or feel it to be a Quixotic extravagance, a freedom ride is a noble enterprise. Compared to them, the individual boy or girl on a solitary journey must seem an anachronism. Such a youngster has very little place in our way of life. And of all the criticisms that might be directed against that way of life, this is the harshest.

4

Joseph Adelson

THE MYSTIQUE OF ADOLESCENCE

Adelson says that the image of the ·adolescent in fiction and mass media could be called the Fool, who "inhabits an Eden of prerexponsibility." Supersed-ing the Fool are two new images: the Visionary, who possesses some especially pure and perceptive moral vision; and his antitype, the Victimizer, who is "Leather-jacketed, cruel, sinister, and amoral. . . ." Neither of these images is correct, says Adelson. Instead, perhaps there is a new type, whose passions and vivacity are being strangled in the "false adulthood of the adolescent teen culture."

In recent years the adolescent has come to weigh oppressively on the American consciousness. Just a few years ago he was of little substance in our collective imaginings, in fiction, and in the mass media. He was represented as a figure of fun: callow, flighty, silly, given to infatuations, wild enthusiasms, and transient moodiness. His prototype was Andy Hardy, Henry Aldrich. Or he was sometimes seen as a latter-day and rather harm-less Werther: sensitive, emotionally afflicted, overly sentimental. In either case the figure was seen as lovable, though sometimes exasperating, and not to be taken too seriously. He would get over it—whatever *it* might be— in time. I shall call this type the adolescent as Fool.[1] The Fool exists outside the world of adult happenings; he is blessedly innocent of compli-cation, guilt, or responsibility. He is a fool not in being duped, but because he is unrelated to the intrigues and corruptions, or the moral seriousness, of adulthood. He inhabits an Eden of prerexponsibility.

These days two new images, weightier and more ominous, have super-seded the Fool figure, and between them they divide the contemporary sense of the adolescent. One of these I shall call the adolescent as Vision-ary. He is distinguished by a purity of moral vision which allows him to perceive or state the moral simplicity hidden by adult complication. In the way of prophets, he is also a Victim. He is betrayed, exploited, or neglected

From Joseph Adelson, "The Mystique of Adolescence," *Psychiatry,* Vol. 27 (1964), pp. 1–5. Reprinted by special permission of The William Alanson White Psychiatric Foundation, Inc.

[1] Compare Orrin E. Klapp, *Heroes, Villains, and Fools: The Changing American Character,* Englewood Cliffs, N. J., Prentice-Hall, 1962.

by the adult world. His needs go unrecognized by adults too busy in their own affairs; or as an innocent bystander he may be victimized by adult corruption. The prototypes here are J. D. Salinger's adolescents, Holden Caulfield or Franny Glass. Whereas the Fool is essentially unrelated to the adult world, the Visionary-Victim is connected to it in being passive and powerless. Perceptive, articulate, morally precocious, his only resources are insight and knowledge, and the strength which may eventually accrue from them.

The antitype to the Visionary is the newest and most disturbing representation of the adolescent, as Victimizer. Leather-jacketed, cruel, sinister, and amoral, he is the nemesis-hero of a new genre of fiction and film. Here, as one example, is the plot of a typical fiction of the genre. A man accidentally incurs the hatred of some hoodlum youths who threaten to kill him. He appeals to the police for protection, but they are impotent to help him. The story ends as the night closes in, and the man, alone and helpless, awaits his death at the hands of the youths. The story's mood is paranoid; this adolescent stands in utter contrast to the Visionary; one is innocent, the other evil; one is powerless, the other omnipotent.

The emergence of these images makes it clear that the adolescent occupies a peculiarly intense place in American thought and feeling.[2] As prophet and victim, he joins and replaces the child-innocent who once played these roles exclusively. As victimizer, he is the carrier of the society's projections; sadistic and sexual motives are imputed to him, and he joins or replaces the gangster, the Negro, and other projective enemies. Nor is it only in our dark imaginings that these adolescent types hold so central a place. A good deal of recent social thought sees in the adolescent's character and situation the key to our moral and social pathology. Curiously, it is in their response to the adolescent that the social criticism of the Left is joined by the social criticism of the Right. Both see our youth as reflecting what is most ignoble and most portentous in our time.

I have stressed this mystique of adolescence because it has influenced both work and thought in the social sciences. The attention of social scientists has been captured by two conspicuous but atypical enclaves of adolescence, drawn from extreme and opposing ends of the social-class continuum, and representing exceptional solutions to the adolescent crisis. The victimizer corresponds, of course, to the delinquent. The visionary-victim corresponds—though this may not be apparent at first—to the sensitive, articulate, intense, intelligent type of upper-middle-class adolescent on whom the psychoanalytic theory of adolescence is almost exclusively based.

<hr />

[2] Yet this is not to say that these motifs have been restricted either to American thought, or to the representation of adolescence. The themes of saintliness and violence have been endemic in recent European writing as well, and have also figured in the depiction of postadolescent prototypes—for example, the Beats as "holy barbarians." An interesting variation is seen in the effort to fuse saintliness and violence, as in the writings of Jean Genet, Norman Mailer, and William Burroughs.

Now in most ways these two adolescent types could not be more dissimilar. The estranged lower-class youngster relies largely on alloplastic solutions to the adolescent crisis, living out mutely, in urgent yet aimless acts of violence or bravado, a sullen resentment against the middle-class world and its values. The estranged upper-middle-class youngster is largely autoplastic in response, subject to acute intrapsychic upheavals which are expressed in neurotic symptoms, affect storms, character eccentricities, and a general value ferment. Paradoxically, these two extremes are alike, and their alikeness is in being different from the normative adolescent—that is, the socially modal adolescent. The extremes are alike in showing an unusual degree of independence from the family; they are alike in disaffection, in acting out or thinking out a discontent with the social order; they are alike, above all, in their adoption of radical solutions to that key problem of adolescence, the task of ego-synthesis. I want to suggest that one cannot generalize these processes to the adolescent population at large. The adolescent at the extremes responds to the instinctual and psychosocial upheaval of puberty by disorder, by failures of ego-synthesis, by a tendency to abandon earlier values and object-attachments. In the normative response to adolescence, however, there is more commonly an avoidance of inner and outer conflict, premature identity consolidation, ego and ideological constriction, and a general unwillingness to take psychic risks.[3]

Now having stated my thesis, let me pause here to say something about its origins. These conclusions derive from a national survey of adolescent boys and girls.[4] A colleague and I studied, by means of a rather extensive semistructured interview, 3,000 youngsters, including about 1,000 boys between 14 and 16, and about 2,000 girls between 12 and 18. Let me say at once that we were very much aware of the limitations of this sort of interview; one must write questions suitable for the lowest common denominator, and the interview setting is one which maximizes cautious, shallow, and platitudinous responses. But we were, if anything, hypersensitive to these problems, and mined the questionnaire with a great number and variety of projective items. Thanks to IBM technology we were buried in data; but I want to bypass a discussion of specific findings and approach these interviews as personal documents, to consider them impressionistically, discursively, clinically. The great advantage of this kind of project is that it permits study of those adolescents who make up the middle majority, who evoke neither grief nor wonder, and who all too often escape notice. When one looks at the normative forms of the adolescent experience, one is led to think twice about the received version of adolescence.

[3] It should be clear that I am speaking here of institutionalized patterns, rather than voluntaristic "choices."

[4] A full report on this research, in co-authorship with Elizabeth Douvan, will be published shortly by John Wiley. A report on one aspect can be found in Douvan and Adelson, "The Psychodynamics of Social Mobility in Adolescent Boys," *Journal of Abnormal and Social Psychology*. (1958) 56:31–44.

Let me begin with the question of autonomy and conflict. Many writers take the position that at puberty the child is under great pressure to detach himself from the family emotionally, to find a pattern of disengagement. The instinctual revival brings with it a return of Oedipal dangers and temptations. The home is a hothouse and the youngster must discover a way out, a means of escaping his dependent status in the family, and even more urgently, the dimly recognized drives and feelings toward his parents. The psychosexual irritation pushes the child from home, leading him to negotiate or battle with the parents for greater freedom. The conflict of generations is joined. Theorists add to this the psychosocial pull of the child's need to be his own man, to forge an individual identity—those needs which draw him toward the future. These forces give the adolescent peer group its critical importance. Peer group and culture supplant the family as the locus of authority and the giver of norms. Through his immersion in the peer group, through the incorporation of peer ideals and values, the youngster gains the support he needs to win autonomy from the family. And the peer group provides a haven in which the delicate task of self-exploration and self-definition can be accomplished.[5]

This view of adolescence has a good deal to recommend it, but my reading of the interviews suggests that it needs revision in some important particulars. It exaggerates the degree of conflict between parent and child; it wrongly estimates the autonomy issue; and it misinterprets the role of the peer group. The normative adolescent tends to avoid overt conflict with his family. This is not to say that conflict is not present, but it is largely unconscious conflict—undersurface resentments which do not necessarily liberate or enlarge the personality, but which, paradoxically, increase the child's docility toward his parents. Even when one does find overt conflict one senses that it has an *as if* quality to it, that it is a kind of war game, with all the sights and sounds of battle but without any bloodshed. More often than not the conflicts center on trivia, on issues of taste—clothing, grooming, and the like. It can be argued that these issues are trivial only to the adult, that they are of great symbolic importance in the adolescent's quest for autonomy. True; but one can reply that parent and child play out an empty ritual of disaffection, that they agree to disagree only on token issues, on teen issues, and in doing so are able to sidestep any genuine encounter of differences.

Much the same is true of autonomy. There are autonomies and autonomies. The American adolescent asks for and is freely given an unusual degree of behavioral freedom—the right to come and go, to share in setting rules, and so on. But it is far more problematic whether he asks for or

<hr/>

[5] A full yet succinct review of this general position can be found in Leo Spiegel, "A Review of Contributions to a Psychoanalytic Theory of Adolescence: Individual Aspects," in *Psychoanalytic Study of the Child* 6:375–393; New York, Internat. Univ. Press, 1951.

achieves a high degree of emotional autonomy, and it is even more doubt-ful whether he manages much in the way of value autonomy. Indeed, the ease with which the adolescent acquires behavioral freedom may tend to interfere with the achievement of emotional and ideological freedom, for reasons I will mention in a moment. As to the peer group, its supposed functions—as an arena for the confrontation of the self, for the testing and trying out of identities—are present for many adolescents, but for many more the peer group is used for the learning and display of sociability and social skills. The peer culture is all too often a kind of playpen, designed to keep children out of harm's way and out of parents' hair. It may not work out this way; the children may begin throwing toys at each other, or —what is worse—may begin throwing them at the grownups in the living room. But generally it does work out just this way. The peer group, with its artificial amusements and excitements, more often than not acts to hinder differentiation and growth.

This is especially evident in the area of values and ideology. The traditional idea of the adolescent experience holds that the youngster be-comes involved in an intense concern with ethics, political ideology, reli-gious belief, and so on. The moral parochialism of early childhood was thought to be smashed by the moral fervor and incipient cosmopolitanism of adolescence. The youngster's need to detach himself from the family and its view of the moral and social order, his need to redo the egosuperego constellation, his need to find new and more appropriate ego ideals, his need to use ideology as a solution for instinctual problems—all these needs came together, so it was thought, to produce a value crisis somewhere in the course of the adolescent career. This pattern can be found in adoles-cence, but it is found in a bold, sometimes stubborn, often unhappy mi-nority. Our interviews confirm a mounting impression from other studies that American adolescents are on the whole not deeply involved in ideology, nor are they prepared to do much individual thinking on value issues of any generality. Why is this so? I would guess because to think anew and differ-ently endangers the adolescent's connection to the community—his object attachments—and complicates the task of ego synthesis.

Let me sum up in the language of personality theory. The inherent tensions of adolescence are displaced to and discharged within the matrix of peer-group sociability. Intrapsychically the defenses and character posi-tions adopted are those which curtail experience and limit the growth and differentiation of the self—repression, reaction-formation, and certain forms of ego restriction. These modes of dealing with inner and outer experience join to produce a pseudo-adaptive solution of the adolescent crisis, marked by cognitive stereotypy, value stasis, and interpersonal conformity. It is a solution which is accomplished by resisting conflict, resisting change, resisting the transformation of the self. It settles for a modest, sluggish resynthesis of the ego that closely follows the lines of the older organization of drives, defenses, values, and object-attachments. It is characterized by an avoidance of identity-diffusion through identity-coarctation.

One is left to wonder whether this form of adolescence is a new thing in this country, or whether Americans have always been falsely bemused by one or another mystique of adolescence. Of course we cannot know; if, as this paper has suggested, today's adults have egregiously misunderstood the adolescents they see before their very eyes, then it would be prudent, to say the least, to avoid generalizations about historically earlier patterns of adolescence. In all likelihood, the degree of tension and disorder has always been more apparent than real. It is always more likely that passion, defiance, and suffering will capture the fancy, and that the amiable, colorless forms of adaptation will be ignored.

And yet—and yet—one feels, nevertheless, that the contemporary modes of adolescence do involve something new, that Friedenberg,[6] among others, is correct in saying that adolescence is disappearing as the period during which the individual can achieve a decisive articulation of the self. If this is so—and granting how large an *if* this is—then perhaps one important reason that can be singled out is the extraordinary attenuation of today's adolescence. Given the long preparation required for advanced technical training, given the uselessness of the adolescent in the labor market, parent and child settle down for a long, long period of time during which the child will, in one way or another, remain a dependent being. Traditionally, adolescence has been the age in which the child readied himself to leave home; accounts of adolescence in the earlier part of this century often describe a decisive encounter between father and son, a decisive testing of wills, in which the son makes a determined bid for autonomy, either by leaving home, or threatening to do so, and meaning it. The adolescent then had little of the freedom he has today; he was kept under the parental thumb, but he used his captivity well, to strengthen himself for a real departure and a real autonomy. Nowadays the adolescent and his parents are both made captive by their mutual knowledge of the adolescent's dependency. They are locked in a room with no exit, and they make the best of it by an unconscious *quid pro quo,* in which the adolescent forfeits his adolescence, and instead becomes a teen-ager. He keeps the peace by muting his natural rebelliousness, through transforming it into structured and defined techniques for getting on people's nerves. The passions, the restlessness, the vivacity of adolescence are partly strangled, and partly drained off in the mixed childishness and false adulthood of the adolescent teen culture.

[6] Edgar Z. Friedenberg, *The Vanishing Adolescent;* Boston, Beacon, 1959.

5

Herbert A. Otto
Sarah T. Otto

A NEW PERSPECTIVE OF THE ADOLESCENT

Society, say Otto and Otto, has shaped a traumatized image of the teenager who proceeds to live up to the label. A new perspective of the adolescent is offered "as a means of regenerating the image of the teen-ager and as an opening wedge toward breaching the cultural conspiracy." In the new image, the adolescent is portrayed as clarifying and developing his identity, and making substantial progress in self-actualization. He is perceived as "a growth catalyst" who represents "the wave of the future."

In a society which is "image-conscious" the image of the adolescent has become succeedingly less favorable over the years. The words "adolescent" and "teenager" are increasingly associated with "juvenile delinquent" and "trouble-maker." The public media of communication have contributed materially to the shaping of a traumatized or deformed image of the teenager. To cite but one example which could be duplicated on a national scale many times: a recent dance in Salt Lake City attended by over 3,000 adolescents resulted in fights, which police estimated involved about sixty persons. Approximately two per cent of those attending were therefore involved in what the newspapers subsequently headlined as a "Full-Scale Teenage Riot." The (sometimes) unwitting but consistent shaping of a distorted image of the teenager by the media of communications raises a number of questions: (a) Does the distorted image of the teenager fostered by the public media affect the self-system and self-image of our young people? (b) Does the adult perception of the adolescent erect a barrier between him and the adult world? and (c) Does this barrier impede the development of both the adolescents' and adults' potential? A new perspective of the adolescent is long overdue.

As a part of the Human Potentialities Research Project at the University of Utah, a number of studies (Healy, 1965; Souba, 1965) have

From Herbert A. Otto and Sarah T. Otto, "A New Perspective of the Adolescent," [*Psychology in the Schools,* Vol. 4, No. 1 (1967), pp. 76–81.] Reprinted from *Psychology In The Schools,* 1967, *4,* 76–81.

been conducted to determine the nature of the adolescent's strengths and personality resources. One outcome of these studies was the gradual emergence of a new perspective of the adolescent.

The role of the adolescent in contemporary culture has been both misunderstood and distorted. *We can speak of a cultural conspiracy in the sense that major "culture carriers," the adults, appear to enter into a tacit agreement to stereotype and label the adolescent. The adolescent keeps his part of the agreement by conforming to the label.* A vicious cycle is thus set in motion. Our lack of understanding of what the adolescent *can* contribute denies him his true function in relation to society and social institutions. We have closed our eyes to the fact that the adolescent has a vital function in relation to our institutions. Equally important, by not understanding the essential nature of the adolescent's role, *the adult denies himself a substantial measure of growth which is possible through his relationship to the adolescent.*

The image of the teenager combined with the culture conspiracy operate to suppress the development of human potential both in the adolescent as well as the adult. The following New Perspective of the adolescent is suggested as a means of regenerating the image of the teenager and as an opening wedge toward breaching the cultural conspiracy.

The Adolescent Is Fully Engaged in the Process of Clarifying and Developing His Identity—He Issues the Challenge That Identity Formation Is a Life-Long Undertaking

There is a growing awareness in professional and lay circles that identity formation is an integral part of adult existence and does not cease until death. This process is often referred to as "the search for identity." It would be more correct to call it *"the ongoing development of identity."* This ongoing development of identity involves the searching out of latent and unrealized aspects and fragments of the self, thus bringing greater wholeness to the total self structure.

Closely related to this process is the concept of the open-self system. The open-self system is characterized by an attitude toward self and life which has the qualities of open-endedness and flexibility. Flexibility and being accessible to new ideas, new experiences, new viewpoints is an index to the individual's psychological health.

The measure of health is flexibility, the freedom to learn through experience, the freedom to change with changing internal and external circumstances, to be influenced by reasonable argument, admonitions, exhortation and the appeal to emotions; the freedom to respond appropriately to the stimulus of reward and punishment, and especially the freedom to cease when sated. The essence of normality is flexibility in all of these vital ways. The essence of illness is the freezing of behavior into unalterable and insatiable patterns (Kubie, 1958, pp. 20–21).

The self of the teenager particularly has the elements of an open-ended system. Many aspects of his functioning have not as yet become frozen and are highly labile. Much of what appears to be erratic functioning is actually *purposive and developmental,* a manifestation of the open-self system in an accelerated state of growth. If we accept the view that identity formation (the ongoing unfoldment of our uniquely individual abilities and powers) is a life-long process, *then the adolescent becomes the highly visible symbol of a challenge.* He challenges us to enter more fully into the searching out of that which is latent and unfulfilled; he challenges us to enter more fully into this process which brings wholeness to the structure of the self and which is a means of developing our identity.

As a part of developing his identity, the adolescent is engaged in an ongoing search for truth, for the meaning of life and death.[1] The adolescent is involved in searching out the meaning of existence. In contradistinction, for many adults the search for the meaning of existence is frozen into systems and certainties, *whereas it is the quality of search which lends vitality and joy to life.* The adolescent's quality of search can, for the adult, become a source of stimulation and inspiration.

The Adolescent Is at a Point of Major Impetus in Self-Actualization and Unfoldment—He Symbolizes the Human Potential Actively Committed to Self-Realization

Many well-known behavioral scientists (Gordon Allport, 1955; Carl Rogers, 1961; Abraham Maslow, 1964; Margaret Mead, 1966; and Gardner Murphy, 1958, to name only a few) subscribe to the hypothesis that the average healthy human being is functioning at a fraction of his potential. This recognition is not restricted to this country. There is a clear awareness by Russian scientists of the importance of the human potential. In an official publication of the U.S.S.R. dated November, 1964 reporting the work by Vasili Davydov of the Moscow Institute of Psychology, we find the following under the heading of "Inexhaustible Brain Potential":

The latest findings in anthropology, psychology, logic and physiology show that the potential of the human mind is very great indeed. "As soon as modern science gave us some understanding of the structure and work of the human brain, we were struck by its enormous reserve capacity," writes Yefremov.

[1] In 1954 suicide was the fifth-ranking cause of death in the age brackets fifteen to nineteen. By 1962 it was the third most common killer of youth.

(Ivan Yefremov, eminent Soviet scholar and writer) "Man, under average conditions of work and life, uses only a small part of his thinking equipment . . .

"If we were able to force our brain to work at only half its capacity, we could, without any difficulty whatever, learn 40 languages, memorize the Large Soviet Encyclopedia from cover to cover, and complete the required courses of dozens of colleges."

The statement is hardly an exaggeration. It is the generally accepted theoretical view of man's mental potentialities.

How can we tap this gigantic potential? It is a big and very complex problem with many ramifications. (*U.S.S.R.*, 1964, pp. 42–43.)

The recognition that healthy humanity is operating at 10 to 15 per cent of its potential represents the major challenge of this age. Yet very few people consciously select the development of their potential as a life goal and then systematically and planfully proceed to actualize this potential.

The adolescent is, for the most part, clearly aware that a great deal is potential within him and that the realization of this potential will determine the course of his future. He is at the same time instrumentally engaged in self-actualization and in becoming what he can be. He represents to everyone the human potential energetically engaged in self-realization, self-actualization and unfoldment.

The Adolescent Is a Growth Catalyst

The teenager extends an invitation to adults to participate in growth. If this invitation is accepted and the adult is able to open himself, the teenager by the quality of his being and the nature of his interaction can trigger growth in adults. Since the essence of his being is growth and *becoming,* the adolescent offers both a challenge and opportunity to grow with and through him.

If we grant that the matrix of interpersonal relationships is the major medium of personality growth and if we acknowledge that the multiple and complex relationships between family members are for both parents and children a means of development and fulfillment, then it becomes clear that what the adolescent brings to the family is of a high order of quality. He offers parents an opportunity to break established and restricted habit patterns, habitual modes of perception and habitual modes of relating. By the keen and discerning nature of his observations and the honesty of his confrontations ("Mother, you are often afraid of life," "Father, you are too much of a stick-in-the-mud.") he brings into existence a moment which can be grasped for insight and self-understanding—an opportunity to root out cherished yet destructive stereotypes one has about oneself.

The teenager in the home through the quality of his relationships presents to his parents the chance to regain the spontaneity, freshness and vitality so often buried beneath the cares and routines of adult existence. This, for the parents, usually comes at a time of life when it is most needed.

Unless the adult acquires the perspective or recognition that the adolescent functions as a catalyst, minimal change in the adult can be expected. *Outlook inevitably determines outcomes.* The very same principle also holds for the professional. His perceptions and emotional meanings (how he sees the adolescent and what he means to him) determine whether in the course of the professional relationship with the adolescent the professional will open himself to growth.

The adolescent by the nature of his qualities, his fundamental honesty, idealism and by virtue of his capacity to ask searching questions of life and experience creates multiple occasions for the examination, reassessment and regeneration of adult and familial values. Finally, the ideational flow or wealth of ideas of the adolescent (if allowed to proceed unimpeded) can lead to creative exchange and better communication between all family members. If understood and allowed to function in his natural role, the adolescent becomes a growth catalyst par excellence for parents and for the family as a whole.

The Adolescent Represents a Force for Social and Institutional Regeneration

It has long been recognized that the teenager is a very astute critic of our social and institutional structures and is able to ask penetrating questions and raise fundamental issues. Unfortunately, this ability has largely been dismissed as a manifestation of "rebellion" and "revolt against authority." This is the equivalent of throwing out the baby with the bath water.

The adolescent brings to the social scene an idealism, integrity and commitment to values which penetrate to the very heart of dysfunctional institutions and social structures. He contributes a fresh viewpoint and often shows a keen ability for organizational analysis. If an institution shows lack of soundness in its functioning, the teenager will not accept this as the status quo but will ask "Why?" and call for change and reform. Perhaps more than the adult, the teenager recognizes the extent to which personality is indebted for its functioning to the social structures and inputs which form its environment. *The rebellion of the adolescent against institutions may stem from an awareness that social disorganization is related to personal disorganization and that a healthy self demands a healthy society.*

The adolescent represents a vital resource which has never been adequately tapped for institutional regeneration and renewal. There appears to be a partial awareness that the adolescent *can* make a contribution toward our institutional structures. In recent times a growing number of mayors of municipalities (and even governors and legislative bodies of states) have voluntarily relinquished their offices for a day to teenagers. Many of these officials have found it profitable to listen to the comments and suggestions of teenagers following their "term" in office. In the process of institutional evaluation and renewal, the adolescent represents a much neglected resource: he can make a significant contribution as co-investigator and partner, in efforts directed toward the study, improvement and the regeneration of our institutions.

The Adolescent's Healthy Body Sense and Capacity for Sensory Awareness Is an Indicator of Individual Potential

The adolescent is noted for a *healthy narcissism,* a healthy pride in his growing, developing body. He is also noted for his ability to enjoy fully the sights, sounds and smells of the wonderful world which surrounds him. This heightened sensory awareness, *joie de vivre,* and life-affirmative outlook need not be restricted to the period of adolescence. There is every indication that adults whose physical systems suffer from lack of proper exercise (with a consequent dulling of sensory capacities) can regain healthy body tonicity and body sense and experience an increase in sensory function by entering into a regime of physical conditioning and sensory awareness training. For the adult, the regaining of a healthy body sense usually brings with it not only an increased enjoyment of life and living, but also increased energy, drive and interest—qualities for which the teenager is noted.

It has been a finding from the Human Potentialities Research Project (Otto, 1964) that the development of a healthy body sense via a physical conditioning regime appears to have a markedly positive affect on the self-image and self-concept as well as the self-confidence of adults. The adolescent through his healthy body sense and quality of sensory functioning, issues an invitation to the adult to regain a soundness of physical well-being, pride in the body and increased enjoyment of living which is the potential of every man and woman.

The Adolescent Represents the Wave of the Future

In many ways the adolescent is a cultural innovator. For example, the widespread acceptance by the adult world of the "new sound" and the plethora of new dances (the frug, the watusi) had their origin in an extended period of teenage enthusiasm and support of these forms of expression and communication. Certain styles of apparel and popular sports (surfing, for example) have first found favor with the teenager and then been adopted by the adult world. The innovative contribution of the adolescent to the cultural mainstream is much more pervasive than suspected—and largely ignored.

Ignoring the contribution of the adolescent is but another subtle manifestation of the conformity pressures which are exerted on youth with special care. Among the institutions our educational system plays a dominant role in delimiting the development of the individual's unique capacities. This fact is repeatedly rediscovered by investigators, most recently by Friedenberg's research (1963) which makes clear that "through pressures both direct and indirect the schools encourage or demand that the student relinquish his autonomy, sacrifice his personal desires and often reject his particular excellence on behalf of institutional and social considerations which themselves are often trivial." One step in the right direction is the recognition by some professionals that *adolescenthood* just as *adulthood* is a distinct entity rather than a period of transition. "As long as adolescence is conceptualized as an in-between stage, the adolescent has no status in his own right" (Maier, 1965). And we might add, we attach minimal worth and dignity to an in-between stage.

The adolescent symbolizes and is the wave of the future. The nature of his being and *the quality of his developing self* foreshadow the man of tomorrow. He is the citizen and leader of the years to come and should be the pride and hope of the generation which is moving into his shadows. The tragedy of this generation is that through its distorted view of the teenager it is both shaping him and inviting the anger and contempt which will be an inevitable harvest.

True understanding of the close *interrelationship between all members of the family called man must lead to the development of a new perspective of the teenager* which more accurately reflects his real function and contribution. The adolescent is the living symbol of man's unfolding possibilities —of the human potential actively engaged in the process of self-realization.

REFERENCES

Allport, G. W. *Becoming: basic considerations for a psychology of personality*. New Haven: Yale University Press, 1955.
Friedenberg, E. Z. *Coming of age in America*. New York: Random House, 1963.
Healy, S. L. Adolescent strengths: strength concepts of adolescents. Unpublished master's thesis, Graduate School of Social Work, University of Utah, 1965.

Kubie, L. S. *Neurotic distortion of the creative process.* Lawrence, Kansas: University of Kansas Press, Porter Lectures, Series 22, 1958.

Maier, H. W. Adolescenthood. *Social Casework,* 1965, *46,* 3–6.

Maslow, A. H. *Toward a psychology of being.* New York: Van Nostrand, 1962.

Mead, M. Culture and personality development: human capacities. In H. A. Otto (Ed.), *Explorations in human potentialities.* Springfield, Ill.: Charles C Thomas, 1966.

Murphy, G. *Human potentialities.* New York: Basic Books, 1958.

Otto, H. A. The personal and family strength research projects—some implications for the therapist. *Mental Hygiene,* 1964, *48,* 447–450.

Rogers, C. R. *On becoming a person.* Boston: Houghton Mifflin, 1961.

Souba, C. E. Revision of inventory of personal resources, form "A." Unpublished master's thesis, Graduate School of Social Work, University of Utah, 1965.

U.S.S.R., Soviet life today. Pedagogical quests, 1964 (Nov.), 42–45.

ADDITIONAL READINGS

Bittner, Guenther. The pedagogical and medical care of youth. *Adolescence,* Summer 1966, **1** (N 2) 112–125. The author states as his purpose "to define the image of youth as it appears in the medical literature and to suggest where it might be improved by consideration of sociological and educational aspects." Then he discusses how physicians and educators may, through "mutual speculation," help in the current crisis situation of youth.

Denney, Reuel. American youth today. In Erik H. Erikson (Ed.), *Youth: change and challenge.* New York: Basic Books, 1963. Pp. 131–160. Denney describes today's youth as being of various types, and relates their attitudes to current social factors. He sees the sex roles as converging, and the majority of adolescents as somewhat conventional. He suggests that current types of youth reflect the changing times.

Gladston, Richard. Adolescence and the function of self-consciousness. *Mental Hygiene,* April 1967, **51** (2), 164–168. The writer expands on the theme that the adolescent's most compelling task is the establishment of a sense of self-confidence in place of reliance upon parental faith. The key to understanding the many deviations in adolescents lies in self-consciousness.

Hess, Robert D. & Goldblatt, Irene. The status of adolescents in American

society: a problem in social identity. *Child Development,* 1957, **28**
459–468. The authors see adolescents' position in society as ambiguous.
Adolescents and adults rated both teen-agers and adults on a 7-point
scale. The data suggested that each group distrusts the other. Adolescents and their parents expressed mildly favorable opinions of adolescents, while the latter tended to idealize adults.

Hurlock, Elizabeth B. American adolescents today—a new species. *Adolescence,* Spring 1966, **1,** 71–79. Hurlock portrays American adolescents
of today as a new species, different from those of other times and other
places in the world. She sees them as knowledgeable and sophisticated,
but also as bored, unhappy, lazy, and neurotic. She analyzes some of
the factors accounting for this unhappy situation.

Naegele, Kasper D. Youth and society: some observations. *Daedalus,* 1962,
91 (1), 47–66. The author portrays adolescence as a stage in development and delineates various images of youth. He is concerned with the
relation between life cycles and changes in social patterns.

Preston, Caroline E. Self-perceptions among adolescents. *Psychology in the
Schools,* 1967, **IV** (3), 254–256. This investigation of the hypothesis that
there would be demonstrable differences in how adolescents perceived
themselves or their situations, depending on their current situations, was
confirmed for girls and to a lesser extent for boys. An important part of
the adolescent image is the way the adolescent perceives himself.

Rosenberg, M. *Society and the adolescent self-image.* Princeton, N.J.:
Princeton University Press, 1965. Rosenberg made an extensive study
of adolescent self-esteem and related it to achievement and interpersonal
skills. Adolescents with high and low self-esteem described themselves
somewhat differently.

III. The Significance of
Pubertal Rites

In our society, there is no single criterion or set of rituals for heralding the arrival of adulthood. True, in our upper classes the girl comes out, implicitly into the marriage market, at age eighteen. Also, we have certain religious rites, such as the Bar Mitzvah, and graduation exercises from school, which have connotations of progression toward maturity. Otherwise, progression from one age-stage to another is vague and ambiguous. It is unclear exactly when the child becomes an adolescent, and even more so when the adolescent becomes an adult. Tokens of maturity are varied, and individuals report having first perceived themselves as adults at widely different ages, and for widely varied reasons. One boy may consider himself a man at age 16 after his father dies. Another may feel like an adolescent at 21 because he still lives at home and is supported by his parents. Others recall having come to feel adult by degrees, with various events contributing to the progression: the first ownership of a car, the first date, or the first lipstick.

By contrast, in most primitive cultures attainment of adult status is related to pubescence; and graduation from childhood is achieved as the climax of initiation ceremonies involving traditional ordeals and rituals. These rites mark definite shifts in the social and economic status of the individual. All the procedures involved collectively encourage the attitudes required for the adult role, including conformity to property and sex rights, and assuming the particular role assigned by the established authority.

Various issues relate to such rites, for instance, what accounts for their near universality in primitive cultures, and their absence in modern society? What explains the differences in such rituals for the sexes? Many theories, varying widely, propose explanations of pubertal rites. In certain basically Freudian theories male rites are perceived as instrumental in loosening the son's oedipal ties to his mother, and reducing hostility toward his father. An alternative explanation, by Frank Young, interprets initiation ceremonies as a mechanism for maintaining the consensus among males. Thus, if boys did not undergo initiation, and if some were permitted to avoid it, the male definition of the male's situation would be weakened. Initiation becomes the first and perhaps the most memorable step in a continued participation in an organized system.[1]

[1] Frank W. Young, "The Function of Male Initiation Ceremonies: A Cross-Cultural Test of an Alternative Hypothesis," *American Journal of Sociology,* Vol. 67 (January 1962), pp. 379–394.

In certain cultures, a succession of rites mark the passage from youth to adulthood. This is the case among the Hopi: the transition from youth to adulthood is marked, not by a single crisis, as in the passage from childhood to adolescence, but by a series of crises involving adolescence and marriage ceremonies.[2] Typically, pubertal rites for boys are more complex and difficult than for girls; in some primitive cultures, rites for girls are absent altogether. The reasons for this differentiation are obscure. Perhaps males need some event of consequence to match the adolescent female's drama of menstruation. More likely, the concentration on boys indicates the greater importance attached to their growing up. Significantly, initiation ceremonies for the girl grow more complex and differentiated in cultures in which her economic functions are more important. Occasionally, as in some West African tribes, puberty rites exist for girls only.[3]

Another question is this: would such rituals assist our own youth, by institutionalizing their status; or would they prove dysfunctional? Perhaps in a society so complex, with so many subcultures, no single time or set of criteria for attaining adulthood would be appropriate. Youth expecting to fulfill more responsible roles may require a longer apprenticeship. Again, the farm boy may well be accorded a freedom which, if accorded the city youth, would expose him to forces he is unprepared to handle. Actually, we need more adequate study of how particular experiences in Western society hasten or retard attainment of maturity. Meantime, most studies of *rites de passage,* including the selections that follow, concern primitive tribes. Our first selection, by Burton and Whiting, is about male initiation rites, and is Freudian in flavor. Initially, the male child sleeps with his mother, developing strong dependency feelings which must somehow be broken. Otherwise, the boy's reliance on his mother and hostility toward his father would be disruptive to society. The pubertal rites are designed to pry him loose from infantile ties.

The second selection, by Judith Brown, concerns initiation rites of girls. She indicates how such rites vary with time and place. Recently, many new theories have developed on this topic, and she provides an insightful interpretation of the more significant views.

[2] Laura Thompson and Alice Joseph, *The Hopi Way* (Chicago: University of Chicago Press, 1944), pp. 55–64.
[3] P. Radin, *Primitive Religion: Its Nature and Origin* (New York: Viking, 1957).

6

Roger V. Burton
John W. M. Whiting

THE ABSENT FATHER AND CROSS-SEX IDENTITY[1]

As an infant, the individual is cared for and identifies with his mother. Beginning in childhood, however, he perceives his father's favored status. Male initiation rites at puberty sever this less acceptable female identification and reinforce his need for the male's higher status. Presumably, our society fosters little sex-identity conflict; hence, there is no need for initiation ceremonies.

In this paper, we shall present evidence on the effect of the father's position in the family as it relates to the growing child's learning by identification and to the development of his sex identity. This evidence consists first of a cross-cultural study done at the Laboratory of Human Development, Harvard University,[2] and second, a review of recent research in the United States and Europe, relevant to our theory of identification, on the effect of father absence in the household.

THE STATUS ENVY HYPOTHESIS

Before presenting this evidence, however, we would like to state our view on the process of identification and the development of identity. This view we would like to call the *status envy hypothesis*. This hypothesis may

From Roger V. Burton and John W. M. Whiting, "The Absent Father and Cross-Sex Identity," *Merrill-Palmer Quarterly of Behavior and Development*, Vol. 7, No. 2 (1961), pp. 85–95. Reprinted by permission.

[1] This paper is a shortened revision of the paper read at the symposium.

[2] The first portion of this paper constituting the theoretical formulation and supporting cross-cultural material is based on a presentation of the status envy hypothesis given by John W. M. Whiting at Tulane University as part of the Mona Bronsman Sheckman Lectures in Social Psychiatry, March 17–19, 1960. These lectures, called "Social Structure and Child Rearing: A Theory of Identification," provide a more extended presentation of this material and will be published as a monograph at a later date.

be summarily stated as follows: The process of identification consists of the covert practice of the role of an envied status. Identification consists of learning a role by rehearsal in fantasy or in play rather than by actual performance, and this rehearsal is motivated by envy of the incumbent of a privileged status.

Let us consider the mother-infant relationship in which the mother attempts to satisfy all of the infant's needs. According to our theory, if it were possible for the mother to supply everything the infant wanted, he would not identify with her as he already occupies the privileged status. Some learning does, of course, take place in such a complementary relationship. The child learns to give the proper signals when he wants something and to accept and consume it when it is offered. Furthermore, he learns to predict certain sequences of events determined by his mother's behavior. In other words, he has cognizance of his mother's role. Although this cognizance may provide some savings in later learning, if and when he is motivated to perform her role, we would like to distinguish cognizance of a complementary role from identification with its incumbent.

To clarify our view of the motivation leading to identification, we would like to introduce the concept of a resource. A resource is anything, material or nonmaterial, which somebody wants and over which someone else may have control. Resources include food, water, optimum temperature, freedom from pain, and the derived symbolic resources such as love, solace, power, information, and success. Were these resources inexhaustible, and equally and completely available to all, there would be no such thing as status envy and, by our hypothesis, no learning by identification. Such, however, is not the case. As part of the cultural rules of every society, there is a status system which gives privileged access to resources for some positions in the system and, at the same time, disbars other positions from controlling and consuming them.

Returning to our mother-child example: As soon as the mother withholds a resource from her child and, by virtue of her position in the family, either herself consumes it or gives it to someone else, the conditions for status envy obtain. Even during infancy in societies where an infant occupies the most privileged status, complete nurturance is practically impossible. No matter how much a mother might wish to be ever-loving, the exigencies of life are such that there are times when she must withhold some resource that the child wants.

This is particularly true during the process of socialization. By definition this process involves teaching the child to delay gratification and to defer to the rights of others. More specifically, socialization involves teaching the child the privileges and disabilities which characterize the social structure of his society.

We may now restate our major hypothesis: If there is a status that has privileged access to a desired resource, the incumbent or occupant of such a status will be envied by anyone whose status does not permit him the control of, and the right to use, the resource. Status envy is then a motivational component of status disability, and such motivation leads to learning by identification.

This view differs from some other theories of identification in that we hold that a completely satisfying complementary relation between two people will not lead to identification. By this hypothesis, a child maximally identifies with people who consume resources in his presence but do not give him any. He does not identify with the people he loves unless they withhold from him something he wants. Love alone will not produce identification. Thus, the status envy hypothesis advanced here makes identification with the aggressor just a special case, and the Oedipal situation is also simply a special case.

The actual process of learning by identification consists of the covert practice in fantasy or in play of the role of the envied status. So when the child wants to stay up late, for example, and his parents make him go to bed while they themselves stay up, the child says to himself, "I wish I were grown up. Perhaps if I acted as they do I would be grown up," and he goes to sleep rehearsing, in fantasy, grown-up behavior.

ATTRIBUTED, SUBJECTIVE, AND OPTATIVE IDENTITY

We would now like to present our views on another concept which we believe will be useful in distinguishing households with fathers absent from those with fathers present. This is the concept of identity.

In every society, statuses have names or labels. In our society, for example, there are familiar kinship statuses of mother, father, uncle, aunt, brother, sister; the age-determined statuses of infant, child, adolescent, adult, and aged; the occupational statuses of doctor, lawyer, clerk, workman, etc.; and, especially important to our thesis, the sex-determined statuses of male and female.

We would like to define a person's position or positions in the status system of this society as his identity. Furthermore, we would like to distinguish three kinds of identity: attributed, subjective, and optative. *Attributed identity* consists of the statuses assigned to a person by other members of his society. *Subjective identity* consists of the statuses a person sees himself as occupying. And finally, *optative identity* consists of those statuses a person wishes he could occupy but from which he is disbarred. It is this last kind of identity that is most important for this paper.

Obviously, one's optative identity derives from status envy, and nothing much would be added to our theory by introducing this concept if one's optative identity were always objective and realistic. The wish being father to the thought, however, this is frequently not the case, and people often feel "I am what I would like to be." In such a case, the subjective and optative identities merge and become discrepant with the attributed identity.

It is our thesis that the aim of socialization in any society is to produce an adult whose attributed, subjective, and optative identities are isomorphic: "I see myself as others see me, and I am what I want to be." It is further presumed, however, that such isomorphism can only be achieved by passing through a stage in which there is status disbarment, status envy, and thus a discrepancy between one's optative and attributed identities. That is, to become such an adult, a person must have been deprived of the privileged consumption of resources accorded only to adults. This disbarment results in his wanting to be a member of that class. When society then permits him to occupy this privileged status, there is agreement in what he wants to be, in what society says he is, and in what he sees himself to be.

CROSS-CULTURAL EVIDENCE

Having briefly presented our views on learning by identification and on identity, let us now turn to the consideration of some empirical data which may provide a test of these notions. The first such test will be cross-cultural. The independent variables are judgments as to the distribution of resources during infancy and during childhood. Specifically, social structure of a sample of societies was judged for the degree to which the father and adult males in general, or the mother and adult females in general, occupied privileged or equivalent statuses as perceived by the infant and later by the child. Arrangements in infancy lead to *primary identification;* whereas those in childhood lead to *secondary identification.*

It is our assumption, and this has been supported by a previous study (14), that sleeping arrangements provide the best index of status envy during infancy. The bed seems to be the center of a child's world during the first year or two of his life. This is where the resources of greatest value to him are given or withheld, and those who share this setting with him become the models for his first or primary identification.

In most societies the world over, an infant sleeps during the nursing period either in his mother's bed, or in a crib or cradle right next to it, and within easy reach. Of over 100 societies on which we have data on sleeping arrangements, the American middle class is unique in putting the baby to sleep in a room of his own.

For our purposes, the big difference lies in whether or not the father also sleeps with the mother. In a sample of 64 societies which we would like to report now, 36 of them have the pattern of the father and mother sleeping apart, and the infant thus has the exclusive attention of the mother at night. In the remaining 28 societies, the infant either shares his mother's bed with his father or in a few instances sleeps alone. According to our theory, these two arrangements should be profoundly different in their effect on the infant's first or primary identification.

In the exclusive mother-infant case, the mother should be seen as all-powerful, all-important, and, insofar as she sometimes withholds resources, the person to be envied; and we predict the infant will covertly practice her role, and this optative identity will be female. In societies where the father sleeps with the mother, quite a different picture obtains with respect to valued resources. In this instance, both parents give and withhold important resources. Under these conditions, therefore, we assume the envied status to be that of a parent of either sex. For the infant, the juxtaposition of privilege is seen as between self and adult, rather than between self and female.

Thus the male infant in societies with exclusive mother-child sleeping arrangements should have a primary cross-sex optative identity, whereas the boy reared in societies in which the father sleeps with the mother should have a primary adult optative identity.

After a child is weaned and becomes what Margaret Mead calls a yard child, conditions may change drastically from those of infancy. Privilege may now be defined by marital residence. Three major patterns emerge in our samples of societies: patrilocal, matrilocal, and equilocal.

In societies with patrilocal residence, a man will remain throughout his life in or near the house in which he was born, his wife or wives moving in from another village. In such societies, the domestic unit consists of a group of males closely related by blood, and a group of inmarrying and interloping females. Prestige and power are clearly vested in this group of men, and adult males are the ones to be envied.

Societies with matrilocal residence are a mirror image of the patrilocal case. Here the daughters stay at home and their husbands are the interlopers. In such societies, by contrast with the patrilocal, women occupy the privileged and envied statuses.

Equilocal societies are more familiar to us. Here a young husband and wife set up a household of their own apart from the parents of either, as is generally the case in our own society; or they may choose between, or alternate between, living with the wife's parents and the husband's parents. In this instance, residence does not automatically give advantage to either men or women, and sex identity is thus not an important issue.

Thus residence patterns may provide the conditions for the envy of males or the envy of females; or sex-determined statuses may be relatively unprivileged. This distribution of resources in the domestic unit provides the conditions for what we would like to call secondary identification.

SOME PRIMARY AND SECONDARY
OPTATIVE IDENTIFICATION COMBINATIONS

Although the two types of sleeping arrangements and three residence patterns yield six combinations of conditions for primary and secondary identification, we would like here to concentrate on only two of them in contrast to all others. These are, first, the societies which should produce the maximum conflict between primary and secondary optative sex identity: e.g., societies with both exclusive mother-infant sleeping arrangements, which should lead a boy initially to wish he were feminine, and patrilocal residence patterns, which should lead him subsequently and secondarily to want to be masculine. The other societies of interest to us are those which promote feminine identification, both initially and secondarily; that is, societies with both exclusive mother-child sleeping arrangements and matrilocal residence.

Having described our independent variables, let us now turn to the dependent variables which should be predicted by our theory from (a) maximum conflict in optative sex identity and (b) maximum feminine optative sex identity.

Initiation Hypothesis

In a previous study (14), male initiation rites at puberty were shown to be strongly associated with exclusive mother-child sleeping arrangements and a long post-partum sex taboo. Although cross-sex identification was mentioned in a footnote as a possible interpretation of these findings, the authors' major explanation was based on the assumption that these conditions exacerbated the Oedipal conflict, and that initiation rites were the symbolic expression of resolution of this conflict.

We now believe, and would like to present evidence, that the sex identity interpretation is the more valid and fruitful. We would like to present the cross-sex identity and initiation hypothesis explicitly as follows: In societies with maximum conflict in sex identity, e.g., where a boy initially sleeps exclusively with his mother and where the domestic unit is patrilocal and hence controlled by men, there will be initiation rites at puberty which function to resolve this conflict in identity.

This hypothesis suggests that the initiation rites serve psychologically to brainwash the primary feminine identity and to establish firmly the secondary male identity. The hazing, sleeplessness, tests of manhood, and painful genital operation, together with promise of high status—that of being a man if the tests are successfully passed—are indeed similar to the brain-washing techniques employed by the Communists. Indicating how traumatic these rites may be, one ethnographer (11) reports that boys returning home after initiation did not know their village or recognize their parents.

Native theory also supports our interpretation. In most societies with elaborate initiation rites at puberty, there are two terms labeling one's sex identity which are different from the ones with which we are familiar. One term refers to all women and uninitiated boys, whereas the other refers to initiated males only. In these societies, according to native theory, a male is born twice: once into the woman-child status, and then at puberty he symbolically dies and is reborn into the status of manhood.

Let us now turn to our data. In our sample of 64 societies, there were 13 in which there were elaborate initiation ceremonies with genital operations. All 13 of these had the exclusive mother-infant sleeping arrangements which we predicted would cause a primary feminine identification. Furthermore, 12 of these 13 had patrilocal residence which we predicted would produce the maximum conflict in identity and hence the need for an institution to help resolve this conflict. A chi-square test of the association is fantastically beyond chance. Expressed simply, 87½ per cent of the 64 societies fall in the cells predicted by our hypothesis.

But what of societies where the female status is seen as privileged both in infancy and childhood, where the infant sleeps exclusively with his mother and in childhood moves into a world controlled by his mother, his aunts, and his tyrannical maternal grandmother? Here our theory would predict that a man would have a strong optative feminine identity, and the society should provide him some means to act out, symbolically at least, the female role.

From the beginnings of ethnographic reporting, a strange custom has been described for various societies over the world. This custom consists of the husband going to bed and undergoing all the same taboos as his wife during the time she is in labor. This custom is known as the *couvade* and has long been a favorite example for undergraduate texts in anthropology to exemplify the curious customs of primitive peoples. As a test of our hypothesis, however, the couvade is most apt. What event more than childbirth defines that part of a woman's role that is uniquely feminine? It seems to us, at least, that when a man attempts to participate in the birth of his child by closely imitating the behavior of his wife, this should be a good index of his wish to act out the feminine role and thus symbolically to be in part a woman.

Our hypothesis is again strongly confirmed by the data. Of the 12 societies with couvade in our sample, 10 had exclusive mother-child sleeping arrangements and 9 had matrilocal residence. Again, the results are highly significant statistically. In this instance, 90 per cent of the cases fall in the predicted cells.

AMERICAN CULTURE EVIDENCE

Cross-cultural evidence thus seems to confirm the status envy hypothesis with respect to sex identity. Now let us turn to other studies done within our own cultural context which seem relevant and yet were not specifically designed with this theory in mind. A recent book by Rohrer and Edmonson, *The Eighth Generation*(8), seems especially significant. This study is a follow-up twenty years later of the people described in *Children of Bondage* by Davis and Dollard(2). The problems of identification and identity are stressed throughout, and the importance of what we have called primary feminine identification clearly presented.

The girls raised in the matriarchy, which coincides with our exclusive mother-infant case, are very likely to establish a matriarchal home of their own and to live with their mothers or very close to them. The boys from this kind of household also seem to conform to our theoretical expectations. If the boy finds that he falls under the dominance of older men when he leaves his house, in these cases a gang of older boys, he shows evidence of a sex role conflict in compulsive denial of anything feminine. Rohrer and Edmonson conclude that "the gang member rejects this femininity in every form, and he sees it in women and in effeminate men, in laws and morals and religion, in schools and occupational striving"(8, p. 163).

This compulsive masculine behavior is also described by Walter Miller(6) in his discussion of the "focal concerns" of the lower-class culture. He emphasizes that the "female-based" household and "serial monogamy" are characteristics of the "hard core" of this lower class and closely associated with delinquent gang behavior. He argues that delinquent acts function as means of resolving dominant motivational themes in the lower-class community, which he views as "long-established, distinctively patterned tradition with an integrity of its own—rather than a so-called 'delinquent subculture' which has arisen through conflict with middle class culture" (6, pp. 5–6).

In Miller's writings and in *The Eighth Generation* are descriptions of the requirements for gang membership, requirements which closely resemble the attributes of the initiation ceremonies of primitive societies, especially the "tests of manhood." Miller specifically relates the focal concern of "toughness" to conflict over sexual identity:

. . . Among its [toughness] most important components are physical prowess, evidenced both by demonstrated possession of strength and endurance and athletic skill; "masculinity," symbolized by a distinctive complex of acts and avoidances (bodily tattooing; absence of sentimentality; non-concern with "art," "literature," conceptualization of women as conquest objects, etc.); and bravery in the face of physical threat (6, p. 9).

The attributes of this male model are seen in the prototypical "private eye" of television: "hard, fearless, undemonstrative, skilled in physical combat," and irresistible as a Don Juan(6, p. 9). Behavior deviating from this stereotype is evidence of one's being a homosexual. Miller also attributes the genesis of this obsessive concern with masculinity to a cross-sex primary identification and considers the behavior a type of compulsive reaction formation. This interpretation is, of course, closely attuned to the status envy hypothesis we have described.

In their study of delinquency, the Gluecks report that more of the delinquent boys, as compared with the nondelinquents, came from homes "broken by desertion, separation, divorce, or death of one or both parents, many of the breaches occurring during the early childhood of the boys"(3, p. 280). They further indicate that the fathers of the delinquents tend to be irresponsible in family matters and to have far poorer work habits than the fathers of the nondelinquents. If many of these broken homes were actually exclusive mother-infant or female-based households, and it seems from most reports on the lower class that this is a fairly safe assumption, these results are consonant with Miller's interpretation that delinquent acts conform to the focal concerns of boys raised in the mother-child household.

Concentrating on the "good" boy in a high delinquency area, Reckless, Dinitz, and Murray(7), and more recently Scarpitti(9), found that the nondelinquent boy comes from an intact family which is quite stable. These boys also felt accepted by their parents and expressed acceptance of them. These relationships with their parents were markedly different from those of a group of boys being held in a detention home.

The studies we have just considered found family structure an important factor in the early lives of the subjects. This relationship was found as a result of the analyses of the data which the investigators had gathered in order to study the culture as a whole or with special focus on delinquency. Let us now turn to some investigations which have the presence or absence of the father as the selected variable for study.

FATHER ABSENCE AND PRESENCE

The draft at the beginning of World War II made possible several studies comparing middle-class children from father-absent homes with those from father-present households(1, 10, 12). These studies indicated that boys from father-absent households behaved like girls both in fantasy behavior and overt behavior, especially with respect to producing very little aggression. Investigating the effect on the child of the father's return, Stolz(12) found that boys whose fathers had been absent but were then returned, continued to be effeminate in overt behavior, but there was a marked change in their fantasy behavior. This group now produced the maximum amount of aggression in fantasy. These conditions of father absence for the initial years and then control by an adult man are the conditions we have indicated should produce conflict over sexual identification.

The influence of father absence on the child has also been studied in Norway(4, 5, 13). The families of sailors were compared with other families of the same social class in which the fathers were present. The absence of these fathers often extended for two or more years. The results showed the wives of the sailors were more isolated from social contacts, more overprotective, and more concerned with obedience rather than happiness and self-realization for their children than were the nuclear household mothers, i.e., mothers whose husbands were not away from the household. The boys of the sailor families tended to be infantile and dependent and to manifest conflict over identification through compensatory or overly masculine behavior as compared with the father-present boys.

These data are suggestive for our theory, but we would also be interested in what happens to those boys later on. It would be interesting to know whether or not these boys themselves tend to become sailors, an occupation which would be suitable for a man who places a high value on obedience and also permits a man to perform acts of the female role in cleaning his quarters, sewing, etc., that are necessary on an extended sea voyage. The age of their first voyage and a description of the treatment accorded them as novitiate seamen would be pertinent. We would not be surprised, according to our theory, if these boys from sailor households themselves became sailors, made their first voyage during adolescence, and underwent a rather severe initiation ceremony on their first trip.

These studies, then, seem generally consistent with our cross-cultural findings in that the absence of the father produces in the boy cross-sex identification which is either acted out or, more usually, defended against by exaggerated masculine behavior. Although the conditions differentiating primary and secondary identification are not as clearly specified in these studies as in the cross-cultural study, it does seem clear that the gang is an institution with a function similar to that of initiation, and that at least certain types of delinquent behavior are equivalent to the tests of manhood in those societies with conflict in sex identity.

Further Research

Although the general effect of father absence seems evident, the details of the process are not. For example, are there critical periods when the absence of a father is more crucial than other times? How long does it take for a child to establish identity? What are the relative effects of a weak father and an absent father? What is the effect of the absent father on the development of a girl?

Some of these details are being investigated at the Laboratory of Human Development at Harvard University, and others at the National Institutes of Health at Bethesda, Maryland, but these studies are not far enough along to warrant reporting here. It seems to us, however, that the effect of the household structure on the process of identification provides a very fruitful area for research.

REFERENCES

1. Bach, G. R. Father-fantasies and father-typing in father-separated children. *Child Develpm.*, 1946, **17**, 63–79.
2. Davis, A. and Dollard, J. *Children of bondage.* Washington: American Council on Education, 1941.
3. Glueck, S. and Glueck, Eleanor T. *Unraveling juvenile delinquency.* New York: Commonwealth Fund, 1950.
4. Grønseth, E. The impact of father absence in sailor families upon the personality structure and social adjustment of adult sailor sons. Part I. In N. Anderson (Ed.), *Studies of the family.* Vol. 2. Gottingen: Vandenhoeck and Ruprecht, 1957. Pp. 97–114.
5. Lynn, D. B. and Sawrey, W. L. The effects of father-absence on Norwegian boys and girls. *J. abnorm. soc. Psychol.*, 1959, **59**, 258–262.
6. Miller, W. B. Lower class culture as a generating milieu of gang delinquency. *J. soc. Issues,* 1958, **14**(3), 5–19.
7. Reckless, W. C.. Dinitz, S. and Murray, Ellen. Self concept as an insulator against delinquency. *Amer. sociol. Rev.*, 1956, **21**, 744–746.
8. Rohrer, J. H. and Edmonson, M. S. *The eighth generation.* New York: Harper and Bros., 1960.
9. Scarpitti, F. R., Murray, Ellen, Dinitz, S. and Reckless, W. C. The "good" boy in a high delinquency area: four years later. *Amer. sociol. Rev.*, 1960, **25**, 555–558.
10. Sears, Pauline S. Doll play aggression in normal young children: influence of sex, age, sibling status, father's absence. *Psychol. Monogr.*, 1951, **65**, No. 6 (Whole No. 323).
11. Staub, J. Beitrage zur Kenntais der Materiellen Kultur der Mendi in der Sierra Leone (Contributions to a Knowledge of the Material Culture of the Mende in Sierra Leone) Solothurni Buchdruckerei Vogt-Schild, 1936, p. 61. Translated for the Human Relations Area Files by Cecil Wood.
12. Stolz, Lois M. *Father relations of warborn children.* Palo Alto: Stanford Univer. Press, 1954.
13. Tiller, P. O. Father absence and personality development of children in sailor families: a preliminary research report. Part II. In N. Anderson

(Ed.), *Studies of the family*. Vol. 2. Gottingen: Vandenhoeck and Ruprecht, 1957. Pp. 115–137.

14. Whiting, J. W. M., Kluckhohn, R. and Anthony, A. The function of male initiation ceremonies at puberty. In Eleanor E. Maccoby, T. M. Newcomb and E. L. Hartley (Eds.), *Readings in social psychology*. New York: Holt, 1958. Pp. 359–370.

7

Judith K. Brown

FEMALE INITIATION RITES: A REVIEW
OF THE CURRENT LITERATURE[1]

In this article prepared especially for this volume, Dr. Brown, one of the foremost authorities on female initiation rites, takes a critical look at major theories relevant to the topic and indicates the major sources of controversy. The author says female rites are not merely pale reflections of male pubertal rites, but reflect customs of the particular societies involved. Where such customs are missing, as in our country and Samoa, female initiation rites simply do not exist.

Travellers and missionaries offered accounts of initiation ceremonies among the far-flung tribal societies of the world long before anthropology, the scientific study of man and his works, was born. These rites seemed inexplicable and exotic because analogous observances in our own Western tradition were absent. Descriptions of the initiation of girls, plucked out of context, were utilized by "butterfly collectors" of human behavior such as Frazer, Crawley and Ploss.[2] Early in this century, Van Gennep (1909), in a work which is still highly regarded,[3] attempted to fit all initiation rites into a general theoretical framework. His book represents the beginning of the scientific study of the initiation of girls. Somewhat later there were descriptive distributional studies like those of Du Bois (1932) and Driver (1941), which were followed by more psychoanalytically oriented words like those of Bonaparte (1950) and Bettelheim (1954).[4]

The present paper offers a review of the current literature dealing with the initiation of girls. It will begin with a brief resumé of the controversy which has developed in the literature dealing with the male initiation rites.

[1] I am indebted to the Radcliffe Institute for the generous support which has made this research possible. I would like to thank Paul Shankman for his helpful comments on portions of the manuscript.

[2] An extensive review of the literature dealing with initiation rites is contained in Brown (1962).

[3] An explication and elaboration of Van Gennep's ideas may be found in Gluckman (1962).

[4] Bettelheim's (1954) basic thesis that genital mutilations are motivated by the unconscious desire for the genitals of the opposite sex was not well substantiated. A recent article by Singer and Desole (1967) suggests that envy of the bifid penis of the kangaroo may underlie certain Australian male genital mutilations.

The initiation of boys has always received more scholarly attention than the initiation of girls. This is because male ceremonies have been more fully described in the ethnographic literature, and because such ceremonies are often more dramatic than female rites. The latter are by no means always a mere pale reflection of those celebrated for boys, as some writers have maintained. However, theories concerning female rites are often simply a by-product of theories dealing with male rites.

The volume of speculation and theory concerning initiation ceremonies increased sharply after the publication, in 1958, of Whiting, Kluckhohn and Anthony's article "The Function of Male Initiation Ceremonies at Puberty." This paper proved to be a seminal influence partly because of the explanation that it offered, and partly because of the method used to substantiate it. The initiation rites for boys celebrated in certain societies, were seen by these writers as the solution to psychological problems inherent in certain customs related to child rearing. A mother-child household and a long post-partum sex taboo—both customary in certain societies —result in unusually strong emotional dependence of the boy upon the mother, and the attendant hostility to the father. At adolescence incestuous approaches to the mother and open rivalry with the father are potentially disruptive. They are counteracted by rites that subject the youth to painful hazing, isolation from women, trials of manliness and genital operations. The authors were able to explain the absence of such rites in societies like ours by absence of the child-rearing conditions which exacerbate the Oedipal conflict.

To test their hypothesis, Whiting, Kluckhohn and Anthony used the so-called cross-cultural method (see Whiting, 1968). Briefly, the method involves the use of a large sample of preliterate, peasant and industrial societies, each rated for the relevant variables on the basis of ethnographic accounts. An attempt is made to select societies representing different linguistic groups as well as widely separated geographical areas within each of the six major culture areas of the world: Africa, Circum-Mediterranean, Eastern Eurasia, Island Pacific, North America and South America. This is done to obtain a sample of cases as independent as possible in spite of the ever-present contaminating historical factors of diffusion and common origin. The rated variables are coded, and an attempt is made to see if the relationships among the variables are those that might arise by chance alone, or if they achieve statistical significance.

The paper by Whiting, Kluckhohn and Anthony has generated a host of criticisms and alternate theories. Norbeck, Walker and Cohen attempted to replicate the ratings on a small sub-sample. They pronounced the ratings unreliable, and felt that distortion had been introduced by removing information from its ethnographic context. Young (1962, 1965) rejected the psychological explanations of essentially anthropological phenomena. His alternative explanation and that of Cohen (1964a, 1964b) will be considered below. Whiting, Kluckhohn and Anthony's original hypothesis received some modification in an overly brief article by Burton and Whiting (1961). The emphasis was shifted from Oedipal strivings to sex identity conflict.[5] A subsequent paper by Whiting, "Effects of Climate upon Certain Cultural Practices," (1964) presents an elaborate version of the Whiting hypothesis, and a rebuttal to Young. Whiting's conclusions are as follows:

> In summary, some ecological reasons for the biased geographical distribution of circumcision rites have been presented. Starting with the findings of former research that exclusive mother-infant sleeping arrangements, a long postpartum sex taboo, and patrilocal residence are associated with circumcision rites, it has been shown: 1. that exclusive sleeping arrangements are influenced by winter temperature . . . ; 2. that a long postpartum sex taboo is influenced by protein deficiency which, in turn, is related to rainy tropical climates . . . ; and 3. that patrilocal residence is associated with polygyny which is, in turn, associated with a long postpartum sex taboo . . . the above associations are for the most part statistically significant . . . (Whiting, 1964: 523)

In answer to the critics of his methodology, Whiting includes not only a table of ratings on which the findings are based, but also excerpts from the ethnographic reports from which the ratings were made.

The controversy has not yet ended. Cohen (1966a) has published another criticism, and more recently Ember (1967) has suggested still another alternative explanation. According to Ember, male initiation rites and their antecedents are all related to the variable "internal warfare," which he defines as "fighting between communities that belong to the same language group, such fighting occurring at least every one or two years" (Ember, 1967: 3). Koch (1968) has suggested a possible synthesis of the Whiting, Young and Cohen hypotheses, which he views as complementary rather than conflicting.

The most interesting recent criticism of the Whiting, Young and Cohen studies has been made by Shankman (1966). He has noted that these authors rely on a method which looks at synchronic correlations, from which, according to Shankman, a sequence leading to initiation rites is inferred. He suggests that it is illogical to use these methods to explain the origin, persistence or change in the rites, because the way in which institutions develop cannot necessarily be deduced from what they are at present. According to Shankman, the conditions specified by Whiting, Young and Cohen should have a bearing on actual historical events. Shankman tests their theories on historical case material dealing with the adoption of male genital mutilations by certain Australian tribes, and finds none of the theories relevant. Shankman's paper is provocative because of the

---

[5] This concept is fully explained in Whiting (1960), and has received interesting application by Beatrice Whiting (1965).

tests he suggests for hypotheses previously substantiated by the cross-cultural method and because of the unusual case material he supplies. Although his paper deals with rites for males, it is relevant for studies dealing with rites for females. No historical case material dealing with the adoption of female initiation rites exists. However, the gradual modification or abandonment of initiation ceremonies for girls after prolonged Western contact has been reported. A diachronic analysis of such cases might be instructive.

Whiting himself has not published on the subject of female initiation rites;[6] however Brown, in "A Cross Cultural Study of Female Initiation Rites" (1963) offers hypotheses and uses a method which leans heavily on Whiting's works. Her definition of an initiation is as follows:

. . . it contains one or more prescribed ceremonial events, mandatory for all the girls of a given society, and celebrated between their eighth and twentieth years. The rite may be a cultural elaboration of menarche, but it should not include betrothal or marriage customs . . . A rite which meets the above specifications is not excluded if it happens to be celebrated for both sexes . . . (Brown, 1963: 838)

Brown suggests that those ceremonies which meet her definition are not all similar in character:

There are differences from society to society in the actual practices: sometimes the initiate is isolated, sometimes she is the center of attention; sometimes she feasts, sometimes she fasts. There are differences in the sanctions that apply to these practices: some threaten terrible consequences, some promise great benefits. And there are differences in the elaborateness of the ceremonies: some take years to complete and require extensive preparation; others are brief and performed without much to-do. (Brown, 1963: 842)

Due to the diversity of the ceremonies, no one ethnographic account can be singled out as representative, nor can a composite description be drawn with any accuracy. However, the following account by Powdermaker (1933) of an initiation in Lesu, New Ireland, provides an illustration of a fairly typical rite:

Tsuros has her first menses, and the news spreads eagerly through the village. It is talked about as a great event. Immediately bananas are brought by the women of both moieties and buried in the sand by the men, in preparation for the feast which will soon be held.

There is no seclusion for the girl during this period of her first menses, at the end of which is her ritual washing. Just before sunrise she is washed in the sea by an old woman, who holds in her hand a branch of the tree *tsil*. The girl and the old woman stand in the rather shallow water just off the reef as

[6] However, he has published on the subject of menarcheal age (Whiting, 1965).

the old woman dips the leaves in the sea and then waves them over the girl, touching the various parts of her body with the wet leaves. As she does so she says the following spell:

> Leaf, leaf, I wash her,
> Soon her breasts will develop,
> I take away sickness of blood.

Then the leaves are mixed with white lime and rubbed all over the body of the girl by the same old woman, and after that she paints the girl's hair red . . . Should the ritual washing of the girl not occur, it is thought that her breasts will not develop, and she would therefore lack the symbols of womanhood.

A feast is held on the day of the ritual washing. The village women of both moieties come, bringing their taro to the hamlet where the girl lives, and there they prepare it to be baked in the *liga*. The girl herself is present, but does not help in the preparations. (Powdermaker, 1933: 141–142)

Powdermaker continues with a description of the distribution of the food. A special song is sung. "Each group eats a little, and then loads the remainder in their baskets to carry home, where the whole family get their share." (Powdermaker, 1933: 142)

Brown's analysis of female initiation rites (1963) attempts to answer two major questions: first, why are these ceremonies celebrated in some societies but not in others; second, why are there such marked differences in the character of the rites which are observed? Brown suggests three hypotheses (each confirmed to a statistically significant degree) to answer these questions. First, the typical female initiation rite is celebrated in those societies in which the young girl is likely to remain in the same household unit with her mother even after marriage. The rite, according to Brown, emphasizes to the girl and to her family that she is now grown up. Such rites are unnecessary in those societies in which the young girl changes residence at marriage, either to live with her husband's kinsmen or to set up a new household unit with her husband. Since the latter condition, though rare among the societies of the world, is the usual one in our own society, the theory explains the absence of female initiation rites in the United States. Second, certain female rites, a few in number, but widely dispersed geographically, subject the initiate to extreme pain (usually in the form of a genital operation). According to Brown, these rites are an attempt to deal with the sex identity conflict. This concept, developed by Whiting (1960, Burton and Whiting, 1961) suggests that exclusive mother-child sleeping arrangements in infancy, followed by residence in a patrilocal society, steeps the child in a situation that is ambiguous for sex-role identification. In order to force the young on the threshold of adulthood to make the proper sex-role identification, these very dramatic and painful ceremonies are performed.[7] Finally Brown sees initiation rites as characteristic of those societies in which women make a sizable contribution to subsistence. The rites are celebrated in order to insure the initiate and those around her of her proficiency. A number of writers have emphasized the educative function of initiation rites, without explaining why some societies do not observe these ceremonies. In societies like our own, in which women's role in the economic organization is not crucial, such observances are unnecessary.

Brown's paper suggests that female initiation rites, far from being exotic customs inflicted upon adolescent girls in some societies, are to be understood as a response to specific cultural conditions which are absent in our own society. Two of these conditions, life-long residence in the domestic unit of the mother, and a considerable economic contribution by women, may be described as conditions which generally elevate the position of women. Of the former, Mead writes:

. . . we may speak of matrilocal society, in which house and land are owned by women and pass from mother to daughter, and husbands move in and move out. This system is . . . less compatible with the exercise of very much authority by the husband-fathers, who live under their mother-in-law's roof. (Mead, 1949: 301)

A large economic contribution by women can also result in high female status, when it coincides with feminine control of the economic organization of the tribe (Brown, 1969).

Brown's hypotheses gain added support because they are confirmed in the writings of anthropologists of varied nationality and theoretical persuasion. A posthumously published work by Schmidt, *Das Mutterrecht* (1955), deals with the initiation of girls within the framework of his *Kulturkreis* theory. According to Schmidt, such ceremonies are observed in societies characterized by *Mutterrecht,* a concept which includes elements of matrilineality, matrilocality and subsistence based on *Pflanzenkultur* [8] (i.e. horti-

[7] Brown noted that during the initiation rite of the Gusii (which involved a genital operation), the women's desire to be men was openly expressed, and the women indulged in masculine and other inappropriate behavior. Gluckman (1963) mentions cattle herding, a male activity, by women in the puberty ceremony of the Transkeian Thembu. Gluckman classes the latter as a "ritual of rebellion," which he defines as follows: . . . these ritual rebellions proceed within an established and sacred traditional system, in which there is dispute about particular distributions of power, and not about the structure of the system itself. This allows for instituted protest, and in complex ways renews the unity of the system. (Gluckman, 1963: 112) The masculine behavior by women during these initiation ceremonies can be interpreted both within the sex-identity conflict context, and within the rituals of rebellion context.

[8] Peuckert (1951) also notes a relationship between horticulture and initiation rites for girls. Although not specified in the ratings used by Brown to devise her scores, many of the societies that she scored as having a sizable contribution to subsistence made by women, are indeed horticultural.

culture, as opposed to *Ackerbau,* the cultivation of broadcast cereals in large fields). Although Schmidt's formulations are based on a very different theoretical and methodological orientation, with far less reliance on recent ethnographic materials published in English, they essentially accord with Brown's findings.

Basically similar conclusions are also suggested by Audrey Richards in *Chisungu* (1956), a work which takes its title from the female initiation rite of the Bemba of Northern Rhodesia. A portion of the book is devoted to an extensive description of the rite that Richards witnessed in 1931. She gives a detailed interpretation of this ceremony in terms of its expressed purposes, its relation to tribal dogma and values, the unconscious tensions and conflicts the rite expresses, and its pragmatic effect. Richards analyzes the ethnographic accounts of female initiation rites of other Bantu groups, but the information is far too scant to make comparisons with her own detailed interpretations possible. She writes:

> It is not possible to answer all the questions I asked as to the possible connections between chisungu rites on the one hand and matrilineal structure, marriage by service and uxorilocal residence on the other . . . . (Richards, 1956: 185)

Richards' term "uxorilocal" is used by the English school of social anthropology to indicate that the groom moves into the home of the bride's family at marriage. In other words, Richards also notes the relationship between female initiation rites and life-long residence by the girl in the domestic unit of her mother.

Gough (1955) offers a detailed description of the initiation of girls practiced by several groups on the Malabar Coast of India. Her interpretations are psychoanalytic, and it is difficult to predict their possible usefulness if applied to the few equally detailed accounts of girls' initiation rites elsewhere. According to Gough, the motivating forces behind the ceremonies she describes are a strong fear of incest and of defloration. The rite contains a symbolic defloration, and a pre-menarcheal mock menstruation seclusion because, Gough suggests, "this rite issues out of the marked horror of incest in these castes, which makes it necessary for natal kinsmen of a woman to renounce the rights in her mature sexuality before she is in fact mature" (Gough, 1955: 64). Because the virgin is unconsciously associated with the mother, who is also a forbidden sex object, defloration is an "unclean thing." However, Gough states that the natal kinsmen retain strong rights in the girl throughout life, and that the girl's residence after marriage is usually among these same kinsmen. Gough states that "this (initiation) rite marks a change in the etiquette of behaviour between a girl and her natal kinsmen" (Gough, 1955: 77). Although this is the focus of

Gough's interpretation, it marks a certain similarity to Brown's formulations.[9]

Eliade, who considers himself a historian of religion, has written extensively on the subject of initiation. He unwisely attempts a composite description of a female initiation rite, but he recognizes the purpose of the ceremony, stating, "It (the initiation of the girl) is a ceremonial announcement that the mystery has been accomplished. The girl is *shown* to be adult, that is, to be ready to assume the mode of being proper to woman." (Eliade, 1958: 43)

Two recent papers that deal with the ritual genital mutilation of girls deserve mention. That by Meinardus (1967) deals with clitoridectomy in Egypt, and offers no new interpretations of this practice. Another paper by Herrmann (1961) offers an explanation that is essentially akin to Whiting's sex-identity hypothesis. Herrmann views the genital mutilation of both sexes as *erzieherische psychotherapie* (educative psychotherapy), a ritual which helps to establish manliness in boys and womanliness in girls. To answer the important questions of why these rites occur where they do, and why they are absent in most societies, Herrmann invokes an explanation which is, in essence diffusionist. In summary, striking similarities occur in much of the current speculation concerning female initiation rites.

The next two works to be considered offer alternative explanations for female initiation rites. They differ in their definitions of these rites from that used by Brown, but like Brown, they use the cross-cultural method to substantiate their findings. Young's theory concerning initiation ceremonies represents a reaction against Whiting's "psychogenic explanation of cultural phenomena," and embodies a distrust of the interdisciplinary approach to the understanding of human behavior. The theory reserves "Anthropology for the Anthropologists." Young (1962, 1965) suggests that initiation rites are a device for status dramatization in those societies that practice sex-group solidarity. Although such sex-group solidarity for males is not infrequent, very few cases of community-wide female sex solidarity actually occur. Thus Young suggests that institutionalized household solidarity predicts female initiation. Such solidarity is indicated by the presence of female work groups organized around household tasks and by the presence of the focused or bounded household unit. Although Young does not apply any

[9] In a recent article, Rigby (1967) offers a detailed description and a sociological interpretation of the initiation of girls among the Gogo to Tanzania. He criticizes Gough's approach as follows, "By concentrating upon the psychic fears engendered by the internal structuring of kin groups, she neglects the importance of the 'external' relationships created or given potential by the rites" (Rigby, 1967: 442). Female initiation rites in Ugogo, according to Rigby, are neighborhood celebrations which emphasize the availability of the girls for marriage, and "relegate to less importance the interests and obligations of dispersed categories of kinsmen 'lineal' or otherwise" (1967: 440).

test statistic to his findings, the distribution of the numerical frequencies in his tables is not convincing. A curvilinear relationship occurs, which Young explains with difficulty, summarizing, "When a more sensitive measure of female solidarity is devised, it should reduce the variability of this relationship" (1965: 111).

Another cross-cultural study, that of Cohen, (1964b) contains a very complicated seven-point definition for initiation rites. The rites for both sexes are treated as a single phenomenon, a questionable procedure. In the opening sentence of this book, Cohen states the focus of his research:

> The goal of this book is to learn why there are two distinct notions of liability in the legal systems of different societies. (Cohen, 1964b: 11)

These two forms of liability are several and joint liability. Cohen continues:

> The specific ways in which different societies cope with the transition from childhood to adolescence will be examined because it is during this passage that a sense of responsibility, consonant with the goals of the society, is implanted in the growing child. . . . The ways in which the incest taboos are taught constitute one of the crucial modes by which a sense of responsibility is implanted within an individual during his transition from childhood to adolescence. (1964b: 11)

According to Cohen, joint liability is characteristic of those societies in which the larger kin group supplies emotional anchorage for the individual. In order to inculcate the latter, the child is brought up by the nuclear family *and* by members of the larger kin group. These societies practice "extrusion" (compelling the child to sleep away from his own family, in the home of a relative or in a special youth house), brother-sister avoidance and initiation ceremonies. The purpose of these practices is to make the child less dependent upon his nuclear family, and more dependent upon the larger kin group, by disrupting his emotional relations with the former. In those societies where the nuclear family supplies the emotional anchorage for the individual the child is brought up by his parents and non-members of a larger kin group. These societies will not practice extrusion, brother-sister avoidance nor initiation rites, and are characterized by several liability.

Cohen considers initiation rites as less significant for both the individual and for the society than the practices which precede them: extrusion and the observance of rules of brother-sister avoidance. These take place in what Cohen calls the first stage of puberty, a period marked by internal physiological change, which is not externally apparent. At this time the child is especially vulnerable, and Cohen considers extrusion and brother-sister avoidance far more shattering and impressive than the more "dramatic" ceremonies at the second stage of adolescence, when secondary sex characteristics appear. Cohen concludes, "fewer societies will take formal and explicit steps in connection with the second stage of puberty than with the first." (Cohen, 1964b: 113)

Cohen attempts to explain why this is so, but it is not entirely clear why initiation ceremonies are observed at all, as their purpose is the same as that of extrusion and brother-sister avoidance. Why do certain societies carry on this redundant custom, while other societies observe such customs only for the first stage of adolescence? Furthermore, Cohen's concept of joint liability needs some refinement in its application to women. Most of the instances in this custom which he cites apply to crimes by males. It is not clear why extrusion, brother avoidance and/or initiation rites to which girls are subjected should predict a custom which, from the cited evidence, pertains almost entirely to men. Cohen's theory is elaborate and interesting, and receives statistically significant support. However, his hypotheses are neither proven nor disproven due to the methodological inadequacies in his application of cross-cultural techniques.[10]

The present review has summarized a number of hypotheses concerning the initiation of girls. Brown's approach stresses the impact of these rites on the girl and those around her. Young and Cohen stress the relationship of the rites to other customs of the societies in which they take place. Both approaches leave a number of questions unanswered, as Shankman has pointed out. For example, one might ask if the observance of rites would alleviate the stress of girls' adolescence in our own society. In a brief article dealing with girls' adolescence, Margaret Mead (1958) points out that initiation rites are not observed among the Samoans nor among ourselves. In the former society, female adolescence is a period of tranquility, whereas among ourselves it is a period of strain. Among the Manus, where elaborate rites are held, the observances do not coincide with periods of stress and conflict in women's lives. Mead writes:

Most of the factors which complicate the lives of the adolescent: changing sex mores, the present economic system, the heterogeneity of American society, are hardly subject to manipulation by the most earnest social legislator or purveyor of panaceas. (Mead, 1958: 348)

[10] Although his theory is provocative, Cohen's lapses in sampling cannot, as he suggests (Cohen, 1964b: 202) be condoned. Drawn from all the major culture areas of the world, the sample over-represents the Island Pacific area. Societies supposedly representing all of Central and South America contain proportionately too many cases from the Carribean. The Circum-Mediterranean area is represented by only three cases, two of which are from Eastern Europe. Cohen has been cavalier about the possible contamination of his findings by diffusion. He does not seem to be cognizant of the fact that in all his major dichotomizations, all his Central and South American cases fall on only one side, while all his African cases but one fall on the other. His results might be interpreted as reflecting diffusion. Cohen does provide the reader with the ethnographic information on which his ratings are based, a fact which would make replication on a larger, more representative sample possible. Both Young and Cohen have restricted themselves almost entirely to ethnographic sources in English, a fact which is regrettable.

Further evidence for the inappropriateness of initiation ceremonies for our own society can be inferred from a composite description of those societies that observe such rites. Such a profile emerges from a recent study by Textor (1967). By means of a computer, Textor examined the interrelationships among many variables for which cross-cultural ratings were available. Although Textor warns against the uncritical use of the results, it is instructive to examine some of the variables that appear in relationship with female initiation rites. (Brown's ratings were used, but only 65 societies of her original sample were included.) Societies that observe these ceremonies are those in which social stratification is absent, occupational specialization is low, superordinate justice is absent, codified laws are unimportant or absent, individual rights in real property and rules for inheritance are absent, religious specialists are part-time rather than fulltime, and sorcery is important. Strong menstrual taboos and male initiation rites are also observed. These generalizations, when coupled with those of Brown, suggest that these rites have little to do with the pan-human physiological facts of female adolescence. The rites are part of a coherent cluster of customs, none of which are characteristic of our own society.

BIBLIOGRAPHY

Bettelheim, Bruno. *Symbolic wounds*. Glencoe, Ill.: The Free Press, 1954.

Bonaparte, Marie. Notes on excision. In Géza Róheim (Ed.), *Psychoanalysis and the social sciences*. Vol. II. New York: The International Universities Press, 1950.

Brown, Judith K. *A cross cultural study of female initiation rites*. Unpublished Doctoral Dissertation, Harvard Graduate School of Education, 1962.

Brown, Judith K. A cross cultural study of female initiation rites. *American Anthropologist*, 1963, **65**, 837–853.

Brown, Judith K. Economic organization and female status among the Iroquois. *Ethnohistory*, 1969, in press.

Burton, Roger and Whiting, John W. M. The absent father and cross-sex identity. *Merrill-Palmer Quarterly*, 1961, **7** (2), 85–95.

Cohen, Yehudi. The establishment of identity in a social nexus: the special case of initiation ceremonies and their relation to value and legal systems. *American Anthropologist*, 1964, **66**, 529–552. (a)

Cohen, Yehudi. *The Transition from Childhood to Adolescence: Cross Cultural Studies of Initiation Ceremonies, Legal Systems, and Incest Taboos*. Chicago: Aldine Publishing Co., 1964. (b) For review see Ember, 1965.

Cohen, Yehudi. On alternate views of the individual in culture-and-personality studies. *American Anthropologist*, 1966, **68**, (1), 355–361. (a)

Cohen, Yehudi. Review of Frank Young, 1965. *American Anthropologist*, 1966, **68**: 776–778. (b)

Driver, Harold. Culture element distributions: XVI. Girls' puberty rites in Western North America. *Anthropological Records*, 1941, **6** (2): 21–90. Berkeley and Los Angeles: University of California Press, 1941.

Du Bois, Cora. *Girls' adolescence observances in North America.* Unpublished Doctoral Dissertation, University of California, Berkeley, 1932.

Eliade, Mircea. *Birth and rebirth: the religious meanings of initiation in human culture.* Willard R. Trask (Trans.) New York: Harper & Row, 1958.

Ember, Melvin. Review of Yehudi Cohen, 1964b. *American Anthropologist,* 1945, **67**, 1039–1040.

Ember, Melvin. Still another interpretation of male initiation ceremonies. Paper presented at the 66th annual meeting of the American Anthropological Association, Washington, D.C., December, 1967.

Gennep, Arnold Van. *Les rites de passage.* Paris: Émile Nourry, 1909.

Gluckman, Max. Les rites de passage. In *Essays on the ritual of social relations.* Manchester: Manchester University Press, 1962. Pp. 1–52.

Gluckman, Max. Rituals of rebellion in South-East Africa. In *Order and rebellion in tribal Africa.* New York: The Free Press of Glencoe, 1963. Pp. 110–136.

Gough, E. K. Female initiation rites on the Malabar Coast. *The Journal of the Royal Anthropological Society of Great Britain and Ireland,* 1955, **85**, 45–80.

Herrmann, Ferdinand. Die Beschneidung: zur Frage ihrer Deutung. In *Beiträge zur Völkerforschung.* Veröffentlichungen des Museums für Völkerkunde zu Leipzig, Heft 11. Berlin: Akademie-Verlag, 1961. Pp. 243–253.

Koch, Klaus-Friedrich. Personal communication, 1968.

Mead, Margaret. *Male and female.* New York: William Morrow, 1949.

Mead, Margaret. Adolescence in primitive and in modern society. In Eleanor Maccoby, Theodore Newcomb and Eugene Hartley (Eds.), *Readings in social psychology.* (3rd ed.) New York: Henry Holt, 1958. Pp. 341–349.

Meinardus, Otto. Mythological, historical and sociological aspects of the practice of female circumcision among the Egyptians. *Acta Ethnographica Academiae Scientiarum Hungaricae,* 1967, **16**, 387–397.

Norbeck, Edward, Walker, Donald, and Cohen, Mimi. The interpretation of data: puberty rites. *American Anthropologist,* 1962, **64**, (3, Part 1), 463–485.

Peuckert, Will-Erich. *Geheim Kulte.* Heidelberg: Carl Pfeffer Verlag, 1951.

Powdermaker, Hortense. *Life in Lesu: the study of a Melanesian society in New Ireland.* New York: W. W. Norton, 1933.

Richards, Audrey. *Chisungu: a girl's initiation ceremony among the Bemba of Northern Rhodesia.* New York: Grove Press, 1956.

Rigby, Peter. The structural context of girls' puberty rites. *Man,* 1967; **2** (3), 434–444.

Schmidt S.V.D, Wilhelm. Dass mutterrecht. *Studia instituti anthropos.* Vol. 10. Vienna: Verlag der Missionsdruckerei St. Gabriel, 1955.

Shankman, Paul. Initiations and mutilations: esoteric and erotic. Mimeograph. Department of Social Relations, Harvard University, 1966.

Singer, Philip, Desole, Daniel. The Australian subincision ceremony reconsidered: vaginal envy or kangaroo bifid penis envy. *American Anthropologist,* 1967, **69**, 355–358.

Textor, Robert. *A Cross-Cultural Summary.* New Haven, Conn.: HRAF Press, 1967.

Whiting, Beatrice. Sex identity conflict and physical violence: a comparative study. *American Anthropologist*, 1965, **67** (6) Part II, 123–140. (Special publication)

Whiting, John W. M. Resource mediation and learning by identification. In Ira Iscoe & Harold Stevenson (Eds.), *Personality development in children*. Austin, Texas: University of Texas Press, 1960. Pp. 112–126.

Whiting, John W. M. Effects of climate on certain cultural practices. In Ward Goodenough (Ed.), *Explorations in cultural anthropology*. New York: Mc-Graw-Hill, 1964. Pp. 511–544.

Whiting, John W. M. Menarcheal age and infant stress in humans. In Frank Beach (Ed.), *Sex and Behavior*. New York: John Wiley, 1965. Pp. 221–233.

Whiting, John W. M. The cross-cultural method. In Gardner Lindzey (Ed.), *Handbook of Social Psychology*, 1968, in press.

Whiting, John W. M., Kluckhohn, Richard, & Anthony, Albert. The function of male initiation ceremonies at puberty. In Eleanor Maccoby, Theodore Newcomb, & Eugene Hartley (Eds.), *Readings in Social Psychology*. (3rd ed.) New York: Henry Holt, 1958. Pp. 359–370.

Young, Frank. The function of male initiation ceremonies: a cross-cultural test of an alternative hypothesis. *American Journal of Sociology*, 1962, **67** (4), 379–396.

Young, Frank. *Initiation ceremonies: a cross-cultural study of status dramatization*. Indianapolis: Bobbs-Merrill, 1965.

ADDITIONAL READINGS

Bettelheim, Bruno. *Symbolic wounds*. New York: The Free Press, 1954. Bettelheim's presentation is one of many attempts to explain pubertal rites from the psychoanalytic point of view. Basing his conclusions on observations of emotionally disturbed children and a small sampling of ethnographic literature, Bettelheim suggests that an unconscious desire for the genitals of the other sex explains rituals characterized by genital mutilation. He suggests that this desire is universal, but pubertal rites themselves are not.

Brown, Judith K. Adolescent initiation rites among preliterate peoples. In Robert E. Grinder (Ed.), *Studies in Adolescence*. New York: Macmillan, 1963. Pp. 75–85. The writer considers various hypotheses relating to the significance of adolescent initiation rites. She discusses the Oedipal complex, the stabilization of sex role, and sex identity conflict as possible explanations of pubertal rites.

Cohen, Yehudi A. The establishment of identity in a social nexus: the special case of initiation ceremonies and their relation in value and legal systems. *American Anthropologist,* June 1964, **66** (3) Part I, 529–552. The author first reviews the most important theories concerning the significance of pubertal rites, and then offers his own views: He proposes that initiation ceremonies "help to establish a sense of social-emotional anchorage for the growing individual." The establishment of this anchorage and of a sense of social-emotional identity and self-hood is effected through society's manipulations of the child's relationships with his family, as in pubertal rites.

Norbeck, Edward, Walker, Donald E., & Cohen, Mimi. The interpretation of data: puberty rites. *American Anthropologist,* June 1962, **44** (3) Part I. These researchers rejected the conclusions of Whiting, Kluckholn and Anthony (see reference below) after replicating their ratings on seven of the societies in the sample. They criticized the earlier study on various statistical grounds.

Whiting, J. W. M., Kluckhohn, R. C., & Anthony, A. The function of male initiation ceremonies at puberty. In Eleanor Maccoby, T. M. Newcomb & E. L. Hartley (Eds.), *Readings in social psychology.* New York: Holt, Rinehart and Winston, 1958. Pp. 359–370. The writers try to explain why some societies have male pubertal rites and others do not. They base their hypothesis on the psychoanalytic formulation of the Oedipus complex. Where the mother-son affectional bond is particularly strong, and the father-son rivalry acute, initiation rites are performed to forestall the son's incestuous approaches to his mother and aggressive acts toward his father.

Young, Frank W. The function of male initiation ceremonies: a cross-cultural test of an alternate hypothesis. *American Journal of Sociology,* January 1962, **97** (4), 379–396. Young interprets the concept of pubertal rites broadly, including such practices as tattooing, fasting, special taboos, tooth filing, and change of name. Young rejects the hypothesis that such rites are related to events in earlier life, and proposes that such ceremonies serve to stabilize the boy's sex role as he enters adult life. It is the presence of a high degree of male solidarity that best explains the initiation of adolescent boys.

IV. Early Versus Late Maturers

Considerable research has been directed toward determining what bearing early- or late-maturing has on adjustment. Both short-term and long-term studies concerning boys have fairly consistently reported negative effects of late maturing, and positive ones for early maturing. Jones and Bayley reported that early maturers are treated by adults as more mature.[1] As compared with late maturers, they have less need to strive for status. By contrast, late maturers manifest more undesirable compensatory behaviors, including greater activity and striving for attention. A follow-up study of the same group at about age 33 showed no substantial changes in these differentials.[2] Physical differences had tended to disappear, but personality differences remained much the same. Early maturers made higher scores on "good impression" and "socialization." The investigators concluded that for many boys late puberty is a handicap, and rarely offers special advantages. In our culture, early maturing provides boys with competitive status, but sometimes requires rapid reorientation to others' revised expectations of them. Similarly, Corboz's study of late maturing boys revealed "depression, social withdrawal, paranoid ideation, patterns of delinquent behavior, and sexual inadequacy." What difficulties were involved in negotiating a change in body image remain unknown.[3]

Since the negative effects of late-maturing boys are acknowledged, why not provide hormonal therapy to hasten maturation? Several arguments oppose such a plan: an adolescent may feel that his sexual endowment is artificial; or the rapid appearance of secondary sex characteristics may intensify incipient neurotic patterns. Actually, tentative findings suggest that such complications do not arise if therapy is made available at appropriate periods.[4]

Where females are concerned, effects of early or late maturing are more variable. One study found that early-maturing girls are more mature

[1] Mary Cover Jones and Nancy Bayley, "Physical Maturing Among Boys as Related to Behavior," *Journal of Educational Psychology*, Vol. 41 (1950), pp. 129–148.

[2] Mary Cover Jones, "The Later Careers of Boys Who Were Early- or Late-Maturing," *Child Development*, Vol. 28 (1957), pp 113–128.

[3] R. J. Corboz, "Psychological Aspects of Retarded Puberty," *Adolescence*, Vol. 1, No. 2 (Summer 1966), pp. 135–139.

[4] Robert S. Stempfel, "The Question of Sex-Hormone Therapy in Cases of Delayed Puberty," *Journal of Pediatrics*, Vol. 70, No. 6 (1967), pp. 1023–1024.

in personality.[5] However, Jones says the very early-maturing girl suffers disadvantages. She may feel physically conspicuous, and find breast development a handicap in active games. She acquires interest in boys, but boys her age are unreceptive. Nor is she prepared, in over-all maturity, to cope with older boys.[6]

The late-maturing girl has her troubles, too. She often possesses a negative self-concept, experiences social rejection, and difficulties in competitive athletics.[7] In sum, both early- and late-maturing girls experience special problems; however, on balance, early maturers seem less handicapped.

Despite a considerable amount of research on this topic, many questions remain to be answered. To what extent are problems of maturity biologically caused or socioculturally determined? What about less extreme degrees of early or late maturing? If boys profit from early maturing, does it follow that the boy who matures slightly early is more fortunate than one who matures slightly late, or at the average time? What accounts for the differences in research reported for girls and boys? What, if anything, may be done to assist individuals to adapt to advanced or late maturity? On the physical level, should efforts be made to determine the optimum age for puberty, and to induce or delay puberty, as the case suggests? What other assistance, either preventive or remedial, may be advised? For example, should experiences be arranged to increase the late maturer's feelings of independence and competence? Should early-maturing girls receive special counseling with sex problems?

By far, most research on this topic applies only to boys. However, our first selection, by Faust, relates age of maturing to girls. The second article, by Frisk, Tenhunen, Widholm, and Hortling, reports results consistent with the majority of studies. For both sexes, late maturing seemed disadvantageous, while early maturing proved helpful for boys, but often difficult for girls.

[5] C. P. Stone and R. G. Barker, "Aspects of Personality and Intelligence in Postmenarcheal and Premenarcheal Girls of the Same Chronological Ages," *Journal of Comparative Psychology,* Vol. 23 (1937), pp. 439–455.

[6] Harold E. Jones, *The Family in a Democratic Society.* In Anniversary Papers of the Community Service Society of New York, pp. 70–82.

[7] Paul Henry Mussen and Mary Cover Jones, "Self-Conceptions, Motivations, and Interpersonal Attitudes of Late- and Early-Maturing Boys," *Child Development,* Vol. 28 (1957), pp. 243–256.

8

Margaret Siler Faust * [1]

DEVELOPMENTAL MATURITY AS A DETERMINANT IN PRESTIGE OF ADOLESCENT GIRLS [2]

It has been clearly established that early maturity relates to prestige in boys; however, the relationship between early maturing and prestige for girls has been unclear. In this study, level of maturity was not a single factor constituting prestige but was an important part of a composite of factors affecting a girl's reputation.

The factors involved in gaining and maintaining prestige during adolescence are still obscure, despite the numerous investigations which have sought to define them. Of the physical characteristics which have been studied in relation to prestige, level of maturity consistently has been found to be significant for boys (6, 8, 10). It has been clearly established that early-maturing boys command an advantage in social relations, not only during adolescence (2, 10), but in the later years of life, as well (13). The gains in strength and physical ability which accompany puberty (6, 7, 15) provide an advantage for the early-maturing boy in at least one important avenue for gaining prestige, i.e., athletics (6, 17, 18).

For girls, however, the relation between developmental maturity and prestige is less evident and has not been clearly established. While early maturing provides no obvious prestige-gaining advantage for girls (such as competence in athletics brings for boys), it seems reasonable to expect that the rate and timing of physical changes at adolescence would have significant concomitants in the behavior and reputations of adolescent girls

Margaret Siler Faust, "Development Maturity as a Determinent in Prestige of Adolescent Girls," *Child Development,* Vol. 31 (1960), pp. 173–184. Reprinted by permission of The Society for Research in Child Development, Inc. Copyright 1960.

* 1100 Harvard, Claremont, California.
[1] At the Department of Child Study, Vassar College, 1959–1960.

[2] A paper reporting a portion of this research was presented at the 1957 meetings of the American Psychological Association. The paper and article are based upon a dissertation submitted in partial fulfillment of the Ph.D. requirements at Stanford University. The author is grateful to Dr. Lois Meek Stolz, chairman of this dissertation committee, for her continued interest and help in the research.

(4, 16). One means of determining whether early puberty, with its concomitants, is advantageous or deleterious to the social status of girls would be to analyze Guess Who reputations of adolescent girls in terms of the girls' level of physical development during adolescence.

It is the purpose of the present research to determine for girls whether developmental maturity is a determinant in prestige during adolescence. The study is an extension of Tryon's *Evaluations of Adolescent Personality by Adolescents* (17), in which she noted differences between 12-year-old and 15-year-old boys and girls in their evaluation of traits with respect to prestige. In the present study of adolescent girls four consecutive grades have been included in the analysis in order to see more clearly the relationship between developmental maturity and the evaluations of prestige and other traits during this phase of adolescence. The period from the sixth to the ninth grades is generally a time of rapid physical changes for girls, and it might be expected that developmental differences among girls would be systematically associated with certain trait scores of the Guess Who test. Some traits or reputations might be ascribed characteristically to the more mature rather than to the less mature girls. On the other hand, it is possible that, as the level of maturity of the girls changes from one grade to the next, their evaluations of traits and of developmental maturity may undergo progressive changes as well. In order to see more clearly the changing relationship between developmental maturity and the reputations of adolescent girls, the present analysis is undertaken for each grade separately. This may help to clarify the meaning which early and late development has for girls at various times during the adolescent period.

SUBJECTS

The subjects were 731 girls enrolled in the sixth, seventh, eighth, and ninth grades in a suburban school community.[3] Girls in the three upper grades attended junior high school, while the sixth graders attended various elementary schools, all of which were within the junior high school attendance area. The population represents roughly 96 per cent of the girls enrolled in the classes selected for the study.

PROCEDURE

The test used in this investigation was a duplication of the Guess Who test which Tryon (17) employed, with the addition of the following pair of items, which were designed to measure prestige:

[3] The author is deeply grateful to Supt. Norman O. Tallman and to school principals Messrs. Wood, Post, Niedermeyer, and Wise of the Montebello (California) Unified School District for their cooperation in this research.

Here is someone whom everyone thinks a lot of, who influences the group. What he (or she) says or does is important to the group.

Here is someone whom no one thinks much of; what he (or she) says or does matters little to the group.

The Guess Who test, comprised of 21 pairs of trait descriptions, was administered in the natural classroom setting to both boys and girls, although only the scores of the girls were analyzed for the present purpose.

Following Tryon's procedure, the sixth graders were instructed to mention on the test anyone within their classroom, while in the three junior high school grades the pupils were instructed to mention anyone within their whole grade.[4]

Scoring the Guess Who Test

For every girl the number of mentions received on the positive and the negative item of each trait pair was summed algebraically, following Tryon's procedure. A score of zero was assigned to anyone who was mentioned on neither item of a trait pair or who received an equal number of positive and negative mentions. Self-mentions were excluded.

For the sixth grade girls each score was expressed as a proportion of the number of mentions received relative to the number of possible mentions (girls in the class). This gave scores which were comparable among the seven sixth grade classes, which varied considerably in size.

Scoring Developmental Maturity

Developmental maturity was assessed by means of menarcheal age scores, the data for which were obtained by the school nurses for the sixth grade girls and by the women's physical education staff for the three junior high school grades. The data were obtained at a time when the girls were in a health class or physical education class separate from the boys, and when it would seem very natural for the staff to obtain such developmental data.

Subsequently, the girls were classified into four developmental groups. Girls who had not reached menarche were considered "Prepuberal," while girls who had reached menarche within a year of the time of testing were classified "Puberal." Girls who had reached menarche more than one year and less than three years prior to the testing were called "Postpuberal." All

[4] See Faust (3) for detailed description of administration, tabulation, and scoring procedures.

others were considered "Late Adolescent." The distribution of girls in each developmental group is given in Table 8–1 for the four grades.

Table 8–1   Classification into Developmental Groups

Grade	Prepuberal	Puberal	Postpuberal	Late Adolescent	Total
Sixth	96	29	5	0	130
Seventh	66	99	53	3	221
Eighth	17	45	104	27	193
Ninth	4	16	106	61	187
Total	183	189	268	91	731

Analysis of Data

Pearson product-moment correlations between *prestige* and each of the other Guess Who traits were computed for each of the four grades separately, and the findings are presented in Table 8–2. The close correspondence between Tryon's prestige-lending traits and the traits yielding the highest correlations with *prestige* by the present method is discussed elsewhere (3).

Before testing whether Guess Who scores were a function of developmental maturity, it was necessary to ascertain whether the various developmental groups within each grade were of comparable CA. Analysis of variance revealed that, at each grade, the developmentally more mature girls were significantly older than the less mature girls. Therefore, it became necessary to determine whether CA differences within a grade were related to Guess Who test scores. Twenty-one correlations between CA and Guess Who scores were computed for each grade. Of these 84 correlations, only one reached significance at the .05 level of confidence, and one is fewer than would be expected on a chance basis alone! Therefore it was unnecessary to use a covariance method of holding CA constant while analyzing the effect of developmental maturity upon Guess Who scores, since CA differences within a grade were found to be unrelated to trait scores. Thereupon, an analysis of variance (12, p. 261 ff.) was conducted for each grade to determine whether any given trait was more closely associated with one level of development than with another. Some developmental groups in certain grades were not large enough to warrant their inclusion in the statistical analysis (*see* Table 8–1). Table 8–3 shows the mean score of developmental groups on the Guess Who items upon which significant differences among the developmental groups were revealed by this analysis.

Table 8-2   Correlations Between Prestige and Other Guess Who Traits
Within Each Grade

	Sixth N = 130	Seventh N = 221	Eighth N = 193	Ninth N = 187
Restless	−.42**	−.31**	−.15*	−.12
Talkative	−.01	.08	.15*	.05
Active-games	.18*	.27**	.42**	.34**
Humor-jokes	.23**	.34**	.29**	.35**
Friendly	.68**	.73**	.68**	.68**
Leader	.48**	.46**	.67**	.63**
Fights	−.27**	−.15*	−.10	−.05
Assured-class	.43**	.33**	.55**	.34**
Daring	.47**	.39**	.41**	.50**
Tidy	.57**	.48**	.48**	.35**
Older friends	.20*	.17*	.27**	.05
Humor-self	.35**	.35**	.75**	.59**
Grown-up	.33**	.25**	.19**	.20**
Attention-getting	−.23**	−.09	−.18*	−.33**
Assured-adults	.57**	.41**	.45**	.48**
Popular	.68**	.80**	.93**	.82**
Happy	.43**	.62**	.67**	.58**
Good-looking	.65**	.42**	.42**	.54**
Enthusiastic	.65**	.56**	.67**	.61**
Bossy	.15	−.01	−.03	−.12

* Significant at .05 level.
** Significant at .01 level.

Table 8-3   Average Score for Individuals on Items Which Differentiated
Significantly Among the Developmental Groups

	Prepuberal	Puberal	Postpuberal	Late Adolescent	p
Grown-up					
Sixth	0.1	4.3	*	*	.05
Seventh	−1.1	0.4	1.2	*	.001
Eighth	−2.0	−1.1	0.5	2.2	.001
Ninth	*	−0.8	0.2	0.8	.01
Older Friends					
Seventh	0.0	0.8	1.4	*	.001
Eighth	−0.2	0.4	0.9	2.6	.001
Daring					
Ninth	*	−0.2	0.7	0.6	.01

*Group not large enough to be included in the analysis.

RESULTS

At every grade the more mature girls received progressively higher mean scores on the item *grown-up* than did their less mature classmates. Similarly, on the item *older friends* consistent differences among the developmental groups were observed at each grade, although only in the seventh and eighth grades did the differences reach statistical significance. While CA differences with a grade were unrelated to trait scores, developmental differences significantly affected the opinions which girls had of their peers on these traits.

On the other hand, the differences among developmental groups on the trait *daring* reached the .01 level in the ninth grade only. Since the differences on the trait *daring* were significant only in this grade and since they do not reflect a consistent trend in mean scores for the developmental groups, it is difficult to determine whether or not the differences might have resulted from chance alone.

Differences in mean scores among developmental groups were not great enough to reach significance on the other traits. However, the differences in mean scores for developmental groups on many of the items followed a consistent pattern within each grade. A consideration of the mean scores of developmental groups on the prestige-lending traits alone (*see* Table 8–2) suggests that level of development had some effect upon Guess Who evaluations. Considering only the item *prestige* and the items correlated significantly with *prestige,* it is apparent that one developmental group at each grade received more than a chance allotment of high scores on these favorable traits. At each grade the developmental group which received the highest mean score on *prestige* tended to receive high scores also on the items which correlated positively with *prestige* and to receive low scores on the items which were negatively correlated with *prestige* for that grade.

By means of the binomial test it was determined that at each grade one developmental group was attributed more of the prestige-related traits than was a likely occurrence on the basis of chance (*see* Table 8–4). For the three junior high school grades the most mature groups consistently received the highest mean scores on *prestige* and on items significantly correlated with it, such as *popular, friendly,* and *assured-adults.* While girls in the later stages of development were favored during the junior high school years, this was not the case for the sixth grade girls. Instead, the least mature girls, the prepuberal group, received favorable scores on most of the desirable traits in the sixth grade.

In the sixth grade a prepuberal girl is developmentally "in phase" with the majority of her classmates, and being at the prepuberal stage of development seems to be an asset in prestige in sixth grade. However, in the seventh grade the average girl is in the puberal group (*see* Table 8–1); yet

Table 8–4 Distribution of Favorable Scores on Prestige-Lending Traits
for Developmental Groups in Each Grade

Grade	No. of Traits Significantly Correlated with *Prestige*	Pre- puberal	Puberal	Post- puberal	Late Adolescent	p
Sixth	18	15	3	*	*	.003
Seventh	17	4	$3\frac{1}{2}$	$9\frac{1}{2}$	*	.035
Eighth	18	1	3	1	13	.00003
Ninth	15	*	$1\frac{1}{2}$	$5\frac{1}{2}$	8	.05

Note.—When two developmental groups received the same high mean score, each was given credit for one-half.

* Group not large enough to be included in the analysis.

the prestige-lending traits are most frequently ascribed to the postpuberal girls. In both eighth and ninth grades, when the average girl is in the postpuberal group, the desirable traits are most frequently ascribed to girls in the late adolescent group (four to six years beyond menarche).

DISCUSSION

A girl's level of physical maturity is not the only determinant in her scores on the Guess Who items, but, together with associated emotional, social, sexual, and personality changes, level of maturity does contribute significantly to the reputation which a girl has in her social group. Although puberal development contributes only a small amount of variance to the Guess Who trait scores, it does seem to contribute enough to give slight but consistent direction to the mean trait scores.

Adolescents' awareness of developmental differences is clearly revealed in their evaluations on certain Guess Who traits. While CA bore no significant relation to scores on the items *grown-up* and *older friends,* at every grade the more mature girls received progressively higher mean scores than did their less mature classmates on these items. Thus, developmental differences were more significant than CA differences in affecting these scores. It is evident that the more mature girls are taller, on the average (14), and that they appear more "grown-up" in terms of secondary sex characteristics (5). These associated factors of development may be the basis for the girls' evaluations on the trait *grown-up.* The possible relation of developmental maturity to the scores on *older friends* is likewise evident. For the more mature girls to seek out comparably mature girl friends of a higher grade in school is reasonable and is consistent with Jones' finding (9) that level of maturity is a factor in friendship selection. In addition, level of development is related to maturity of interests and activities (16), and common interests are known to be important in establishing friendships (1). The evaluations on the trait *older friends* may indicate, on the other hand, that the more mature girls are judged as having boy friends in a higher grade in school. Since the boys of a given grade mature later than the girls, the girls of advanced physical maturity may find satisfaction of their hetero-sexual interest in dating older boys. However, by ninth grade, associating with older friends is no longer judged as being prestige-lending ($r = .05$). Perhaps, as the discrepancy in physical maturity between boys and girls diminishes, the prestige-lending nature of dating older boys is concomitantly reduced to insignificance.

According to Jones and Bayley (10), the traits *grown-up* and *older friends* were two of the Guess Who items upon which the early- and the late-maturing boys received significantly different scores. Consistently on six testings throughout the adolescent period the group of late-maturing boys were seen as less "grown-up" and less likely to have "older friends" than were the early maturing boys. These findings correspond with those found here among the girls: *grown-up* and *older friends* were characteristic of the more mature girls at each grade.

Although the scores of physically immature boys and girls are similar on these two traits, their scores on the other Guess Who traits show a marked sex difference. Jones and Bayley (10) report that the late-maturing boys received above-average scores on *attention getting, restless, assured-class,* and *talkative,* while the evidence from the present study is that the less mature girls *in junior high school* were characterized by the traits *non-attention getting, quiet,* and *avoids fights.* According to Jones and Bayley, boys seem to defend themselves against the anxieties of late development by compensation for inferiority, expressed in attention-getting mannerisms. However, for girls the defense against immature physical status in junior high school seems to be more of a withdrawal and an attempt to be incon-spicuous in the group. Both of these patterns seem to represent a persever-ation of certain components of the respective, sex-appropriate, preadolescent pattern, which was prestige-lending for neither boys nor girls at this level.

The findings of this study suggest that for girls level of development is a factor in the assignment of traits during adolescence. Although the single trait *prestige* is not significantly associated with level of physical maturity, the high scores on this item are consistent with the pattern of high scores on the other desirable traits; i.e., one developmental group at each grade received more of the favorable scores than would be expected on a chance basis. When all of the prestige-lending traits of a given grade are considered as a whole, it appears that prestige is more likely to surround those in the sixth grade who are developmentally "in phase" (prepuberal), whereas during the junior high school years being ahead of the group developmentally seems to be an advantage. While prepuberal status may be hazardous for girls in junior high school, it is not considered "immature" nor undesirable in sixth grade. A prepuberal girl in sixth grade is developmentally "in phase" with the great majority of her classmates, while a prepuberal girl in ninth grade is a "developmental isolate." A girl's level of physical maturity is not only relative to the development of others in the class, but it is seen against a background of developmental differences within the whole school. Being at the prepuberal level of development seems to lend different qualities to the composite picture of an individual in elementary school than it does to one in the junior high school grades.

Although the evaluations of traits in relation to *prestige* were much the same for sixth and for seventh grade girls (rho = .90), the actual traits were attributed to a developmentally different group of girls. In the one year from sixth to seventh grade, the prestige-lending qualities shift from the prepuberal to the postpuberal girls, a developmental difference of two to three years. Moreover, in the eighth and ninth grades it is the late adolescent group, girls from four to six years beyond menarche, who are at the favored developmental level. This discontinuity between rate of developmental change and rate of change in prestige-lending evaluations suggests that a girl who is prepuberal in sixth grade cannot remain in the favored developmental position in junior high school, because her level of maturity cannot keep pace with the *rate* at which peer evaluations change with respect to developmental maturity.

This discontinuity suggests that for girls neither physical acceleration nor physical retardation is consistently advantageous. It is not until the junior high school years that the early-maturing girl "comes into her own" and reaps the benefit of her accelerated development. Until that time her precocious development is somewhat detrimental to her social status. The adjustments which inevitably must be made to losses and gains in status during the adolescent period (18) may be partly a function of this discontinuity in the relationship between developmental maturity and prestige during the adolescent period. Tryon alluded to this discontinuity and its significance when she described Case 29 (17), a girl who commanded prestige at 12 years of age, but who at age 14 or 15 was still developmentally immature. Tyron noted that in the ninth grade "she is now one of the very few little girls; she seemed like a child in the midst of adults with a group of girls; tended to avoid large mixed groups of boys and girls and their activities". . . . The emotional hazard of losing status during adolescence because of relative physical immaturity is not infrequently noted in case studies and observed in child guidance clinics. Contrariwise, as the findings of this study suggest, precocious physical maturity may possess its hazards, particularly in the period before entrance to junior high school.

After the transition to junior high school, girls begin to ascribe prestige to classmates who have been physically mature for a longer period of time and to girls whose interests and activities are undoubtedly more advanced. Perhaps these more mature girls satisfy a requirement for prestige in the group because of their "advanced standing" with respect to the new developmental tasks which the less mature girls are facing.

The significance of the present research is in its clarification of the changing relationship between developmental maturity and social prestige during adolescence. The findings of this study do not support Jones' assertion that "the very early maturing girl . . . is in many respects in a disadvantageous position" (8). From an unpublished study arising from the Adolescent Growth Study, Jones states that *"when we compared them* (italics the writer's) . . . we found that the early-maturing (girls) were below average in prestige, sociability, and leadership; below average in popularity; below average in cheerfulness, poise, and expressiveness." Perhaps the discrepancy between the present study and the one which Jones reports lies in the phrase "when we compared them," for it is apparent that the present findings for *sixth* grade girls are not unlike the H. Jones quotation. However, the present findings indicate that early-maturing is indeed advantageous in all three junior high school grades. By junior high school accelerated development has taken on a prestige-lending connotation. The favorable position of the early-developing girl is generally consistent with other of the California Growth Study findings, although not with the citation above of H. Jones. M. C. Jones and Mussen (11) report: "Although the differences were not consistent in all categories, the early-maturing girls tended to score more favorably than the slow-maturing on 'total adjustment,' and also on family adjustment and feelings of personal adequacy. These data from the self-report inventory seem to be generally consistent with the findings from the TAT". . . .

The findings of the present research point out the complex nature of variables which interact in producing a girl's reputation during adolescence. The data support the hypothesis by Jones and Mussen (11) that early and late development may mean different things at different times during adolescence. The discontinuity between rate of change in evaluations of prestige and rate of physical changes during adolescence means that, for girls, accelerated development is not a sustained asset throughout the adolescent period, as it is for boys. Accelerated development for girls is somewhat detrimental to prestige status before the junior high school years, while it places a girl in a very favorable social position throughout the junior high school years.

SUMMARY

The purpose of the present study was to ascertain for girls whether level of physical maturity is a determinant in prestige during adolescence. Tryon's Guess Who test, including an additional pair of items designed to measure prestige, was administered to 731 girls in the sixth, seventh, eighth, and ninth grades. Correlations between prestige and the other 20 traits were computed for each grade separately, and the correlations were tested for significance.

Level of physical maturity was assessed by means of menarcheal age scores, which were obtained by the school nurses for the sixth grade girls and by the women's physical education staff for the three junior high school grades. On the basis of the menarcheal age data girls at each grade were classified into four developmental groups.

In order to determine whether CA differences within a grade were related to Guess Who scores, correlations between CA and each of the 21 Guess Who traits were computed for each grade. No significant relation was found between CA differences within a grade and Guess Who trait scores.

An analysis of variance based upon developmental groups revealed that the developmentally more mature girls at each grade received significantly higher scores on the items *grown-up* and *older friends* than did their less mature classmates. Differences in mean scores among developmental groups were not great enough to reach significance on the other traits. However, one developmental group at each grade received the highest scores on more of the prestige-related traits than would be expected on the basis of chance. By means of the binomial test, it was determined that *prestige* and the significant prestige-related traits were more frequently ascribed to sixth grade girls who were developmentally "in phase" (pre-puberal), while in all three junior high school grades girls who were physically accelerated and were in the most mature developmental groups received more of the favorable reputation scores. Thus, for girls precocious physical development tends to be a detriment in prestige status during sixth grade, while it tends to become a decided asset during the three succeeding years.

The findings indicate that level of development is not a single factor in determining a girl's status in the group, but it is an important part of a composite of factors in creating a girl's reputation during adolescence. A discrepancy between rate of developmental change and rate of change in prestige-lending evaluations during adolescence was noted and was interpreted in terms of the different meanings which early and late development have for girls at different times during adolescence. After the transition to junior high school, the more favorable reputation scores were ascribed to the physically accelerated girls.

REFERENCES

1. Bonney, M. E. A sociometric study of the relationship of some factors to mutual friendships in the elementary, secondary, and college levels. *Sociometry,* 1946, 9, 21–47.

2. Bower, P. A. The relation of physical, mental, and personality factors to popularity in adolescent boys. Unpublished doctoral dissertation, Univer. of California, Berkeley, 1941.

3. Faust, Margaret S. Developmental maturity as a determinant in prestige of adolescent girls. Unpublished doctoral dissertation, Stanford Univer., 1957.

4. Frank, L. K. Personality development in adolescent girls. *Monogr. Soc. Res. Child Develpm.,* 1953, 16, No. 53.

5. Greulich, W. W. Physical changes in adolescence. *Yearb. nat. Soc. Stud. Educ.,* 1944, 43(I), 8–32.

6. Jones, H. E. *Development in adolescence.* New York: Appleton-Century-Crofts, 1943.

7. Jones, H. E. *Motor performance and growth.* Berkeley: Univer. of California Press, 1949.

8. Jones, H. E. Adolescence in our society. In *The family in a democratic society: anniversary papers of The Community Service Society of New York.* New York: Columbia Univer. Press, 1949. Pp. 70–82.

9. Jones, Mary C. Adolescent friendships. *Amer. Psychologist,* 1948, 3, 352. (Abstract)

10. Jones, Mary C., & Bayley, Nancy. Physical maturing among boys as related to behavior. *J. educ. Psychol.,* 1950, 41, 129–148.

11. Jones, Mary C., & Mussen, P. H. Self-conceptions, motivations, and interpersonal attitudes of early- and late-maturing girls. *Child Develpm.,* 1958, 29, 491–501.

12. McNemar, Q. *Psychological statistics.* New York: Wiley, 1955.

13. Mussen, P. H., & Jones, Mary C. Self-conceptions, motivations, and interpersonal attitudes of late- and early-maturing boys. *Child Develpm.,* 1957, 28, 243–256.

14. Shuttleworth, F. K. Sexual maturation and physical growth of girls age six to nineteen. *Monogr. Soc. Res. Child Develpm.,* 1937, 2, No. 5.

15. Stolz, H. R., & Stolz, Lois M. *Somatic development of adolescent boys.* New York: Macmillan, 1951.

16. Stone, C. P., & Barker, R. G. The attitudes and interests of premenarcheal and postmenarcheal girls. *J. gent. Psychol.,* 1939, 54, 27–51.

17. Tryon, Caroline. Evaluations of adolescent personality by adolescents. *Monogr. Soc. Res. Child Develpm.,* 1939, 4, No. 23.

18. Tryon, Caroline. The adolescent peer culture. *Yearb. nat. Soc. Study Educ.,* 1944, 43(I), 217–239.

9

M. Frisk
T. Tenhunen
O. Widholm
H. Hortling

PSYCHOLOGICAL PROBLEMS IN ADOLESCENTS SHOWING ADVANCED OR DELAYED PHYSICAL MATURATION

On the basis of their data, these researchers concluded that both rate and stage of maturation are significant for personality. Among boys, early development proved advantageous except in unusual cases, while among girls early development often led to problems. Delayed development presented problems for both sexes but especially for boys.

Opinions differ in regard to the effect of a nonpathological deviation in physical development, on personality development and the mental condition. Reiss, (9) for instance, stated that a discrepancy between chronological age and mental and physical maturity often seems to be a significant factor in the development of psychiatric disturbances. By contrast, Eichorn (3) doubted that the metabolic variables, e.g. endocrinological, through which the skeletal and somatic effects are mediated, have much direct influence on personality characteristics. Steinwachs (11) emphasized the effect of asynchronism on the mental condition and the fact that the classification into accelerated and retarded development yields heterogeneous groups, which include individuals with "asynchronous" development.

Adolescents with accelerated or retarded development have to cope with a variety of problems. Macfarlane (7) found that tall, early-maturing boys and short, late-maturing girls tended to have an easier time than their opposites, and Schneider (10) observed disharmonious precocity and early psychosexual tendencies in early-maturing girls. According to Breckenridge, (1) late maturing seems to create concern for both sexes, though in a more

From M. Frisk, T. Tenhunen, O. Widholm and H. Hortling, "Psychological Problems in Adolescents Showing Advanced or Delayed Physical Maturation," *Adolescence*, Vol. 1, No. 2 (Summer 1966), pp. 126–140. Reprinted by permission.

acute form for the boys, who find themselves underdeveloped. A disturbance of maturation impairs their ability to adjust themselves to their environment and predisposes to mental breakdown. (9) Their feelings of inferiority and dependency have a realistic basis for many years, (3) particularly as long as the developmental deviation manifests itself as a pronounced physical deviation.(1)

In the present study an attempt was made to find out whether deviations in physical development are exceptionally frequent among adolescents showing mental symptoms, and whether a disturbance of maturation can thus be regarded as a factor contributing to the development of mental problems. Furthermore, attention was directed to the effect of the deviation on personality development and the symptomatology.

MATERIAL

Two groups of adolescents, one showing markedly advanced and the other markedly delayed maturation, were selected among the patients examined for various reasons at the outpatient clinic for teenagers of the Samfundet Folkhälsan. A discrepancy of ≥ 1.5 years between the bone age and the chronological age was considered as the criterion of marked development deviation. This principle of selection was adopted because bone age is regarded as a useful indicator of physical developmental deviation. (8)

The scheme of the investigation included a general somato-endocrinological and psychiatric examination. The somatic examination was supplemented by certain laboratory tests, e.g. the determination of SPI and basal metabolism and the oestrogen effect in vaginal smear. Bone age was determined according to Greulich and Pyle's Atlas (4) by double checking. This method takes into account the different developmental levels of boys and girls. (13) The clinical psychiatric examination was supplemented by history-taking which included interviews with the parents, and frequently also by psychological tests. In all cases a clinical neurological pilot examination was performed, and when indicated an EEG was taken.

The series consisted of 596 teenagers. Most of them belonged to the urban population, and over half were secondary school pupils. Advanced development was observed in 26 cases, delayed development in 66 (Table 9–1). The largest group consisted of late-maturing boys.

Table 9–1 Distribution of Developmental Deviations in the Series

	Girls	%	Boys	%	Total	%
Advanced development	11	3.4	15	5.5	26	4.4
Delayed development	18	5.6	48	17.5	66	11.1

Age Distribution

The early-maturing girls were mostly aged 12 or 14–15 years, while the early-maturing boys were evenly distributed over the whole range of teenage. By contrast, the late-maturing girls were mainly found in the older age groups, with peaks at 15–16 and 19 years, while the majority of the late-maturing boys were aged 14–17 years.

RESULTS

Physical condition. It is noteworthy that 50 per cent of the patients in the group were tall for their age. By this is implied a deviation of $\geq$ 5 per cent from the mean value for the age group in question as indicated by Leena Bäckstrom-Järvinen. (2) The frequency of overweight was also striking, 64 per cent of the girls and 73 per cent of the boys exceeding by $\geq$ 7 per cent the normal weight for the height in question according to the scale of Lichtenstein. (6) (Table 9–2)

Table 9–2   Advanced Development and Somatic Findings

	Girls	%	Boys	%	Total	%
Tall/age	5	46	8	53	13	50
Obese/height	7	64	11	73	18	69
Allergic disposition	6	55	7	47	13	50
Low Hb values	5	46	1	7	6	24
Functional somatic symptoms						
Total	4	36	10	67	14	54
Fatigue	2	18	6	40	8	31
Sleep disturbances	3	27	4	27	7	27
Digestive disturbances	–	–	2	13	2	6
Central nervous dysfunction						
Total	1	9	8	53	9	CE
Of lesional origin	1	9	7	47	8	31

*Approximate percentages are given in order to facilitate comparison of the groups.

Half these patients were found to have an allergic disposition. This estimate was based on actual allergic manifestations or on the presence of two of the following factors: heredity, previous allergic manifestations and elevated blood eosinophil values. Furthermore, among the girls there was a high frequency of low haemoglobin values (Hb $\geq$ 11.1 g) although definite anemia was present in only one case.

Among the boys, in particular, there was a high frequency of functional somatic disturbances. The main symptoms, sometimes concurrent in one and the same patient, were fatigue, sleep disturbances and digestive disturbances. Among the girls a tendency towards sleep disturbances was the main symptom.

Somatic disease of a serious nature was rare in this group. One girl and one boy obviously had somewhat impaired thyroid function with low SPI values, though in the normal range. In two cases Besnier's prurigo was observed.

In the group of boys, the neurological aspect was more serious. Signs of cerebral dysfunction were strikingly frequent. Half the early-maturing boys exhibited a neurological status deviating from the normal, often characterized by motoric disturbances and pathological changes of the EEG. In all cases except one, a cerebral lesion was regarded as responsible for the disturbance. Symptoms like dyslexia, speech defects, enuresis, etc., were rather common.

Mental condition. The frequency of neurotic symptom was striking, and the girls, in particular, showed failure of adjustment. (Table 9–3)

The main neurotic symptoms were poor concentration, depression, hypochondria and various disturbances such as tics, nail-biting, etc. These were more common among the boys than among the girls. By contrast, the girls more often exhibited poor family adjustment. Furthermore, disturbances of a slightly asocial character occurred in the form of various manifestations of dishonesty. None of the early-maturing individuals in the present series showed complete emotional equilibrium.

Often a variety of symptoms occurred in one and the same case, but sometimes neurotic symptoms occurred alone, and three girls showed failure of adjustment alone. The smokers were relatively few in this group. As compared with the boys, the early-maturing girls smoked more often, although their mean age was lower. Among the early-maturers, strikingly many had problems relating to relationships with peers. Almost half the boys and two girls were continually ill-treated.

Since the subjective experiences of deviating from age mates is of essential significance from the standpoint of psychological adaption, those who showed deviations in height or weight from the standards for the age group were compared to those who were normal in regard to body build despite the deviation in age.

From the standpoint of symptomatology, there were certain differences between those who were *tall* for their age and those who were *of normal height*. Among the girls, both groups showed failure of adjustment, but those who were of normal height more often exhibited a tendency towards asocial behavior and poor school adjustment. On the whole, the boys showed failure of adjustment to a lesser degree, and this symptom was particularly infrequent in the group of tall boys. By contrast, this group showed a high frequency of neurotic disturbances consisting of nail-biting and tics. Other functional somatic disturbances were also common. Furthermore, in comparison with those of normal height, the tall boys more often showed hypochondria and feelings of physical inferiority, and were more

Table 9–3   Advanced Development and Psychological Observations

(a) The various symptom groups present in individual cases

	Girls	%	Boys	%	Total	%
Failure of adjustment, neurotic symptoms and functional somatic disturbance	2	18	2	13	4	15
Failure of adjustment and neurotic symptoms	2	18	1	7	3	12
Failure of adjustment and functional somatic disturbance	1	9	1	7	2	8
Failure of adjustment	3	27	–	–	3	12
Neurotic symptoms	3	27	4	27	7	27

(b) Frequency of the various symptoms in the group

	Girls	%	Boys	%	Total	%
Failure of adjustment						
Total	8	73	4	33	12	46
Conflict with parents	4	36	3	20	7	27
Failure of school adjustment	3	27	2	13	5	19
Asocial behavior	3	27	1	7	4	15
Neurotic symptoms						
Total	7	64	14	93	21	81
Depression	7	64	10	67	17	65
Poor concentration	3	27	8	53	11	42
Tics, nail–biting	3	27	3	20	6	23
Feelings of physical inferiority	–	–	2	13	2	8
Hypochondria	–	–	1	7	1	4
Smoking	4	36	3	20	7	27
Badly treated by peers	2	18	7	47	9	35

often ill-treated. In general, those of normal height seemed to react more aggressively, whilst the tall individuals were more neurotically inhibited. In the group exhibiting *overweight* there was as relatively greater number of patients with a tendency towards neurotic disturbances. In addition, restlessness and aggressiveness occurred. Among both the obese patients and those of normal weight, functional somatic symptoms were common, but the obese individuals exhibited, in addition, feelings of physical inferiority, and they were more often badly treated by their peers.

Delayed Development

Physical condition. In this group one-fourth of the girls and half the boys were short for their age. Obesity was of rare occurrence. Underweight ($\geqq$ 7 per cent deviation) was somewhat more often observed (Table 9–4).

An allergic disposition was only observed in a few of the boys. Among the girls, in particular, low haemoglobin values were strikingly frequent. Definite anaemia was only noted in one girl and three boys, however.

Table 9–4   Delayed Development and Somatic Findings

	Girls	%	Boys	%	Total	%
Short/age	5	28	24	50	29	44
Obese/height	4	22	10	21	14	21
Slender height	5	28	15	31	20	30
Allergic disposition	7	39	10	21	17	26
Low Hb values	11	61	13	27	24	36
Functional somatic symptoms						
Total	11	61	23	48	34	52
Sleep disturbances	11	61	12	25	23	35
Fatigue	9	50	10	21	19	29
Headache	6	33	12	25	18	27
Digestive disturbances	4	22	6	13	10	15
Dysmenorrhoea	5	28				
Central nervous dysfunction						
Total	4	22	24	50	28	42
Of lesional origin	1	6	12	25	13	20

In this group, too, various functional somatic symptoms were common, particularly among the girls. The most common symptoms were sleep disturbance and fatigue, but headache, digestive symptoms and dysmenorrhoea, were also frequent. Clinical disease in the form of anorexia nervosa was present in one girl, Turner's syndrome (mosaic) in one, and gastritis in one. In addition, two girls exhibited low SPI values, though in the normal range. Among the boys there were two cases of a syndrome resembling adiposogenital dystrophy associated with obesity and delayed puberty, but not with any detectable central nervous lesion, and one case of severe malabsorption. Furthermore, one boy had bronchial asthma and two had low SPI values, though in the normal range.

As evaluated on the basis of the neurological findings, disturbances of the central nervous system were frequent. Mostly, the disturbances seemed to be analogous with the general retardation of maturing, but among the boys, in particular, a lesion aetiology seemed probable in many cases. Dyslexia and poor motoric skill leading to difficulties in gymnastics and athletics were of frequent occurrence. These boys often had a history of protracted enuresis and speech difficulties. In the cases interpreted as dysmature, dyslexia and a history of enuresis were likewise frequent, and a tendency toward maladjustment and problems in the relations with the parents was often observed. In regard to athletics, these boys often chose to go in for heavy branches. The group of girls was small, but it exhibited similar tendencies and problems.

Mental condition. Various neurotic symptoms were frequent and often occurred in conjunction with functional somatic disturbances. In the whole group only two girls were considered to be in mental balance. A striking feature was the tendency towards maladjustment observable among the boys (Table 9–5).

Table 9-5   Delayed Development and Psychological Observations

(a) The various symptom groups present in individual cases

	Girls	%	Boys	%	Total	%
Failure of adjustment, neurotic symptoms and functional somatic disturbances	3	17	12	25	15	23
Failure of adjustment and neurotic symptoms	2	11	14	29	16	24
Failure of adjustment and functional somatic disturbances	1	6	1	2	2	3
Neurotic symptoms and functional somatic disturbances	7	39	5	10	12	18
Failure of adjustment	–	–	4	8	4	6
Neurotic symptoms	3	17	7	14	10	15
Functional somatic disturbances	–	–	5	10	5	8

(b) Frequency of the various symptoms in the group

	Girls	%	Boys	%	Total	%
Failure of adjustment						
Total	6	33	31	65	37	56
Conflict with parents	4	22	15	31	19	29
Failure in school adjustment	1	6	16	33	17	26
Asocial behavior	–	–	15	31	15	23
Neurotic symptoms						
Total	15	83	37	77	52	79
Poor concentration	7	39	24	50	31	47
Tics, nailbiting, enuresis	3	17	19	40	22	33
Depression	8	44	10	21	18	27
Feelings of physical inferiority	3	17	9	19	12	18
Hypochondria	–	–	2	4	2	3
Smoking	3	17	23	48	26	39
Badly treated by peers	3	17	9	19	12	18

Among the girls in this group neurotic and functional somatic symptoms were particularly frequent. The boys showed a high frequency of problems of adjustment, often in conjunction with neurotic and functional somatic symptoms. Smoking was common among the boys, and relatively many of both the boys and the girls were continually ill-treated by their peers.

Maladjustment was equally frequent among the *short* boys as among those *of normal height,* while the short girls seemed to exhibit a stronger tendency towards poor adjustment than the girls of normal height. In regard to the nature of the problems there were obvious differences between the two categories of boys. The short boys mostly had conflicts in their homes, while the late-maturing boys of normal height had more serious problems and showed asocial tendencies. Neurotic and somatic functional symptoms occurred in both groups, and there was a general tendency towards feelings of physical inferiority. The short boys were more often exposed to continuous ill-treatment by their peers; and neurotic mechanisms, regression in particular, seemed to be more common in this group. Smoking was not noticed among the short girls, but the short boys often smoked, although not so often as the boys of normal height. *Obese* individuals with delayed development were particularly often badly treated. The boys had problems of adjustment. Psychosomatic symptoms, feelings of inferiority and a high frequency of smokers characterized this group.

Discussion and Further Differentiation of the Factors Conductive to the Mental Disturbances

In a previous study, performed by the team of workers from the Teenager Clinic on a normal secondary school class of pupils aged 15–16 years, advanced development was observed in 2.4 per cent of the girls and 8.6 per cent of the boys, and delayed development in 2.4 and 14.3 per cent, respectively, using the same criteria as in the present study. (5) Hence, it appears that the physiological variations in a general population are rather wide. That delayed development was more common than advanced may in part, at least, be due to the method of investigation. According to Koski, (6) Finnish adolescents lay some seven months behind the average bone age as indicated in Greulich and Pyle's Atlas. If this observation holds good, the consequence must be a decreased frequency of individuals showing advanced development. However, as compared with the above-mentioned normal school class, the present series which consisted of adolescents who had sought medical aid at the Teenager Clinic with its team of workers with both medicoendocrinological and psychiatric competence exhibited an increased frequency of early maturing girls and of girls and boys showing delayed maturation and late-maturing boys constituted the largest group. This seems to be evidence in favor of the hypothesis that a deviation in physical maturation can be a cause of mental problems. Owing to the smallness of the groups no statistical significance could be demonstrated, but a tendency was clearly discernible.

In regard to *mental symptoms* failure of adjustment was typical of the early-maturing girls and the late-maturing boys. Among these individuals it was striking that those girls and boys who differed in habitus from their age mates showed a reactive pattern characterized by neurotic inhibition and poor family adjustment, whilst those with a normal habitus often exhibited more aggressively asocial maladjustment. It is in agreement with this observation that the proportion of smokers was greater in the latter group. Although the social standards relating to smoking are dependent on age, it seemed obvious that the personal problems connected with the developmental deviation predisposed to early smoking.

Neurotic features were common in the whole series. Depressive symptoms were more often dominant among the girls, whilst the boys attempted to repress such symptoms by compensatory and denial mechanisms. Feelings of physical inferiority were, however, common in the whole group of late-maturing individuals, but also occurred among the boys showing advanced development. In these cases such feelings mainly originated in a complicated psycho-physical constitution.

Those girls and boys who differed unfavorably from their age mates in regard to psycho-physical equipment were often badly treated by their peers. Some boys tried to compensate for their inferiority by going in for particularly heavy forms of athletics, such as boxing and ice-hockey. In other cases the situation resulted in disharmonious self-assertion. These observations applied in particular to short and physically weak boys. But early-maturing tall and weak boys and those with overweight were also in an unfavorable position.

It thus seems that the type of developmental deviation influenced the pattern of the mental disturbance.

The developmental deviation was not the only factor, however, that constituted a source of problems. On the basis of the psychological, social and physical data recorded in the individual cases, an attempt was made to find out *which factor or factors had been conducive to the development of the mental symptoms*. Since an evaluation of this kind always is difficult and the risk of erroneous interpretations is great, the conclusions drawn can only be regarded as tentative. The following groups of causative factors were distinguished:

External cause of long standing tending to produce neurosis or an acute external cause.

Internal cause in the form of a failure of ego-adaptation or in the form of a previous experience of being different.

Problems mainly connected with puberty.

Among the individuals showing *advanced development* the three above-mentioned groups were fairly evenly represented (Table 9–6), al-

Table 9-6 Distribution of the Patients with Advanced and Delayed
Development According to the Factors Regarded as Causative

	Advanced development						Delayed development					
	Girls	%	Boys	%	Total	%	Girls	%	Boys	%	Total	%
External, internal and puberty problems	1	9	–	–	1	4	–	–	2	4	2	3
External and puberty problems	–	–	2	13	2	8	5	28	5	10	10	15
External and internal problems	–	–	1	7	1	4	1	6	2	4	3	5
Internal and puberty problems							–	–	11	23	11	17
External problems	2	18	1	7	3	12	3	27	5	10	8	12
Internal problems	1	9	9	60	10	39	6	33	14	29	20	30
Puberty problems	6	55	2	13	8	31	3	17	8	17	11	17

though the disturbance often seemed to be due to the combined influence
of external and internal causes. The largest group consisted of boys with
symptoms due to internal factors. In 53 per cent of these, cerebral dysfunction, probably of lesional origin, seemed to be the main cause of the
mental or emotional symptoms. Among the girls, on the other hand, the
advanced development was frequently found to cause special problems
during puberty. One group consisted of cases in which the environment was
mainly responsible for a conflict situation and disturbed mental balance.

In the group, showing *delayed development,* too, both external and
internal factors and mechanisms were of importance. It was striking that in
some cases the general delay in development, as a rule in combination with
a retarded development of the nervous system, resulted in protracted in-
sufficiency of physical performance. In the boys this led to doubts about
the sexual role, a sensation of failure and fear of "not being a man" (Table
9-6). On comparing the girls and the boys it seemed that the disturbed mental balance of the former was more often due to external factors alone or

in combination with other causes, whilst in regard to the boys a psycho-
physical deviation of long standing caused persistent problems or accentuated the problems connected with puberty. As compared with the
short individuals, those of normal height had often external factors as the
only cause, or as a contributory cause, of their mental condition. By contrast, among the short individuals problems relating to identity were more
frequent, originating in the physical deviation. Among the boys, cerebral
dysfunction was more common among those or normal height. This seems
to indicate that a short statute constituted a major problem from the
standpoint of personal experience and therefore caused difficulties in
adaptation.

In regard to *social background* in the group with *advanced development* it is noteworthy that broken homes were a frequent external cause
in the group of boys, and that the situation was more often due to divorce
than to the death of the father. In the group of girls the environmental
situation was different in that it was characterized by marital conflicts or by
a peculiar attitude towards the daughter. The mother's attitude reflected her
uneasiness on account of the daughter's early maturing, which she feared
might involve sexual tendencies and their possible consequences. As a rule,
a tendency towards excessive demands was more common than an overprotective parental attitude. In some cases this seemed to be due to the fact
that these adolescents were regarded as older than their real age, which led
to insufficient emotional interaction. Emotional deprivation resulted, owing
to which both girls and boys were inclined to look for tenderness elsewhere,
and started "going steady," for instance.

The social background in the group with *delayed development* showed
broken homes due to divorce in the group of boys, whilst marital conflicts
between the parents were somewhat more often encountered as a causative
factor among the girls. Conflicts in the home relating to upbringing were
also of common occurrence. In particular, the fathers often placed excessive
demands on the boys, asking for performances which were above the level
of the latter. In regard to the girls in this group it was noteworthy that social
stress in the form of illness of the parents, economic difficulties or alcohol-
ism in the father was of rather common occurrence. On the whole, circumstances tending to cause social insecurity were frequently noted.

A deviation in development was often concurrent with a *disturbance
of the central nervous system.* The individuals with delayed development
exhibited both lesional cerebral conditions and neurogenous dysmaturity,
probably associated with the disturbed development. The disturbances of
the central nervous system seemed to predispose to certain mental problems and to produce certain primary symptoms and handicaps. At school,
poor motoric skill, reading and writing difficulties, etc. played a significant
part. The problems occurring in the group of advanced development were
mainly caused by an ego handicap due to cerebral lesion.

A relationship often seemed to exist between the disturbed mental balance and the disturbance of maturation. The present observations could indicate that early-maturing boys have a fair chance to a favourable mental development but in the other groups the developmental deviation seemed to cause mental stress. In this connection particular significance was accorded to the external deviations, the experience of being different or handicaps, also in regard to motoric skill, although in many cases other external or internal factors were of greater importance. The developmental deviation was in some cases the main cause, in others it was regarded as a primarily disturbing factor leading to social complications, or as a weakness in the personality and a contributory cause when physic stress resulted from external factors. Various mechanisms could be distinguished. *Problems relating to identity formation* during puberty played the most significant role for a long period of time. In the girls showing advanced development the early physical maturation led to a deviation in habitus from those of the same age. Menarche and growing sexual tension caused anxiety and restlessness. In the absence of compensatory emotional maturity or social security it was difficult to integrate the developmental deviation with the ego. The result was a pronounced crisis during early puberty, which diminished the capacity for family and school adjustment. Problems of identity were common in connection with delayed development, too. In the boys, in particular, late maturing significantly influenced the ego experience throughout the period of development, but particularly during the critical stage of puberty. The experience of a handicap, partly in the form of an external physical deviation, partly in the form of poor performances, rendered adequate establishment of male identity more difficult and led to feelings of inferiority. The father's attitude of disapproval and excessive demands often made the situation worse and enhanced the experience of inadequacy. Delayed development in combination with shortness meant that one was a "kid." In such cases the demands of the environment were better adapted to the actual level of development than in the case of late-maturing individuals of normal height. The latter had an obvious subjective handicap from their disturbed development, and their psychic reactions were more aggressive in nature. In this group primary or secondary social stress of an external character was, moreover, more common, which in part explains the situation and behavior of these individuals.

A disturbed emotional child-parent interaction constituted a problem in the group of early-maturing girls, in particular, but also among the early-maturing boys. Owing to their rapid growth, these individuals had at an early age been deprived of their position as children, with access to manifestations of tenderness and care. This led to a state of emotional deprivation, which increased the need for "going steady" which in turn, enhanced the mother's anxiety on account of her daughter's early development and its secondary sexual manifestations. The mother's anxious and suspicious attitude often became a serious cause of aggressiveness and failure of family adjustment.

Delayed development, like other handicaps, led to an increased *need for security and care*. Hence, external circumstances tending to cause insecurity came to be of great importance. In the case of late-maturing boys, the lack of a father implied both insecurity and lack of a suitable model for identification. There had been conflicts prior to the breaking of the home by divorce, and now that only one parent was there, its whole existence was threatened. This social insecurity seemed to be the main cause of the mental condition in the group of late-maturing girls. They were afraid of losing their homes, which they felt an acute need for owing to their infantile dependency and their lack of assurance. External factors causing stress, e.g., marital conflicts or illness of the parents, were often noted in these cases. Problems relating to identity were of secondary importance in this group of girls.

The deviation in physical development also influenced *peer- and school-adjustment*. The early-maturing girls felt a need for older friends, and this necessitated adaptation to the standards and ways of the latter. The result was often a pronounced conflict with what was considered proper for the girl's chronological age. School adjustment was rendered more difficult. School seemed childish and uninteresting, these girls often felt sick of it. In the group of late-maturing boys the problems were even greater. Self-esteem was undermined by failure among their peers in connection with athletics and by physical weakness, and the belief in being a man was shaken. Various, often unsuccessful, attempts at self-assertion and the continuous ill-treatment by age mates caused further complications. Difficulties in gymnastics and the reading and writing difficulties often seen in conjunction with a developmental deviation rendered it impossible for these pupils, already hampered by feelings of inferiority, to obtain even a moderate degree of compensation by good school performances.

SUMMARY

It was established that a disturbance of the process of maturation sometimes renders psychological adaptation more difficult temporarily, at least, during the critical period of puberty. Both the rate and the stage of maturation must be regarded as significant from the standpoint of personality development as a whole. Developmental deviations were found to be more frequent in a series of adolescents exhibiting various psychic problems. The proportions of early-maturing girls and late-maturing boys were particularly high. Among the boys, advanced development could be regarded as an advantage except in complicated cases, whilst among the girls early maturation often led to a crisis in connection with the development to womanhood. Delayed development constituted a problem for both girls and boys, but particularly for the latter. It seems obvious that a delay in maturation constitutes a punctum minoris resistentiae from the standpoint of personality development. Late-maturing girls and boys have an increased need for care and external security. Thus, problems are more likely to result if the outer, social conditions are unsatisfactory. An important mechanism consists of the experience of being different—before puberty owing to failure in various psycho-physical performances, during puberty owing to a deviation in the development to womanhood or manhood—which interferes with the establishment of identity. Furthermore, it appears that the different types of developmental deviation tend to produce different reactive patterns.

REFERENCES

1. Breckenridge, N. E. & Vincent, E. L. Child Development. W. B. Saunders Comp. Philadelphia, London, 1960.
2. Bäckström-Järvinen, L. Heights and Weights of Finnish Children and Young Adults. H:ki 1964.
3. Eichorn, D. H. Child Psychology. National Society for the Study of Education. The University of Chicago Press. Chicago 1963.
4. Greulich, W. W. & Pyle, S. I.: Radiographic Atlas of the Skeletal Development of the Hand and Wrist. Stanford University Press 1959.
5. Hortling, H., de la Chapelle, A., Frisk, M. & Widholm, O. The Syndromes of Obesity and Delayed Growth in Adolescence, Acta Medica Scand. Suppl. 412. 109. 1954.
6. Koski-Haataja-Lappalainen. Suomalaisten lasten käden ja ranteen luuston kehityksestä. Suomen hammaslääkäriseuran toim. 4. 1959.
7. Lichtenstein, A. Den fysiska utvecklingen under uppväxtåren och särskilt under skolåren. Skolhygien, page 63. Svenska Bokförlaget 1947.
8. Macfarlane, J. W. The significance of early or late maturation in physical and behavioral growth. Report of the 26th Ross Pediatric Research Conference. San Francisco, Oct. 1957. Columbus Ohio, Ross Laboratories 1958.
9. Miller, E. Individual and Social Approach to the Study of Adolescence, Brit. J. Med. Psychol. 35.211 1962.
10. Reiss, M. Psychoendocrinology. Grune and Stratton. New York and London 1958.
11. Schneider, K. Das seelische Bild der Accelerierten im Spiegel der Tat. Prax. Kinderpsychol. & Kinderpsychiatrie 10 1955.
12. Steinwachs, F. Körperling-seelische Wechselbeziehungen in der Reifezeit. S. Karger, Basel/New York 1962.
13. Tanner, J. M. Wachstum und Reifung des Menschen. Georg Thieme Verlag, Stuttgart 1962.
14. Wasz-Höckert, O. & Eklund, J. Järnbristanemi hos flickor i läroverksåldern. Finska Läkaresällskapets Handlingar 106, 129. 1962.

ADDITIONAL READINGS

Jones, Mary Cover. Psychological correlates of somatic development. *Child Development,* 1965, **36,** 899–911. Jones discusses the personality characteristics of men in the Berkeley Growth Study who were early or late maturers in adolescence. Early developers were socially successful in adolescence and continued to be in adulthood. The later maturer appeared to have used adaptive compensations; he was insightful, exploring, independent, and impulsive.

Jones, Mary Cover & Mussen, Paul Henry. Self-conceptions, motivations, and interpersonal attitudes of early- and late-maturing girls. *Child Development,* 1958, **29,** 491–501. The data presented in this study supported the researchers' hypothesis that early-maturing girls would experience negative self-feelings and less fortunate interpersonal attitudes. However, contrary to their predictions, early-maturing girls proved to have better self-concepts than late-maturing girls. It was concluded that late-maturing adolescents of both sexes had less adequate self-concepts, slightly poorer parent-child relationships, and tendencies toward stronger dependency needs than early maturers.

Mussen, Paul Henry & Bouterline-Young, H. Relationships between rate of physical maturing and personality among boys of Italian descent. *Vita Humana,* 1964, **7,** 186–200. Early-maturing Italian boys demonstrated lower self-concepts than their American counterparts but felt warm and affectionate toward their parents; while early-maturing American boys were more self-confident and less rebellious toward their parents. The rate of maturation proved less important for the Italian boys, suggesting that body build is more important for American youth.

Mussen, Paul Henry & Jones, Mary Cover. The behavior-inferred motivations of late- and early-maturing boys. *Child Development,* 1958, **29,** 61–67. On the basis of data obtained at the Institute of Child Welfare, University of California, the writers conclude that early-maturing boys attain greater athletic prowess, higher heterosexual status, more favorable heterosexual status, and greater esteem from peers than late-maturing boys. In the study described here, physically accelerated and retarded boys were compared in a wide variety of situations.

Stempful, Robert. The question of sex hormone therapy in cases of delayed puberty. *Journal of Pediatrics,* 1967, **70** (6), 1023–1024. Problems of delayed puberty are considered, as well as the feasibility of using hormonal therapy to accelerate sexual maturation.

Weatherley, D. Self-perceived rate of physical maturation and personality in late adolescence. *Child Development,* 1964, **35,** 1197–1210. Weatherley reports that late-maturing males tend to be less dominant than early maturers, and consider themselves as more divergent in attitudes from their parents and peers. Personality differences between early- and late-maturing girls are less clear.

Woronoff, Israel. An investigation of the relationship of some pre-adolescent developmental factors to adolescent adjustment. *Journal of Educational Research,* 1962, **56,** 164–166. An hypothesis relative to social adjustment of slow and rapid growing adolescents was explored in this study. Little or no relationship was found between rate of growth and social adjustment scores or sociometric ratings.

Two

Stage Theory
Versus Adolescence

V. Persistence of Personality: Significance for Adolescence

Most studies reveal considerable persistence of basic personality traits. Such studies embrace periods of varying length, at various stages of life. A study spanning two years of infancy indicates stability of such "primary reaction characteristics" as activity level, rhythmicity, approach or withdrawal, adaptability, intensity of reaction, threshold of responsiveness, quality of mood, distractibility, attention span, and persistence.[1] Other studies reveal a similar consistency, at least for certain traits, over longer periods of time. For men, traits which have proved stable from early childhood to maturity, include "ease of anger arousal" and "sexual behavior"; for women "passive withdrawal from stressful situations" and "dependency on the family."[2]

In another study, stability of cognitive style, especially as revealed in field-behaviors, was studied for one group, from age 8 to 13 years, in another from 10 to 24 years. A progressive increase in field dependence was evident up to age 17, with no further change from then until 24. In a field-dependent mode of perceiving, perception is dominated by the over-all organization of the field. There is relative inability to perceive parts of a field as discrete. Thus, field dependent persons have limited ability to differentiate experiences in the world about them.[3]

For some traits, adolescence seems to be critical; that is, characteristics which stabilize during this period persist into adulthood and even beyond. Moreover, certain traits, apparent in adolescence, prove more predictive of later personality than do childhood manifestations of these traits. In a study at Fels Institute, the correlation of birth-to-age-three ratings on "aggressive retaliation" was only .19, but by the age period 10 to 14, it rose to .47.[4] Behaviors relating to sex and dependency, in particular, stabilized in early adolescence and remained highly persistent through early adult-

---

[1] H. G. Birch, A. Thomas, S. Chess and M. E. Hertzog, "Individuality in the Development of Children," *Development Medicine Child Neurology*, Vol. 4 (1962), pp. 370–379.

[2] Marjorie P. Honzik, "Prediction of Behavior from Birth to Maturity," *Merrill-Palmer Quarterly*, Vol. 12 (1965), p. 81.

[3] Herman A. Witkin, Donald R. Goodenough, and Stephen A. Karp, "Stability of Cognitive Style from Childhood to Young Adulthood," *Journal of Personality and Social Psychology*, Vol. 7, No. 3 (1967), pp. 291–300.

[4] Jerome Kagan and Howard A. Moss, *Birth to Maturity* (New York, Wiley, 1962).

hood. Behaviors which deviated from social norms were correspondingly less stable. Thus, aggressive behaviors in women and dependent behaviors in men, both frowned upon in our society, indicated less stability from adolescence to maturity than did the same traits in the other sex. Adolescent behaviors that were not subject to strong social pressures were often apparent ten or fifteen years later. For example, intellectual striving and mastery behaviors, which are accepted for both sexes, proved highly persistent from high-school years through early adulthood.

Similarly, a study of the same students, first in the sixth grade and later as high-school seniors, revealed that girls became more socially oriented and boys more personally oriented, with the years. Self-esteem, which is less dependent on changing concepts of sex role, proved independent of sex.[5]

An interesting finding in the Fels study was the so-called sleeper effect. A trait, apparently dormant for a while, would reappear. For instance, the degree of passivity and fear of bodily harm, as demonstrated during the age period birth-to-three years proved more predictive of love-object dependency in adult men than did later assessments of these traits. In another study, the pace of prepubescent growth in height correlated more closely with final adult height than did the pace of pubertal growth.[6]

The factor, the special significance of adolescent experience for adult personality, has been accorded little attention. Recently, we have been disposed to think of personality as stabilized almost beyond possibility of fundamental change by late childhood. However, some data indicate that adolescent behavior patterns are still fluid, thus simultaneously presenting a challenge and opportunity to secondary-school teachers.[7]

One especially comprehensive and well-known study, begun more than forty years ago, concerns individuals originally testing in the top one per cent of the population. Extensive data have been kept on this group, involving all sorts of behaviors. A comparison of the interests, abilities, and personality characteristics in childhood and youth revealed few significant changes. All the evidence has indicated that the superior child becomes the superior adult. However, women have lived up to their vocational potential far less so than men, reflecting their different role.[8]

Such findings suggest various questions with regard to adolescents. Is the persistence of traits due to genetic factors or to constant factors in

[5] Rae Carlson, "Stability and Change in the Adolescent's Self-Image," *Child Development*, Vol. 36 (1965), pp. 659–666.

[6] R. D. Tuddenham and Margaret M. Snyder, "Physical Growth of California Boys and Girls from Birth to Eighteen Years," *University of California Publications in Child Development*, Vol. 1, No. 2 (1954).

[7] R. D. Hess, "High School Antecedents of Young Adult Achievement," in Robert Grinder, (ed.), *Studies in Adolescence* (New York, Macmillan, 1963), pp. 401–414.

[8] Melita H. Oden, "The Fulfillment of Promise: 40-Year Follow-up of the Terman Gifted Group," *Genetic Psychology Monographs*, Vol. 77 (1968), pp. 3–93.

the environment? Might not undesirable, yet stubbornly persistent traits, be altered, given proper environmental engineering? If certain apparently less desirable traits do resist change, how best may the individuals involved be helped to adapt to them? Might not schools reward a broad range of achievement, so that fewer adolescents would find themselves disadvantaged? For example, if it be conceded that relatively passive boys are unlikely to transform into aggressive ones, why not somehow make participation in less active pursuits as rewarding as football or boxing? Again, might not it be well to reserve judgment, if boys and girls indicate a lapse in certain approved traits, such as dependability? Might it not be a case of "sleeper effect?" Perhaps certain internal readjustments are taking place, and more stable characteristics will reappear. Of course, such reappearance should not be taken for granted, and warrant attention if they are unusually delayed.

Moreover, to the extent that traits first apparent in adolescence persist into adulthood, should we not determine how such long-lasting traits are formed? That is, what sort of experiences seem to have an unusual "stamping-in" effect? If intellectual attitudes established during the teens tend to persist, then it becomes imperative to learn how to establish favorable attitudes.

Remember, also, that certain traits prove more persistent in some children than in others. How may teachers and parents learn to distinguish between children whose traits can and should, or cannot or should not, be changed? Sometimes a socially deviant trait, such as a considerable degree of introversion, may be optimum for the individual concerned. Perhaps the child is a researcher-in-the-making, who will be compelled to spend long hours alone. Or perhaps a somewhat dependent boy may make his best long-term adjustment through continuing to play a passive role. Any effort to make him assertive might simply leave him anxious and discontent with himself.

The first selection, by Kagan and Moss, summarizes research from the Fels study, quoted above. It treats the persistence of certain behaviors from birth through adolescence. The second selection, by Tuddenham, considers the persistence of traits from adolescence into adulthood. These selections are merely typical of many similar studies today, some devoted to determining the persistence of particular traits, others to the durability of several traits, perhaps as they relate to each other.

10

Jerome Kagan
Howard A. Moss

THE STABILITY OF PASSIVE AND DEPENDENT BEHAVIOR FROM CHILDHOOD THROUGH ADULTHOOD

This article reports the results of a study of a group of "normal" adults from the Fels longitudinal research population for whom data were available from birth through adolescence. Specifically, the findings relate to stability of passive and dependent behaviors. Such behaviors proved quite stable for women, but minimally stable for men, reflecting differential pressures on the sexes.

A basic assumption of developmental theory is that adult behaviors are often established in early childhood. Although retrospective reports obtained from the verbal protocols of adults support this assumption, it has been difficult to produce a more objective demonstration of the long term stability of childhood behavior patterns. This unhappy state of affairs is a consequence of the expense and difficulty associated with collecting long term longitudinal information on a large sample of children. Only extensive, longitudinal research programs, as exemplified by the Berkeley Growth Study or the Fels Research Institute, can furnish the answers to this developmental problem.

This paper presents one set of results which have emerged from a recent study of a group of "normal" adults from the Fels longitudinal research population for whom extensive information was available from birth through adolescence. The findings deal specifically with the long term stability of passive and dependent behavior in the face of situations which are frustrating and/or demand problem solving activity. This particular behavioral variable was chosen for initial analysis because theoretical essays on personality development emphasize that the early dependence of the child on the parent is of the utmost importance in shaping his future personality. That is, the development of a variety of adult motives and behav-

From Jerome Kagan and Howard A. Moss, "The Stability of Passive and Dependent Behavior from Childhood Through Adulthood," *Child Development,* Vol. 31 (1960), pp. 577–591. Reprinted by permission of The Society for Research in Child Development, Inc. Copyright 1960.

iors are based on the quality and intensity of the dependent relationship with the mother and mother-substitute figures. Further, psychological symptoms are theoretically attributed to inconsistency in the gratification of the child's dependent overtures and/or to denial or inhibition of dependent motives or behavior.

In addition to the longitudinal material, each subject was recently assessed during early adulthood by means of both interview and test procedures. The adult assessment was focused on the behavior variables of dependency, aggression, achievement, and sexuality and on the degree of conflict and type of defensive responses associated with behavioral strivings in these areas. It was anticipated that there might be important sex differences with respect to occurrence of these behaviors, and the assessment procedures were designed to detect these potential sex differences.

METHOD

The Sample

The subjects (Ss) in this analysis were 27 male and 27 female Caucasian adults born between 1930 and 1939 who had recently been through a comprehensive assessment program which included an average of five hours of tape recorded interview and a variety of test procedures. The Ss were between 20 and 29 years of age at the time of the assessment. In addition, these Ss had fairly complete longitudinal records from 3 to 10 years of age. The Ss were predominantly middle class but came from a variety of vocational backgrounds including agricultural, skilled labor, tradesmen, and professional groups. The religious affiliations of the group included 43 Protestants, 10 Catholics and 1 Jewish subject. The mean Wechsler-Bellevue IQ of the group was 120 with an IQ range of 97 to 142.

Interview Variables: Adult Assessment

Each S was interviewed by the senior author for approximately five hours over two to three sessions. *The interviewer had absolutely no knowledge of any of the longitudinal information on the Ss.* Since these Ss had been studied by psychologists for over 20 years, rapport was usually excellent, and defensive and evasive answers were infrequent. Following the interviews, each S was rated (7-point scale) on 59 variables. Six of these adult interview variables dealt specifically with passive and dependent behavior; abridged definitions of these variables follow:

Degree to which dependent gratifications were sought in choice of vocation. This variable assessed the degree to which security was an important aspect of job choice, the degree to which the subject looked to his employer for gratification of his dependent needs, reluctance to shift jobs because of temporary loss of security. For nonworking women, emphasis was placed on her attitudes about the importance of security in her husband's job.

Degree of dependent behavior toward a love object. This variable assessed the degree to which the subject sought advice and emotional support from a love object (sweetheart, husband, wife), degree to which the subject looked for stability and wisdom in a love object, degree to which responsibility for decision making was given to love object.

Degree of dependent behavior with parents. This variable assessed the degree to which the subject looked for advice, support, emotional encouragement, and nurturance from one or both parents.

Degree of dependent behavior toward nonparental figures. This variable assessed the degree to which the subject sought advice, emotional support, and nurturance from nonparental figures who were not love objects, e.g., friends, relatives, and teachers.

Tendency to display behavioral withdrawal in the face of anticipated failure. This variable assessed the frequency and consistency with which S tended to withdraw from tasks and situations which he thought were difficult to master and in which failure was anticipated.

Degree of conflict over dependent behavior. This variable assessed the degree to which the subject avoided placing himself in dependent positions, his derogation of dependent behavior in self and others, and his emphasis on the value and importance of independent behavior.

A random sample of 32 taped interviews were independently studied and rated. The interrater reliabilities for the six dependency variables ranged from .63 to .82 with an average coefficient of .74.

Procedure for Evaluation of Childhood Behavior

The junior author, who had no knowledge of the adult psychological status of the Ss, evaluated narrative reports based on direct observation of the child in a variety of situations. Summaries of interviews with the child and the mothers were also available. The observation reports were based on (a) semiannual visits to the home in which a staff member observed the child interact with mother and siblings for a two to four hour period, (b) semiannual or annual observations of the child in the Fels experimental nursery school and day camp settings, (c) interviews with the child, and (d) observations of the child in the classroom. After studying this material, the psychologist rated each child for a comprehensive set of variables (7-point scale). The rater studied the material for each S for ages 3 to 6 and made his ratings. Following a period of interpolated work, he then studied all the material for each S for ages 6 to 10 and again made the ratings. A period of approximately six months intervened between the evaluation of the material for any one child for ages 3 to 6 and 6 to 10. The rater felt that retroactive inhibition was sufficiently intense to mask any halo effect of the preschool ratings upon the later ratings made for 6 to 10 years of age. That is, the amount of material studied and the large number of variables rated militated against the recall of specific ratings over such a long period of time. In addition, the high degree of interrater reliability for these ratings supports the above statement. Independent ratings of the four childhood dependency variables by a second psychologist produced satisfactory interrater reliabilities. The product-moment correlations for each variable were all in the .80's with an average reliability of .86. The four childhood variables which involved passive and dependent behavior were defined as follows:

Tendency to behave in a passive manner when faced with environmental obstacles or stress (rated for ages 3 to 6 and 6 to 10). This variable assessed the degree to which the child was behaviorally passive in the face of external frustrations and failed to make any active mastery attempts to obtain desired goal objects following frustration. The rating of a passive behavioral reaction emphasized withdrawal from the frustration but included whining, crying, and soliciting help.

Tendency to seek support, nurturance, and assistance from female adults when under stress: general dependence (rated for age 3 to 6). This variable assessed the S's behavioral tendency to obtain assistance, nurturance, or affection from mother and other female adults when confronted with a threat to his well-being, a problem, or loss of a desired goal object. Dependent behavior included seeking out adults when faced with a problem or personal injury, reluctance to start a task without help or encouragement, seeking assistance of others, seeking affection from and close contact with female adults.

Tendency to seek affection and emotional support from female adults (rated for ages 6 to 10). This variable assessed the degree to which the child sought affection or emotional encouragement from mother or mother substitute figures. Evidence included kissing, holding hands, clinging, seeking encouragement or proximity to female adults.

Tendency to seek instrumental assistance from female adults (rated for ages 6 to 10). This variable assessed the degree to which the child sought instrumental help with specific problems from mother, teachers, or other female authority figures. Instrumental dependent acts included seeking help with tasks, seeking help when physically threatened.

As mentioned above the average interrater reliability for these four variables was +.86.

The distributions for both the childhood and interview variables were normal. Product-moment correlations were computed between each of the childhood variables and the six interview based dependency variables obtained in adulthood with separate analyses for males and females.

Tachistoscopic Perception

After the interviews and interview ratings were completed, each adult
S was seen for a variety of test procedures, one of which was a tachistoscopic perception task. A series of 14 scenes were drawn to suggest action
in the areas of dependency, aggression, sexuality, and physical danger.
Three motivationally neutral, control pictures were also included.[2] For nine
of the 14 pictures, separate pairs of illustrations were made for males and
females so that the sex of the central figure was the same as the sex of the
subject. The pictures were black and white line drawings with minimal
background details. A brief description of the three dependency pictures
follows:

1. A young adult in the foreground (male for male Ss and female for
female Ss) is on his knees clutching to the waist of a figure of the same age
but of opposite sex who is standing and looking forward. The figure on the
floor is looking up at the face of the standing figure.
2. A young adult in the foreground (male for male Ss and female for
female Ss) has his arms extended in an imploring gesture toward an adult of
the same sex who is standing in the background with his back to the figure in
the foreground.
3. A young adult (male for male Ss and female for female Ss) is seated
on a chair with head buried in the abdomen of an adult of the opposite
sex who is standing and comforting the seated figure.

The 14 pictures were presented seven times at seven different exposure
speeds and in six different orders. The seven speeds ranged from .01 to 1.0
seconds. The pictures were shown initially at the fastest exposure (.01 second), and each succeeding series was presented at a slower exposure speed.
All exposures were above threshold and all Ss reported seeing something at
each exposure. The S sat in a light-proof room, 22 in. from a flash-opal
milk glass screen. The image was projected from the back of the screen, and
the field was constantly illuminated by a 35 mm. projector (30 ft.-candles
at the screen). The subject was told to state for each picture (a) the sex of
each figure, (b) the approximate ages of each figure, and (c) what each
figure on the picture was doing. The S was given three practice pictures to
adapt him to the task and its requirements, and the entire protocol was
electrically recorded and transcribed verbatim.

The protocols were scored for recognition threshold for each picture.
Recognition threshold was defined as the first series at which the picture
was described accurately and all succeeding trials were accurately described. The distribution of recognition thresholds differed among the 14
pictures and were markedly skewed either to the low or high end of the

[2] Photostats of the 14 stimuli are available upon request.

Table 10–1 Correlations Between Passive-Dependent Behavior in Childhood and Adulthood

Childhood Variables	Adult Dependency Variables											
	Dependency in Vocation		Dependency on Love Object		Dependency on Parents		Dependency on Others		Withdrawal to Failure		Dependency Conflict	
	M	F	M	F	M	F	M	F	M	F	M	F
Passivity (ages 3 to 6)	−.07	.24	.10	.23	−.28	.25	.04	.19	.06	.26	.03	.01
Passivity (ages 6 to 10)	.11	.73**	.25	.36*	−.20	.54**	.04	.06	.21	.52**	−.26	−.63**
General Dependence (ages 3 to 6)	−.06	.21	.13	.20	−.07	.07	.11	−.06	.12	.00	.05	.26
Emotional Dependence (ages 6 to 10)	.21	.08	.18	.37*	.02	.51**	−.02	.06	.35*	.37*	−.12	−.31
Instrumental Dependence (ages 6 to 10)	.19	.39*	.06	.58**	.14	.32	.37*	.01	.09	.39*	−.04	−.17

* $p < .05$, one tail.
** $p < .01$, one tail.

scale. Thus, the distribution of recognition thresholds for each picture was divided at the median into early and late recognition groups for statistical operations.

RESULTS

Stability of Dependent Behavior

Table 10–1 presents the product-moment correlations between the childhood and adult ratings of passive and dependent behavior.

The major result is that passive and dependent behaviors were fairly stable for females but not for males. For girls the ratings of passivity during ages 6 to 10 correlated significantly with the adult ratings of a dependent orientation in vocational choice, dependency on love object, dependency on parents, and withdrawal to failure. Childhood passivity was inversely correlated with adult conflict over dependent behavior. That is, females who were passive as children were apt to accept the dependent behavior in adulthood and show minimal anxiety over their dependent motives. Only dependent behavior toward nonparental figures failed to show a significant, positive correlation with the childhood ratings of passivity. Similarly, the childhood ratings of both instrumental and emotional dependency on female adults, for girls aged 6–10, predicted adult ratings of dependency on love object, dependency on parents, and withdrawal to anticipated failure situations.

For the men there were only two significant correlations between the childhood dependency ratings and those based on the adult interview. Boys who were high on instrumental dependency for ages 6 to 10 were high on dependent behavior towards nonparental figures in adulthood. Second, emotional dependence during ages 6 to 10 was positively correlated with adult withdrawal to failure.

Of the 18 correlations between each of the three childhood variables for ages 6 to 10 and the six adult variables, 60 per cent were significant in the expected direction for females, while only 9 per cent were significant for the men.

Tables 10–2 and 10–3 present the intercorrelations among the childhood and adult interview variables respectively.

The correlations among the passive and dependency variables between ages 3 to 6 and 6 to 10 were generally more consistent for girls than for boys. That is, for girls the correlations among passivity and general dependence for ages 3 to 6 and the three variables for ages 6 to 10 were all consistently high. For boys the stability of the passivity rating for ages 3 to 6 and 6 to 10 was quite high. However, the relationships between

Table 10-2 Intercorrelations Among Childhood Dependency Variables

	Passivity (6 to 10)		Gen. Dep. (3 to 6)		Emot. Dep. (6 to 10)		Instr. Dep. (6 to 10)	
	M	F	M	F	M	F	M	F
Passivity (3 to 6)	.82**	.76**	.74**	.83**	.26	.80**	.38	.79**
Passivity (6 to 10)	—	—	.40*	.63**	.43*	.65**	.53**	.61**
General Dependence (3 to 6)	—	—	—	—	.37	.61**	.38*	.63**
Emotional Dependence (6 to 10)	—	—	—	—	—	—	.60**	.79**
Instrumental dependence (6 to 10)	—	—	—	—	—	—	—	—

* $p < .05$, two tails.
**$p < .01$, two tails.

Table 10-3 Intercorrelations Among Adult Dependency Variables

	Dependence Love Object		Dependence Parents		Dependence Others		Withdrawal		Dependence Conflict	
	M	F	M	F	M	F	M	F	M	F
Dep. vocation	.61**	.42*	.53**	.49**	.12	−.10	.41*	.50**	−.61**	−.56**
Dep. love object	—	—	.24	.54**	.48**	.16	.54**	.49**	−.66**	−.50**
Dep. parents	—	—	—	—	.39*	.03	.44**	.57**	−.59**	−.71**
Dep. others	—	—	—	—	—	—	.38*	−.15	−.46**	.15
Withdrawal	—	—	—	—	—	—	—	—	−.57**	−.70**
Dep. conflict	—	—	—	—	—	—	—	—	—	—

* $p < .05$, two tails.
**$p < .01$, two tails.

passivity for 3 to 6 and the two dependency behaviors for 6 to 10 were not as high as they were for girls. This finding suggests that overt seeking of affection and/or instrumental aid in school-age boys begins to be dissociated from a passive withdrawal reaction to problem situations.

The intercorrelations among the adult dependency variables were generally positive for both sexes. Dependency on parents and dependency on love objects were each associated with withdrawal to failure and negatively related to conflict over dependency. It is interesting to note that women who are dependent on their parents tended to be dependent on their love object but not on friends or authority figures. Men, on the other hand, who were dependent on their parents tended to be dependent on friends and authority figures rather than on a love object. Dependency on parents and friends usually involves instrumental aid with problems, while dependency on a love object more often included the soliciting of emotional support and affection. It will be recalled that one of the two significant correlations for males between childhood and adult dependency involved instrumental dependency for ages 6 to 10 with adult dependency on nonparental authority figures. Emotional dependency for boys age 6 to 10 showed no correlations with the adult dependency variables. Thus, male dependent behavior is apt to emphasize the seeking of instrumental assistance with problems, while females are likely to seek affection and emotional support in addition to instrumental aid.

It is important to note that passive and dependent behavior for ages 6 to 10 showed a better relation to adult dependent behavior than the ratings for 3 to 6 years of age. This finding indicates that important age changes occur between ages 3 and 10 and that behavior displayed during the first few years of school is a better index of adult functioning than the earlier preschool behavior patterns.

Tachistoscopic Perception of Dependent Pictures

There were significant sex differences in recognition threshold for the three dependency pictures with the females recognizing all three pictures earlier than the males. The scene that depicted a person imploring a same sexed adult (. . .) yielded the most significant sex difference ($p < .001$, two tails). The picture of the adult on his knees clutching on to an opposite sexed adult (. . .) and that of the seated adult holding on to an opposite sexed adult (. . .) yielded sex differences significant at the .005 and .08 levels, respectively, for two tails. The aggressive pictures, on the other hand, produced opposite results, for the females recognized two of the four aggression pictures significantly later than the men ($p < .01$, two tails). There were no significant sex differences for the sex, physical danger, or three neutral scenes.

There was not a highly consistent relationship between recognition threshold for the dependent scenes and the interview ratings of dependency conflict. Only recognition of the scene that illustrated a man on his knees in front of a woman (. . .) showed a relation to dependency conflict, and this held only for males. The males who were above the median in recognition threshold for this scene (late recognition) were rated as more conflicted over dependent behavior than males who recognized this picture early ($p = .07$, two tails). For the females, recognition threshold for the dependency pictures showed no significant relation to ratings of dependency conflict.

DISCUSSION

The results support a basic hypothesis of developmental theory which states that the acquisition of certain adult response patterns begins in early childhood. The differential stability of passive-dependent behavior for men and women is probably the result of several factors. However, one set of processes which may contribute to this phenomenon is derived from the commonly accepted hypothesis that passive and dependent behavior is less punished in females than in males. Further, females are often encouraged to be passive while men are expected to be independent and autonomous in the face of frustration. Parental and peer group punishment for passive and dependent behavior should result in some inhibition of this behavior in males. Thus, we would not accept this class of behavior to be as stable for men as for women. Studies of both overt behavior and fantasy (2, 3, 4, 6, 7) all indicate that dependent responses are more frequent for girls than for boys. Further, the sex stereotypes presented by communication media fit this description. The analysis of children's books by Child, Potter, and Levine (1) indicated that girls are portrayed as passive while boys are presented as independent and heroic. Finally, a study of the likes and dislikes of 10-year-old children (5) confirms the belief that girls accept passive behavior as more appropriate for their sex role than do boys.

The present tachistoscopic threshold data support the notion that men are more conflicted over dependent behavior than women. It will be recalled that the women recognized all three scenes depicting dependent behavior much earlier than the men. This finding suggests that the tendency to perceive dependent behavior in adults is much weaker in men than it is in women. One possible cause of this "weaker perceptual hypothesis" is that dependent action is less acceptable to men, i.e., that men are more conflicted over dependent behavior. This conclusion finds support in the correlation, for men, between late recognition of dependency (. . .) and the interview rating of dependency conflict.

Detailed analysis of the 54 cases indicates that there was a greater proportion of men, than women, who shifted from high dependency during childhood to independent behavior as adults. The women tended to be either dependent or independent for both childhood and adulthood. For example, in comparing emotional dependence for ages 6 to 10 with adult dependency on parents, not one female showed a major shift from high dependency in childhood to low dependency in adulthood. For the men, however, 20 per cent were rated very dependent during the ages 6 to 10 and very independent in adulthood.

The authors do not suggest that passive and dependent behavior in girls is rigidly fixed at school age and that change is a rare or unusual phenomenon. It must be kept in mind that the social milieu of these particular subjects remained rather constant throughout their lives. Their familial and extrafamilial environments were not disrupted to any marked degree. The parents and peers of these Ss retained their same values, their reference groups remained constant, and, in most cases, their geographical travel was limited. Thus, the degree of behavioral stability obtained for these females might not hold for populations that are more mobile or transient, for different ethnic or class samples, or for people subjected to major traumata during adolescence and early adulthood.

Implicit in these results is a strategy for certain research problems in developmental psychology. It would appear that a select group of theoretically relevant behaviors become clearly established as preferential response tendencies as early as 6 to 10 years of age. This means that one can study the child longitudinally without having to wait 15 or 20 years before asking important questions of the data. Since the current philosophy of financial support for research allows an investigator to chart a 5 to 10 year program, it is now feasible for one investigator to see the products of a longitudinally oriented project in a reasonable length of time.

Although case history material can never prove an hypothesis, it often facilitates scientific communication by placing some flesh on the skeleton of a correlation matrix. The following case material is presented to give the reader a clearer picture of the material upon which our childhood evaluations were based and to illustrate dramatically the degree of constancy of behavioral passivity for two specific individuals.

Case A. Miss A is a 21-year-old, unmarried woman, who was in her senior year in an Eastern college. She was one of the most independent women in our sample and one who showed a strong reaction against dependent behavior in a wide variety of situations. As an adult she was described as a woman with a very strong need for recognition by others combined with a striving for achievement related goals. She had a strong desire to nurture others and often sought out situations in which she could give advice, support, and encouragement to peers. Miss A stated during the interview that she liked to keep her personal problems to herself. She did not like to discuss her personal problems because she felt that this behavior made her appear "helpless and weak." Statements like this indicate very strong conflict and anxiety over being in a passive-dependent position with other people. She was trying to sever any semblance of a dependent relation with her mother and derogated the latter because the mother seemed to be dependent upon her for companionship. Miss A sometimes felt lonely but said that she fights these feelings and tries to be able to live with them, for she does not like to admit that she needs friends or companionship. Her relationship with men seems to be consistent with the above pattern, for she tends to withdraw from heterosexual relationships that become too intense. Miss A said that she does not like men that make demands upon her, and she avoids men who attempt to place her in a passive role or position.

The following material represents selected verbatim excerpts from the longitudinal material on this subject.

Age 3 years, 4 months: Summary of Fels Nursery School Observations. S seems to be able to control and channel her behavior so that she got done just what she wanted to get done. In this activity she was very independent and capable. She was very social but also had a streak of aloof self-sufficiency, and she always made her individuality felt. She was what might be called a strong personality, often very intense, quite stubborn. . . . Her most outstanding characteristic was her consistent independence and integrity. In spite of the fact that she imitated and followed certain boys, she seemed to do this very much from her own choice, and she never lost the flavor of her individuality. She was capable of being social and seemed to enjoy contacts but at all times she was her own master. She would often withdraw from play and go on in her own direction at any time that she wished. . . . She was independent with adults and at times negativistic just to be devilish. She seemed somewhat self-conscious and had some cute little tricks. . . . In all, she could be characterized best by being called "tough minded." She shows determination and will, originality and spark, curiosity and interest in factual detail. She likes to quibble and argue, to verbalize, to construct, to accomplish. She is an individualist, independent and stubborn.

Age 5 years, 4 months: Fels Nursery School Observation. S seems to be vigorous, ruthless, competitive, highly sensual young woman, but one felt quite often that antagonism toward others was simply a direct response to their behavior. . . . She has grown far more social and also popular with an increasingly large crowd of special friends in a gang. She could be, when she chose, quite a successful leader, forging ahead and organizing a group on a hike, directing them and arranging things, and particularly keeping order in a fair sharing of the tools in the carpentry shop. . . . Many of S's conflicts with the adult world seemed a direct imitation of a certain boy. She needed a chance to grumble, would scornfully refuse any adult suggestions or orders, would usually go officially ahead to carry them out. She was quite demanding, often shouting an order to an assistant. . . . With her other work the same drive for strong achievement was also evident, sticking to anything until it was finished, whatever the group stimuli. S still had real trouble in fine motor coordination, would growl as she worked, "I'm doing this as well as I can steer my pencil." For all her teeth gritted effort, the final results would still be relatively crude. She was very skilled in the use of puzzles and interested in the problems of designs and the way things fit together. She scorned any of the ready-made designs for the Christmas tree decorations.

Age 7 years: Observation in Fels Day Camp. S came accompanied by one friend. S did not seem overwhelmed by the large proportion of adults around, but in her sturdy self-sufficient manner went ahead with her own activities. Her friend was at first rather shy and withdrawn and S, with her usual confident bullying and bossing of the adults, tended to take the girl under her wing and make sure she had a good time. S remains an exceptionally eager, imperturbable young woman. On a number of small issues she did insist on her own way, on just how long she would stay in the gym and play before lunch, but was quite reasonable about making compromises. She chose a rather difficult necklace to make and got quite mad when it didn't work out well. She kept doggedly with it, very self-sufficient, and continuing all on her own after getting some initial advice. . . . Her major effort was put on self-appointed tasks, to be able to master jumping over the horse at the gym where she took numerous tumbles until she succeeded. In spite of her distractability and preference for the apparatus she did set herself to learning the new skills required there.

Age 9 years: Report from Teacher. S is one of the most responsible children in the group. . . . She is self-reliant, independent, and knows how to plan her time well. She enters all games with enthusiasm, is very well coordinated, is full of personality and "joie de vivre."

Case B. Miss B is a 23-year-old, unmarried woman, who is working and living with her parents. She was one of the most overtly dependent women in the sample. During the interview she was very dependent on the interviewer for structure and was rather mild and meek. Her most typical reaction to failure or stressful situations is to deny or to withdraw and she says quite blithely, "I'm not a worrier." She is very sensitive to the opinions of other people and usually conforms with their expectations for her. She accepts her passive-dependent role with authority people and with love objects. *S* tends to be very dependent on peers for advice, likes being close to the family, and tends to see herself as inadequate in the face of problem situations.

Following are selected excerpts from her longitudinal records:

Age 2 years, 6 months: Fels Nursery School Observation. At the first day of nursery school, *S* seemed rather frightened and very reluctant to leave her mother this morning. The mother had to carry her and hold her in the car until the door was shut. For the first few miles she cried and then suddenly stopped and began to take an interest in the various animals and objects. She cried when she reached the nursery school but stopped as soon as she left the other children. On the second day of nursery school she cried again but seemed much less frightened and more angry. During the nursery school she stood watching the other children and at one point ran to another girl and stood beside her. The other little girl paid no attention, and *S* trailed after her. *S* wandered around and, when the teacher went to the house, *S* rushed to follow her and stood around the teacher. *S* tagged after another little girl all morning. During the nursery school two-week period she was timid and tense.

Age 3 years: Fels Nursery School Summary. At first, *S* was timid and tense and was gathered under the wing of another peer and her cohorts. From then on she was "at home" with the group. She followed another girl's lead and joined in the activities the other girl organized. On days when this girl was absent she was at loose-ends and tended to return to her original dependence on an adult. Several weeks after her nursery school stay she visited the school one morning for several hours. She was a little apprehensive at first but made no real protest. She stood around not joining in the play until an adult suggested an activity.

Age 4 years: Fels Nursery School Summary. S cried the first day of nursery school after she saw another girl cry. She stayed close to the teacher the first few days and watched the other children with a worried expression on her face. Indoors she chose small blocks or color cubes to play with. In the yard *S* was very cautious about trying out the apparatus, particularly when there was any balancing involved. She has a high, whining nasal voice, and several letter substitutions made her speech rather difficult to understand. She was quite complying with adult requests. Frequently, she appealed to adults for help in conflicts, such as getting a turn to slide, which is a situation she could have handled for herself.

Age 6 years: Visit to the School. S is retiring, quiet, and shy. She doesn't show the enthusiasm that most of the children in the class do. She seems content. . . . She goes to the teacher for suggestions and skips to her seat jubilantly with a word of approval from the teacher. S recites a bit timidly in front of the whole class but accepts the teacher's support and gets through successfully. Her voice is a little soft and her enunciation is not clear. S volunteers information a bit tentatively and without enthusiasm. The teacher reports that S is about the brightest of the average group. S is not a leader but she is very sweet and cooperative and is never any trouble.

Age 6 years, 6 months: Summary of Fels Day Camp Observations. S was outclassed in almost every respect in this group but fluttered happily about after the others doing the best she could. She occasionally withdrew or grew silent but, when encouraged by an adult, she soon recovered. She was not insensitive and did not seem to have her security disturbed more than momentarily. She seems to feel a great confidence and trust in adults and could always be bought off or led along. She lacked initiative in almost every way. She could not go ahead on any craft project nor could she assert herself socially. She needed help and encouragement, hung about the adults, not exposing herself to the center of the group. She is essentially a conformist and wanted only to do what was right. She got into no mischief and had little sense of fun. She was happiest when settled into a situation that was approved and guided by an adult, and at these times she would proddle along very happily. Her main interests lay in conforming to any plans laid by adults and working on simple handcrafts. She was rather unsure in her accomplishments. She was often physically apprehensive.

Age 7 years, 6 months: Summary of Fels Day Camp Observations. The most characteristic aspect of S's day camp behavior was her ability, high conformity, and social reticence. She did not participate in social activities to any extent and was generally ignored by the other children. She clung to adults, wanted to assist them when possible, and wanted their approval and comforting in all her activities. She seemed to be somewhat apprehensive of physical contacts, especially if they became at all rough. She was apprehensive about almost any physical danger. Her actual physical ability was not particularly poor, and, when she was put into athletic situations, she did surprisingly well. Her general lack of physical participation seems not to be due to poor ability as much as to lack of motivation and apprehension.

Age 8 years: Visit to the School. S is always anxious to do what is right all of the time. She is not a discipline problem. S shows no interest in physical activities. Initially, she is lost at school work and takes some time to adjust to new work. S was pretty tentative in her first attempt to get the teacher's attention and held up her paper hesitantly. She was very pleased when the teacher came to her. She was uncertain about the problems although they had similar ones before.

Age 8 years, 8 months: Fels Day Camp Summary. S is a small, dark looking girl, bent over, with thick dark hair and a tired face. Her voice is high but with no force; her hands hanging limp at the wrists. Much of this lack of force seemed related to her personality, and at the races she surprised us by doing remarkably well. *S* obeyed adults implicitly and wanted to have their sanction for even small acts which the group had already been given permission for. She was a rather cringing, servile manner. This clinging around adults was particularly marked the first day when she ate her lunch with them.

Age 9 years, 8 months: Fels Day Camp Summary. S is a rather pathetic looking little girl. Rather thin, droopy eyed, clammy handed, somehow reminiscent of an orphan in an old melodrama. She seems nearer to seven or eight than her actual age and with a kind of naivete and unsureness about all she did. She was an exceedingly compliant child in taking the tests, even the reading tests which she obviously disliked, without a murmur.

SUMMARY

This paper summarized some results from a larger investigation of the stability of behavior in a group of subjects who were part of the Fels Research Institute's longitudinal population. This report dealt specifically with the long term stability of passive and dependent behavior from childhood through adulthood.

The *S*s were 27 males and 27 females for whom extensive longitudinal information was available from birth through adolescence. One psychologist studied narrative reports based on observations of the child in various settings and rated each child on four variables describing types of passive and dependent behavior for ages 3 to 6 and ages 6 to 10. A second psychologist, who had no knowledge of the childhood data, interviewed each *S* in adulthood and rated each *S* on six variables related to aspects of adult passive and dependent behavior. In addition, each adult *S* was administered a tachistoscopic perception task in which scenes illustrating dependent activity were presented at seven different exposure speeds.

The results revealed that passive and dependent behaviors were quite stable for women, but minimally stable for men. Over 60 per cent of the correlations between the childhood (ages 6 to 10) and adult ratings of dependency were statistically significant for females, while only 9 per cent were significant for men. For example, the correlation between passive withdrawal from problem situations for ages 6 to 10 and adulthood was .52 ($p < .01$) for women and .21 for men. Similarly, the correlation between emotional dependence for ages 6 to 10 and adult dependency on parents was .51 ($p < .01$) for women and .02 for men. The correlations between the ratings for ages 3 to 6 and adulthood were considerably lower and not statistically significant.

It was suggested that environmental disapproval and punishment of dependent behavior in young males led to inhibition of and conflict over dependency in the growing boy. The social acceptance of passive and dependent behavior in females would be expected to result in greater stability for this class of responses for women than for men. The fact that females recognized the tachistoscopically presented dependency scenes earlier than the men was interpreted as support for this explanation.

Case history material for two female subjects was presented to illustrate the type of information utilized in this study.

REFERENCES

1. Child, I. L. Potter, E. H., & Levine, Estelle M. Children's textbooks and personality development: an exploration in the social psychology of education. *Psychol. Monogr.*, 1946, **60**, No. 279.
2. Hattwick, Bertha. Sex differences in behavior of nursery school children. *Child Develpm.*, 1937, **8**, 323–355.
3. Kagan, J. The stability of TAT fantasy and stimulus ambiguity. *J. consult. Psychol.*, 1959, **23**, 266–271.
4. Sanford, R. N., Adkins, M. M., Miller, R. B., & Cobb, E. N. Physique, personality and scholarship: a comprehensive study of school children. *Monogr. Soc. Res. Child Develpm.*, 1943, **8**, No. 1.
5. Tyler, Leona E. The development of vocational interests. I. The organization of likes and dislikes in ten year old children. *J. genet. Psychol.*, 1955, **86**, 33–44.
6. Watson, R. I. *Psychology of the child.* New York: Wiley, 1959.
7. Whitehouse, Elizabeth. Norms for certain aspects of the Thematic Apperception Test on a group of nine and ten year old children. *J. Pers.*, 1949, **1**, 12–15.

11

Read D. Tuddenham

CONSTANCY OF PERSONAL MORALE OVER A FIFTEEN-YEAR INTERVAL

This article compares matters of personal morale relating to the same sub-jects originally tested as high school seniors in 1938 and again fifteen years later. There was a modest degree of constancy, with changes greater on certain items than others.

The psychological literature is rich in studies on the measurement of personality attributes, but few studies have been concerned with the stability of measurements over appreciable intervals of time. Exceptions are the reports of Strong on interests (7), of Crook (2, 3), and Kelly (5) on self-report inventory responses, and of Bender (1) and Nelson (6) on attitudes. More recently, the author described the constancy of a wide array of ratings by observers, based on a sample of the Oakland Growth Study (8).

The present paper is concerned with the temporal stability of self-report responses to a brief morale questionnaire administered to the same Oakland Growth Study subjects in 1938 when they were high school seniors and again in the course of a follow-up investigation after a 15-year interval marked by a great war and a considerable change in the economic and psychological climate. The bulk of this follow-up was completed during 1953. A few cases residing outside the San Francisco Bay Area, and hence not available, were tested at various times between 1953 and 1958 upon the occasion of visits to Berkeley. These cases have been added to augment the group, giving a total of 51 men and 41 women.

METHOD

The Questionnaire

The original questionnaires administered in 1938 consisted of 20 items in each of two forms. All items were in multiple choice format with the

From Read D. Tuddenham, "Constancy of Personal Morale Over a Fifteen-Year Interval," *Child Development*, Vol. 33 (1962), pp. 663–673. Reprinted by permission of the Society for Research in Child Development, Inc. Copyright 1962.

stem cast usually as a question, and four declarative sentences arranged below as response alternatives. In 1944 the two questionnaires were combined, and half the items eliminated for an opinion-change investigation conducted on another group of high school seniors and repeated on still another group in 1947 (4). This shortened version was the basis for the 1953 revision, but obsolete items and those inappropriate for adults were dropped and replaced by others. After these changes, 14 items remained in substantially the same form in 1953 as in 1938. The sequence of items and the ordering of response alternatives from optimistic to pessimistic varied somewhat in different versions of the questionnaire, but, throughout this paper, items are grouped by content and alternatives ordered uniformly from optimistic to pessimistic.

Statistical analysis. The questionnaire as a whole was originally intended to measure various aspects of personal morale or optimism, but the items were quite heterogeneous in content. Ten of the 14 retained items seemed to have something in common, in that they referred either to personal satisfactions or to attitudes where an underlying dimension of personal optimism vs. pessimism could be assumed, though the manifest content involved judgments about society. Distributions on these 10 items were combined to yield an over-all measure of changes in the morale of the group. Also, the scores of individual subjects were summed over these 10 items, and the correlations calculated separately by sex between the total scores earned in 1938 and those earned in 1953.

In addition to this analysis, all 14 items were studied separately. Four-step frequency and percentage frequency distributions of responses were prepared separately by sex and occasion for each item. Next, Pearson product-moment correlations were calculated separately for men and women between the 1938 responses and those made 15 years later. To throw more light on the *direction* of opinion changes in the group as a whole, a χ^2 test was made for each item of the number of individuals changing in a positive direction vs. those changing in the opposite way over the 15-year interval. The significances of sex differences in response distributions were evaluated by χ^2 for the 1938 and also for the 1953 data.

RESULTS AND DISCUSSION

Differences between subjects' morale in adolescence and in adulthood, based on the mean of the 10 "optimism" items, are summarized in Fig. 11–1. As the charts make clear, the adults of both sexes gave fewer pessimistic responses and more optimistic ones in 1953 than they did as adolescents in 1938. However, optimistic responses were much more numerous at both age levels than were pessimistic ones. The parallelism between results

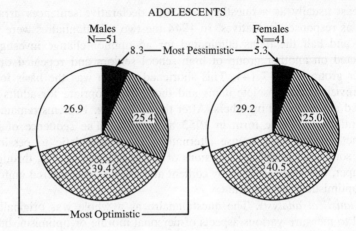

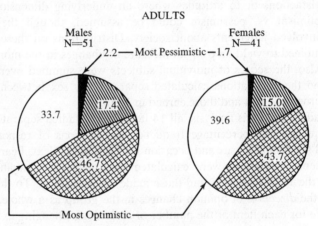

Fig. 11–1. Percentages in four levels of response.

for men and for women was close, and such sex differences as obtain were not significant, in contrast to the age differences.

It would be reassuring to conclude that increased optimism is a usual concomitant of passage from stormy adolescence to serene maturity. However, in our study, personal maturation is confounded with historical change. The world of 1938, still economically distressed and trembling on the brink of World War II, may well have justified much less optimism than that of 1953 to 1958.[1]

[1] Using different, but comparable samples of high school seniors on each of three occasions, Jones (4) found morale was somewhat higher in 1942 than in 1938, despite the uncertainties of a world at war. By 1947, morale was back to about the same level as in 1938, though in all groups most students tended to be optimistic. Corresponding data for adults are not available.

Although the group as a whole grew decidedly more "optimistic" over the 15-year interval, there was little consistency in the relative position of individuals, the correlations between adolescent and adult scores summed over the 10 items being only .09 for women and .25 (significant at the 5 per cent level) for men.

Considering the 14 items individually, the stability correlations were on the whole low, ranging from near 0 to .47. However, 12 of 14 were positive in sign for men, and 13 of 14 for women. The median correlation for men of .23 reached almost the 5 per cent level (one tail), but the women's median was only .15 and the distribution of correlations for women was more variable. These median values are lower than those reported by Kelly (5) for self-ratings (.30) and by Tuddenham (8) for ratings by observers (.27 and .24 for men and women, respectively).[2] However, Kelly's subjects were somewhat older on the first occasion, and Tuddenham's results are values for pooled pairs of observers. The present data are in most instances at least consistent with the other studies in support of the popular view that inconstancy and variability are more characteristic of women than of men!

Although the separate items are characterized by relative instability through time and by absence of significant sex differences on either testing occasion, they reveal temporal shifts in group opinion, in certain instances significant, that throw light on the difference between the adolescent and adult perspectives of our subjects.

Four of the items refer directly to the respondent's appraisal of his own life and happiness (see Table 11–1). In this group, the increased optimism of adults is consistent, though in certain instances they favor the less extreme of the two positive alternatives. Statistically significant shifts toward optimism occur only in the data for men: on value of present activities (1 per cent level) and expectation of getting one's wants from life (5 per cent level). In both instances, a parallel shift among women is not significant. Through-time correlations are positive though modest in magnitude, suggesting some degree of stability in personal morale. Significant levels are reached only on the item concerning worries for the future. Sex differences are small and nonsignificant at both age levels.

Value of present activities. Men were significantly more likely to report as adults than as schoolboys that their time was profitably spent. Women showed this tendency in a lesser degree, and for them the through-time correlation was 0.

Is it fun just to be alive? Both age groups tend to be optimistic. Fewer adults than adolescents "enjoy life so much it is really fun just to be alive," but, also, fewer emphasize the disappointments of life. This trend toward philosophi-

---

[2] Higher correlations have been reported for scores on attitude or neuroticism inventories, e.g., Nelson (6) and Crook (3), but, since such scores are based on item composites, they are not comparable to these results for single items.

Table 11-1 Responses to Items on Personal Life and Happiness

	Men		Women	
Alternatives	1938	1953–8	1938	1953–8
Value of present activities				
1. Most of my time is quite profitably spent	29%	55%	26%	47%
2. Many of the things I do will someday be useful to me	49	39	58	34
3. Only a few of the things I do will be useful to me later on	20	4	11	16
4. Most of the things I do are really quite useless	2	2	5	3
Temporal stability †	$r =$ .18		$r =$ .02	
Temporal shift ‡	$\chi^2 =$ 10.32**		$\chi^2 =$ .76	
Is it fun just to be alive?				
1. I enjoy life so much that it is really fun just to be alive	41%	29%	45%	30%
2. There are only a few things in life that are very disappointing	43	67	38	60
3. There are many things in life that are disappointing	12	4	7	8
4. Sometimes life seems to be just a series of disappointments	4	0	10	2
Temporal stability †	$r =$ .10		$r =$ .19	
Temporal shift ‡	$\chi^2 =$ .04		$\chi^2 =$ .76	
Do people of your age worry about the future?				
1. I never worry about the future	4%	6%	10%	2%
2. I seldom worry about the future	47	61	51	59
3. I quite frequently worry about the future	43	33	32	37
4. Very often the future looks pretty hopeless to me	6	0	7	2
Temporal stability †	$r =$ .31*		$r =$ .29*	
Temporal shift ‡	$\chi^2 =$ 3.38		$\chi^2 =$ .01	
Will people of your age get the things they want most in life?				
1. I expect to get almost all of the things I really want in life	24%	35%	24%	37%
2. I will probably get more of the things I want than not	33	45	42	45
3. There are several things I want in life that I will probably never have	41	18	34	18
4. I will probably never have most of the things I really want in life	2	2	0	0
Temporal stability †	$r =$ .23*		$r =$ .08	
Temporal shift ‡	$\chi^2 =$ 5.28*		$\chi^2 =$ .70	

† Stability coefficients significantly greater than 0 (one tail) are marked by an asterisk for 5 per cent level, a double asterisk for 1 per cent level.

‡ Chi square is a measure of the net shift of opinion in the groups as a whole from 1938 to 1953. It is based on the number growing more optimistic as compared with the number growing more pessimistic. Significance levels are indicated by asterisks as above.

cal acceptance is consistent in both sexes. Failure to identify this finding at a statistically significant level may follow from use of an index which measures net shift rather than convergence.

Do people of your age worry about the future? Although there is an increase in guarded optimism in adults as compared with adolescents, significant through-time correlations are obtained for both sexes. Worrisomeness seems to be a more stable tendency than most other factors in morale.

Will you get most of the things you want in life? Both sexes show increased optimism, though the shift approaches significance only for men. The through-time correlation reaches the 5 per cent significance level only for men. One is led to speculate to what degree the increased expectations of our adults of getting most of the things they want follow from redefinitions of wants in a more modest and realistic direction.

Two items overtly require subjects to compare their own generation to the preceding one, but the latent dimension of personal optimism is apparent (*see* Table 11–2).

Table 11-2   Responses to Items on Differences Between Generations

	Men		Women	
Alternatives	1938	1953–8	1938	1953–8
What about opportunities?				
1. There are actually a great many more good opportunities today than ever before	18%	53%	23%	67%
2. There are at least as many good opportunities today as ever	33	43	20	31
3. Good opportunities are not so numerous nowadays as they used to be	39	4	54	2
4. There aren't many good opportunities today	10	0	3	0
Temporal stability†	$r =$	$-.07$	$r =$	$.11$
Temporal shift‡	$\chi^2 =$	$20.10**$	$\chi^2 =$	$18.90**$
How many people of your age have as good a time as the people in your parents' generation did?				
1. Probably all of us do	57%	63%	61%	64%
2. Many of us do	33	31	23	28
3. Some of us do	8	4	8	8
4. Probably very few of us do	2	2	8	0
Temporal stability†	$r =$	$-.03$	$r =$	$.11$
Temporal shift‡	$\chi^2 =$	$.90$	$\chi^2 =$	$.46$

† Stability coefficients significantly greater than 0 (one tail) are marked by an asterisk for 5 per cent level, a double asterisk for 1 per cent level.

‡ Chi square is a measure of the net shift of opinion in the groups as a whole from 1938 to 1953. It is based on the number growing more optimistic as compared with the number growing more pessimistic. Significance levels are indicated by asterisks as above.

Table 11–3   Responses to Items on Attitudes Toward Society

	Men		Women	
Alternatives	1938	1953–8	1938	1953–8
How important is any given individual?				
1. Every individual is important to the whole of society	60%	53%	73%	75%
2. An individual is usually important to most of the people who know him	16	27	17	10
3. An individual is usually important only to his family and a few friends	14	18	10	15
4. An individual is really not important to anybody but himself	10	2	0	0
Temporal stability[†]	$r =$	.29*	$r =$	.05
Temporal shift[‡]	$\chi^2 =$	.04	$\chi^2 =$	.01
Most people can be trusted				
1. I agree quite definitely with this statement	12%	25%	10%	33%
2. On the whole I agree with the statement	72	63	70	65
3. On the whole, I disagree with the statement	10	12	18	0
4. I strongly disagree with the statement	6	0	2	2
Temporal stability[†]	$r =$	.03	$r =$	.45**
Temporal shift[‡]	$\chi^2 =$	2.22	$\chi^2 =$	10.32**
Are all men equal before the law? The average citizen—				
1. Is treated as justly in the courts as the most influential citizen	10%	6%	13%	29%
2. Is usually treated fairly in the courts	35	70	52	71
3. Is frequently handicapped in getting justice in the courts	26	18	24	0
4. Is not treated as justly in the courts as he would be if he were famous or important	29	6	11	0
Temporal stability[†]	$r =$	.25*	$r =$	.45**
Temporal shift[‡]	$\chi^2 =$	9.04**	$\chi^2 =$	14.08**

Sex difference in 1953 data is significant (χ^2 test) at 1 per cent level.

Table 11–3 *(Continued)*

What determines whether a person will have "social prestige"? In determining social prestige—				
1. Personal qualities and not money are what really count	14%	12%	7%	12%
2. Personal qualities are usually more important than money	31	21	34	34
3. Personal qualities (pleasantness, ability, etc.) are important but less influential than money	43	59	52	46
4. Money is much more important than personal qualities	12	8	7	8
Temporal stability†	$r =$	.40**	$r =$	.05
Temporal shift‡	$\chi^2 =$	.64	$\chi^2 =$	.34

† Stability coefficients significantly greater than 0 (one tail) are marked by an asterisk for 5 per cent level, a double asterisk for 1 per cent level.

‡ Chi square is a measure of the net shift of opinion in the groups as a whole from 1938 to 1953. It is based on the number growing more optimistic as compared with the number growing more pessimistic. Significance levels are indicated by asterisks as above.

What about opportunities? This item shows a highly significant shift for both sexes (.1 per cent level) toward a more optimistic appraisal. This change may well owe more to the altered economic climate than to personal psychodynamics. Through-time correlations are very small and sex differences minor at both levels.

How many people of your age have as good a time as the people in your parents' generation did? This item showed a very small shift in the optimistic direction, but even among adolescents the model choice was the most positive of the four. Stability coefficients are near 0. Sex differences are small and nonsignificant at either age level.

The remaining four items in the morale group involved less self-reference and tapped instead attitudes toward society and its institutions (*see* Table 11–3). In this area, the subjects tended to show more consistency of judgment across the 15-year interval, though significant stability coefficients for one sex were sometimes coupled with near-0 values for the other. While responses of adults were slightly more positive than those of adolescents, they often reflected a more guarded position. Rather consistently the men gave tough, realistic judgments more frequently and expressed conventional ideals less often than did the women. Among adolescents this trend is weaker.

How important is any given individual? The most frequent choice of both adolescents and adults was for the view that everyone is important to the whole of society. Girls and women were more nearly unanimous than were men and boys, and, whereas this sentiment occurred more often among women than among girls, it occurred less often among men than boys. These trends do not reach statistical significance. The through-time correlation is significant for men but not for women.

Most people can be trusted. Optimism increased among both sexes, significantly among women. Consistency of opinion among women yielded one of the largest stability coefficients (.45), but the corresponding value for men was near 0.

Are all men equal before the law? Adults of both sexes are significantly more likely than adolescents to credit the basic fairness of the courts; and women are more likely than men to reject the negative alternatives and to accept the conventional ideal, the only significant sex difference found in the entire test. Temporal stability coefficients are significant for both sexes and reach the 1 per cent level in the women's data.

What determines whether a person will have social prestige? This item is unusual in that the most frequent response of both men and women, adolescent and adult, was the mildly pessimistic opinion that personal qualities are important, though less influential than money; but, whereas the stability coefficient for women is near 0, that for men is .40 (significant at 1 per cent level).

The residual items in the questionnaire were four dealing with attitudes toward aspects of school and education. In this area, points of view tended to show significant correlation across the 15-year interval. Sex differences were significant at neither age level (*see* Table 11–4).

Do you feel that your education helps you to earn a living? Do you feel that your education helps you to enjoy life more? These items, phrased in the future tense in 1938 and the present tense in 1953, show similar trends. Significant correlations through time were obtained for both sexes, .27 and .24 for men and women on the first named, .24 and .32, respectively, on the second. Sex differences in judgment were not significant on either item on either occasion. All groups value education more for earning a living than for enjoying life.

Is it important to make good grades? This item showed the greatest constancy of any in the set, with through-time correlations of .33 (1 per cent level) and .47 (1 per cent level) for men and women, respectively. Despite the evidence for a significant degree of individual consistency through time, opinions of the adults, especially the men, were less positive than were those of adolescents about the subsequent value of good grades. The shift was not significant for women, but reached the .1 per cent level for men. Differences in judgment between men and women were not significant on either occasion.

Are social cliques a good thing in high school? The stem of this item was rephrased from the 1938 version, but the response alternatives were not changed. This item was of interest to the staff of the Oakland Growth Study because of recurring controversy over the proper role (if any) of fraternities and sororities in the high schools attended by Study subjects. Generally speaking, disapproval of cliques is greater among the adults, but men are more inclined than women to minimize their importance. Sex differences are not significant nor are through-time correlations.

Table 11–4 Responses to Items on School and Education

	Men		Women	
Alternatives	1938	1953–8	1938	1953–8
Do you feel that your education helps (will help) you to earn a living?				
1. I think it is (will be) a very great help	55%	63%	45%	63%
2. It is (will be) a considerable help	33	27	35	27
3. It helps (will help) me in a few respects	10	10	18	10
4. I think it is (will be) very little help	2	0	2	0
Temporal stability†	$r =$	.27*	$r =$	.24*
Temporal shift‡	$\chi^2 =$	.38	$\chi^2 =$	2.46
Do you feel that your education helps (will help) you to enjoy life more?				
1. It is (will be) a most important factor in the enjoyment of life	47%	33%	32%	37%
2. It is (will be) a great help	41	45	44	50
3. It is (will be) a fair amount of help	12	16	21	8
4. It has (will have) little effect on my enjoyment of living	0	6	3	5
Temporal stability†	$r =$	.24*	$r =$	.32*
Temporal shift‡	$\chi^2 =$	3.22	$\chi^2 =$	.56
Is it important to make good school grades?				
1. It is extremely helpful later on	55%	16%	44%	41%
2. It is helpful later on	33	66	36	49
3. It really isn't of great help later on	10	14	18	8
4. It is no help later on	2	4	2	2
Temporal stability†	$r =$	.33**	$r =$	.47**
Temporal shift‡	$\chi^2 =$	12.04**	$\chi^2 =$	.21
Are social cliques a good thing in high school? (Does social cliquiness make school life unpleasant?)				
1. Exclusive social cliques are a good influence on students, because it is an honor to belong to them	16%	0%	10%	2%
2. Social cliques exist, but have little effect on most students' happiness	54	53	39	27
3. Exclusive social cliques do affect rather unpleasantly the lives of the students outside the cliques	22	33	34	61
4. Social cliques (such as fraternities and sororities) are harmful in school, because they make the school lives of those outside the cliques unhappy	8	14	17	10
Temporal stability†	$r =$	.18	$r =$	−.16
Temporal shift‡	$\chi^2 =$	5.34	$\chi^2 =$	1.04

† Stability coefficients significantly greater than 0 (one tail) are marked by an asterisk for 5 per cent level, a double asterisk for 1 per cent level.

‡ Chi square is a measure of the net shift of opinion in the groups as a whole from 1938 to 1953. It is based on the number growing more optimistic as compared with the number growing more pessimistic. Significance levels are indicated by asterisks as above.

SUMMARY

Responses to a brief morale questionnaire showed a modest degree of temporal constancy across an interval of 15-plus years involving the age range from 18 years to 33 years. Items tapping attitudes toward education were most constant, yielding consistently significant correlations ranging in the twenties and higher. Opinions on other topics, e.g., the fairness of the courts, the importance of the individual, etc., were less constant, yielding significant stability coefficients for one sex and not for the other. Items relating more to the individual, especially if the content referred to mood or feeling tone, were notably lacking in temporal constancy.

Sex differences were small, both in the high school and in the adult data, but conventional, positive clichés tended more often to be offered by women. "Realistic," tough-minded responses were more often given by men. There was a general tendency for adult judgments to be more homogeneous than was true of the adolescents. Also, while they were inclined to avoid extreme statements, the adults were more optimistic and confident than they had been as adolescents—an outcome probably not unrelated to changes in the economic climate between 1938 and 1953. In general, the constancy of these questionnaire responses was lower, but not notably different from that reported for observers' ratings on the same group.

REFERENCES

1. Bender, I. E. Changes in religious interest: a re-test after 15 years. *J. abnorm. soc. Psychol.,* 1958, **57**, 41–46.
2. Crook, M. N. Retest correlations in neuroticism. *J. gen. Psychol.,* 1941, **24**, 173–182.
3. Crook, M. N. Retest with the Thurstone Personality Schedule after 6½ years. *J. gen. Psychol.,* 1943, **28**, 111–120.
4. Jones, H. E. Attitude changes of high school youth over a nine year period. *Amer. Psychologist,* 1948, **3**, 352. (Abstract)
5. Kelly, E. L. Consistency of the adult personality. *Amer. Psychologist,* 1955, **11**, 659–681.
6. Nelson, E. N. P. Persistence of attitudes of college students fourteen years later. *Psychol. Monogr.,* 1954, **68**, No. 2 (Whole No. 373).
7. Strong, E. K., Jr. Permanence of interest scores over 22 years. *J. appl. Psychol.,* 1951, **35**, 89–91.
8. Tuddenham, R. D. The constancy of personality ratings over two decades. *Genet. Psychol. Monogr.,* 1959, **60**, 3–29.

ADDITIONAL READINGS

Bronson, Wanda C. Central orientations: A study of behavior organization from childhood to adolescence. *Child Development,* 1966, **37,** 125–155. This investigation was designed to determine behaviors which are most consistent throughout the developmental span. Measures which proved most predictive and persistent for both sexes were found to fall in three dimensions: withdrawal-expressiveness, reactivity-placidity, and passivity-dominance. However, the meaning and expression of such traits may vary with shifting environmental demands.

Carlson, Rae. Stability and change in the adolescent's self-image. *Child Development,* 1965, **36,** 659–666. This article reports changes in the structure of the self-image of students studied in the sixth grade and again as high-school seniors. Boys increased in personal orientation, girls in social-personal orientation.

Costanzo, Philip R. & Shaw, Marvin E. Conformity as a function of age level. *Child Development,* 1966, **37,** 967–975. An experiment confirmed the hypothesis that conformity develops in two stages, increasing to adolescence and decreasing thereafter. Subjects were exposed to erroneous judgments in a simulated conformity situation.

Engel, M. The stability of the self-concept in adolescence. *Journal of Abnormal and Social Psychology,* 1959, **58,** 211–215. Engel reported that self-concepts of 172 middle-class junior-high and high-school students correlated .78 after an interval of two years. In general, their self-concepts improved as they moved through adolescence.

Kellmer, Pringle M. L. and Gooch, S. Chosen ideal person, personality development and progress in school subjects: A longitudinal study. *Human Development,* 1965, **8,** 161–180. A group of fourth year secondary pupils were asked to write a description of their ideal person, and give reasons for their choice. The same group had performed the same task four years earlier in junior high school. A longitudinal comparison indicated definable stages in the choice of the ideal person. A developmental pattern, which attempted to encompass the findings of other workers was outlined, characterizing choice of "ideal person" from 8 years into adolescence.

Jones, Mary Cover. A study of socialization patterns at the high school level. *Journal of Genetic Psychology,* 1958, **93,** 87–111. On the basis of data from the Adolescent Growth Study, University of California, Jones compares students who participate heavily in extracurricular activities with those who do not participate, in terms of intellectual, social, and physical characteristics. In general, patterns of social participation persisted into adult life, although some decided shifts took place.

Witkin, Herman A., Goodenough, Donald R., & Karp, Stephen A. Stability of cognitive style from childhood to young adulthood. *Journal of Personality and Social Psychology,* 1967, **7,** (3), 291–300. The development of differentiation, as reflected in cognitive style, was followed longitudinally in two groups, one from 8 to 13 years, the other from 10 to 24 years. A progressive increase in field independence was evident to age 17, with no further change to age 24. Individuals showed marked stability over the years in extent of field dependence. Data from other studies are in the same direction.

Yarrow, Leon J. (Ed.) Symposium on personality, consistency and change: perspective from longitudinal research. *Vita Humana,* 1964, **7,** 65–146. In this issue, representatives of three well-known longitudinal studies (the Berkeley Growth Study, the California Guidance Study, and the Fels Study of Human Development) and of one nonlongitudinal study (the Topeka "Coping Project") presented selected findings and interpretations. The papers were introduced by Yarrow and discussed by Schaefer and Honzik.

VI. Two Related Concepts: Stage Theory and Critical Period Hypothesis

In recent years psychologists have paid considerable attention to the related concepts of *stage theory* and *critical period*. In stage theory, human development is perceived as progressing by stages, each of which possesses a certain distinctiveness. However, there is considerable disagreement concerning how discrete such stages may be, the exact duration of such stages, and the particular significance of each stage. The critical period hypothesis suggests that certain times in life are especially critical for the acquisition of particular sorts of experience. A critical period may span varying lengths of time—hours, days, months, or years. There may be different critical periods for different functions. If the critical period for acquiring a particular function is missed, presumably a similar experience at a later date will have much less, if any, impact. Also, learning acquired during a critical period tends to persist. Thus, if childhood be deemed critical for establishing the concept of self as male or female, once established the feeling is difficult, and perhaps impossible to change.

Where adolescents are concerned, stage theory involves several issues. Is adolescence a "natural" stage in development, or merely an artefact of modern society? Are experiences during adolescence in any sense critical for what happens later on? Perhaps infancy and childhood are the truly critical stages, so that by the teens an individual's course is set, and subject to little modification.

The first selection that follows, an article written by the editor of this volume, relates age-stage theory and critical period hypothesis to adolescence. The second selection, by Douvan and Adelson, treats adolescence as the stage for establishing an identity, as described in the first selection. Concepts of identity, as interpreted by Douvan and Adelson, are empirically based; however, their data concern only American teen-agers. The application of their concepts of identity to adolescents of other cultures would make an interesting study.

Several important questions about stage theory and critical periods remain unanswered. Might experiences be so manipulated that children would proceed through life stages at a faster pace than generally believed possible, or perhaps skip some stages altogether? Also, might experiences in adolescence be so engineered that the period would assume more significance than it presently does? Certainly much research remains to be done concerning life stages to resolve the considerable confusion that surrounds this important topic.

12

Dorothy Rogers

STAGE THEORY AND CRITICAL PERIOD AS RELATED TO ADOLESCENCE

In the following, the author reviews certain of the better known stage theories and relates them to adolescence. She also makes critical observations concerning them, both individually and collectively. The writer concludes that adolescence may indeed have distinctive features, but much of its significance depends on the way specific individuals experience it.

Among the longer-standing controversies in developmental psychology is whether individuals maintain the same basic sequences in their patterns of development. This question gave rise to the age-stage hypothesis, which suggests that children manifest various behaviors sequentially in the course of their development, and progress through increasingly mature and relatively well-defined stages.

. . . The idea of life stages was pursued in earnest at the University of Vienna in the 1930's. The Vienna writers, especially Charlotte Bühler, postulated five principle stages.* During the first stage, childhood, an individual lives at home, and is dependent on his family. From age 12 to about 28, the individual engages in exploratory and preparatory activities, while deciding what to do with his life and establishing his independence. A person performs his major work in life from about age 28 to 50, after which his activities decline. At 65 he retires, gradually restricting his activities and loosening his ties.[1]

SEVERAL WELL-KNOWN STAGE THEORIES

Some writers concentrate on certain life-stages in particular; others indicate how the various life-stages fit together and attempt to define the special significance of each. Let us now look at certain of the more influential views concerning life-stages viewed developmentally, beginning with Piaget.

* C. Bühler, *Der Menschliche Lebenslauf als Psychologisches Problem.* Gottingen: Verlag für Psychologie, 1959.
[1] Dorothy Rogers, *Child Psychology* (Belmont, Calif., Brooks-Cole Publishing Co., 1969).

155

Piaget perceived children as progressing through sequential stages of development, for example, in morals.[2] In the first stage, until age 7, the child is a moral realist, and judges deviant acts in terms of damage done. Finally, after certain intermediate stages, the child learns to apply principles differentially and to realize that rules can be altered. At the later stage, intent matters more than damage done. At the early stage, the child who breaks fifteen cups is judged more wicked than one who breaks one cup, even though the first child's mishap was completely accidental while the second child's involved disobedience.

Another stage concept, by Henry Stack Sullivan, suggests how adolescence relates to earlier life stages.[3] After infancy, he distinguishes two stages of childhood. The young child has clear interpersonal relations, but is still so young that such experiences are largely confined to the home. Later childhood, roughly what Freud called the latency period, Sullivan refers to as the juvenile era. In this period the child must deal as an individual with strangers, and cope with the gap between his image of himself and others of him, and between what he needs and what they give. When he begins seeing others as competitors, childhood is at an end. Maturity becomes a matter of individual psychodynamics, not biological age. Thus, childhood may end earlier for a lower-class child, who may have to fend for himself almost as soon as he can walk. Adolescence, says Sullivan, is distinguished from earlier stages by the warp of tenderness, but fibers of social experience tie the personality together. Other people come to matter as individuals, and not merely as sources of support or obstructions to impulse. The adolescent learns to love, and to value others for their personalities.

HAVIGHURST'S DEVELOPMENTAL TASK THEORY

Havighurst and Erikson base their stage theories on the need for continuous mastery of new tasks, appropriate for successive age-stages. Implicit in such developmental task theories is the idea that an individual must resolve certain conflicts, or acquire certain skills at a given stage if he is to fulfill successfully the obligations of the next age level. Certain developmental tasks, maintains Havighurst, originate chiefly from physical maturation, others primarily from cultural pressures.[4] Learning to write is required by social pressure, while establishing satisfactory heterosexual re-

[2] *Ibid.*

[3] Henry Stack Sullivan, *Interpersonal Theory of Psychiatry* (New York, Norton, 1953).

[4] R. J. Havighurst, *Human Development and Education* (New York, Longmans, 1953).

lationships depends on physical maturation. A third source of developmental tasks is the individual's value system. Whether a girl spends her time learning to knit or to operate a computer may depend on whether she aspires to a domestic or career role in the future.

ERIKSON'S EIGHT STAGES OF MAN

Erikson defined life tasks in terms of personality characteristics.[5] He portrayed life as consisting of eight periods, ideally beginning with the establishment of *basic trust* in infancy. The quality of the maternal relationship is perceived as crucial for creating in the child a feeling that others can be trusted. In the second stage, the child begins establishing a sense of *autonomy*. In the process of developing basic patterns of eating, sleeping, or toilet training he is permitted certain alternatives and choices, which result in feelings of freedom. In the third stage the child develops *initiative*. At this time, he gains a sense of responsibility, especially through contact with ideal adults. Next comes the stage when the child gains a sense of the technological ethos of his culture. He attends school and gains *respect for industry and its tools*. The fifth stage, adolescence, is a period of *identity* versus role diffusion. Faced with "physiological revolution" within him, and with tangible adults ahead of him, the adolescent becomes preoccupied with how he appears to others compared with what he believes he is, and with how roles and skills cultivated earlier will articulate with "occupational prototypes of the day." The great danger is role confusion; and where such confusion is based on doubt as to one's sexual identity, delinquent and psychotic episodes occur. For most young people, the confusion occurs over the occupational role.

In a strenuous effort to maintain his integrity, the adolescent over-identifies, almost to the point of losing his identity, with cliques and crowds. This involvement of the self with others leads to "falling in love," which is an attempt to define the identity rather than a sexual matter. Clannishness becomes adolescents' defense against identity confusion. They help each other through a period of great discomfort by stereotyping themselves. Nevertheless, the youth searches for social values to guide his identity, and yearns to believe that those who succeed in the adult world also shoulder the obligation of being the best sort of people.[6]

Next comes the sixth stage, adulthood, and with it marriage and the *need for intimacy*. In a culture which subordinates sexuality to duty, work, and worship, the sense of intimacy does not come easily. Also involved in marriage is the need for *parental sense,* which may never be acquired if

[5] E. H. Erikson, *Childhood and Society* (New York, Norton, 1963).
[6] E. H. Erikson, *Childhood and Society* (New York, Norton, 1963), pp. 247–274.

the parent exploits his children. The crises of development is the last stage—adulthood. In this period, Stage 7, the individual attains *generativity, or accomplishment*—the reverse of stagnation. Finally, in old age, comes ego *integrity,* the culmination of the life stages, and with it fulfillment instead of despair. Only through integrity is an individual capable of defending his own life style.

A special deficit in Erikson's theory is the lumping of males and females together. For instance, adolescent girls may not have the vigorous need for identity that males do. Girls play nurturant, autonomous roles, boys an instrumental one. A vigorous sense of self may actually obstruct or interfere with the girl's subordinating her own needs to those of her husband and the needs of her children.

CRITICISM OF DEVELOPMENTAL TASK THEORY

Theories such as Havighurst's and Erikson's may help to order life's tasks but present certain dangers as well: mastery of specific tasks may indeed be more crucial at certain stages; however, such tasks should not be thought of as discrete and belonging solely to a specific stage. A task can hardly be mastered successfully if the groundwork for its accomplishment is not laid earlier. For example, an adolescent will hardly establish an identity at adolescence unless he has made considerable progress toward that goal earlier. The developmental task theory also encourages the perception of development as a lock-step process. One performs Task No. 1, then Task No. 2, and so on, in that order. Actually, progress in mastering developmental tasks is overlapping and relatively continuous, though setbacks are normal. Moreover, the identification of such tasks, in so precise a fashion, tends toward crystallizing the life-curriculum prescribed for children, thereby obstructing the sort of critical reexamination and continuous modification needed in a rapidly changing society. For instance, we may assign the goal—to establish satisfactory heterosexual relations—to adolescence. However, if the child society continues its present trend toward embracing both sexes in childhood activities, then tomorrow's child, in order to be well adjusted socially, may need increased interaction with opposite-sex peers at an earlier age.

Finally, the concept of developmental tasks may be wrongly interpreted as implying that each life stage is simply an apprenticeship for what follows. Thus, the child's role would simply be an audition for the role he will play as an adult. Instead, each stage is important for its own sake but should provide a healthy base for later stages.[7]

[7] Rogers, *op. cit.*

PSYCHOANALYTIC STAGE THEORY

Traditional psychoanalytic stage theory has been especially significant in determining popular concepts of adolescence. In the Freudian tradition, adolescence is portrayed as the period when sexual interest and activity re-awaken in the pubescent boy or girl after a prolonged latency period, during which infantile sexual drives have been repressed or sublimated into other areas. Presumably, the growing individual passes through oral, anal, and genital stages of sexuality, in turn directing erotic impulses toward self, the parent of the same sex, and the parent of the opposite sex. In late infancy, when the boy is between the ages of three and six, his sexual urges are said to be genitalized and are directed toward the mother, representing the so-called Oedipal situation, or the desire for sexual union with the mother and recognition of the father as a rival and of a desire for his death. At the same time, the son justifies his hostility toward his father by presuming that his father wishes to castrate him for his incestuous desire for his mother. However, the boy's identification with the father serves to introject within him the father's restrictions and taboos, and bring the Oedipal stage to a close. Sexual feelings toward the mother become sublimated into affection.

Now comes the latency period of late childhood, which is terminated by pubescence. Strong hormonal influences operate to reawaken the sex urges, and heterosexual impulses come to the fore and demand satisfaction. Sex feelings now become so strong that the *ego,* or self, is pictured as constantly in danger of being overcome by *id* (primitive urges) and disregarding the *superego* (conscience). Some writers have advocated imposing strict environmental limits as a means of helping the adolescent hold his sex impulses in check, and of helping him sublimate repressed id drives into art, social life, athletics, or other interests.[8] *Sublimation* refers to substituting for socially disapproved outlets, socially approved ones which satisfy the same need. However, others warn that over-repression may lead to rigidity of the personality disturbances, and stress that the ego should serve as mediator between superego and id.

The psychoanalysts also considered adolescence as the critical period for establishing proper sex-role patterns of male or of female, and for the achievement of normal heterosexuality. Various factors might, however, cause the individual to fixate at an earlier psychosexual level, forever thwarting normal progression to mature heterosexuality. For instance, the young boy might become so attached to his mother that he never marries and continues to live in the maternal home the rest of his life.

There are various criticisms of psychoanalytic stage theory. For one thing, infants lack the hormonal base to support sexual feelings, in the

[8] F. J. Hacker and E. R. Geleerd, "Freedom and Authority in Adolescence," *American Journal of Orthopsychiatry,* Vol. 15 (1945), pp. 621–630.

sense that adults interpret them. Moreover, adolescent sexuality is no mere continuation of earlier stages but differs from them in intensity and quality due to the enormously increased hormonal production. When the body attains its distinctive sexual secondary sex characteristics, the adolescent must incorporate a greatly revised physical self-image.

Ausubel questions the psychoanalytic contention that most adolescent interests and activities are merely sublimated products of sex drives.[9] Merely in the process of establishing social status, an individual becomes involved in a host of activities and relationships. Since other motives for such activities are readily apparent, it is simply unnecessary to think of them as being powered by repressed sex needs. Does the boy shoot basketballs into the basket because this activity constitutes a sublimation of the sex act, or merely because he wins applause and a higher social status for so doing, besides gaining a feeling of physical exuberance? Moreover, it is questionable how completely the sex impulses are repressed, especially among males. More or less regular outlets are found in masturbation, petting, and intercourse.

Consider next the psychoanalytic concept of adolescent literary and artistic productions as a means of sublimation of sex drives. Since such activities involve a great deal of symbolism they would seem to qualify very nicely for indirect outlets. However, adolescents' increased emotionality in the broader sense, and not merely sex feeling, may lead to producing such creations. It is difficult to perceive in all the adolescents' creative endeavors evidence of repressed sex feelings. Besides, it is hardly tenable that painting a picture or growing flowers will somehow drain off pent-up sex feelings.

Rankian theory, as stated or interpreted by Otto Rank and his followers, originated in the psychoanalytic tradition, but stressed the individual's conflicting needs for dependence and independence. Society demands of the adolescent that he become independent, but nevertheless makes it very difficult for him to become so.[10] The adolescent fights against his own sexual urges because he fears that to surrender to them will threaten his hard-won independence. It becomes a major developmental task of the adolescent to establish a wholesome balance of dependence and independence in dealing with adults and peers. He must acknowledge his dependency on others while not becoming unduly manipulated by them.

QUESTIONS POSED BY STAGE THEORY

Stage theory has given rise to many questions, some of them stated or implicit in the foregoing. One question relative to adolescence as a stage

[9] D. P. Ausubel, *Theory and Problems of Adolescent Development* (New York, Grune & Stratton, 1954), p. 28.

[10] D. Hankins, "The Psychology and Direct Treatment of Adolescence," *Mental Hygiene,* Vol. 27 (1943), pp. 238–247.

is this: *is it a true stage in itself, or is it merely a prolonged transition from childhood to adulthood?* Sorenson calls adolescence "much more than one rung up the ladder from childhood." [11] It is a built-in, necessary transition period for ego development. It is a "leave-taking of the dependencies of childhood and a precocious reach for adulthood." He also calls it "an intermission between earlier freedoms . . . a last hesitation before . . . serious commitments concerning work and love."

If adolescence is to be considered significant in its own right, perhaps it should be institutionalized. *Institutionalization* would imply establishing pretty clear guidelines for adolescents, including definition of responsibilities and privileges. Such a clarification, it is argued, would relieve much of the adolescent's anxiety. As it is, he has difficulty defining himself vis-à-vis an ambiguous situation. Also, institutionalization would assist parents by indicating how the older and younger generations should relate to each other.

Others argue against institutionalization, claiming that it would obstruct regular examination of age-graded tasks, in terms of their functionalism for society or for the individual. For instance, in this culture Americans place a high value on popularity, and it becomes incumbent on the adolescent to learn to get along with his age-mates. But does confronting him with the task of getting along interfere with getting ahead? Does the adolescent sell a bit of himself, at too dear a price, to gain acceptance by others simply because this aspect of adolescence has become confirmed? Also, if adolescence receives too much recognition as a stage, then youth may feel constrained to remain rooted in it. Stone and Church call it a "way station" in development and as such, its most "universal and pervasive feeling is of being out of step." [12] Perhaps feeling out of step may help motivate the adolescent to become adult. If he settled too comfortably into adolescence he might forever remain just partly grown up.

Also implicit in stage theory *is society's task of articulating each stage with what follows.* Should rural youth be trained for city-type living, simply because most of them will eventually live in the city? Or should they simply adjust as well as possible to rural living, on the assumption that what they need most to transfer to adult life is a general way of adjustment rather than specific behaviors? Again, should adolescents be encouraged to substitute serious group endeavors for the many light-hearted pastimes of the youth culture, in order to adapt more easily to the adult responsibilities that follow? Or may the fun culture of youth be an appropriate preparation for an adult world where the work week is shrinking and adults are confronted with increasingly larger chunks of leisure time?

Another question originating in age-stage theory is this: *to what ex-*

[11] R. Sorenson, "Youth's Need for Challenge and Place in Society," *Children*, Vol. 9 (1962), pp. 131–138.

[12] L. J. Stone and J. Church, *Childhood and Adolescence* (New York, Random House, 1957).

tent are life stages genetically or socioculturally derived? If they are genetically based, it would seem that life tasks must somehow be accommodated to them. If they are sociocultural creations, then such tasks might be ordered to fit a particular society or individual. One way to answer this question is to determine factors common to the various life stages in cultures around the world. Such an examination yields this conclusion: that development in all cultures does indeed proceed by more or less distinctive stages, but that there is very wide variation in the definition and significance of those stages. For one thing, age stages may be defined differently from one culture to another. Infancy may be prolonged where breast-feeding is lengthened, or accelerated where women must work in the fields. In some backward countries, where there is much illness and malnutrition, old age begins much earlier than in countries where vigor is maintained longer.

Again, life in some cultures is more rigidly defined in terms of age-stages than others. In primitive cultures, ceremonies mark the end of childhood and adulthood begins, thus bypassing adolescence. Individuals simply glide from childhood into adulthood. There was no moratorium called adolescence, no twilight zone between childhood and adulthood. By contrast, preparation for adult life in complicated societies requires a distinguishable period with its own rules, customs and relationships. For example, in the British public school, adolescence was more than an interregnum; it was an epoch. Such schools were tough; they defined the content of adolescence, and gave the adolescent something to be adolescent about.[13]

ADOLESCENCE AS A CRITICAL PERIOD

Cross-cultural comparisons justify another conclusion: that particular life-stages, either universally or within particular societies, become critical, in certain respects, for the stages that follow. This concept, called the *critical period hypothesis,* suggests that similar experiences, either at an earlier or later stage, would have less effect where particular functions are concerned. Unless the infant has established a satisfactory relationship with his mother, perhaps he will be unable to establish satisfactory heterosexual relationships later on.[14] Unless a child has unhampered chances to manipulate objects, perhaps he will forever sacrifice optimal neuromuscular development in later years.[15]

[13] Edgar Z. Friedenberg, *The Vanishing Adolescent* (Boston, Beacon Press, 1959).

[14] Harry F. Harlow and Margaret F. Harlow, "The Effect of Rearing Conditions on Behavior," *Bulletin of the Menninger Clinic,* Vol. 26 (1962), pp. 213–224.

[15] J. McVicker Hunt, "The Psychological Bases for Using Preschool Enrichment as an Antidote for Cultural Deprivation," *Merrill-Palmer Quarterly,* Vol. 10 (1964), pp. 209–248.

Adolescence itself has been viewed critical in various ways. Ausubel declares adolescence to be universally a time of extensive personality reorganization. Because of sharp distinctions between child and adult status, profound changes are required in an individual's attitudes and behaviours.[16] According to Friedenberg, two aspects of growth essential to self-definition are climactic in adolescence.[17] One is a capacity for tenderness, fired by sexuality, which produces a pattern of life not wholly cynical or expedient. Adolescents are passionate, and their passion is no less real when directed toward a hot-rod, a popular singer or the leader of a black jacketed gang. Also, the adolescent acquires a respect for competence both in himself and others. This respect is crucial, because a youngster who does not know what he is good at will not be sure what he is good for.

Many writers, including Friedenberg, believe adolescence critical for establishing identity; but certain forces seem dedicated to destroying identity. For example, America once prided itself on being a land of self-fulfillment; but now Madison Avenue, via Mass Media, is subordinating individuals to social goals. The dominant middle-class individual is "other directed," unthinkingly obtaining his aspirations and goals from his social class, and concerned only with adjustment and popularity.

If adolescence is critical, is one part of this period more important than the other? Often writers have remarked on the pubertal period as a time of special "storm and stress," but late adolescence may be no less critical, in certain ways. According to Hess, successful performance in the early twenties, as evaluated by occupational commitment, social skill, and psychological health, is more closely related to events and experiences that occur *after* high school than to high school behavior.[18] *Moreover,* these data demonstrate the fluid and unstable nature of adolescent behavior patterns, and provide an empirical basis for the belief that the processes of identity that make for stable adult behavior and personality behavior and personality continue well past high school.

APPLICATIONS OF STAGE THEORY

Various groups have adapted the stage concept of development to their own needs and goals. The business world has capitalized on life-stages by popularizing the notion that individuals must have distinctively different material goods—clothes, sports equipment, and the like—for each age-

[16] D. P. Ausubel, *Theory and Problems of Adolescent Development* (New York, Grune & Stratton, 1954), pp. 22–23.

[17] E. Z. Friedenberg, *The Vanishing Adolescent* (Boston, Beacon Press, 1959).

[18] Robert D. Hess, "High School Antecedents of Adult Achievement," in Robert E. Grinder (Ed.), *Studies in Adolescence* (New York, Macmillan, 1963), pp. 401–414.

stage. The youth must have his collegiate attire; the young business man must put away his college clothes and look the part of an adult.

Educators have attempted to organize the curriculum in terms of stages in cognitive development. For example, Cross emphasizes that educators must consider the "individuality, self-assertiveness, and uniqueness" of adolescents. Adults should consider the way adolescents perceive their own values, and not merely try to get the young person to endorse their own.[19] Unless adults can change their own traditions and policies to accommodate adolescents' characteristics, then youth will initiate change themselves, through rebellious social movements such as the college drug craze and the "hippie movement." In the meantime, considerable talent is lost to the propertied traditionalists. For, as Timothy Leary warns, those youths who have "turned on, tuned in, and dropped out," will make neither soldiers nor executives to carry on middle-class traditions.

INDIVIDUAL EXPERIENCE WITH ADOLESCENCE

A glaring lack in research concerning age-stage theory is phenomenological evidence. How do individuals differ in their own perceptions of the stages through which they pass? Erikson claims that adolescence is the period, par excellence, for establishment of identity; but is that the way adolescents themselves—or older persons in retrospect, perceive it? In an informal test of this question, the writer asked a group of college students to answer this question: "In your life, in what respects have you found childhood distinctive from adolescence, and adolescence, in turn, different from adulthood—if indeed you feel you have moved beyond adolescence?" There was little conscious awareness of the need to establish identity, except indirectly. Girls often mentioned growing social obligations, boys an awareness of broadening responsibilities and sex consciousness. However, there was a great diversity of replies, pointing up the highly individual ways that different individuals experience adolescence. Here are several replies:

> During adolescence I developed independence, and this caused friction within my close-knit family. I also developed a self-consciousness because of a complexion problem and braces. During the two years I have been married I have developed a concept of what things are really valuable to me, and what things are simply attractive because they are "in." I have become less fashion-conscious and more academically-oriented. I have learned diplomacy and social graces, and I have acquired many new interests, and I have developed self-confidence and the ability to be aggressive when necessary. (Female)

[19] Herbert J. Gross, "Conceptual Systems Theory—Application to some Problems of Adolescents," *Adolescence*, Vol. 2, No. 6 (Summer 1967), pp. 153–166.

I don't feel that I suddenly went from childhood to adolescence. As an adolescent, I was more socially conscious—wanting to be popular, wanting approval from my peers. I also became much more sexually aware. Still, this was only a magnification of what I was in childhood—there was no sudden jump from one to the other.

As with childhood, I have gradually reached adulthood—there was no sudden jump between adolescence and adulthood. For me, the main difference is that in adulthood, I am much more self confident and independent in thought. I am also much more socially aware, about world problems, etc. (Female)

Adolescence for me was different from childhood in that I became much more aware of *everything*. Childhood was like a merry-go-round. Nothing had meaning or significance. Adulthood, to me, is an unpleasant step, but a step I know I must take. It encompasses responsibility, something I am not yet sure I can handle. (Male)

In childhood one accepts, in adolescence one criticizes. The distinction is quite apparent for thinking is more dynamic in adolescence. The adolescent makes his own concepts and his parents no longer do his thinking for him. (Male)

The only difference in childhood, adolescence, and adulthood is added responsibilities. More is expected of you at each stage. Also, antisocial behavior among children or adolescents is not judged as hard as if an "adult" did it. I do not feel like an adult because in some situations I am still talked down to and treated like a child. (Male)

From the foregoing several conclusions seem justified. First, all societies appear to be divided according to age-grades and stages, but large variations occur. Adolescence is judged as being significant, even critical in certain ways, but just how is not entirely clear. It is most popularly interpreted as the time for establishing an identity. However, stage theories are too numerous and varied to justify sweeping conclusions, either as to how human development proceeds throughout life, or during adolescence in particular. Badly needed is some theory which ferrets out, synthesizes, and integrates into one overall empirically based theory the major thinking and research that exists on this topic. Such a theory might, in fact, be something completely new, only vaguely resembling the present day formulations of human age-stage progression.

13

Elizabeth Douvan
Joseph Adelson

THE SELF AND IDENTITY

In this excerpt from the report of a nation-wide study of adolescents, the writers consider the nature of self and identity, the tempo of identity crystallization, and various kinds of identities. They distinguish between normative, negative, achieved, and ascribed identities, and also between feminine and masculine identities. Social status is seen as a critical component in the sense of identity.

At adolescence the self is, perhaps for the first time, felt to be tractable. The youngster can step away from himself, separate into subject and object, a "me" and an "I," and then hope and intend to change himself. The self is no longer the implacable being it has been up to this point, and we sometimes find not merely a belief in the possibility of self-transformation, but a passionate wish for it. Thus we find the adolescent changing clothes, hair style, accent, manners, mannerisms, posture, muscles, figure, attitudes, beliefs. The self is Procrustean.

This yearning to change the self is one reflection of the heightened self-consciousness of adolescence. Everything in adolescence contributes to self-awareness. The body is in constant, bewildering change; new wishes and feelings emerge; psychosocially the youngster is transitional, in a status between statuses. Add to this the fact that other people are instinctually needed, and yet out of reach. Instinctual energy flows back to the self, contributing to the irritating and often insufferable vanity and exhibitionism we find among so many adolescents. Not that we find the entrenched narcissism common to certain character neuroses; adolescent narcissism is a variable and transient phenomenon. The self is not set apart from others. Indeed, there is the constant temptation (and danger) to lose the self in others, to merge with others psychologically, by taking in the ego qualities of others in radical acts of internalization, by the extraordinary empathy the adolescent is sometimes capable of, by putting oneself psy-

From Elizabeth Douvan and Joseph Adelson, "The Self and Identity," in *The Adolescent Experience* (New York, Wiley, 1966), pp. 14–19. Reprinted by permission.

chically in thrall to the other. Introjections and projections, infatuations and sudden revulsions, intense closeness and utter detachment—these oscillations reflect the unsteady state of ego and self during adolescence.

Our understanding of the adolescent self has been enhanced through the invention, by Erik Erikson, of the concept of ego identity (Erikson 1950, 1956). The concept "self" is rather closely tied to consciousness; the identity concept encompasses this sense of the self, and includes unconscious determinants and aspects of self, ego, and character. Technically speaking, the identity concept is not altogether satisfactory, since it is allusive, complex, and connotative. Its connotativeness is explicitly recognized by Erikson, who prefers to let "the term identity speak for itself in a number of connotations. At one time, then, it will appear to refer to a conscious *sense of individual identity;* at another to an unconscious striving for a *continuity of personal character;* at a third, as a criterion for the silent doings of *ego synthesis;* and, finally, as a maintenance of an inner solidarity with a group's ideals and identity."

Identity does not begin at adolescence. The child has been formulating and reformulating identities throughout his life. As significant identifications succeed and overlap each other, as psychosexual crises are traversed, as ego qualities arise and are absorbed, as environmental demands are encountered, childhood identities are constantly changing. At adolescence, however, the commitment to an identity becomes critical. During this period, the youngster must synthesize earlier identifications with personal qualities and relate them to social opportunities and social ideals. Who the child is to be will be influenced (and in some cases determined) by what the environment permits and encourages: identity possibilities for the lower-class Negro adolescent (of whatever capacity) are different from those for the white upper-middle-class Protestant youngster. Identity is influenced as well by the child's talents, needs, sublimations, and defenses. The girl who discovers that she is attractive to boys will define herself differently than will the girl who senses (or mistakenly assumes) that she is not. The highly intelligent youngster is confronted with identity opportunities (and pressures) different from those which will be met by the youngster of average intellectual competence. The identity concept, in short, concentrates on the fusion of these elements (identifications, capacities, opportunities, and ideals) into a viable self-definition.

THE TEMPO OF IDENTITY CRYSTALLIZATION

Adolescents vary in the pace of identity formation. It is impossible to discover a "normal" pattern here, but *is* possible to speak of premature and delayed crystallizations. Some children crystallize identity too early and too narrowly; the motive in some cases is to avoid the anxiety inherent in identity diffusion; in other cases the impetus is to settle an instinctual conflict quickly and decisively. When we find unusual endowments supported environmentally, as for example, the star athlete who gains much attention from his activities, the youngster may be tempted to define himself exclusively along the lines of a special but narrow skill. Or we may have the young "genius," of a clever turn of mind, who cathects intellectuality in order to ward off the dangers of interpersonal intimacy. At other times the child may rush prematurely into a "normative" identity in order to avoid a tempting and feared identity alternative.

At the other extreme we find those cases marked by a delay in identity crystallization, those adolescents who cannot "find themselves," who keep themselves loose and unattached, committed to a bachelorhood of preidentity. Erikson sees the late adolescent period, in our times, as a "psychosocial moratorium," a time set aside for the youngster to try out identities, to discover what fits him best, to find the articulation between identifications and talents on the one hand, and role opportunities on the other, which can be synthesized into a satisfactory sense of inner coherence. In a number of cases the period is insufficient. The youngster resists crystallization and seeks out enclaves where noncommitment is possible. As Erikson puts it: "They come, instead, to psychiatrists, priests, judges and (we must add) recruitment officers in order to be given an authorized if ever so uncomfortable place in which to wait things out."

There are any number of causes for delayed identity crystallization. Often the reasons are those we have become familiar with in clinical work with adolescents: the feasible identities are those which seem to involve instinctual danger, as in the case of the boy who delays "growing up" because it involves the unconscious danger of replacing his father. In other cases, however, instinctual conflict, while it may be present, is not the central motive for delay. The youngster may feel unable to actualize his capacities; he feels unused and unrealized. The roles which seem available do not engage his true talents or do not gratify his need-linked capacities. In these cases the youngster may give the appearances of identity, dutifully going through the motions, but betraying, if only in his mechanicalness or lack of zest, the absence of genuine identity engagement. In other similar instances the youngster may sense where his dispositions lie but feel pressured to achieve an occupational or social identity which cannot utilize them.

IDENTITIES: NORMATIVE, NEGATIVE, ACHIEVED, ASCRIBED

Identity formation is also influenced by the normativeness of the identity chosen. Certain identities are well defined, common, and socially approved. In certain milieux the youngster is under almost unbearable pressure to choose these, and to develop within a fairly limited range of possibilities. In these cases the socialization processes are so closely articulated with socially defined ideals and opportunities that identity choice is automatic. We are likely to find an easy crystallization toward a well-defined social identity—as we have it, let us say, in the "golden youth" of American society—the upper-middle or upper-class youngsters who pass from the best preparatory schools to the best colleges to the best brokerage houses. In such instances we can speak of the identity as ascribed. Within certain social strata and ethnic groups we are likely to find that identities are both normative and ascribed. An identity which for some individuals is ascribed may for others have to be achieved, generally through upward social mobility. Those individuals whose ascribed identities are normative may find themselves during adolescence striving to achieve socially deviant identities. In the extreme instances (described brilliantly by Erikson) the youngster may feel that he can be something, or be himself, only by the choice of a deviant identity. The child may in fact be driven to the choice of a negative identity, composed of feared, yet fascinating, qualities. Ordinarily, however, the choice of socially deviant identities is made, we feel, to actualize inner potentialities which cannot be realized in the normative and ascribed identity; thus we see the scion of an aristocratic family choosing a Bohemian or other deviant role.

MASCULINE AND FEMININE IDENTITIES

The process of identity formation in boys and girls are in fact much more dissimilar than the discussion so far has suggested. The problem of sex differences is both complex and largely unexplored, and we shall only concentrate on some aspects of it. Boys tend to construct identity around the vocational choice; in most cases the girl does not. For most boys the question of "what to be" begins with work and the job, and he is likely to define himself and to be identified by occupation. But there is more to the total identity than occupation, and the stress placed on vocation tends to conceal, both from the onlooker and the child himself, some of the vicissitudes of identity formation. Through a precocious vocational choice the child may factitiously crystallize identity. The necessary delays, the necessary diffusion and confusion of the adolescent period may be forestalled, an outcome which may either hinder the full development of personal qualities or simply postpone the identity crisis until a later and more inappropriate moment. The precocious choice may produce a narrowed, overdefined personality, impoverished through a premature foreclosure on experiment and experience; postponement may produce those cases marked by late anguish, where the person sees himself boxed into a life path he does not feel com-

mitted to, filled with bewilderment or disgust, or trying abortively to retrace
the path or undo it.

The boy tends to concretize identity through anchoring it in an (often
premature) vocational choice; the adolescent girl does not ordinarily have
this opportunity. Girls tend to keep identity diffuse, and misty. The boy is
made to feel (however much he may doubt it, deep down) that his identity
is in his own hands, that the choice of vocation and with it, of a life style,
will define him. The girl cannot count on this degree of active preferment
in identity; her identity is bound up not so much in what she is as in what
her husband will be. Someone has spoken of marriage as a "mutual mobility
bet." We may add that for the girl it is equally an identity bet. It is for this
reason that the girl, unless she is one of the rare ones who remain committed to a work ideal, seems unrealistic and romantic, often foolishly so,
when asked to imagine a future life for herself. She tends to retreat into
stereotyped notions of the future, imagining a life of suburban idyl. She
seems more comfortable in the present; her vision of the future is necessarily dim; and to this extent identity formation (so far as it depends on an
anchorage to the future) is likely to remain incomplete.

SOCIAL CLASS

A central component of the sense of identity is the sense of social
status. However we define ourselves, whether we imagine ourselves as we
are, or were, or will be in the future, the sense of ourselves carries with
it some placing of the self in the social system. At adolescence the child
loses whatever innocence about social class he had remaining to him; the
period is, if anything, more class- and status-sensitive than any other. The
youngster plunges into the dead-serious game of grading and appraising
himself and others; he does so on a hundred dimensions, but the most important, perhaps, is social status. The status game at adolescence can be
cruelly damaging; the youngster is as vulnerable as he will ever be, and it
is his very vulnerability which causes him to turn status against others
heartlessly.

It is not only social class as such which enters into identity; it is, quite
as saliently, social class-to-be—involving expectation, hope, and dread. The
child's emergent sense of himself reaches into the future; the identity is, let
us say, not so much "electrician's son" as it is "electrician's son who will
be an electrical engineer"; or "sales clerk's daughter who will marry a
junior executive"; or even "doctor's son who will not be good enough to
be much of anything." Identity, then, encompasses both the past-in-present
("What I am through what my parents are") and the leap from present to
future ("What I deeply hope to be, what I deeply dread being"). Fantasies
and imaginings of social class and social mobility reflect some of the earliest
identities of childhood—that is, class mobility (aside from their objective

significance) are the media through which the adolescent expresses yearnings and despairs rooted in the object ties of childhood: to rise, to fall, to maintain oneself—behind these and informing these are those constructions of the self which began in the Oedipal situation, and earlier. . . .

REFERENCES

E. Erikson. *Childhood and society,* New York: Norton, 1950.
E. Erikson. The problem of ego identity. *Journal of the American Psychoanalytic Association,* 1956, 4, 56–121.

ADDITIONAL READINGS

Boyd, Robert D. Analysis of the ego-stage development of school-age children. *Journal of Experimental Education,* 1964, **32,** 249–257. The author investigated ego-stage development, as defined by Erikson's stages, through using an interview or projective technique. The results supported Erikson's concept that there is a developmental trend through Stage 8.

Brim, Orville G. Adolescent personality as self-other systems. *Journal of Marriage and the Family,* May 1965, **27** (2), 156–162. Brim and his colleagues explored the organization of the adolescent personality and conceptualized it as a self-other system including reference groups, role prescription, and self-conceptions among its components. Their ultimate objective is a fully developed theory of adolescent personality from the sociological perspective.

Cross, Herbert J. Conceptual systems theory—application to some problems of adolescents. *Adolescence,* Summer 1967, **2** (6), 153–165. The author describes how children's behaviors and thinking differ at five stages of conceptual development. He suggests that adolescents vary greatly in their conceptual level, and that learning environments should be adapted accordingly.

Douvan, Elizabeth. Sex differences in adolescent character processes. *Merrill-Palmer Quarterly,* July 1960, **6,** 203–211. Girls have much less pressure placed on them than boys do to establish an identity. In fact, there is pressure on the girl not to establish an identity until after adolescence. By maintaining a fluid personality she is better able to adapt to the needs of her future husband.

Elkind, David. Egocentrism in adolescence. *Adolescence,* December 1967,

38 (4), 1025–1034. Elkind describes the forms of egocentrism characteristic of the major stages of cognitive growth designated by Piaget. Adolescent egocentrism is seen as giving rise to two mental constructions, the imaginary audience and the personal fable, which in turn affect adolescent behaviors.

Erikson, Erik H. *Childhood and Society.* (2nd ed.) New York: Norton, 1963. In Chapter 7 Erikson outlines the eight ages of man. He portrays adolescence as the stage for establishing an identity (pp. 261–263). In Chapter 8, "Reflections on the American Identity," he pays special attention to familial and societal factors which impinge on the male adolescent and modify his identity.

Heilbrun, A. B., Jr. Conformity to masculinity-femininity stereotypes and ego identity in adolescence. *Psychological Reports,* 1964, **14,** 351–357. Heilbrun found that sex identity relates to self-concept, though the nature of the relationship was different for males and females. The more masculine males felt more consistent. The young woman's self-consistency was related either to strong feminine or to strong masculine self-concepts. The author presents an hypothesis to account for this apparently ambiguous finding about females.

Kohlberg, Lawrence. The development of children's orientation toward a moral order: I. Sequence in the development of moral thought. *Vita Humana,* 1963, **6,** 11–33. Boys of three age levels (10, 13, 16) were interviewed concerning hypothetical moral dilemmas modeled after those devised by Piaget. The results partially supported Piaget's contentions concerning stages of moral development.

Marcia, James E. Development and validation of ego identity status. *Journal of Personality and Social Psychology,* 1965, **3,** 551–558. The author describes four ways of reacting to the late adolescent identity crisis. Criteria for these statuses were the presence of crisis and commitment in the areas of occupation and ideology. Subjects higher in ego identity performed better on a concept attainment task; those in the status characterized by adherence to parental wishes set goals unrealistically high and subscribed more to authoritarian values.

McNassor, Donald. Social structure for identity in adolescence: Western Europe and America. *Adolescence,* Fall 1967, **2** (7) 311–334. This paper compares Western European and American youth with regard to schooling, age of maturity, peer groups, relationship to authority, and identity.

Muus, Rolf E. Jean Piaget's cognitive theory of adolescent development. *Adolescence,* Fall 1967, **2** (7), 285–310. The author summarizes the basic concepts in Piaget's cognitive theory, which he believes to be of utmost importance for the understanding and education of adolescents. He describes Piaget's outline of developmental stages and suggests educational implications.

VII. Adolescence: A Period of
Storm and Stress

The concept of adolescence as a period of storm and stress raises several questions. First, is adolescence particularly stressful, or conspicuously more so than other age periods? If it be conceded that adolescence *is* stressful, then how stressful is it? Is such stress attributable to physical changes that occur, or to society's failure to adapt to adolescents' needs? How do the sexes differ in degree and type of stress? How does stress vary from early to late adolescence? Finally, what special measures, if any, should be taken to prevent or alleviate such stress?

The concept of adolescence as a period of storm and stress was popularized around the turn of the century by G. Stanley Hall. Hall, often dubbed the Father of Child Study in America, portrayed pubertal changes as so marked, and so catastrophic, as to be upsetting. Since Hall's time, most writers on adolescence have expressed similar views. For example, Stone and Church [1] call adolescence a "vulnerable period" involving painful adolescent problems and the reawakening of past developmental issues only partially resolved. It is during adolescence, they point out, that a true schizophrenic breakdown may first occur. Many normal adolescent traits, in their extreme form, approximate schizophrenic behavior. Such characteristics include persistent feelings of dislocation and estrangement, total docility or exaggerated rebelliousness, emotional volatility, feelings that everybody is against one, talk of suicide, and intense idealism. Breakdowns are most likely to take such forms as schizophrenic delusions, sexual deviations, and psychosomatic disorders. Fortunately, conclude Stone and Church, most adolescents have developed "a tough core of security, and an anchorage in reality, that permit them to withstand and thrive on the stresses of this period."

Traditional psychoanalytic theorists also play up the traumatic features of adolescence. Individuals are said to proceed through certain stages— oral, anal, phallic, latent, and adolescent—then into adulthood. The late childhood or latency period comes to an abrupt end at puberty. According to Blum,[2] sex maturity "brings in its wake a wave of disturbance, not only

[1] L. Joseph Stone and Joseph Church, *Childhood and Adolescence* (New York, Random House, 1957), pp. 369–370.
[2] G. S. Blum, *Psychoanalytic Theories of Personality* (New York, McGraw-Hill, 1953), pp. 136–155.

in the sexual area, but also in the broader realm of social behavior." The adolescent, "flooded by his own resurgent impulses, must regroup the defensive forces of his ego in an attempt to meet this new onslaught."

Similarly, Robert Nixon [3] speaks of the "shock of puberty" which we all remember as a stage of anxiety. The adolescent spends hours in deep, and usually secret, preoccupation with the physical and psychological changes going on inside him. In time, he accepts himself as a teen-ager and the anxiety subsides, only to be reawakened, in full force, at around age 14, when peer groups divide into males and females. Another burst of anxiety, says Nixon, occurs at about 16, when the adolescent is assailed by doubts concerning all sorts of issues that adults prefer to leave unquestioned.

According to psychoanalytic theory, individuals at any age may experience an inability to handle impulses, subdue anxieties, or to delay gratification; but the maturation of sexual impulses makes adolescence especially stressful. Others, including Jersild,[4] note that every age has its problems. Nevertheless, adds Jersild, the fact that adolescents typically have problems is more significant than deciding whether their lives are more stressful than those of persons older or younger.

A review of research suggests that adolescent girls experience more emotional disturbances than boys.[5] However, Friedenberg [6] believes boys are more emotional and females less emotional than commonly believed. Boys are "moodier, more intense, more mystical almost," he says. Watch a basketball player's face and you will see moments of ecstacy and transfiguration. The female's reputed emotional instability is simply her defense against male domination, and otherwise is absent. If either sex experiences stress, what sort of help is required? Is it society itself that needs adjustment for its failure to provide adolescents a suitable niche? Some people believe adolescence is simply a disease to be gotten over. "He—or she—will outgrow it," is their stock reply. Others believe in full-blown guidance programs, designed to anticipate and prevent, as well as to treat problems.

However, not all authorities agree either that storm and stress is inevitable within our own culture, or universal among all cultures. Bernard [7] suggests that emotionality may be heightened at adolescence but hardly enough to justify calling adolescence a period of storm and stress.

---

[3] Robert E. Nixon, "Psychological Normality in Adolescence," *Adolescence,* Vol. 1, No. 3 (Fall 1966), pp. 211–223.

[4] A. T. Jersild, *The Psychology of Adolescence,* 2nd ed. (New York, Macmillan, 1963), p. 17.

[5] D. Rogers, *Psychology of Adolescence* (New York, Appleton-Century-Crofts, 1962), pp. 145–146.

[6] Edgar Z. Friedenberg, *The Vanishing Adolescent* (Boston, Beacon Press, 1959).

[7] Harold Bernard, *Adolescent Development in American Culture* (New York, Harcourt, Brace & World, 1957).

Others believe the *Sturm and Drang* of adolescence simply a sociocultural creation. They point out that youth in primitive societies glide smoothly from childhood into adulthood. Such cultures are continuous, writes Benedict,[8] in that children's activities often constitute a true apprenticeship for adulthood. By contrast, in Western society, adult activities demand traits interdicted in the child. Moreover, adults blame the child when he fails spontaneously to adopt mature behaviors.

Some writers stress that emotionality is inherent in puberty itself. Buxbaum[9] states that, unconsciously, first menstruation is experienced as an injury to the genitals, as a castration, and as punishment for masturbation. Another view, that stress reflects rapid shifts in hormonal balance, is challenged by Garn.[10] Twenty milligrams of testosterone, he observes, is not unsettling except to a few dozen sebaceous glands. Moreover, rebellion occurs in hypogonadal boys as well as in normal boys. Nor does adolescence result in awkwardness. The vicissitudes of adolescent growth stem neither from genes or glands but from society's failure to provide a meaningful status for the adolescent.

Polar extremes of the storm-and-stress question are represented in the two selections that follow. The first, by Gustin, presents the psychoanalytic point of view, that adolescence is indeed traumatic, and that stress is an inherent aspect of adolescence. In the second selection, Bandura challenges this view. At least among middle-class boys, he found little evidence of trauma. However, until Bandura's point of view gains greater acceptance, society will continue to act on the belief that adolescents are somewhat upset and unstable.

8 Ruth Benedict, *A Study of Interpersonal Relations,* Patrick Mullahy, ed. (New York, Hermitage Press, 1949).
9 Edith Buxbaum, "Angstäusserungen von Schulmädchen in Pubertätsalter," Z. psa. Padagogik, VII (1933).
10 S. M. Garn, "Growth and Development," in E. Ginzberg, Ed., *The Nation's Children,* Vol. 2 (New York, Columbia University Press, 1960), pp. 24–42.

14

J. C. Gustin

THE REVOLT OF YOUTH

A psychoanalytic writer portrays the adolescent as "racked by sexual desire frustrated by outer prohibitions and inner inhibitions; desperately longing for independence yet fearful of isolation; eager for responsibilities yet fraught with anxieties about inferiority . . ."

One of the most poignant moments in the psychology of man is the scene between the adolescent and the parent, glaring at each other with hopeless despair. They yearn for each other with aching desperation; they long for the familiar signs of understanding. Instead, they find that they no longer speak the same language, perceive the same dangers nor accept the same values. At the precise moment when each needs the reassuring warmth of the other, there is a breakdown of communication as though a bolt of lightning had cut the lines that bound them together. It is at this moment that they become aware of how widely they are separated by the distance of a generation. The twenty-odd years that divide them suddenly become an unbridgeable chasm.

This bleak and disheartening scene is not particularly unique to our time. "What is happening to our Modern Generation?" is an imperishable cliché which has always plagued and baffled parents, teachers, social workers, ministers, judges, psychologists and—not least of all—the youths themselves. The lament, the complaints, the bills of indictment may change like seasons but the cold (and often hot) war between adults and adolescents is as certain as springtime.

Throughout history, even to the best-intentioned, most enlightened and understanding parents, the antics, the behavior and "acting out" of their younger generations has seemed to be incomprehensible at best and, most of the time, quite bizarre. To the stuffy, inhibited, puritanical parents of the 1920's, the gin-swizzling, rowdy, belligerent, sexually-promiscuous adolescent was a shameful enigma. That was indeed a "Lost Generation" which could be found in illegal speakeasys or in the indelible pages of F. Scott Fitzgerald. Nor was the serious-minded, socially-conscious adolescent

From J. C. Gustin, "The Revolt of Youth," *Psychoanalysis and the Psychoanalytic Review*, Vol. 98 (1961), pp. 78–90.

of the 30's any less of a mystery to his adult contemporaries. The fact that he denounced capitalistic society from corner soap-boxes, crusaded on picket lines and wrote inflammatory poetry was a bitter thorn in the side of his depression-plagued, morally-repressed and rigidly conformist parent. In the 40's, the alumni of the firebrand, rebellious "Lost Generation"—now paunchy and middle-aged—despairingly found that they had spewn forth a generation of spineless, "adjusted" jellyfish who worshipped security above ambition; silence above protest; rank above rancor; prudence above principle; status above stature; certainty above adventure. [The children read Herman Wouk, the high priest of conformity, rather than the protestant polemics of Fitzgerald, Hemingway and Dos Passos that had been pre-scribed fare among their parents.] As inexplicable seeds of the "Lost Generation," they have been variously dubbed the "Unlost Generation," the "Conformists," the "Unangry Ones," and so forth.

The 1950's has had its share of quickly shifting generations that are equally as unintelligible to their grown-ups. How many parents could take more than an amusedly tolerant attitude toward their bobby-socked daughters who were cutting classes to hysterically throw themselves in the aisles at the Paramount? Or the blue-jeaned, sideburned counterparts charging to do wild battle on their fiery motorscooters? And how many adults can tolerate—no less understand—the bleating, beating rock-and-roll rhythm that is the folk music of the "shook-up" generation. And how many of us really "dig" the "coolest cat" of them all: the "hipster" of the Beat Generation. Talking a language of its own, charged by its esoteric jazz and poetry, drugged by a sexless philosophy of indifference, these "cats" leave their square, punch-drunk, befuddled parent "way out there."

But the adolescents that have come in for the greatest amount of publicity have been the violent dissenters, the psychopaths, the rebels-without-a-cause, the juvenile delinquents. Ever since the "Blackboard Jungle" became a Hollywood *cause celebre,* these teenage terrors have become a school-yard scandal, a neighborhood menace and a national disgrace. The newspaper exposés and court records are glaring testimonials to the break-down of mutual understanding between this group of youths and their adult world.

Parents are old-fashioned. Everyone knows and says that. Furthermore, it is almost an American tradition to expect the young to protest and, in the name of progress, overthrow some of the stale and tired values of their parents. But, inevitably, both get more than they bargained for. The protest is ubiquitous and usually either shockingly unexpected or unexpectedly shocking. It may be rage or resignation; violence or avoidance. Its forms are many, its methods varied. But what is constantly present and painfully clear is that the rift between the parent and the adolescent is fraught with unhappiness, bewilderment, disappointment, unrest; in short, very little mutual understanding.

What is it about adolescence that makes it the most fractious period in the relationship between the parent and child? Is there an inborn instinct which comes alive at puberty? Is this teen-age ferment a symptom of social unrest, a form of mass psychopathy; or is it a healthy revolt against rigid conformity and constricting authority?

There are some answers, particularly in relation to schoolyard violence and teen-age sexual aggressions—the most dramatic forms of protest. First, we are quickly reassured that the great majority of school children are decent and law-abiding and that the trouble-makers are just an infinitesimal fraction of the whole; a few rotten apples in a barrel full of rosy-cheeked, bright-eyed, wholesome kids who innocently drink Coca Cola while doing the Lindy. It is the hardened "problem" children—estimated at 1 per cent —who get the attention of sociologists, social workers and psychologists. The explanations offered include such well-known platitudes as "bad housing . . . bad neighborhoods . . . poverty . . . broken homes . . . parental neglect . . . breakdown of morality . . . lack of discipline . . . too much rod . . . too little rod . . . too much love . . . too little love and, perhaps the greatest cliché of them all, unhappy childhood." There is general agreement that these sociological, environmental and somewhat psychological factors can influence and do contribute to the dismal picture. But those who are equipped to listen with more than two ears hear the eruptions of violence, the underground rumblings of a more serious and universal disturbance that affect every child. It is with the use of the tools we have inherited from Sigmund Freud—the exploration of unconscious motivations—that we may hope to arrive at a deeper understanding of the gap between the parent and the adolescent.

Puberty is that period of human development when sexual maturation is brought to its biological conclusion. Natural hormonal changes effect drastic changes in the structure of the body and produce an intensification of the instincts. After the deceptive calm of a relatively blissful period of latency, a libidinal bomb drops with a violent explosion that shakes the very foundation of the personality. All hell breaks loose—and the adolescent finds himself in the grip of the most crucial time of his life.

In this lurid twilight of sexual maturity, the adolescent finds that, along with the dramatic physical changes that have swept over his body, there has been an inner sexual revolution that keeps him under constant bombardment. Oedipal strivings—long dormant—are reawakened but, this time, being vitalized with a genital charge, make demands upon an ego that is not yet too far removed from childhood naiveté. Under the cloud of incestuous guilt, he turns to masturbation, homosexuality or phantasied sexual perversions. Anna Freud describes some of the changes that take place at this time: "Aggressive impulses are intensified to the point of complete unruliness, hunger becomes voracity and naughtiness becomes criminal behavior. Oral and anal interests, long submerged, come to the surface again.

Habits of cleanliness, laboriously acquired during the latency period, give place to pleasure in dirt and disorder and instead of modesty and sympathy we find exhibitionistic tendencies, brutality and cruelty to animals."

How to cope with the increased pressures of his sexual and instinctual drives may be the primary preoccupation of the adolescent, but it is not the only one. The demands and expectations of the world around him—parents, teachers, society—confront him with further complications. Poised as he is on the threshold of manhood, the boy trembles at the thought of adult responsibilities. He may long desperately for independence to show how grown-up he is, but he has serious doubts about his capacities. He is further confused by the fact that, although he has the physical equipment for an adult sexual relationship, he is not encouraged to enter the state of marriage and is furthermore, firmly exhorted not to engage in premarital sexuality. The fact that he does so (as Kinsey has shown) indicates that the urge of the instinct is greater than the prohibition of society. But the Kinsey report does not indicate the enormous price the adolescent has to pay in feelings of guilt and self-hatred. Society also confuses him in relation to aggression. The same society that compels him to curb his aggressive instincts also demands that he exercise them in cases of national defense.

The role of the young female also undergoes subtle as well as intense changes. She is told, in a thousand different ways, that she must become more passive, more "ladylike," more aware of her feminine charms but must not, under any circumstance, surrender her pre-marital chastity.

As one might have guessed by now, the life of an adolescent is not a particularly happy one. Buffeted from within by powerful impulses and pushed from without by a strange, unfriendly world, the adolescent must find some new ways to make his life tolerable. To put it technically; the ego, threatened by a reawakened and irrepressible id and alienated from the superego, must establish new defenses to maintain itself. Among these defensive maneuvers you find the strange and sometimes bizarre behavior patterns we associate with adolescence. Unbridled righteous dogmatism, dream-like states, intellectualizations in the form of discussions about esoteric philosophies and the meaning of life serve as ways of diverting volatile energy to harmless pursuits. Athletics and interests in poetry, music and art transform phantasy into reality with the blessing of the ego. Asceticism, which is commonly associated with adolescence, has, as its purpose the denial of instinctual needs. It is as though the adolescent says to the world, "Me? I don't need sex. I don't need love. I don't need nothin.' " The apostles of the Beat Generation have made a dogma of it. It is sinful to show emotion. "You just play it cool, Man."

These are just a few typical defenses among many that the adolescent adopts in an attempt to release the tensions within him. While these defenses help him maintain a balance, they tend to alienate the adolescent from himself and the world around him. Changes in object relationships are an outstanding feature and an absolute must in adolescence. Embroiled as he is in the violent revival of the oedipal conflict, he must break with the object of this dangerous state. He renounces (or, more accurately, represses) his incestuous strivings for the parent by withdrawing from the old familiar contact with them. This contributes to the feelings of loneliness and isolation.

In an attempt to break away from his parents and yet reduce the pain of isolation, the adolescent joins with others to form groups—even anti-social groups such as the familiar "gangs." Among his peers he feels equal; a man among men. Since misery loves company, the young adolescent also diminishes the anxiety that comes from sexual and aggressive impulses by sharing it with his fellow-sufferers.

Lost, baffled, no longer a child and not quite a man, the adolescent is in a hopeless state of confusion. Living under the domination of a society that demands compulsive morality and mechanization of natural impulses, he finds the gap between his instincts and the appropriate circumstance for outlet ever widening. Should he yield to the incitement of his awakened sexuality or keep himself in a state of grace by renouncing or replacing his needs?

In this murky atmosphere, and out of habit, he turns to the one who has always been there to help him before. More than ever, the adolescent yearns to be held and comforted and encouraged. But the parent has now become the symbol of his shame and guilt. The parent, as the object of unconscious oedipal love, represents danger and must be avoided at all costs. This often leads to feelings of disappointment, disenchantment and even disgust. The parent is divested of the exaggerated power and the magical omnipotence which had been so important in building the self-esteem of the child. But, even though the separation from the parent is imperative, the need (for the parent) continues to exist. This leads to feelings of inconsistency and ambivalence. His attitudes turn to (simultaneous) hate and love; truculence and compliance; mistrust and hope; indifference and longing. (The anxiety stirred by this ambivalence can explain the indolence and frequent depressions that are so characteristic of this period.) As a matter of fact, the more the adolescent declares his independence from the family the more alienated he feels and the more he struggles (inwardly) to repair the ruptured relationship to the parental image. The stronger his denial, the greater his need.

Picture our adolescent now poised at the brink of adulthood. Racked by sexual desire, frustrated by outer prohibitions and inner inhibitions; desperately longing for independence yet fearful of isolation; eager for responsibilities yet fraught with anxieties about inferiority; flooded by irrational impulses yet committed to rules of propriety, he is hopelessly and helplessly confused and an enigma to everyone and himself.

The inescapable fact is that this is everyone's dilemma at adolescence. No one is exempt—no matter how warm and understanding the family background. The comfort and security of having been loved may help sustain the adolescent in this moment of terror, but no parent, however devoted and well-intentioned, can spare his child this frenzied conflict. For this conflict follows the law of nature. It is the self-actualizing principle that provides the impetus toward growth; the dialectical development by which individual consciousness progresses from innocence to maturity; from boy to man, from girl to woman.

But while the adolescent is trying to pull himself up on the unyielding bar of manhood, writhing in his tortured state and trying to make sense of the turbulent "mish-mash" of his feelings, the parent has not been simply an innocent, helpless bystander. If guilt or blame is involved, the parent must be prepared to accept his share. The influence of paren's upon children is as old as the history of man. It *is* the history of man. But no history is complete without understanding the unconscious forces that shape it, and the parental attitude, particularly at the pubescence of the child, undergoes great unconscious stress and change.

The same earthquake that rocks the adolescent at puberty shakes the personality foundation of the parent as well. The parents' own repressed, unresolved conflicts re-emerge, seeking to find vicarious release through their children. Psychoanalytic experience has produced overwhelming evidence of the fact that parents unconsciously saddle the children with their own conflicts. The most innocuous suggestion carries a powerful imperative. In a thousand ways, parents encourage the "acting out" and give unwitting sanction by making remarks like "You are just like your father," "You'll wind up in the gutter," or "You would if you loved me," etc. Excessive permissiveness or irrational opposition is dictated more by the anxiety of the parent than by the need of the child or the merit of the situation. This often leads to peculiar and irrational acts on the part of the parent. An extreme example would be the mother who held her child's hand over a flame to teach it the lesson of honesty. How strange are the ways of love!

The changing demands on the part of the growing child call for changing attitudes on the part of the parent. What happens, for example, to the paunchy, middle-aging father who uncomfortably senses the vigorous, potent, sexual vitality of his young son? Or even as he becomes equally aware of the budding sensual changes in his young pubescent daughter? If he has not, with some degree of success, come to terms with his own feelings of guilt, his unconscious is in for a mighty uncomfortable time. The anxieties these changes arouse can force him to behave in ways that are strange and unpredictable.

And take mother who is, by this time, beginning to worry about the lines around her eyes and her sagging skin and is buying stronger and tighter girdles. It is a well-known fact that many women go into deep depressions when their daughters reach the age of sexual availability. What mothers have done to their sons has been frighteningly described by such writers as D. H. Lawrence and Philip Wylie. Some social scientists blame mothers for the demasculinization and fear of homosexuality that plague American men.

The anxieties that are aroused in the parents by the re-emergence of their own buried conflicts lead to changes in their behavior toward the strife-torn child. You find awkwardness, self-consciousness, denial, fault-finding, irritability, projection and many other mechanisms of defense that are quite independent of the needs of the child but rather designed to still their own uncertainty. Nevertheless, the child is often left with the feeling of being responsible, which amplifies his already over-burdened sense of guilt.

It is not difficult to see the dilemma of the adolescent at puberty. Not only must he cope with the unleashed sexual and instinctual drives that torture him, but he has to attempt to find a place in a cold, disapproving world whose total aim seems to be to deny him pleasure and force him to become a "well-adjusted" automaton. In this climate of conflict, he desperately turns to his parents for comfort but finds that he cannot ask for help out of the embarrassment of his own guilt feelings and because he senses in them an awkward self-consciousness. Turning away from the parent, joining "gangs," sublimating, intellectualizing and making use of other defense mechanisms offer him some temporary solutions but he is left with the feeling of alienation and isolation. In addition, he must face the problem of his place in society or, more succinctly, his role as a man and a member of society.

Most adolescents, in a terrifying attempt to find a way out of this wilderness, seek a solution that will restore to them a feeling of unity; an attempt to reconcile the conflicts within them and to dissolve the painful ambivalences. They seek a solution that will enable them to deal with the parent (and society, which is an extension of the parent) with whom they have no choice but to live. So, they can either fight them or join them. They can rebel and run the risk of being disapproved-of trouble-makers, or they can conform and take the risk of losing their sense of individuality and self-respect.

Conformity is about as dirty a word as can be used in some circles. It is held to be synonymous with stagnation, suffocation, resignation, demoralization, Babbitism, robotism, puppetism, and so on. The "Organization Man" is easily recognizable as our neighbor and we tremble at what the "Hidden Persuaders" may be implanting in our subliminal consciousness. Who among us has not shuddered at the prospect of a "Brave New World" or an Orwellian "1984"?

There is no question about it. Conformism can be like a cancer slowly eating away the flesh and bowels of individuality. It is an acid that can dissolve the spine, pollute the blood and destroy the guts of man. It is the great neutralizer that can turn a piquante and exciting life into a bland, spiritless existence.

The danger is clear. It is familiar to everyone who has been commanded to take some action or perform a deed against his will. But conformity is an essential dimension of mankind. Without it, life, as we know it, would cease. The will to conformism is a flight from flux; an attempt to turn uncertainty to stability, convulsion to quiescence, chaos to order. The very act of love demands it. Take any expression you like; if love includes concern with the other person it then, by definition, makes demands to which one is expected to conform. In our society it is customary for lovers to kiss one another on the lips. As far as I know, there is no inborn lip-kissing instinct. It is purely a social custom, albeit a delightful one. But a rabid, professional rebel would not dare kiss his girl in this way for fear of being called bourgeois or "square" or conformist.

The love of man for man as well as the hatred of man for man; in short, the Brotherhood of Man, binds us together in a reflected resemblance to each other. To the extent that we are each part of the other, to that extent we strive to achieve oneness by stimulating uniformity. By acting like each other, we commit ourselves and conform to a common brotherhood.

Rebellion, too, is an essential dimension of life. Life without the protest against serfdom, the search for new directions would indeed be gruesome—if conceivable. The dream of overthrow, the promise of change, the discovery of the unusual, the joy of creation is the hope that continues to pump the blood in our veins and makes life worth struggling for.

But rebellion is not an end in itself. It is not the panacea that will cure the evils of the world and remove conflicts from the hearts of men. Many writers try to make a secular cult of rebellion. They worship at the altar of defiance and proclaim the holiness of riot. Conformism is the Devil; Rebellion the Saviour. They speak of school, family, church, society as organized gangs who are out to dragoon innocent, helpless dupes, to stamp out resistance and create an indistinguishable mass. The sad fact is that these charges have the sound of truth. Anyone who works with patients psychoanalytically sees the ravages of the repressive influences of authority upon the personality. But what is overlooked is that these are not enemy forces outside of ourselves. They are us. We are they. We are the forces that demand our own imprisonment as well as our own liberation. To call conformism evil without acknowledging the psychological need that creates and perpetuates it is naive. No man is an island, says the poet.

Rebellion, like conformity, may not be an end in itself, but it is a necessary means toward growth and a reaching beyond man's grasp to capture a bit of heaven. It is a necessary ingredient which enables the ego to stretch its muscles and mature. The infant crawls until the walking muscles are developed to a point where they push the child to attempt the walk. In the same way, the ego needs the expansion of rebellion to push it onward toward individuation. Needless to say, if the push is too strongly smothered, you have the basis for a neurosis. Rebellion can help the personality be different without being alien; dissident, without being nihilistic; destructive, but not without loving.

"The Rebel is a man who cares. Rebellion is an act of love and a confirmation that existence is worth fighting for. It is an aspiration toward clarity, unity and order. Rebellion is not an act of hating unless it is also an act of loving." So writes Albert Camus, one of the sensitive thinkers of our time.

Aimless rebellion that takes as its goal ravage and destructiveness without creating something new in its place is nihilistic and as deadening to the sensibilities as senseless conformity. We need our artists to remain disaffiliated from all deadening influences in order to provide us with a spirit of intransigence; we need an *avant garde* that will keep alive experimentation and search. But the anti-social defiance of Bohemianism is as significant as the marauding of juvenile delinquents is criminal. Wearing a beard or starving in a garret may be romantic rebellion, but it does not guarantee artistic talent or produce a single creative act. Rebellion, to be a positive force, must be an act of conviction, or belief, of love for others.

Rebellion versus Conformity is not the issue. The adolescent who seeks safety in one or the other is doomed to another disappointment. The presence of one demands the presence of the other. It is the dialectic—the very conflict between the two that insures the continuity of life. Without rebellion, life would be reduced to a meaningless, mundane existence. Without conformity, there would be a regression to an archaic, anarchic jungle where annihilation and destructiveness would be the only aim of man. It is the nature of man to encompass—no, to transcend—both.

It is generally acknowledged that the feeling of isolation is one of the most painful states a human can endure. That is, alienation from himself and his fellow-man. Conformity or rebellion—each is an excessive attempt to attain unity, to still uncertainty, to feel one again, to belong, either to oneself or to another or to all others.

One must not deplore conflict but realize that out of this furnace of conflict comes the well-tempered steel that binds human relationships. Psychological differences are not only unavoidably accessory to personality development but also essentially ingredient to growth. The psychological struggle between teen-age children and their parents may be painful to behold and even more painful to endure, but life without it would be unimaginable. Parents and children are natural enemies with instincts to destroy the other. But they are also enduringly and forever bound together in common need.

More than ever before, the parent needs the child to make life endurable. At this moment in history, when man is little more than a cipher, a statistic whose number may be coming up on the wings of a guided missile from a misguided enemy, when even the dignity of personal death has been denied and one can look forward to the ignominy of mass radioactive extinction, he needs to be reminded of the purposefulness of living. The child offers the parent perpetual youth and immortality—the most potent force against the inexorable advent of death. Only because of our young can we continue to live, with some degree of equanimity, in the shadow of death. Only because of their unending vitality and regenerating vigor can we feel new strength and new hope in our tired, aging psychic muscles. They offer promise of flexibility to chronically rigid character patterns and attitudes. Their trust and belief can melt the hardness we build inside ourselves in the course of daily living. Coming home to the child at the end of the day makes the day endurable.

In a similar way, the parent can offer the child the courage to face the future and the feeling that the struggle is worth the effort. Remember the dreary dilemma of the adolescent. Caught in a vise of his rampant sexuality, at odds with a repressive society, unsure of himself and seriously wondering what life is all about, he sees in his parents stability, responsibility and a reverence for life. They represent contiguity in an atmosphere of isolation. They seem to offer cohesion to feelings of impermanence, an oasis in the desert of loneliness. Parents may seem to have their own troubles but—to the youngsters, at least—they appear to have mastered uncertainty and have crystallized into a distinguishable way of life. They offer definition, stillness from want, established values and orderly routine. To a jittery adolescent, this can appear like a life-saver.

The sad and glorious fact is that children and parents cannot live without each other. The mutual need that binds them carries the seeds of life and death. Each is responsible for the destruction as well as the perpetuation of the other. It is this conflict, this internal contradiction that gives meaning to life. The energy that motivates life is in the striving to achieve a moment of unity out of this discord.

What is the solution? Can the relationship between the adolescent and the parent ever be a good one? Can they ever reconcile their natural differences? How can they help each other?

The solution is in striving, striving—with kindness and faith—for that one moment of sublime closeness and understanding in which all differences are dissolved. There is an absence of tension, a cessation of hostilities, a meshing of gears—what the artist calls a "moment of truth." All dialectics are suspended. Call it Zen. Call it Nirvana. All is forgiven. All is one. There is that moment when the opposites take shape in concordant harmony.

Parents must not deplore what they see in their adolescent children for what they see in their own past and their future. Parents must forego the luxury of righteousness and be scrupulously aware of the responsibility of the authority they wield. Their longer years and sadder experiences have not necessarily given them greater wisdom nor granted them the privilege of dictating the terms by which a younger individual must live. Guidance should be offered with sensitivity and must never be used to imprison a spirit that cannot remain captive. There are some (so-called "wise" men) who think that by reforming our education program, by establishing clinics, by more progressive or restrictive methods, they will cure our children of "aggressiveness" and in this way outlaw opposition. We must guard against such blind sanctimony. The rebellion of adolescence may be born out of trapped despair but it is not only a hostile act of destructiveness—it is also a pungent statement of affirmation. It is a desire to fight for life-producing forces against elements of repression—and that is everyone's fight. Modern youth is not only angry, incorrigible and rebellious. It is also the vitality which produces new directions in art, literature and music. To the extent that we hinder and dampen this enthusiasm and experimentation, to that extent we sign our own death warrant.

And the love we bear our children is love only to the extent that it guarantees them freedom and not smothering, dignity and not degradation, honor and not disrespect, life and not death. The desire to endure may lead to a feeling of possessiveness but the total possession of another human being is an impossible dream.

The adolescent brings with his advent to adulthood the responsibility of examining his own attitudes and the irrationality of his demands. Understanding is a two-way street. He must recognize that, even though he may have become disenchanted with his parents and no longer sees them as "the coolest," that they have not lost all human shape and feelings. Nor should he be too intolerant of their values. Ezra Pound once wrote, "There is no reason why a man should like the same book at 18 and at 48."

Adolescence must also take a responsible attitude toward its spirit of rebellion. Rebellion is a heritage and privilege that must not be abused. It must be carefully screened as to values, convictions, taste, decency, morality. It must not be confused with senseless plunder, meaningless destruction and wanton annihilation. We all carry within ourselves our private crimes and our secret plots to murder. But our task is not to unleash them upon the world; it is to fight them within ourselves and wherever we discover them in others.

Only with respect for the integrity and individuality of ourselves and all others—only with the deepening capacity to live with good will and encouragement of healthy, natural impulses—can we hope to achieve a more harmonious unification of opposing forces. We must recognize in our children the innate desire to live spontaneously and to grow in accordance with their own biological and psychological needs. We must not, under any circumstances, interfere with or destroy this tropism but, above all, we must cherish it. For therein lies the hope of the future for peace and life-positive growth. Added to this is the knowledge that life struggles irrepressibly toward greater freedom, as living plants turn to the sun.

15

Albert Bandura

THE STORMY DECADE: FACT OR FICTION?

The writer first describes the traditional storm-and-stress image of adoles-cence, then compares this popular version of adolescence with research by him-self and Walters. In a study of middle-class families of adolescent boys they found little to support the traditional view. They examine reasons for the faulty image and discuss its unfortunate effects.

If you were to walk up to the average man on the street, grab him by the arm and utter the word "adolescence," it is highly probable—assuming he refrains from punching you in the nose—that his associations to this term will include references to storm and stress, tension, rebellion, de-pendency conflicts, peer-group conformity, black leather jackets, and the like. If you then abandoned your informal street corner experiment, and consulted the professional and popular literature on adolescence, you would become quickly impressed with the prevalence of the belief that ado-lescence is, indeed, a unique and stormy developmental period (Gallagher & Harris, 1958; Hurlock, 1955; Josselyn, 1948; Mohr & Despres, 1958; Parsons, 1950; Pearson, 1958).

The adolescent presumably is engaged in a struggle to emancipate himself from his parents. He, therefore, resists any dependence upon them for their guidance, approval or company, and rebels against any restrictions and controls that they impose upon his behavior. To facilitate the process of emancipation, he transfers his dependency to the peer group whose val-ues are typically in conflict with those of his parents. Since his behavior is now largely under the control of peer-group members, he begins to adopt idiosyncratic clothing, mannerisms, lingo, and other forms of peer-group fad behavior. Because of the conflicting values and pressures to which the adolescent is exposed, he is ambivalent, frightened, unpredictable, and often irresponsible in his behavior. Moreover, since the adolescent finds himself in a transition stage in which he is neither child nor adult, he is highly confused even about his own identity.

Reprinted from PSYCHOLOGY IN THE SCHOOLS, 1964, *1*, 224–231.

The foregoing storm and stress picture of adolescence receives little support from detailed information that Dr. Walters and I obtained in a study of middle class families of adolescent boys (Bandura & Walters, 1959). Let us compare the popular version of adolescence with our research findings.

Parental Restrictiveness

At adolescence, parents supposedly become more controlling and prohibitive. We found the very opposite to be true. By the time the boys had reached adolescence, they had internalized the parents' values and standards of behavior to a large degree; consequently, restrictions and external controls had been lightened as the boys became increasingly capable of assuming responsibility for their own behavior, and in directing their own activities. The parents were highly trustful of their boys' judgment and felt that externally imposed limits were, therefore, largely unnecessary. The following interview excerpts provide some typical parental replies to inquiries concerning the restrictions they placed on their boys:

M. (Mother). I don't have to do anything like that any more. I think he's getting so mature now, he's sort of happy medium. I don't have to do much with him.

I. (Interviewer). What are some of the restrictions you have for him? How about going out at night?

F. (Father). We trust the boy. We never question him.

I. Are there any things you forbid him from doing when he is with his friends?

F. At his age I would hate to keep telling him that he mustn't do this, or mustn't do that. I have very little trouble with him in that regard. Forbidding I don't think creeps into it because he ought to know at 17, right from wrong.

I. Are there any friends with whom you have discouraged him from associating?

F. No, not up to now. They are very lovely boys.

I. How about using bad language?

F. Only once, only once have I; of course I'm a little bit hard of hearing in one ear, and sometimes he gets around the wrong side and takes advantage of that.

The boys' accounts were essentially in agreement with those given by the parents. In response to our questions concerning parental demands and controls, the boys pointed out that at this stage in their development parental restraints were no longer necessary. An illustrative quotation, taken from one of the boys' interviews, is given below:

I. What sort of things does your mother forbid you to do around the house?

B. Forbid me to do? Gee, I don't think there's ever anything. The house is mine as much as theirs. . . Oh, can't whistle, can't throw paper up in the air, and can't play the radio and phonograph too loud. Rules of the house; anybody, I mean, it's not just me. . .

I. Are you expected to stay away from certain places or people?

B. She knows I do. I'm not expected; I mean, she figures I'm old enough to take care of myself now. They never tell me who to stay away from or where. Well, I mean, they don't expect me to sleep down on Skid Row or something like that. . .

Since the boys adopted their parents' standards of conduct as their own, they did not regard their parents and other authority figures as adversaries, but more as supportive and guiding influences.

Dependence-Independence Conflicts

The view that adolescents are engaged in a struggle to emancipate themselves from their parents also receives little support from our study.

Although the boys' dependency behavior had been fostered and encouraged during their childhood, independence training had begun early and was, therefore, largely accomplished by the time of adolescence. A similar early and gradual decrease in dependency upon adults is reported by Heathers (1955), who compared the dependency behavior of two-year-old and of five-year-old children. He found that, even over this small age range, dependency on adults had declined, whereas dependency on other children had increased.

For most of the boys that we studied, the emancipation from parents had been more or less completed rather than initiated at adolescence. In fact, the development of independence presented more of a conflict for the parents, than it did for the boys. Some of the parents, particularly the fathers, regretted the inevitable loss of the rewards that their sons' company had brought them.

I. Do you feel that you spend as much time with Raymond as other fathers do with their sons, or more?

F. I would say about average, but perhaps I should spend more time with him, because as the years go by, I see that he's growing into manhood and I'm losing a lot of him every year. When he was younger, I think I was with him more than I am now. I think, as he gets older, he's had a tendency to get his pleasures from people his own age, this is fine as long as he makes home his headquarters. That's all I want.

Although the boys devoted an increasing amount of time to peer-group activities, they nevertheless, retained close ties to their parents and readily sought out their help, advice, and support when needed.

Parent Peer-Group Conflicts

The boys' primary reference groups were not selected indiscriminately. Since the adolescents tended to choose friends who shared similar value systems and behavioral norms, membership in the peer-group did not generate familial conflicts. In fact, the peer-group often served to reinforce and to uphold the parental norms and standards of behavior that the boys had adopted. Consequently, the parents were generally pleased with their sons' associates because they served as an important source of control in situations where the parents could not be present.

An essentially similar picture of adolescence, based on an intensive study of middle class families, has been presented by Elkin and Westley (1955; 1956). They summarize their findings as follows:

Family ties are close and the degree of basic family consensus is high. The parents are interested in all the activities of their children, and the adolescents, except for the area of sex, frankly discuss their own behavior and problems with them. In many areas of life, there is joint participation between parents and children. . . In independent discussions by parents and adolescents of the latters' marriage and occupational goals, there was a remarkable level of agreement. The adolescents also acknowledged the right of the parents to guide them, for example, accepting, at least manifestly, the prerogatives of the parents to set rules for the number of dates, hours of return from dates, and types of parties. The parents express relatively little concern about the socialization problems or peer group activities of their children (1955, p. 682).

SOURCES OF THE
ADOLESCENT MYTHOLOGY

What are the origins of the mythology about adolescence, and why does it persist?

Overinterpretation of Superficial Signs
of Nonconformity

The view that adolescence is a period of rebellion is often supported by references to superficial signs of nonconformity, particularly adolescent fad behavior.

It is certainly true that adolescents frequently display idiosyncratic fashions and interest patterns. Such fads, however, are not confined to adolescent age groups. Several years ago, for example, coon skin caps and Davy Crockett apparel were highly fashionable among pre-adolescent boys. When Davy Crockett began to wane a new fad quickly emerged—every youngster and a sizeable proportion of the adult population were gyrating with hoola-hoops. The hoola-hoop also suffered a quick death by replacement.

If pre-adolescent children display less fad behavior than do adolescents, this difference may be primarily due to the fact that young children do not possess the economic resources with which to purchase distinctive apparel, the latest phonograph records, and discriminative ornaments, rather than a reflection of a sudden heightening of peer-group conformity pressures during adolescence. The pre-adolescent does not purchase his own clothing, he has little voice in how his hair shall be cut and, on a 15-cent a week allowance, he is hardly in a position to create new fads, or to deviate too widely from parental tastes and standards.

How about adult fad behavior? A continental gentleman conducts a fashion show in Paris and almost instantly millions of hemlines move upward or downward; the human figure is sacked, trapezed, chemised, or appareled in some other fantastic creation.

At a recent cocktail party the present writer was cornered by an inquiring lady who expressed considerable puzzlement over adolescents' fascination for unusual and bizarre styles. The lady herself was draped with a sack, wearing a preposterous object on her head, and spiked high heel shoes that are more likely to land one in an orthopedic clinic, than to transport one across the room to the olives.

Fashion-feeders determine the styles, the colors, and the amount of clothing that shall be worn. It would be rare, indeed, to find an adult who would ask a sales clerk for articles of clothing in vogue two or three years ago. As long as social groups contain a status hierarchy, and tolerance for upward mobility within the social hierarchy, one can expect imitation of fads and fashions from below which, in turn, forces inventiveness from the elite in order to preserve the status differentiations.

Mass Media Sensationalism

The storm and stress view of adolescence is also continuously reinforced by mass media sensationalism. Since the deviant adolescent excites far more interest than the typical high school student, the adolescent is usually portrayed in literature, television, and in the movies as passing through a neurotic or a semi-delinquent phase of development (Kiell,

1959). These productions, many of which are designed primarily to generate visceral reactions or to sell copy, are generally viewed as profound and sensitive portrayals of the *typical* adolescent turmoil. Holden Caulfield, the central character in *The Catcher in the Rye* (Salinger, 1945), has thus become the prototypic adolescent.

Generalization from Samples of Deviant Adolescents

Professional people in the mental health field are apt to have most contact with delinquent adolescents, and are thus prone to base their accounts of adolescence on observations of atypical samples. By and large, the description of the modal pattern of adolescent behavior fits most closely the behavior of the deviant ten per cent of the adolescent population that appears repeatedly in psychiatric clinics, juvenile probation departments, and in the newspaper headlines.

Our study of the family relationships of adolescents also included a sample of antisocially aggressive boys. In the families of these hyper-aggressive adolescents there was indeed a great deal of storm and stress for many years. The boys' belligerence and rebellion, however, was not a unique product of adolescence. The defiant oppositional pattern of behavior was present all along, but because of their greater size and power the parents were able to suppress and to control, through coercive methods, their sons' belligerence during the early childhood years. By the time of adolescence, however, some of the boys had reached the stage where they were almost completely independent of the parents for the satisfaction of their social and physical needs. Moreover, they had developed physically to the point where they were larger and more powerful than their parents. With the achievement of the power reversal and the decrease of the parents' importance as sources of desired rewards, a number of the boys exhibited a blatant indifference to their parents' wishes about which they could now do little or nothing.

I. What sort of things does your mother object to your doing when you are out with your friends?

B. She don't know what I do.

I. What about staying out late at night?

B. She says, "Be home at 11 o'clock." I'll come home at one.

I. How about using the family car?

B. No. I wrecked mine, and my father wrecked his a month before I wrecked mine, and I can't even get near his. And I got a license and everything. I'm going to hot wire it some night and cut out.

I. How honest do you feel you can be to your mother about where you've been and what things you have done?

B. I tell her where I've been, period.

I. How about what you've done?

B. No. I won't tell her what I've done. If we're going out in the hills for a beer bust, I'm not going to tell her. I'll tell her I've been to a show or something.

I. How about your father?

B. I'll tell him where I've been, period.

The heightened aggression exhibited by these boys during adolescence primarily reflected response predispositions that became more evident following the power reversal in the parent-child relationship, rather than an adolescence-induced stress.

Inappropriate Generalization from Cross-cultural Data

It is interesting to note that many writers cite cross-cultural data as supporting evidence for the discontinuity view of child development in the American society. The reader suddenly finds himself in the Trobriand Islands, or among the Arapesh, rather than in the suburbs of Minneapolis or in the town square of Oskaloosa.

In many cultures the transition from child to adult status is very abrupt. Childhood behavior patterns are strongly reinforced, but as soon as the child reaches pubescence he is subjected to an elaborate ceremony which signifies his abrupt transformation into adult status. Following the ceremonial initiation the young initiate acquires new rights and privileges, new responsibilities and, in some cultures, he is even assigned a new name and a new set of parents who undertake his subsequent social training in the skills and habits required to perform the adult role.

In our culture, on the other hand, except for the discontinuities in the socialization of sexual behavior, there is considerable continuity in social training. As was mentioned earlier, independence and responsibility training, for example, are begun in early childhood and adult-role patterns are achieved through a gradual process of successive approximations. This is equally true in the development of many other forms of social behavior.

It should be mentioned in passing, however, that cross-cultural studies have been valuable in demonstrating that stresses and conflicts are not inevitable concomitants of pubescence, but rather products of cultural conditioning. Indeed, in some societies, adolescence is one of the pleasant periods of social development (Mead, 1930).

Overemphasis of the Biological Determination of Heterosexual Behavior

With the advent of pubescence the adolescent is presumably encumbered by a powerful biologically determined sexual drive that produces a relatively sudden and marked increase in heterosexual behavior. The net result of the clash between strong physiological urges demanding release and even more substantial social prohibitions, is a high degree of conflict, frustration, anxiety and diffuse tension. In contrast to this widely-accepted biological drive theory, evidence from studies of cross-species and cross-cultural sexual behavior reveals that human sexuality is governed primarily by social conditioning, rather than endocrinal stimulation (Ford & Beach, 1951).

The cross-species data demonstrate that hormonal control of sexual behavior decreases with advancing evolutionary status. In lower mammalian species, for example, sexual activities are completely regulated by gonadal hormones; among primates sexual behavior is partially independent of physiological stimulation; while human eroticism is exceedingly variable and essentially independent of hormonal regulation. Humans can be sexually aroused before puberty and long after natural or surgical loss of reproductive glands. Thus, one would induce sexual behavior in a rodent Don Juan by administering androgen, whereas presenting him lascivious pictures of a well-endowed mouse would have no stimulating effects whatsoever. By contrast, one would rely on sexually-balanced social stimuli, rather than on hormonal injections for producing erotic arousal in human males.

The prominent role of social learning factors in determining the timing, incidence and form of sexual activities of humans is also clearly revealed in the wide cross-cultural variability in patterns of sexual behavior. Sex-arousing properties have been conditioned to an extremely broad range of stimuli, but the cues that are sexually stimulating in one culture would, in many instances, prove sexually repulsive to members of another society. A similar diversity exists in the timing of the emergence of sexual interest and in the choice of sexual objects. In cultures that permit and encourage heterosexual behavior at earlier, or at later, periods of a child's development than is true for American youth, no marked changes in sexual behavior occur during adolescence.

It is evident from the foregoing discussion that "sexual tensions" are not an inevitable concomitant of pubescence. Furthermore, any significant increase in heterosexual activities during adolescence is due more to cultural conditioning and expectations than to endocrinal changes.

Stage Theories of Personality Development

Until recently, most of the theoretical conceptualizations of the developmental process have subscribed to some form of stage theory. According to the Freudian viewpoint (1949), for example, behavioral changes are programmed in an oral-anal-phallic sequence; Erikson (1950) characterizes personality development in terms of an eight-stage sequence; Gesell (1943) describes marked predictable cyclical changes in behavior over yearly or even shorter temporal intervals; and Piaget (1948, 1954), delineates numerous different stages for different classes of responses.

Although there appears to be relatively little consensus among these theories concerning the number and the content of stages considered to be crucial, they all share in common the assumption that social behavior can be categorized in terms of a relatively prefixed sequence of stages with varying degrees of continuity or discontinuity between successive developmental periods. Typically, the spontaneous emergence of these elaborate age-specific modes of behavior is attributed to ontogenetic factors. The seven-year-old, for example, is supposed to be withdrawn; the eight-year-old turns into an exuberant, expansive and buoyant child; the fifteen-year-old becomes remote and argumentative; parents are finally rewarded at sweet sixteen (Ilg & Ames, 1955). In truth, all seven-year-olds are not withdrawn, all eight-year-olds are not exuberant, expansive and buoyant, nor are all fifteen-year-olds aloof and argumentative. I am also acquainted with sixteen-year-olds who are anything but sweet. The withdrawn five-year-old is likely to remain a relatively withdrawn eight, nine, and sixteen-year-old unless he undergoes social-learning experiences that are effective in fostering more expressive behavior.

Although the traditional stage theories of child development are of questionable validity (Bandura & McDonald, 1963; Bandura & Mischel, 1963; Bandura & Walters, 1963), they have nevertheless been influential in promoting the view that adolescence represents a form of stage behavior that suddenly appears at pubescence, and as suddenly disappears when adulthood is achieved.

Self-fulfilling Prophecy

If a society labels its adolescents as "teen-agers," and expects them to be rebellious, unpredictable, sloppy, and wild in their behavior, and if this picture is repeatedly reinforced by the mass media, such cultural expectations may very well force adolescents into the role of rebel. In this way, a false expectation may serve to instigate and maintain certain role behaviors, in turn, then reinforce the originally false belief.

In discussing our research findings with parents' groups I have often been struck by the fact that most parents, who are experiencing positive and rewarding relationships with their pre-adolescent children are, nevertheless, waiting apprehensively and bracing themselves for the stormy adolescent period. Such vigilance can very easily create a small turbulence at least. When the prophesied storm fails to materialize, many parents begin to entertain doubts about the normality of their youngster's social development.

In closing, I do not wish to leave you with the impression that adolescence is a stress- or problem-free period of development. No age group is free from stress or adjustment problems. Our findings suggest, however, that the behavioral characteristics exhibited by children during the so-called adolescent stage are lawfully related to, and consistent with, pre-adolescent social behavior.

REFERENCES

Bandura, A., & McDonald, F. J. The influence of social reinforcement and the behavior of models in shaping children's moral judgments. *J. abnorm. soc. Psychol.*, 1963, **67**, 274–281.

Bandura, A., & Mischel, W. The influence of models in modifying delay-of-gratification patterns. Unpublished manuscript, Stanford Univer., 1963.

Bandura, A., & Walters, R. H. *Adolescent aggression.* New York: Ronald, 1959.

Bandura, A., & Walters, R. H. *Social learning and personality development.* New York: Holt, Rinehart & Winston, 1963.

Elkin, F., & Westley, W. A. The myth of adolescent culture. *Amer. sociol. Rev.,* 1955, **20**, 680–684.

Erikson, E. H. *Childhood and society.* New York: Norton, 1950.

Ford, C. S., & Beach, F. A. *Patterns of sexual behavior.* New York: Harper, 1951.

Freud, S. *An outline of psychoanalysis.* New York: Norton, 1949.

Gallagher, J. R., & Harris, H. I. *Emotional problems of adolescents.* New York: Oxford Univer. Press, 1958.

Gesell, A., & Ilg, Frances. *Infant and child in the culture of today.* New York: Harper, 1943.

Heathers, G. Emotional dependence and independence in nursery school play. *J. genet. Psychol.,* 1955, **87**, 37–57.

Hurlock, Elizabeth B. *Adolescent development.* New York: McGraw-Hill, 1955.

Ilg, Frances L., & Ames, Louise B. *Child behavior.* New York: Harper, 1955.

Josselyn, Irene M. *Psychosocial development of children.* New York: Family Service Assoc. of America, 1948.

Kiell, N. *The adolescent through fiction.* New York: International Univer. Press, 1959.

Mead, Margaret. Adolescence in primitive and in modern society. In V. F. Calverton, & S. D. Schmalhausen (Eds.), *The new generation*. New York: Macauley, 1930.

Mohr, G. S., & Despres, Marian A. *The stormy decade: adolescence*. New York: Random House, 1958.

Parsons, T. Psycho-analysis and social structure. *Psychoanal. Quart.*, 1950, **19**, 371–384.

Pearson, G. H. J. *Adolescence and the conflict of generations*. New York: Norton, 1958.

Piaget, J. *The moral judgment of the child*. New York: Free Press, 1948.

Piaget, J. *The construction of reality in the child*. New York: Basic Books, 1954.

Salinger, J. D. *The catcher in the rye*. Boston: Little, Brown, 1945.

Westley, W. A., & Elkin, F. The protective environment and adolescent socialization. *Social Forces*. 1956, **35**, 243–249.

ADDITIONAL READINGS

Adams, James F. Adolescents' identification of personal and national problems. *Adolescence,* Fall 1966, **1** (3) 240–250. Four thousand girls and boys, aged ten to nineteen, were asked to name their own personal problems, those of their peer group, and the major problem facing the country. In addition they were asked to suggest solutions to these problems. The most frequently named personal problems related to school, interpersonal relationships, the family, and financial matters. Boys reported more school and financial problems, girls more interpersonal and family problems.

Allport, Gordon W. Crises in normal personality development. *Teachers College Record,* 1964, **66** (1) 235–241. The author, an outstanding personality theorist, reports that the role of the teacher is most vivid to middle and late adolescents. From biographical data obtained from his students Allport defines the nature of the adolescent's crises and outlines the major crisis areas involved. Freudian interpretations seemed to fit well those adolescents who were disturbed but not the vast majority who are reasonably well adjusted. He suggests that personality theory for guidance not be drawn from the more "lurid" components of Freudian theory.

Koupernik, Cyrille. Refusal of an adolescent to accept the modern world. *Journal of Child Psychology and Psychiatry,* 1967, **8**, 233–240. The

case history is presented of a 16-year-old boy who refuses "frantically"
all that is modern, including airplanes, missiles, nuclear bombs, liberal
trends in the Catholic Church, pop singers, and everything that is exotic.
Reference to these topics leads to anxiety and he resorts to conjuratory
rites to avoid contamination.

Nixon, Robert E. Psychological normality in the years of youth. *Teachers
College Record,* October 1964, **66** (1) 71–79. The writer declares that
psychological normality in youth is recognizable, and makes it possible
to distinguish the abnormals, the conformists and rebels who make up
the majority. Few of us, he asserts, had a chance as adolescents to discover our own normality. He describes cases of particular adolescents
to make his points.

Three

Issues in Self-actualization

VIII. Schools for Adolescents

Those individuals who prescribe for adolescents' education usually begin—and sometimes end—by deploring today's version as grossly inadequate. Such criticisms take many forms. Some critics—for example, Patricia Sexton—deplore the school's failure to discharge its commitment to opportunity and equality.[1] Culturally deprived children, she claims, are unprepared to compete in schools which pursue middle-class goals and reward middle-class values. Frustration, maladjustment, and early dropouts are the inevitable outcomes. On the other hand, Koerner laments that the schools fail all intellectually capable students.[2] Still others—among them Jules Henry, Paul Goodman, and Edgar Friedenberg—are disturbed about the damage schools do to apparently successful students. What disturbs them is the way the school sets out, and succeeds in, molding youth to fit passively into the culture.

Specifically, Henry claims that schools are highly efficient in destroying youth's individuality and creative potential. The real offender is society, which designs schools in the interests of its own perpetuation. Schools have considered industry's needs, pursues Henry, and not the child's. ". . . I am not convinced, [he adds], that what is good for General Motors is good for our children. Even less am I convinced that what is good for Missile Dynamics is good for our children, or what is good for the Pentagon is good for them." Our love for our children, he goes on, is lifted by our love for fun and high-rising living standards. In consequence, the educational system, pressured by interest groups of various sorts, simply breaks one form of incompetence after another." [3]

Another problem, says Henry, is the all-too-ubiquitous incompetent teacher, who thanks heaven for a system which provides meek students. Such children "permit him to grow old without too much intellectual stir—without making him feel vulnerable." Bright teachers often find intolerable the "embalmed curriculum" and required textbooks forced upon them. Only through threatening to fail children does the school manage to motivate them at all. Remove the fear of failure, asserts Henry, and American education "would stop as if its heart had been cut out." [4]

[1] Patricia Sexton, *Education and Income* (New York, Viking Press, 1961).

[2] James Koerner, *The Miseducation of American Teachers* (Boston, Houghton Mifflin, 1963).

[3] Jules Henry, *Culture Against Man* (New York, Random House, 1963).

[4] Jules Henry, "Vulnerability in Education," *Teachers College Record,* Vol. 48, No. 2 (November 1966), pp. 135–145.

Friedenberg considers the school's success in helping adolescents to clarify values, on balance, poor. Administrative experience outweighs human considerations. Confidentiality of students' records is violated, making it dangerous for students to deal honestly with counselors. The schools also act as if America were still a melting pot, says Friedenberg, encouraging uniformity—not merely external, but also internal—more than individuality. Standards are fragmentary and incoherent. The lack of a philosophical structure obstructs developing curricula which utilize the best cultural resources to help youth make sense out of their lives. Those who buck the system feel anxious and guilty.[5] Nor are schools to be exonerated for these failings, but must bear their responsibility. After all, the school more than any other social institution, is the standard-bearer of the Western liberal tradition. Schools are bound by an intellectual tradition and a moral ideology that limits the kind and degree of complicity in cultures that they may accept.[6]

Goodman points out that one of the school's most obvious functions, of which talent search is a part, is to train prospective employees for private enterprise and public expense. Thus, schools teach children "the niceties and not-so-niceties" of corporate conduct, and compile dossiers of children's social or anti-social tendencies. Children are not only compelled to attend schools, but to become what the schools want to make them.[7]

Undergirding much controversy is a persistent issue: should schools attempt to produce the cultivated man or the specialist? [8] Should students attend a liberal arts college or a professional school? Within hybrid-types of institutions, what should be the balance of academic to professional courses? Some colleges clearly dedicate themselves to the one goal or the other. One college is tough, selective, and demanding, producing professionalized specialists. Another is tender rather than tough, with a dilletantish concern for liberal arts.

A related controversy is whether schools should be "Rickover-like" in rigor, modelled after the British public schools, or latter-day offshoots of Dewey progressivism and permissivism. Also, should the school simply mirror the society it serves or should it attempt to effectuate social change? Practically speaking, local school boards insist on societal conversation as a goal, while various philosophers and critics insist that the schools must become the "pivotal agent of social amelioration and change." The school,

[5] Edgar Z. Friedenberg, "The Impact of the School," *The Vanishing Adolescent* (Boston, Beacon Press, 1959).

[6] Edgar Z. Friedenberg, "New Value Conflicts in American Education," *The School Review*, Vol. 74, No. 1 (Spring 1966), p. 66.

[7] Paul Goodman, *Compulsory Mis-Education* (New York, Horizon Press, 1964).

[8] Joseph Gusfield and David Riesman, "Academic Standards and the Two Cultures" in the Context of a New State College," *The School Review*, Vol. 74, No. 1 (Spring 1966), pp. 95–115.

according to this view, should be open around the clock and become a resource for bettering the entire community.[9]

One major question today is the school's role in dealing with children whose parents differ from the dominant society in terms of culture, economic resources or values. In this area, questions proliferate like weeds in a tropical garden. How can peer relationships in the school be utilized to modify anti-social group norms? What sorts of reinforcement are needed to produce socially acceptable behaviors? What sort of rapprochement should be made between the child's own cultural norms and the school's middle-class values? Is the child hung up between two cultures worse off than the child with a firm foothold in his own minority culture? [10]

In the first selection, Dr. James S. Coleman suggests ways in which the school may pursue a more effective role in preparing children for society. Dr. Coleman argues that students will pursue goals which adequately prepare them for a productive life in society *only* when schools find ways of rewarding such efforts.

In the second article, Dr. Herbert J. Klausmeier pleads for balance in secondary school education. The diversity of human abilities and interests indicate that curricula should embrace non-verbal, fine arts, and vocational subjects along with more abstract subjects. Requirements should be flexible and adapted to the needs of all students involved.

[9] Michael D. Usdan and Raphael O. Nystrand, "Towards Participative Decision-Making: The Impact of Community Action Programs," *Teachers College Record,* Vol. 68, No. 2 (November 1966), pp. 95–106.

[10] George Henderson, "Opportunity and Alienation in the Public Schools," *Teachers College Record,* Vol. 69, No. 2 (November 1967), pp. 151–158.

16

James S. Coleman

ADOLESCENCE AND SECONDARY
EDUCATION IN MODERN SOCIETY

After reporting data obtained from a study of ten high schools represent-ing a range of environments from farm to city to suburb, the writer recom-mends ways that the school may function more effectively in modern society He points out that the school has assumed an increasingly significant place in the adolescent's life, and that adolescent society should be used to further the ends of education. He believes that present motivations used by the school are often unhealthy and suggests instead the use of creative games and contests.

The author has documented the character of the adolescent society in ten high schools. These schools do not represent the whole United States, but they cover a wide range of living conditions—from farm to city to suburb; from working class to executive class. Most important, it includes segments of American society likely to be representative of the future, es-pecially in the affluent suburb of Executive Heights.

The results of this research are disturbing to one concerned with the ability of an open society to raise its children today and in the future. This was once a task largely carried out within the family or in local places of work, a task with which the larger society had little need to concern itself. But the rationalization of society more and more inhibits the "natural" processes, by separating the adolescent off into institutions of his own, and insulating him from adults' work and adults' perspective. The adolescent remains in these institutions, treated as a child, for a longer and longer period, while he gains social sophistication earlier and earlier. If there was one striking difference between the adolescents of Marketville or Farmdale and those of Executive Heights, it was the greater social sophis-tication of the latter. They were more nearly teen-agers, less children; their own peers were of more importance to them, and their parents of less importance. Yet most of them would be forced to remain in school, as chil-dren, longer than their small-town counterparts. . . .

From James S. Coleman, "Adolescence and Secondary Education in Modern Society," in *The Adolescent Society* (New York, The Free Press of Glencoe, 1961), pp. 311; 314–324. Reprinted by permission.

The rewards and punishments dispensed by the adolescent society to its members are largely incorporated in the status system. The adolescent society has little material reward to dispense, so that its system of rewards is reflected almost directly in the distribution of status. This is the reason for our focus on the status system among adolescents . . . —because this status system shows the pattern of rewards and punishments dispensed by the adolescent society.

Several attributes of a status system have been examined here, all of them important to our inquiry:

1. The *content* of those activities which are rewarded and those which are punished. This content varied somewhat from one school to another, but in all cases athletics was extremely important for the boys, and social success with boys was extremely important for girls. Scholastic success received differing amounts of rewards, and sometimes punishments, in the different schools.

2. The degree of *ascriptiveness* of a system: whether status was awarded because of who a person *is*, or because of what he *does*. The schools differ sharply in the importance of family background for the status system, with family background generally being more important in schools which have a high component of upper-middle-class children. In such systems, where social acceptance depends upon a person's fixed attributes rather than what he *does,* there are many people whose efforts are dampened completely, since these efforts can gain them nothing.

3. The *range* of activities rewarded. In some schools, such as Green Junction, a single activity (e.g., football) completely dominates the status system. In others, like Marketville, a boy can be *either* a scholar or an athlete, and receive the rewards of his peers. In still other schools, like Maple Grove and Executive Heights, the range of rewarded activities is just as narrow as in Green Junction, but the rewarded "activity" includes a combination of elements: a boy must be an athlete *and* a reasonably good student *and* have social sophistication *and* have enough money to dress well and meet social expenses. The system is no more pluralistic than that of Green Junction in the activities it rewards; it is the special combination called the "all-around boy" that is rewarded.[1]

How then can the status systems among adolescents be changed? There have been many clues throughout the preceding chapters, and it will be the intent of the succeeding sections to examine the implications of these clues.

---

[1] There are numerous important variations in status systems which remain unexamined. For example, there has been no examination of the question of whether all students in school award status on the same bases, or whether these bases differ from group to group. Is the school broken down into relatively separate status systems, or does it have a single, all-encompassing one?

THE OPPORTUNITY FOR
RESPONSIBLE ACTION

One of the most important recent changes in adolescents has been their increasing social sophistication. They are no longer content to sit and be taught. It is Executive Heights, not Farmdale, where the "brilliant student" image is most shunned by girls; it is Executive Heights where the boys are uninterested in the quiet, conforming, studious girl, obedient to teachers' and parents' demands. Modern adolescents are not content with a passive role. They exhibit this discontent by their involvement in positive activities, activities which they can call their *own*: athletics, school newspapers, drama clubs, social affairs and dates. But classroom activities are hardly of this sort. They are prescribed "exercises," "assignments," "tests," to be done and handed in at a teacher's command.[2] They require not creativity but conformity, not originality and devotion, but attention and obedience. Because they are exercises prescribed for all, they do not allow the opportunity for passionate devotion, such as some teen-agers show to popular music, cars, or athletics. Compare again, for example, the diversity among students in time spent watching television with their homogeneity in time spent on homework, as shown in Figure 2–1. Television apparently "captures" some adolescents and pulls them further and further, while homework captures no one, but remains compressed toward an average level. Jacques Barzun, discussing the school-work carried out by students, notes this lack of passionate devotion:

No, it is at best industry, a virtue not to be despised, but lacking the essential element of work, which is passion. It is passion in work and for work that gives it its dramatic quality, that makes the outcome a possession of the worker, that becomes habit-forming and indeed obsessional. Of all the deprivations that modern life imposes on intellectual man, the abandonment of work is the cruellest, for all other occupations kill time and drain the spirit, whereas work fills both, and in the doing satisfies at once love and aggression. That is the sense in which work is "fun," with an irresistible appeal to man's love of difficulty conquered.[3]

Barzun writes of college students, where the problem exists as it does in high schools. In college as well as in high school, the opportunity for passionate devotion to scholarly work is nearly absent. The structure of

[2] I do not mean to suggest that all schoolwork is of this sort. Some teachers are able to devise projects involving positive, responsible, creative action of the sort I suggest below. However, these are sporadic cases, dependent on the special abilities of a teacher. The problem is to build a structure of education in which the ordinary teacher can easily develop such activity.

[3] Jacques Barzun, *The House of Intellect* (New York: Harpers, 1959), p. 125.

education puts both a floor and a ceiling upon scholarly effort, and prevents scholarship from truly competing for an adolescent's energy.[4]

In part, the floor and the ceiling are established by the prescribed "assignments"; in part by the norms of the adolescent community against excessive effort. Not only do these "exercises" seldom provide the opportunity for passionate devotion by a boy or girl; when they do so, his efforts are purely individual, and contribute nothing to the adolescent community as a whole. Instead, they make matters more difficult for others, who must work harder to keep up with this "curve-raiser." The norms of the adolescent community, damping down such excessive effort, are merely a response to this situation.

Another consequence of the passive, reactive role into which adolescents are cast is its encouragement of irresponsibility. If a group is given no authority to make decisions and take action on its own, the leaders need show no responsibility to the larger institution. Lack of authority carries with it lack of responsibility; demands for obedience generate disobedience as well. But when a person or group carries the authority for his own action, he carries responsibility for it. In politics, splinter parties which are never in power often show little responsibility to the political system, a party in power cannot show such irresponsibility. In an industrial plant, a group of workers that has no voice in decisions affecting it is purely irresponsible; a stable union with a role in decision-making is responsible. An adolescent society is no different from these.

In the history of education in America, this fact is exemplified well. One of the major avenues for positive action, for passionate devotion to a task in high schools and colleges, is in athletic contests. However, colleges and high schools did not always have such contests. Their introduction had a great impact upon discipline problems in school. As one pair of authors notes, "The early history of American colleges, before the advent of organized sports, is full of student violence, directed at each other, at the faculty, the institution, and the townies." [5] Organized athletics provided an avenue for positive action of the student body as a unit, and this action carried its own discipline with it. It is likely that without organized athletics, some of the high schools in this research would show violence and rebellion of the sort described above. In other schools, there are enough different extracurricular avenues to capture this energy. But in none of the schools is this possibility for positive, responsible action built

---

[4] For a discussion of education and the competition for energy, see James S. Coleman, "The Competition for Adolescent Energies," *Phi Delta Kappan*, 1961.

[5] Burton R. Clark and Martin Trow, "Determinants of College Student Subculture," in *The Study of College Peer Groups*, Theodore Newcomb, ed., 1961. See also Richard Hofstadter, "Part One: The Development of Higher Education in America," in R. Hofstadter and C. Hardy, *The Development and Scope of Higher Education in the United States* (New York: Columbia University Press, 1952).

into the purely scholarly activities—except in isolated examples, like debate teams.

The present research, and more particularly this chapter, cannot lay out a concrete plan for a structure of education which answers this problem. The above paragraphs state the problem, and the comments below indicate possible means of partial solution.

COMPETITION

Competition in schools has always had an ambiguous position. It has always been explicitly utilized as a motivating device in scholastic activities through the use of grades. It has at times been utilized in other ways, such as spelling bees, debates, and other contests. Yet some educational theory, particularly that of recent years, has emphasized the psychological ill effects which competition, and the resultant invidious comparison, can bring about. Thus the movement in education in the 1930's, 40's, and 50's has been away from scholastic competition, toward a minimization of differences in achievement. At the same time, the attempt to do away with grades has never met with success, and even in the recent anti-competition climate of public education, the use of I.Q. tests has come to be greater than ever.[6]

The attempt to do away with competition as a motivating device in schools is based on three important misconceptions, as follows:

1. There is a failure to recognize that the fundamental competition among children, adults, or anyone, is a competition for respect and recognition from others around them. In different systems, different achievements will bring this respect and recognition. The removal of scholastic achievement as a basis of comparison does not *lessen* the amount of competition among adolescents; it only *shifts* the arena from academic matters to non-academic ones. There is nothing so awesome as the competition between two girls for the attention of a boy; there is nothing so cruel as the world of a girl who's been rejected by a crowd she aspires to. Thus the psychological ill effects of competition are fully as present in a school where there are no grades and no possible comparison of scholastic achievement, as in a school where such criteria are in full view. There are no fewer psychological effects of competition in Green Junction than in Marketville, no fewer in Executive Heights

[6] It can probably be easily shown that I.Q. and achievement tests in school serve primarily two purposes, and have increased in use as these two purposes have become more important: as classification devices, for allocating students to classes grouped by achievement level, and as protective devices, to give the teacher an objective standard to justify to parents the poor performance of a child. For example, Executive Heights, in which these needs are greatest, administered a multitude of standardized tests to parents; Farmdale, where these needs are least great, administered almost none.

than in Midcity. It is only the *bases* of competition which are different.

2. Learning never takes place without a challenge, that is, a discrepancy between a desired state and one's existing state. A "satisfied" person does not learn, as the similarity of this word to the concept of "satiation" in learning theory suggests. The remarkable strides of young children derive in large part from the wide discrepancy between their present state and an ability to cope with the social world.

Competition is a major means by which such a challenge occurs. Competition against nature, against other persons, against other groups constitute attempts to overcome obstacles. If such competition is removed and no other challenge is substituted, then learning will not take place at all. Because of this, most attempts to do away with competition in schools through a removal of grades have failed, because no substitute challenge was provided. There has been much talk of substituting cooperation for competition, with little recognition that cooperation is not a substitute for competition as a motivating device. It is a tribute to the inconsistency of American ideology that Americans can extol "free competition" as the only device for generating economic enterprise, and at the same time deplore the existence of competition in the classroom, attempting to replace it by communal cooperative efforts.

3. In pointing to the psychological ill effects of the invidious comparisons produced by differential achievement, there is usually a failure to realize that these invidious comparisons are not due to competition itself, but to the *structure* of competition. A person is psychologically hurt when he fails *relative to those around him*. Thus when he fails relative to his friends, when they progress and he stays behind, his psychological equilibrium must be upset. Or when he succeeds while his friends fail, the relation between him and his friends is eroded. Interpersonal competition, and the resulting distinctions it creates between potential friends, undercuts bonds between people.[7]

---

[7] This is evidenced in numerous areas of life. Two examples of research illustrate this well. In the American Army during World War II, the morale of different army units was studied. It was found that Military Police noncommissioned officers had greater satisfaction with the promotion system than did Air Force noncommissioned officers, although their rate of promotion was less. Further investigation indicated that the faster rate of promotion created invidious comparisons among the Air Force officers, and left them dissatisfied. Where almost no one was promoted, in the Military Police, then everyone was doing as well as those around him, and there was satisfaction with the system. See S. A. Stouffer, et al., *The American Soldier,* Vol. 1 (Princeton: Princeton University Press, 1949), pp. 250–254.

A study of the system of ranks and levels among sales clerks in department stores shows the proliferation of minute gradations, each level with its own title. The study shows how these gradations and frequent tiny promotions undercut the development of strong communal relations among the clerks, and reduce the possibility of collective bargaining or union formation. See Carl Dreyfuss, "Prestige Grading: A Mechanism of Control," in R. K. Merton et al., *Reader in Bureaucracy* (Glencoe: Free Press, 1952), pp. 258–264.

However, such erosion of interpersonal ties stems not from competition, but from the *interpersonal* structure of scholastic competition. When a boy or girl is competing, not merely for himself, but as a representative of others who surround him, then they support his efforts, acclaim his successes, console his failures. His psychological environment is supportive rather than antagonistic, is at one with his efforts rather than opposed to them. It matters little that there are others, members of other social communities, who oppose him and would discourage his efforts, for those who are important to him give support to his efforts.

Another element in the structure of competition also shapes its psychological consequences. This is the source of the reward. If the win or loss depends upon subjective judgment of a "judge," then there can be maneuvering for position, claims of unfairness, attempts to gain favor of the judge, conformity to the judge's (i.e., teacher's) wishes rather than an all-out attack on the problem, and numerous other degrading activities. Yet when the win or loss stems truly from the activity at hand, as in a footrace, a game of football, or a game of chess, no such subjective judgment occurs. Thus the degrading activities so familiar in the classroom (where teacher is judge and student is competitor for a grade) are absent in other competitions where the race itself decides the winner.

In sum, then, the criticism of scholastic competition in education has been misplaced on several counts. And while this criticism developed, competition of the kind whose effects are most deleterious continued unabated in schools, both in the scholastic arena and in the social arena. It has continued in the scholastic arena simply because educators have found no alternative to it as an energizing device—just as economic systems, including those in Communist countries, have found no substitute for it. The proposals below do not attempt to do away with scholastic competition, but even to increase it in some areas (thus draining off the abscess of purely social competition, with its ill effects). The proposals are aimed at the *structure* within which competition takes place.

INTERSCHOLASTIC COMPETITION, AND THE CHANNELING OF EFFORT

One approach is made obvious by the dominant role of interscholastic athletics in the schools studied here. It is evident in the chapters above that it is the interscholastic structure of athletic competition that directs so much energy toward athletics. It is evident also that part of the reason for less ascriptiveness in the boys' status system is the lack of anything for girls comparable to interscholastic athletics.

Similarly, it is possible to substitute interscholastic (and intramural) competition in scholastic matters for the interpersonal competition for grades which presently exists. Such a substitution would require a revision of the notion that each student's achievement must be continually evaluated or "graded" in every subject. It would instead make such evaluations infrequent or absent, and subsidiary to contests and games, both within the school (between subgroups) and between schools.

Such a change from interpersonal to intergroup competition would also make it necessary to create, with considerable inventiveness, the vehicles for competition: intellectual games, problems, group and individual science projects, and other activities. Yet there are some examples which show that it can be done: debate teams, music contests, drama contests, science fairs (though science fairs as now conducted lack one crucial element, for they are ordinarily competitions between individuals, and not competitions between schools, thus lacking the group reinforcement which would go along with "winning for the school"). There are, in one place and another, math tournaments, speaking contests, and other examples of interscholastic competition.

In other places, one can find the bases from which to develop new kinds of scholastic competition. For example, Rand Corporation sociologists have developed "political gaming," in which teams represent policymakers in various countries. An international situation is set up, the policy-making teams respond to it and to one another's moves (under the supervision of referees), and a game is pursued in earnest. It is not too difficult to see how this, and modifications of it to include legislative politics, union-management bargaining, and other such situations, could be brought to the high school level and used in interscholastic competition. (Rand reports that an experiment in political gaming at MIT induced such interest among the student players and spectators that for weeks afterwards they avidly followed international news events, to see how their moves corresponded with actual policies as they developed.)

As another example, business executives are now being trained in a few companies by "management games," in which hypothetical situations are set up requiring teams of executives to make decisions and take the consequences. Electronic computers provide the hypothetical situation, and teams of executives "play games" in which each team is a firm in competition with the other. With effort and ingenuity, such games could be adapted to training in high school, not only in business economics, but in other areas.

A similar example is a political game recently devised at Johns Hopkins University in conjunction with the 1960 election. A sample of voters was interviewed to determine their attitudes toward various issues. Then processes by which these attitudes could affect vote intentions were programmed on an electronic computer. A class was divided into two sets of campaign strategists (a "Nixon team" and a "Kennedy team") and each team made campaign decisions in an attempt to influence the electorate.

These decisions were fed into the computer, which gave back preliminary vote intentions. New decisions were made, and their consequences assessed. After a fixed number of decisions, the campaign was ended, and the candidate with most votes was the winner. In one use of this game, the class learned far more about election processes than in previous courses using ordinary techniques. In part, they taught each other, through their meetings and discussions of strategy. In part they were taught by the results of their previous decisions, as manifested in the effect on the electorate.

There are many examples in high schools which show something about the effects interscholastic competitions might have. When I was attending a small-town school in Ohio, a slight, unprepossessing senior boy placed among the first ten in a state-wide physics competition. From that day, the senior boy—and physics as well—enjoyed a prestige and a prominence neither would have otherwise had. Rather than ridicule or indifference, his efforts were treated with respect and encouragement—for he was bringing glory to the school.

It is true that many of the examples and experiments mentioned above have had far less effect in bringing informal social rewards, encouragement, and respect to participants than the present analysis would suggest. The reason is clear, however: such social rewards from the student body as a whole are only forthcoming in response to something the individual or team has done for *them,* such as bringing glory to the school by winning over another school. If the activity, whether it be debate or math competition or basketball, receives no publicity, no recognition in the newspapers and by the community generally, then its winning will have brought little glory to the school, and will bring little encouragement to the participants. If it does receive recognition, it will encourage not only the participants, but those on the sidelines as well. In many high schools, boys not on the basketball team shoot baskets at noontime; every football team has its "Monday-morning quarterbacks"; a chess game has its kibitzers. In such ways, the energies of even the non-participants turn toward the game activity.

Sporadic and infrequent cases of interscholastic competition in non-athletic activities, with no attention to promotional activity, have little effect. However, if there were systematically organized games, tournaments, and meets in all activities ranging from mathematics and English through home economics and industrial arts to basketball and football, and if promotional skills were used, the resulting public interest and student interest in these activities would undoubtedly increase sharply. Suppose such a set of activities culminated in a "scholastic fair," which like a state fair included the most diverse exhibits, projects, competitions, and tournaments, not between individuals, but between *schools.* I suspect that the impact upon student motivation would be remarkably great—an impact due to the fact that the informal social rewards from community and fellow-students would reinforce rather than conflict with achievement.

These are simply examples of what might be done to change the structure of rewards in high schools—to shift from interpersonal competition, with its conflict-producing effects, to intergroup competition, in which group rewards reinforce achievement. More important than these examples, however, is the general principle—that motivations may be sharply altered by altering the structure of rewards, and more particularly that among adolescents, it is crucial to use the informal group rewards to reinforce the aims of education rather than to impede them.

CONTESTS, GAMES, AND THE ABSENCE OF JUDGES

Even when games and contests are interpersonal, rather than interscholastic, they constitute an important difference from the present structure of competition in the classroom. For another deleterious consequence of competition as it exists in the classroom is the prevalence of subjective judgment to decide a student's success. Teachers are forced, by the system which exists, to be judges as well as teachers. Much of the rebellion and the conformity, the alienation and the subservience of students can be traced to this role of the teacher. A system which eliminates these judgments would restore the role of teacher *as* teacher, remove from the teacher the onus of sorting and grading students, and allow a boy or girl to see far more clearly the relation between his work and his resulting success. This is the virtue of contests and games which provide their own criterion of success. In the games described above, the outcome of the game provides the success or failure; no intermediate judgment of a teacher is necessary. To be sure, it is difficult to devise such games in certain areas (e.g., creative writing); but it is not impossible. And even in such areas, the existence of contests (such as debates) makes more explicit the criteria of success, so that attempts to influence the teacher (or judge) can have far less effect.

In general, games and contests, with their explicit (and usually intrinsic) criteria of success remove the ill effects of a teacher's subjective judgment. No longer do the rewards go to the quiet little girl in the front row who makes no trouble for the teacher and is always ready with the "right" answer; the rewards are directly linked to achievement.

Two recent researches are relevant in illustrating the difference between these two kinds of competition. John Holland has studied creativity of National Merit Scholarship winners. He found that among the winners, there was no correlation between scores on tests of creativity and grades received in school. On the other hand, there was a correlation between creativity scores and success in various contests of skill during high school;

winning music, speech, art, writing, or science contests, writing something which was published, etc. Those students who had *won* in some such contests of skill were not generally students with the highest grades, but were students with a high potential for creativity. Further, the creative students showed such personal traits as independence, intellectuality, low sociability, while those with high grades showed perseverance, sociability, responsibility, and were rated high on "citizenship" by teachers.[8]

In another study, Getzels and Jackson compared two groups of students: those high in scores on creativity tests, but not especially high in scores on I.Q. tests; and those high in I.Q., but not especially high in scores on creativity tests. Although the two groups were nearly identical in their performance on standardized achievement tests, they differed sharply in other respects: the highly creative were far less interested in conforming to the teacher's demands, were far more imaginative, more given to humor, more wide-ranging in their interests. The personal traits they preferred for themselves were negatively correlated with those they felt teachers preferred, while the personal traits preferred by the high I.Q. students were highly correlated with those they felt teachers preferred. Correspondingly, the teachers in fact preferred the high I.Q. students to the highly creative ones.[9]

The results of these two studies suggest that the teacher's role as judge tends to inhibit creativity, and to systematically underselect creativity. This could hardly be otherwise, for teachers must also be disciplinarians, and their judgments must reward conformity as well as achievement. Creativity can be troublesome to a teacher confronted with classroom discipline. When the outcome is intrinsic to the competition, however, the pure achievement, unadulterated with conformity, is rewarded. At the same time, the contest provides its own discipline for the highly creative, who must organize their energies to succeed, and cannot get by with uncoordinated flashes of brilliance or with mere verbal adroitness.

Games have also a peculiar motivating quality, quite apart from the above considerations. This perhaps derives from the close connection they provide between action and outcome. A player sees the consequence of his moves, and is immediately able to test them against a criterion: the moves of the opponent. An economist has this to say about games and motivation:

Most human motives tend on scrutiny to assimilate themselves to the game spirit. It is little matter, if any, what we set ourselves to do; it is imperative to have some objective in view, and we seize upon and set up for ourselves objec-

[8] John L. Holland, "Creative and Academic Performance among Talented Adolescents," submitted for publication to *Journal of Educational Psychology*.
[9] J. W. Getzels and P. W. Jackson, "The Study of Giftedness: A Multidimensional Approach," in *The Gifted Student*, Cooperative Research Monograph No. 2, U.S. Department of Health, Education, and Welfare (Washington: United States Government Printing Office, 1960), pp. 1–18.

tives more or less at random—getting an education, acquiring skill at some art, making money, or what-not. But once having set ourselves to achieve some goal it becomes an absolute value, weaving itself into and absorbing life itself. It is just as in a game where the concrete objective—capturing our opponents' pieces, carrying a ball across a mark, or whatever it may be—is a matter of accident, but to achieve it is for the moment the end and aim of being.[10]

Unfortunately, the game spirit induced by the present structure of competition in high schools is often a game between students and teachers, the students devising strategies (individual and collective) to reduce the effort necessary for a grade, and the teacher devising strategies to increase this effort.

[10] Frank H. Knight, *Risk, Uncertainty and Profit* (Boston: Houghton Mifflin, 1948), p. 53.

17

Herbert J. Klausmeier

BALANCE IN HIGH SCHOOL EDUCATION

Dr. Klausmeier deplores restricting high-school education to the nar-rowly conceived subject orientation of the late nineteenth century, and recom-mends instead a comprehensive curriculum embracing non-verbal arts, as well. Besides traditional subjects, he would specifically include vocal music, dra-matics, and vocational education. Academically talented students would have a flexible program, tailored to their needs.

According to Lawrence A. Cremin (3), educational leaders in the early 1900's were successful in overcoming the narrowness and formalism of a curriculum that had prevented American high school education from being of value to many youth. During the early twentieth century many new subjects, especially vocational, were added to the high school curriculum; a much higher per cent of all students attended high school; and teaching methods became less formal, less repressive. The high school seemed to be progressing successfully to meet social needs. By the late 1940's, how-ever, it was apparent that education was no longer keeping up with the transformation of American society.

The effects of World War II upon education cannot yet be clearly established; but, in the 1950's high school education was regressing to the narrowly conceived subject orientation of the late nineteenth century. Some lay persons and professors emphasized only one function of the high school for all students, namely, developing the ability to think. In order to develop that ability, it was said, learning should be hard and painful, and all high school students should take the same subjects: English, foreign languages, mathematics, science, and social studies, especially history. A highly vocal group urging that these subjects dominate the high school curriculum for all students is the Council for Basic Education (6).

James B. Conant, unlike the Council for Basic Education, has vigor-ously defended the continuation and strengthening of the American compre-hensive high school, including its role in vocational education. However, he

From Herbert J. Klausmeier, "Balance in High School Education," *Teachers College Record,* Vol. 67, No. 1 (October 1965), pp. 18–25. Reprinted by permission.

proposes a very narrow curriculum in the five "academic" subjects for academically talented students (2). Although he would have academically talented students take 20 units in mathematics, science, English, social studies, and foreign languages prior to any electives in art, music, or vocational subjects, he insists that the majority of high school students should learn a marketable skill through a program of vocational education. For girls he suggests such courses as home economics, typing, stenography, or the use of clerical machines; for boys, vocational courses such as auto mechanics or machine-shop.

OBJECTIONS TO VERBAL CONCENTRATION

That many high school students during and immediately after World War II took too little work in the academic subjects is not debated. The critical point is that a desirable balance in education cannot be achieved by eliminating the non-verbal, fine arts and vocational subjects from the curriculum, as is now happening in many schools. Quality education cannot be exclusively verbal. Thinking critically about many significant problems requires some use of non-verbal symbols, often some actual psychomotor activity. To recommend only the five academic subjects for all high school students, including the academically talented, suggests ignorance of the diversity of human abilities and interests, lack of respect for the contribution of the non-verbal arts and work to the individual and society, and distrust of the democratic principle of freedom to choose from among various alternatives. One student may eventually achieve self-realization and make a maximum contribution to society as a scientist, another as an artist, another as a secretary, another as an auto mechanic, another as a homemaker. A balanced education, not an identical group of subjects, must be available in the secondary school for all these students and many others.

VOCATIONAL EDUCATION REAPPRAISED

Since 1960, several conditions have resulted in a reappraisal of vocational education in the high school. Unemployment of young people, age 18 to 24, is as alarmingly high as the unemployment of older persons that is attributed to automation. Many college students quit prior to graduation for lack of money. The home is increasingly unable to provide vocational education. Personality deterioration may be related to the false value that through education one can avoid work. Chase has recently stated the case for vocational education (1):

Unless interest in vocational education is awakened on a massive national scale, the United States will lose a crucial lap in "the race between education and catastrophe"—in H. G. Wells' annually more apt definition of history.

. . . Today rational education must include training for the 80 per cent of all young Americans who enter the labor market without college degrees. To ignore their vocational training is a reverse twist on the Eskimos' fabled custom of pushing their unproductive senior citizens onto the ice pack. That practice at least has a certain economic logic. Our system is managing to be at once inhumane and economically suicidal.

Recent information about our population and jobs dramatizes the need for vocational education. Out of every 10 youngsters now in grade school, three will not finish high school. Seven will be graduated from high school. Three will go to work, some as wives and mothers. Four will continue into higher education but only two will finish college.

Twenty-six million young workers will have started work between 1960 and 1970. The most rapidly expanding occupations for the decade are, in this order: professional and technical, clerical and sales, service, skilled workers and proprietors, managers about equally, and semi-skilled last (4).

The changing picture of both jobs and labor force suggests a need for the reappraisal of the entire field of vocational education, similar to what is occurring in the academic subject areas. Although this is the case, the comprehensive high school should now have a strong program in business education and in distributive education. Technicians, machine operators, mechanics and others in jobs related to the production, operation, and maintenance of machines will be needed in increasing numbers. Schools should be equipped immediately to teach general shop skills, psychomotor skills, knowledge, and attitudes which have transfer value for the jobs enumerated. The future of home economics and agriculture is uncertain, inasmuch as life in the home and on the farm is changing so rapidly. Fewer persons will work on the farms; more women will work outside the home. There is clearly a greater need for other types of vocational education.

In spite of the need for appraisal, we cannot afford to eliminate vocational education from the comprehensive high school. On the contrary, it should be possible for any student, including the academically talented, to pursue a major of three units in a vocational field. The larger high school might profitably have at least four general vocational programs, two particularly appropriate for girls and two for boys. Not every student should be required to take even one semester in a vocational subject, but a major of three units should not be denied to any student who desires to elect it. It is possible, of course, that many academically talented students will elect courses in the non-verbal fine arts rather than in a vocational field.

MANUAL LABOR BY
UNDERGRADUATES

Vocational education is not solely for students who do not attend college. Many college students require vocational education because their families cannot support them. Lins studied students' expenses and sources of income on the Madison campus of the University of Wisconsin for the academic year 1960–61 (7). Information from his study is presented only for the *unmarried, undergraduate students who were residents of Wisconsin and not living at home*. The average cost of university attendance was $1,485 for these students, and their average total income was $1,619. Men received 31.7 per cent and women received 57.3 per cent of their income from family contributions. The average income from various sources was scholarships $82, work during the year $154, summer work $398, savings $169, loan $74, family contribution $660, and others including ROTC and military reserves $82.

About 46 per cent of the men and 42 per cent of the women worked. Of the working freshmen 50 per cent or more worked 8.5 or more hours per week; of the working seniors 50 per cent worked 12.5 or more hours per week. The average pay per hour was $.99 for freshmen and $1.38 for seniors. Ninety per cent of the working freshmen earned between $.59 and $1.22 and ninety per cent of the seniors earned between $.90 and $3.29 per hour. The minimum pay by the University for student hourly help was $.96 per hour.

Thirty-five per cent of the parents of males and 22 per cent of the parents of females earned less than $6,000 during 1960. About one-third of the mothers were working in occupations other than in the home. Twenty per cent of these students received no family support. Slightly above 16 per cent were in debt. Of all sophomores, juniors, and seniors who had been out of school for one semester or more since entrance, about two-thirds gave finances as the first or second reason for drop-out.

The Director of Student Employment at the University of Wisconsin states that the principal employment of males during the academic year, on and off campus, is in kitchens and dining facilities, laboratories, and libraries doing odd jobs, mostly *unskilled manual labor*. Males could be employed in clerical and to a lesser extent distributive occupations, if they had the skills. The principal employment of females is in clerical jobs, dining and kitchen facilities, and library and laboratories. The supply of typists who can type at moderate speeds nearly meets the demand in University jobs; the supply of stenographers who can take shorthand at moderate speeds is far short of the demand. The supply of all jobs is, on and off campus, less than the demand.

The urban family experiences unsurmountable difficulty in providing household chores, much less work experience and vocational education, for children. Parents find it nearly impossible to locate work activities, in or outside the home, with or without pay, that is suited to the interests and abilities of adolescent boys, age 13 to 18. High school girls who baby sit, clean house, and prepare meals get little or no satisfaction from these activities, when repeated year after year. Manual labor tasks, distasteful to adults or for which the hourly rate is exceedingly low, are about the only ones available to high school students, and to able college students, as was shown previously. Even these jobs for youth are disappearing as chronic unemployment of unskilled and semi-skilled adults increases.

Education about work and careers also is meager in the modern home. The son usually does not see his father at work, much less learn the job from him. The same is true of the girl whose mother works. Most parents are only semi-literate about economic affairs, apparently preferring to permit others to manipulate much of their economic life. So poor is the total program of vocational education in the home and school that many unmarried female college graduates with majors in one of the liberal arts or sciences enroll in a business college in order to prepare themselves for a job. Also many industries employ some of the liberal arts graduates for less money than they pay equally young skilled workers—high school graduates with four years of work experience.

PERSONALITY, CULTURE, AND WORK

Work is closely related to individual personality and to culture. Man has progressed from prehistoric times to his present state only as he has been able, through work, to change the environment so that his many abilities might emerge and develop. His evolution is not so much a process of adjusting to the environment as adjusting the environment to suit his needs and emergent abilities.

Smith points out that most capitalist and socialist writers have treated work behavior narrowly either as a means of production, as a source of wealth, or as a limited aspect of technology, but not as a critical aspect of human behavior and adjustment (8). He then develops a comprehensive theory to explain work as the primary determinant of the human condition. In this comprehensive theory, he relates how work in man has contributed to his evolution, how its feedback effects define the personality of each individual, how it has provided the dynamic human motivation toward social and economic development, and how its behavior mechanisms are regulated.

From a biosocial account of work, Smith theorizes how the feedback effects of occupation determine the specific properties of individual adjustment, mental health, motivation, social integration, aging, and individual behavior resources. In referring to work and personality he says:

> Throughout the ages of man's civilized existence, the events of work have borne an interacting relation to what is called personality. This relation at times has been decisive not only in structuring the human condition of existence and aspiration, but in specifically determining the social circumstances of individuality. In ancient periods, occupation determined class, caste, and the dominant personality association of each. . . . As the structure of institutional organization in industry has become more complex, the pattern of individual social behavior within the organized work systems has become more stylized and group-structured, leading to greater emphasis than heretofore on both the assessment and control of the over-all pattern of social-emotional behavior.

This approach to work behavior bears analysis, not only in America but throughout the world. Until recently, a minority in most nations of the Western world has argued successfully for liberal education of a wealthy elite ruling class, educated to accrue wealth, to rule, to lead, and on the other hand, low-cost, technical education or no education for the masses of working people. Until recently, America has successfully pursued a different course through its comprehensive high school, which has included vocational education as a primary objective.

VALUES OF NON-VERBAL ARTS

Instrumental music, the visual arts, and dance are relatively non-verbal in comparison with English, mathematics, science, social studies, and foreign languages. Vocal music and dramatics are also non-verbal in many respects. The content of these non-verbal arts may not be selected intelligently and the courses may not be taught well in many high schools at the present time. Though this is the case, it is almost unbelievable that liberally educated persons are recommending, explicitly or implicitly, that academically talented high school students should not take work for credit in these arts. The truly educated person appreciates the cultural heritage more fully through understanding at least one of the non-verbal arts. He has liberated himself from ignorance about a most important area of human activity and has also learned to control his own instrumental acts in an individually and socially constructive manner. A kind of blindness concerning the purpose of man and civilized society has led some to treat the non-verbal fine arts as non-essential to liberal education.

Taking a course in painting or instrumental music for credit can be defended as readily as taking a course in a modern foreign language if the

primary purposes of the foreign language are to learn to understand and
speak the language, to read and write it, and to understand the culture of
other people who speak the language. Learning to express oneself with a
musical instrument is a more complex psychomotor skill; but understanding
music notation and composition is as worth while an intellectual operation
as is understanding the grammar of the language. Great musical composi-
tions are understood by people from many lands and are part of the culture
of many nations. Music and visual arts are surely more nearly universal
than is any verbal language.

The greatest value to be derived from acquiring competence in one of
the arts is the ability to express one's feelings and ideas in a medium other
than words. The need to achieve is very strong in our society. Many students are frustrated in connection with their perceived lack of competence
in one or another academic subject or in other daily affairs. Gaining mastery
over self, over the musical instrument or art medium, and over the self-
medium relationship should not be underestimated as a means of achieving
self-realization.

To propose that instruction in the arts should be at the expense of the
parents is to deny most high school students the instruction. To propose that
this work can be taken solely in the summer or as extracurricular activity
is to indicate that one's value system is negatively oriented toward the
arts. The many liberal arts colleges, public and private universities, and
state colleges which offer majors in music and art are tangible evidence that
these subject fields have a substantial content and should not be dismissed
as frills, unworthy of credit in the high school.

Unless there is some threat to national security of which the writer is
unaware, the taking of twenty units of work in the five academic subjects
prior to any work in the fine arts cannot be justified. On the contrary,
every academically talented student should be permitted to take a full major
of three units or years of work in one of the non-verbal arts, or three years
in a combination of them. Every high school should offer at least three
years of work in music and three years in the visual arts. There also should
be course work, to be counted toward high school graduation, in dance and
in dramatics. It is possible, of course, that the content and methods of
instruction in the non-verbal arts need thorough revision.

RECOMMENDATIONS FOR BALANCE

Although vast changes should be made in secondary schooling in the
next decades, let us assume that the majority of high school students will
spend from three to five years completing what are now normally Grades
9 through 12 in a comprehensive high school. The balance to be achieved

in high school is among the three main objectives: general education, incorporated in the required program for all students; vocational education, including the acquisition of a marketable skill or the beginning of it; and education to prepare for college attendance.

The general education requirement for all students might be 9 years or units: 3 in English, 2 in social studies, 1 in each mathematics, science, and a fine art, and 1 additional unit in one of the first four subject fields. The student who does not plan to go to college might take the remaining 7 of 16 units in any combination of subjects but should probably take at least three in a vocational area.

The academically talented students need a different, but flexible program. It is the academically talented who are now being put on a diet of only academic subjects. Further, even the oldest, brightest students are forced to stay in high school for four years, instead of being permitted to graduate after three or three and one-half years, in order to complete 18 to 20 units in the five academic subjects. The six recommendations which follow are intended to provide for balance in the program for academically talented high school students (5).

1. Every student identified as academically talented in English, foreign languages, mathematics, science, or social studies toward the end of Grade 6 or the beginning of Grade 7 or 8 should be given the opportunity to take condensed work in each subject in which he is superior and should receive full credit toward high school graduation for any work of high school caliber completed by the end of Grade 8, up to a total of four units. The student superior in all subjects should complete any four of the following subjects, normally ninth-grade subjects, by the end of Grade 8; general science, algebra, civics or some other social studies, Grade 9 English, and Grade 9 foreign language. The student superior in one, two, or three fields should complete one, two, or three units in the respective subjects by the end of Grade 8.

2. The academically talented student should be permitted to take five courses, in addition to physical education, during each year, Grades 9–12, and should be required to take at least four courses.

3. The academically talented student who completes 6 to 9 units required for high school graduation by the end of Grade 9 should have the following options available in the senior high school (Grades 10–12):

a. Attend senior high school for three years and take one or more courses designed specifically for admission to college with advanced standing.

b. Attend senior high school for three years and take for college credit one or more courses at an easily accessible local university or college during the senior year.

c. Attend senior high school for two or two and one-half years, be graduated, and then enter an easily accessible local university or college full time.

d. Attend senior high school for two or two and one-half years, be graduated, and then enter any university or college of the student's choice full time.

e. Attend senior high school for three school years but take no course designed specifically for college admission with advanced standing (no acceleration involved).

f. Attend senior high school for three years but have released time for part time employment in the senior year (no acceleration involved).

4. Each student identified as academically talented as early as Grade 10 should be required to complete at least 12 units in the academic subjects and at least a total of 17 units in all subjects for high school graduation, excluding physical education. The 12 units required in the academic subjects should be distributed as follows: 3 in English, 2 in mathematics, 2 in foreign language, 2 in science, 2 in social studies, and 1 additional unit in any of the five subject fields. Each academically talented student should thus be required to complete a minor of 2 units in four academic subjects and a major of 3 or 4 units in one, or a major of 3 units in two subjects and a minor in each of the other three. The 5 additional elective units might be totally in the nonverbal arts and/or vocational subjects or they might be distributed among the academic subjects, the non-verbal arts, and vocational subjects as outlined in the next recommendation.

5. The academically talented student should be required to take one unit in the non-verbal arts and/or vocational subjects for each unit above fourteen taken in the academic subjects. Thus, the student graduating with 18 units should be permitted to take a maximum of 16 units in the academic subjects and should be required to take a minimum of 2 units in the non-verbal arts and/or vocational subjects; the student graduating with 20 units should be permitted to take a maximum of 17 units in the academic subjects and should be required to take a minimum of 3 units in the fine arts and/or vocational subjects.

6. The academically talented student should complete 4 units in at least three subject fields before completing 5 units in any field, and should not be permitted to complete more than 6 units in any subject field during Grades 8–12. The student completing 22 units, 18 in the academic subjects and 4 in the fine arts and vocational subjects, could take 3 units in each of two academic subjects and 4 in each of the other three for a total of 18; or he might take 2 units in each of two subjects, 4 units in each of two others, and 6 in the fifth for a total of 18 units in the academic subjects. The 4 units in the fine arts and/or vocational subjects likewise could be distributed or all in one subject.

If college-bound students are permitted to acquire a saleable skill at a beginning level or to pursue a non-verbal art, there is some hope that vocational education and the non-verbal arts will survive in the comprehensive high school for the non-college bound students. We should not expect the fine arts or any vocational subject to survive when the many students who think they will go to college, the high school counselors, principals, and teachers in the academic subjects shun them as unworthy of serious study, unworthy of credit toward graduation. Unless the non-verbal arts, as well as vocational education, receive proper attention in arranging a balanced education for each student, our system will not only be inhumane and economically suicidal, as Chase has pointed out, it will also be culturally sterile.

REFERENCES

1. Chase, E. T. Learning to be unemployable. *Harper's*, 1963, **226**, 33–40.
2. Conant, J. B. *The American high school today.* New York: McGraw-Hill, 1959.
3. Cremin, L. A. *The transformation of the school: Progressivism in American education.* New York: Knopf, 1961.
4. Haines, P. G. (Ed.) A time for professional statesmanship. *Delta Pi Epsilon J.,* 1963, **5** (No. 2), 33.
5. Klausmeier, H. J. *Desirable education for high school students of superior learning abilities.* Madison: Wisconsin Improvement Program, 1962, 38–43.
6. Koerner, J. D. (Ed.) *The case for basic education.* Boston: Little, Brown, 1959.
7. Lins, L. J. *Student expenses and sources of income 1960–1961. University of Wisconsin, Madison Campus.* Madison: Univer. Wisc. Off. Inst. Studies, 1961.
8. Smith, K. U. *Behavior organization and work.* Madison, Wisc.: Coll. Printg. Typ. Co., 1962.

ADDITIONAL READINGS

Coleman, James C. *The adolescent society: The social life of the teenager and its impact on education.* New York: Free Press, 1961. This important book analyzes the social systems of ten high schools, all in Northern Illinois, but otherwise varying in size, social-class composition, and community setting. Coleman's chief concern is to account for the importance of athletic and other nonacademic values and the downgrading of intellectual values. He suggests ways in which academic achievement may be increased. The book affords insights into social systems of American high schools and the influences of their interpersonal relationships.

Coleman, James S. *Adolescents and the schools.* New York: Basic Books, 1965. Coleman portrays the American high schools as a compulsory closed society, which coexists with the world of the adolescents outside the school. The school is at a great disadvantage in having to compete with out-of-school distractions. Football, popularity, good looks, and having a good time are reported as more important to teen-agers than academic achievement.

Friedenberg, Edgar Z. The modern high school: A profile. In *Dignity of Youth and Other Atavisms*. Boston: Beacon Press, pp. 79–95. The author describes a typical working-class high school which he calls Milgrim High, and a typical middle-class one, Hartsburgh High. At Milgrim discipline is everywhere evident, initiative is squelched, and the general atmosphere is drab and prison-like. Hartsburgh High is much more pleasant, but there is still the same pattern of control, distrust, and punishment. Friedenberg deplores the school's encroachment on students' dignity and privacy, and its assumption of custodial control.

Gusfield, Joseph & Riesman, David. Academic standards and "the two cultures" in the context of a new state college. *The School Review,* Spring 1966, **74** (1), 95–120. This paper tells of a university college founded with the ideal of providing an elite education, with few concessions to a student body with minimal experiences of high culture, either in their homes or in their secondary schools. Slack standards and vocationalism were alike taboo. The authors reject such a rigorous program as unwise and offer alternate suggestions.

Jencks, Christopher & Riesman, David. The war between the generations. *Teachers College Record,* October 1967, **69** (1), 1–21. The writers discuss the relationship between students and faculty down through the years and into the present. The problems of various types of youth are discussed along with problems they pose for the colleges.

Kvaraceus, William C. Teacher and pupil in the technological culture of the school. *Phi Delta Kappan,* February 1965, XLVI (6), 269–272. The writer discusses some of the implications for teacher and learner of accelerating technological change in the school apparatus as seen particularly in highly automated classrooms (some even containing classroom computers and information retrieval systems).

Kysar, John E. Social class and adaptation of college students. *Mental Hygiene,* July 1966, **50** (3), 398–405. The author cites research relating social class to mental health, and describes problems faced by students from lower socioeconomic levels and minority groups in higher education. He stresses the need for research in this area.

McDill, Edward L., Meyers, Edmund D. Jr., & Rigsby, Leo C. Institutional effects on the academic behavior of high school students. *Sociology of Education,* Summer 1967, **40** (3), 181–199. This study was designed to assess the influence of different pedagogical and social dimensions of school environment on the achievement of students while controlling relevant personal variables.

Newcomb, Theodore M. & Wilson, Everett R. (Eds.). *College peer groups: Problems and prospects.* Chicago: Aldine Publishing Company, 1966. A collection of essays, mostly methodological, considers ways of studying how the college changes students.

Tuel, John K. & Wursten, Rosemary. Dimensions of the educational environment. *California Journal of Educational Research,* 1965, **16,** 175–188. The writer considers how various factors affect the climate of learning, including the home, the classroom (methods, evaluation techniques, group structure), and the school (values, social pressure, and peer-group influences).

IX. The Adolescent and Creativity

Until recently, any child with a high IQ was deemed gifted, but a distinction is now made among such aspects of giftedness or talent as intelligence, musical and artistic ability, creative writing, and even social leadership. Distinctions between giftedness and high IQ have become so confused that the term "gifted" has been all but abandoned. It is accepted that children with special talents may or may not earn high IQ scores.

Numerous definitions of creativity may be found. Guilford, a pioneer in the field, speaks of "originality" as the production of "unusual, far-fetched, remote, or clever responses." An idea is novel if it is new so far as the particular individual is concerned.[1] Paulston sees creativity as "a form of energy of the psyche released when there is a healthy relationship between the conscious and unconscious. This energy, the source of creativity, grows with use and contributes to the health of the psyche, just as the healthy psyche releases energy for creative activity."[2] Writers differ in defining creativity in terms of process or product. Developmental studies have typically dealt with process. Torrance, for example, defines creative thinking as "the process of sensing gaps or disturbing missing elements; forming new hypotheses concerning them; testing these hypotheses and communicating the results, possibly modifying and retesting the hypotheses."[3]

Many studies have involved determining what creative individuals are like. In studies by Hammer and by Parloff and Datta, creative adolescents are described as having a high degree of emotional strength, determination, and ambition, accompanied by sensitivity and intuition.[4,5] Mac-Kinnon describes eminent architects as being self-confident, imaginative, non-conforming, and possessing inner ethical and artistic standards; they also score low on various anxiety scales.[6] A byproduct of such studies is the

[1] J. P. Guilford, *Teachers College Record,* Vol. 42 (1962), pp. 380–392.

[2] Christina Bratt Paulston, "On Creativity and Teaching," *Teachers College Record,* Vol. 69, No. 4 (January 1968), p. 370.

[3] E. P. Torrance, *Education and the Creative Potential* (Minneapolis, Minn., University of Minnesota Press, 1963), p. 80.

[4] E. F. Hammer, "Creativity and Feminine Ingredients in Young Male Artists," *Perceptual Motor Skills,* Vol. 19 (1964), p. 414.

[5] M. B. Parloff and L. Datta, "Personality Characteristics of the Potentially Creative Scientist," in J. H. Masserman (Ed.), *Science and Psychoanalysis,* Vol. 8 (New York, Grune & Stratton, 1965), pp. 91–106.

[6] D. W. MacKinnon, "Personality and the Realization of Creative Potential," *American Psychologist,* Vol. 20 (1965), pp. 273–281.

realization that non-cognitive factors, especially those concerned with motivation and personality, are important correlates of creativity. These factors include non-conformity, freedom of expression, playfulness, and curiosity.

Since all these factors are largely determined by environment, especially the home, researchers have attempted to establish relationships between creative development and patterns of child rearing. In one such study, where creativity was related to dimensions of authoritarian-control, hostility-rejection, and democratic attitudes, only authoritarian-control factors proved significant. Authoritarian attitudes of the mother related negatively to creativity and originality in the child.[7] Other studies by Nichols, and by Getzels and Jackson, demonstrated that the parents of highly creative adolescents were not authoritarian, and stressed openness to experience and enthusiasm for life. By contrast, parents of highly intellectual, but not creative, youths promoted "good" or conforming behavior and studiousness in their children.[8, 9]

Creativity also varies by sex and age, even in early grades. By grade 3, reports Torrance, boys score higher than girls on creative tasks, because even small girls are trained to accept things as they are.[10] However, if girls have access to scientific toys they, too, will make progress in scientific thinking. The important factor, where age is concerned, is what experiences the passage of time involves. The boy, on the other hand, who becomes concerned over his masculine image may become less creative because he represses sensitive feelings. Both sensitivity and independence are important components of creativity.[11]

Findings like these raise significant questions where adolescents are concerned. Can losses in creativity, sustained earlier, be restored? If not, should curricula be modified to accommodate all children, regardless of creative potential? Should girls be encouraged to be creative; or is creativity maladaptive for their future, a largely nurturant role?

Studies indicate that the teacher's role is especially important in the pupils' creative development. Most teachers classify as a behavior problem the creative child who is manifestly bored by classroom routines. In a study by Torrance, pupils of highly creative teachers, as determined by various objective tests, demonstrated a considerable gain in creative writing ability

[7] Robert C. Nichols, "Parental Attitudes of Mothers of Intelligent Adolescents and Creativity of Their Children," *Child Development*, Vol. 35 (1964), pp. 1041–1049.

[8] *Ibid.*

[9] J. W. Getzels and F. W. Jackson, "Family Environment and Cognitive Style: A Study of the Sources of Highly Intelligent and of Highly Creative Adolescents," *American Sociological Review*, Vol. 26 (1961), pp. 351–359.

[10] E. P. Torrance, "Factors Affecting Creative Thinking in Children: An Interim Research Report," *Merrill-Palmer Quarterly*, Vol. 7 (1961), pp. 171–180.

[11] E. P. Torrance, "Changing Reactions of Preadolescent Girls to Tasks Requiring Creative Scientific Thinking," *Journal of Genetic Psychology*, Vol. 102 (1963), pp. 217–223.

in a three-month period, while those who had less creative teachers showed no improvement.[12]

Even less able teachers, it is argued, may learn how to encourage creativity. One method, says Paulston, is to scold conformity and praise disagreement. Students should be taught to question intelligently their own perceptions, their teachers, and their textbooks. "It's so because the textbook says so," should become an obsolete argument.[13] Paul Torrance, an outstanding authority on creativity, also proposes techniques for encouraging creativity. Dr. Torrance, who is quoted in the first selection, believes the development of creativity to be an important obligation of the schools.

Authorities differ somewhat on whether creative potential may be produced, or simply discovered and developed. Ausubel argues that the widespread challenge, to teach for creativity, is based on several untenable propositions. It assumes that every child has potentialities for creative production provided they are not stifled by the educational system. Even if the child has no such potential, inspired teaching may somehow "instill" it. Moreover, all creativity is assumed to be of one piece, instead of diverse and of many sorts. However, says Ausubel, the school can help children who possess unique creative potential by arranging opportunities for spontaneity and individuality, rewarding creative accomplishment, and providing suitable guidance and encouragement.[14]

Unlike Ausubel, Robert J. Havighurst (quoted in the second selection) believes the production of mentally superior individuals a matter of social engineering rather than one of discovery and exploitation of natural resources. His point of view, if valid, holds great promise for disadvantaged groups.

[12] E. P. Torrance, "Education and Creativity," in C. W. Taylor (Ed.), *Creativity: Progress and Potential* (New York, McGraw-Hill, 1964), pp. 50–128.

[13] Paulston, *op. cit.,* p. 371.

[14] David P. Ausubel, "Creativity, General Creative Abilities, and the Creative Individual," *Psychology of the Schools,* Vol. 1, No. 4 (1964), pp. 344–347.

18

E. Paul Torrance

FOSTERING CREATIVE THINKING
DURING THE HIGH SCHOOL YEARS

*The writer deplores the lack of scientific data about creative thinking at
the high school level and discusses four ways in which high schools can foster
creative thinking: 1. provide opportunities for students to learn and think creatively; 2. develop skills in creative thinking or problem-solving; 3. reward creative thinking, and 4. reduce the common inhibitors of creative thinking.*

We have less scientific information about fostering creative thinking
during the high school years than for any other educational level. We have
information about fostering creativity during the pre-school and elementary-
school years, because it has been considered legitimate to stimulate the
"creative imagination" of children. The development of "creative imagination," however, is not generally accepted among the legitimate objectives
of the high school. We have information about fostering creative thinking
during the college years, because it has been deemed appropriate for colleges and universities to produce professional workers capable of making
creative contributions. No such expectations exist for high schools.

Actually the fostering of creative thinking *can* be considered a legitimate concern of the high school, *if* we examine carefully the most widely
accepted goals of all education—including the high school. High schools are
legitimately concerned about the *mental health* of students. There is little
question but that the stifling of creative thinking cuts at the very roots of
satisfaction in living and eventually creates overwhelming tension and breakdown. Creative thinking is a most important resource in coping with life's
daily stresses.

High schools maintain that they are concerned about the *full intellectual development and functioning* of students. Certainly a person is not fully
functioning mentally, if his skills in creative thinking remain undeveloped
or if his creative thinking abilities are paralyzed.

From E. Paul Torrance, "Fostering Creative Thinking During the High School
Years," *The High School Journal,* Vol. 45 (April 1962), pp. 281–288. (Reprinted by
permission of The University of North Carolina Press.)

The high school's concern about *solid educational achievement* is un-disputed. High school teachers and guidance workers are urged to help underachievers to achieve in line with their potentialities and to aid over-achievers to become "better rounded" personalities. Recent research (Get-zels and Jackson, 1958; Torrance, 1960) on creative thinking calls for a revision of the traditional concepts of under- and over-evaluation. The crea-tive thinking abilities contribute importantly to the acquisition of informa-tion and even the traditionally measured educational skills. They become even more important when the material is taught in such a way that youngsters have a chance to use these abilities.

High schools are interested in the *vocational success* of their pupils. It has long been recognized that creativity is a distinguishing characteristic of outstanding individuals in almost every occupational field. We are dis-covering now that creative thinking is important even in some of the most common occupations, such as selling in a department store, even in sales jobs considered "routine" (Wallace, 1961).

Finally, high schools are legitimately concerned that their graduates *make useful contributions to society*. Graduates conditioned for "brain-washing" and paralyzed in their creative thinking are not likely to make the contributions needed now by our society.

If high school educators can accept the fostering of creative thinking as a legitimate goal, they have already taken the first big step! What else can they do? As I add up the scattered evidence, it seems to me that the most important things they can do are:

1. Provide opportunities for students to learn and think creatively
2. Develop skills in creative thinking or problem-solving
3. Reward creative thinking
4. Reduce as many as possible of the common inhibitors of creative thinking

OPPORTUNITIES FOR LEARNING AND THINKING CREATIVELY

In a recent review of some of the experimental high school programs in physics, chemistry, biology, and mathematics, Ornstein (1961) described what he termed "a classroom revolution which is turning up talent that old methods could not touch." Many students with mediocre scores on tests of scholastic aptitude are outstanding in achievement. It is difficult to explain the many scholastic reversals which Ornstein describes until we recognize that the experimental courses and the teaching methods which they demand provide a better chance for youngsters to learn and think creatively. Thus, they use abilities not usually measured by tests of intelligence and scholas-tic aptitude and abilities not very valuable in learning by authority. The same hypothesis might be advanced to explain Rosenbloom's finding that students low on traditional measures of scholastic aptitude by comparison profit more from the new mathematics courses (School Mathematics Study Group) than do students in the upper brackets of scholastic aptitude. This is especially interesting in view of the fact that many teachers thought that these experimental materials would be appropriate only for high ability students. Apparently these new materials bring into play kinds of abilities which are not especially useful in mastering traditional materials.

Perhaps I should attempt to explain how learning creatively differs from learning by authority. One learns creatively by questioning, inquiring, searching, manipulating, experimenting, guessing, testing the limits and risking, even playing around, but always trying to find out the truth. Learning and thinking creatively begins when the student starts sensing difficulties, problems, missing elements, or gaps in his knowledge. The process continues as he starts making guesses or formulating hypotheses about these deficiencies and is impelled to test these guesses or hypotheses, possibly revising and retesting them. The process is not completed and the tension is not eased until the results are communicated. Strong fundamental needs are involved in all four of these stages.

We learn by authority when we accept something as true because some authority or power figure says so. This authority may be a teacher, a parent, a textbook, a newspaper, an encyclopedia, a minister or priest. It is frequently the tyranny of the consensus of the peer group.

On the high school scene, new developments in the mathematics (SMSG, University of Illinois, etc.) and the sciences (Physical Science Study Committee, Biological Sciences Curriculum Study, Chemical Education Materials Study, etc.) seem to be leading the way in providing opportunities for learning and thinking creatively. Promising trends have also been apparent in art education. The social studies, language arts or English, and other areas of the curriculum have shown no such vigorous signs.

SKILLS IN CREATIVE THINKING

Since at least as early as 1898 with the work of Royce, experimenters have been demonstrating the effectiveness of deliberate efforts to develop skills in creative thinking, creative problem-solving, or originality. Slosson and Downey in 1922 and Mearns in 1929 (reprinted, 1958) reported pioneering efforts. Currently the work of Parnes and Meadow (1959, 1960), True (1956), Nicholson (1959), Maltzman (1960), Hyman (1960), Torrance (1961), and numerous others is continuing to demonstrate that it is possible through deliberate methods to develop and/or increase skills in creative thinking.

234 Issues in Self-actualization

In spite of this rather convincing accumulation of scientifically-developed information, educators continue to rely upon chance when they ask students to produce original ideas. Of course many of the clues obtained from these experimental studies need to be translated into materials and methods in the high school curriculum and re-tested. Such studies provide at least a basis for getting started. Some time ago, I attempted to summarize the clues as I interpret them in the form of twenty suggestions to classroom teachers for developing skills in creative thinking. In summary, these are as follows:

1. Value creative thinking.
2. Help students become more sensitive to environmental stimuli.
3. Encourage manipulation of objects and ideas.
4. Teach how to test systematically each idea.
5. Develop tolerance of new ideas.
6. Beware of forcing a set pattern.
7. Develop a creative classroom atmosphere.
8. Teach students that their ideas have value.
9. Teach students skills of avoiding or coping with peer sanctions against originality without sacrificing their creativity.
10. Teach students the nature of the creative process.
11. Dispel the sense of awe of masterpieces.
12. Encourage and evaluate self-initiated learning.
13. Create "thorns in the flesh," making students aware of unsolved problems and gaps in knowledge.
14. Create necessities for creative thinking.
15. Provide for both active and quiet periods, recognizing that thinking is a legitimate "activity."
16. Make resources available for working out ideas.
17. Encourage the habit of working out the full implications of ideas, pushing thinking as far ahead as possible.
18. Develop skills of constructive criticism—not just criticism.
19. Encourage acquisition of knowledge in a variety of fields, along with a constructive attitude towards such knowledge.
20. Be adventurous-spirited yourself, letting one thing lead to another, being alert to ideas when they come.

REWARDING CREATIVE THINKING

Repeatedly and consistently, research has shown that individuals tend to learn and to develop along whatever lines they find rewarding. Thus, my associates and I have spent considerable time in developing and attempting to test a set of principles for rewarding creative thinking in the classroom. Briefly, these principles are as follows:

1. *Be respectful of unusual questions.* Nothing is more rewarding to the person who asks a question than to find an answer to his question. Questions reflect a "mind hunger" and this hunger must be satisfied lest the mind be starved. Although the need should be met immediately, there is much that high school teachers can do to enrich the period between the question and the answer. In general, they should tell students only what they cannot learn for themselves. This means that students need to be taught the skills of inquiry and research. They need to learn how to sustain a question, to play with it, toss it back and forth, refine it, and accept the questioning mood without the need for ready-made answers from the teacher.

2. *Be respectful of the unusual ideas of students.* Students who are stimulated by creative approaches will see many relationships and significances that their teachers miss. They will present ideas and solutions which their teachers will not be able to evaluate. Thus, it is extremely difficult for teachers properly to reward such thinking and it is usually the more creatively talented youngsters who suffer most such unrewarded effort.

3. *Show students that their ideas have value.* In showing adolescents that their ideas have value, the trouble is that many teachers do not believe that adolescents are capable of thinking of ideas that have value. Such teachers obviously will not be able to reward creative thinking in adolescents. I would suggest that teachers who do not genuinely believe that the ideas of their students have value, be on the alert for a few days to recognize new ideas among students. They can be shown that their ideas have value, if teachers listen to their ideas, consider them, test them, use them, communicate them to proper individuals or groups, give students the credit for them, and the like. Teachers need to give more attention to the lure of discovery and the role of curiosity and interest in motivating learning.

4. *Provide opportunities for self-initiated learning and give credit for it.* An old principle of learning is: "Excite and direct the self-activities of the learner and tell him nothing that he can learn for himself." Almost all children have strong curiosity and exploratory tendencies. The problem of high school teachers is to keep these tendencies alive or reawaken them. Overly detailed supervision, too much reliance upon prescribed curricula, failure to appraise and give credit for growth resulting from the student's own initiative, and attempts to teach too many subjects and cover too much material may seriously interfere with such attempts.

5. *Provide for periods of non-evaluated practice or discovery.* There is a need for periods when students can learn and discover without threats of immediate evaluation. External evaluation is always a threat and creates a need for defensiveness. This makes some portion of the individual's experiencing or sensing denied to awareness (Rogers, 1954). Thus, there is lacking the openness which is so necessary in the production of new ideas.

INHIBITORS AND FACILITATORS

After summarizing the accumulated information (Torrance, 1961), it seems to this writer that there are certain forces in our culture which inhibit creative thinking at all ages. The following are some of the more important of these forces: an extremely peer-oriented culture, sanctions against questioning exploration, overemphasized or misplaced emphasis on sex roles, the equation of divergency with abnormality or delinquency, and a work-play dichotomy. Many of the common facilitators have been mentioned in the foregoing sections. Others include: rewarding a variety of kinds of talent and achievement, helping highly creative individuals become less obnoxious without sacrificing their creativity, reducing the isolation of creative individuals, providing sponsors and patrons for creative students, helping them to develop values and purposes, and helping them learn to cope with the fears and anxieties which arise from so frequently being a minority of one.

In studies involving high school students, many of the inhibiting and facilitating factors listed above are reflected in the work of Getzels and Jackson (1958), Coleman (1961), Drews (1961), and others.

Some educators maintain that there must be fundamental changes in the ways schools are organized, if they are to foster creativity, achieving such objectives as developing independent responsibility for learning, inquiring minds, and ability to solve problems in contrast to emphases on familiarity with facts. Some, like J. Lloyd Trump (1959), have suggested organizations involving team teaching, varied class-size, provisions for individual study, resource centers and programs which emphasize creativity and develop independence in learning. Evaluations of programs such as those proposed by Trump and others should include assessments of creative growth and achievement.

Many high school teachers and administrators feel that they are "in a steel box" in attempting to make changes in the direction of a more creative kind of education because of the domination of the colleges. Recently there have been a number of eloquent pleas for colleges to recognize and make a place in college for superior divergent students as well as the superior convergent thinker. Among these has been that of Getzels (1960) who has charged that the usual criteria of admissions—tests, recommendations, and rank in class—are all biased in favor of the student with "convergent" intellectual ability and social interests.

Taylor (1960) has pointed out some of the possible negative and positive effects of new instructional media on creativity. He points out that it is quite unlikely that areas heretofore neglected in education will automatically be taken care of with the emergence of new instructional devices. He emphasized the need for deliberate techniques for developing creativity and to determine which instructional media might be most effective in developing various characteristics, including creativity. The Philosophy of Education Association has also called attention to the need for determining whether or not some of the new instructional media can be used in such a way as to stimulate creative thinking. Unless attention is given to these problems through research, many of the new teaching media can become inhibitors rather than facilitators of creativity.

At least as recently as 1952 and 1957 (Mead and Métraux, 1952; Heath *et al.,* 1957; Remmers, 1957) the image of the scientist among high school students could be counted as a serious inhibitor of creativity. In a study by Mead and Métraux, using projective material, and in a national survey by Remmers and his associates, it was found that high school students have a very unfavorable image of the scientist. The nature of this unfavorable image is such that it is likely to create an unfavorable reaction to almost any career requiring a high degree of creativity.

CONCLUSION

An attempt has been made to show that the fostering of creative thinking *is* a legitimate concern of high school educators and that creative thinking can be fostered among high school students by providing opportunities for them to learn and think creatively, developing skills in creative thinking or problem-solving, rewarding creative thinking, and reducing as many as possible of the common inhibitors of creative thinking.

REFERENCES

Coleman, J. S. *The Adolescent Society.* New York: Free Press, 1961.

Drews, Elizabeth M. A Critical Evaluation of Approaches to the Identification of Gifted Students. In A. Traxler (Ed.) *Measurement and Evaluation in Today's Schools.* Washington, D.C.: American Council on Education, 1961. Pp. 47–51.

Getzels, J. W. Non-IQ Intellectual and Other Factors in College Admission. In *The Coming Crisis in the Selection of Students for College Entrance.* Washington, D.C.: American Educational Research Association, 1960.

Getzels, J. W. and P. W. Jackson. The Meaning of "Giftedness"—An Examination of an Expanding Concept. *Phi Delta Kappan,* 1958, **40,** 75–77.

Heath, R. W., M. H. Maier, H. H. Remmers, and D. C. Rodgers. *High School Students Look at Science.* Lafayette, Ind.: Division of Educational Reference, Purdue University, 1957.

Hyman, R. *Some Experiments in Creativity.* New York: General Electric Services, 1960.

Maltzman, I. On the Training of Originality. *Psychological Review,* 1960, **67,** 229–242.

Mead, Margaret and Rhoda Métraux. Image of the Scientist Among High School Students. *Science,* 1952, 126. Pp. 384–390.

Mearns, H. *Creative Power.* New York: Dover, 1958.

Nicholason, P. J., III. An Experimental Investigation of the Effects of Training Upon Creativity. Doctoral dissertation, University of Houston, 1959.

Ornstein, J. A. New Recruits for Science. *Parent's Magazine,* February 1961, **36, 42,** 101–103.

Parnes, S. J. and A. Meadow. Effects of "Brainstorming" Instructions on Creative Problem Solving by Trained and Untrained Subjects. *Journal of Educational Psychology,* 1959, **50,** 171–176.

Parnes, S. J. Evaluation of Persistence of Effects Produced by a Creative Problem-Solving Course. *Psychological Reports,* 1960, **7,** 357–361.

Remmers, H. H. Factors in the Early Motivation of Scientists. In *Strengthening Science Education for Youth and Industry.* New York: New York University Press, 1957. Pp. 79–90.

Rogers, C. R. Toward a Theory of Creativity. *ETC: A Review of General Semantics,* 1954, **11,** 249–260.

Royce, J. The Psychology of Invention. *Psychological Review,* 1898, **5,** 113–144.

Slosson, E. E. and J. E. Downey. *Plots and Personalities.* New York: Century, 1922.

Taylor, C. W. Possible Positive and Negative Effects of Instructional Media on Creativity. Paper prepared for seminar on theory of instructional materials. St. Louis, Mo., April 19–23, 1960. Dittoed.

Torrance, E. P. *Educational Achievement of the Highly Intelligent and the Highly Creative: Eight Partial Replications of the Getzels-Jackson Study.* Minneapolis: Bureau of Educational Research, University of Minnesota, 1960.

Torrance, E. P. *Status of Knowledge Concerning Education and Creative Scientific Talent.* Minneapolis: Bureau of Educational Research, University of Minnesota, 1961.

True, G. H. Creativity as a Function of Idea Fluency, Practicability, and Specific Training. Doctoral dissertation, Iowa University, 1956.

Trump, L. J. Images of the Future. Washington, D.C.: National Association of Secondary-School Principals, 1959.

Wallace, H. R. Creative Thinking: A Factor in Sales Productivity. *Vocational Guidance Quarterly,* Summer 1961, 223–226.

19

Robert J. Havighurst

CONDITIONS PRODUCTIVE OF SUPERIOR CHILDREN

The writer discusses the influences of social class, urbanization, and family background on mental superiority and suggests steps which might be undertaken to produce greater numbers of mentally superior children. Specifically, he proposes improving cultural opportunities for the disadvantaged and teaching in a manner which stimulates highly creative, intellectual accomplishments.

Children become mentally superior through a combination of being born with superior potential and being raised in a superior environment. Nobody knows the relative importance of these two factors. Certainly, biological intelligence is too low in some children to permit them to develop even average mental ability. Probably a severe environmental handicap can prevent the potentially most able child from showing more than average mental ability.

It seems probable that our society actually discovers and develops no more than perhaps half its potential intellectual talent. Some evidence for this statement lies in the fact that former immigrant groups, which at one time did the heavy labor of America, at first produced very few mentally superior children; but after a sojourn in this country of two or three generations, they have produced large numbers of mentally superior people. They did this through bettering the environment in which they reared their children. The same process is now going on in the underprivileged groups of today—the Negroes, the Puerto Ricans, the rural southern whites—as they secure better economic conditions and then create a more favorable environment for the mental development of their children.

There is some validity to a view of the production of mentally superior people as a *processing* of human material. Some of this material is of better biological quality than other parts of it, but it all depends heavily on social processing for the quality of the final product.

From Robert J. Havighurst, "Conditions Productive of Superior Children," *Teachers College Record,* Vol. 62 (1961), pp. 524–531. Reprinted by permission.

In this paper we shall deliberately ignore the biological element in the production of mentally superior children and consider only the cultivation of mental superiority through the family, the school, and the community. We shall try to answer the question: What kind of social environment produces mentally superior children most efficiently, and how can we expand this environment and make it more effective?

SOCIAL CLASS AND CITIES

Mentally superior children come in relatively high proportions from upper and upper-middle class families and in relatively lower proportions from lower working class families. This fact has been affirmed in dozens of studies of the relations between IQ and socio-economic status.

Some idea of the relative efficiencies of the various social classes in processing their children for mental ability is given in Table 19–1, which comes from a study of all the children in the sixth grade of the public schools of a medium-sized mid-western city. The upper and upper-middle classes, combined, produced 1.8 times as many children in the upper quarter of the IQ distribution as they would if all social classes had been equally efficient at this, and only .4 times as many children in the lowest quarter. The lower working class showed a reversal of these efficiency ratios.

Table 19–1   Efficiencies of the Various Social Classes in the Top and Bottom Quarters of IQ Distribution

(Sixth Grade in River City)

Social Class	Percentage Distribution of Children	Efficiency Ratio[1] in Producing Children in	
		Top Quarter	Bottom Quarter
Upper and upper middle	10	1.8	.4
Lower middle	27	1.5	.6
Upper lower	39	.8	1.1
Lower lower	24	.4	1.6

[1]These ratios indicate the relative efficiencies of the various social classes. If all classes were equally efficient in producing children of a given quartile in IQ, the ratios would all be 1.

If all four socio-economic groups had been as efficient as the upper and upper-middle class groups in providing children with IQ's in the top quarter (above about 110), there would have been 180 children with IQ's over 110 in this community for every 100 such children today. In other words, the numbers of mentally superior children would have been almost doubled, and the intelligence level of the child population would have been lifted enormously.

Similar conclusions arise from a study of high school seniors in a city of 500,000. Roughly 5 per cent of the seniors were selected by a systematic screening program as being "academically superior." As can be seen in Table 19–2, the various high schools contributed to this total in rough proportion to the socio-economic status of the parents. The school with highest socio-economic status contributed 19 per cent of its seniors to the select group. Within this group, 92 per cent of the fathers were high school graduates; 65 per cent were college graduates. The three schools with lowest socio-economic status contributed 1.5 per cent of their seniors to the select group. Less than 40 per cent of the fathers of the superior students in these three schools were high school graduates. If all schools had contributed as efficiently as School A to the production of superior students, there would have been 532 instead of 194, or almost three times as many. Probably the reason this proportion is higher than the proportion reported in Table 19–1 is that Table 19–1 refers to sixth graders, Table 19–2 to twelfth graders. The cultural advantages of the higher status children probably cumulated between the sixth and twelfth grades to give them even greater superiority over their less privileged age-mates.

Table 19-2 Efficiencies of Schools of Various Socio-Economic Levels in Producing Academically Superior High School Seniors

(Data from an American City of 500,000 Population)

	High School						
	A	B	C	D	E	FGH	Total
No. of graduates	412	392	325	71	400	1,203	2,803
No. of superior students in graduating class	77	45	30	5	17	20	194
Per cent of superior students	19	12	9	7	4	1.5	5.1
Rank in socio-economic status	1	2	3	4	5	7	
No. of superior students if A ratio prevailed	77	74	62	14	76	229	532

Granted the assumption we are making in this paper—that mental superiority is largely a product of social environment—the mental level of the population would be raised very greatly if we could give all children the kinds of social environment which upper middle class children have today.

Mentally superior children also tend to come from urban and suburban communities, rather than from rural communities. This is not as pronounced an effect as the social class effect, but it seems to indicate that the urban-suburban environment is more stimulating mentally than the rural environment.

Within the families lower on the socio-economic scale, there is enough production of mentally superior youth to indicate that socio-economic status alone is not what makes the difference between a good and poor environment for mental growth. It is probably certain cultural and motivational deprivations that often go with low socio-economic status that reduce the efficiency of lower status families. Whenever a very bright boy or girl is discovered in a family of low economic status, it turns out that this family has unusual characteristics which give the youth an advantage. These characteristics may consist of thrift and ambition or of an interest on the part of the mother or father in literature, art, or science.

Summing up the argument thus far, it seems that boys and girls who are mentally superior have become so because of 1. a home and school environment which stimulated them to learn and to enjoy learning; 2. parents and other significant persons who set examples of interest and attainment in education which the children unconsciously imitated, and 3. early family training which produced a desire for achievement in the child. When these influences act upon a child with average or better biological equipment for learning, the child will become mentally superior. They are sometimes found in unexpected places.

For instance, Paul is a very good student in high school. His mother has worked as a waitress for years, since her husband deserted her, to support herself and Paul. She placed Paul in a boys' home sponsored by a church, and he has lived there from the age of 8 until his present age of 18. He says, "My father and mother never went to college. I thought I'd like to do better in life than they did." At the boy's home, the superintendent and the teachers were demanding but warm. Under them, Paul performed well in the elementary school until time for senior high, when he went to the local public school. Here he had some difficulty at first. He says, "English was about my worst subject. The teacher helped me though, and I improved a lot. I consider her an important person in my life." A careers unit in civics helped him to decide on engineering or mathematics, and he will go to college with scholarship help. Two of his closest friends have college plans. The superintendent of the home has urged him to go. "He told me to go to college. He said I was a good student, and I ought to go to college."

DIVERGENT THINKERS

Among the mentally superior part of the population some people are creative and some are not. Much attention has been paid recently to the quality or qualities of creativity on the assumptions that our society needs not only intellectually facile people but, more especially, creative people, and that a high IQ does not guarantee creativity.

Guilford and others have made a distinction between "convergent thinking" and "divergent thinking." The person with "convergent" intellectual ability is retentive and docile. He tends to seek the single, predetermined "correct" answer to an intellectual problem. On the other hand, the "divergent" thinker is constructive and creative. He tends to seek the novel, experimental, and multiple answer to an intellectual problem.

Guilford has devised a number of tests of creative intelligence which have only a low positive correlation with the usual intelligence tests. Getzels and Jackson (3), using these tests, picked out a group of high school pupils who were high in IQ (average 150) but not especially high in creative thinking for comparison with a group high in creative thinking but lower in IQ (average 127). The two groups did equally well in achievement tests, but the high intelligence, non-creative group were preferred by their teachers as the kind of students they liked to have in their classes. The high creative group, in freely-written stories, showed more humor, more unexpected endings, more incongruities, and generally a freer play of fantasy. Similarly, Cattell and Drevdahl (2) compared outstanding research scientists with outstanding teachers and administrators in the same fields on the 16 P.F. Personality Inventory. They found the researchers to be more self-sufficient and schizothymic (introverted), to have a greater drive for mastery, and to entertain more radical ideas.

We know relatively little, as yet, about creative people and even less about what makes them creative. If it proves to be true that some or all of the qualities of creativity can be taught, this will become another goal in the society's processing of mentally superior children.

THE UNDER-ACHIEVERS

In the study of intellectually superior children, attention has been called to a substantial group whose educational performance falls below what might reasonably be expected from their performance on intelligence tests. These mentally superior under-achievers are people with biological or environmental superiority who have not put their superiority to use in school. They may be regarded as products of an inadequate processing in the home, the community, or the school. This conclusion emerges from a number of recent studies of bright under-achievers.

Thus, Terman and Oden, in their study of adults whom they had followed from childhood as gifted children (8), compared the 150 men in their sample who had been most successful in their occupations with the 150 least successful men. As children, these men all had IQ's of 135 or higher.

The more successful group had had an average IQ of 155 in 1922, while the less successful had had an average of 150. However, there were considerable differences in other respects between the two groups. Ninety per cent of the more successful had been graduated from college, compared with 37 per cent of the less successful. Fifty per cent of the fathers of the more successful group were college graduates, compared with only 16 per cent of the fathers of the less successful. In occupation, 38 per cent of the fathers of the more successful were professional men, compared with 19 per cent of the fathers of the less successful.

Terman concludes, "Where all are so intelligent, it follows necessarily that differences in success must be due largely to non-intellectual factors"; and "Everything considered, there is nothing in which the (more successful and less successful) groups present a greater contrast than in drive to achieve and in all-round social adjustment. . . . At any rate, we have seen that intellect and achievement are far from perfectly correlated."

Most of the studies of under-achievement have been made on boys rather than girls, because bright boys are under-achievers in school much more frequently than girls are. The many studies have produced substantially similar results and point to under-achievement as a form of personal and social maladjustment. In one or another of these studies, the following characteristics of under-achieving able students appear:

1. They see themselves as inadequate persons.
2. They have lower aspirations than achievers.
3. They do not like school as well as achievers do.
4. They do not enjoy learning from books.
5. They have lower popularity and leadership status in the eyes of their age-mates.
6. They tend to come from homes that are broken or emotionally inadequate in other ways.
7. They tend to come from homes of low socio-economic status.
8. Their vocational goals are not as clearly defined as those of achievers.
9. Their study habits are not as good as those of achievers.
10. They have narrower interests than those of achievers.
11. They have poorer personal adjustment than that of achievers.

Haggard (6), comparing high with low achieving high IQ children, found that the high achievers had better mental health. In particular, the high achievers in arithmetic, "had by far the best-developed and healthiest egos, both in relation to their own emotions and mental processes and in their greater maturity in dealing with the outside world of people and things." Haggard concluded, "Our findings indicate that the best way to produce clear thinking is to help children develop into anxiety-free, emotionally healthy individuals who are also trained to master a variety of intellectual tasks."

Much the same conclusion is expressed by Gowan (4) after reviewing a number of studies of under-achievement. He says, "To summarize, achievement is an indication that the individual has successfully transferred a large enough portion of his basic libidinal drives to areas of cultural accomplishment so that he derives a significant portion of his gratification from them."

Although the general proposition seems justified that high IQ under-achievers are people with inadequate socialization and poor personal-social adjustment, there are two major exceptions to this generalization. One exception refers to a group of high IQ boys with a limited horizon. They are well-adjusted within a small world which does not require more than average school achievement and does not require a college education. Take Kenny, for example. With an IQ of 145, Kenny found school work easy and more or less coasted through his studies, doing enough work to get fairly good grades, but falling down somewhat in high school, where he graduated at about the middle of his class. Kenny's parents were earnest people, good church members, with little formal education. They did not read very much and had no intellectual interests. They were satisfied with Kenny's report cards and pleased that he was going further in school than they had gone. They were especially pleased with Kenny's interest in earning money. He always had several jobs waiting for him and showed great enterprise as a salesman. During his later years in high school, he worked in a shoe store where his employer was so pleased with his work that he offered Kenny a full-time job and a chance to buy into his business when he was graduated from high school. This seemed good to Kenny, and he is now getting along well as junior partner in the store.

The other exception refers to a rather large group of girls with high intelligence who achieve very well up to the end of high school, when their grades fall off and they show little or no interest in going to college. These girls either get married as soon as they finish high school or they take a job in an office or a shop for a few years until they marry. Girls do not generally show as under-achievers because their school grades are pretty well maintained until the end of high school. But they would be called under-achievers if under-achievement were defined as failure to go as far in education as one's abilities would justify.

With this broad definition of under-achievement, one can say that the gifted under-achievers have not been effectively processed by the society for maximal or optimal educational achievement for one or more of the following reasons:

Inadequate home environment leaves them personally maladjusted and unable to use their intellectual ability.

Inadequate home environment limits their horizon and fails to stimulate them to use education for vocational achievement, although they are personally well adjusted.

Inadequate home environment fails to instill in them a deep drive or need for achievement.

School and home together fail to instill in them an intrinsic love of learning.

The social role of wife and mother is seen by some girls as more important than that of student; and the home, school, and community have caused them to see a conflict between marriage and a home, on the one hand, and continued educational achievement on the other.

INCREASING THE SUPPLY

Holding to our tentative assumption that production of mentally superior people is more a matter of social engineering than of discovery and exploitation of a rare natural resource, we may essay an answer to the question of how to increase the supply of mentally superior children who are well motivated to achieve in school and college.

First, it must be remembered that our culturally deprived families, both in the big cities and in isolated rural areas, have always in the past improved themselves as producers of superior children when they had economic opportunity. The same process of improvement is evident today among working class Negroes, Puerto Ricans, and white emigrants from the rural South. It is to these groups that we may look for an increased supply of able youngsters, and the rate of increase is likely to be considerably facilitated by increasing their degree of economic opportunity and enriching their cultural environment. This point is a central one for those social policies related to our long-range needs for manpower and for school programs aimed at the underprivileged and academically impoverished. Within the schools, there is a grave need for greater attention to rewards for achievement within these groups, for a keener recognition of developing intellectual effort, and for a greater responsiveness to embryonic academic motives.

Second, counseling and guidance services could usefully focus on increasing educational motivation among superior pupils. The well adjusted child with limited horizons, like Kenny, represents a kind of national loss. If education is concerned with the actualizing of individual potentialities, then special attention to youngsters of this kind is more than warranted. A sound argument can be made for the school counselor's devoting more of his time to this sort of developmental enterprise than to the remediation of "problem cases" and to the support of the pathological, the delinquent, and the dull. Both kinds of service are desirable and necessary, of course; but we may have overemphasized the guidance worker's obligation to the educationally handicapped to the serious neglect, both in training and in on-the-job functionings of his potentialities for working productively with the superior child with low academic motivation.

Third, studies of the unconscious drive for achievement, like those by McClelland (7) and Rosen (8), indicate that the early training of boys in the home has a great deal to do with their motivation to use their mental ability for school achievement. Closer collaboration between school and home, especially with lower class parent groups, can be helpful here. Even more, an explicit and articulate concern with the development of intellectual motivations in the earliest school years could possibly harvest a more widespread drive for academic achievement and a deeper channeling of intellectual capacities into school work and the kinds of goals that our schools and colleges represent. It is not so much that boys lack a need to achieve, but they often find little reward in harnessing their motives to the activities of the conventional classroom or school.

Fourth, the demonstration that intellectually superior and "creative" abilities are not the same thing suggests that we could profitably expand our search for the gifted to include the "divergent thinker." More clarity and precision in our methods of identifying creative youngsters with above-average but not extremely high IQ's, and more imagination and effort in our attention to such children might yield a happy increment in the numbers of those able to think inventively about important problems. This approach requires, of course, that we reward the innovator, the person with new and deviant ways of dealing with the world; and while this requirement is one to which we all pay lip service, it is one that is likely to entail trouble and inconvenience if it is realistically met. That the trouble and inconvenience will be worth the result is highly probable, but the result hardly alters, although it may more than justify, the cost.

Finally, the most potent means of increasing the numbers of mentally superior children that lies at hand for teachers is to teach so that learning is made more attractive to children. This alone will cause children to increase their own mental abilities. For example, the experiment in Manhattanville Junior High School and the George Washington Senior High High School in New York City is having this effect (1). Boys and girls from culturally deprived families are getting an enriched program, combined with guidance and attempts to improve the home environment. This program has kept pupils in school longer, and there has been a measurable increase in IQ points for these children as they have progressed from the sixth to the ninth grades.

REFERENCES

1. Board of Education of the City of New York. Demonstration guidance project: Junior High School 43, Manhattan and George Washington High School. *Third Annu. Progr. Rep.,* 1958–59.
2. Cattell, R. B., & Drevdahl, J. E. A comparison of the Personality Profile (16 P.F.) of eminent researchers with that of eminent teachers and ad-

ministrators, and of the general population. *British J. Psychol.,* 1955, **46,** 248–261.

3. Getzels, J. W., & Jackson, P. W. The highly creative and the highly intelligent adolescent. In *Third University of Utah Research Conference on the Identification of Creative Scientific Talent.* Univer. of Utah Press, 1959. Pp. 46–57.
4. Gowan, J. C. Factors of achievement in high school and college. *J. counsel. Psychol.,* 1960, **7,** 91–95.
5. Guilford, J. P. The structure of intellect. *Psychol. Bull.,* 1956, **53,** 267–293.
6. Haggard, E. A. Socialization, personality, and academic achievement in gifted children. *School Rev.,* 1957, **65,** 388–414.
7. McClelland, D. C., Atkinson, J., Clark, R., & Lowell, E. The achievement motive. New York: Appleton-Century-Crofts, 1953.
8. Rosen, B. C., & D'Andrade, R. The psychosocial origins of achievement motivation. *Sociometry,* 1959, **22,** 185–218.
9. Terman, L. M., & Oden, Melita. *The gifted child grows up.* Stanford, Calif.: Stanford Univer. Press, 1947.

ADDITIONAL READINGS

Cashdan, Sheldon & Welsh, George S. Personality correlates of creative potential in talented high school students, *Journal of Personality,* 1966, **34,** 445–455. In a study of the personality patterns of creative adolescents, the High Creative adolescent "emerged as an independent, nonconforming individual who seeks change in his environment and whose interpersonal relationships are open and active. The Low Creative adolescent, particularly the male, emerged as a somewhat compulsive individual with a strong desire to achieve." Findings indicated that creative adolescents are similar despite sex or specialty differences.

Clarke, H. Harrison & Olson, Arne L. Characteristics of 15-year-old boys who demonstrate various accomplishments or difficulties. *Child Development,* June 1965, **36** (2), 559–567. Boys who were especially outstanding and boys who were poor students or presented delinquency symptoms were compared with other boys their age. The only common trait which characterized all types of outstanding boys was intelligence. Boys who excelled in athletics, science, fine arts, leadership, and scholarship differed in other traits measured. Delinquent boys were not distinguished from other boys by any of the characteristics investigated.

Getzels, Jacob W. & Jackson, Philip W. Family environment and cognitive style: A study of the sources of highly intelligent and of highly creative adolescents. *American Sociological Review,* 1961, **26,** 351–359. Highly intelligent and highly creative adolescents were found to differ both in intellective and social behaviors in family environments. The high IQ's home environment was distinguished by parental vigilance over academic performance, the high creative's by focus on less visible qualities, including the child's openness to experience his values, interests, and enthusiasms.

Guilford, J. P. Factors that aid and hinder creativity. *Teachers College Record,* 1962, **63,** 380–392. The writer, a foremost authority on creativity, discusses the basic facts concerning the nature of creative thinking and of more creative persons. He describes creative behaviors, and the relationship of IQ, temperament, and motivational qualities to creativity.

Hammer, Emanuel F. Personality patterns in young creative artists. *Adolescence,* Winter 1966–67, **1,** (4), 327–350. The author's expressed aim is to formulate hypotheses, on the basis of his research, about which traits, feelings, or attitudes correlate with creativity. In short, in what personality soil does creativity grow?

Holland, John L. Creative and academic performance among talented adolescents. *Journal of Educational Psychology,* 1961, **52,** 136–147. Holland reports the results of a study designed to determine what highly talented adolescents are like, what their teachers think of them, and the nature of their family background. The findings suggest that traditional predictors of scholastic aptitude are of little or no value for predicting creativity among students of superior scholastic aptitude.

Nichols, Robert C. Parental attitudes of mothers of intelligent adolescents and creativity of their children. *Child Development,* 1964, **35,** 1041–1049. Child-rearing attitudes of high-ability high-school seniors were rated in terms of authoritarian control, hostility-rejection, and democratic attitudes. Authoritarian child rearing proved to be negatively related to the child's creativity and originality but positively related to academic performance.

X. Determinants of
Achievement Motivation

Achievement motivation suggests a tendency to define one's goals according to some standard of excellence in performance attained. In general, a child is classified as an under- or over-achiever if he seems to fall below, or to surpass, his potential. Studies of achievement orientation are based on certain assumptions, one being that the youngster who engages in particular sorts of behaviors is "achieving." Another is that achievement involves attainment of goals judged worthwhile by society. Certainly every child's behaviors achieve something, if only the minimal adjustments required to live. Another assumption is that striving, for its own sake, is good. In some cultures, children might well be non-achievers, in the sense of making little effort, and still be well adjusted. In fact, a "striver" in such a culture might appear grossly maladjusted. Even in this culture, the girl achiever may earn social disapproval, especially if she lets her striving show, or if her goals are deemed more appropriate for boys.

The dominant factors in determining achievement orientation are culture (including sub-culture), family, school, and—to an unknown degree—heredity. The relationship of heredity to achievement-orientation has been largely overlooked. Such data as exist indicate a positive, though indirect, relationship. Various traits having genetic components, including anxiety, energy level, agility, and body size, are obviously related to achievement.[1]

Unlike heredity, culture is fully recognized for its effect on achievement. In Western society, achievement-orientation is deemed a basic essential for boys, and somewhat less so for girls. Unless an individual strives, he may fail rapidly enough or effectively enough to establish the basic requirements for accomplishment, either of personal or socially encouraged goals. Therefore, parents set about inculcating achievement early, especially in boys. In fact, many studies indicate method of child training to be a critical factor. In general, children who are trained to be independent, self-reliant, self-confident and competent, become motivated to achieve.[2] At school, different climates apparently stimulate children to varying degrees of industry or apathy.

[1] Sandra Scarr, "Genetic Factors in Activity Motivation," *Child Development,* Vol. 37, No. 3 (September 1966), pp. 663–673.
[2] M. L. Goldberg, "Motivation of the Gifted," *National Society for the Study of Education,* 57th Yearbook, Part 2 (1958), pp. 87–109.

Apparently, such motivation is acquired early in life. Changes may occur later, but prove less significant. High levels of achievement behavior, at ages 6 to 10, correlate highly with achievement in adulthood.[3] Moreover, mothers of high-achievement sons tend to demand achievement of their sons earlier than do mothers of low-achievement sons.[4]

Especially as children move into adolescence, achievement orientation becomes linked with social mobility, which suggests movement upward or downward on the social scale. A particular social class involves individuals having certain features in common which designate that particular category or "class." The group an individual normally moves in, and is accepted by, governs his social class. In turn, his own characteristics— manners, education, family, and the like—determine his access to particular groups.

Factors within the individual determine to what extent environmental influences take hold. Adler suggested that individual striving stems from a need to overcome deep-seated feelings of inferiority. These inadequacies, in turn, originate in frustrations encountered in the process of need fulfillment.[5] The *manner* of striving is a highly individual matter. Some individuals appear motivated by fear of failure, others by pleasure in success.

Various issues relating to achievement orientation remain unresolved. For example, how do various types and levels of achievement affect individual adolescents? Do some individuals incur a lifetime of stress because of too persistent a need to succeed? Is the stress on achievement a factor in the relatively high incidence of teenage schizophrenia? Should schools utilize positive forces, such as ego-building and making sure of the intrinsic worth of subject matter, instead of negative motives like fear and anxiety, as incentives to achievement?

A related, and often neglected, issue is this: what goals should adolescents seek to achieve? Some of the most avid achievers madly pursue goals to their own and others' ultimate disadvantage. How may the adolescent be led to distinguish between goals suitable for him and those thrust on him by family, peers, and society? While the meaning of success varies, group values are well known by adolescents and modify their interpretations of success.[6] This subject will be considered later in the topic, "Youth's Values."

Another question is this: should girls, as well as boys, be stimulated to achieve? It has been suggested that achievement-orientation may prove

[3] L. W. Sontag and J. Kagan, "The Emergence of Intellectual Achievement Motives," *American Journal of Orthopsychiatry*, Vol. 33 (1963), pp. 532–534.

[4] M. R. Winterbottom, "The Relation of Need for Achievement to Learning Experiences in Independence and Mastery," in *Motives in Fantasy, Action, and Anxiety*, J. W. Atkinson, Ed. (Princeton, N.J., Van Nostrand, 1958) pp. 453–478.

[5] A. Adler, *Individual Psychology* (New York, Harcourt, Brace & World, 1924).

[6] F. M. Katz, "The Meaning of Success: Some Differences in Value Systems of Social Classes," *Journal of Social Psychology*, Vol. 62 (1964), pp. 141–148.

maladaptive for girls. Highly motivated mothers may never quite resign themselves to the routines that domestic life entails. Also, they project a need-to-strive onto their husbands, thus imposing a burden of stress. Women who never marry, and compete with men in the business world, feel unusual anxiety if they are highly motivated to succeed. Since they inevitably face discrimination, especially ambitious women are often doomed to frustration and disappointment.

Where current literature is involved, the dominant issues are these: what are the characteristics of achievers and under-achievers; and what sort of factors, personal or experiential, promote the attitudes and skills required to achieve? The first selection, by Rosen, concerns those family factors which are basic to establishing achievement-orientation. In the second article, Krauss relates achievement to social class, a matter of great current concern. His discussion provides a helpful background for understanding problems related to social-class composition of school populations and to youth's aspirations for higher education.

In conclusion, many questions about achievement-orientation remain to be answered. Often we make unwarranted assumptions, later disproved by empirical data. In one study, good achievers in reading proved *less* satisfied with themselves than teachers expected, and poor achievers *better* satisfied. The one clear implication of this finding, decided Otto, was that we should examine our notions about the attitudes of good and poor achievers.[7]

[7] Wayne Otto, "Yes, Virginia, There is An Achievement Dilemma," *Psychology of the Schools,* Vol. 2, No. 4 (1965), pp. 329–333.

20

Bernard C. Rosen

FAMILY STRUCTURE AND ACHIEVEMENT ORIENTATION

Rosen considers how various factors relate to achievement orientation, including family size, mother's age, the child's ordinal position, and social class. Patterns of training for achievement orientation varied from family to family, and the researcher concluded that no one demographic factor should be singled out as explaining achievement orientation.

This paper is a study of the relationship of certain demographic factors to family structure and personality development. Specifically, it examines the ways in which family size, ordinal position, mother's age, and social class influence the quality and quantity of patterned parent-child interaction and their impact upon the development of achievement motivation.

Achievement motivation has been defined as the redintegration of affect aroused by cues in situations involving standards of excellence.[1] Such standards are typically learned from parents who urge the child to compete against these standards, rewarding him when he performs well and punishing him when he fails. In time parental expectations become internalized, so that when later exposed to situations involving standards of excellence the individual re-experiences the affect associated with his earlier efforts to meet them. In our culture, the behavior of people with strong achievement motivation is characterized by persistent striving and general competitiveness.

Recent empirical data show that strong achievement motivation tends to develop when parents set high goals for their child to attain, when they indicate a high evaluation of his competence to do a task well, and impose standards of excellence upon problem-solving tasks, even in situations where such standards are not explicit. This complex of socialization prac-

From Bernard C. Rosen, "Family Structure and Achievement Orientation," *American Sociological Review*, Vol. 26 (1961), pp. 574–585. Reprinted by permission of The American Sociological Association.

[1] D. C. McClelland, J. Atkinson, R. Clark, and E. Lowell, *The Achievement Motive*, New York: Appleton-Century-Crofts, 1953.

tices has been called *achievement training*. Also related to achievement
motivation is another set of socialization practices called *independence
training*. This type of training involves expectations that the child be *self-
reliant* in situations where he competes with standards of excellence. At the
same time the parent grants him relative *autonomy* in problem-solving and
decision-making situations where he is given both freedom of action and
responsibility for success or failure. The role of independence training in
generating achievement motivation is exceedingly complex and can only be
understood in the context of what appears to be a division of labor between
the fathers and mothers of boys with high achievement motivation. Observation of parent-child interaction in an experimental problem-solving
situation has shown that both of the parents of boys with high achievement
motivation stress achievement training. When compared with the parents
of boys with low achievement motivation, it was found that the fathers and
mothers of boys with high achievement motivation tend to be more competitive and interested in their sons' performance; they set higher goals
for him to attain and have a greater regard for his competence at problem
solving. They also react to good performance with more warmth and
approval, or with disapproval if he performs poorly. The pattern changes
with respect to independence training. Much of this type of training comes
from the father, who (in an experimental situation at least) expected his
son to be self-reliant in problem solving, and gave him a relatively high
degree of autonomy in making his own decisions. The mothers of boys
with high achievement motivation, on the other hand, were likely to be
more dominant and to expect less self-reliance than the mothers of boys
with low motivation.

It appears that the boy can take, and perhaps needs, achievement
training from both parents, but the effects of independence training and
sanctions (a crucial factor determining the child's affective reaction to
standards of excellence) are different depending on whether they come from
the father or mother. In order for strong achievement motivation to develop, the boy seems to need more autonomy from his father than from his
mother. The authoritarian father may crush his son—and in so doing
destroy the boy's achievement motive—perhaps because he views the boy
as a competitor and is viewed as such by his son. On the other hand, the
mother who dominates the decision-making process does not seem to have
the same effect, possibly because she is perceived as imposing her standards
on the boy, while a dominating father is perceived as imposing himself on
his son. It may be that mother-son relations are typically more secure
than those between father and son, so that the boy is able to accept higher
levels of dominance and hostility from mother than father without adverse
effect upon his achievement motivation. It should be remembered, however, that while the mother of a boy with high achievement motivation is
willing to express hostility at poor performance she is also more likely to

show approval and warmth when he does well than is the mother of a boy with low motivation.[2]

A number of investigators have remarked upon the differences in parent-child relationships associated with certain demographic characteristics of the family. It has been said that life in a small family is more competitive than in a large family, and that the parents of the former are more likely to have higher aspirations for their children and to place a greater stress upon personal achievement. Furthermore, fathers of small families, particularly in the middle class, are described as less authoritarian than those of large, lower class families. With respect to the variable of ordinal position, early born children are said to be reared more anxiously, to be more "adult-oriented," and to command more of their parents' attention than later born. And as regards parental age, it has been noted that parents as they grow older have less energy to enforce their socialization demands. They are also said to be more indulgent and solicitous, placing less emphasis upon self-reliance and achievement in child rearing. For these and other reasons which will be spelled out in more detail, this study hypothesized that (a) children from small families will tend to have stronger achievement motivation than children from larger families, (b) early born (first or only) would tend to have higher achievement motivation scores than later born, and (c) children of young mothers would tend to have higher motivation than the children of old mothers.

RESEARCH PROCEDURE

The data for this study were collected from two independent samples. The first was a purposive sample of 427 pairs of mothers and their sons who resided in four Northeastern states. This sample (which we will call Sample "A") was deliberately designed to include subjects from a very heterogenous population.[3] The interviewers, all of whom were upperclassmen enrolled in two sociology courses, were instructed to draw respondents from six racial and ethnic groups: French-Canadians, Greeks, Italians, Jews, Negroes, and white Protestants, as well as from various social classes. Most of the mothers and all of the sons were native-born. The boys ranged in age from 8 to 14, with a mean age of about eleven. At a later date, a second group of respondents (Sample "B") was obtained in connection with another and larger research program by interviewing systematically virtually the entire universe of boys, nine to eleven years of

[2] The above two paragraphs are paraphrased from B. C. Rosen and R. D'Andrade, "The Psychosocial Origins of Achievement Motivation," *Sociometry*, 22 (September, 1959), pp. 185–218.

[3] Cf. B. C. Rosen, "Race, Ethnicity, and The Achievement Syndrome," *American Sociological Review*, 24 (February, 1959), pp. 47–60.

age, in the elementary schools of three small Northeastern Connecticut towns. This sample of 367 subjects had a mean age of about ten years, and was much more homogeneous with respect to race and ethnicity. All the respondents were white, and predominantly Protestant or Roman Catholic. Also, the interviewers were two carefully trained graduate assistants employed specifically for this purpose. For both samples, the respondent's social position was determined by a modified version of Hollingshead's Index of Social Position, which uses the occupation and education of the main wage-earner, usually the father, as the principal criteria of status. Respondents were classified according to this index into one of five social classes, from the highest status group (Class I) to the lowest (Class V).

A measure of the boy's achievement motivation was obtained by using a Thematic Apperception-type test.[4] This projective test involves showing the subject four ambiguous pictures and asking him to tell a story, under time pressure, about each one. The stories are then scored by counting the frequency of imagery about evaluated performance in competition with a standard of excellence. This test assumes that the more the individual shows indications of connections between affect and evaluated performance in his fantasy, the greater will be the degree to which achievement motivation is a part of his personality. The boys in both samples were given this test privately and individually. In the case of the first sample the testing was done in the home; in the second at school in a private office. The subject's imaginative responses were scored by two judges, and a product-moment correlation between the two scorings of .86 for the first sample and .92 for the second was obtained.

For Sample "A", information about the size of the family, ordinal position of the boy, mother's age, and occupation-education characteristics of the father was obtained from the mother in personal interviews in the home. In the case of Sample "B", these data were secured from the boy through questionnaires administered in the classroom. Data on the age of mother are lacking for subjects in Sample "B", as the boys were frequently uncertain of their mother's age.

RESEARCH FINDINGS

Family Size and Achievement Motivation

Considering the sociologist's traditional and continuing concern with group size as an independent variable (from Simmel and Durkheim to the

---

[4] The test was administered under neutral conditions, using pictures 33, 26, 9, 24 in that order. For more information about this test see, D. C. McClelland, *et al.*, *op. cit.*

recent experimental studies of small groups), there have been surprisingly few studies of the influence of size upon the nature of interaction in the family. However, such studies as do exist (Bossard's work especially) strongly point to the importance of family size as a variable affecting the socialization process in ways that are relevant to the development of achievement motivation. In fact, when comparing small and large families, investigators tend to regard what we have called achievement and independence training as among the more important criteria differentiating one type of family from the other.[5]

The small family has been described as a planned unit driven by ambition. Middle class small families are regarded as particularly oriented towards status striving and upward mobility. To achieve this end, the parents stress planning and achievement not only for themselves but for their children as well. Considerable attention can be given to the child's progress in the small family since its limited size affords the parents a relatively greater opportunity to devote more of their time and effort to each child than would be possible in the large family. In fact, life in many small families seems to be organized around plans for the child's development and future achievement. There may be, for example, an intense concern with his performance in school. In such families, parental reaction to the child's success or failure in competition with his peers is frequently immediate and strong. Evidences of achievement are likely to be lavishly applauded and rewarded, while failure will elicit numerous signs of parental disappointment or displeasure. Of course, the parent's motives are not always altruistic. In some cases the child's achievements serve to improve the family's status or may represent the working out through the child of the parent's unfulfilled personal aspirations. McArthur suggests that children in small families are sometimes "exploited to fulfill the expectations, even the frustrated desires of the parents."[6] Whatever the motives may be, and surely they are many and complex, it seems safe to say that in cases where parents are ambitious for themselves and their children, we may expect to find much emphasis upon standards of excellence, coupled with expectations for high achievement and intense parental involvement in the child's performance. Competition with standards of excellence, and rivalry with peers and siblings are, in fact, oft noted charac-

[5] See, for example, J. H. Bossard, *Parent and Child,* Philadelphia: University of Pennsylvania Press, 1953; J. H. Bossard and E. S. Boll, "Personality Roles in the Large Family," *Child Development,* 26 (March, 1955); D. E. Damrin, "Family Size and Sibling Age, Sex, and Position as Related to Certain Aspects of Adjustment," *The Journal of Social Psychology,* 29 (February, 1949), pp. 93–102; R. Stagner and E. T. Katyoff, "Personality as Related to Birth Order and Family Size," *Journal of Applied Psychology,* 20 (May–June, 1936), pp. 340–346.

[6] C. McArthur, "Personalities of First and Second Children," *Psychiatry,* 19 (February, 1956), pp. 47–54.

teristics of the behavior of children from small, particularly middle class, homes.[7]

The pattern of independence training known to be related to the development of achievement motivations is also believed to be more characteristic of life in the small family. The achievement-oriented values of parents of small families and their recognition of the importance of self-reliance *in situations where he competes with standards of excellence.* Also, the small family is said to be more democratic and relatively free from the authoritarian, patriarchal leadership that is more common to the large family. In the small family, particularly in the middle class, the parent typically seeks to obtain the cooperation of the child through the employment of conditional love and the manipulation of guilt feelings rather than by the use of coercion. Of course, the very intensity of parent-child relations in this type of family, especially between mother and son, sets definite limits to the child's freedom of action. But an intensely involved, "pushing" mother appears to promote the development of achievement motivation in boys. It is the authoritarian father, not the mother, who represents a greater threat to the boy and inhibits the development of achievement motivation.

The large family is a different social system, both qualitatively as well as quantitatively. The larger number of persons in the group creates a greater degree of interdependence between members and an increased need for cooperative effort and consensus. The precarious equilibrium of the large family would be threatened by excessive emphasis upon competition and achievement. Rivalry exists, of course, but it must be muted. Hence, in contrast to the small family, the large family is more likely to value responsibility above individual achievement, conformity above self-expression, cooperation and obedience above individualism. Children are more likely to be disciplined for the sake of family harmony than to assure their meeting achievement goals. Bossard maintains that there is a greater degree of specialization of roles in the large family. Each child tends to become functionally specialized, his behavior being more influenced by the family division of labor than by parental aspirations for achievement. He notes that his material on the large family contains "little mention of a child who excels at large, as is so common with small family children; there is

---

[7] Cf. M. Mead, *And Keep Your Powder Dry,* New York: William Morrow and Co., 1943, especially Chapters VI–VII. The variables examined in this paper do not, of course, exhaust the list of possible causal factors. It is quite possible that other demographic factors, such as the number and ordinal position of male and female siblings and the number of years separating each child, may also be important. Furthermore, non-demographic factors, such as parental values, could also play a significant role in the development of achievement motivation. Thus family size and achievement motivation may *both* reflect the achievement oriented values of the parents. We know, also, that other persons besides parents, for example, peers, play an important part in the socialization process. Cf. B. C. Rosen, "Multiple Group Membership: A Study of Parent-Peer Group Cross-Pressures," *American Sociological Review,* 20 (April, 1955), pp. 155–161.

little comparison with neighbor's children; there is emphasis on duty, not spectacular achievement." [8]

As the size of the family increases, better internal organization and a higher degree of discipline are required. It is perhaps for this reason that the authoritarian father is often associated with the large family system. But in families where the father is overly-dominant the amount of autonomy permitted the son will be severely curtailed. The child will have little opportunity to experience the pleasures of autonomous mastery that appear important to the development of strong achievement motivation. On the other hand, although the child may not be granted very much autonomy in the large family, he typically receives considerable training in self-reliance. In the large family, the child normally receives a smaller amount of attention and surveillance from his parents than would be the case in the small family. Hence, he is expected to be self-reliant, but usually in areas involving self-care-taking (e.g., feeding, dressing, amusing and defending oneself) rather than in situations where he competes with standards of excellence. Research has shown that self-reliance training in care-taking areas is not related to high achievement motivation.

In view of these differences between the socialization practices of parents with families of different sizes, we predicted that the children from small families would tend to have higher achievement motivation than those from large families. To test this hypothesis, we divided the families into three groups. Families with one or two children were called "small," those with three or four children "medium," and those with five or more children "large." This procedure was performed for both samples. In Table 20–1 are shown the boys' mean achievement motivation scores, cross-tabulated by family size and social class [9] for samples "A" and "B". The data tend to support our hypothesis, especially for subjects in sample "A". Considering for the moment only the means for family groups without regard to social class, we find a clear inverse relationship between family size and achievement motivation: the mean score for boys from small families in sample "A" is 5.43, medium families 4.64, and large families 2.48. Thus, the mean score of boys from small families is more than twice as great as that of boys from large families, and the mean score of boys from medium size

[8] J. H. S. Bossard, *The Large Family System,* Philadelphia: University of Pennsylvania Press, 1956.

[9] An analysis was made to determine the relationship of religion and race to family size, since achievement motivation is known to be related to these factors. (See footnote 3.) It was found that Roman Catholics and Negroes have larger families than white Protestants, Greeks, and Jews. But these differences virtually disappear when social class is controlled. For example, in the middle class the average number of children in Negro families is 3.0, Catholic families 2.7 as compared with 2.5 for Greek, 2.6 for Jews, and 2.8 for white Protestants. In the lower class the differences are somewhat larger but not statistically significant: Jews 2.1, Greek 2.4, white Protestants 3.0, Catholics 3.3, and Negroes 3.6. This finding is one reason why social class was introduced as a controlling variable throughout this study.

Table 20-1   Mean Achievement Scores by Family Size and Social Class

Social Class	Sample A*				Sample B**			
	Family Size				Family Size			
	Small	Medium	Large	x̄	Small	Medium	Large	x̄
I–II	5.20	6.41	2.33	5.46	7.28	7.93	2.25	7.11
III	6.49	6.14	5.83	6.28	7.67	7.36	6.13	7.32
IV	5.06	3.40	2.82	4.00	6.33	6.15	7.29	6.29
V	4.37	3.67	1.48	3.31	4.15	5.00	2.00	4.69
x̄	5.43	4.64	2.48		6.61	6.57	6.22	
N	178	193	54		155	166	45	

* Information lacking for two cases.
**Information lacking for one case.

families almost twice as great. The difference between the scores of boys from large families and those from medium and small families is statistically significant at the .001 level. However, the difference between small and medium families is not statistically significant. Social class is also related to achievement motivation, as has been reported elsewhere,[10] and, in fact, accounts for more of the variance ($F = 5.67$, $P < .01$) than family size ($F = 3.70$, $P < .05$). However, for sample "A", the relationship between family size and achievement motivation tends to persist even when social class is controlled. An internal examination of the table reveals that for each social class, in eleven out of twelve cells, the boys from small families have the highest mean scores, with somewhat lower motivation scores for boys from medium size families, while the scores of boys from large families are the lowest in every social class.

For sample "B", the relationship of family size to achievement motivation is also an inverse one (small family 6.61, medium 6.57, large 6.22), but the differences between groups are small and statistically insignificant. Social class continues to be related significantly to achievement motivation—this time at the .05 level—and displays a pattern identical to that found in Sample "A": the highest score is in class III, a somewhat lower score in Class I–II, with progressively declining scores in classes IV and V.

There are other similarities between samples "A" and "B". For example, the *rank* of mean scores for class I–II and III are similar for both samples. That is, in class I–II the relationship between family size and motivation is curvilinear: highest score in medium size families, a somewhat lower score in the small family and a considerably lower score in large

[10] See B. C. Rosen, "The Achievement Syndrome: A Psychocultural Dimension of Social Stratification," *American Sociological Review*, 21 (April, 1956), pp. 203–211.

families. In class III there is an inverse relationship between motivation and family size: the smaller the family the larger the motivation score. Furthermore, in both samples the large size families in classes I–II and V have the lowest scores of all groups. Why should this be so? Perhaps because at both extremes of the status continuum the pressure to excel is not so intense; there may be less stress on striving, less emphasis on standards of excellence and fewer pressures on the child to compete with them, possibly because in one class the need to succeed is not as great, and in the other because the objective possibility is so limited.

Generally, then, boys from large families tend to have lower achievement motivation than those from small and medium families (with one exception: class IV in sample "B"), but it must be added that any statement about the relationship of family size to achievement motivation would be on firmer ground if the F ratio for sample "B" had been statistically significant.

Birth Order and Achievement Motivation

Influenced, perhaps, by Freud's observation that "a child's position in the sequence of brothers and sisters is of very great significance for the course of his later life," [11] a considerable number of researchers have studied the relationship between ordinal position, socialization and a variety of personality characteristics. Though sometimes conflicting, many of their findings have relevance for a study of the development of achievement motivation.[12]

A disproportionate degree of attention has been concentrated on the first born, so that an impressive amount of data has been collected on this position. While the term "achievement training" is not used explicitly, several studies indicate that the first born child (i.e., eldest child in a family containing two or more children) typically receives more achievement training than the later born. To begin with, the amount and degree of interaction between parent and first born is likely to be large and intense. Also, as the only child (at least for a time), he is the sole object of parental expectations. These tend to be high, and sometimes involve an overestimate of the child's abilities, in part because there are no other children to provide a

[11] S. Freud, *A General Introduction to Psycho-Analysis*, Garden City, N.Y.: Doubleday & Co., 1938, p. 182.

[12] A. Adler, "Characteristics of First, Second, and Third Child," *Children, the Magazine For Parents,* 3 (May, 1928), pp. 14–52; H. E. Jones, "Order of Birth," in *Handbook of Child Psychology,* C. Murchison, editor, Worcester: Clark University Press, 1933; M. H. Krout, "Typical Behavior Patterns in Twenty-six Ordinal Positions," *Journal of Genetic Psychology,* 55 (September, 1939), pp. 3–30; J. P. Lees, "The Social Mobility of a Group of Eldest-born and Intermediate Adult Males," *British Journal of Psychology,* 43 (August, 1952), pp. 210–221; R. R. Sears, "Ordinal Position in the Family as a Psychological Variable," *American Sociological Review,* 15 (June, 1950), pp. 397–401.

realistic standard against which his performance may be evaluated. This may lead the parent to accelerate his training, a process which receives further impetus with the arrival of younger siblings. Thus, it has been noted that the first born child tends to talk earlier than the later born. Koch has found that first born children are more competitive than the later born.[13] Furthermore, in part because of his greater access to his parents, the first born tends to become intensely involved with them and very sensitive to their expectation and sanctions. The first born child has been described as "adult-oriented," serious, conscientious and fond of doing things for his parents, while the second born is said to be more "peer oriented." [14] Of course, this close association may make him more dependent upon his parents, although with the advent of younger siblings he is likely to receive considerable and even abrupt independence training. Frequently, where the family is large, the oldest child will act as a parent-surrogate, and is given very early self-reliance training, so that at times he may behave more like a responsible little man than a child. However, in the absence of achievement training this type of self-reliance training is likely to generate a personality oriented more towards accepting responsibility than striving for achievement.

In the beginning, the positions of the oldest and the only child are identical—neither have siblings, and one would expect that their socialization experiences would be similar. This is likely to be the case with respect to achievement training, although the only child will miss the extra push that the oldest child receives with the advent of the next-born. The major difference seems to be with respect to independence training. Only children are said to be anxiously trained: some are reared over-strictly, others are excessively indulged. They run the risk of being "smothered" by their parents and of becoming excessively dependent. An over-dominated child may be only externally driven and "run out of gas" as soon as parental pressures are removed. The excessively indulged child may simply not internalize the expectations of his parents. Thus, Sears reports that "high conscience" is found more frequently in children whose parents employed both rewards and punishments than among children who experienced only rewards.[15] In either event, the only child is not likely to receive the training in self-reliance and autonomy that is more frequently the experience of the oldest child with several siblings.

The socialization experiences of the youngest child may involve considerable achievement training, for with approaching freedom from child

[13] H. L. Koch, "Some Personality Correlates of Sex, Sibling Position and Sex of Siblings Among Five and Six Year Old Children," *Genetic Psychology Monographs,* 52 (August, 1955) pp. 3–50.

[14] C. McArthur, *op. cit.,* p. 54.

[15] R. R. Sears, E. E. Maccoby and H. Levin, in collaboration with E. L. Lowell, P. S. Sears and J. W. M. Whiting, *Patterns of Child Rearing,* Evanston: Row, Peterson, 1957.

care the mother tends to accelerate the youngest child to the level of mastery attained by his elder siblings. Thus, Lasko found, in comparing second children who are youngest with second children who have younger siblings, that parents tend to accelerate the younger in a two-child family to the level imposed upon the oldest child.[16] Where there were younger sibs no such attempt was made, since the parents were able to estimate more realistically the child's capabilities. The youngest child, however, does run considerable risk with regard to independence training. Research in this connection indicates that parents are more warm and solicitous towards the youngest child than towards other children in the birth order. The youngest child is likely to be pampered, over-protected, and over-indulged, not only by his parents but also by elder siblings. Such indulgence and over-protectiveness is antithetical to the development of achievement motivation, which requires that parents set and enforce high expectations for achievement, self-reliance, and autonomy.

Very little has been written about the socialization of the intermediate child in the birth sequence. Perhaps this is because the intermediate child is not so much a fixed position in the birth order as a residual category. The intermediate child could be any one of several children in the ordinal sequence; e.g., the second child in a three-child family, the third or fourth child in a five-child family, and so on. Despite this ambiguity, there has been some speculation that the position of the intermediate child is the most comfortable in the birth order.[17] There is less pressure on the intermediate child to conform to the levels of mastery attained by his siblings and less anxiety about his development. Furthermore, the intermediate child is more likely to come from a large family than a small family; he must, of course, come from a family with at least three children. It is probable, then, if our observations about socialization in the large family are correct, that his training will involve a greater emphasis upon cooperation and responsibility than on achievement.

Given these descriptions of the socialization experiences associated with different positions in the birth order, we predicted that achievement motivation would be highest among boys who are oldest in the birth sequence, somewhat lower among only and youngest children, and lowest among the intermediate boys. As can be seen in Table 20–2, the data do not confirm our hypothesis. It is true that the mean score for oldest boys in sample "B" is higher than those for other ordinal positions, as predicted. But, unfortunately for our hypothesis, the oldest boys in sample "A" have a lower mean score than only or youngest although the differences between the positions are very small and statistically insignificant. The intermediate

[16] J. K. Lasko, "Parent Behavior Towards First and Second Children," *Genetic Psychology Monographs*, 49 (February, 1954), pp. 97–137.

[17] W. Toman, "Family Constellation as a Basic Personality Determinant," *Journal of Individual Psychology*, 15 (November, 1959), pp. 199–211.

Issues in Self-actualization

boys in sample "A" have the lowest mean score, again as predicted, but in sample "B" their mean score is higher than that for only or youngest boys. Most significant is the fact that an analysis of the variance for each sample revealed that the effects of ordinal position are not statistically significant. The effects of the social class, however, are statistically significant; at the .01 level for sample "A", and the .05 level for sample "B".

Table 20-2 Mean Achievement Scores by Birth Order and Social Class

| | Sample A* | | | | | Sample B** | | | | |
| | Birth Order | | | | | Birth Order | | | | |
Social Class	Only	Old-est	Inter-mediate	Young-est	$\bar{x}$	Only	Old-est	Inter-mediate	Young-est	$\bar{x}$
I–II	3.50	6.03	4.28	5.34	5.46	5.33	7.76	5.76	8.29	7.11
III	8.50	6.38	5.61	5.62	6.28	9.83	6.63	7.16	7.88	7.32
IV	2.92	3.73	4.02	4.70	4.00	3.91	7.36	7.27	4.29	6.29
V	4.14	3.36	2.89	4.95	3.31	4.28	5.84	4.21	2.66	4.69
$\bar{x}$	5.08	4.97	3.45	5.12		5.41	7.02	6.59	5.97	
N	36	162	103	124		31	139	106	90	

* Information missing for two cases.
**Information missing for one case.

Since family size has been shown to be related to achievement motivation, it occurred to us that the difference between these two samples might be a function of the effects of this variable. That is, perhaps the oldest boys in sample "A" come from large families, while those from sample "B" tend to be from small families. Similarly, youngest and intermediate boys in the two samples might also come from families of markedly different size. We decided to introduce family size as a test variable. Table 3 shows the relationship between birth order and achievement motivation with family size and social class controlled. Class III has been grouped with classes I–II, and class IV with class V in order to reduce the number of cells without cases. We will call the former group middle class, the latter group lower class. Only the data derived from sample "A" are presented. Unfortunately, the smaller number of cases in sample "B" made a multivariate analysis of this complexity impossible—there proved to be too many empty cells or cells with very few cases—so we were not able to test our hypothesis about the different composition of the two samples. Only children, for whom of course family size is not a variable, are also not included.

Table 20-3 shows how perilous it is to speak about the relationship of birth order to achievement motivation without taking into account the influence of family size and social class. For each ordinal position, with the exception of only two out of seventeen cells, achievement motivation declines as the size of the family increases. The decline is greatest and most consistent in the lower class. For example, the mean score for oldest children from small families is 4.31, medium families 2.86 and large families 1.00. Similar consistent declines also apply to lower class intermediate and youngest children. The motivation score of the youngest child is most consistently affected by family size: the mean scores for both middle and lower class boys who are youngest in the birth sequence decline as the size of the family increases. In the middle class, the mean score for youngest boys from small families is 5.94, from large families 2.00. In the lower class the score for youngest boys from small families is 5.93, from large families 2.84. On the other hand, only in the lower class does family size affect the scores of the oldest child. In the middle class, the mean motivation scores for oldest boys increase from 5.82 in small families to 7.52 in medium families and drop negligibly to 5.75 in large families. But in the lower class the scores for oldest boys drop rapidly as family size increases: small family 4.31, medium 2.86, large 1.00.

Table 20-3   Mean Achievement Motivation Scores by Birth Order,
Family Size and Social Class

| | Social Class I-II-III | | | Social Class IV-V | | |
| | Family Size | | | Family Size | | |
Birth Order	Small	Medium	Large	Small	Medium	Large
Oldest	5.82	7.52	5.75	4.31	2.86	1.00
Intermediate	*	5.44	10.00	*	3.43	1.96
Youngest	5.94	5.21	2.00	5.93	3.90	2.84

*There are, of course, no intermediate children in a two-child family.

Why should family size have this differential effect? Probably because the socialization practices associated with ordinal position vary with the size of the family and its social class. We have noted that oldest children in large, lower class families are often expected to be parent-surrogates, performing some of the child-rearing duties for which the overburdened parents have neither the time nor energy. This condition is especially likely to occur when both parents are working (as is increasingly the case for both middle and lower class families), and are unable or unwilling to hire help. In situations where the mother is absent from the home, or where one parent is missing for some reason, the oldest child must frequently assume her functions. Often he must defer his own ambitions and gratifications in order to help raise the family and to insure the education of younger siblings. Under these conditions a concern with training him for achievement may go by the board. In the middle class, however, financial pressures are not as likely to force parents to place so much of the burden of child-rearing on the oldest child. If the mother is working, it is usually possible for the family to hire someone to perform some of her functions.

The situation is quite different for the youngest child. In large families the youngest child is frequently indulged, over-protected, and may in general be exposed to few of the socialization experiences associated with the development of high achievement motivation. *In this connection it is particularly interesting that the impact of family size on achievement motivation scores of boys who are youngest in the birth order appears to be more important than social class.* The pervasive achievement orientation of the middle class, which may have been responsible for the maintenance of relatively high scores among oldest boys of large middle class families, seems *not* to have had the same effect on the youngest child; i.e., the youngest child from a large family has a lower mean achievement motivation score than any other middle class group.

Social class seems clearly to influence the impact of family size on ordinal position and achievement motivation. As we have noted, *in the lower class* the scores for oldest, intermediate, and youngest children all decline as family size increases. This decline is more precipitate among oldest than intermediate or youngest children. Also the mean motivation scores of the youngest and intermediate boys are higher than those for oldest children. Thus in the lower class the mean scores for youngest boys is as follows: small family 5.93, medium 3.90, large 2.84. The scores for oldest boys are consistently lower: small family 4.31, medium 2.86, large 1.00. But *in the middle class* the scores for oldest children are higher than those for intermediate and youngest, except in small families where the score for youngest children is slightly and negligibly higher.

It is difficult to assess the relative effects of these three variables—ordinal position, family size, and social class—since unfortunately the empty cells in this table make an analysis of variance impracticable. But it appears probable that social class is the greatest and most consistent factor, followed by family size and ordinal position.

Mother's Age and Achievement Motivation

When considering the relationship of mother's age to the achievement motivation of the child, the question arises as to the nature of the changes that occur in the socialization process with increments in the parent's age. Systematic data on this factor are exceedingly skimpy, although the frequent use of such terms as "young mother" or "old mother" suggest that the parent's age is commonly considered important.[18]

[18] See J. H. S. Bossard, *Parent and Child,* Philadelphia: University of Pennsylvania Press, 1953.

Perhaps the most obvious difference between young and older women is that of sheer physical stamina. Older mothers on the average have less energy to cope with very young children, who normally seethe with activity, and may have difficulty enforcing their socialization demands. It is said, also, that older mothers tend to be more solicitous and indulgent towards children than their younger counterparts. The older mother, particularly where the child represents a long delayed fulfillment, may be unwilling to make strong demands upon her child for self-reliance and achievement. Or, if the demands are made, she may not enforce them with the negative sanctions that appear important to the development of achievement motivation. The tendency for the young mother, on the other hand, especially in the middle class, to be intensely competitive about the speed with which her child learns to master his environment—as compared with his peers—has excited frequent and disapproving comment. She may, for example, constantly compare her child's skill in walking or talking with that of his playmates. Later in school, his performance relative to that of his peers is closely watched and strong pressure may be exerted if he falls behind. Where the competitive spirit is not a factor, the young mother may accelerate her child's training simply through inexperience and an inability to correctly gauge his abilities. It was for these reasons that we hypothesized that children of younger mothers would tend to have higher achievement motivation than those of older mothers.

In order to test this hypothesis the mothers were divided into three age groups: mothers 34 years of age or less are called "young," those between 35 and 44 "middle age," and those 45 years or more "old." These data were obtained only from subjects in sample "A", where is was possible to interview the mother personally.

Table 20–4 shows the relationship between mother's age and the boy's achievement motivation with social class controlled. An analysis of variance

Table 20–4   Mean Achievement Motivation Scores by
Mother's Age and Social Class

Social Class		Young	Middle	Old	$\bar{x}$
I–II		5.00	5.57	6.50	5.65
III		9.14	5.78	6.18	6.32
IV		2.37	4.78	3.58	4.01
V		0.57	4.33	2.87	3.43
	$\bar{x}$	3.61	5.09	4.75	
	N	75	266	69	

Information missing on seven cases.

of the data revealed that mother's age is significantly related to achievement motivation (F = 5.56, P < .01). The effects of social class are also significant (F = 5.79, P < .01): *within all mother's age groups* the boy's mean achievement motivation scores decline as the mother's status decreases, except for a slight increase from class I–II to class III. However, our hypothesis that the children of young mothers would have higher achievement motivation scores than those of older mothers was not confirmed. Disregarding social class, the relationship between mother's age and the boy's motivation is curvilinear: children of young mothers have the lowest mean scores (3.61), those of middle age mothers the highest (5.09), and the sons of old mothers the intermediate score (4.75). However, when social class is controlled the picture becomes quite confused. In class I–II, the achievement motivation scores of the boys increase as mother's age increases—just the opposite of what we had predicted. However, in class III, the reverse is true: the boys of younger mothers have higher scores than those of old mothers.

Some of this confusion is reduced when family size is introduced as a specifying variable. The data in Table 20–5 show the relationship of mother's age to son's achievement motivation when the variables of social class and family size are controlled. In small size families the sons of young mothers

Table 20-5   Mean Achievement Motivation Scores by Mother's Age, Family Size and Social Class

Mother's Age	Social Class I-II-III			Social Class IV-V		
	Family Size			Family Size		
	Small	Medium	Large	Small	Medium	Large
Young	7.64	7.33	*	4.32	0.02	0.33
Middle	5.79	5.70	4.50	5.58	4.29	2.70
Old	5.86	7.60	5.33	3.81	3.53	2.36

*No cases.

have higher mean scores than the sons of old mothers, but this relationship is reversed as the size of the family increases. In medium and large size families of both the middle and lower classes, the sons of old mothers have higher scores than the sons of young mothers. The effect of increased family size, however, is much greater in the lower than in the middle class and greatest of all upon the sons of young, lower class mothers. Thus, the mean scores of the sons of young, lower class mothers drop precipitately as the size of the family increases: from 4.23 in small families to 0.02 in medium size, and 0.33 in large families. The mean scores of the sons of older mothers also decline as family size increases, but the drop is more modest; i.e., small family 3.81, medium family 3.53, large family 2.36. Why should the motivation scores of sons of young mothers be so much more adversely affected by increased family size than are the scores of sons of older mothers? Perhaps because the children of a young mother with a large family are all young, so that the older children are not able to provide much help in taking care of younger siblings. In this case the young mother, particularly if she is lower class and unable to obtain help, may simply be overwhelmed. She will have little time or energy for the supervision and complex training in achievement that the development of achievement motivation requires.

The introduction of family size as a specifying variable requires a rephrasing of our original hypothesis about the relationship of mother's age to achievement motivation. Our prediction that the sons of young mothers would have higher motivation than the sons of old mothers is correct *but only when the family is small and primarily when the parents are middle class.* As the family increases in size, the motivation scores of children of older mothers are higher than the scores of children of younger mothers, and indeed in the lower class the sons of middle age mothers have the highest scores of all.

CONCLUSION

Perhaps the most important generalization to be drawn from this study is that it is exceedingly unwise to single out any one demographic factor as an explanation of achievement motivation. It is true that social class is consistently related to achievement motivation: the data show that the motivation scores of classes I–II–III boys are significantly higher than are the scores of boys from classes IV–V. Also, we have noted time and again that boys from small families tend to have higher achievement motivation than their peers from large families. But the effects of social class and family size, as well as the impact of birth order and mother's age, can only be properly understood in a large context in which all of these variables (and others, undoubtedly) interact.

For example, the impact of family size on the boy's achievement motivation varies with his social class. It was shown that while, in general, motivation scores decline as family size increases, the effect of family size on motivation scores is much greater at the upper-middle (class I–II) and lower class (class V) levels than at the lower-middle (class III) and upper-lower class (class IV) levels. Furthermore the effect of birth order is intimately related to family size and social class. Hence it is not very helpful in predicting an individual's achievement motivation to know his position in the birth order—indeed this information may be misleading rather than useful—unless the social class and size of his family of orientation are also known. In small middle class families, for example, the effect of ordinal position seems to be relatively unimportant: the oldest and youngest child in a two-child, middle class family have almost identical motivation scores, but *as the size of the family increases* the scores for the oldest child *in the middle class* become higher than those for the youngest child. However, *in the lower class* the reverse is true: the youngest child has a higher achievement motivation score on the average than the oldest child—a position that is maintained even when the size of the family increases. Similarly, the effect of mother's age upon the child's achievement motivation varies with the size of her family and social class. Thus the hypothesis that the sons of young mothers would have higher achievement motivation than the sons of old mothers proved to be correct, *but only when the family is small.* As the size of the family increases, *particularly in the lower class,* the scores of sons of young mothers drop rapidly and are surpassed by the scores of sons of middle age and old mothers.

These data, then, indicate that the demographic factors examined in this study have relevance for the development of achievement motivation, but their effects are complicated, interconnected, and interdependent upon one another, and difficult to assess individually.

21

Irving Krauss

SOURCES OF EDUCATIONAL ASPIRATIONS AMONG WORKING-CLASS YOUTH *

A comparison of data on working-class and middle-class high school seniors reveals that the following conditions influence working-class students' college aspirations: the mother has "married down," either the father or the mother has a white-collar job, family members or friends of the family have white collar experience, the father or mother has a high status occupation. Important, too, are the student's acquaintances, participation in extra-curricular activities, and attendance at predominantly middle-class schools.

Characteristic of industrial society is growth in the proportion of better paid and more prestigeful occupations, increased educational requirements for the more desirable jobs, and greater availability of education. These conditions encourage individuals to develop mobility aspirations, and increasingly education is a primary channel for upward movement.[1] Yet, as is well known, only a limited proportion of working-class youths take advantage of this source of mobility.[2]

From Irving Krauss, "Sources of Educational Aspirations Among Working-Class Youth," *American Sociological Review*, Vol. 29 (1964), pp. 867–879. Reprinted by permission of The American Sociological Association.

* The data in this paper are from a thesis submitted in partial fulfillment of the requirements for the Ph.D. in the Department of Sociology, University of California, Berkeley. A grant of funds from the Committee on Research at the University of California helped defray research expenses. I wish to thank Seymour M. Lipset for several helpful suggestions, which were incorporated into this paper.

[1] These phenomena are examined by Seymour M. Lipset and Reinhard Bendix in *Social Mobility in Industrial Society*, Berkeley and Los Angeles: University of California Press, 1959. See also Pitirim A. Sorokin, *Social and Cultural Mobility*, New York: The Free Press, 1959.

[2] See William H. Sewell, Archie O. Haller and Murray A. Strauss, "Social Status and Educational and Occupational Aspiration," *American Sociological Review*, 22 (February, 1957), pp. 67–73 and Robert J. Havighurst and Robert P. Rogers, "The Role of Motivation in Attendance at Post-High School Educational Institutions," in Byron S. Hollinshead (ed.), *Who Should Go To College*, New York: Columbia University Press, 1953, pp. 135–165.

Many of the numerous studies of determinants of mobility have focused on lower-status youths.[3] In this paper I shall further probe the sources of educational aspirations among working-class youngsters, concentrating on five areas: 1. discrepant situations in the family of orientation; 2. the experience of family members and friends; 3. the relative status of the working-class family; 4. the influence of peers and participation in the school culture, and 5. working-class students' attitudes and middle-class values.

THE DATA

A precoded questionnaire was administered to 706 high school seniors in four San Francisco Bay Area high schools, approximately three weeks prior to their graduation in June, 1959.[4] The students were categorized ac-

[3] The literature is summarized by Lipset and Bendix, *op. cit.*, pp. 227–259. Recent studies include Richard L. Simpson, "Parental Influence, Anticipatory Socialization, and Social Mobility," *American Sociological Review,* 27 (August, 1962), pp. 517–522 and Robert A. Ellis and W. Clayton Lane, "Structural Supports for Upward Mobility," *American Sociological Review,* 28 (October, 1963), pp. 743–756.

[4] All the students in several classes in each school completed questionnaires, and of the 706 returned, 52 were not used: father's occupation was unclear for 38 respondents, 8 fathers were farmers, and six questionnaires were defaced or unanswered. Of the remaining 654 respondents, 387 whose fathers are in blue-collar work were defined as working-class, and 267 whose fathers are in white-collar occupations were defined as middle-class. The distinction was based on the U. S. Census classification of blue-collar and white-collar occupations. Evidence that this distinction is a meaningful one is summarized by Lipset and Bendix, *op. cit.*, pp. 14–17, 156–157 and 165–171. Cf. Peter M. Blau, "Occupational Bias and Mobility," *American Sociological Review,* 22 (August, 1957), pp. 392–399 and Robert S. Lynd and Helen M. Lynd, *Middletown,* New York: Harcourt, Brace, 1929, pp. 22–23.

Father's occupation was determined by responses to the following questions: "What is your father's occupation? Be as specific as possible. (If he is deceased, say what his occupation was.) *Tell exactly what he does* (for example, 'sells clothes,' 'operates a lathe,' etc.)," "In what kind of place does he work (for example, 'a department store,' 'a factory,' etc.)?" and, "Is he self-employed or does he work for someone else?" No distinction was made between employed and unemployed fathers, although my impression is that practically all were working at the time. The fathers of 20 working- and 13 middle-class students were deceased or out of contact, and these questionnaires are included.

Schools with a substantial number of working class students were sought. A list of approximately 50 schools was compiled, excluding those whose students came almost entirely from upper middle-class neighborhoods. Because our resources were limited, we selected four schools on the basis of willingness to participate. The percentages of working-class fathers were 68, 62, 56, and 45. Students in all programs of study— college preparatory, commercial and vocational—were surveyed. Questionnaires were administered in mixed and in all-male classes, such as personal hygiene, where it was felt that the bases for segregation would not introduce bias. Thus 59 per cent of all respondents are working-class; 69 per cent of the working-class, and 67 per cent of the middle-class students are boys. Working-class students' post-high school plans,

cording to their potential mobility, as expressed in their plans for *college, technical school,* or *no further education.* The most mobile students plan to enter a regular four-year college, or to attend junior college for two years and then transfer to a four-year institution. The students whose potential mobility is more limited plan to learn a trade or receive other training in a technical school, or in the vocational program of a junior college, where they will be one or two-year terminal students. Those who are likely to be the least mobile have no definite plans for education after they leave high school. Some stated that they might seek additional schooling in the future, and the rest indicated that they definitely do not plan to obtain further education.

Table 21-1, which contrasts the post-high school plans of working- and middle-class students, shows that the educational aspirations of the working-class students are much lower than those of the middle-class students. While 64 per cent of those from middle-class homes plan to attend college, only 41 per cent of the working-class youths have similar plans.

Table 21-1   Post-High School Plans of Working-Class
and Middle-Class Students

(In Percentages)

Student's Post-High School Plans	(N)	Working-Class Students (387)	Middle-Class Students (267)
College		41	64
Technical school		30	20
No further education		28	16
	Total	99	100

This is a considerable, though not unexpected, proportion of the working-class students: what are the sources of their educational aspirations? That is, to what extent do the same conditions influence both working-class and middle-class youths to seek higher education? To what extent are the conditions most important for working-class students of limited significance for those from middle-class homes?

for boys and girls respectively, were: *college,* 43 and 37 per cent; *technical school,* 31 and 29 per cent, and *no further education,* 25 and 34 per cent. For middle-class students' these percentages were: *college,* 66 and 61; *technical school,* 20 and 20, and *no further education,* 14 and 19. Since these sex differences were not large, male and female students were analyzed together to permit more detailed cross tabulations.

SOURCES OF EDUCATIONAL ASPIRATIONS

Discrepant Situations

Among the possible sources of mobility aspirations are conditions or experiences that lead to dissatisfaction with a present status and interest in a new one.[5] Modern social conditions favor such dissatisfaction, while certain types of family structure may strongly encourage active interest in mobility. Previous research suggests that status discrepancies between husband and wife may be one of the structural factors responsible for mobility aspirations.[6]

Nearly one-fourth of the working-class mothers are employed in non-manual occupations. Fifty-three per cent of the children from these families plan to attend college, compared with only 29 per cent from families in which mother's occupation is manual. In fact, working-class students whose mothers are in manual occupations are less likely to have college plans than youngsters from homes in which the mother is not employed. Only ten middle-class students have mothers in manual occupations; of these, four have college aspirations, in contrast to 67 per cent from middle-class families where the mother's employment is non-manual, and 63 per cent where the mother does not work. (See Table 21–2.)

The working-class mother whose occupational status is higher than her husband's is likely to come in contact with middle-class persons and to acquire middle-class values. If her husband's status seems unlikely to improve, she may attempt to realize her aspirations through her children by encouraging them to develop middle-class interests and objectives.

Working-class students whose mothers were employed *prior* to marriage were more likely to express college aspirations, though mother's occupational level was not significant, if she did work. Perhaps employment prior to marriage indicates achievement motivation, which these working-class mothers may have passed on to their children. In middle-class families,

[5] The process of breaking away from one group and entering a new one, of which this dissatisfaction is probably a part, has been examined in the framework of reference group behavior by Robert K. Merton, *Social Theory and Social Structure* (rev. ed.), New York: The Free Press, 1961, pp. 225–386. Other researchers who have studied this phenomenon with special reference to social mobility include Seymour M. Lipset, "Social Mobility and Urbanization," *Rural Sociology*, 20 (September–December, 1955), pp. 220–228; Lipset and Bendix, *op. cit.*, pp. 256–259 and Ralph H. Turner, "Reference Groups of Future-Oriented Men," *Social Forces*, 34 (December, 1955), pp. 130–136.

[6] Jean E. Floud, F. M. Martin and A. H. Halsey, "Educational Opportunity and Social Selection in England," *Transactions of the Second World Congress of Sociology*, 2 (1954), pp. 203–204.

Table 21–2   Students' Post-High School Plans
by Mother's Current Occupational Status

(In Percentages)

Student's Post-High School Plans	(N)	Working-Class Students			Middle-Class Students		
		Mother Currently Employed		Mother Does Not Work	Mother Currently Employed		Mother Does Not Work
		In Non-Manual Work	In Manual Work		In Non-Manual Work	In Manual Work	
		(91)	(55)	(235)	(100)	(10)	(149)
College		53	29	39	67	(4)[a]	63
Technical school		23	44	30	16	(5)	20
No further education		24	27	30	17	(1)	16
Total[b]		100	100	99	100	(10)	99

[a] Numbers rather than percentages are given whenever the total number of cases is 15 or less.
[b] In this and in succeeding tables, unless otherwise noted, variations from the totals in Table 21-1 are due to omission of cases for which data were unavailable.

whether the mother worked prior to marriage is not important; if she *was* employed, however, then her occupational level is strongly associated with her child's college aspirations. Among those whose mothers were in manual occupations, only 50 per cent have college aspirations, in contrast to 72 per cent among those whose mothers were in non-manual work.[7] (See Table 21–3.)

Another indicator of the wife's status relative to her husband's is the educational level of each at the time of marriage. Premarital educational differences were significant in working-class families, but only under certain circumstances. When the working-class father has not completed high school the mother's educational achievement does not influence the youngster's post-high school plans. But when the father is a high school graduate, mother's education strongly affects the child's interest in college. For where the mother has married "down," as indicated by her having had more education than her husband, 76 per cent of the offspring plan to attend college —a larger percentage than among students whose fathers went to college. Where mother and father are both high school graduates, 44 per cent of the children plan on college. But where the mother married "up," that is, has had less education than her husband, only 29 per cent of the children have college aspirations. . . .

[7] Interpretation of these data must be tentative because of the number of mothers whose premarital occupational level is not clear.

Table 21-3   Student's Post-High School Plans by Mother's
Occupational Status Prior to Marriage
(In Percentages)

Student's Post-High School Plans	(N)	Working-Class Families		Mother Worked in:		
		Mother Worked (191)	Mother Did Not Work (196)	Non-Manual Occupation (71)	Manual Occupation (71)	Occupational Level Not Clear (49)
College		48	35	48	51	43
Technical school		28	33	28	28	29
No further education		24	32	24	21	29
Total		100	100	100	100	101

Student's Post-High School Plans	(N)	Middle-Class Families		Mother Worked in:		
		Mother Worked (179)	Mother Did Not Work (88)	Non-Manual Occupation (116)	Manual Occupation (32)	Occupational Level Not Clear (31)
College		64	65	72	50	48
Technical school		19	22	16	25	26
No further education		17	14	12	25	26
Total		100	101	100	100	100

In middle-class families, students whose fathers have had college training but whose mothers have not, are less likely to have college plans than those whose mother and father have both gone to college (70 compared with 82 per cent). These students from status discrepant families, however, are more likely to plan to go to college than those whose parents are both high school graduates. Mothers who married "down" are numerous only among students whose fathers did not complete high school; these students are only a little more likely than their working-class counterparts to plan to attend college.

The significance of a working-class mother's educational achievement may be in the more important role she plays in child-rearing.[8] A college-trained mother may share her values and her aspirations for her child with middle-class college-educated people even if she went to college for only a short time. Consciously or unconsciously, she may encourage her child

[8] See Ellis and Lane, op. cit., p. 747.

to develop college aspirations rather than more limited working-class values. In working-class families in which the father has not completed high school, however, such factors as low occupational and income level may limit the effect of mother's greater education.

Another possible source of college aspirations may be the status of the preceding generation. Information on grandfather's occupational level was available for 71 per cent of the middle-class and for 65 per cent of the working-class students. Seventy per cent of the middle-class adolescents with at least one grandfather in a non-manual occupation planned to attend college, compared with only 54 per cent of those whose grandfathers were both manual workers. In middle-class families, college expectations for the children may be reinforced by white-collar occupational experience in the preceding generation.

In working-class families, having had at least one grandparent in a non-manual occupation also favors college aspirations. Fifty-six per cent of such students plan to attend college, compared with 41 per cent whose grandfathers were both manual workers. . . . This may be a result of different factors, however, for these working class families have been downwardly mobile. Lipset and Bendix suggest the parents in such a family may be expected to compensate by encouraging their children to rise, and they cite Elizabeth Cohen's research.[9] My data support this thesis to some extent, although they are limited by the substantial number of students for whom information on grandparents' occupation was not available.[10]

College Experience of Family Members and Friends

Working-class students whose relatives or family friends have attended college may be encouraged to develop middle-class aspirations, including the desire for higher education. In this context, the college experience of parents, siblings and friends of the family is relevant.

Working-class parents who have attended college have not only been exposed to middle-class values that influence their children to seek further schooling, but in addition their having gone to college, even if for a limited

[9] Lipset and Bendix, op. cit., p. 238. Also see Elizabeth G. Cohen, "Parental Factors in Educational Mobility," unpublished Ph.D. dissertation, Harvard University, 1958. Wilensky and Edwards show that the fathers in such families identify with the middle class, hold middle-class aspirations for themselves and have middle-class expectations for their children. See Harold L. Wilensky and Hugh Edwards, "The Skidder: Ideological Adjustments of Downward Mobile Workers," American Sociological Review, 24 (April, 1959), pp. 215–231, especially Table 1, pp. 221–225.

[10] Another source of mobility aspirations may be a working-class father's previous middle-class status. I have no data to prove this, but Wilensky and Edwards (op. cit.) found that these fathers are strongly middle-class oriented and expect their children to achieve middle-class status.

time, may suggest to their offspring that such aspirations are not unreasonable. In addition, these parents know the requirements and procedures for entering college. Thus, in working-class families in which the father has college training, 61 per cent of the children plan to obtain higher education; in contrast, only 35 per cent of the youngsters whose fathers did not complete high school plan to attend college. . . .

Middle-class students whose fathers did not complete high school are only a little more likely than their working-class counterparts to plan to attend college. On the other hand, 74 per cent of those whose fathers experienced higher education, and 66 per cent of those whose fathers completed high school, have college aspirations.

The effects of mother's education are almost identical with those of father's education. As noted earlier, mother's education affects college aspirations most strongly when it differs from father's.

Students whose older siblings have attended college are, in working-class families, more likely to plan on college themselves. Where no older sibling has any higher education, only 26 per cent of the youngsters studied planned to attend college, while among those with one or more siblings who have gone to college, 53 per cent expected to go themselves. . . .

A working-class child whose brothers or sisters have gone to college can benefit from their experience in coping with entrance requirements and the mechanics of enrolling. His siblings have demonstrated that college is attainable for a working-class child, they may provide a model for him, and their college experiences may allow him to participate vicariously in some aspects of middle-class life.

Older siblings who have gone to college have a less striking effect on the aspirations of a middle-class student. Seventy-six per cent of the middle-class students who have at least one older brother or sister with college training plan to obtain higher education themselves; but 61 per cent of those without a college-trained older sibling also have college aspirations.

The working-class student *and* his siblings may develop an interest in college for other reasons, of course, but an older sibling's college experience is clearly more relevant for the working-class than for the middle-class child, and probably reinforces other conditions favorable for college aspirations.

Of the working-class students who report that most of their parents' close friends are college graduates, 53 per cent plan to attend college, in contrast to 41 per cent in families where none of the close friends are college graduates. In middle-class families, all but one of the 20 students who report that all of their parents' close friends are college graduates have college plans, in contrast to 56 per cent where none of the close friends are college graduates.[11]

[11] Having uncles or aunts who are college graduates did not affect working-class students' post-high school plans. Having friends who are college graduates may

Father's Occupational Status. Of the 387 working-class students, 49 per cent have fathers who are craftsmen or foremen, and 36 per cent have fathers who are semi-skilled workers. The remainder include protective service workers (5 per cent), other service workers (6 per cent) and laborers (3 per cent). Forty-seven per cent of the students whose fathers are craftsmen or foremen plan to attend college, in contrast to 36 per cent whose fathers are in semi-skilled, service, or laboring work.[12]

Regardless of father's educational achievement, the children of foremen and craftsmen are more likely than the children of other manual workers to have college plans. . . . This relationship, however, is strongest when the father is a high school graduate.[13] Where the father has some college education, the percentage planning to attend college among children of lower-level manual workers is relatively high. And where the father has less than a high school education, the difference between the children of craftsmen and foremen and the children of other manual workers is not very great; the father's limited education mitigates against the family's developing values that might encourage the child to seek a college education.

As the elite of the working class, craftsmen and foremen have greater prestige and higher incomes than other manual workers.[14] In consumption patterns and aspirations for their children, the high status blue-collar family may to some extent approximate the middle-class ideal and therefore develop middle-class aspirations, provided it is not handicapped by very little education.

For middle-class students, father's occupational level does not affect college aspirations, even in the college-educated group, the only one in which a substantial number of fathers have professional-level occupations.

---

indicate parents' interest in mobility either for themselves or for their children. Thus they may have sought such friends, or if other considerations were the basis for friendship, acquaintance with college graduates may have resulted in the development of interests encouraging the children to seek college training. Status differences involving relatives may be a greater barrier to association than those involving friends, so that the latter may have more influence on the children's post-high school plans.

Middle-class students who reported that at least some of their uncles and aunts are college graduates were more likely to have college plans themselves, compared with those who reported that none of their uncles or aunts are college graduates.

[12] Cohen, *op. cit.,* also found that the status level of father's work affected college aspirations among working-class sons.

[13] Cf. Alan B. Wilson, "Residential Segregation of Social Classes and Aspirations of High School Boys," *American Sociological Review,* 24 (December, 1959), p. 841.

[14] See Albert J. Reiss, Jr., *Occupations and Social Structure,* New York: The Free Press, 1961, pp. 95–97 and Appendix B. The median income of craftsmen and foremen is higher than that of many white-collar workers and small businessmen. Figures for 1960, for year-round, full-time male workers are: craftsmen, foremen and kindred workers, $5,905; self-employed managers, officials and proprietors (excluding farm), $5,396; clerical and kindred workers, $5,328. U. S. Bureau of the Census, *Statistical Abstract of the United States: 1962,* Washington, D. C.: U. S. Government Printing Office, 1962, p. 336.

The Peer Group, and Participation in
Extra-Curricular Activities

College-oriented students may be expected to gravitate toward others with similar interests, and such associations are likely to reinforce college aspirations. While our data do not indicate how friends are selected, they show that working-class students whose acquaintances plan to go to college are more likely to plan to go themselves.[15] Among those who report that all their acquaintances are going to college, 81 per cent have similar plans, while only 6 per cent do not expect to obtain additional education. On the other hand, among those who report that none of their acquaintances plan to go to college, only 10 per cent expect to go themselves, while 45 per cent do not plan to obtain additional education. A similar relationship holds for middle-class students. . . .

Previous research has shown that participation in the school culture is closely related to class position, and that participants are disproportionately from high-status families.[16] Working-class students who participate in extra-curricular activities have an opportunity to associate with middle-class students, most of whom plan to enter college, and as a result may be encouraged to develop interests leading them to seek higher education. Or, the association may reinforce pre-existing tendencies.

Both working-class and middle-class students who are extremely active in extra-curricular activities tend to have college aspirations: 74 and 80 per cent, respectively, plan to attend college. Only 28 per cent of the non-active working-class youngsters have college aspirations, however, compared with 55 per cent of the non-active middle-class students.[17] . . . These data suggest that although active participation in extra-curricular activities encourages or reinforces all students' interest in college, such participation is more important for working-class youths.

The working-class student's peer group, and the extent to which he participates in extra-curricular activities, appear to be related to the development of college aspirations, but the context in which such behavior takes place is also important. That is, the atmosphere of the school and the general student body background are likely to affect working-class students'

[15] Undoubtedly some choose friends who plan to go to college because they have similar aspirations, while others may develop an interest in college *after* associating with college-oriented students.

[16] See August B. Hollingshead, *Elmtown's Youth,* New York: John Wiley, 1959, esp. pp. 201–203, and Floud *et al., op. cit.,* p. 204.

[17] In "The Pattern of Postponability and its Relation to Social Class Mobility," *Journal of Social Psychology,* 44 (August, 1956), pp. 33–48, Harry Beilin reports that of the lower-class high school boys in his study who planned to attend college, 84 per cent participated in extra-curricular activities, in contrast to 38 per cent of those who did not expect to go to college. See also Richard L. Simpson, *op. cit.,* pp. 519–520.

college aspirations. Alan Wilson suggests that students from working-class homes who attend a predominantly middle-class school are prone to identify with the middle-class.[18] He found that 59 per cent of these students plan to go to college, in contrast to 33 per cent of the working-class students in predominantly working-class schools. These findings are quite similar to those reported here. . . .[19] The importance of school milieu for the development of college aspirations is also indicated by its effect on middle-class students in both surveys: those who attended a predominantly middle-class school were much more likely to have college aspirations than those who were in a predominantly working-class school.[20]

CHARACTERISTICS OF THE COLLEGE-ORIENTED STUDENTS

The sources of educational aspirations among working-class youth suggested by these data are largely structural in nature. That is, they refer mainly to the family's life conditions and only to a limited extent to the students' own attitudes and behavior. Yet several researchers have reported, and perceptive high school teachers have observed, that in many ways college-oriented working-class students resemble middle-class much more than other working-class youngsters. In . . . the college-oriented and non-college-oriented working-class students are compared with their middle-class counterparts on a number of selected characteristics. The similarities between the college-oriented working-class and the college-oriented middle-class students are striking in regard to occupational preference, income expectations, belief in the existence of opportunity, interest in national and international affairs, interest in classical or serious music, and the number of books recently read. In political preference and attitude toward labor, the college-oriented working-class students are more "conservative" than other working-class youths, but less so than college-oriented middle-class

[18] Wilson, *op. cit.*, pp. 836–845.

[19] Wilson's eight schools cover a wider range than ours, for we sought mainly working-class schools. The data in Table 12 represent the "most" middle-class and the "most" working-class among the four schools in the present study, using basically the criteria Wilson used. (See *ibid.*, pp. 837–838, and notes in Table 12 below.)

[20] Wilson found that among boys from professional homes who attended a predominantly middle-class school, 93 per cent planned to attend college, whereas this was true of only 64 per cent of those in a predominantly working-class school. Among boys from white-collar homes, the percentages with college aspirations are 79 per cent of those attending a middle-class school and 46 per cent of those in a working-class school. And among boys whose fathers were self-employed, 79 per cent of those in a middle-class school have college plans, in contrast to 35 per cent of those in a working-class school (see *ibid.*, p. 839). In the present sample, 80 per cent of the middle-class children attending a predominantly middle-class school plan to attend college, whereas 59 per cent of those in a predominantly working-class school have college aspirations.

youths. In their attitude toward the role of government, college-oriented working-class students were somewhat closer to the college-oriented middle-class youngsters than to other working-class students.

How do these college-oriented working-class students come to have middle-class values? To what extent are these values responsible for interest in college—or, to what extent does interest in college encourage the development of these values? Status discrepancies between parents, familial contact with middle-class groups and the youngsters' association with other middle-class children may have encouraged them to take the college-oriented middle-class students as their reference group. And the middle-class interests and values shared by the working-class students who plan to attend college, as well as such behavior as participation in extra-curricular activities, may reflect anticipatory socialization. As Merton and others have pointed out,[21] taking on the values and forms of behavior of another group facilitates entry into that group.

SUMMARY AND CONCLUSIONS

My analysis has revealed two major sources of educational aspirations among the 387 working-class youths in this sample: primarily certain conditions in the family, and secondarily, the nature of the student's peer associations and his participation in school activities.

Significant influences in the family include the following: (a) *Status discrepancies,* especially where the working-class mother is currently holding a non-manual job, and also where the mother has had some college training while her husband has completed high school only. A history of downward mobility in the family, as indicated by a grandfather whose occupation was non-manual, also favored working-class youngsters' college aspirations. (b) *Family members, or friends of the family who have gone to college:* If parents, older siblings, or friends of the family have had college experience, the working-class student is more likely to have college aspirations. Such a person can furnish practical information about higher education, or, possibly, he may serve as a model for the child. (c) *Father's occupational status:* High occupational status within the working-class is associated with college aspirations in the offspring, and this relationship is strongest when the father has completed high school. If he has less than a high school education, high occupational status has little effect on children's college plans, whereas if he has gone to college, that experience appears to be more influential than high occupational status.

As for the student's peer associations and participation in extra-curricular activities, these influences were significant: (a) College-oriented

---

[21] See especially Merton, *op. cit.,* pp. 265, 290–291 and 384–385, and Lipset and Bendix, *op. cit.,* pp. 257–259.

working-class students were very likely to have acquaintances who also have college aspirations. (b) They tended to be extremely active in extra-curricular activities. (c) They were more likely to be attending a predominantly middle-class than a predominantly working-class school.

In certain interests, values and activities, the college-oriented working-class youths were very similar to the college-oriented middle-class students. Reference group behavior may be involved, particularly anticipatory socialization.

Viewed from the perspective of familial responses to thwarted upward mobility, or attempts to arrest downward mobility, several of these findings may take on added meaning. For example, a wife's employment in a non-manual occupation, or a husband's employment in a high-status manual occupation, may reflect upward striving in the working-class family. In both cases upward mobility is limited by the husband's manual occupation, and the wife may attempt to realize her aspirations through her child. Hence educational attainment is encouraged. Similarly, families where the wife has more education than her husband, or where a grandfather was in a non-manual occupation, may have experienced downward movement and attempt to realize mobility aspirations through the children.[22]

ADDITIONAL READINGS

Alexander, C. Norman & Campbell, Ernest G. Peer influences on adolescent educational aspirations and attainments. *American Sociological Review,* 1964, **29,** 568–575. Male seniors in thirty high schools are studied in terms of their effect on each others' educational aspirations and achievements.

Clarke, H. Harrison & Olson, Arne L. Characteristics of 15-year-old boys who demonstrate various accomplishments or difficulties. *Child Development,* June 1965, **36** (2), 559–567. This study contrasted the physical,

[22] Not to be overlooked is the possibility of the husband rising or returning to a non-manual status. The data of Wilensky and Edwards, *op. cit.,* and Seymour M. Lipset and Reinhard Bendix, "Social Mobility and Occupational Career Patterns," *American Journal of Sociology,* 57 (January and March, 1952), pp. 366–374, 394–504 and Reinhard Bendix, Seymour M. Lipset and F. Theodore Malm, "Social Origins and Occupational Career Patterns," *Industrial and Labor Relations Review,* 7 (January, 1954), pp. 246–261, show that a considerable number of working-class men make such moves at some time in their careers. Thus a family's response to thwarted upward mobility or attempts to arrest downward mobility may involve the husband as well as the children.

mental, and interest characteristics of 15-year-old boys who demonstrated certain accomplishments or difficulties in high school with the same characteristics of other boys of their age. The similarities and differences of the two groups are summarized.

Douvan, Elizabeth & Adelson, Joseph. The psychodynamics of social mobility in adolescent boys. *Journal of Abnormal and Social Psychology,* 1958, **56,** 31–44. The writers distinguish varieties of mobility behavior, and hold that upward-mobile boys are characterised by effective, autonomous ego functioning, downward-mobile boys by demoralization. The two types of boys are different in activity level, time perspective, self-esteem, and family milieu.

Drews, Elizabeth Monroe. The development of talent. *Teachers College Record,* December 1963, **65** (3), 210–219. The author, who has been involved in experimental efforts to teach adolescents more creative ways of confronting problems, both cognitive and effective, summarizes the convictions born of her extensive experience. She also discusses parallel ideas in the growing literature on creativity.

Fink, Martin B. Self-concept as it relates to academic underachievement. *California Journal of Educational Research,* 1962, **63,** 57–62. Fink reports a study which confirmed his hypothesis that self-concept would relate to academic underachievement. He cites research indicating that underachievement relates to certain specific personality traits as well.

Hess, Robert D. High school antecedents of young adult achievement. In Robert E. Grinder (Ed.), *Studies in adolescence.* New York: Macmillan, 1963. Pp. 401–414. Hess finds that successful achievement in the early twenties, as judged by occupational commitment, psychological health, social accomplishment, and skill, proves more closely related to events and experiences that occur after high school than to high school behavior. The data also suggest that the processes of identity that make for stable adult personality continue well past high school. Perhaps, concludes Hess, late adolescence and early adulthood may be a more critical period than early or middle adolescence.

McDill, Edward L. & Coleman, James. High school social status, college plans, and interest in academic achievement: A panel analysis. *American Sociological Review,* 1963, **28,** 905–918. A freshman-to-senior panel analyzes data obtained from students of six midwestern high schools, and discusses the relations between status in adolescent social systems, college intentions, and academic achievement orientations. Students of high social status seemed more likely to shift to a positive orientation toward attending college and a negative orientation toward scholastic achievement than those of lower status. Various processes are perceived as accounting for interrelationships among factors involved.

McDill, Edward L., Meyers, Edmund D., & Rigsby, Leo C. Institutional effects on the academic behavior of high school students. *Sociology of*

Education, Summer 1967, **40**, (3), 181–199. This article reports a study of the dimensions of school environment having significance for students' performance. The results indicate that school environments in which achievement, intellectualism, and competition are stressed by faculty and students are conducive to high achievement on the part of individual students.

Moss, Howard A. & Kagan, Jerome. Stability of achievement and recognition seeking behaviors from early childhood through adulthood. *Journal of Abnormal and Social Psychology,* 1961, **62**, 504–513. Basing their conclusions on data obtained at the Fels Research Institute at Yellow Springs, Ohio, the authors consider the stability of achievement and recognition seeking behaviors from early school years through young adulthood. Intellectual rather than athletic activities, between the years 10 to 14, proved positively correlated with achievement in adulthood.

Moulton, Robert W. Effects of success and failure on level of aspiration as related to achievement motive. *Journal of Personality and Social Psychology,* 1965, **1**, 399–406. Atkinson's hypothesis that individuals high in fear of failure and low in need for achievement would react in an atypical manner to success or failure experience; i.e., they would raise their level of aspiration following failure and lower it after success, was confirmed.

St. John, Nancy Hoyt. The effect of segregation on the aspirations of Negro youth. *Harvard Educational Review,* 1966, **36**, 284–294. The author's findings failed to support her hypothesis that segregation would lower the aspiration level of Negro students. She suggests reasons for this unexpected finding.

Turner, Ralph H. *The social context of ambition: A study of high-school seniors in Los Angeles.* San Francisco: Chandler Publishing Company, 1964. This volume reports an extensive field study designed to explore the social context in which ambition is nurtured. Facets studied include the stratification system in the area, the family of orientation, the neighborhood, the youth subculture, and characteristics of the individuals involved.

Wilson, Alan B. Residential segregation of social classes and aspirations of high school boys. *American Sociological Review,* 1959, **24**, 836–845. This paper treats the influence of the school society on teen-agers' educational and occupational aspirations and political party preferences. Wilson reports that sons of manual workers were more likely to adhere to middle-class values and aspirations if they attended a predominantly middle-class school rather than a predominantly working-class one.

XI. Issues Relating to Youth-Versus-Vocation

A youth's problem of establishing a vocational role originates in the home, the school, society at large, and himself. In the past, a boy learned his occupation directly from his father, but now the son often has only a vague idea of his father's work environment, which may be miles from home. Nevertheless, the father may assume an important role in his son's vocational choice, perhaps in ill-advised ways. The father is of another time, and does not see the world through the eyes of the new generation. He himself struggled hard to get ahead, and has trouble accepting his son's apparently casual attitude. Finally, the son settles on some secure, pleasant sort of work, which violates his father's view of what is either masculine or worthwhile. If the father lacks a son, he may project his dreams onto a daughter, only to find that girls of her generation are still more marriage- than career-minded.

Vocational problems are also linked with adjustment at school. Ideally, the school should fit the child, not the other way around. However, children who cannot adapt to an inflexible and uncongenial school setting, simply quit and go to work. The question arises: how may schools readjust to hold such youth? What sort of work-study arrangement may permit continued education, while providing for present and future vocational needs?

A partial answer, with advantages for potential dropouts and college-bound youth alike, lies in part-time jobs. Ideally, such employment fulfills several requirements: establishment of emotional autonomy from parents, achievement of socially responsible behaviors, preparation for future employment, and provision of spending money for current demands. Most youth do, in fact, indicate that odd jobs and vacation employment yield real benefits; however, others fail to find full satisfaction. For one thing, child labor laws may obstruct obtaining the sort of jobs required to lay the foundation for particular occupations. Instead, young teenagers are largely confined to such odd jobs as cutting lawns, shoveling snow, and baby sitting, and older ones to waiting on tables at local cafés or summer resorts, or clerking in stores. Such jobs may provide little practical experience for the work role that follows. Typically, they lack the complexity, continuity, or stability of adult work roles. However, such work may prove more functional than it seems. The youth who establishes a satisfactory combination of part-time work and leisure-time pursuits may have an easier time adjusting to a future consisting of ever-increasing leisure and ever-decreasing work than the youth who works full-time.

However, the youth who remains in school does run certain risks. He lingers in a sort of hiatus between youth and adulthood, unable to establish a firm grip on maturity. If the youth is middle- or upper-class, his parents continue to support him for as long as he remains in school, even after he marries. Although vocational preparation is thus expedited, problems of dependency and emotional entanglements often result.

Meantime, the school's counseling service does what it can, but faces difficult tasks in acquainting the youth with the range of work open to him. In so diversified a society, the variety is truly bewildering and constantly changing. A type of work is here today, and altered beyond recognition tomorrow. Certain of the more esoteric, significant occupations are hard to describe in realistic fashion. Exactly how does a counselor get across what it is like to do computer programming, social science research, or metallurgical engineering? Also, how early should such counseling begin? Is there a danger of precipitating children into making too early a choice? Perhaps an early choice helps to focus the individual's interests and to motivate his efforts. However, it is a cliché of vocational guidance, says Sing-Yan Fen, that early adolescence should be a period of exploration, never of decision. Even the gifted should be permitted to "simmer" and weigh the alternatives of becoming a Ph.D. at twenty or a scientist with a poetic vision.[1] For any youth, early choice may interfere with acquiring the broad background needed for adjustment to a complex, rapidly changing society. Besides, early choice is based on the child as he now is, and does not take into account later growth.

Schools also attempt to ease youth's transition to the adult work-world. Somehow the young worker must be prepared to adapt to long hours, rigid schedules, hierarchical industrial structures, and repetitive routines. Apprenticeships may sometimes be arranged, but often become overly standardized. Vocational courses help, too, but there is a gap of indefinite proportions between what transpires in the classroom and in the world of work.[2] A youth must also be prepared to face the question: what experience have you had? No matter how competent he may be, his age becomes a status depressant. Often, the teenager is relegated to the meanest tasks. Even the college graduate may begin on the lowest rung of the occupational ladder.

Many of youth's problems arise from modern man's changing relationship to his work. In earlier generations, society relied for its very survival on each individual's making his contribution to the economy. Nowadays

[1] Sing-Yan Fen, "Junior High School and the Open Road," *Teachers College Record,* Vol. 48, No. 4 (January 1967), p. 331.
[2] H. Kirk Dansereau, "Work and the Teen-Ager," in *Teen-Age Culture,* ed. Jessie Bernard, Philadelphia: The American Academy of Political and Social Science, Vol. 338 (November 1961) pp. 44–52.

many workers suspect that their work could be done as well by machines, and fear ultimate displacement by them. In such a situation, it is hardly ego-building to perceive that one's contributions are non-essential. At the same time, note the effects of the curtailed work-day. Vocation once was the core of the adult male's existence. Through attaining and advancing in a good job he validated his masculinity. But now men have far more leisure time. The world of work has shrunk in their personal universe. Another effect of the shortened work week is the male's return to the family. He now has far more time to spend with the children. As a result, changes are taking place in family patterns as men assume a more active father role.

The issue arises: what effects may such trends have on adolescents? Boys' futures will be drastically altered, and girls' more indirectly, but no less fundamentally, affected. Perhaps a boy's job choice will be less critical than formerly simply because a smaller portion of his future destiny will depend upon it. He can afford to spend a part of himself each day at a relatively mundane job, simply because many hours remain for him to use as he wishes.

Changes in the vocational picture will alter youth's outlook in other areas as well. Since the teenage boy can look forward to having more free time as an adult than his forebears did, he must develop a more complete personality. If he is to handle free time intelligently, so that it contributes to his continuing growth as a person, he needs a broad education. To what extent vocational training might be correspondingly curtailed is debatable. In fact, the amount of vocational training needed by a youth is a basic issue. And what type should it be?

Can the suggestion that vocational choice has become less critical go unchallenged? Perhaps it is as vital as ever. As machines take over much of the purely routine work, and industry grows more sophisticated, more individuals will be required to be equipped for new types of creative jobs. Even if hours spent on the job may be less, the work performed may be on a higher level than formerly. Brighter individuals, especially, will be in demand for programming and organizing the features of a space-age society.

However, the same trends will create problems for less intelligent, less advantaged groups. As machines displace routine tasks, the low-IQ individual becomes superfluous in the job market. What can be done about him? Also, as more jobs require advanced education, what is to be done about school dropouts? Will they become professional rioters, delinquents, and welfare cases?

Another problem derived from rapid change is this: how can a youth establish a stable vocational identity in a fluid economy? In the past, it was easy for a youngster to visualize himself as a general practitioner of medicine, as a teacher or lawyer, or whatever. Occupational roles were relatively well defined. But how can the modern youth define himself vis-à-vis a job, whose nature is constantly changing, and may even disappear in years to come. What, for example, may be the effect on the librarian's work of the mechanization and computerization of library services? What sort of teachers will be able to cope with the proliferation of knowledge and with programmed instruction? A current trend is to help the adolescent think of changing self in relation to changing vocation. He projects himself into the future to consider how he may adapt to, and grow with, a changing job.

Many a youth's problems are specific to himself. Perhaps he has physical or mental deficiencies which make him virtually unemployable. He may have personality traits which make it difficult to match him with a congenial job. Besides, he may still be too immature to know if he will like a particular job in later years. Sometimes a youth may become so wrapped up in the process of decision-making that it is difficult for him to take an objective view of his vocational assets and liabilities. At other times, a combination of sexual maturity and desire for independence may precipitate a youth's dropping from school and seeking a job. Society faces a challenge in helping him adjust until he is prepared for the mature role he seeks. Consequently, considerable research nowadays concerns the adolescent's ego-involvement in vocational decisions.[3]

Most of what is written about youth and vocations, including the foregoing, relates more specifically to boys, though somewhat to girls. The girl shares many of the boy's vocational problems, besides having special ones of her own. The types of occupations open to her are limited and allow less opportunity for personal growth. Many parents do little to encourage their daughters, who then work out their vocational destiny as best they can. Both the larger society, and the particular families that compose it, make less effort to provide girls with the advanced education required for high-status jobs. Even if a girl attains a good job, she continually encounters often subtle, and sometimes open, discrimination. Another problem the girl faces is the uncertainty of what her work role will be. As an adolescent, she does not know whether a vocation will constitute her main role, an auxiliary role, or no part of her role at all. Even as an adult, she may constantly waver between full-time, part-time, or no outside employment.

Actually, the topic of vocation, and its relation to adolescence, involves problems and issues so numerous we can barely touch upon them here. For example, how well have we defined the more subtle, but no less significant, factors affecting a child's vocational attitudes and ultimate vocational choice? How should child training, both at home and school, be modified to assist the child in choosing and preparing for his later vocational role? The selections that follow represent a miniscule sample of the vast amount of literature on youth-versus-vocation. The first article, by O'Hara and Tiedemann, treats the development of vocational attitudes and concepts in terms

[3] Hugh M. Bell, "Ego Involvement in Vocational Decisions," *Personnel and Guidance Journal,* Vol. 38 (1960), pp. 732–736.

of stages. One aspect of youth's progress in this definition of self is establishment of a vocational identity. This approach relates to our earlier topic on adolescence as a stage in development.

The second article, by Matthews, is one of the relatively few which concern the girl's special problems of vocation. Matthews considers the childhood antecedents of typical feminine vocational patterns, and how such factors interrelate. Often such articles reflect the author's bias either toward career as either a major or a secondary way of validating the female personality. In this regard, Matthews states no clear definite position; however, her discussion suggests that a strong career commitment for women is atypical.

22

Robert P. O'Hara
David V. Tiedeman [1]

VOCATIONAL SELF CONCEPT IN ADOLESCENCE

In this article, O'Hara and Tiedeman report on an investigation which, they assert, demonstrated the existence of stages in the development of occupational choice. These stages, in turn, relate to successive clarifications of a vocational self-identity. The findings here corroborate and expand upon Ginzberg's stage concept of development as related to vocational choice.

SELF CONCEPTS AND OCCUPATIONAL CHOICE

The process of occupational choice may be characterized as that of developing a vocational identity. The "Self" is the central concern of identity. The concepts of identity and self are intuitively satisfying means of attributing motivation for occupational choice to the person choosing.

Super and his associates say that the "self concept seems to lend itself admirably to the formulation of broad principles explanatory of occupational choice and vocational adjustment" (Super, *et al.,* 1957). They do, however, express some doubt about the merit of using the term self concept because of the difficulties encountered in making the term operational. Despite their doubts they formulate the general principle: "Self concepts begin to form prior to adolescence, become clearer in adolescence and are translated into occupational terms in adolescence."

From Robert P. O'Hara and David V. Tiedeman, "Vocational Self Concept in Adolescence," *Journal of Counseling Psychology*, Vol. 6, No. 4 (1959), pp. 292–301. Reprinted by permission of the American Psychological Association.

[1] *Harvard Studies in Career Development, No. 7.* This work was supported in part by the Office of Naval Research, Department of the Navy, Contract Nonr-1866(31) and in part by the School-University Program for Research and Development, Graduate School of Education, Harvard University. Reproduction in whole or in part is permitted for any purpose of the United States Government. The authors are indebted to the faculty and students of Boston College High School for their wholehearted collaboration in this project.

In an attempt to give an empirical formulation to self concept theory in the realm of vocational development, we have defined self concept as *an individual's evaluation of himself*. Using this definition we have investigated the areas of aptitude, interest, social class, and values. Previous research has shown that these areas are important in the development of careers. The research reported here not only measures the individual's standing in these four areas but adds a further dimension—a measure of the person's *ability to evaluate his standing*. Such a dimension is essential to an understanding of the way in which a person solves the occupational choice problem which he is facing. Hence it was felt that analysis of the evaluations individuals had of themselves in these areas would further illuminate the influence of these factors in occupational choice.

The relative independence of the dimension we are considering is apparent from several related studies. In the area of aptitude, inventoried assessment is only moderately related to self evaluation of aptitude (Arsenian, 1942; Brinn, 1956; Coffee, 1957; Matteson, 1956). "In terms of common elements, perhaps no more than between 25 and 50 per cent of the factors associated with expressed interests are associated with measured interests," according to Berdie (1950). This conclusion seems valid also for the areas of social class (Hollingshead, 1949; McArthur, 1954; McArthur & Stevens, 1955) and values as well (Stanley, 1951).

The above studies merely indicate that some awareness of vocationally-relevant attributes does exist during adolescence and early adulthood. None of them investigated the *clarification* of self concepts implied in Super's proposition. A study by Schulman (1955) and another by Anderson (1948) do provide evidence on this score in the areas under consideration. However, the two studies are limited to single areas, and each deals with a different set of fine points.

STAGES IN THE CLARIFICATION OF SELF CONCEPTS

In 1951, Ginzberg, Ginzburg, Axelrad and Herma set forth the theory that occupational choice progresses through three periods: fantasy choice, tentative choice, and realistic choice. The tentative choice period is subdivided into four stages: interest, capacity, value, and transition. Each of these names designates an element presumably dominant in occupational choice at a particular time. Ginzberg emphasized the developmental nature of his findings. He says that boys pass through the stages in the above order within rather regular age limits; interests, 11–12; capacities, 13–14; values, 15–16; transition, 17–18. Data for his study were derived from intensive analysis of interviews of eight individuals at each of eight periods in the educational process, starting with the sixth grade in elementary school, through the eighth, tenth, and twelfth grades in high school, freshman and senior years in college, first year graduate study and advanced graduate study.

In defining the stages of interest, capacity, value, and transition in the period of tentative choice, Ginzberg uses two approaches. The first approach involves the concept of maturity. However, little research evidence is presented for determination of the stages in explicit terms of maturity or quality of the subject's statements about his occupational choice.

The second approach to stages is found throughout Ginzberg's consideration of the tentative period. The criteria for the stages in this period are those factors which the interviews reveal to be the *basis for choice* by the boys at each age level.

Fig. 22–1 represents graphically the stages of interest, capacity and value as enunciated by Ginzberg. All factors are present to awareness at all stages. At three grade levels the awareness comes into focus on one factor and this factor is used as the basis for making vocational choices during that period. Ginzberg made no effort at graphical presentation of his periods and stages. Hence our representation may do injustice to Ginzberg's ideas even though we have tried to present his words pictorially as faithfully as we can.

Whether our representation of Ginzberg's periods and stages is accurate or not, the fact remains that we have been unable to locate any work on the mathematical representation of the "periods" or "stages" of vocational development. The expression in the mathematical idiom of phases of development supposedly relevant for occupational choice is one of the major purposes of this study.

Although the concepts of "period" and "stage" are frequently used in regard to career development, they are difficult to define. However defined though, both words ordinarily connote a time interval in which something is prevalent which is not prevalent at another time. Thus, "period" and "stage" suggest discreteness, dominance, and irreversibility. Discreteness is indicated by Fig. 22–1 by the precipitous change in the line for an area of discourse when it becomes the basis for choice. Dominance is implied when a line for an area exceeds lines for other areas, i.e. when the area becomes the basis for choice. Irreversibility suggests that a line, once advanced, never recedes. Ginzberg is not clear about irreversibility in this sense. He suggests that earlier considerations remain "constructive forces" in the differentiation of occupational intent but implies that they never again reach the eminence of being the sole "basis for choice" once having been so. To us this implies the *reversibility* depicted in Fig. 22–1. Adolescent imbalance causes an element to be the sole basis for choice but, having been so, the element returns to the more mature position of being a constructive force operating simultaneously with others to effect differen-

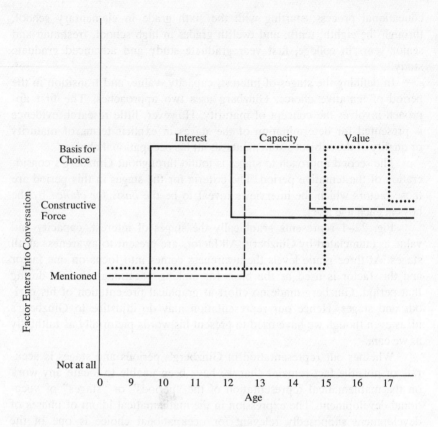

Fig. 22–1. Stages in the tentative period [after Ginzberg (1951)]

tiation of occupational choice. This may result from an adolescent's increasing *ability to estimate* the reality of his interests, aptitudes, and values through his widening experience in school and work.

SEMANTIC PERSPECTIVE

This investigation relates the subjects' estimates of their present status with regard to aptitudes, interests, social class, and values to assessments of their standing in each of these categories as revealed by tests or statements of preference.

In the area of *aptitude* the following five scales of the Differential Aptitude Test: Form A (Bennet, Seashore & Wesman, 1947) were used: verbal reasoning, numerical ability, mechanical reasoning, space relations, and abstract reasoning. The ten scales of the Kuder Preference Record, Vocational, Form CH (Kuder, 1948) delimited the area of interests. The

Home Index of Gough (1949) defined the area of social class. A modification of the Study of Values (Allport, Vernon, & Lindzey, 1951) which provided scales in each of the six areas of this inventory, was the setting for the study of general values. The Work Values Inventory, (Super, 1955) distinguished the area of work values.

For every variable, the self estimate requested was oriented by adaption of the definition provided by the test or inventory. A copy of the self-estimate questionnaire used is available upon request. The questionnaire gives the actual definitions of variables for which subjects provided self-estimates. Authors' definitions of variables were followed as exactly as possible.

SUBJECTS

Data were collected at a private Catholic day school in Boston staffed by the Fathers and Scholastics of the Society of Jesus (Jesuits). There were 1021 boys in the sample, 160 Seniors, 264 Juniors, 276 Sophomores, and 321 Freshmen. The four grades are homogeneous by sex, intelligence, and religion by virtue of administrative policy. Our data revealed that the boys in the several grades also had similar distributions of verbal ability, numerical ability, and social class. The tests of this study were administered over a period of a week and a half in the latter part of March, 1958. Each boy contributed 8 hours of his time providing data.

Admission to the school is competitive and selective. As a result, the classes are above average in scholastic aptitude, yet a fairly high fraction of the boys who are admitted leave before graduating. The attrition, however, was independent of verbal ability and of social class in this sample.

ANALYSIS

Results are summarized by *grade* since grade was the sampling unit of this investigation. Strictly speaking, development should be expressed as a function of *age*. Age was *not* the unit of sampling in this case, however, because the necessary complicated administrative arrangements did not yet seem justifiable. In addition, although we had no way to substantiate the supposition, we felt that clarification of self knowledge in these vocationally relevant areas is a function of the curriculum more than it is a function of length of life. These considerations dictated choice of *grade* as the unit of development *for this investigation*.

Ours is the cross-sectional method of studying development. With this method tests of significance are made relative to the variations of individuals around the parameters one is interestsd in testing rather than relative to the variations within individuals. If this less sensitive test permits rejection of the null hypothesis, one may be assured that the more sensitive test available from longitudinal data would reject the same null hypothesis.

For the data of each grade, the relationships between self-estimates and estimates provided through inventories are summarized for each area (aptitude, interest, general values, and work values) by means of the canonical correlation coefficient (Hotelling, 1935). These canonical correlation coefficients give in each case the maximum correlation between a *linear* composite of the self estimates in an area and a linear composite of the estimates provided through the analogous inventory. Clearly, nonlinear composites of either or both of the estimates provided by rating and test can be more highly correlated than the linear composites investigated. However, relating linear composites introduces sufficient complexity into the current state of our knowledge of the clarity of perception of vocationally relevant attributes.

Since the social class area provided only a single estimate from both self and test, these estimates were related by means of the product moment correlation coefficient which is the analogue of the canonical correlation for this class of data.

DEVELOPMENT OF KNOWLEDGE OF SELF IN VOCATIONALLY RELEVANT AREAS

Fig. 22–2 depicts over-all relationships between self estimates and test estimates for each of the four grade levels in the five areas: aptitude, interest, social class, and general and work values. The correlations themselves are given in Table 22–1.

Except for the area of social class, the increasing congruence of self-estimates and test estimates with increasing grade level is apparent from a glance at Fig. 22–2. Since we knew of no test for the significance of the difference in canonical correlations at the time of this investigation, we could not determine whether the trends for interests, work values, and aptitudes were significant or not. In view of the large number of subjects and of the characteristics of the three curves, however, it seems likely that at least these three trends are significant. The trend for general values is perhaps not significant but manifests the same upward tendency. Congruence in the social class area does not seem to increase appreciably in these grades.

There is a test of significance of the difference between zero-order correlation coefficients and this test was applied to the difference between the correlation of self estimate and test estimate for the ninth-grade data and for the twelfth-grade data as obtained on each of the variables of the several areas. As is indicated in Table 22–2, 17 of the 37 correlations differed

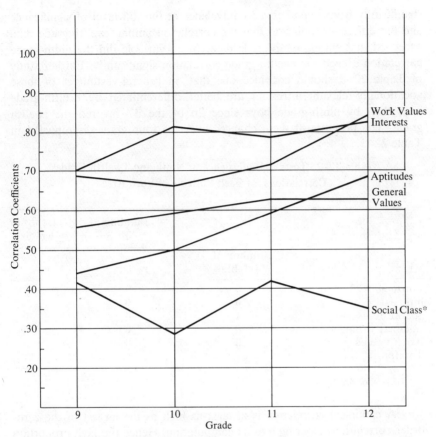

* Product moment correlations. All others are economical correlation coefficients.
Fig. 22–2. Correlations of text scores and self estimates by grade.

Table 22-1   Correlations of Test Scores and Self Ratings by Grade

	Fresh. (N-321)	Soph. (N-276)	Jun. (N-264)	Sen. (N-160)
Aptitudes	.44	.50	.59	.69
Interests	.70	.81	.79	.83
Social class*	.42	.29	.42	.35
General values	.56	.59	.63	.63
Work values	.69	.67	.71	.84

*Product moment correlations. All others are canonical correlation coefficients n explanation given in text.

significantly from hypothesized equivalence at the .05 level of significance and the difference indicated that the correlation among twelfth-grade data exceeded that among ninth-grade data. In no variable did the ninth-grade correlation exceed the twelfth-grade correlation significantly. Further study of Table 22–3 should convince one that, in general, estimates of these vocationally-relevant attributes are better differentiated by twelfth-grade boys than by ninth-grade boys since 26 of the 37 favored the twelfth grade. The progress of these changes over the four grades is reported in Table 22–3.

Table 22-2   Tests of Equivalence of Ninth and Twelfth Grade
Correlations for Each Variable of Each Area

| | | Number of rejections* of $H: \rho_9 = \rho_{12}$ in which | |
Area	Number of Variables	$r_9 > r_{12}$	$r_9 < r_{12}$
Aptitude	5	0	2
Interest	10	0	6
Social class	1	0	0
General values	6	0	4
Work values	15	0	5
Totals	37	0	17

* .05 level of significance.

A canonical correlation is at least as high as the largest of the zero-order correlations entering into its computation. Hence the high proportion of rejection of the hypothesized equivalence of ninth- and twelfth-grade correlations reported in Table 22–2 suggests that the ninth- and twelfth-grade canonical correlations reported in Table 22–1 are significant, particularly since the diminution of degrees of freedom contingent upon the fitting of constants in the computation of the canonical correlations is small relative to the sample sizes of the two grades.

Fig. 22–2 also reveals that the relative *order* in the relationship between self estimates and test estimates of the several areas is approximately the same for the first three years of high school. Interest test scores are most highly related to their respective self ratings with correlations for work values, general values, aptitudes and social class following in that order. Only in the twelfth grade is the order changed. By the senior year the relationship of aptitudes to self ratings of aptitudes surpasses that of general values to self ratings of those values.[2]

[2] As in the case of multiple correlation, canonical correlation tends to increase with an increase in the number of variables. The patterning of the canonical correlations in relation to the numbers of variables entering into each causes us to consider this an unlikely explanation of the results, however.

Table 22-3   Correlation of Self Estimate and Test Estimate by Area and Grade

Area	Variable	Grade 9	Grade 10	Grade 11	Grade 12
Aptitude	Verbal reasoning	.30	.26	.31	.26
	Numerical ability	.32	.40	.43	.51
	Mechanical reasoning	.26	.38	.41	.58
	Space relations	.24	.24	.26	.18
	Abstract reasoning	.19	.08	.03	.13
Interest	Outdoor	.50	.48	.47	.50
	Mechanical	.49	.58	.57	.66
	Computational	.58	.60	.60	.69
	Scientific	.51	.54	.46	.68
	Persuasive	.24	.53	.48	.32
	Artistic	.59	.48	.43	.50
	Literary	.41	.43	.54	.57
	Musical	.59	.63	.61	.65
	Social service	.44	.45	.60	.60
	Clerical	.32	.32	.37	.50
Social class	Social class	.42	.29	.42	.35
Values, general	Theoretical	.19	.16	.10	.18
	Economic	.22	.30	.25	.44
	Aesthetic	.32	.37	.43	.46
	Social	.19	.37	.46	.45
	Political	.28	.36	.27	.28
	Religious	.23	.31	.32	.46
Values, work	Creative	.42	.50	.45	.57
	Aesthetic	.39	.36	.44	.39
	Planning	.19	.25	.25	.28
	Theoretical	.33	.27	.32	.40
	Variety	.44	.37	.52	.47
	Independence	.27	.34	.33	.30
	Supervision	.12	.10	.14	.09
	Work conditions	.15	.07	.22	.20
	Associations	.24	.18	.19	.35
	Way of life	.23	.33	.35	.40
	Social welfare	.46	.55	.57	.61
	Security	.28	.28	.35	.48
	Material	.38	.38	.52	.56
	Prestige	.23	.31	.19	.35
	Mastery	.08	.07	.07	.04

To this point then, the analysis of the data clearly reveals that self concepts in the areas of interests, aptitudes, and work and general values are clarified as boys pass through grades nine to twelve.

STAGES IN THE CLARIFICATION OF
VOCATIONAL SELF CONCEPTS

A major purpose of this investigation was to assess evidence for the existence of *stages* in the development of occupational choice within the context of congruity of self estimates and test estimates of vocationally-relevant attributes. At the outset we suggested that "period" or "stage" should connote discreteness, dominance, and/or irreversibility. Therefore, let us now consider Fig. 22–2 in these terms.

Criterion of Discreteness

Some developments are characterized by surges which are followed by quiescence during which gains are consolidated. Development of this nature, when represented by a growth function, is indicated by a line, parallel to the time axis for a period, which rises sharply from time to time without regression. These surges are indicative of some kind of discreteness in the growth function. It is unclear, however, whether the stage should be denoted by the sequence, surge followed by quiescence, or quiescence followed by surge. It is a matter of whether a stage involves anticipation or not and also of whether consolidation must be included or not. Because of this ambiguity, *we shall refer only to the surge itself as a stage*.

Fig. 22–2 indicates possible nonlinearity in the progress of clarification of self knowledge. *Setting consideration of sampling variability aside* momentarily, the relationship of self estimates to test estimates in the interest area is best represented as a parabolic function of grade: were a parabola to be fitted to the data for interest, it would curve *markedly* in the range from grade 9 to grade 10 and start to become asymptotic to the grade axis even within the range indicated. This suggests some form of discreteness in the differentiation of interest, sampling considerations being ignored, with an *interest stage* that seems to *terminate* by grade 10. Our data do not permit inference of the grade at which this possible stage originates.

The area of work values also approximates a parabolic function when possible sampling variations are ignored. The function, however, seems to be the mirror image of that of interest. In the work values area, the developmental function will be approximately asymptomatic to the grade axis in grades 9-11 and curve upward markedly between grades 11 and 12. Ignoring sampling variation then, work values become more differentiated through grade 12. This may well be a *secondary* phase for the differentiation of work values. Since the asymptote defined by the range *of these data* is relatively high for the area, there must be an earlier grade at which *primary* differentiation of these work values occurs in order for the relationship to have reached .69 by grade 9. We might speculate also that periods of gestation are required before surges of progress in awareness of self concepts can occur.

If sampling variations are completely ignored, progress in the differentiation of general values is also a parabolic function. The function, when fitted, would have a shallower curve than would those for interests and work values. This would suggest that progress in the development of general values is continuous through grades 9 and 10 and that a plateau in progress occurs in grades 11 and 12. Our data would then suggest that the stage of differentiation of general values is in progress through grades 9 and 10.

Since the surges of progress in differentiation of general values are not as precipitous as they are for the differentiation of work values and interest, we are inclined to consider the apparent surge in the general values curve attributable to sampling variation. In this case progress in the differentiation of general values is more likely a straight line within this range of data. *In this event, we would characterize differentiation of general values as that of continual progress rather than as that of a stage.*

Sampling variation notwithstanding, progress in differentiation of perceptions of aptitude is definitely linear rather than parabolic. *Within this grade-range there is not an aptitude stage* of differentiation of perceptions. Rather there is continual progress in the attainment of differentiated perceptions of aptitude.

The correspondence of self ratings and inventory estimates of social class seems to reflect only sampling variation about a line of zero slope. There seems to be no gain in awareness of social class in these grades.

The Criterion of Dominance

The criterion of dominance in the definition of a stage usually implies that one aspect overrides another or others. Ginzberg (1951) says that interests, aptitudes and values dominate boys' talk about their occupational choices in that order. This research interprets dominance in terms of the *ability of the boys to estimate* their interests, aptitudes, values, and social class. According to this interpretation, congruence of self-estimates and test-estimates is greatest in the area of interest throughout the grade-range except in grade 12 when it is tied by the area of work values. In addition, maximum congruence is achieved earliest in the area of interest, namely in grade 10. Throughout grades 9 through 12, congruence of estimates in the areas of interest and work values eclipses congruence of estimates in the area of general values and aptitudes.

Congruence in the aptitude area is singularly low in grades 9, 10, and 11 when pupils are presumably making a number of tentative decisions about work which we would prefer to have based upon accurate perceptions of capability. Only in grade 12 does congruence in the area of aptitude exceed that in any area and then only that of the area of general values. This unawareness of aptitude in these grades may explain why assessments of aptitude predict curriculum choice only poorly in junior high school and high school (e.g., Cass, 1956; Kugris, 1956).

The Criterion of Irreversibility

A third connotation of stage is that of irreversibility. In the sense that the congruence of self-estimates and test-estimates is a monotonic increasing function of grade, our data provide concrete evidence that the developmental function in each of the areas except that of social class is irreversible. Only in this connotation of stage do general values and aptitudes emerge as stages. Awareness of social class does not regress but neither does it progress.

The increasing ability to evaluate these vocationally-relevant factors could be responsible for the reversibility in the stages as outlined by Ginzberg earlier. The imbalance which resulted in one factor being the sole basis for choice is gradually redressed under the force of the always increasing clarification of vocationally-relevant self concepts so that at the end of the tentative period all factors become constructive forces in the career development process. The grade limitation of our data does not allow us to estimate at what future point the ability to evaluate these factors converges. However we feel that the location of this point is important for the estimation of vocational maturity. However, it may well be that there is no point of convergence but that there always remains a differential hierarchy of ability to evaluate one's self in these areas.

GENERALIZATION

Our purpose has been to establish empirically the existence of clarification of self concepts in areas of relevance to vocational choice, and through study of this clarification to introduce more precise means of identifying and describing the stages of occupational choice. Our contribution lies both in the methods we have introduced and in the conclusions drawn from the analysis of our data. The method opens a way for other investigations which are necessary before our conclusions are generalizable.

Dominance of areas was investigated by comparison of the general *level* of the congruence of test-estimates and self-estimates as revealed by canonical correlation. Irreversibility was equated with the monotonic increasing nature of the function relating congruence of estimates and grade level. Finally, a stage was taken to be represented by a monotonic increasing, non-linear function whose level exceeded that of other functions at some time.

The above definitions were applied to the self-estimates and test-estimates provided by 1021 boys in attendance at a private Catholic day school in Boston. From the milieu of an academically well-qualified Catholic boy living in Greater Boston and receiving his education in the scholastic tradition of the Jesuits, *our data indicate increasing clarification of self concepts in four vocationally relevant areas. Further, our data identify an interest stage seemingly terminated by grade 10 and a work-values stage probably proceeding through a secondary phase in grade 12.* Differentiation of perception in the areas of aptitude and of general values progresses continuously and concomitantly with differentiation in the areas of interest and work values. No clarification of social class occurs during high school.

These data in no way contradict the stages of development proposed by Ginzberg. Ginzberg identified his stages in the *talk* of boys who were asked to consider themselves in relation to school and work. Interest, aptitudes, and other values became a part of this talk, in that order, as he moved from boys in grades 8 and 9, to boys in grades 10 and 11, and to boys in grade 12. Our data do, however, indicate that this sequence is not applicable to the *quality* of estimates of vocationally-relevant attributes. A difference of particular importance is that reporting the *quality* of estimates of aptitude. *Aptitude is relatively poorly perceived throughout grades 9 through 12 even by academically able boys.*

REFERENCES

Allport, G. W., Vernon, P. E., & Lindzey, G. *A study of values* (rev. ed.). Boston: Houghton Mifflin, 1951.

Anderson, Rose G. Subjective ranking versus score ranking of interest values. *Personnel Psychol.*, 1948, 1, 349–355.

Arsenian S. Informing college freshmen of their test scores. *J. educ. Psychol.* 1942, 33, 291–302.

Bennett, G. K., Seashore, R. G., & Wesman, A. G. *Differential aptitude tests.* New York: The Psychological Corp., 1947.

Berdie, R. F. Scores on the Strong Vocational Interest Blank and the Kuder Preference Record in relation to self ratings. *J. appl. Psychol.*, 1950, 34, 42–49.

Brinn, O. G., Jr. College grades and self-estimates of intelligence. *J. educ. Psychol.*, 1956, 45, 477–484.

Cass, J. C. Prediction of curriculum choice in Maine secondary schools. Unpublished Ed.D. dissertation, Harvard Graduate School of Education, 1956.

Coffee, J. Occupational realism: An analysis of factors influencing realism in the occupational planning of male high school seniors. Unpublished doctoral dissertation, Graduate School of Education, Harvard Univer., 1957.

Ginzberg, E., Ginsburg, S. W., Axelrad, S., & Herma, J. L. *Occupational choice*. New York: Columbia Univer. Press, 1951.

Gough, H. G. A short social status inventory. *J. educ. Psychol.*, 1949, **40**, 52–56.

Hollingshead, A. E. *Elmtown's youth*. New York: Wiley, 1949.

Hotelling, H. The most predictable criterion. *J. educ. Psychol.*, 1935, **26**, 139–142.

Kuder, G. F. *Kuder Preference Record—Vocational—Form CH*. Chicago: Science Research Associates, 1948.

Kugris, Violet. A study of the allocation of differential aptitudes to various high school curricula in terms of pupil choice and counselor opinion. Unpublished Ed.D. Dissertation, Harvard Graduate School of Education, 1956.

Matteson, R. W. Self estimates of college freshmen. *Personnel guid. J.*, 1956, **34**, 280–284.

McArthur, C. Long-term validity of the Strong test in two sub-cultures, *J. appl. Psychol.*, 1954, **38**, 346–353.

McArthur, C., & Stevens, Lucia B. The validation of expressed interests as compared with inventoried interests: A fourteen-year follow-up. *J. appl. Psychol.*, 1955, **39**, 184–189.

Schulman, J. A comparison between ninth and twelfth grade students on self estimates of abilities and objective scores on the Differential Aptitude Tests. Unpublished Doctoral dissertation, New York Univer., 1955.

Sinnett, E. R. Some determinants of agreement between measured and expressed interest. *Educ. psychol. Measmt.*, 1956, **16**, 110–118.

Stanley, J. C. Insight into one's own values. *J. educ. Psychol.*, 1951, **42**, 339–408.

Super, D. E. *Notes on Career Pattern Study Tests*. New York: Columbia Univer., February, 1955. (Mimeographed.)

Super, D. E., *et al. Vocational development: A framework for research*. New York: Columbia Univer. Bureau of Publications, 1957.

23

Esther Matthews

CAREER DEVELOPMENT OF GIRLS

The writer traces the antecedents of the typical girl's career interests, from early fantasy career choices to later patterns of single or dual role commitment (marriage and/or career). Finally, she suggests principles for counseling girls in such matters.

Counselors have long recognized that career development differs in boys and girls. They also have recognized that counseling practice, in the area of career development, is not based upon a definitive body of knowledge.

However, while research * in career development theory is of comparatively recent origin and is based almost entirely upon the study of boys, it has resulted in profound alterations in conceptual approaches to the whole matter of the human career (2, 6, 7). Prediction of a specific career, or even of a career field, is becoming of less concern than is an understanding of the *process* of decision-making that results in the presence or absence of a career.

One fundamental fact, applicable to both boys and girls, has emerged from research to date. That central fact is that career development, like personality development, is a life-long process. Should this finding *alone* become rooted in a counselor's way of relating with a student, important progress would have been made. This vista of evolving life carries hope for the future and denial of the irrevocability of the past. Allport's (1) concept of "Becoming," and Murphy's (5) stress upon "Human Potentialities" emphasize this trend of thinking.

Are there any gross, tentative, descriptive accounts of career development in girls and women that can aid counselors' general understanding, without obscuring the individual differences in girls? It is vital to consider the descriptions that follow as observations drawn from knowledge and

Matthews, E. Career Development for Girls. *Vocational Guidance Quarterly,* 2, 4, 1963, 273–277. Reprinted by permission.

Esther Matthews is Head Counselor, Newton South High School, Newton, Massachusetts, and Lecturer on Education, Harvard University.

* The original paper, prepared for ASCA at the 1963 APGA Boston Convention, contains a summary of research on girl's career development.

experience that must be subjected to careful research. The descriptive stage generates hypotheses usually preceding a deeper level of inquiry into the dynamics of process.

ANTECEDENTS IN INFANCY

Career development, as counselors observe it during adolescence, has its antecedents in the infancy stage. The attitudes of a girl's parents regarding her birth condition her acceptance or rejection as a girl and as a *person.* An essentially emphatic, feminine mother and a protective, masculine father will not only accept, but will welcome the birth of a girl baby. They will give her a feminine name rather than deny her sex by the use of a masculinized name. On the other hand, parents expecting and desiring a son, and only pretending to value the birth of a daughter, endanger her emotional security and her subsequent sex identification.

The infant's interpersonal orientation or view of the world is conditioned toward love, happiness, and curiosity; or toward fear, mistrust, and hostility, by the presence or absence of warm, protective care, both physical and emotional, during the early dependent months and years of life. A positive life orientation is crucial to the evolving acceptance at various age levels of the *full human role,* which is dominated for many women by the traditional feminine role exclusively.

It is important to stress that sex role identification cannot be ignored in our society. Sex role identification is unmistakably a part of everyone's life agenda; it is a way station on the road to full humanness. It is not better or worse to be a man or a woman but it *is* different. There is a subtle balance over the years between the parent's recognition of a daughter as not only a potential and inevitable occupant of a sex role but also as an individual with possible needs for personal occupational fulfillment.

The young girl moves from a phase of loving imitation of her mother to a more persistent seeking of her father's attention and an intermittent withdrawal from her identification with her mother. If her mother can understand and accept this temporary development, another firm commitment toward unconscious acceptance of feminine identity has been established. If the mother resents and rejects the little girl, or if the father is over-encouraging in perpetuating this phase of development, the little girl may experience sex identity confusion.

In the latency period, although direct interest and concern over matters pertaining to sex subside, the little girl's energies are absorbed in feminine identification with her mother and with gradual repression of her overtly expressed, aggressive tendencies. For most girls the values of femininity outweigh the appeal of the active, aggressive role of the boy. Gradually most girls become more submissive and introspective. It is during these years that society exerts a constricting effect upon the privilege and "rightness" of *full* human development for many girls.

Paradoxically, at this very age, girls are competing in a co-educational system with boys. Girls, since they mature more rapidly, often surpass boys in early school learning. These differences in early achievement confuse both boys and girls. In boys, the groundwork for resentment toward occupational competition with women in later years may be laid at this time. In girls the mainspring of tense competition is wound so tightly that there may be some unconscious unwillingness to accept the cooperation aspects of marriage and family responsibilities.

FANTASY CAREER CHOICES

Both girls and boys in the early puberty period express fantasy career choices. The psychological import of their fantasy choices differ in boys and in girls. Boys' early puberty fantasy choices seem vitally related to the crystallization of masculine identity rather than bearing any firm relationship to actual abilities or talents that will affect ultimate career selection.

On the other hand, girls' fantasy choices at early puberty must be studied from a different frame of reference because girls' maturation rates have placed them at a life developmental stage that boys will reach about two years later. Girls' career concerns in early puberty may be psychological strategies designed to channel unconscious desires for marriage and children which may not be realized until a later period in our culture. (Counselors will note the adventurous, masculine type of girls' early puberty fantasy choices such as reporter, explorer, and space scientist.) The fantasy choices may thereby serve not only as a denial of unconscious wishes that may not be fulfilled until a later time but also as a last fling of aggression before adopting the more passive feminine role. Perhaps they are accepting a role that may or may not be the most rewarding and sensible for their lives; a role that may or may not be demanded of women by an evolving society.

DECLINING CAREER INTEREST

Observation of girls' later high school years reveals a pattern of sharply declining career interest on the part of many girls. This decline of career interest as marriage interest rises is obscured by the scholastic success of girls. There is reason to believe that the schools reward girls' conscientious submission to academic authority.

As the high school years draw to a close, boys are becoming involved in the necessity, and even desirability of making a career decision, while girls are increasingly drawn toward the marriage goal. Girls express a variety of marriage-career and goal patterns: marriage after high school; a job then marriage; college or post-high school education followed by a brief work experience, then marriage; college and marriage at the same time; and occasionally, career goal without marriage.

In a very few years after high school a majority of girls are married. With the period of the twenties and early thirties being devoted to raising of children. These active and fruitful years show a woman's need to be busy and useful. However, the trend toward early marriage means that a woman past the middle thirties, faces a readjustment as her last child enters school and her husband's career direction becomes established.

Some women face this life period constructively through: increased civic activity; return to partial or full employment; enrollment in school or college; or resumption of earlier hobbies and interests.

BEING USEFUL AND NEEDED

Probably the most critical aspect of this period in a woman's life is not her individual pattern of adaptation, but rather the necessity for recognition by husbands, employers, and educators of the fact that she has an intense desire to be useful and needed in order to experience satisfaction.

The intelligent woman of the middle thirties has a highly developed sense of values, a wealth of life experience, a much better idea of where she would like to fit into the world of work, and a capacity for greater commitment to professional life since the marriage-family goal has been accomplished.

The middle and late years of a woman's life may bring a new sense of personal fulfillment through professional service. New areas of respect and understanding may enrich the love between husband and wife. Children may be granted the freedom of developing their own lives and, in turn, family patterns, without the loving constriction of the idle, middle-aged parent.

The customary pattern of women's lives is a product of relatively comfortable acquiescence to biological, cultural, and social forces. Highly educated women seem to face, to some degree, a conflict between marriage and career. The natural desire for marriage runs counter to the societal press for the professional services of the educated. Such women may experience guilt at the fulfillment of their fundamental wishes for marriage and family, and, conversely, resentment over the abandonment of a promising career. This resentment may be repressed and diverted into impaired relationships with husband and children. Considerable research is needed on these problems, alone. How do women who complete a professional education differ from women of equal intelligence who fail to consider or who neglect to complete a professional education? Have we underestimated the level of life energy necessary for dual role commitment?

DUAL ROLE COMMITMENT

What of the educated woman who does combine marriage and career successfully? Her life pattern would not appear to differ substantially from the customary life development previously recorded. It would seem to be rooted in a normal existence characterized by warm, satisfying emotional and physical care during infancy and childhood, and a normal sequence of sex identification.

However, there may be important *additional* influences in such a person's life—familial acceptance of and encouragement of strong interest and motivation toward a career as well as toward marriage; a marked superiority in life energy, persistence, and personal attractiveness. There may be a mother who successfully combines both roles. In addition, there may be a husband who is so personally secure and occupationally competent that he is free to encourage the growth of his wife's full human career —as wife, mother, and productive member of a profession. This is a prime research frontier.

SINGLE ROLE COMMITMENT

The next life pattern of feminine, nurturant career, without marriage, is probably more difficult to understand. One possibility may be an infancy stage of warm and satisfying emotional and physical care from a mother intensely preoccupied with the infant to the exclusion of the father. If such a mother also withdrew love at any sign of the child's normal movement toward a father fixation, a pre-oedipal stage might be maintained. This would result in an internalization of only part of the feminine adaptation, the maternal or nurturant aspect without the balance of opposite sex involvement at appropriate stages.

In another type of situation, progress may seem to be normal until adolescence. At that time the girl's feminine image must receive strong reinforcement from parents and peers. Unless she feels attractive, lovable, and socially accepted, her energies may be diverted toward compensatory retreat into career involvement.

The final pattern of the truly aggressive, masculine, competitive career *may* differ at every stage from the previous descriptions. In infancy maternal rejection may combine with paternal indifference and/or rejection. A desire for a son may force a daughter into the hopeless struggle to gain attention by being as much like a boy as possible. Such girls generally show marked confusion and anxiety over sex role identification. Unconscious resentment over the denial of the right to be a girl may be built into career as a form of retaliation for lack of approval of the woman's major role. This prevents a free and creative career commitment.

Major influences on both of the last two life patterns—the feminine nurturant career and the aggressive masculine career—may also be drawn from unresolved traumas of childhood and adolescence. During these years the girl is gradually crystalizing her own conception of the meaning of being a woman, a wife, and a mother. Parental experiences of pain, hatred, cruelty or violence witnessed or even remotely inferred by a girl may paralyze normal movement toward full acceptance of the adult feminine role.

As you can see, there is a great deal of research to be done in the study of women's career development and in the evolution of the concept of the full human career for women.

THE COUNSELOR'S RESPONSIBILITIES

What, then, are some of the counselor's responsibilities in the light of this discussion?

To provide a setting in which a girl may freely examine her inner feelings and needs and gain respect for her own decision-making power.

To integrate into one's counseling framework extensive knowledge of human development over the life span and to be particularly aware of the tasks of development faced at each stage of life (for example, the search for identity in adolescence).

To accept the girl as a "special" kind of person (just as the boy is) with a "special" kind of contribution to make in her total career development as a complete human being.

To realize the naturalness of girls' shift in energies from career-directed goals to marriage-directed goals in late adolescence.

To recognize the variety of combinations of patterns of career and marriage that a woman may follow over her life span.

To understand the derivation and meaning of varying life patterns in the development spectrum.

To acknowledge the existence of marriage-career conflict in some girls—and as importantly—the absence of this conflict in other girls.

To be aware of and to avoid cultural biases that discourage able girls from seriously considering careers not regarded as "feminine."

To realize that rational discussion of women's employment statistics—as a concrete evidence of their changing role—carries little psychological meaning for girls as they make life decisions.

To support the emerging dual life plan of marriage and career when it does exist.

To identify neurotic, and even pathological, deviations in life planning and to help such girls to seek appropriate psychological help.

To reinforce the individual girl's sense of personal worth and to re-affirm her right of choice, whatever that choice may be.

To widen girls' horizons as to the many possible life plans they may consider.

To contribute, directly or indirectly, to research on girls' career development by actually conducting research or by communicating observations and insights to researchers.

Counselors need to be aware that girls may fulfill their lives in many ways. The role of the counselor is not to determine which way of life is best for any person. The role of the counselor is to provide a knowledgeable, sensitive, and empathic relationship that will enable each student to make a truly free and informed set of evolving life decisions.

REFERENCES

1. Allport, Gordon. *Becoming: Basic Considerations for a Psychology of Personality*. New Haven: Yale University Press, 1955.
2. Field, Frank L., Kehas, Chris D., & Tiedeman, David V. "The Self Construct in Transition," *Harvard Studies in Career Development, No. 24.* (Duplicated) Cambridge, Mass., 1962.
3. Matthews, Esther. "The Marriage Career Conflict in the Career Development of Girls and Young Women." Unpublished Ed. D. dissertation, Harvard University, 1960.
4. Matthews, Esther & Tiedeman, David V. "The Imprinting of Attitudes Toward Career and Marriage upon the Life Styles of Young Women," *Harvard Studies in Career Development, No. 18.* (Duplicated) Cambridge, Mass., 1962.
5. Murphy, Gardner. *Human Potentialities*. New York: Basic Books, 1958.
6. Tiedeman, David V., & O'Hara, Robert P. "Differentiation and Integration in Career Development," *Harvard Studies in Career Development, No. 23.* (Duplicated) Cambridge, Mass., 1962.
7. Tiedeman, David V., & O'Hara, Robert P. "The Harvard Studies in Career Development in Retrospect and in Prospect," *Harvard Studies in Career Development, No. 15A.* (Duplicated) Cambridge, Mass., 1960.

ADDITIONAL READINGS

Cohen, Eli E. The employment needs of urban youth. *Vocational Guidance Quarterly,* Winter 1962, **10** (2), 85–89. Topics considered in this article are: the unique nature of youth's employment problems, the impact of automation, problems of school dropouts and minority youth, the bleak, long-term outlook, and government work programs.

Douvan, Elizabeth & Adelson, Joseph. *The adolescent experience.* New York: Wiley, 1966. Chapter 3 treats adolescent vocational aspirations in terms of social mobility. Social mobility was found to relate to sex, intelligence, social status, personality traits and education of parent.

Eppel, E. M. & Eppel, M. *Adolescents and morality: A study of some moral values and dilemmas of working adolescents in the context of a changing climate of opinion.* New York: Humanities Press, 1967. An empirical study of the young worker's character and values. See especially Chapter 5 which compares results from several studies.

Falk, Laurence I. Occupational satisfaction of female college graduates. *Journal of Marriage and the Family,* May 1966, **28** (2), 177–185. Role analysis was used to determine whether males differ from females in their satisfaction with their occupational and avocational uses of their college training. Although housewives proved more satisfied with their vocation than did males, they seemed less satisfied with the application of their academic training in the home than males did with their vocational uses of academic training. There was some support for concluding that both sexes engage in avocational activities as a partial solution to occupational dissatisfaction.

Freedman, Marcia K. Perspectives in youth employment. *Children,* March–April 1965, **12** (2), 75–80. The writer examines the problems and dilemmas involved in the efforts of young people to find a niche in society. The problem of youth unemployment is pinpointed and its significance discussed.

Gribbons, Warren D. & Lohnes, Paul R. Shifts in adolescents' vocational values. *Personnel and Guidance Journal,* November 1965, **44,** 248–251. Changes in value hierarchies of youth were analyzed over five years of development, in the 8th, 10th, and 12th grades. A constancy of values was revealed which indicated a maturity of self-concepts early in the 8th grade. Some sex differences were noted, but similarities outweighed differences.

Harris, Dale B. Work and adolescent transition to maturity. *Teachers Col-*

lege Record, 1961, **63,** 146–153. In this article, Harris considers the significance of work experience in the socialization of adolescents. He indicates how such factors as responsibility, wages, status, and attitudes toward work participate in the socialization process.

Havighurst, Robert J. Counseling adolescent girls in the 1960's. *Vocational Guidance Quarterly,* Spring 1965, **13** (3), 153–160. The writer asserts that the pathways to adulthood and problems of identity achievement are different for the sexes. He outlines acceptable career patterns for girls and discusses deviant behaviors which may be associated with these career patterns.

Little, J. Kenneth. The occupations of non-college youth. *American Educational Research Journal,* March 1967, **4** (2), 147–153. This study, involving a state-wide inquiry among graduating seniors in Wisconsin, answers the questions: What is the occupational destiny of youth with differing levels of education? For what part of the occupational world is attainment dependent upon education beyond high school? What are the characteristics of youth who reach differing levels of occupational attainment?

Mulvey, M. C. Psychological and sociological factors in prediction of career patterns of women. *General Psychology Monographs,* 1963, **68,** 310–386. The research presented here supports the common belief that the average woman's perception of her role as homemaker is central to her personality. However, the findings further suggest that woman's work role is more significant to her existence and more internalized than many writers suggest. The woman's self-perception in the social structure has not yet been adequately defined.

Nelson, Richard C. Early versus developmental vocational choice. *Vocational Guidance Quarterly,* Autumn 1962, **11** (1), 23–27. The writer examines certain common assumptions and considers the relative effects of making either early or developmental career choices. He emphasizes the process of choosing and the importance of long-term goals.

Sewell, William H. & Orenstein, Alan M. Community of residence and occupational choice. *American Journal of Sociology,* March 1965, **70** (5), 551–563. This research tests the hypothesis that there are differences in occupational choices of individuals reared in rural and urban communities. The hypothesis held true for boys but not for girls.

Shuval, Judith T. Occupational interests and sex-role congruence. *Human Relations,* May 1963, **16** (2), 171–182. Shuval considers the recruitment of women to sex-linked occupations in the Israeli context. She reports that religiously oriented girls tend to adhere to traditional female role patterns and choose female identification figures.

Super, Donald E. A developmental approach to vocational guidance: Recent theory and results. *Vocational Guidance Quarterly,* Autumn, 1964, **13** (1), 1–10. Super defines the differences between occupation and career, and then reviews major approaches and trends in the psychology of occupations. Important current research deals with translating self-concepts into occupational terms.

Werts, Charles E. Career choice patterns. *Sociology of Education,* Fall 1967, **40** (4), 348–358. Werts reports on an investigation among college freshmen, and of how their father's education and high school grades were related to career choice. Career choices were found to vary with the father's education, especially among women with non-traditional careers.

Four

Issues in Peer Relations

XII. Youth Culture—A Myth?

Some years ago, Murray and Kluckhohn wrote that major discrepancies exist in all cultures between the ideal patterns for various age groups.[1] This differentiation tends to isolate age groups from each other and to produce characteristic ways of life. Among American adolescents, especially, youth's way of life, or culture, has assumed features distinctive from those of the larger culture—perhaps for several reasons. For one thing, peer-group activities help offset the discipline and strains imposed by modern schools. Also, in free democratic societies youth are left largely to themselves, which permits developing distinctive groups. In such societies, the adult is expected to be free-thinking and independent, and youth groups help overcome the dependency of early childhood. In contrast, totalitarian societies attempt to bring youth under centralized control through officially organized, adult-directed youth organizations. A final factor is affluence, for, in cultures of poverty, children are too involved in helping with family chores to participate in peer-group activity.[2]

Only recently, and still largely within the western world, has society been able to afford a large leisure class of adolescents, who have enough money to be consumers on a large scale. This money, in turn, finances the material aspects of their culture, which gives it much of its flavor. Clothes, especially, are important, and teenagers are encouraged to have distinctive outfits for various occasions. Designers constantly introduce new styles, producing continuing obsolescence. Cosmetics are important, and advertisers have begun successfully to tap the male market. The trick is to make cosmetics and deodorants especially for men, so that boys may use them without forfeiting a self-image of masculinity. Nor can we overlook the automobile, which is a staple item in male-adolescent consumption and also important, though less so, to girls.

Non-material features of the teen culture are no less significant. Teenagers speak their own tongue, a blend of accepted usage and their own special modifications. Their idiom is constantly changing so that even recent alumni of the teen culture may have trouble understanding siblings in the younger set.

Youths also have their tribal customs. Parking in lovers' lanes and lingering in teen hangouts are among favorite pastimes. The hangout may

[1] Clyde Kluckhohn and Henry A. Murray, eds., *Personality in Nature, Society and Culture* (New York: Alfred A. Knopf, Inc., 1948), p. 22.
[2] S. N. Eisenstadt, *From Generation to Generation* (Chicago: The Free Press of Glencoe, Illinois, 1956).

be a soda fountain, a juke joint, or a college snackbar. Teen culture, like
the larger culture that surrounds it, is stratified by social class. Until recently, social class roughly divided high-school students into college bound
students and vocational-commercial students. Each social class has its
subtle differences in dress, personal ideals, and sex practices. However,
nowadays many youngsters with lower-class background are going to college. Some of these are absorbed into the older collegiate version of the
youth culture. Others have a strong occupational orientation and are intent
on preparing for adult roles.

The composition of the teen culture is somewhat uncertain, and certainly changing. Formerly, the youth culture was almost wholly a middle-
and upper-class culture, except in the very early teens. Children of the
lower class entered the adult world hardly before puberty ended. However,
a combination of welfare assistance and higher wages for less skilled labor
now prolong lower-class children's tenure in school, and permit participation in youth culture.

At least four models of student culture have been distinguished.[3] The
collegiate culture is the world of football, Greek letter societies, cars, and
drinking; while courses and college professors occupy a dim place in the
background. Adolescents following this culture are not hostile to college;
they simply evade its more serious demands. This sort of culture has flour-
ished on the campuses of large state universities.

The vocational culture prevails in urban colleges and universities attended chiefly by students of lower middle-class families. They are custom-
ers, not in a luxury market, but in a diploma market, says Bernard.[4] Many
are married, and working hard—hence, their way of life is not teenage in
nature.

A third type, the academic culture, has learning as its major value.
Practitioners of this culture identify with the faculty and their goals. Neither
the academic culture nor the vocational culture are teen-type cultures in
character. A fourth type possesses various blends of the intellectual, the
radical, and the alienated Bohemian. When students' intellectual and cultural interests are at odds with those held by their teachers or parents, they
become alienated from their own groups. Members of the academic subculture pursue their goals within a formal educational framework; these
non-conformists outside it.

[3] Burton R. Clark and Martin Trow, "Determinants of College Student Sub-
culture," in *The Study of College Peer Groups: Problems and Prospects for Research*
(Ann Arbor: Social Science Research Council) as reported in Jessie Bernard, ed.,
Teen-Age Culture, Philadelphia: The American Academy of Political and Social
Science, Vol. 338 (November 1961), pp. 10–11.

[4] Jessie Bernard, "Teen-Age Culture: An Overview," in Jessie Bernard, ed.,
Teen-Age Culture, Philadelphia: The American Academy of Political and Social
Science, Vol. 338 (November 1961), pp. 1–12.

Formerly, the collegiate culture was dominant, but now the other three have attained greater significance. The influx of the lower classes into college have accented vocational values; while a complex, rapidly changing culture has produced stresses and strains, and with them non-conformist groups.

The topic, teen culture, subsumes many issues; for example, what are its more subtle traits? Also, what is its over-all effect on the youth himself and his society? Is its residual impact beneficial or otherwise? Furthermore, what is youth culture in the process of becoming? Will it spread through the world—or will it ultimately disappear? Perhaps the concept of a teen culture is a myth anyhow. If it reflects the larger culture can it be truly classified as "a culture" in its own right?

Some writers argue that youth's way of life is not sufficiently distinctive to deserve the designation, "youth culture." Among these is David Epperson, a selection by whom follows. Ernest Smith takes the opposite view and, in our second selection, describes the teen culture as it applies to "youth who are American, white, urban, middle-class, post-pubertal, not yet fulfilling adult roles." In the third selection, Dr. Eldon Snyder reviews both positions and concludes that youth indeed have a distinctive culture. However, youth culture is no homogeneous entity, but possesses considerable diversity according to socioeconomic, sexual, ethnic, and other factors.

24

David C. Epperson

A REASSESSMENT OF INDICES OF PARENTAL INFLUENCE IN THE ADOLESCENT SOCIETY *

Epperson challenges Coleman's conclusion that adolescents live in a distinct subculture, in effect cut off from the adult culture. Epperson concludes that we need a "conceptual scheme that takes into consideration the multiple loyalties of the teen-ager and the relation of these loyalties to specific situations."

Coleman's study of the adolescent society presents evidence of the centrality of the peer group in teenage life.[1] He suggests that

. . . in a rapidly changing, highly rationalized society the "natural processes" of education in the family are no longer adequate. They have been replaced by a more formalized institution that is set apart from the rest of society and that covers an ever longer span of time. As an unintended consequence, society is confronted no longer with a set of individuals to be trained toward adulthood, but with distinct social systems, which offer a united front to the overtures made by adult society.[2]

Some commentators have considered the concept of a distinct adolescent peer culture a myth,[3] while recent evidence suggests that adolescents tend to be peer-conforming in making certain kinds of choice and parent-conforming in other kinds of choice.[4]

From David C. Epperson, "A Reassessment of Indices of Parental Influence in the Adolescent Society," *American Sociological Review*, Vol. 29 (1964), pp. 93–96. Reprinted by permission of the American Sociological Association.

* The critical comments and suggestions for revision made by Professor R. Murray Thomas are gratefully acknowledged.
[1] James S. Coleman, *The Adolescent Society,* New York: The Free Press of Glencoe, 1961.
[2] *Ibid.,* p. 4.
[3] Frederick Elkin and William A. Westley, "The Myth of the Adolescent Peer Culture," *American Sociological Review,* 20 (December, 1955), pp. 680–684.
[4] Clay V. Brittain, "Adolescent Choices and Parent-Peer Cross Pressures," *American Sociological Review,* 28 (June, 1963), pp. 385–391.

As indices of the emergence of an adolescent subculture, Coleman used a question about teenagers' relations with parents, teachers, and peers and a question about teenage boys' attitudes toward going into father's occupation. The findings presented below suggest that a distinct adolescent subculture may indeed exist, but the present data require a qualification of the conclusions that Coleman drew from his study. The transition from a life primarily oriented toward parents to one that is more oriented toward peers undoubtedly occurs, but evidence from the present study indicates that the teenage group is in some respects no more estranged from adults than the pre-teenage group and that standards set in the family may *not* have been replaced by peer group standards in the high school context to the degree that Coleman implied.

When Coleman's methods and interpretations are inspected more closely, it appears that 1) some of his results may be artifacts of the way he phrased his questions and 2) other interpretations can account for certain of his findings as logically as his.

Coleman asked adolescents whether they would be more disturbed by their parents' disapproval or by breaking with their closest friend. He interpreted *disapproval* as the emotional equivalent of *breaking*. Such an equation is questionable. And before we may accept Coleman's conclusion, that his respondents' answers revealed a distinct adolescent subculture, it must be demonstrated that pre-adolescents would answer the questions in a significantly different manner.

In addition, the manner in which Coleman gathered data about the perceived desirability of going into father's occupation, as well as the way in which he interpreted these findings, leave some doubt as to whether his data give substantial support to his thesis.

To challenge the adequacy of Coleman's approach, the present writer asked 619 preadolescent and 159 adolescent pupils a series of questions that conveyed Coleman's apparent intention in a form that seemed more appropriate. The responses to these questions indicate that a conceptual model for adolescent behavior ought to provide adequately for the adolescent's attachment to the adult culture.

CONCERN OVER THE DISAPPROVAL OF OTHERS

Coleman's data show that about 43 per cent of secondary school students say that *breaking* with a friend would be harder to take than being *disapproved* by either their parents or their favorite teacher. These data were presented to support the emergence of an adolescent subculture in industrial society. But one could question the emotional equivalence of *disapproval* by either parents or teacher and *breaking* with one's closest friend. Parent and teacher disapproval are undoubtedly frequent in the life of a young person, whereas a break with his closest friend is probably less frequent, involving a much greater psychological investment on the part of the student. The alternative posed by Coleman may have contributed to the large number who selected breaking with one's peers as having more serious consequences for them.[5]

To overcome this apparent weakness the following question was constructed: "Which one of these things would make you the most unhappy?" (a) If my parents did not like what I did, (b) If my (favorite) teacher did not like what I did, (c) If my best friend did not like what I did.[6] Table 1 compares the responses to this question with the distribution obtained by Coleman.

The differences between the two samples are quite marked. The answers to Coleman's questions favored the hypothesis that a distinct subculture has emerged, while my data show that over 80 per cent of the sample said it would make them most unhappy if their parents did not like what they did.

In view of Brittain's findings [7] about the situation-specific nature of adolescent conformity, the absence of a specific decision in my more generalized question might have contributed to the differences reported in Table 24–1. Or, it might be argued that the preponderance of students choosing parental disapproval as making them most unhappy represents a general predisposition to respond to parental wishes especially in new and indeterminant situations where the student has no cues to guide him. This interpretation supports Brittain's conclusions without requiring complete rejection of Coleman's findings.

Since children begin their lives very much integrated into the family group and remain closely linked to it during their childhood, one might expect, under the hypothesis that there is a distinct adolescent subculture, a decided difference between elementary and secondary school pupils in the degree to which they are concerned over the disapproval of their parents. Using the generalized question, however, there is no evidence that secon-

[5] Coleman's question asked which would be the hardest to take: 1. parent disapproval, 2. teacher disapproval, 3. breaking with a friend. This question followed three others, asking whether they would join a club in school if 1. their parents didn't approve, 2. parents approved but favorite teacher didn't, 3. parents and teacher approved but joining would mean breaking with closest friend.

[6] The phrase "like what I did" could have been interpreted as referring to a vocational choice in the context of the other questions. This possibility was checked with a sample of the subjects, and the question seemed to have a more generalized meaning to most subjects. With any general question, however, proximal stimuli potentially provide a set for the respondent. This weakness in the question should not call for a revision in the conclusions drawn. Whatever the student meant by "what I did," he was more concerned with the approval of his parents than with the approval of his peers.

[7] Brittain, op. cit.

Table 24–1 Others: Epperson Data Contrasted with Coleman Data[a]

Evaluating Agent	Boys		Girls	
	Epperson[b]	Coleman[c]	Epperson[b]	Coleman[c]
	%	%	%	%
Parent	80.4	53.8	80.5	52.9
Teacher	3.6	3.5	1.2	2.7
Best friend	15.8	42.7	18.1	43.4
Number of cases (excluding non-responses)	82	3,621	77	3,894

[a] Coleman, *op. cit.*, p. 5.
[b] This sample, drawn from a comprehensive high school of 2,200 in a medium size city (pop. 60,000), is approximately 50% 10th graders, 42% 11th graders, and 8% 12th graders.
[c] This sample includes students from all ten of Coleman's schools, representing small-town, rural, city and suburban high schools with enrollments ranging from 150 to 1950.

dary pupils are less concerned over parental disapproval than elementary school pupils. Table 24–2 contrasts the responses of 3rd, 4th, 5th, and 6th grade pupils with the responses of 10th, 11th, and 12th graders. Since there were no significant differences among grades at either the elementary or pared as a group with the elementary grades.

Table 24–2 Others: Epperson Elementary School Data
Contrasted with Epperson Secondary School Data

Evaluating Agent	Boys		Girls	
	Elementary	Secondary	Elementary	Secondary
	%	%	%	%
Parent	73.1	80.4	75.8	80.5
Teacher	8.9	3.6	9.2	1.2
Best friend	17.9	15.8	14.9	18.1
Number of cases (excluding non-responses)	312	82	302	77

Secondary school pupils appear to be more, rather than less concerned about parental reactions.[8] The elementary school pupils, however, appear to be more concerned over their teachers' disapproval, possibly because

[8] This small difference may be accounted for by the secondary school pupils' higher socio-economic level as approximated by father's occupation. Fifty-three per cent of the secondary school sample were from white-collar homes in contrast to 40 per cent of the elementary school sample. In addition the secondary school questions were presented in a context that differed in two ways from the elementary school context: there were fewer questions and the questions were in a different order.

Issues in Peer Relations

they spend more time with teachers than secondary school pupils spend with even their favorite teachers. Since opportunities for loyalties to develop are significantly different, these data provide no basis for saying that secondary school pupils are more estranged from the adult culture.

DESIRE TO FOLLOW FATHER'S OCCUPATION

Coleman's data show that boys infrequently choose to follow their father's occupations. He interpreted this finding as support for his argument that a separate subculture has emerged, assuming that: 1. his data represent a valid assessment, 2. not choosing to follow one's father's occupation evinces rejection of adult cultural values, and 3. this rejection of the father's occupation is a phenomenon that did not exist during childhood, but newly arises at adolescence. Let us inspect the validity of these assumptions.

Coleman asked students to specify their father's occupations and also to indicate their own occupational preferences. Comparison of the two responses indicated whether the student desired to go into the same occupation as the father. This comparison was scored in an all or nothing fashion, that is, the student's choice had to be definitely the same. In the present study, the boy's degree of interest in going into his father's occupation was elicited by asking "When you grow up would you like to do the same kind of work that your father does?" The pupils selected one of the following alternatives: Yes, Maybe, I don't think so, No. Table 24–3 contrasts Coleman's findings with the present ones.

Table 24–3 Occupational Preferences of Secondary School Boys by Type of Father's Occupation: Epperson Data Contrasted with Coleman Data[a]

Boy's Occupational Preference	Epperson Father's Occupation		Coleman Father's Occupation
	Blue Collar	White Collar	White and Blue Collar
	%	%	%
Same occupation	35.7	28.9	9.8
Different occupation	64.3	71.1	90.2
Number of cases (excluding non-responses)	42	38	2,177

[a] Coleman, op. cit., p. 7. These data represent his sample from city and suburban schools. His small-town sample was not included for comparison because it does not approximate my medium-size city sample.

Conceivably, the difference in the method of assessing the student's desire to go into his father's occupation accounts for the difference between the two samples. All students who said "Yes" (3.6 per cent) or "Maybe" (27.4 per cent) when asked whether they wanted to go into their fathers' occupations were grouped together for comparison with Coleman's results, as were all those who answered "I don't think so" (15.5 per cent) and "No" (53.6 per cent).

However one chooses to view the data from both studies, they show that a large number of adolescent boys do not want to do the same kind of work their fathers do. This could be interpreted as an indicator of adolescent estrangement from the adult culture, but other interpretations seem equally plausible. It is possible that the students prefer a different occupation because they have internalized aspirations to upward mobility from their parents and hence prefer jobs with higher status than the kind of work their fathers do. The present data do not permit evaluating this possibility.

An analysis of the elementary data suggests still other explanations of Coleman's occupational choice findings. Comparison of the elementary school data with the secondary school data in Table 24–4 reveals a trend toward less desire to follow one's father among the secondary school pupils.

Table 24–4 Occupational Preferences of Elementary and Secondary Boys: Epperson Elementary and Secondary Data Contrasted

Desire to Follow Father's Occupation	Elementary	Secondary
	%	%
Yes	25.8	3.6
Maybe	27.8	27.4
I don't think so	12.9	15.5
No	33.4	53.6
Number of cases (excluding non-responses)	302	84

This shift may or may not reflect the emergence of a distinct adolescent subculture. It could be argued that as the child grows older he confronts more directly the realities of the requirements and relative status of jobs; hence he is more likely to make a realistic appraisal of the kind of work for which he will be best suited. This factor alone could account for the differences between the elementary and secondary school groups.

Occupational choice must be analyzed in relation to both the occupational structure of society and the social-psychological processes of aspiration setting. Factors such as the changing balance of occupational roles, the visibility of alternative occupations, the frequency with which the pupil interacts with his parents, the socioeconomic status of parents, and the achievement level of the pupil must be considered in any effort to understand the significance of occupational choice. Before occupational choice can be admitted as evidence for the existence of an adolescent subculture, the role of these variables in setting occupational goals should be empirically assessed. In view of the complexity of the phenomenon, it is doubtful that any measure of desire to follow father's occupation, no matter how well constructed, can be interpreted as a reliable index of decreasing parental influence. Even if one admits lack of desire to follow father's occupation as evidence of decreasing parental influence, the present findings suggest that Coleman's index has serious limitations.

SUMMARY

The data reported in this study require a reassessment of potential indices of the emergence of an adolescent subculture. No observer of adolescent behavior could deny Coleman's suggestion that the adolescent child is not as closely related to his family as he was earlier or that today's adolescent is less involved in family life than the adolescent of generations past. But one may ask whether it is useful or appropriate to think of adolescents as comprising distinct social systems without taking account of both the student's attachment to his family and, as Brittain has suggested, the nature of the decision-making situation. Coleman's work has drawn attention to the importance of the teenage peer culture in adolescent behavior, but we still need a conceptual scheme that takes into consideration the multiple loyalties of the teenager and the relation of these loyalties to specific situations.

25
Ernest A. Smith

CHARACTERISTICS OF AMERICAN YOUTH CULTURE

Smith argues that youth have a distinctive culture and describes its major characteristics. He shows how adult norms relate to those in the youth culture. Also, adult attitudes toward various youth practices, including petting and courtship, are examined. Smith pays special attention to conformity and secrecy as fundamental aspects of the youth culture.

. . . Informal and intimate relations of course—whether of youth or adult culture—appear in all societies. This aspect of youth culture is a universal phenomenon. The emphasis in this analysis is that, whether or not its characteristics are universal, youth culture in America is distinguishable from adult culture.

One of the characteristics that seem to be universal is the tendency for all members of all age-sex categories above the infant level to develop solidarity and conceal behavior from other age-sex levels (Linton, 1936, p. 590).

Solidarity and concealment of behavior, therefore, may be viewed as universal characteristics of youth culture. Simmel asserts that the principle of secrecy, implicit in concealment of behavior, is a universal sociological form appearing in youths in all cultures, subcultures, and groups within a culture (Simmel, 1906, pp. 462–463).

The universality of secrecy suggests that in various cultures youth will manifest varying degrees of withdrawal from adult socializing institutions. This implies a degree of withdrawal of association and confidences from adults, and consequent obstacles to communication between youth and adults. The activities and interactions of youth will be hidden behind a veil of secrecy erected to escape the supervision and control of adults.

Although the peer associations of youth may largely evade adult control, there are several pervasive areas within which youth behavior is patterned by adult norms and institutions. The broadest areas, involving political, religious, property, and linguistic systems, need only be noted.

Adult cultures will pattern youth behavior in status associations, which are a by-product of the ascribed family position. Sex-typing, which influences hair and dress styles, as well as posture, gait, and voice tone, is also a general factor. Implicit in this is the conditioning toward hetero-sexual relations, which, in our culture, is codified in monogamy, romantic love, and the glamour role of the female. The universality of familial sex controls, as evidenced by sex and incest taboos, appears here (Murdock, 1949, Table 1, p. 12; pp. 284–285).

All of the behavior areas mentioned set limits to approved youth behavior. The standards are mediated through the adult socializing institutions, and the effectiveness of this mediation varies from culture to culture. Some of the factors influencing the degree of effectiveness revolve around both the age of initiation into adult status-roles, and the degree of withdrawal from adult associations, as well as the impediments to communication between youth and adults. Also involved is the degree of integration, opposition, or conflict of youth and adult norms and institutions.

In order to compare the relative effectiveness of adult socializing institutions, it is necessary to make cross-cultural studies. This is beyond the scope of this book, which is limited to American youth. The characteristics of contemporary American civilization are, however, sufficiently distinctive to merit a general assumption that the norms, institutions, and behavior of American youth are sufficiently distinctive to set them off from the youth culture of other societies. In other words, in contrast to the universal characteristics that appear in all youth cultures, there seem to be certain variable characteristics that mark and set off American youth culture from other youth cultures as well as the American adult culture. In this study, "youth culture," both as a term and as a subject for analysis, will be limited largely to youth who are American, white, urban, middle-class, and post-pubertal, not yet fulfilling adult roles. Occasionally, contrasting class and sex patterns will be introduced for purposes of comparison and differentiation. Where this is done, they will be so identified.

Characteristics Distinctive of American Youth Culture

As has been pointed out, there are certain values and behavior patterns in youth culture, such as religion and politics, which are patterned by adult culture. Mead places these within the realm of "ultimate values," or communal norms governing formal morality and family life (Mead, 1943, p. 597). There are also certain values and behavior patterns in American youth culture which are modifications or adaptations of adult values and behavior, and to this extent they appear as distinctive characteristics. Mead calls these "immediate values," dealing with peer behavior, appearance, and dress (Mead, 1943, p. 597). These characteristics are found to be sufficiently well defined to justify dealing with American youth culture as a distinct subculture within the context of American society.

The youth norms and behavior patterned by the adult culture first appear in connection with political democracy and the Judeo-Christian religious tradition. These norms, in addition to the economic norms of private property and occupational aspirations, are transmitted mainly through the adult socializing institutions of the family, school, and church. As these norms are pertinent mainly to adult institutions, they do not provide a dominant focus in youth culture. One exception is found in the norms of competition and individual success, norms that are emphasized in the adult culture and are reflected in youth culture by dominating the dating pattern (Waller, 1937, p. 731). In view of the fact that the school and church are socializing institutions dominated by adults, and not constituting an integral part of the informal institutions of American youth culture, their treatment in this survey is minimal.

Another set of adult norms is mediated to the members of youth culture through the parental family, which is an institution of adult culture. The parental family acts as a primary field of socialization as well as the source of continuous material subsistence for youth. It also provides an enduring frame for youth relations and virtually inalienable affectional ties with its members.

The parental family also ascribes social class position to its youth—a factor that influences their peer associations as well as their educational aspirations and achievements. Although the relations between young people are class-selective, youth modify these adult norms by muting economic differences and covering a wide class-spread in their associations.

Probably the most important area within which adult norms attempt to dominate youth behavior is that of sex—particularly in regard to sex-typing, sex taboos, and hetero-sexual relations. Much of the secrecy and concealment connected with youth culture appears to protect youth from adult sanctions, where their sex behavior violates adult norms.

The norms of sex-typing and sex taboos are initiated during the primary period of socialization in the parental family. This infancy period precedes the appearance of youth culture. With the maturation of youth, these norms are reinforced by youth culture. The institutions of youth culture, therefore, strengthen the adult-initiated sex differences in the realm of clothing styles, hairdress, posture, and gait, as well as vocabulary, voice tone, and pitch. The monosexual youth clique is an important institution in the differential patterning of behavior and emotions of the two sexes (Mead, 1949, pp. 278–279).

The adult sex taboo on premarital sex relations is also reinforced in youth culture, particularly for middle-class youth. Youth are taught by

adults to believe that all sex is wicked, but youth approve various deviations
and conceal them from adults. Petting is one of these approved deviations,
a pattern that will be discussed later. By means of the petting pattern, youth
maintain the taboo against premarital relations during the dating period
(Christensen, 1950, p. 226). The commitment relations of older youth, on
the other hand, permit a gradual relaxation of this taboo, although this, too,
is disapproved by adults.

A broader area of sex behavior within which youth behavior is patterned by adult norms is the emphasis upon couple relationships in the
compulsive context of romantic love. Romantic love, and the glamour pattern
that preoccupies American girls and fills the reverie of their boy friends, are
pervasive norms greatly enhanced by youth culture.

YOUTH CULTURE AS A
DISTINCT CULTURE

The main theme of this survey, that there exists in America a distinct
youth culture, is supported by the fact that many of the characteristics that
distinguish a culture are to be found in youth culture. Elkin and Westley,
after making a study of twenty boys· in a privileged Montreal suburb, attacked the notion of a distinctive youth culture. If most of the activities of
these youth are approved and directed by adults, it shows only that the characteristics of youth culture are much less clearly revealed in a Canadian
suburb than in American communities (refer: Westley, 1955, p. 680, and
p. 249). Coleman, in contrast, asserts not only that do most students of
adolescent behavior agree on the existence of an adolescent subculture,
but also that his study of over 8,000 American youth indicates that youth
culture is becoming stronger in modern middle-class suburbia (Coleman,
1961, p. 3). Youth culture enforces a conformity upon its members, which
is intensified by the withdrawal of youth from adult socializing institutions
(Eisenstadt, 1955, p. 305) and by the resulting secrecy, which acts as an
obstacle to the supervision and control of adults over youth activities.
From this secrecy, there arises the series of conflicts between youth culture
and adult culture that is characteristic of American society.

Youth Culture Norms

Youth culture has been shown to dominate youth behavior in those
areas most seminal to peer relations and appearance. Youth culture initiates
and perpetuates norms that pre-empt the loyalty of youth and pattern their
sentiments and behavior, particularly in relation to sex activities. Youth culture teaches and approves norms of sexual intimacy that are tabooed by

adult norms. In effect, this youth-approved behavior significantly modifies the formal adult norms. An important example is that of petting, which involves a degree of sexual intimacy tabooed by adult norms. Most parents and other adults disapprove of petting (Folsom, 1943, p. 548), yet it is a widespread activity in the dating and courtship of middle-class youth.

Such aspects of the youth culture are judged by adult norms to be undesirable and destructive, and are rejected by formal adult society (Davis, 1944, p. 14). In several instances, however, such as in dating and courtship, adults encourage and aid youth, while exercising minimal supervision and control over these activities.

The date, a major institution of youth culture, has been initiated and perpetuated by youth, who elaborate norms and sentiments independent of, and even conflicting with, adult norms (Waller, 1937, p. 728). The incompatibility of competitive date norms with marital norms is so great that the more successful youth are in dating, the less prepared they may be for marital adjustment (Taylor, 1946, p. 68).

The socially proscribed adult sex norms include premarital chastity, marriage, mutual affectional commitment focused on romantic love and children. In contrast, the norms of the competitive-date phase of youth culture emphasize concurrent or sequential dating partners, no mutual affectional commitment, mutual exploitation, and petting as a sexual release (Waller, 1938, p. 230).

There are of course regions and communities, or ethnic and class groups, where the competitive-date phase is brief or even is bypassed. Yet the evidence available on middle-class urban youth indicates that this phase is conventional, if not actually universal, among American middle-class youth. Williams' study shows that parents often do not understand this aspect of the dating situation (Williams, 1949, Table 3, p. 28), and are therefore unable to give youth guidance and training in dating behavior. Where parents do attempt to intrude, youth of both sexes attempt to evade their supervision by not talking about and concealing dating behavior.

There may, indeed, be adults who project the dating and petting behavior of their own youth culture experience into the marital period. These patterns, of course, violate family norms, lead to tension and discord, and may result in the breakup of the marriage.

Petting in the date is particularly subject to adult censure because it violates modesty and threatens the taboo against premarital intimacy. In consequence, petting is carried on by youth only in secrecy (Hollingshead, 1949, pp. 288–289). This is maintained both by silence about such behavior and by avoiding adult observation. The automobile is particularly useful in giving this necessary privacy, mobility, and anonymity to dating couples.

Current courtship and engagement behavior, characteristic of youth culture, are incompatible with the adult tradition—which has become largely obsolete. Courtship permits a series of progressive intimacies through petting, and engagement gives tacit approval to premarital relations, both of which threaten or violate the adult sex taboos. Adult institutions no longer dominate courtship and engagement, as couples withdraw from both family and friends into a relatively autonomous relationship (Waller, 1938, p. 273).

The clique, another major institution of youth culture, sets norms that are often the highest authority for its members and may take precedence over both family and other adult norms. It is a fundamental sentiment-binding group, its relationships being based on norms and strong affectional ties among its members. The clique, then, acts as a protective structure, which may oppose and evade adult authorities and sanctions (Zachry, 1940, pp. 281, 346–347). Cliques will, in fact, discipline youth who accept or practice disapproved adult norms (Demerath, 1943, p. 517).

This opposition to adult norms results in deviations from adult-approved behavior (Warner, 1940, p. 187). Such opposition is directed against adults in positions of authority, such as parents, teachers, and police. In cases of extreme conflict, the group most effective in applying sanctions will dominate. Lower-class youth norms, for example, dominate gang youth in slum areas, for such youth have superficial involvement in middle-class norms and institutions. Gang youth emphasize and enforce antagonism towards parents, school, police, and law, as well as other middle-class institutions (Shaw, 1931, p. 76-n).

Youth Culture Conformity

A basic characteristic of a culture is that it forces the individual into conformity, so that most of its members think, act, and believe largely in accordance with its norms. In a complex society, such as America, this conformity may be patterned by a subculture possessing its own norms.

A fundamental evidence of the existence of youth culture is the compulsive conformity required of its members (Pearson, 1958, p. 88). Talcott Parsons states that one of the most basic needs of members of youth culture is to be accepted and identified with given youth groups. This acceptance requires rigid patterning of behavior (Parsons, 1949, b, pp. 196–197). This rigorous youth conformity may in turn be preparatory to the compulsive conformity found on the adult level, which Riesman states is becoming characteristic of modern America (Riesman, 1950, passim).

This emphasis on rigid conformity is linked, in one aspect, to emotional insecurity. One analysis of college-girl dress styles reveals the domination of mass standards of dress and behavior in an attempt to ameliorate the insecurity and lack of confidence arising from the exaggerated competition of campus life (Blake, 1946, p. 23). Linked to this is the pressure from advertisers and manufacturers, which highlights the seasonally changing styles for young people. . . . Mass standards are enforced by the ruthless application of informal sanctions common to all cultures—mainly teasing, ridicule, and even ostracism.

Tests made by Havighurst and Taba show that adolescents fear and shun the holding of positions deviant to those of their peer groups (Havighurst and Taba, 1949, p. 87). If the youth norms diverge from adult norms, conformity will be away from adult patterns and toward peer-group behavior. Clothing, for example, is a conventional symbol of social class membership, yet teenage styles minimize class standards and maximize conformity to peer styles (Silverman, 1945, p. 117). . . .

REFERENCES

"A Caste, A Culture, A Market 1," *New Yorker* (November 29, 1958), p. 73.

Patricia Blake, "Why College Girls Dress that Way," *New York Times Magazine Section* (April 7, 1946), p. 23.

Harold T. Christensen, *Marriage Analysis* (New York: The Ronald Press Co., 1950), p. 226.

James S. Coleman, *The Adolescent Society* (New York: Free Press of Glencoe, 1961), p. 3.

Kingsley Davis, "Adolescence and the Social Structure," *Annals of the American Academy of Political and Social Science,* Vol. 236 (November 1944), p. 14.

N. J. Demerth, "Adolescent Status Demands and Student Experiences of Twenty Schizophrenics," *American Sociological Review,* Vol. 8 (October 1943), p. 517.

Joseph Kirk Folsom, *The Family and Democratic Society* (New York: John Wiley & Sons, Inc., 1943), p. 548.

Robert J. Havighurst and Hilda Taba, *Adolescent Character and Personality* (New York: John Wiley & Sons, Inc., 1949), p. 87.

August B. Hollingshead, *Elmtown's Youth* (New York: John Wiley & Sons, Inc., 1949), pp. 288–289.

Ralph Linton, *The Study of Man: An Introduction* (New York: D. Appleton-Century Co., Inc., 1936), p. 590.

Margaret Mead, "Problems of a Wartime Society—The Cultural Picture," *American Journal of Orthopsychiatry,* Vol. 13 (October 1943), p. 597.

Margaret Mead, *Male and Female* (New York: William Morrow and Co., 1949, a), pp. 278–279.

George P. Murdock, *Social Structure* (New York: The Macmillan Co., 1949), pp. 284–285.

Talcott Parsons, "The Social Structure of the Family," *The Family: Its Function and Destiny,* edited by Ruth Nanda Anshen (New York: Harper and Brothers, 1949, b), pp. 196–197.

Gerald H. J. Pearson, *Adolescence and the Conflict of Generations* (New York: W. W. Norton and Co., 1958), p. 88.

David Riesman, *The Lonely Crowd: A Study of the Changing American Character* (New Haven: Yale University Press, 1950).

Clifford R. Shaw, *The Natural History of a Delinquent Career* (Chicago: The University of Chicago Press, 1931), p. 76.

Sylvia Susan Silverman, *Clothing and Appearance: Their Psychological Implications for Teen-Age Girls* (New York: Bureau of Publications, Teachers College, Columbia University, 1945), p. 117.

Georg Simmel, "The Sociology of Secrecy and of Secret Societies," *American Journal of Sociology,* Vol. 11 (January 1906), pp. 461–463.

Donald C. Taylor, "Courtship as a Social Institution in the United States, 1930 to 1945," *Social Forces,* Vol. 25 (October 1946), p. 68.

Willard Waller, "The Rating and Dating Complex," *American Sociological Review,* Vol. 2 (October 1937), p. 731.

Willard Waller, *op. cit.,* p. 728.

Willard Waller, *The Family: A Dynamic Interpretation* (New York: The Dryden Press, 1938), p. 230.

Willard Waller, *op. cit.,* p. 273.

Melvin J. Williams, "Personal and Familial Problems of High School Youths and Their Bearing Upon Family Education Needs," *Social Forces,* Vol. 27 (March 1949), p. 28.

Caroline B. Zachry, *Emotion and Conduct in Adolescence* (New York: D. Appleton-Century Co., Inc., 1940), pp. 281, 346–347.

26

Eldon E. Snyder *

SOCIOECONOMIC VARIATIONS, VALUES, AND SOCIAL PARTICIPATION AMONG HIGH SCHOOL STUDENTS

Two contrasting points of view are presented in the sociological literature regarding a youth subculture. One view is that the youth subculture is a reflection of the larger society. A second view is that the youth subculture is distinct from the adult society and has separate norms which emphasize fun, popularity, and conformity. The position taken in this paper is that a youth subculture does exist, but it has several different dimensions and is not characterized by conformity in values and behavior. This position is supported by socio-economic variations, values, social participation, and sexual differences which were studied among high school students.

In the literature dealing with the sociology of adolescence there are two contrasting points of view regarding the presence of a youth subculture, in which context subculture refers to values and behavior that differ from those of the adult society.[1] The first view is that adolescents constitute a subculture that emphasizes conformity in the peer group and values that are contrary to adult values. The adolescent subculture is centered within the high school and constitutes a "small society, one that has most of its important interactions *within* itself, and maintains only a few threads of connection with the outside adult society." [2]

The second view is best characterized by Frederick Elkin and William Westley, who studied forty middle class youth in suburban Montreal. Elkin

From Eldon E. Snyder, "Socioeconomic Variations, Values, and Social Participation Among High School Students," *Journal of Marriage and the Family,* Vol. 28, No. 2 (May 1966), pp. 174–176. Reprinted by permission.

* Eldon E. Snyder, Ed.D., Associate Professor of Sociology, Bowling Green State University, Bowling Green, Ohio.

[1] See David Gottlieb and Charles Ramsey, *The American Adolescent,* Homewood, Ill.: The Dorsey Press, 1964, pp. 29–33.

[2] James S. Coleman, *The Adolescent Society,* Glencoe, Ill.: The Free Press, 1961, p. 3 (author's italics). See also Talcott Parsons, "Age and Sex in the Social Structure of the United States," *American Sociological Review,* 7 (October, 1942), pp. 604–616.

and Westley conclude that the youth in their study do not reject values; thus, they challenge the youth subculture notion.[3]

The issue of a youth subculture is probably not as clear-cut as these two polarized points of view would suggest. A third alternative regarding a youth subculture might be the most feasible position, given the regional, social class, and ethnic differences to be found with all theories. This writer's position is an eclectic approach that rests somewhere between the two extremes outlined above. As with most social phenomena, the youth subculture, upon closer scrutiny, has more layers of reality than the first observations suggest. Certainly, adolescents do interact together under circumstances that result in the development of norms, dress, and language that vary somewhat from the adult society. No doubt some adolescent differences are a reflection of the psychophysical and role changes that take place during the adolescent period in modern urban societies.[4] On the other hand, adolescent values are often merely distortions of adult values. The characterization of adolescent values that stresses fun, popularity, and conformity also represents a significant segment of the adult society. Even the teenage daughter's style of dress and language are often diffused into the adult society by her middle-aged mother.

Thus far the two extreme positions have tended to be reductionistic. The diversity and heterogeneity that exists among adolescents have been largely ignored because several important sociological concepts have not been utilized. This paper is not designed specifically as a refutation of the Elkin-Westley thesis. The predominance of opinions by sociologists seems to be in favor of accepting the notion of some form of distinct youth subculture.[5] However, the position taken by the writer is to promote the eclectic thesis by pointing out several additional factors that suggest greater diversity among adolescents than is frequently recognized by those who wholeheartedly accept the youth subculture thesis.

SAMPLE

Data were collected on 592 sophomore and junior students attending the only high school in a midwestern community of 38,000 population. The community is diversified, having education, agriculture, and light industry represented. The student population would be representative of many similar communities in the Midwest. The sample included all usable questionnaires collected from students in the sophomore and junior classes who

[3] Frederick Elkin and William A. Westley, "The Myth of Adolescent Culture," *American Sociological Review*, 20 (December, 1955), pp. 680–684.

[4] Observers have noted youth subcultural similarities in England and Europe; see John Barron Mays, "Teen-Age Culture in Contemporary Britain," *The Annals*, 338 (November, 1961), pp. 22–32.

[5] Gottlieb and Ramsey, *op. cit.,* p. 32.

were present when the questionnaire was administered. Information was gathered regarding student values, social participation, social class, and sex. Social participation was determined by combining the degree of involvement and the prestige of the activity of organization within the school culture. A modification of Chapin's Social Participation Scale was used in this analysis.[6] Students were divided into high and low social participation groups using the median social participation score as the dividing point. Socioeconomic status was determined by using father's occupation and subdivided into three categories—upper, middle, and lower statuses.

FINDINGS

Socioeconomic Status, Social Participation, and Sexual Differences

Studies have well documented the relationship between socioeconomic status and student social participation in formal activities of the school.[7] In the present study this relationship was highly significant for the girls beyond the .001 probability level, the upper and middle socioeconomic statuses showing high social participation. The boys at all status levels participated less in school activities than girls; and for them, the association between socioeconomic status and social participation was significant at the .05 level of confidence in the expected direction.

Socioeconomic Status, Student Values, and Sexual Differences

In studying student values a central question used by Coleman was employed.[8] Students were asked the following question: "If you could be remembered at your high school for one of the three things below, which one would you want it to be?" Boys were given the alternatives of brilliant student, most popular, or athletic star; girls, the choices of brilliant student, most popular, or leader in extra-curricular activities. The percentage of responses (Table 26–1) to these three images approximates the responses Coleman received in his study except that Coleman's research showed a higher total response by boys who wish to be remembered as athletic stars.

[6] F. Stuart Chapin, *Experimental Designs in Sociological Research,* New York: Harper Brothers, 1955, pp. 276–278.

[7] Note August B. Hollingshead, *Elmtown's Youth,* New York: John Wiley and Sons, 1949; W. Lloyd Warner, Robert J. Havinghurst, and Martin B. Loeb, *Who Shall Be Educated?* New York: Harper Brothers, 1944; Hilda Taba, *School Culture,* Washington, D.C.: American Council on Education, 1955.

[8] Coleman, *op. cit.,* p. 28.

Table 26-1 Relationship Between Socioeconomic Status, Student Values, and Sexual Differences

Socio-economic Status	Boys' Values			Girls' Values			Boys' and Girls' Values		
	Brilliant Student	Most Popular	Athletic Star	Brilliant Student	Most Popular	Activities Leader	Brilliant Student	Most Popular	Activities Leader–Athletic Star
Upper	28	26	22	22	38	31	50	64	53
Middle	54	52	43	54	57	48	108	109	91
Lower	14	20	21	14	29	19	28	49	40
Total	96 (34.2)*	98 (34.8)	86 (30.6)	90 (25.5)	124 (39.5)	98 (31.2)	186 (31.3)	222 (37.4)	184 (30.9)
	Males Total N = 280			Females Total N = 312			Total N = 592		
	$x^2 = 2.84$; P = N.S.			$x^2 = 4.73$; P = N.S.			$x^2 = 5.12$; P = N.S.		

*Figures in parentheses indicate the total percent of boys or girls in each column.

The responses by 3,696 adolescents in the first interview by Coleman were as follows: boys—brilliant student, 31 per cent; athletic star, 43.6 per cent; most popular, 26 per cent; girls—brilliant student, 28.8 per cent; leader in activities, 36.1 per cent; most popular, 35.2 per cent.[9]

The present study provides the additional analysis of student values by socioeconomic status. The student values do not show a significant relationship with socioeconomic status. The responses to value orientations seem to cut across status levels. This lack of relationship between social class and values is contrary to the theoretical expectation. However, Ralph Turner has pointed out that frequently such relationships in the past have been quite modest; furthermore, recent studies of child-rearing practices reveal less class difference than was previously supposed.[10] Apparently the three value images in the high school studied cut across socioeconomic lines and thus provide an additional dimension of heterogeneity apart from socioeconomic status within the youth subculture. Also youth probably differ in the degree to which they feel a value has relevance to them.

Student Values, Social Participation, and Sexual Differences

The analyses thus far have indicated a significant positive relationship between socioeconomic status and social participation and a lack of association between socioeconomic status and student responses to selected student values. When student values and social participation were studied, a statistically significant relationship beyond the .001 level prevailed for the girls. Those girls who preferred to be remembered as popular and leaders in activities were high in social participation. The analysis of the same variables among the boys indicated no relationship between those who preferred to be remembered as brilliant students, popular, or star athletes and their degree of social participation in school activities.

These differences between the boys and girls of the high school in student values and social participation suggest that another and perhaps the most obvious source of heterogeneity within the youth culture is a sexual differentiation. Apparently there is a difference between the sexes in their value orientation toward scholarship, popularity, and school activities as this orientation relates to social participation in the school.

SUMMARY AND CONCLUSIONS

Previous studies of adolescents have tended to embrace the notion that the youth subculture is a reflection of the adult society or the more popular position, that this subculture is largely separated from the adult society in

[9] *Ibid.*, p. 30.
[10] Ralph H. Turner, *The Social Context of Ambition*, San Francisco, Chandler Publishing, 1964, pp. 213–214.

values, behavior, and overall social interaction. The position taken in this paper is that an intermediate position is probably a closer representation of reality in most Midwestern communities.

Upon close scrutiny of adolescent interaction within the high school studied by this writer, there was a considerable degree of segmentation within the student subculture. The diversity might be summarized as follows:

1. Socioeconomic differences are well-documented within school environments. The amount and kind of social participation is usually found to be associated with socioeconomic status. The present study noted a similar relationship.

2. The values that students aspire to achieve in regard to scholarship, popularity, and athletic and other extracurricular activities in this study did not show significant socioeconomic differences. Apparently the value structure cuts across some of the socioeconomic categories. Additional questions might be raised, however, regarding differences in the relevance of values to one's behavior. Such differences might be based on socioeconomic, sexual, ethnic, or other factors.

3. When student responses to values were compared with social participation, the girls who showed a desire to be remembered as popular and leaders in activities ranked high in social participation. The same relationship did not hold true for the boys.

The term *youth subculture* is probably justified in analyzing the behavior and values of adolescents. However, the youth subculture cannot be characterized by internal solidarity and conformity. The high school students studied by this writer revealed a heterogeneity within the subculture that reflected variations of socioeconomic status values, social participation, and sex. A more rigorous analysis of these and other sociological variables probably would divulge additional variations within the adolescent subculture.

ADDITIONAL READINGS

Berger, Bennett M. On the youthfulness of youth cultures. *Social Research,* Autumn 1963, **30,** 319–342. Berger describes various kinds of teen cultures and the basic characteristics of each. He contrasts young people who engage in frivolous and antisocial activities with those actually preparing for adulthood, such as the Boy Scouts or the Future Farmers of America.

Bernard, Jessie. Teen-age culture: An overview. In Jessie Bernard (Ed.), *Teen-Age Culture*. Philadelphia: The Annals of the American Academy of Political and Social Sciences, November 1961, **338**, 2–12. Bernard portrays the teen culture as a product of affluence. In the lower teens it is typically lower class, in the later teens upper-middle class. She describes both material and nonmaterial aspects of this culture, in terms of social class and age levels of the teen-age participants.

Blum, Lucille Hollander. The discothèque and the phenomenon of alone-togetherness: A study of the young person's response to the frug and comparable current dances. *Adolescence,* Winter 1966–67, **1** (4), 351–366. Findings in this study are related to adolescents' self-indulgence and impulse release. Blum concludes that the abandon experienced in such dances as the frug serves as a release for pent-up tension, which might otherwise take some undesirable form.

Burke, Ronald S. & Grinder, Robert E. Personality-oriented themes and listening patterns in teen-age music and their relation to certain academic and peer variables. *School Review,* Summer, 1966, 74 (2), 196–211.
A review of themes in teen-age music suggests that a relatively beneficient view of youth culture is justified. Perhaps youth's participation in youth culture reflects the attractiveness of that culture rather than a rebellion against the adult culture.

Parsons, Talcott. Youth in the context of American society. *Daedalus,* 1962, **91** (1), 97–123. Parsons first describes the American value pattern, then considers youth's position in the culture. Finally, he outlines significant characteristics of the current youth culture.

Schwartz, Gary & Merten, Don. The language of adolescence: An anthropological approach to the youth culture. *The American Journal of Sociology,* March 1967, **72** (5), 455–468. This paper portrays youth culture as a genuinely independent subculture. Adolescents' special social terminology provides them with their own "world view, life styles, and moral standards."

Sherif, M. & Sherif, G. W. *Reference groups.* New York: Harper & Row, 1964. The Sherifs observed adolescent boys in natural settings for a period of five to seven months. They identified factors associated with power in the group, conformity to group norms, and homogeneity of values.

XIII. Alienated Youth

The term "alienated youth" suggests youth who reject normal patterns of growing up in favor of atypical behaviors more congenial to their needs and temperament. Several major issues relate to alienated youth groups. What are they like? What is their effect on society and on the individuals who compose them? What should be done about them? What causes them to exist?

Various reasons have been suggested to explain them. For one thing, a small, static society is generally capable of providing for all its members; but a changing specialized society often generates social isolates.[1] Moreover, present-day society provides little opportunity for children's groups to learn how to get along with each other. Increasingly, children are finding it difficult to be together, as streets become hazardous and sidewalks disappear. Social activities, especially arranged for children, lose their spontaneous quality. Also, as society grows more complex, and population more dense, the government must exercise greater control over the compulsive life of its citizens, thus creating more repression and discontent. Those individuals who fail to fit neatly into the mold resent the restraints imposed by a conservative, middle-of-the-road majority. Moreover, youth are overwhelmed by bigness. Society is large-scale, and so are the forces that run it. Very few are granted active roles in decision-making, making the ordinary individual feel frustrated and helpless. The result may be withdrawal into mutually supporting groups. Finally, the schools do their part in producing alienation. Many teachers fail to respect the child's value system, or they may fail to bridge the gap between values of home and school. Moreover, children often fail to understand the schools' goals or how to attain them.[2]

Evaluations of alienated groups mirror the attitudes and personalities of their critics. A minority defend them, or at least explain them; and a smaller minority praise them, or at least certain things they represent. Adolescence, says Friedenberg, is not merely a physical process but a social process, whose fundamental task is establishing self-identification. A society that is hostile to clarity and vividness may undermine the process. We err in labelling as aberrant the fully human adolescent, who faces life with love and defiance. We treat our silent, alienated, or apathetic youth as

[1] Louis Goldman, "Varieties of Alienation and Educational Responses," *Teachers College Record,* Vol. 69, No. 4 (January 1968), pp. 331–339.
[2] Philip W. Jackson, "Alienation in the Classroom," *Psychology in the Schools,* Vol. 2, No. 4 (1965), pp. 299–308.

problems, an attitude which is unreal.[3] Raywid insists that behaviors of alienated youth often pose no danger for the community; on the contrary, they may constitute a healthy reaction against conformity. For instance, such groups may express their protest against society by symbolic acts, such as wearing long hair and deviant styles of clothing. How can schools that forbid independent ideas about hair, dress, and grooming succeed in encouraging unorthodox minds? If blind conformity is dangerous, should we not do what we can to *counteract* such tendencies, rather than formalizing group behaviors? [4]

Still others defend patterns of alienation as "natural." Youth need their fling; and youth is not youth without rebellion. The youthful rebel almost always settles down, and is the wiser for having sown his wild oats. Adverse criticism of such groups also reflects the critic. The conventional person is repelled by anything, however harmless, which is different. However, quite liberal critics may deplore much that is done in the name of individualism. Specific criticisms depend on the group under consideration. For example, Parkinson [5] appraises the Beatnik, so dubbed by San Francisco columnist Herb Caen. Beatnik life, says Parkinson, became "a nexus of jazz, Buddhism, homosexuality, drugs and squalor." It is not easy to estimate the importance of this "extra-official" mode of life. Is it "spindrift" or "the point of an iceberg," the emergence of resentment? Is it merely American Bohemia in a new garb? The true rebel, pursues Parkinson, does not merely protest the present order but suggests an ideal one. However, the Beats manifest little interest in modern society's major problems—fallout, population explosion, legal justice, civil rights—except when these problems somehow impinge on "printing books with taboo words, on problems of dope addicts cut off from their supply, or on rights of poets to slander policemen." Otherwise, they are "sardonic, apocalyptic, or impudent."

In several respects the Beatniks are not merely beat but also Bohemian. Both groups are rebels, not revolutionists. They loaf and feast their souls in some congenial atmosphere, manifesting an evasive rather than destructive attitude toward society. They possess the egotistic view of Christ-as-Beatnik, ranch house and pad, cocktails and marijuana. Essentially, Bohemians of succeeding decades are the same, and apparent differences are merely reflections of the times.

Bennett M. Berger describes another group, the hippies of America in the 1960's, and tells how they have adapted eight basic points of Bohemian doctrine, as outlined by Malcolm Cowley in *Exile's Return*.[6] The first is

[3] Edgar Z. Friedenberg, *The Vanishing Adolescent* (Boston, Beacon Press, 1959).

[4] Mary Anne Raywid, "The Great Haircut Crisis of Our Time," *Phi Delta Kappan,* Vol. 48 (December 1966), No. 4, p. 155.

[5] Thomas Parkinson, "Phenomenon or Generation," in Thomas Parkinson (Ed.), *A Case Book on the Beat* (New York, Crowell, 1961), pp. 276–290.

[6] Bennett M. Berger, "Hippie Morality—More Old than New," *Trans-Action,* Vol. 5, No. 3 (December 1967) pp. 19–26.

the idea of salvation by the child. The analogues are the hippies' innocence, flower power, and the educational revolution. The Bohemians' second idea, of self-expression, is identical with the hippies' moral injunction to "do your thing." The Bohemian idea of paganism is manifest in their overpowering eroticism—the baring of female flesh, the symbols of male strength (beards, boots and motorcycles). "The idea of living for the moment," is converted to "being super WOW where the action is in the NOW generation." Point five, the Bohemian's idea of liberty, is revealed in hippie movements to legalize marijuana and to render ecstacy respectable. The idea of female equality means, for the hippies, permitting equality in smoking, drinking, and love-making. Another point in Bohemian doctrine, the idea of psychological adjustment, is sought by hippies through yoga and LSD. The last point, the idea of changing place (they do better things in "you-name-it") emerges in the hippies' fascination by such places as Tahiti, Tangier, and Paris.

In the first selection, Dr. David Matza describes three major categories of alienated youth—radicals, bohemians, and delinquents. Rebellion, he holds, has always been a part of youth, and part of the subterranean tradition. In part of the article, deleted because of space limitations, Matza suggests that youth's alienation may be somewhat reduced by the current widespread adult tolerance and the waning of youthful frustrations. However, he advises a systematic arrangement for integrating youth's potential as an alternative to less healthy subterranean adaptations. Note that such an arrangement existed at *Summerhill,* described by A. S. Neill. This institution was committed to overcoming alienation in two ways: first through creating a permissive, though responsible educational environment, with minimal repression; and second to providing therapy for those who became hurt by too much repression.

The second article, by Gerald Pine, describes delinquents who do not simply evade society's dictates, or seek to change them, but violate them. By contrast, Bohemian-type groups typically register their protest inside, and sometimes on the fringe of, the law rather than outside it. The delinquent has been around a long time, and has inspired endless efforts dedicated to his cause and cure. What is new about him is this: his number has increased. Often he is affluent, and increasingly a suburban or small town dweller instead of the traditional slum dweller. Dr. Pine relates delinquency to such factors as affluence, social class, and social mobility.

27

David Matza

SUBTERRANEAN TRADITIONS OF YOUTH

*Tensions in American society have led to a variety of deviant patterns,
the three major forms being delinquency, radicalism, and Bohemianism. The
delinquency pattern is characterized by a spirit of adventure, disdain of work,
and aggression; radicalism by apocalyptic vision, and evangelism; Bohemianism
by romanticism, expressive authenticity, and monasticism. Only a small minority of youth participate in these "subterranean" patterns, but many more
are vulnerable.*

This essay attempted to describe features of rebellious youth during the
late '50s. With the development of a movement in civil rights, the widespread protest against the war in Vietnam and the appearance of fiery
rebellion in American cities—all inspired by segments of youth—the
shape, texture and magnitude of the matters under consideration have
shifted significantly. Rebellious youth have escaped the condition of partial insularity—the condition by which they were more or less controlled
during the fifties—and have emerged as a potent and forceful vanguard
of political and cultural revolution. In that sense, American youth have
transcended their historical limitations, inspired a world-wide movement;
and, much less significantly, they have exposed many shortcomings in the
essay that follows.

The rebellious character of youth has periodically troubled serious-
minded adults since the appearance of modern civil life. While the major
purpose of this paper is to describe some patterns of youthful rebelliousness,
and not to inquire into their causes, it will be useful to begin with a brief
discussion of some theories regarding youth's vulnerability to rebelliousness,
and the evidence on which theories presumably rest.

THE VULNERABILITY OF YOUTH

The primary object of Kingsley Davis' two essays on youth written
some twenty years ago was to explain the rebelliousness of youth in modern

From David Matza, "Subterranean Traditions of Youth," in *Teen-Age Culture*,
Jessie Bernard (Ed.), 1961, pp. 103–118. (Reprinted by permission of the author
and publisher.)

society as contrasted with the docility allegedly found in more primitive societies.[1] Among the reasons given was the fact that, although parents and youth remain together, the viewpoints of parents are primarily shaped during their own childhood; thus, friction is likely whenever the rate of change in customary attitudes is rapid. Furthermore, Davis suggested that the contemporary domination of the principle of merit results in tension and frustration by providing the basis for dispute regarding rightful incumbency in scarce positions and relative claims over scarce rights and perquisites. Moreover, he argued that adults tend to realism because of their greater stake in the system and because they are implicated in the compromises necessary in any ongoing social order. Youth, standing outside the establishment and not responsible for its defects, is likely to oscillate between what seems to adults an overdemanding idealism and a merciless cynicism.

Other writers have indicated additional sources of tension in the position of youth. Benedict, Erikson, Bloch and Niederhoffer, and many others, have stressed the crisis of identity inherent in a society which defines adolescence and youth ambiguously.[2] Parsons has emphasized the effects of an adult stress on performance.[3] Some have stressed the frustrating effects of a puritanical repression of sexuality, and others, of the post-Kinsey era, lament the effects of the stimulation provided by a sex-obsessed culture.[4] Whatever the difference in opinion regarding the source, there seems to be a general consensus that something requires explaining, and this something usually turns out to be youthful rebelliousness.

Most empirical evidence seems to support this consensus, provided we limit our assertions in two ways. First, we may not contend that extremist versions of youthful rebelliousness characterize anything like a majority of the youthful population. Rather, it seems that the great majority of American youth behave either in a conventional manner [5] or participate in conventional versions [6] of deviant youth traditions; this, despite the fact that many youths are vulnerable to rebelliousness. Second, there seems no

[1] Kingsley Davis, "Sociology of Parent-Youth Conflict," *American Sociology Review,* Vol. 5 (August 1940) and "Adolescence and the Social Structure," *The Annals of the American Academy of Political and Social Science,* Vol. 236 (November 1944).

[2] Ruth Benedict, "Continuities and Discontinuities in Cultural Conditioning," *Psychiatry,* May 1933; Erik Erikson, in *New Perspectives for Research in Juvenile Delinquency,* eds. Helen Witmer and Ruth Kotinsky (Publication No. 356; Washington, D. C.: Children's Bureau, 1956); Herbert Bloch and Arthur Niederhoffer, *The Gang* (New York: Philosophical Library, 1958).

[3] Talcott Parsons, "Age and Sex in the Social Structure of the United States," *American Sociological Review,* October, 1942.

[4] Pitrim Sorokin, *The American Sex Revolution* (Boston: Sargent, 1956).

[5] Frederick Elkin and William A. Westley, "The Myth of Adolescent Culture," *American Sociological Review,* December 1955; also, Bennett M. Berger, "On the Youthfulness of Youth Cultures" (unpublished manuscript).

[6] Conventional versions of deviant traditions are discussed in the final section of this paper.

reason to believe that there have been any long-run increases or decreases in rates of youthful rebelliousness during the modern era. Rather, it seems likely that rates of some forms of youthful rebelliousness have increased somewhat over the last twenty-five years, whereas rates of other forms have declined. Even in those modes of rebelliousness like delinquency, where rates during the last twenty-five years have apparently increased, there is some evidence that rates fifty years ago were higher than those currently experienced.[7] During the decade of the fifties, a decline in youthful radicalism gave rise to the feeling that an age of conformity was upon us. There seems no firm ground for this suspicion. Periods of prosperity have often signaled a decline in radical activity.

What may we contend? First, within the life cycle, the apex of rebelliousness is reached during the period of youth, before and after which rates of rebelliousness seem considerably lower.[8] This holds, by hypothesis, for the three modes of youthful rebelliousness to be discussed in this paper: delinquency, radicalism, and Bohemianism. This means that the youthful spirit of rebelliousness coincides more or less with chronological youth.[9] Second, we contend that because of the persistent vulnerability of youth, traditions of each mode have emerged; distinctive viewpoints have remained relatively stable in content and location.[10] And, finally, that these traditions

[7] Negley K. Teeters and David Matza, "The Extent of Delinquency in the United States," *The Journal of Negro Education* (Summer 1959), pp. 210–211; also, Henry McKay's unpublished data on Chicago delinquency rates, cited in Albert K. Cohen and James F. Short, "Juvenile Delinquency," in *Contemporary Social Problems,* eds. Robert K. Merton and Robert A. Nisbet (New York: Harcourt, Brace and World, 1961), p. 84.

[8] Evidence of this using national delinquency statistics may be found in most standard textbooks and the *Uniform Crime Reports* of any year. For instance, Cohen and Short, *op. cit.,* p. 85. More reliable evidence of "maturational reform," based on cohort analysis, appears in William McCord, Joan McCord, and Irving Zola, *Origins of Crime* (New York: Columbia University Press, 1959), p. 21; Jessie Bernard, *Social Problems at Midcentury* (New York: Dryden, 1957), pp. 421, 444; W. H. Dunham and M. E. Knauer, "The Juvenile Court and its Relationship to Adult Criminality," *Social Forces,* March 1954. The evidence for radicalism and Bohemianism are necessarily more impressionistic. For supportive but inconclusive evidence of "maturational defection" in radicalism, see Gabriel A. Almond, *The Appeals of Communism* (Princeton: Princeton University Press, 1954), pp. 218–220; James A. Wechsler, *The Age of Suspicion* (New York: Random House, 1953), p. 84; Robert E. Lane, *Political Life* (Glencoe: Free Press, 1959), pp. 216–217; Morris L. Ernst and David Loth, *Report on the American Communist* (New York: Holt, 1952). For impressionistic evidence on the drifting from Bohemianism with the gaining of adulthood, see Thomas Parkinson, "Phenomenon or Generation," in *A Casebook on The Beat,* ed. Thomas Parkinson (New York: Crowell, 1961), pp. 277–278; Albert Parry, *Garrets and Pretenders: A History of Bohemianism in America* (New York: Covici-Friede, 1933), p. 12.

[9] Bennett Berger, *op. cit.,* rightly distinguishes between youthfulness in the spiritual sense and chronological youth. He suggests that there is no necessary correlation between the two. I agree but suggest that there is a rough empirical correlation.

[10] The content of these viewpoints will be discussed below. With regard to stable ecological anchoring, the evidence varies in reliability. The ecological anchoring of the delinquent tradition has been documented in Clifford H. Shaw and Henry D.

of youthful rebelliousness—delinquency, radicalism and Bohemianism—
are in the nature of subterranean traditions in American life.

THE SUBTERRANEAN TRADITION

The major contribution of sociology to the understanding of deviance
has consisted of two fundamental insights. First, persistent deviance is
typically not a solitary enterprise; rather, it requires and most often receives
group support. Second, deviance does not typically represent an historical
innovation; rather, it has a history in particular neighborhoods and locales.
Thus, the individual deviant is linked to the society in minimal fashion
through companies of deviants and through localized traditions. To speak
of subterranean traditions is to extend the notion of linking to the wider
social system; it is to posit connections between localized deviant traditions and the broader traditions of conventional society. The notion of subterranean implies that there is an ongoing dialectic between conventional
and deviant traditions and that, in the process of exchange, both are modified.[11]

Subterranean traditions of youth have a number of common aspects
which suggest a definition of the concept. First, they are traditions which
are publicly denounced. Second, the extreme versions of these traditions are
adhered to by only a small proportion of the youthful population. Third,
these traditions are familiar to and tolerated by broad segments of the
adult population. Fourth, conventional versions of these traditions are
experienced by broad segments of the youthful population. Fifth, these
traditions are viewed with ambivalence in the privacy of contemplation by
a majority of adults, and, thus, public reactions are subject to faddish oscil-
lation ranging from sympathetic tolerance to outright suppression.[12] To
point to the existence of subterranean traditions is to suggest that no one

McKay, *Juvenile Delinquency and Urban Areas* (Chicago: University of Chicago
Press, 1942); Albert K. Cohen, *Delinquent Boys* (Glencoe: Free Press, 1955). The
widespread impression that youthful radicalism has been stably located on the campuses of a handful of typically large, prestigious, and cosmopolitan universities and
colleges receives adequate documentary confirmation in Robert W. Iversen, *The
Communists and the Schools* (New York: Harcourt, Brace, 1959), Chap. 6. The
widespread impression that American Bohemianism has located in run-down sections
of large cities or in areas adjacent to cosmopolitan campuses remains largely undocu-
mented. However, there seems no urgent reason to qustion this impression.

[11] Reinhard Bendix and Bennett Berger, "Images of Society and Problems of
Concept Formation in Sociology," in *Symposium on Sociological Theory,* ed. Llew-
ellyn Gross (Evanston: Row, Peterson, 1959).

[12] Fads often involve the brief elevation of modified elements of subterranean
traditions, most notably Bohemian traditions, to the status of eccentric but partially
acceptable behavior. Perhaps the classic example of this in the United States was the
"Trilby" fad in the 1890's when a modified form of female Bohemianism came in
vogue. For a discussion of "Trilby," see Parry, *op. cit.,* Chap. 9.

in any society is fully socialized or fully respondent to public expectations; [13] as a consequence, whenever there are available counterthemes, there will be varying degrees of indulgence in these traditions ranging from relatively complete immersion to occasional vicarious appreciation.

SUBTERRANEAN TRADITIONS OF YOUTH

Delinquency, radicalism, and Bohemianism are the extremist versions of subterranean youth traditions. They impart a spirit of rebelliousness and impetuosity that seems consistent with the sort of tensions ordinarily attributed to the position of youth. These kinds of behavior exhibit what is frequently termed immaturity or irresponsibility.[14] However, the lumping together of delinquency, radicalism, and Bohemianism requires more systematic justification. Thus, it will be useful to briefly discuss their similarities, over and above their apparent temperamental affinity, and to specify the differences between them.

Similarities

First, the traditions in question seem to have a greater appeal to youth than to the population at large. Second, all three have distinct anticivil implications, at least over the short run. All three are "threats" to the stability and order of an ongoing system. Third, all three are specifically anti-bourgeois, although in different ways. The delinquent, for instance, does not denounce bourgeois property arrangements, but he violates them. He does reject the bourgeois sentiments of methodism and routine, particularly as they are manifested within the school system. The Bohemian's attitude toward bourgeois property arrangements is typically one of indifference, although he is appalled by the commercialization ordinarily associated with these arrangements. His ire is especially reserved for the puritanical and methodological elements of the bourgeois ethos. Moreover, the Bohemian is typically antagonistic to recent trends in bourgeois society. He is opposed to the mechanized, organized, centralized, and increasingly collectivized nature of modern capitalism. The radical tradition envisages a less general denunciation. Particularly in the varieties of revolutionary Marxism, which represent the most important examples of modern radicalism, the primary focus of radical attack has been on the capitalist system of political and economic domination and on the imperialist role allegedly played by such systems in international affairs. The

[13] Dennis Wrong, "The Oversocialized Conception of Man in Modern Sociology," *American Sociological Review*, April 1961.
[14] Parsons, *op. cit.*

methodical, the puritanical, and, especially, the industrial aspects of the bourgeois order have been more or less embraced.

Thus, we see that each subterranean tradition has been hostile to the bourgeois order, but each has followed a somewhat different line of attack.

Differences

First, delinquency differs from both radicalism and Bohemianism with respect to the specific age of vulnerability. However, the stage of education seems a more decisive point of division than age per se. Delinquency is a high school phenomenon; it seems most pronounced among that section of youth which terminates its education during or at the end of high school. Radicalism and Bohemianism, particularly in the United States, are apparently enmeshed within the system of higher education. Its adherents are typically drawn from those whose education terminates during college, with the attainment of a bachelor's degree, or with some graduate work of indeterminable duration.

Second, they differ with respect to the degree of self-consciousness attained. Radicalism and Bohemianism are intellectually self-conscious and represent explicit and reasonably coherent critiques of modern society; the delinquent critique tends to be implicit. Furthermore, radicalism and Bohemianism possess a written literature; delinquency is almost by necessity an oral tradition.

Third, the modes of rebelliousness differ with respect to their ambitions. Delinquency has no designs on society; there is no desire on the part of delinquents to reconstruct it. Thus, in Merton's terms, they are aberrant.[15] Radicals, on the other hand, wish to reshape society in the form of their own ideological predilections. Thus, they are the archetype of Merton's nonconformist.[16] Bohemians fall somewhere between, typically wishing to develop a private and insulated way of life but rarely having any aspiration to convert the rest of society.

Fourth, the modes of rebelliousness differ with respect to assessments regarding their normal worth. In the case of delinquency, the judgments of its adherents seem to coincide with those belonging to conventional society.[17] There is no serious belief in either camp in the moral value of the delinquent enterprise. On the other hand, there has been considerable dispute regarding the moral value of radicalism and Bohemianism. Many intellectuals attribute varying degrees of moral value to them; those of lesser intellect have probably been less generous. Moreover, radicals and Bo-

[15] Robert K. Merton, "Social Problems and Sociological Theory," in *Contemporary Social Problems, op. cit.,* pp. 725–727.

[16] *Ibid.*

[17] Gresham M. Sykes and David Matza, "Techniques of Neutralization," *American Sociological Review,* December 1957.

hemians, unlike delinquents, are convinced of the moral value of their enterprises.

Despite these differences, we have suggested that there is a spiritual affinity between delinquency, radicalism, and Bohemianism; all are modes of youthful rebelliousness. Each represents a subterranean tradition of American youth. Thus, an analysis of youthful deviance requires an examination of each tradition. It is to that task that we now turn.

DELINQUENCY: SPIRIT AND SUBSTANCE [18]

There are many perceptive accounts describing the behavior of juvenile delinquents and their underlying values.[19] Although there have been important differences of opinion in the interpretation of this material and in the relative stress placed on various components, there exists a striking consensus on the content of delinquent values. Three themes describing the spirit of the delinquent enterprise and two defining its substance, or business, seem implicit in these accounts.

The distinctive feature of the spirit of delinquency is the celebration of prowess. Each of the themes in the delinquent tradition develops an aspect of the meaning of prowess. First, delinquents are deeply immersed in a restless search for excitement, "thrills" or "kicks." According to the delinquent code, the approved style of life is an adventurous one. Activities pervaded by displays of daring and charged with danger are highly valued in comparison with more mundane and routine patterns of behavior. Although delinquent acts do not exhaust the field of adventurous activities, they make up an important component of activities that may be feasibly viewed as adventurous. The fact that an activity involves breaking the law is often the fact that lends it its air of excitement. In fact, "kicks" or "action" may come to be defined with clear awareness as "any action tabooed by

---

[18] The following section is, with slight modification, based on David Matza and Gresham M. Sykes, "Juvenile Delinquency and Subterranean Values," *American Sociological Review*, forthcoming.

[19] Frederic M. Thrasher, *The Gang* (Chicago: University of Chicago Press, 1936); Clifford R. Shaw and M. E. Moore, *The Natural History of a Delinquent Career* (Chicago: University of Chicago Press, 1931); Albert K. Cohen, *Delinquent Boys, op. cit.*; Albert K. Cohen and James F. Short, "Research in Delinquent Subcultures," *The Journal of Social Issues*, Vol. 14 (1958), No. 3; Walter Miller, "Lower Class Culture as a Generating Milieu of Gang Delinquents," *The Journal of Social Issues*, Vol. 14 (1958), No. 3; Solomin Kobrin, "The Conflict of Values in Delinquent Areas," *American Sociological Review*, Vol. 16 (1951); Harold Finestone, "Cats, Kicks and Color," *Social Problems*, Vol. 5 (1957); Richard A. Cloward and Lloyd E. Ohlin, *Delinquency and Opportunity* (Glencoe: The Free Press, 1960); H. Bloch and Arthur Niederhoffer, *The Gang, op. cit.*; Beatrice Griffith, *American Me* (Boston: Houghton Mifflin, 1948); Sheldon and Eleanor Glueck, *Unraveling Juvenile Delinquency* (New York: Commonwealth Fund, 1950).

'squares' that heightens and intensifies the present moment of experience and differentiates it as much as possible from the humdrum routines of daily life." [20] In courting physical danger, experimenting with the forbidden, and provoking the authorities, the delinquent is not simply enduring hazards; he is creating them in an attempt to manufacture excitement. For many delinquents, "the rhythm of life fluctuates between periods of relatively routine and repetitive activities and sought situations of greater emotional stimulation." [21]

Second, to attain prowess is to seek and receive the material rewards of society while avoiding, in the manner of a leisure class, the canons of school and work with their implicit commitments to methodism, security, and routine. Thus, delinquents commonly exhibit a disdain for "getting on" in the realms of school or work. In its place, there is a sort of aimless drifting or grandiose dreams of quick success.

However, the delinquent must be financed if he is to attain the luxury of the sporting life. Although some writers have coupled the delinquent's disdain of work with a disdain of money, it seems unlikely that money is renounced in the delinquent code; it would seem more accurate to say it is treated in a special way. Money is valued, but not for purposes of a careful series of expenditures or long-range objectives. Money, for the delinquent, is luxury and not regular income; and the modesty of the sums involved, for what are, after all, children, has obscured this fact. Money is viewed as something to be squandered in gestures of largesse, in patterns of conspicuous consumption. An age-old method of facilitating this is gambling among peers. A major function of this sort of gambling, whatever its motive, is to redistribute scarce finances so that, over the long run, each member of the group may play at luxury. This hardly exhausts the ways in which prowess may be used in the sudden acquisition of "large" sums of money. The other techniques involve incursions on the world of outsiders— the victims.

Simple expropriation—theft and its variants—must be included, of course; but it is only one of a variety of ways of "scoring" and does not always carry great prestige in the eyes of delinquents.[22] Other forms of prowess include chicanery or manipulation which may take the form of borrowing from social workers or more elaborate forms of "hustling"; an emphasis on "pull," frequently with reference to obtaining a "soft" job assumed to be available only to those with influential connections. Thus, there are a variety of means, ranging in legality from theft to the holding

[20] Finestone, *op. cit.*
[21] Miller, *op. cit.*
[22] Finestone, *op. cit.*

of a soft job, all of which are exhibitions of prowess, all of which may be applied in the pursuit of luxury.

A third theme running through the accounts of juvenile delinquency centers on aggression. This is the third component of prowess. The code of the warrior, which in many ways the delinquent code reflects, calls for an aggressive manliness, a reluctance to accept slights on one's honor.[23] The delinquent's readiness for aggression is particularly emphasized in the analysis of juvenile gangs in the slum areas of large cities. It is in such gangs that we find the struggles for "turf," and, thus, it is in these cases that the applicability of the warrior code is most apparent. Cloward and Ohlin have pointed out that we can be led into error by viewing these conflict-oriented delinquents as typical of all delinquents.[24] Yet, the gang delinquent's use of violence for the maintenance of honor, or "rep," and the proof of courage, or "heart," seems to express in extreme form the idea that aggression is a demonstration of toughness and, thus, of masculinity; and it is this idea which pervades delinquent thought. Whatever the degree of differentiation among delinquent subcultures, the concept of *machismo*,[25] of the path to manhood through the ability to take it and hand it out, is foreign to the average delinquent only in name.

Finally, let us turn to the substance of delinquency—the business of the delinquent enterprise. The substance of delinquency is defined by the legal code and contains two major elements. First, there is victimization. This includes larceny and all of its variants, assaults on persons or on property, that is, vandalism, and a host of less frequently committed offenses, all involving victims. Second, there are status offenses, activities which are expressly prohibited for juveniles but which may be performed by adults, within limits, with legal impunity. This includes truancy, drinking, gambling, driving cars, runaway, indulgence in sex, and, in some jurisdictions, smoking, swearing, staying out late, and a host of vaguely defined forms of misconduct. However, while these activities are officially delinquent, the law, particularly at the level of police enforcement, exhibits considerable discretionary tolerance with regard to youngsters exhibiting these forms of behavior, particularly if their dossiers are otherwise clean.[26]

[23] Joseph Margolis, "Juvenile Delinquents: Latter-Day Knights," *The American Scholar,* Spring 1960.

[24] Cloward and Ohlin, *op. cit.*

[25] Griffith, *op. cit.*

[26] Though it may appear obvious or unimportant, it is crucial to specify the substance of delinquency as well as its spirit. The basic process involved in the conventional versions of each tradition is the fortuitous stripping away of its most odious features. Thus, for instance, the conventional version of delinquency, teen-age culture, involves a continuing flirtation with its tolerable components; and among these tolerable components are the status offenses, to be discussed below.

STUDENT RADICALISM: SPIRIT AND SUBSTANCE

Compared to the many accounts of delinquency, there are relatively few systematic descriptions of student radicalism in the United States.[27] Enough exists, however, to proceed with a tentative description of this tradition.[28]

Radicalism among students did not begin in the decade of the Thirties, although there is little question that it reached its height during that period. The Intercollegiate Socialist Society was organized in 1905, and by 1921 Calvin Coolidge decried student radicalism.[29] Despite the internecine struggles within the revolutionary socialist movement since 1905, some aspects of the radical tradition have remained relatively stable. What are the stable components of modern student radicalism?

First, there is the vision of apocalypse.[30] This refers to "the belief that the evil world as we know it, so full of temptation and corruption, will come to an end one day and will be replaced with a purer and better world." [31] This tradition has its origins in the apocalyptic outlook of the prophets of the Old Testament and has been passed down through the early Christians and adherents of heretical sects. Its modern recipients, suggests Shils, are "the modern revolutionary movements and above all the Marxian movements." [32] The tradition is best reflected in "doctrinaire politics, or the politics of the ideal." [33]

Whatever its general importance in revolutionary socialism, the politics of the ideal seems peculiarly well suited to the predispositions of youthful rebelliousness. This sort of politics seems perfectly consistent with Davis' description of youth's mixture of idealism and cynicism. In the politics of the ideal, perception and assessment become bifurcated with respect to idealism and cynicism. On this side of the apocalypse, one views and interprets events critically and cynically; on the other side, or in some contemporary foreshadowing of the future, one views and interprets events idealistically and generously.

---

[27] The most detailed and documented account is found in Iversen, *op. cit.;* for a good impressionistic account, see Wechsler, *op. cit.*

[28] While the Communists have never had a monopoly on student radicalism, their influence, particularly during the Thirties and early Forties, was considerable. Our discussion will focus primarily on Communists partially because of their prominence and partially because their activities have been best documented. See Iversen, *op. cit.,* Chap. 6.

[29] Iversen, *op. cit.,* p. 13.

[30] Edward A. Shils "The Traditions of Intellectuals," in *The Intellectuals,* ed. George de Huszar (Glencoe: Free Press, 1960), pp. 55–61.

[31] *Ibid.*

[32] *Ibid.*

[33] *Ibid.*

The second component of the spirit of student radicalism is populism. "Populism is the belief in the creativity and in the superior worth of the ordinary people, of the uneducated and the unintellectual." [34] Because of the central role of populism in modern radicalism, revolutionary movements have tended to equate the apocalypse with the liberation of the folk. The particular folk celebrated has varied: in the Russian social revolutionary movement, it was the peasant; in traditional Marxism, it is the industrial proletariat; in the anarchism of Bakunin, it tended to be the *lumpenproletariat*. American student radicalism, largely unaware of these esoteric distinctions, has tended to lump these populist ideals together, arriving at a compote consisting of migrant farm workers, unskilled and semiskilled industrial workers, and Negroes.

Among students, the appeal of populism is not simply an outgrowth of traditional radical propensities. Just as the apocalyptic mentality has a special appeal to youth, so, too, does populism. Students have a special affinity for populism because it serves an important function; populism, for students, is an effective attack on the presumption of professorial authority and a neat way of defending against unflattering assessment. For the radical, and for the Bohemian, too, a belief in populism allows students who perceive themselves as vanguard or avante garde to deflect the contrary judgments of their academic elders.

A third component of the student radical spirit is evangelism. Evangelism refers to excursions made by sectarians to the outside world for the purpose of recruiting sympathizers, supporters, and members. It is an intensively active sort of belief. Thus, it is well suited to the exuberance and impetuosity characteristic of rebellious youth. Evangelism plays an especially important role since, compared to Bohemianism, radicalism would otherwise be too serious an enterprise to compete effectively for rebellious youth. Evangelism notwithstanding, student radicalism remains chronically vulnerable to Bohemianism within its ranks.[35] Thus, evangelism seems as important in the bolstering of internal enthusiasm as in its alleged purpose of gaining new adherents. By encouraging excursion, it allows student radicals to stray from the routine of the radical enterprise,[36] and challenges his capacities for argumentation, intimidation, persuasion, and seduction.

The substance of student radicalism is unconventional political action. Its round-of-life consists of taking stands on concrete issues, circulation of

[34] *Ibid.*
[35] The evidence for this is indirect but suggestive. The fear that Bohemianism is infecting the youth is a persistent fear among adult radicals. The classical radical case against Bohemian corruption was made by Lenin in his "sex is not a glass of water" dictum; the classical radical case for Bohemian joy was made by the anarchist, Emma Goldman.
[36] For a discussion of the monotonous character of the round of student radical life, see Wechsler, *op. cit.*

petitions, distribution of leaflets, sale of literature, raising funds, demonstrations and rallies, frequent meetings, discussions, debates, and the like. The mundane character of most of these activities is more or less obscured by the context within which they are viewed. This context is provided by the general characteristics of unconventional politics.

Radical politics is extremist rather than moderate.[37] It is less attentive than conventional politics to the administrative bylaws which govern collegiate activity. Thus, elements of excitement and risk are introduced. Moreover, radical politics is revolutionary rather than simply reformist. A revolutionary orientation adds meaning and drama to concrete activities, and it provides a basis for vicarious excitement by requiring identification with actual revolutions taking place elsewhere. Furthermore, radical politics is ideological rather than "market"[38] politics, and, thus, a sense of moral superiority attaches to the activities of the enterprise. Finally, radical politics is year-round rather than seasonal, and, thus, imparts a sense of urgency rarely apparent in conventional politics. In summary, each of the characteristics of unconventional politics conspires to transform the mundane to the extraordinary. Thus it is that what appears to the uninitiated a serious and dull business is converted to an enterprise with some appeal for rebellious youth.

BOHEMIANISM: SPIRIT AND SUBSTANCE

Bohemianism is a socioartistic enterprise which appeared as a widespread phenomenon in the first part of the nineteenth century in France.[39] Since then, it has spread to many parts of the world, particularly Europe and the United States. Despite indigenous sources in the United States and despite internal influences, the periods of rise and fall have coincided fairly well with its cycles in France.[40] Beat, the most recent expression of American Bohemianism, is best viewed as a response to recurrent internal conditions which have typically favored its resurgence, most notably prosperity of the postwar variety and as a reflection of developments on the French scene, most notably the emergence of *café* existentialism.

The failure to understand the traditional character of Bohemianism in selected American locales and the failure to see its ebb and flow as a reflection of recurrent social process, internal and external, has been largely responsible for alarmist interpretations of beat. Beat has been viewed, alternatively, as a sign of incipient nihilist rebellion and a symbol of hedonis-

[37] Seymour M. Lipset, *Political Man* (New York: Doubleday, 1960).
[38] Daniel Bell, *End of Ideology* (Glencoe: Free Press, 1960).
[39] Parry, *op. cit.*, ix.
[40] Parry, *ibid.*

tic withdrawal from public life. It has been interpreted as a symptom of
some deeper malady and a dark foreboding of what is to come. Interpretations of this sort should be expected whenever deviant patterns are not
viewed in their historical context.[41] What are the persistent components of
the Bohemian tradition, and why may beat be properly viewed as its most
recent American expression?

Romanticism

The first and major component of Bohemianism is romanticism. Romanticism, suggests Shils, "starts with the appreciation of the spontaneous
manifestations of the essence of concrete individuality. Hence it values
originality . . . that which is produced from the 'genius' of the individual
(or the folk), in contrast with the stereotyped and traditional actions of the
philistine." [42] The commitment to spontaneity and originality has had many
manifestations among traditional Bohemians, particularly in the graphic
arts.[43] Among beats, however, greater stress has been placed on development of originality and spontaneity in other art forms. Most notable among
these have been the celebration of improvisation in modern jazz, poetry, and
the novel. For this reason, and for others, jazz and jazz musicians have
occupied an exalted role in the beat point of view. Kerouac, the most
notable literary exponent of improvisation, has occupied a similarly exalted
position.[44]

The exaltation of spontaneity in artistic endeavor is reflected in the
Bohemian view of the folk. Bohemianism, like radicalism, has a distinctive
form of populism, which is best termed "primitivism." Its authentic folk
hero is, of course, the gypsy. Due, perhaps, to the gypsy's chronic unavail-
ability, it was not long before the notion of primitive folk was expanded
to include more visible groupings. The closest approximation that could be
found in urban society was the *lumpenproletariat,* and it is this group that
has occupied a central place in the Bohemian's primitivist mystique.[45] In
the modern rendition of Bohemianism, the mantle of idealized folk has
largely fallen on the lower-class Negro.[46] However, the Negro is not the
first American ethnic group to be granted this dubious honor. East Eu-

[41] John P. Sisk, "Beatniks and Tradition," in Parkinson, *op. cit.*
[42] Shils, *op. cit.,* p. 57.
[43] Harold Rosenberg, *The Tradition of the New* (New York: Horizon, 1959);
also, William Barrett, *Irrational Man* (New York: Doubleday, 1958), Chap. 3.
[44] Jack Kerouac's major publications include *On the Road* (New York: Viking,
1957); *Dharma Bums* (New York: Viking, 1958); *The Subterraneans* (New York:
Grove, 1958); *Excerpts from Visions of Cody,* 1958 (no further citation).
[45] See the critique by Jean Malaquais of Norman Mailer's "White Negro," in
Dissent, Winter 1958.
[46] The most explicit statement of this view is found in Norman Mailer, "The
White Negro," *Dissent,* Summer 1957.

ropean Jews, too, were perceived by previous Bohemians as the incarnation of primitive folk.[47]

Closely connected to the celebration of the primitive is the tradition of dedicated poverty. "A neighborhood where the poor live, the poor who are resigned to their poverty, is the best environment in which to live 'the life.' This is a cardinal principle which the beat share with the Bohemians of the past." [48] Although the dedication to poverty is, in part, a natural outgrowth of a commitment to primitivism, it is simultaneously a conscious way of avoiding the corrupting influence of the commercial world. Among beats, dedicated poverty is taken for granted. It is hardly a subject for debate. What is discussed are "ways of 'making it' . . . with as little commercial work as possible, or ideally, with no commercial work at all." [49]

A final aspect of romanticism seems wholly consistent with primitivism. It consists of a more or less complete rejection of bureaucratic-industrial society. This may be referred to as medievalism and is best described as an apocalyptic view without the apocalypse. Medievalism accepts the first part of the apocalyptic formula, man's fall from grace,[50] but makes no provision, as in radicalism, for man's redemption.[51]

In many respects, the beat's medievalism is similar to a more conventional intellectual view embodied in the theory of mass culture. Shils suggests: [52]

The critical interpretation of mass culture rests on a distinct image of modern man, of modern society and of man in past ages. . . . According to this view, the ordinary consumer of popular culture is something new in the world. He is a "private atomic subject," utterly without religious beliefs, without any private life, without a family that means anything to him; he is standardized, ridden with anxiety, perpetually, in a state of exacerbated unrest, his life emptied of meaning, trivialized, alienated from his past, his community, and possibly from himself, cretinized and brutalized.

Thus, the beat's rejection of modern life [53] is linked to the larger society through its affinity with the theory of mass culture, just as it is linked to the past through the tradition of what we shall call morose Bohemianism.

[47] See Parry, op. cit., p. 35, for a Bohemian's description of East European Jews on the Lower East Side in 1910 that is indistinguishable from the way in which lower-class Negro life is currently romanticized.

[48] Laurence Lipton, The Holy Barbarians (New York: Messner, 1959), p. 59.

[49] Ibid., p. 54.

[50] Typically dating from the Industrial Revolution.

[51] Its only vision of apocalypse is the atomic holocaust, which, in a strict sense, is no apocalypse at all since there is little promise of redemption. See Gene Feldman and Max Gartenberg, The Beat Generation and the Angry Young Men (New York: Dell, 1958), p. 12.

[52] Edward A. Shils, "Daydreams and Nightmares," Sewanee Review, Fall 1957, pp. 596–600.

[53] For a somewhat obscene statement of the beat's rejection of modern progress, see Jack Kerouac, Dharma Bums, op. cit., pp. 38–39; for a discussion of Poe and his rejection of society, see Parry, op. cit., Chap. 1.

Expressive authenticity and the Bohemian moods

The second component of the Bohemian tradition is the insistence on the expression of authentic inner feelings. Thus, Bohemianism has been marked by an intense moodiness. Mood is not to be suppressed or obscured; rather, it is to be indulged, pursued, and exhibited. Mood is a crucial part of inner, or authentic, experience and, thus, deserves unhampered expression. Because of the dedication to the full expression of mood, Bohemianism has always been somewhat perplexing to the outsider who expects some consistency of temperament to accompany a reasonably coherent viewpoint.

Bohemianism has long had two faces which, although they are often combined in the career of the same person, have been manifested in two roughly differentiated streams. There is frivolous Bohemianism, reminiscent in many respects of aristocratic "dandyism"; and there is morose Bohemianism, initiated by Poe and popularized by Baudelaire.[54] After Baudelaire, the two moods persist and are reflected in beat in the modern distinction between "hot" and "cool." [55]

By 1948 the hipsters, or beatsters, were divided into cool and hot. Much of the misunderstanding about . . . the Beat Generation . . . derives from the fact that there are two distinct styles of hipsterism; the cool today is your bearded laconic sage . . . before a hardly touched beer in a beatnik dive, whose speech is low and unfriendly, whose girls say nothing and wear black: The "hot" today is the crazy talkative shining-eyed (often innocent and open-hearted) nut who runs from bar to bar, pad to pad, looking for everybody, shouting, restless, lushy, trying to "make it" with subterranean beatniks who ignore him. Most beat generation artists belong to the hot school. . . . In many cases the mixture is 50–50. It was a hot hipster like myself who finally cooled it in Buddhist meditation, though when I go in a jazz joint I still feel like yelling "Blow, baby, Blow!"

Thus, in the insistence on the authentic display of mood, and in the development of frivolous and morose subtraditions, Bohemianism has pushed to the limits of human expression. It has had a manic and a depressive character.

Monasticism

Even for the morose, however, the solitary life receives little authorization in the Bohemian view. The unfriendly, laconic sage in Kerouac's description had, after all, "made the scene." Bohemias must have "scenes,"

[54] Parry, op. cit., pp. 11–12.
[55] Jack Kerouac, "The Origins of the Beat Generation," in Parkinson, op. cit., p. 73.

since Bohemianism has always referred to a collecting of like-minded eccentrics.[56]

Monasticism, which refers to the formation of insulated communities of adherents, is an explicit attempt on the part of Bohemians to regain the sense of community which, according to their ideology, no longer exists in the broader society.[57] The clubs, *cafés,* dives, or pads, which are their monasteries, are places where the bonds of familiarity can be assumed and, except for the danger of the police interloper, one hardly need "check out" a scene before feeling secure in it. However, not all are welcome in the places of congregation. Monasticism refers to communities of authentic adherents. Thus, theirs is an exclusive community. Bohemians are not evangelists; on the contrary, the newcomer must prove in a variety of ways that he belongs.[58]

Bohemians have long realized that both the unauthentic (pretenders or "phonies") and the outright conventional (tourists or "squares") are greatly fascinated by the Bohemian life.[59] But because of their stress on authenticity, Bohemians have been guarded in their relations with phonies and squares. Moreover, they are guarded because they have been dimly aware of the fate that, sooner or later, befalls all Bohemias. The monasticism of Bohemians, coupled with the persistence with which the squares and phonies discover their haunts, has meant that virtually no Bohemian "monastery" could long survive. Moreover, Bohemian neighborhoods, too, made up of garrets and *cafés,* in traditional Bohemian parlance, or pads and scenes, in modern Bohemian parlance, have been short-lived. When the phonies and squares arrive, some of the most zealous Bohemians leave. From that point on, the process seems irreversible; the phonies move in, the rents increase, many of the remaining Bohemians are forced to leave, and a new pseudo-Bohemia, in the manner of Greenwich village, is created.[60]

Substance

The "business" of Bohemianism has two important and interrelated elements. First, there is the creation of unconventional art which may be distinguished from the conventional variety in three major ways. It is disaffiliated from the major institutions which provide the machinery for the production and distribution of art. Among these institutions are the modern university, with its direct and indirect subsidization of the arts, and

[56] For a discussion of the importance of "scenes," see Francis Rigney and L. Douglas Smith, *The Real Bohemia* (New York: Basic Books, 1961), Chap. 1; also Lipton, *op. cit.,* Chap. 1; and Parry, *op. cit.*

[57] It is because of their peculiar commitment to community that beats often sound like "squares."

[58] Rigney and Smith, *op. cit.*

[59] Rigney and Smith, *op. cit.,* p. 181.

[60] Parry, *op. cit.,* p. 58; Rigney and Smith, *op. cit.,* Chaps. 10–11.

the modern industries of mass communication which, alternatively, deal commercially in art (publishing firms) or deal in commercialized art (advertising). Second, stylistic innovation is characteristic of Bohemian art. In each of the arts, the Bohemian has been an experimenter in new styles of expression.

The third feature of unconventional art applies to its subject matter. Bohemian art has frequently dealt with the forbidden, the censorable. In his attempt to plumb the depths of human existence, the Bohemian has often been guilty of equivocation, of confusing or equating the two meanings of "depths." This equivocation was an outgrowth of the Bohemian's peculiar style of populism in which authentic life coincides with primitive life, with life as it is lived in the lowest orders of society and the underworld. His own descent into the lowest orders, resulting from his dedicated poverty, allowed him to extend the province of his subject matter in an important manner. If the Bohemian feared the *lumpenproletariat*, or if he discovered that their behavior was not always censorable, he could always turn to what is, after all, the most frequent subject matter of Bohemian art—Bohemians. This was fortunate, for if Bohemian life was not sufficiently censorable, there was always the possibility of making it so.

This brings us to the second and interrelated element of the Bohemian enterprise, the pursuit of unconventional personal experience. It is interrelated, because, whatever its motive among Bohemians, it has persistently performed a crucial function for young, aspiring painters, poets, sculptors, and novelists. It has provided them with a subject matter to which to apply their variable talents.

In the pursuit of unconventional personal experience, there is no assurance of success. Some sorts of experience involve higher risks of failure than others—the pursuit of sexual conquest, for instance, is less likely to culminate successfully than the use of alcohol to lessen inhibitions. Thus, a cataloguing of the forms of experience traditionally pursued by Bohemians should not be mistaken for an accurate rendition of what Bohemians typically do. More time seems spent in pursuit than in actual experience.[61]

Two sorts of unconventional experience are pursued. First, there is the pursuit of hedonistic experiences which overlap considerably with activities that are currently deemed illegal in the United States. These are generally nonvictimizing offenses; included are such offenses as sexual excess, homosexuality, intemperate use of alcohol, disturbing the peace, use of narcotics, and speeding in automobiles. Many of these activities received celebration among Bohemians during the nineteenth century.[62] Thus, it should not be

[61] Most novels of beat life written by beats, or those close to beats, confirm this point. Kerouac's novels particularly, may be taken as accurate replicas of beat life. Also, see Chandler Brossard, *Who Walk in Darkness* (New York: New Directions, 1952).

[62] Parry, *op. cit.*, p. 11.

assumed that beats have attained a new threshold of hedonistic experience.

Second, there is a quest for transcendence. This is closely related to the problem of creativity and represents an experimenting with the limits to which human perception may be pushed. It is as an attempt to transcend the mundane limits on human perception that we can best understand three highly esoteric activities of beats: religious mysticism as manifested in Buddhist meditation, or the "Zen kick"; [63] the flirtation with and acceptance of psychosis, or the "insanity bit"; [64] and the hallucogenic use of drugs.[65]

REBELLIOUS YOUTH: RESTORATION AND PREVENTION

The integration of rebellious youth into conventional society hardly seems possible, particularly in view of the eccentricities inherent in each of the subterranean traditions. Yet, the great majority of vulnerable youth are barely touched by these traditions in their full-blown forms and, of those that are, the great majority seem able to re-enter conventional life with the attainment of social adulthood. Two questions must, therefore, be posed. Why, given the vulnerability of youth to modes of rebelliousness, do so few participate in full-blown deviant traditions? And by what process are those who do participate reintegrated into society? The first is the problem of prevention, the second of restoration.

Our concern, here, is not with programmatic solutions which, with respect to the problems of youthful rebelliousness, seem ineffective or non-existent.[66] Instead, we are interested in a process on which the integration of youth seems far more dependent, and that is the crescive and unintended formation of arrangements which fortuitously expedite integration. One such arrangement may be found in the existence of conventional versions of subterranean traditions.[67]

Conventional versions are reasonable facsimiles of subterranean traditions in which their most offensive features are stripped away or tempered. As indicated above, this is not by design, but as a result of emergent

[63] Kerouac, *Dharma Bums, op. cit.*

[64] Seymour Krim, "The Insanity Bit," in *The Beats,* ed. Seymour Krim (Greenwich: Fawcett, 1960).

[65] Lipton, *op. cit.,* p. 178.

[66] The only subterranean tradition for which there is an ongoing correctional apparatus specializing in the restoration of youth is delinquency. Even in that case, however, there is considerable uncertainty as to whether the fact of official correction or the quality of that correction has any effect on the chances of reforming. See Edwin Powers and Helen Witmer, *An Experiment in the Prevention of Delinquency: The Cambridge-Somerville Youth Study* (New York: Columbia University Press, 1951).

[67] Talcott Parsons, *The Social System* (Glencoe: The Free Press, 1951), pp. 305–306; also, Paul Goodman, *Growing Up Absurd* (New York: Random House, 1960); also, Bennett Berger, *op. cit.*

syntheses of conventional and rebellious sentiments or as a consequence of the fortuitous existence of independent traditions.

A conventional version of the delinquent tradition is what has come to be called teen-age culture. Here we find an emphasis on fun and adventure; a disdain for scholastic effort; the more or less persistent involvement in "tolerated" status offenses like drinking, gambling, occasional truancy, "making out" in the sense of sexual conquest, driving cars before the appropriate age, smoking, swearing, and staying out late. The elements of the delinquent tradition that are lacking or tempered are those that are least tolerated. Aggression is considerably tempered, but there is a persistent concern with the credentials on masculinity and femininity. Victimizing crimes are stripped away, and the forms of prowess used for getting money to play at luxury are usually limited to the "conning" of parents.

Many youngsters who would otherwise be vulnerable to the appeals of delinquency get caught up in the teenage round-of-life. Because it has many inherent satisfactions, it tends to maintain the loyalty of its adherents. Furthermore, since it is allegedly capable of deflecting studious teen-agers, it is probably at least as effective in deflecting youngsters who are prone to a tradition with which it has far greater affinity. Moreover, it is likely that the greatest proportion of exdelinquents do not fully reform and become "good boys" in the adult and scholastic sense of the term; more likely, they pass into the ranks of "corner boys" of the lower and middle classes. Thus, although teen-age culture may sometimes act as a preparation for the delinquent tradition, as its critics would have it, there seems little doubt that it often serves the functions of prevention and restoration.

A conventional version of the radical tradition may be found in the longstanding American posture of "doing good." This is a kind of inchoate and uninformed liberalism. It is vaguely radical in that it, too, laments the corruption of society and looks forward to improvement, but it does not envisage apocalypse. It, too, is populist, but only in the limited sense of being for the underdog. It, too, believes in evangelism, but the most frequent expression of its evangelism is guilty inaction. Though this group has long been recognized as a source of sympathizers for radical organizations, its functions in preventing radicalism by providing a tenable alternative, a facsimile, for rebelliously-inclined and idealistic youth has been frequently overlooked; so, too, has its function in the restoration of radical youth. It is not likely that the greatest number of exradicals become either McCarthyites or liberal anti-Communists; more likely, they slip into inactivity, pass into ranks of those committed to doing good, and neutralize the guilt of persistent political inactivity by pointing to the demands of scholarship.

In the Bohemian case, we must proceed cautiously. Because of the great emphasis placed on authenticity and, thus, the great sensitivity and hostility to phonies, the integrative effects of the conventional versions of Bohemianism may be partially neutralized. It is, perhaps, for this reason that Bohemians seem to linger further into the reaches of chronological

adulthood than radicals or delinquents. A Bohemian, because of the stress
on authenticity, is more likely than the radical or the delinquent to perceive
the "duplicity of social systems" that lies behind each of the facsimiles.
While this almost certainly holds with respect to the function of restoration,
it is likely that conventional versions serve to deflect youth who are vulnerable to Bohemianism without yet being aware of its esoteric details. Nonetheless, we must leave open the possibility that, because of the stress on
authenticity, there can be no effective facsimile of Bohemianism.[68] Thus,
it is with some hesitation that we suggest that fraternity life may be viewed
as a conventional facsimile of frivolous Bohemianism and that student
intellectuals stand in a similar relation to morose Bohemianism. Fraternity
life frequently has a quality that is reminiscent of the most frivolous sorts
of Bohemianism. There is the congregating and singing in student taverns,
the round of larks and pranks, the aversion for cerebral activity, the exclusiveness and fraternalism of Bohemian monasticism, the pursuit of "weak"
and typically inoffensive "kicks." The affinity between student intellectualism and morose Bohemianism may be found in the following: the student
intellectual is concerned with creativity and free expression, which may be
taken as a tempering of the Bohemian's commitment to unconventional art;
he is concerned with integrity, which may be viewed as a routinized form of
expressive authenticity; he is unwilling to join his conventional classmates in
the celebration of material success, which is a tempered form of the Bohemian's dedication to poverty; he is prone to the medievalist view of
Bohemians while rejecting primitivist populism; and, finally, he is tempera-
mentally given to seriousness, which is a tempered version of the Bohemian's moroseness.

Our brief discussion of the integration of youth has focused on one set
of mechanisms. These mechanisms, however, operate within a context of
two other important features of modern society. First, there is the widespread sentiment of adult tolerance. Though the strength of this sentiment
varies through time and by section of the population, there is a significant
and influential portion of adult opinion that is ready to embrace prodigal
youth if and when they return. Second, there is the waning of the tensions
and frustrations making for youthful rebelliousness resulting from the onset
of adulthood and the gaining of "first-class citizenship." As important as
these are, they are not sufficient to provide a basis for the integration of
youth. There is the further necessity for some systematic arrangement to
exist through which the integrative potential of adult tolerance and social
maturation of youth may be realized. One such arrangement may be found
in the fortuitous existence of conventional versions of the subterranean
traditions of youth.

[68] This does not mean that Bohemians cannot be restored to conventional society.
There are other integrative processes. Bennett Berger points to the integrative effects
of "youthful" roles within the adult system. See Berger, *op. cit.*

28

Gerald J. Pine

THE AFFLUENT DELINQUENT

Pine cites research which indicates that delinquent behavior is not confined to the culturally and economically deprived. He examines the causes and forms of "affluent delinquency."

At one time or another nearly everyone has assumed the role of delinquency expert. Public and professional comment on juvenile delinquency seems never to die nor fade away. Like sex, religion, sports, politics, and the weather, delinquency can always provide a subject for discussion. One dimension of the delinquency problem which has been a good conversation piece of late is the occurrence of delinquent behavior in the middle and upper classes. Statistics released by the Federal Bureau of Investigation and other governmental agencies, the growing number of newspaper accounts describing the anti-social and aberrant behavior of privileged youth, and the frequency with which delinquency in suburbia is discussed during cocktail *tête-à-têtes* attest to an apparent rising incidence of affluent delinquency.

This paper examines the relationship between delinquent behavior and social class status. Its pivotal concerns are reflected in the following questions:

1. What is the extent of delinquent behavior in the middle and upper classes?

2. How is delinquent behavior treated in the middle and upper classes?

3. Are there any forms of delinquency which are more peculiar to one class than another?

4. What is the relationship between social class mobility and delinquency?

5. What are the factors which generate the affluent delinquent?

In attempting to answer these questions, I have expressed my notions in a series of propositions anchored so far as possible in research findings, in theory, and in my personal experience as a school counselor in an affluent suburban community.

From Gerald J. Pine, "The Affluent Delinquent," *Phi Delta Kappan,* Vol. XLVIII, No. 4 (December 1966), pp. 138–143.

PROPOSITION 1

There is a significant relationship between an increase in a country's economic growth and a rise in delinquent behavior. There is evidence that a significant increase in the gross national product of a nation is accompanied or followed by a significant increase in delinquent behavior. Teenage crime, once little known in France, is up 400 per cent over a decade ago. Prosperous West Germany is becoming concerned about crime by children, especially in the 14 to 18 age groups. Sweden, Denmark, Norway, Holland, and Switzerland all report increased teen-age criminality. Japan, which is enjoying the fastest rate of economic growth in the world, is also experiencing one of the most rapid escalations of delinquency.[1] Such trends offer a sharp contrast to the comparatively low rates of delinquency which appeared in the United States during the depression years.[2]

An increase in economic growth triggers a great deal of social and spatial mobility. The by-products of mobility and their role in delinquent behavior will be discussed in the propositions to follow.

PROPOSITION 2

There has always been a considerable amount of delinquency in the middle- and upper-class segments of our society. Several investigations have attempted to ascertain the frequency and nature of delinquent behavior in the middle and upper classes by using samples vaguely defined as middle- and upper-class in terms such as: "upper-income group," "children of the professional class," "college students," and "group from relatively more favored neighborhoods." In contrast to the evidence based on official records, these studies, notwithstanding the general definition of class, indicate delinquent behavior is more equally dispersed among the various social classes than the average American citizen realizes.

In 1946 Austin L. Porterfield[3] compared the offenses of 2,409 cases of alleged delinquents in the Fort Worth, Texas, area with the admitted conduct of several hundred students at three colleges of Northern Texas. He found that many college students had committed one or more of the "delinquency offenses" but seldom had been so charged as in the case of their less fortunate counterparts.

[1] *Boston Sunday Globe* (UPI), August 22, 1965, p. 53.
[2] Negley K. Teeters and David Matza, "The Extent of Delinquency in the United States," *Journal of Negro Education,* Summer, 1959, pp. 200–213.
[3] Austin L. Porterfield, *Youth in Trouble.* Texas: Leo Potishman Foundation, 1946.

Wallerstein and Wyle [4] distributed to an upper-income group a questionnaire listing 49 offenses under the penal code of the state of New York. All of the offenses were sufficiently serious to draw maximum sentences of not less than a year. Replies were received from 1,698 individuals. Ninety-nine per cent of those questioned answered affirmatively to one or more of the offenses.

In response to a questionnaire which Bloch gave to 340 college juniors and seniors during the period from 1943–1948, approximately 91 per cent admitted that they had knowingly committed offenses against the law, both misdemeanors and felonies. The groups sampled came from considerably better-than-average middle-class homes. Women students were as glaringly delinquent in this respect as men, although the volume of major offenses which they admitted to was somewhat smaller than that for men.[5]

In another study Clinard discovered that of 49 criminology students at a Midwestern university, 86 per cent had committed thefts and about 50 per cent had committed acts of vandalism.[6]

Exploring the implications of "white-collar criminality" in regard to delinquent behavior, Wattenberg and Balistrieri compared 230 white boys charged with automobile theft with 2,544 others in trouble with the Detroit police in 1948. They found the automobile theft group came from relatively more favored neighborhoods and had good peer relations.[7]

An investigation was conducted by Birkness and Johnson in which a group of delinquents was compared with a group of non-delinquents. Each group included 25 subjects. It was found that five times as many of the parents of delinquent children (in contrast with the non-delinquent children) were of the professional class. Almost twice as many parents of the non-delinquents were classified in the manual labor status in comparison with the parents of delinquents.[8]

A study carried out by Nye in the state of Washington revealed that there was no significant relationship between one's position in the social class structure and the frequency and severity of delinquent behavior, i.e., the middle- and upper-class adolescent was involved in as much norm violating behavior as the lower-class adolescent.[9]

In summary, during the past 20 years there has been an accumulation

[4] James S. Wallerstein and G. J. Wyle, "Our Law-abiding Lawbreakers," in *Probation,* 1946, pp. 107–112.

[5] Herbert A. Bloch and Frank T. Flynn, *Delinquency: The Juvenile Offender in America Today.* New York: Random House, 1956, p. 11.

[6] Marshall B. Clinard, *Sociology of Deviant Behavior.* New York: Holt, Rinehart & Winston, 1957, p. 165.

[7] W. W. Wattenberg and J. Balistrieri, "Automobile Theft: A Favored Group Delinquency," *The American Journal of Sociology,* May, 1952, pp. 575–79.

[8] V. Birkness and H. C. Johnson, "Comparative Study of Delinquent and Non-delinquent Adolescents," *Journal of Educational Research,* April, 1949, pp. 561–72.

[9] F. Ivan Nye, *Family Relationships and Delinquent Behavior.* New York: John Wiley & Sons, 1959.

of evidence to demonstrate that delinquency is not the exclusive property of the lower class; it appears to exist to a significant degree in all strata of our society. But if this is the case, why have we only now become so deeply concerned about the affluent delinquent? Certainly if we have been concerned we have not been "publicly" concerned to the degree that we are today. Perhaps the answer lies in the fact that within our social structure there is a protective shield which hides the affluent delinquent and which up to now has served as a curtain of silence making privileged delinquency socially invisible. Nearly 30 years ago Warner and Lunt, in their classic work, *The Social Life of a Modern Community,* observed that the disparity in number of lower- and upper-class arrests is not to be accounted for by the fact that criminal behavior is proportionately higher among lower-class juveniles or that there are more ethnic groups whose children have been imperfectly adapted to city life. It must be understood as a product of the amount of protection from outside interference that parents can give members of their families.

PROPOSITION 3

Official delinquency data has been and is biased in favor of upper- and middle-class youth. Delinquency is usually considered primarily as a lower-class problem. However, the research reporting significant relationships between delinquent behavior and lower socioeconomic status has been characterized by a built-in bias, i.e., the use of official delinquency statistics that do not reflect a considerable amount of upper- and middle-class delinquent behavior. Middle- and upper-class children are less likely to become official delinquency statistics, because their behavior is more frequently handled outside the sphere of formal legal institutions. The middle and upper classes control various means of preventing detection, influencing official authority, and generally "taking care of their own" through psychiatrists, clinics, and private institutions, thus avoiding the police and the courts—the official agencies.

In the following telling and graphic descriptions, Harrison Salisbury [10] describes the classic middle-class way of dealing with anti-social behavior:

If sixteen-year old George and three of his friends "borrow" a nice-looking Pontiac convertible from the country club parking lot and set off on a joyride and are caught speeding by the county police they are taken to the station house all right, but nothing goes on the blotter. The parents come down, there is much talk, the fathers bawl the daylights out of the kids, the boys promise to be good, the owners wouldn't think of making a charge, and by two o'clock

[10] Harrison E. Salisbury, *The Shook-up Generation.* New York: Harper & Bros., 1958, pp. 107–109.

in the morning everyone is back home, peacefully sleeping. There's no case, no records, no statistics, "no delinquency."

When 17-year-old Joan gets pregnant after letting 18-year-old Dennis "fool around" at a beach party one summer night, she isn't sent to the Youth House. Nor is Dennis confronted with the dilemma of marrying the girl or facing a charge of statutory rape. There is an angry dispute between the two families. Joan's family blames Dennis. Dennis's family blames Joan. In the end Joan's father finds a doctor who takes care of Joan for $750. Joan is a month late starting school in the fall because, as her mother explains to the principal, she had a severe reaction from the antibiotics they gave her at the camp up in New Hampshire where she went in August.

In addition to the built-in bias of official delinquency data, studies reporting on the relationship between social class status and delinquent behavior are characterized by another critical shortcoming: a paucity of empirical material on a significant dynamic of social class—social mobility.

PROPOSITION 4

A significant factor related to delinquent behavior in the upper and middle classes is the dynamic of social mobility. What bearing does movement from one social class to another class have on delinquent behavior? What are the implications of vertical movement between classes in regard to norm violations? The question of social mobility has an important place in the study of social class and its impact on delinquent behavior for two reasons:

1. Social mobility introduces a dynamic feature of possible change in a class system, and 2. it can alter the structure and patterns of class relationships as the consequences of mobility introduce changes into those close relationships.

Here I would like to share with you the results of a study designed to determine the significance of the relationships between social class status, social mobility status, and delinquent behavior.[11] The study was conducted to determine the significance of the relationships between social class, social mobility, and delinquent behavior. Data were collected from a population of 683 pupils (grades 9–12) attending an urban high school. Information regarding delinquency was gathered by using a 120-item anonymous "delinquency inventory." The chi-square technique was employed to analyze the data, which showed that, in general, there is no significant relationship between social class status and delinquent behavior. A very strong relation-

[11] Gerald J. Pine, "Social Class, Social Mobility, and Delinquent Behavior," *Personnel and Guidance Journal,* April, 1965, pp. 770–74. See also: Pine's "Occupational and Educational Aspirations and Delinquent Behavior," *The Vocational Guidance Quarterly,* Winter Issue, 1964–65.

ship exists between social mobility status and delinquent behavior. Adolescents moving downward in the social structure are more heavily involved in delinquency; adolescents moving upward are least involved.

The primary conclusion made in this study is that delinquent behavior is less a function of the class an individual is in at the moment and much more a function of the class to which he aspires or toward which he is moving. In examining the relationship between social class and delinquent behavior, it is not only important to know what class an individual is in but perhaps more important to know if he is securely located in the class, if he has just managed a toehold in the class, or if he has just moved down from a class.

The findings indicate delinquent behavior is not a lower-class phenomenon. However, one aspect of the question of class differential in delinquent behavior which invites further investigation is the relationship between value system and delinquency. Social-class status may be more accurately measured in terms of value systems than in terms of economic factors such as occupation, housing, residence, and income. The lower-class boy moving upward into the middle class may be guided in his behavior by a middle-class value system and, therefore, might be more accurately described as a member of the middle class.

The behavior of the middle-class boy moving downward in the social structure may be influenced primarily by lower-class concerns, hence he might be more accurately described as lower class. It is quite possible for a child to live in a lower-class neighborhood and in the midst of a lower-class culture and still be considered middle class.

An explanation of the strong relationship between downward mobility and delinquent behavior may be found in Reissman's hypothesis [12] regarding the psychological consequences of "downward mobility." He suggests that these consequences can be channeled away from the individual to avoid injury to self-conceptions and self-respect. The individual imputes to others the blame for his or his family's descent in the social structure. His frustration and his failure are poured into an explanation that implicates society or society's institutions as the cause of it all. Hostile and negative attitudes toward others and toward authority develop.

If the intensity of the psychological consequences of "mobility failure" is in proportion to the degree of failure, then it is not difficult to understand the strength of the relationship between downward mobility and delinquent behavior. Certainly, downward mobility represents the greatest failure in the mobility process. For, in a culture which highly esteems the success value, what constitutes a greater failure than the failure to at least maintain one's status quo in the social structure?

[12] Leonard Reissman, *Class in American Society*. Glencoe, Ill.: The Free Press, 1959, p. 369.

PROPOSITION 5

Successful social mobility is a breeding ground for the development of delinquent behavior. The research evidence presented in Proposition 3 indicates there is a statistically significant relationship between downward mobility of adolescents and delinquent behavior. Paradoxically, the downward movement of the adolescent may be the consequence of the successful mobility of his parents. Psychological tension and conflict often accompany successful movement in the social structure and may be expressed in delinquent behavior. Successful mobility necessarily involves a major adjustment by the individual. He must reject the way of life of the group he has just left and assume the new way of life of the group he has just entered. It is a process of class "acculturation." Depending upon the change required, the reorientation of the individual can be enormous, depending upon the recency of the change, the reorientation can involve a great deal of insecurity.

"Successful mobility places the individual, for some period of time, in a marginal social position. The individual's former friends and associates may find him threatening: his success is a mark of their failure. His newly created friends and associates produced by his successful move may find him too 'different,' too 'raw,' and 'too recent' to be accepted as a bona fide member. The individual thus finds himself suspended in a 'success limbo.' The insecurity he feels may produce reactions the same as those exhibited by failure." [13]

Not only does the individual experience the results of success or failure but his family does also. Whyte [14] found that the individual's family must become implicated in his success just as they do in his failures.

On a larger scale, our society must experience the consequences for its emphasis upon social mobility, upon seeking and achieving success. Tumin [15] sets forth the following as by-products of the stress placed on social mobility in American society:

1. A "diffusion of insecurity" as more and more people become involved with trying to get ahead rather than developing any lasting and sure sense of the group and its needs. Traditional beliefs and values of society become threatened as behavior is more and more oriented toward "status acceptance and prestige ranking."
2. A "severe imbalance" of social institutions as a result of rapid mobility of the population as religion, education, and the family become tied to the struggle for economic success.

[13] *Ibid.,* pp. 371–72.
[14] W. H. Whyte, "The Wives of Management," *Fortune,* October, 1951; and "The Corporation and the Wife," *Fortune,* November, 1951.
[15] Melvin C. Tumin, "Some Unapplauded Consequences of Social Mobility in a Mass Society," *Social Forces,* October, 1957, pp. 32–37.

3. "Fragmentation of the social order" as more and more individuals become rivalrous with each other. Competition does not always lead to the greatest good for the greatest number.

4. "Denial of work" as the emphasis shifts from the importance of work and striving to the urgency of appearing to be successful. Preference is given to the open portrayal of *being* successful, as measured by the power and property which one openly consumes.

5. "Rapid social mobility" generates in the older portions of the population a cranky and bitter conservatism and worship of the past; and in the new mobile segments a vituperative contempt of traditions.

It is the accumulation and the complex interaction of these social by-products which fertilize the soil for the growth of affluent delinquency.

PROPOSITION 6

The female-based household is a by-product of successful mobility and an important variable in the development of delinquent behavior. Success and the striving for success in the middle and upper classes is frequently the incubator of the female-based household. A number of studies have identified the female-based household as a characteristic of lower-class society and as an influencing factor in the development of delinquent behavior. And yet anyone who has worked with middle- and upper-class youth is keenly aware of the large number of female-dominated families in suburbia. In order to insure and maintain his success, father often becomes a "weekend briefcase-toting visitor" who is either absent from the home, only sporadically present, or when present only minimally or inconsistently involved in the raising of the children. Mother becomes "chief cook and bottle washer," assuming both the maternal and paternal roles.

It is not too difficult to understand how female-centered families in the middle and upper class can produce delinquents, particularly in the male adolescent population.

Because of the inconsistent presence or involvement of an adequate masculine model in the home with whom the suburban boy can identify, many teen-age males develop uncertainties about their masculine identity at a time in their lives when identity is a crucial matter. For the adolescent male who feels insecure about his sex identification, delinquency represents a demonstrative vehicle for asserting his masculinity.

PROPOSITION 7

The emphasis on success in our culture has led to the elongation of adolescence, a contributing factor in the development of delinquent behavior. Another consequence of success in the middle and upper classes is the extension of adolescence as a period of growth and development. The emphasis on success in suburbia is epitomized in the pressures exerted on youth to get into college. For the vast numbers of young boys and girls who do go to college one fact is very clear: Adolescence doesn't end at 18 or 19; it probably ends at 21 or 22; and perhaps even later. Thus for a large number of our privileged youth at least four years have been tacked on to the process of growing up and four years can be a long time to wait to prove yourself—to demonstrate that you are a man or a woman. Four more years of that social limbo we call adolescence are very conducive to intensifying the already existing feelings of anxiety, tension, restlessness, and rebellion so common to high school youth. Adolescence is becoming an "existential vacuum," a social process lacking purpose and meaning. To the degree we elongate the process of adolescence without providing purpose for its existence, to that degree should we anticipate more frequent socially aberrant and rebellious behavior.

PROPOSITION 8

A middle- and upper-class "sheepskin psychosis" nourishes norm-violating behavior. In the middle and upper classes there is tremendous pressure placed upon youth to succeed. These pressures emanate from the dominating concern of parents for achieving and "getting ahead," and the feeling in youth of an ensuing sense of discrepancy between aspiration and achievement. "This strong focus in the middle-class milieu may induce the whole perfectionist-compulsive syndrome, in which children have impossible ideas of what they should accomplish; the result for some individuals is a combination of neuroses built around the individual's inability to achieve internalized goals of various types, e.g., learning to read, being on the honor roll, or getting into the college of first choice. . . . The stresses imposed through the conflict over aspiration and achievement wake a wide variety of symptoms. One of these symptoms may take the form of norm-violating behavior." [16]

PROPOSITION 9

Middle-class values which once served as behavior controls are weakening. One of the identifying characteristics of the middle class is the tradition of deferring immediate gratifications for long-range goals. For years this tradition helped to instill in middle-class youngsters a capacity for self-denial and impulse control. However, there is mounting indication today that the strength of this tradition of focus on achievement, of directed work

[16] William C. Kvaraceus and Walter Miller, Delinquent Behavior: Culture and the Individual. Washington, D.C.: National Education Association, 1959, pp. 99–100.

effort, and deferment of immediate pleasures is diminishing in a number of middle-class sectors. Impulse buying and installment plan financing are very representative of the "have-it-now" pattern of the lower-class culture. Concomitantly, compulsory education and a continuous promotion policy act to keep all youngsters in school regardless of effort, achievement, or future goal. These trends have tended to lessen the view of middle-class youth that success is achieved through deferred gratification, frustration tolerance, directed effort, and self-control. If delinquency is on the rise in the middle class, it may be attributable in part to a diminution in the classical middle-class tradition of "hard work today and rewards tomorrow."

PROPOSITION 10

Middle-class youth behavior reflects lower-class values. Currently, lower-class concerns and values are being sold to and bought by the middle-class consumer. Mass media and the advertising world have dipped deeply into the lower-class culture. Lower-class focal concerns such as force, duplicity, chance, excitement, trouble, autonomy, and "present pleasure" have been mined over and over again for use on the screen, the air waves, the picture tube, and the printed page. The effect of this cultural saturation has been the borrowing of lower-class concerns by middle-class youth. Adolescent fads, jargon, music, and behavior seem to mirror a number of lower-class behavior patterns. It would seem that the interaction of these recently assumed lower-class concerns with the other social and psychological by-products of social mobility constitute a powerful generative force in developing affluent delinquency.

ADDITIONAL READINGS

Henderson, George. Opportunity and alienation in public schools. *Teachers College Record,* November 1967, **69** (2), 151–157. The problem of alienation is defined and related to the programs of the schools. Recommendations are made for curtailing the problems of student alienation.
Keniston, K. *The uncommitted: alienated youth in American society.* New York: Harcourt, Brace & World, 1965. This excellent observational study asks the question: Why are some of our most privileged and talented youngsters disenchanted with American society? Keniston begins with a

psychodynamic analysis of a group of alienated Harvard students. He also appraises the alienating features of American society.

Newman, Fred M. Adolescents' acceptance of authority: A methodological study. *Harvard Educational Review,* 1965, **35,** 303–325. This article involving discussions with adolescents reports a clinical study of criteria which seem to underlie acceptance of authority.

Parkinson, Thomas. (Ed.) *A casebook on the beat.* New York: Crowell, 1961. The essays in this book afford an understanding of the writing relating to the Beat Generation. The first part of the book is composed of poetry, writing, and expository prose; the second part of comment.

Piliavin, Irving & Briar, Scott. Police encounters with juveniles. *American Journal of Sociology,* September 1964, **70** (2), 206–214. This study indicates that policemen exercised wide discretion in dealing with juvenile offenders and were affected in such contacts by a few readily observable criteria including boys' prior offense records, race, grooming, and behavior. The boy is a delinquent because someone in authority has defined him as one, often on the basis of the public face he has presented rather than kind of offense committed.

Schonfield, Jacob. Differences in smoking, drinking, and social behavior by race and delinquency status in adolescent males. *Adolescence,* Winter 1966–67, **1** (4), 377–380. Schonfield summarizes available research on the behavioral characteristics of adolescent smokers, drinkers, and delinquents. He seeks the common core of these findings and interprets them in terms of personality theory.

Shore, Milton F. & Massimo, Joseph L. Comprehensive vocationally oriented psychotherapy of adolescent delinquent boys: A follow-up study. *American Journal of Orthopsychiatry,* 1966, **36,** 609–615. This article reports a follow-up study two or three years after treatment was terminated of boys participating in a comprehensive vocationally oriented psychotherapeutic program. The treated group made major improvements in ego functioning, academic learning, personality attitude, and overt behavior, although the rate of improvement decreased after formal therapy had stopped. The great majority of the untreated boys showed marked and continued deterioration.

Szabó, Denis. The sociocultural approach to the aetiology of delinquent behavior. *International Social Science Journal,* 1966, **18** (2), 176–196. Szabo examines various theories of delinquency, then considers the synthesis of psychology and sociology as an approach. In conclusion, he indicates how criminal behavior can be analyzed by sociologists.

XIV. Dating

Dating is not to be confused with courtship. Courtship is adult-oriented, with marriage as its goal. Dating is present-oriented, and an end in itself. In theoretical terms, dating involves several issues; for example, what is the nature of dating? How do dating patterns vary with time, place, age, and socioeconomic status? Adolescents live in a world largely insulated from the adult, and the dater's world is largely unknown by him. The adult assumes that the same rules of the dating-game apply as in his youth, but do they? Apparently, modifications in dating do occur, often reflecting larger sociocultural change. Today, girls play a more aggressive, and boys a more defensive, role than formerly. Perhaps this change helps account for the increased incidence of going steady, pinning, short engagements, and early marriages. Parents, especially, influence their children's dating patterns. For example, the adolescent who feels particularly obligated to his parents dates less often than normally. Girls date earlier than boys, and marriage-oriented adolescents more frequently than career-directed ones.

Critics differ in their evaluation of dating. Dating is sometimes blamed for wasting time that could better be spent at other pursuits. Moreover, adolescents are considered too immature to handle the intense sex feelings aroused. Dates are also expensive, and encourage boys to drop out of school to finance them. By contrast, defenders of the practice claim that dating constitutes a desirable preparation for marriage. Adolescents receive hetero-sexual experience of a more intimate nature than provided in larger groups.

To the female, dating is especially crucial. The male's adult role is firmly anchored in occupation; but the dominant female role is still that of housewife and mother. Thus, the girl's adult security depends largely on her relation to the particular man she marries. Hence, dating becomes a deadly serious business, and women have higher aspirations for their dating partner than do men.[1]

Another issue is whether "going steady" should be encouraged or deplored. When unchaperoned dating first gained headway in the early part of the century, dating partners changed more often than today. By World War II, steady dating had taken hold, and today most students have had such an experience. Authorities sharply disagree in evaluating the practice. Defenders of going steady argue that more casual dating encourages shallow

[1] Robert H. Coombs and William F. Kenkel, "Sex Differences in Dating Aspirations and Satisfaction with Computer-Selected Partners," *Journal of Marriage and the Family,* Vol. 28, No. 1 (1966), pp. 61–66.

relationships. Adolescents also gain security from having a sure date for attending peer-group functions. Meanwhile, they learn social graces in the process of attending social affairs with their dates. Furthermore, steady dating, more easily than casual dating, permits the simultaneous development of sexual behavior and mutual affection, which is important for the later marital relationship. Finally, since permissiveness-with-affection is an accepted pattern, the girl who goes steady may have sexual experience without jeopardizing her reputation.

Opponents of steady dating say that teen-agers need a more varied heterosexual experience. Before they settle down in marriage they should learn to relate to various types of the other sex. Also, regular dating often merges prematurely into courtship. Moreover, the isolation granted teen daters projects them into situations they are too immature to control. Steady daters, in particular, are likely to risk premarital sex experience by rationalizing that they are in love.

It is commonly assumed that teen-agers are a wild lot sexually, but Reiss disagrees. The coitus rate for females doubles between the ages of 20 and 25. On the basis of available evidence, notes Reiss, teen-agers show greater conservatism and responsibility in sexual codes and behavior than commonly believed.[2]

Other questions about dating are these: how early should parents permit dating? To what extent should parents regulate choice of dating partners? What sex standards should prevail on dates? Where can adolescents gain healthy guidelines for their dating behaviors? To date, researchers have failed adequately to answer these questions. Psychologists, especially, often brush off this aspect of human development as unworthy of serious research. Most available data have come from sociologists. Especially needed are phenomenological studies of what dating means for individual adolescents' development.

In the following selection, Ernest A. Smith, a sociologist, discusses major characteristics of dating as an American pattern. He indicates particular functions of dating, and distinguishes it from courtship. In the second selection, Elizabeth Douvan and Joseph Adelson explore some of the more subtle aspects of dating. Their observations are based on data obtained from two national interview studies conducted by the University of Michigan's Survey Research Center. Both selections indicate dating to possess far more complexities than often assumed. Both also treat it as an integral institution of American adolescence.

[2] Ira L. Reiss, "Sexual Codes in Teen-Age Culture," in Jessie Bernard (Ed.), *Teen-Age Culture,* Philadelphia: The American Academy of Political and Social Science, Vol. 338 (November 1961), pp. 53–62.

29

Ernest A. Smith

THE DATE

Smith discusses the nature and function of dating, different kinds of dating, and the modal pattern of dating in America. Dating is seen as nonfunctional for adulthood, and as distinct from courtship.

The date is a major transitional institution of youth culture and it is the outstanding example of the distinctive institutions developed by middle-class youth. The date, moreover, best illustrates the emergence of a new youth institution in America that functions to provide transition in a new social situation. One discussion of courtship patterns states that the date did not appear as an approved institution until after the 1900's (Merrill, 1949, pp. 8, 20–21). A detailed casenote of the deterioration of a New England community documents the emergence of the exploitative date (Homans, 1950, pp. 334–368, *passim*).

The dating pattern is not only a comparatively recent innovation in youth relations, it is peculiarly typical of America. American youth are often amazed to learn that many contemporary nations and cultures have no dating pattern and strongly resist its introduction.

A most interesting aspect of the date is that, of all youth institutions, it varies most from adult norms. Romantic love is least relevant during dating, although it simulates romantic love by using its language devoid of "meaning." During this period the sex taboos are most rigorously operative, with a gradual relaxation, in terms of increased intimacy, as youth approach marriage. An exception is found in the exploitative cross-class dating carried on by boys.

In terms of the adult norms of marriage and sex relations, the date is aim-inhibited. As a result, it is marked by mutual exploitation. On the other hand, the date is strongly oriented toward the dominant American goals of popularity, achievement, and success.

In view of its distinctiveness and importance in youth culture, the date is an institution particularly relevant to sociological investigation and crucially important to an understanding of youth culture. The date falls within the area of intimate relations, meeting Simmel's criteria of a sexual dyad, or the simplest relational structure dependent on two persons. It is characterized by intimacy and lack of duration (Wolff, 1950, pp. 20, 118, 123, 125–126, 129).

Two different patterns are classified under the date because they both fulfill the function of filling in the interim period prior to courtship. These two patterns, the competitive date and the noncommitment steady date, will be analyzed separately in this section. They are similar in all respects except that the competitive data emphasizes partner mobility, while the noncommitment steady involves only one partner at a time.

The competitive date may be described as a heterosexual pair relationship that is competitive in terms of partners and that stresses no emotional involvement or commitment. This element of noncommitment is a new morality in American premarital relations (Waller, 1937, p. 728). Although dating contravenes adult norms of romantic love and commitment, adults encourage such unchaperoned pair relations and accept the fact that no serious thought of commitment is involved. Youth overwhelmingly conform, as is illustrated by Nimkoff and Wood's study, where 99 per cent of the youth dated (Nimkoff and Wood, 1948, p. 269).

Although there are regional and class variations in dating behavior, there is a broad general pattern emerging, which has a structural form and is reinforced by both communal norms and mass media. There is also a profound culturally determined difference in the goals and behavior of the male and female, which makes it necessary to treat them separately (Winch, 1943, p. 170-n). In this study, the specificities of the date ritual are seen as a male pattern which requires complementary female behavior, but there are significant variations in the goals and behavior of each sex group.

Although the date is a general American pattern, its specific norms are middle-class, particularly because of its transitional function. It is among higher-class youth that the postponement of serious commitment and marriage leads to the emergence of an informal play relationship that provides an outlet for the sex interests of youth. The college campus community being conventionally middle-class, age-selective, and directly affected by postponement of marriage, reveals the mode of the dating pattern. The high school group also is governed by these norms. Both Hollingshead and Winch point out that youth of higher socioeconomic levels date more frequently and more widely than do lower-class youth (Hollingshead, 1949, p. 229; Winch, 1946, p. 337). An analysis of lower-class sex behavior, which violates dating norms, underscores the conclusion that the date is predominantly middle-class, performing a transitional role before courtship, which is a prelude to adult culture. The date is an informal institution of youth culture—perhaps one of the most vital and significant.

The date, as an informal institution of youth culture, has been initiated and perpetuated by youth, who elaborate their own norms and sentiments independently of the adult culture. The fact that dating is mainly characteristic of American youth and is a relatively recent emergent points to its informal structure.

Kingsley Davis points out that the sexual institutions that facilitate reproduction and socialization are given the greatest institutional support. In our culture marriage is the most respectable institution, and the others diminish in respectability as they range away from marriage (Davis, 1937, p. 747). In this sense, the date is far removed from marriage, in that it is oriented neither toward marriage nor children; but it is not socially disapproved. It may be evaluated in terms of its specific function, namely to provide a socially approved outlet for heterosexual interests during a period when the adult status is unattainable. Therefore, the informal norms of youth culture, designed to inhibit a tendency toward mutual affection, marriage, and children, have come to be largely accepted and reinforced by an adult culture that formally condemns such norms. Yet youth, by withdrawal and conspiracy of silence, use the freedom so gained to engage in behavior far removed from the adult-approved norms.

Taylor notes that the date differs from most institutions in that it has no organizations of its own to promote its own goals. It lacks a larger structural control frame, as well as defined stages of ceremonies for entrance into courtship. The date has little control over its technology and material aspects, as in home privacy, automobile, telephone, and finances. Youth often attempt to pre-empt these facilities, a practice that leads to conflict and tension between parents and youth. Consequently, the date pattern does not provide adequate means for meeting partners or for perpetuating such relationships (Taylor, 1946, pp. 66–68).

Landis asserts: "In no field have our social institutions been so negligent of the needs of adolescents and youth" (Landis, 1948, p. 231). Full responsibility for date choices is in the hands of inexperienced youth. In the variants of the pickup, where two unknowns initiate the relationship, and the blind date, where a date between strangers is sponsored by friends or an organization, even less control is exerted (Christiansen and Neumann, 1949, p. 39). Such dating practices are common in an urban, anonymous society and have general approval among youth. Of college students surveyed by Cupps and Hayner, 57.7 per cent of the males and 62.1 per cent of the females approved of the blind date (Cupps and Hayner, 1947, pp. 30–31).

The social life of youth, including dating patterns, is largely independent of adult supervision and control. The clique or crowd often sponsors the date, and recreational activities associated with the date are largely free from parental supervision. The automobile provides mobility in making and keeping dates, as well as complete privacy, which allows an escape from adult observation and chaperonage. Consequently, dates occur under conditions that were considered immoral a generation ago. The dating partners are often virtually unknown to the parents and even to each other, so there can be little parental evaluation of either persons or behavior.

Since dating patterns are relatively independent of adult culture, parents do not influence them. Consequently, youth receive no clear initiation into behavioral norms, and their peers often cannot clear up the confusion. Even if parents were able to give training in dating norms, partners would still face uncertainty and unpredictability in each new dating situation. In spite of parental ignorance, dating youth still get much specific advice on how to act, and mothers tell their daughters just what they should and should not say and do. Frequently, parents view the date as part of the courtship process, instead of recognizing its informal youth culture role. In Williams' study, 73 per cent of the girls and 68 per cent of the boys stated that parents do not understand the dating situation (Williams, 1949, Table 3, p. 281).

Every detail of the dating roles complicates the problem. Youth are confused about when to start dating, methods of meeting and accepting dates, who takes the initiative, who plans activities, the allocation of expenses, what sex behavior is permitted, how late to stay out, and how many dates one may have a week; and they have little guidance in these matters. Williams found that the important problem areas for boys were finding out how to act and finding ways to obtain money and a car. Also, 33 per cent of both boys and girls worried about their behavior, largely in terms of being failures in dating and of being afraid while dating (Williams, 1949, Table 3, p. 281).

Dating Distinguished from Courtship. The norms and behavior of the dating pattern, and their relation to courtship, have influenced analysts to view the date in various ways. Lowrie sees the date as leading to courtship (Lowrie, 1948, p. 90). Winch considers dating as part of the sequence of courtship behavior, ranging from minimum to maximum involvement (Winch, 1943, pp. 165–166). Waller includes dating as part of the courtship process but distinguishes it as "purposeless courtship" in that it is aim-inhibited (Waller, 1938, pp. 227, 235).

However, the date is the antithesis of the romantic love ideal of mutual permanent commitment, while courtship previews ultimate commitment and marriage. The fact that dating activity is correlated with later courtship patterns (Winch, 1943, p. 335) and that dating chronologically precedes courtship, does not mean that they are part of the same process. During "sociological adolescence," created by the discontinuity in formal socializing institutions, age-mates date but continuously change partners on account of their inability to marry. Cuber's study emphasizes that the date

is primarily enjoyed as an end in itself and therefore is not part of courtship (Cuber, 1943, p. 32). On the contrary, it is perhaps the single most
important institution of youth culture, as opposed to courtship, which may
be viewed as a gradual initiation into adult life.

Kingsley Davis points to this difference in noting that although dating
is a sexual institution, along with courtship and marriage, it performs different functions (Davis, 1937, p. 746). Both Mead and Gorer perceive
that dating cannot be identified objectively with either courtship or sex
relations (Mead, 1949, a, p. 285; Forer, 1948, p. 109). Youth itself
clearly perceives and acts on the belief that dating is not part of courtship.
For example, high school girls in New York City openly labeled themselves
available for dating. A blue anklet worn on either leg meant "no boy
friends, but taking date bids," while a red anklet on the left leg meant
"having boy friends and taking date bids" (*The New York Times*, 1953,
p. 25).

Lowrie attempted to test the distinctive criteria of the date by asking
a sample of high school and college students their reasons for dating. He
concluded that the criteria were artificial and contrary to the conceptions
of dating youth. As a result, Lowrie regards dating as a process of mate selection and includes love relations (Lowrie, 1951, p. 340). Several weak-
nesses appear in this analysis. Dating criteria are not invalidated just because
youth do not recognize them. One of the implications of sociological patterns is that people are conditioned by them and certainly need no "reasons"
to explain their behavior. The reasons given by dating youth were not
necessarily sound, yet Lowrie evaluates the date in terms of them.

This difference in analysis has broken into open controversy through
the attack by Burgess and Locke on Lowrie's position, which they feel
makes discriminating research impossible (Burgess and Locke, 1951, pp.
843–844). Lowrie's reply showed that he wants to use the term "date" to
include several phases that can be distinguished within it (Lowrie, 1952,
pp. 364–365). Both analyses take the same position, namely, that pair
relationships pass through different and distinctive phases. The question
resolves itself as to whether the term "date" should be applied to only
one phase, or all phases, of these relationships.

Different analysts use a variety of terms which generally point to the
same characteristics. For example, Hobart distinguishes "no particular
date," favorite date, and going steady (Hobart, 1955, p. 338). Herman
labels the phases: playing the field, going steadily, and going steady (Herman, 1955, p. 36). Hurlock labels the phases: many dates with many individuals, going steady, and an understanding to be married (Hurlock,
1955, p. 391).

An analysis of youth culture as a series of transitional institutions requires that the phases be marked in order to trace the full socialization
process. Independent research indicates that this confusion of concepts may

be cleared up by distinguishing the various phases of the date (Smith, 1955, pp. 92–98, *passim*). For example, the competitive date must be clearly distinguished from the noncommitment steady date and the commitment steady date, since all three phases have different norms and somewhat different functions. The general term "date" is much too broad if it is used to include competitive, noncommitment, and commitment pair relationships. If it is limited to just one phase, say that of "competitive," terms must be found for the other phases. Subsequent analysis of these institutions is designed to do this.

Another confusion arises when an attempt is made to differentiate the phases of dating in terms of subjective motivation. Merrill states that the line between the date and courtship is not clear because the situation will vary depending on each partner's definition of the relationship (Merrill, 1949, pp. 74, 81). Although dating partners may have different attitudes toward the relationship, the institutional phases may be revealed by an analysis of objective factors such as economic-family-class criteria, as well as competition, degrees of commitment, and goal-achievement.

THE DATE AS A TRANSITIONAL INSTITUTION

In general, the date functions as a socially approved transitional institution, directed toward heterosexual association, during the period of sociological adolescence. Since courtship cannot arise where marriage is impossible, the date fills in an extended period of postponed marriage with play relations. The date marks a transitional phase beyond the clique, in which affectional bonds are presumed to be transferred to persons of the opposite sex. The process may be viewed as transitional from one sexual dyad to another, as in son-mother—son-male—son-female—son-wife. Youth formerly went in crowds, but today there may be a tendency to skip the crowd phase (MacKenzie, 1946, p. 34; Folsom, 1943, p. 189).

The date arises to satisfy the maturing need for heterosexual association and intimacy. Youth are dominated by the adult emphasis on couple relationships. Heterosexual interest increases at about thirteen years of age, and its expression in dating starts at that time and increases with age ("Profile of Youth," 1949, f, p. 49). Parents and youth come into conflict over the question of the proper age to start dating. The confused status of youth is revealed by the wide range of ages approved by parents—anywhere from fourteen to twenty years, particularly for daughters. On the other hand, some high school youth set fifteen years as suitable for the first date (Christensen, 1952, pp. 584–585).

REFERENCES

Ernest W. Burgess and Harvey J. Locke, "Comment on Lowrie's 'Dating Theories and Student Responses,'" Letter to the Editor, *American Sociological Review*, Vol. 16 (December 1951), pp. 843–844.

Patricia Christiansen and Margaret Neumann, "Blind Date," *Good Housekeeping*, Vol. 129 (October 1949), p. 39.

John F. Cuber, "Changing Courtship and Marriage Customs," *The Annals of the American Academy of Political and Social Science*, Vol. 229 (September 1943), p. 32.

Rayanne C. Cupps and Norman S. Hayner, "Dating at the University of Washington," *Marriage and Family Living*, Vol. 9 (May 1947), pp. 30–31.

Kingsley Davis, "The Sociology of Prostitution," *American Sociological Review*, Vol. 2 (October 1937), p. 746.

Ibid. p. 747.

Geoffrey Gorer, *The American People, A Study in National Character* (New York: W. W. Norton and Co., Inc., 1948), p. 109.

Robert D. Herman, "The 'Going Steady' Complex: A Re-examination," *Marriage and Family Living*, Vol. 17 (February 1955), p. 36.

Charles W. Hobart, "Romanticism and Marriage Role Opinions," *Sociology and Social Research*, Vol. 42 (May–June 1955), p. 338.

August B. Hollingshead, *Elmtown's Youth* (New York: John Wiley & Sons, Inc., 1949), p. 229.

George C. Homans, *The Human Group* (New York: Harcourt, Brace & Co., 1950), pp. 334–368.

Elizabeth A. Hurlock, *Adolescent Development* (New York: McGraw-Hill Book Co., Inc., 1955), p. 391.

Samuel Harman Lowrie, "Dating, A Neglected Field of Study," *Marriage and Family Living*, Vol. 10 (Fall 1948), p. 90.

Samuel Harman Lowrie, "Rejoinder to Burgess and Locke," Letter to the Editor, *American Sociological Review*, Vol. 17 (June 1952), pp. 364–365.

Samuel Harman Lowrie, "Dating Theories and Student Responses," *American Sociological Review*, Vol. 16 (June 1951), p. 340.

Margaret Mead, *Male and Female* (New York: William Morrow and Co., 1949, a) p. 285.

Francis E. Merrill, *Courtship and Marriage: A Study in Social Relationships* (New York: William Sloane Associates, Inc., 1949), pp. 8, 20–21.

Ibid. pp. 74, 81.

New York Times (April 27, 1953), p. 25.

Meyer F. Nimkoff and Arthur L. Wood, "Courtship and Personality," *American Journal of Sociology*, Vol. 53 (January 1948), p. 269.

Ernest A. Smith, "Dating and Courtship at Pioneer College," *Sociology and Social Research*, Vol. 40 (November–December 1955), pp. 92–98.

Donald C. Taylor, "Courtship as a Social Institution in the United States, 1930 to 1945," *Social Forces*, Vol. 25 (October 1946), pp. 66–68.

Willard Waller, "The Rating and Dating Complex," *American Sociological Review*, Vol. 2 (October 1937), p. 728.

Willard Waller, *The Family: A Dynamic Interpretation* (New York: The Dryden Press, 1938), pp. 227, 235.

Melvin J. Williams, "Personal and Familial Problems of High School Youths and Their Bearing Upon Family Education Needs," *Social Forces*, Vol. 27 (March 1949), p. 281.

Ibid.

Robert F. Winch, "Interrelations Between Certain Social Background and Parent-Son Factors in a Study of Courtship Among College Men," *American Sociological Review*, Vol. 11 (June 1946), p. 337.

Robert F. Winch, "The Relation Between Courtship Behavior and Attitudes Toward Parents Among College Men," *American Sociological Review*, Vol. 8 (April 1943), p. 170-n.

Robert F. Winch, *op. cit.*, pp. 165–166.

Kurt H. Wolff (translator) *The Sociology of George Simmel* (New York: The Free Press of Glencoe, 1950), pp. 20, 118, 123, 125–126, 129.

30

Elizabeth Douvan
Joseph Adelson

AMERICAN DATING PATTERNS

In the following selection excerpted from a nation-wide study already quoted, the writers consider the nature and function of the dating practice in this country. They consider the dating personality, dating as a rite de passage, and developmental patterns in dating. They conclude that the dating practice presents various problems and has certain harmful effects. Specific practices and attitudes are found to vary by age and sex.

Dating is surprisingly complex, and far more difficult to encompass and understand than many discussions of it would make it appear. We have discovered, in talking with people about their dating experiences, that they generally take their own histories to be typical, when in fact their histories were distinctly diverse. We shall speak of the dating pattern but it would be more accurate to make it plural. What we find are many different patterns. Even within the adolescent period, the modes and conditions of dating vary sharply with age. There are local variations and differences stemming from social class. In most cases, the dating institution is loose enough to permit marked individual variations.

Another source of complexity is that the dating mechanism serves a number of functions simultaneously. From the broadest, most telic perspective it is clearly a device for mate selection. From this point of view, dating is to be related to the prevailing ideology of marriage. Our social system stresses love as the motive for marriage, and insists on the free choice of partner. The dating institution, then, is an integral part of the courtship-to-marriage sequence. It offers occasions for falling in love and thus finding a spouse. All of this is obvious enough; but to place too much emphasis on this particular goal of the dating system is to misconstrue its actual workings.

Observers of the American dating system, Waller (1937) and Mead (1955), in particular, have shown graphically that dating absorbs and reflects motives and values somewhat removed from marriage per se. Among other functions, the dating mechanism serves in the finding and testing of

From Elizabeth Douvan and Joseph Adelson, *The Adolescent Experience* (New York, John Wiley, 1966), pp. 203–213. Reprinted by permission.

identity; it is a laboratory for training in the social graces; it provides occasions for sexual experiment and discovery; it is used to chart popularity and success. To be sure these functions are by no means unrelated to the ultimate goal of marital choice, but neither are they isomorphic with it. It is one of the paradoxes of the dating system that its presumably subsidiary goals and values, such as "popularity," become autonomous, lose their connection to the ultimate goal, and may even end in subverting or distorting it. As we shall see, the dating system tends to reward certain personal qualities; these may become entrenched and survive, inappropriately, into marriage. The dating institution encourages certain modes of sexual behavior which, again, tend to survive inappropriately into marriage. It would be both foolish and overfacile to argue that American marital patterns are largely fixed by the rites of dating and by those alone; but there is enough in the relationship between the two to make us want to look closely at dating and its consequences.

Let us begin with an outsider's view. A thoughtful Finnish girl, after a year in this country, tells us she has been unable to feel comfortable about dating. The reason, she has at last decided, is that as a "date" she is not quite herself, not quite allowed to be herself. As a "date" she is, these are her words, a Social Role. "The boy is supposed to bring a date, and it doesn't matter who she is as long as she says and does what's expected of her. The boy brings a date the way he might bring a pair of skis if he were going skiing."

She is being unfair, and we tell her so. She is simply too new to the role, too self-conscious about it, and therefore unable to do much more than discover and try to realize its expectations. The American girl, we say, is socialized to the dating pattern, knows its rules automatically, unconsciously, and so can find within them the elbow room she needs to practice individuality. Our Finn will take some of this reproach, but not much. Yes, there is something in what we say, but on the whole she will let her statement stand. The more sensitive American girls agree with her, and for the rest, they have long since grown into the role, so much so that the role and personality have become hard to separate.

Whatever we may think of this conversation, it does remind us that the dating situation is a social form, governed by a complex and sometimes fiercely constrained etiquette. It is no less formal and ritualized for pretending strenuously that it is not, for appearing to be "free" and "spontaneous." All that merry laughter, all that gay, youthful banter notwithstanding, dating behavior is generally as limited and narrowly focused, as predetermined as the courtship repartee in a Jane Austen novel.[1] That dating is so regulated and constrained does not especially distinguish it; all social behavior follows certain forms and understandings.

[1] Indeed more so, when we come to think of it, and remember the easy play of wit and nuance in the courtship conversations.

388 Issues in Peer Relations

The point our Finnish girl wants to make is that the American dating code, as she has seen it, works to inhibit and destroy the very type of personal relationship it ought to encourage. She means that dating should allow the encounter of selves rather than roles, that it ought to expose rather than conceal individuality.

What are the reasons it does not, when it does not? Here we meet an apparent paradox. We might believe that dating is designed to bring about liaisons marked by increasing intimacy. So they do: sometimes. But dating has another side to it, which is the avoidance of intimacy, or perhaps we should say the control of intimacy. The dating situation is potentially explosive, or at least is felt to possess that potential. The external controls provided by chaperonage are absent; the burden of constraint passes to the actors. One function of the dating role, or the dating persona, is to keep the instincts at bay in a potentially unstable setting. The date will generally have its erotic aspect, but ordinarily it is a token sexuality, implacably fixed in its negotiations, designed less to express the erotic than to bring obligations to account. This is especially true when the boy and girl are new to the game. It is during the early years of adolescence that the dating pattern is a means of shielding the youngster from the demands and anxieties of sexuality.

Another problem is self-esteem, so uncertain during this time even among the better adjusted. Dating is a way of measuring the self through the other's appraisal. All too often the youngster will take his success or failure in dating as a portent of his entire heterosexual destiny. The response of the other is used to predict one's future in affection. With so much felt to be at stake, and knowing easily he can be hurt, the youngster retreats to the safety of the role as a way of hiding the "true self" from the humiliations of social failure.

These vulnerabilities—sexual anxiety, the tenuousness of self-esteem —help us give the dating system its peculiar emotional tone. The problem is to expose the child to these sources of hurt and danger, and yet protect him from being overwhelmed by them. It is something like hyposensitization for an allergy. The trick is in the controlled exposure to a potentially dangerous substance. The dating pattern, particularly in its early stages, immunizes the child, by allowing him to play at and so learn the techniques of social and sexual interaction. The dating code, the implicit prescriptions for behavior and affect, are designed to keep the relationships casual, superficial, emotionally noninvolving.

There develops a kind of characterological fiction—the "good date." Its dimensions vary somewhat with age, social status, and other local circumstances, but generally, the good date is someone skilled in keeping impulses and affects under control in a situation that tends to stimulate them. The good date, male or female, can keep the ball rolling, is amiable and verbally facile. The overt expression of impulse is strictly forbidden.

One must not be directly sensual or aggressive. Indeed, any extreme of be havior, even a "desirable" extreme, is generally felt to be out of place. One ought to be gay and yet not altogether frivolous; one ought to be bright, and yet not serious or intellectual; one is expected to offer comments on the evening's entertainment, the movie, let us say, and yet without vehe- mence. The boy can exercise some inventiveness in arranging the evening's activities, but not to the point of deviation. The girl's behavior is probably more strictly regulated than the boy's; she is to be the audience to the boy's offerings of entertainment, yet she must be at the least polite and if possible enthusiastic about it, whatever her secret inclinations may be. Similarly both sexes must learn to control the moods they may be in as they enter the evening. One cannot settle into a glum silence because one feels out of sorts.

These controls on the free expression of feelings are of course general to social life and are by no means unique to dating. All social intercourse is regulated by expectations and prescriptions of varying degrees of stringency. One does not tell the hostess what one may really think of her meal, nor yawn loudly during a committee meeting, nor do a thousand other things one may want to on public occasions. It is one perspective on social life to see it founded on a complex structure of deceits, hypocrisies, black and white lies, false fronts. In this respect (and allowing for differences in rhetoric) adolescent cynicism-idealism as we see it expressed, for example in the tortured reflections of Holden Caulfield, shows a striking similarity to the solemn observations of an Erving Goffman (1959) on the necessary falsehoods of everyday life. The entry into adolescence brings with it what may appear to be a loss of innocence, in that the child learns to dissemble, and to adjust himself to proprieties which are at the same time, hypocrisies. What the child loses in innocence, he gains in tact. Childhood can also be the age without pity, the age of unconscious and casual cruelty.

It is in this sense that we can see the entrance into dating and the learning of the dating code as functional to adolescent socialization. The youngster acquires a wide array of ego skills appropriate to social inter- action. He may learn to temper whatever projective confusions he has es- tablished concerning the opposite sex. Because dating is to some degree transitory, errors of tact and control are of less permanent consequence than they might otherwise be. The system also provides techniques for terminating unwanted relationships (and for forming new ones) which minimize the loss of face. Later we shall present data which suggest that the girl, as she matures in the dating system, shows a growth in both sensitivity and good sense as regards her relations with boys.

Probably that is the best to be said for the dating pattern as it now exists in this country. There is not much more to be cheerful about. The emphasis on the "dating personality," in a context of intense sexual and personal competitiveness, can drive the American youngster to displays of emptiness, silliness, artificiality, vanity, vulgarity and among girls, outright "tigerish bitchiness," which is truly one of the wonders of the world. Here is a comment from a film review by James Agee:

> The March of Time's issue about teen-age girls is worth seeing in the sense that one might examine with interest a slide of cancer tissue. These girls may be no worse than the teen-age girls of any other country, class, or generation, but I would be sorry really to believe that, and am sorrier still to imagine their children (Agee, 1958).

That is all he has to say. He leaves it to our own experience to fill in the rest, and we find it all too easy to do so. This is, to be sure, the American adolescent at his or her worst, but it is an all too frequent worst, and a worst that is likely to be produced by (and show itself in) the dating context.

One reason that the present dating system is (as we think it is) damaging to character formation is that dating begins so early in this country. Our data show that girls typically begin to have dates at fourteen and fifteen, boys a year or so later. We have been unable to find data for the European countries, but everyone we have talked to reports that dating (or its equivalent) begins several years later in most cases. Indeed, the European observer will generally comment on the tender age at which the American youngster is launched on an independent social career.

One consequence of this early entrance into heterosexual social life is that the youngster will become socially precocious. The American adolescent, put out on his own so soon, will often develop a degree of poise and nonchalance which stands in vivid contrast to the shyness, embarrassment, and even gaucherie of the European youngster of equivalent years. The contrast is perhaps especially marked among girls. One of us taught at an expensive women's college which occasionally enrolled Canadian girls, upper-middle class and raised in the British tradition. These young ladies tended to deviate from the American model in one of two ways: either by a high degree of commitment to the "serious" things of life, and a manner half-bluestocking and half-conventual; or by a brittle primness which, under the stress of heterosexual freedom, quickly gave way to the gigglings, gushings, and grand passions we expect in an American 14-year-old, and even then not commonly. No doubt these differences between the borders are the outcome of differences extending through the full range of socialization; but to some degree at least they stem from the fact that the Canadian girls had had so little immersion in the heterosexual waters, and the American girls so much.

What are the consequences of the American adolescent's social precocity? It seems that the boy and girl readily learn to take command of themselves and each other. They also initiate themselves into the forms of erotic interplay. It is all too easy to imagine that their ease and coolness, their social elan, their erotic dexterity bespeaks a solution of the psychosexual dilemmas of adolescence. On the contrary, we feel that what is learned is only manner-deep, the acquisition of the exterior graces; the deeper bewilderments go untouched. We see a skewed maturation— social maturity preceding psychosexual maturity, and in preceding, influencing it. The American youngster may very well fall back on manner, retreat to the social persona. Initially this is done to temper the anxieties and doubts of sexuality and self-esteem. But the temporary redoubt may become an entrenched position. The adolescent is led to commit much of himself to the achievement of social style, and social style may become a means to delay, inhibit, or distort the psychosexual achievement. The American tendency, we have said, is alloplastic, and it is no more so than in the dating matrix. The American child is led to the use of "external" devices, presentations of the self, as a solution to intrapsychic dilemmas. We have, to be sure, no established way of describing this process metapsychologically, how it is and why it is that the emphases on social face (revealing itself in the stress on popularity, "personality," success), works to abort the subtler, more delicate maturations of character; but something of this sort does seem to take place.

The dating personality is, as we said earlier, a characterological fiction, a beguiling one, a highly cultivated myth of the self, in which only the more agreeable and conflict-free facets of character are shown to the other. Gaiety, charm, masculine poise, or feminine insouciance—these and other ego-ideal qualities are offered for display. The problem, of course, is that these pleasant qualities, so serviceable in casual social interaction, are irrelevant to the needs of marriage. For marriage, more than any other adult relationship, is a projective system within which one's deepest wishes, fears, conflicts, and relational strategies are lived out. Marriage absorbs, reflects, and attempts to settle the object-constellations each partner is burdened with. It attempts to join affection, sexuality, dependency, power (and much else) in a viable mixture, a feat for which there has been no prior preparation, even in the original family setting. Obviously no myth of the self will long survive a relationship so intimate and so geared to unconscious dialectics.

Another dubious consequence of the dating pattern, as Margaret Mead has so perceptively and forcefully observed, is in its influence on marital sexuality. The dating system, as we find it in the middle class, forces its participants to be their own executioners of impulse. The petting pattern involves stimulation without discharge. For this pattern to work there must be a prior socialization against sensuality, directed particularly toward (or against) the girls. Reinforcing it we have peer and adult pressure, expressing itself in the emphasis on good reputation. The girl, if she is to maintain status (and avoid pregnancy) must count on her own ability to check impulse, and to avoid surrender. The boy is expected to get what he can, although it should also be said that the petting code requires the boy not to pressure the girl beyond a certain point. When the girl says "no," the boy must yield, however grudgingly, and despite whatever ritual protests and persuasions he is expected to offer.

That the system breeds its own pathologies, we know well. In the middle class, the boy and girl find their sexuality fixed to the quasi-erotic patterns established by their dating experiences. The young woman, now a bride, will find it difficult to relinquish the habit of constraint. The young man's sexual pattern, as Mead points out, is influenced by the ideal of pure, unchecked potency. The need to meet the ideal is frustrated by his young wife's failure or diffidence in sexual response. This ideal is in any case fantastic enough that any human being would be bound to court disappointment in trying to achieve it. The young man's disappointment and anger may turn inward or outward, and may or may not reach consciousness. The young woman reacts to her husband's resentment and disappointment in any number of ways. In many cases she avoids the bitter sense of her own failure by putting the blame on her husband, relapsing into an aggrieved disappointment of her own which retraces the path of the earlier Oedipal disappointment. Here we have one of the sources of the marital problem so common as to be endemic in the clinical practices that cater to the middle class. The husband fleeing to his work or some other style of acting out, the wife settling into a martyred resignation, or into the sullen conviction that if she were a man she could do it better, or that someone else, a man rather than the child she wed, could really bring out the best in her.

Dating is the closest thing our culture has to a *rite de passage*. The norms for beginning dating are clear and highly specified. Most girls begin dating at fourteen, boys begin between fourteen and fifteen. We have some indications that the form and function of adolescent social life undergo changes in accompaniment to this crucial shift. A change occurs in the activities boys and girls share. Girls under fourteen are more likely to mention sports and physical activities among the things they play with boys (60% of the girls under 14, 40% of those over 14). When they suggest activities for clubs, the older girls make a clearer division in activities depending on whether the club is to be for girls or for both boys and girls. The girls under fourteen suggest essentially the same range of activities for the two settings.

Preference for coed clubs is at its height in the 14 to 16 year age group. Younger girls are more comfortable with girls, while those over sixteen have plenty of boy-girl interaction outside organizational settings, and are not so anxious to use organized groups for this purpose. The 14- to 16-year-old group are not yet firmly established in the dating system and are eager for coed experience. They look for opportunities to meet boys; the organized group offers them this chance, and at the same time does not imply the responsibility of a direct dating relationship. It provides a structure of activities and other companions, both of which act to cushion the anxiety of early heterosexual social encounters.

We find clear developmental patterns in girls' conceptions of dating and attitudes toward boys, corresponding to the three stages of adolescence. The preadolescent group treat dating as a more or less intellectual issue and give no real indication of emotional involvement with boys except for occasional signs of anxiety about their imminent introduction to dating. Early adolescents are very much involved in beginning dating, have considerable anxiety about it, and take a defensive rather than an interactive stance toward boys. Only in late adolescence, as initial anxieties subside, do girls begin to have true interactive relationships with boys, and bring understanding, sensitivity, and feeling to these relationships. In her early dating, the girl is likely to be absorbed with the problem of integrating new role demands and an image of femininity to the self-concept. As she gains some assurance that she is measuring up to a style of feminine behavior, the girl can begin to seek and find emotional gratification in friendships with boys.

Superficiality marks the preadolescent view of boy-girl relationships. Girls at this stage have not begun to date for the most part, and they are relatively unaware of either the bases for boy-girl relationships or the conditions of dating. Their general attitude is unemotional. When asked what they think of the idea of dating, they do not give strong reactions as older girls do, but refer to conditions for dating, particularly the age at which a girl should begin to date. Some of them (23%) indicate anxiety about dating when they stress that girls should not start dating too early, or want to postpone the issue until sixteen or a later age. In general their attitudes are less developed. They give fewer responses than older girls do. They have less formulated views about going steady. Thirty-nine per cent of this group, compared to 74 per cent of the 14- to 16-year-olds and 89 per cent of those over sixteen hold definite opinions about going steady.

The superficiality of the preadolescent view is most clearly seen in answer to the question, "What do you think makes a girl popular with boys?" The modal reaction at this age (56%) is that physical appearance is crucial. They do not stress social skills and the dating personality, nor do they emphasize the girl's sensitivity or interest in the relationship.

They show little conflict about problems that arise in dating, again, doubtless, because these problems have not yet much reality. When confronted with a conflict between loyalty to a girlfriend and a chance for a date, they resolve the issue with minimal conflict. They are much less likely than older girls to try to work out a compromise solution—some arrangement whereby they can meet their obligation to the friend and still have the fun of the date. Although loyalty to the girlfriend is the modal choice for girls all through adolescence, the youngest girls are more likely to make this commitment. Dating is not yet part of their real experience, so their strong loyalty to the girlfriend is not challenged.

Their ideas about the ethics of boy-girl relationships are also undeveloped and simple. The preadolescent girl typically feels that if a boyfriend of hers began paying attention to another girl, she would break her relationship with him. She is not confused by any tendency to look at the issue from his point of view, nor is her investment in the relationship sufficiently great to create a sense of loss at the idea of a summary break.

In an easy reversal, she takes a different stand in the next conflict posed. In this case the issue is criticism. What should a girl do if her fiancé asked her to change certain of her habits and manners? Now the younger girls do not (as we might predict) refuse to enter into the boy's system and break the relationship. Quite the opposite. More often than older girls they unequivocally say that the girl should change to suit her fiancé. They do not surround the change with conditions. They say simply that if the girl loves him, she should do what he wants.

The girl at this age can take a simple, straightforward, uncomplicated view of each issue raised without any complicating context of experience, without any great need for consistency.

At fourteen, when she is launched in the dating market, a girl's thoughts about heterosexual friendship and love are likely to become more subtle and less decisive. Solutions to conflicts are no longer so easy, since the conflicts now have a more striking reality. This greater complexity shows in many ways the answers of the girls in the next age category (14–16). They respond to both dating and the idea of going steady with greater affect than the younger girls. They are more enthusiastic about dating than the younger girls are, and more often have strong feelings about steady dating one way or the other.

The older girls are not so concerned with the age at which a girl should start to date or go steady. Their concerns are more subtle. In the question on steady dating, the girls under fourteen concentrate on the simple age condition, but the girls of fourteen to sixteen talk more about the relationship itself. They think steady dating is acceptable if a boy and girl like each other a great deal, or if they do not get too serious or too sexual. They look at the question from inside the relationship, while the younger girls set up a simple criterion and apply it to individual cases mechanically.

The older girls also take a less superficial approach to the question of attractiveness. They do not emphasize physical appearance as the basis of popularity as much as the girls under fourteen do. They have begun to recognize the importance of the dating personality. They stress the way a girl handles relationships, her social skills, and personal charm. "Good personality" is one of the most common responses to this question for the early adolescent group. They still have little sense of emotional give-and-take in relationships, but they see that attractiveness has something to do with their behavior toward boys.

So girls in early adolescence have some conception of the relationship between a boy and girl. Still, we must recall that many of these girls are in the first uncomfortable stages of dating. The dating institution with its clear definitions and forms serves to relieve them of some of the responsibility and anxiety of their early boy-girl relationships, but it does not wholly dispel anxiety. They are testing themselves in a competitive arena, and we can expect to find some signs of anxiety and defensiveness in their attitudes.

We find, indeed, that this age group is distinguished by a combative image of boy-girl relationships. They show signs of insecurity that are no longer so common in late adolescence, and they do not have the developed emotional interaction with boys that still older girls have. Their defensiveness is most clearly visible in their approach to the question about a girl's fiancé asking her to change. In this group we find the highest proportion of girls who say that the girl should not change, who think that such a criticism is a legitimate basis for breaking an engagement, and who interpret it as a sign that the boy does not love the girl. More often than either younger or older girls, the 14- to 16-year-olds treat the criticism as a threat to the integrity of the girl's self, and react aggressively.

Their anxiety and vulnerability vis-à-vis boys appear in a somewhat different form in response to the question about the boy who starts paying attention to his date's girl friend. First, they are more likely than either of the other two age groups to say that the girl should do nothing, act as though she does not notice, not let the boy know she is jealous. Girls at this age, as we have already noted, are busy building a dating personality—and they base this construction or fiction on a large measure of denial of feeling. They are somewhat less likely than older girls to deal directly with the boy in an effort to solve the problem (for example, by trying to see his side, by talking it over with him, or even by breaking up with him). When they do try to solve it they turn more often to the girlfriend, and try to settle the issue with her. The essential feature of this approach is to manipulate the boy in collaboration with the girlfriend. Along with their stress on social skill as a basis for successful relationships with boys, this finding supports the view that early dating is a manipulative game rather than a real relationship based on mutuality and emotional interaction. It is consistent with many other findings in the area of friendship, and tends to support the observation that in the first stages of dating, girls turn very heavily toward dependence on loyal girl friends. We have noted the importance they attach to loyalty in defining the meaning of friendship. . . .

REFERENCES

James Agee, *Agee on Film* (New York: McDowell, Obolensky, 1958), p. 168.
Erving Goffman, *The Presentation of Self in Everyday Life* (Garden City: Doubleday Anchor, 1959).
Margaret Mead, *Male and Female* (New York: Mentor, 1955).
W. Waller, "The Rating and Dating Complex," *American Sociological Review* (1937), pp. 727–737.

ADDITIONAL READINGS

Bolton, Charles D. Mate selection as the development of a relationship. *Marriage and Family Living,* August 1961, **23,** 234–240. Bolton indicates that little of a scientific nature exists about processes of mate selection in this society. He discusses five types of developmental processes which emerged from the study of a small sampling of cases.

Burchinal, J. G. The premarital dyad and love involvement. In H. T. Christensen (Ed.), *Handbook of marriage and the family.* Chicago: Rand, McNally, 1964. Burchinal reviews research and considers the significance of steady dating, and the social gains accruing to the practice. Since many conclusions about dating are ambiguous, Burchinal suggests that more longitudinal studies are needed to determine the outcomes of different dating histories and patterns.

Coombs, Robert H. Value consensus and partner satisfaction among dating couples. *Journal of Marriage and the Family,* May 1966, **28** (2), 166–173. An empirical study of dating couples found support for the following hypotheses: satisfaction with one's partner increases with an increase in objective value consensus, perceived partner's valuing of self, and ease of communication; ease of communication increases with an increase in objective value consensus and perceived partner's valuing of self.

Duvall, Evelyn. Identifying potential conflict areas in high school dating. *Journal of Marriage and the Family,* 1964, **26,** 103–106. A study within a midwestern high school revealed areas of possible conflict within the social life of the school. Both age and sex proved to be important factors in determining attitudes toward dating and dating practices.

Ehrmann, Winston. *Premarital dating behavior.* New York: Holt, Rinehart and Winston, 1959. The sex aspects of dating behavior are described in terms of various degrees of physical love-making intimacies; the individual's control over this behavior is measured; and ideas about love, sex codes of conduct, and heterosexual behavior are examined. The subjects were a thousand single college students, mostly white, middle class, and Protestant. The author compares his work with that of other researchers, and cites anecdotal material collected from his subjects.

Landis, Judson T. Dating maturation of children from happy and unhappy marriages. *Marriage and Family Living,* 1963, **25,** 351–353. Children of happily married parents tended to have more active dating histories and to have more frequently dated the field rather than concentrating on steady, more serious dating. Also, more often than their opposites, they reported less difficulty relating to the other sex, less often wished to be of the other sex, and reported less about their own chances for a successful marriage.

Lowrie, Samuel Harmon. Early and late dating: some conditions associated with them. *Marriage and Family Living,* August 1961, **23** (3), 284–291. Those adolescents who began dating earlier were found: 1. to be more distinctly American, 2. to have parents with higher education, 3. to have smaller families, and 4. to be of higher socioeconomic class.

Skipper, James K., Jr. & Nass, Gilbert. Dating behavior: A framework for analysis and an illustration. *Journal of Marriage and the Family,* November 1966, **28** (4), 412–413. The writers summarize several researchers' analyses of the functions of dating, and indicate the common elements that seem to exist.

XV. Biological Sex Role

Unresolved questions about psychosexual development abound. What is the origin of sex feelings? How do sex feelings and problems affect males and females differently? Is the double standard fair and reasonable? How much sex expression does a teen-ager need? Common beliefs about such matters are shot through with fallacies. People generally, and psychoanalytic theorists in particular, have assumed that psychosexual development will proceed smoothly, with masculinity and femininity somehow differentiating from an innate, instinctive sexuality. However, the origin and development of psychosexual differentiation are still unclear. On the morphological level—at the prenatal stage—sexual differentiation passes from an original plastic stage to one of fixed immutability. Similarly, though postnatally, psychosexual differentiation proceeds rapidly during infancy, and becomes fixed about the same time that language is acquired. "By school age," asserts Money, "psychosexual differentiation is so complete that sex reassignment is out of the question, save for the rare instances of ambiguous psychosexual differentiation." [1]

Hence, at adolescence, an individual's psychosexual self-perceptions are apparently fixed, and must be dealt with as they are. The question then arises: what should be done about adolescents who have habituated patterns at odds with the approved patterns of society? A boy's erotic feelings may be directed solely to members of his own sex; or he may feel like a girl in a boy's skin, a condition called transsexualism. Some authorities believe such an individual should simply be helped to accept himself and to accommodate to societal standards as best he can. Others believe that society's tolerance in the area of sexuality is too narrow and should be expanded. Still others insist that distortions in psychosexuality are susceptible to modification, under skilled psychiatry.

The first article that follows, by Brown and Lynn, provides a conceptual framework within which such questions may be viewed. These writers, both authorities in this area, clarify certain concepts and terms about which much confusion exists.

Other issues in psychosexual development relate not so much to basic theory as to sexual practices and their implications. Such questions become crucial for adolescents who ordinarily must cope with newly acquired sex

[1] John Money, "Psychosexual Differentiation," in John Money (Ed.), *Sex Research: New Developments* (New York, Holt, Rinehart and Winston, 1965), p. 13.

feelings without adequate sex outlets. But how much is "adequate," and what is the boundary line between "permissible" and "promiscuous" behaviors? College women, asserts Walters, no longer deem premarital chastity a necessary virtue.[2] Is their attitude simply a new standard? There is no clear-cut answer to this, or to a related question: what should be done about unmarried teen mothers and fathers? Should the girls involved remain in school and receive special counseling? Or should they be used as examples of what happens when societal mores are trespassed? Unwed teen mothers have a higher-than-average incidence of malformed babies, a higher incidence of cervical cancer in later life, a higher incidence of non-marriageable husbands, and of marital unhappiness and divorce.[3] Yet society, and its agent the school, continue to play ostrich with the problem of premarital pregnancies.

The current emphasis—to the limited extent that it exists—is on prevention of such eventualities through sex education. However, evidence abounds that teenagers receive insufficient assistance in this area. In one study, typical expressions of girls unprepared for first menstruation were: "I was scared to death"; "I thought I was stabbed and bleeding to death." Similarly, boys unprepared for their first ejaculation, reported: "It scared the hell out of me"; "I thought I had hurt myself"; "I thought I had regressed to the age of four and had wet the bed."

Sex education, as related to parent and child, could involve father and son, father and daughter, mother and son, mother and daughter. However, only between mother and daughter is sex education of any significance at all. About 60 per cent of mothers prepare their daughters for the menarche, but accomplish little else. Children of both sexes resist their parents' discussing reproduction. Perhaps, suggests Shipman, the taboo on parent-child sex behavior is so strong that verbalization about sex in this relationship becomes symbolic incest.[4]

If parents are not doing the job, why not call on the teachers? Teachers themselves believe that the secondary school curriculum should embrace sex education.[5] However, to perform this task adequately teachers need better preparation than presently provided. In a survey of 734 teacher-preparation institutions, only 8 per cent of 250 institutions responding offered courses relating to sex education. About half of such courses are designed for

[2] Paul A. Walters, "Promiscuity in Adolescence," *American Journal of Orthopsychiatry,* Vol. 35 (1965), pp. 670–675.

[3] Gordon Shipman, "Addendum to Adams' Article," *The Family Co-ordinator,* Vol. 17, No. 1 (January 1968), pp. 22–24.

[4] Gordon Shipman, "The Psychodynamics of Sex Education," *The Family Co-ordinator,* Vol. 17, No. 1 (January 1968), pp. 3–12.

[5] "Teacher-Opinion Poll—Sex Education," *NEA Journal,* Vol. 54, No. 2 (February 1965), p. 2.

the secondary education specialist in health education, biology, or home economics (family life), and the remainder for the elementary school generalist.[6]

Inevitably, another question emerges: what should sex education include, and how should it be incorporated into the curricular framework? Many authorities advise playing down the facts of sex and emphasizing interpersonal relationships. Mulholland says that social and psychological aspects of sex are more important in the education of early adolescents than the biologic and physiological ones.[7] Such a philosophy becomes converted into courses called human relations, character education, or family life, one of whose objectives is to educate young people in responsible expressions of sexuality. Fortunately, such topics are often treated in responsible journals, such as *Journal of Marriage and the Family,* from which our second selection, by Luckey, is taken. Luckey, an authority in this field, appraises various problems and issues, and discusses sex education and the multiple problems involved. Actually, issues relating to psychosexual adjustment are so many, and opinions about them so diverse, that the selection of articles for such a book as this are bound to be arbitrary.

[6] James L. Malfetti and Arline M. Rubin, "Sex Education: Who is Teaching the Teachers?" *Teachers College Record,* Vol. 69, No. 3 (December 1967), pp. 213–222.

[7] Walter E. Mulholland, "Sex of Social Education," *The Clearing House,* Vol. 41, No. 6 (February 1967), p. 332.

31

Daniel G. Brown
David B. Lynn*

HUMAN SEXUAL DEVELOPMENT: AN OUTLINE OF COMPONENTS AND CONCEPTS

This paper provides an analysis of human sexual development in terms of three related but independent components: 1. a person's sexual structures and functions (male or female) 2. his sex-role identification and behavior (masculine or feminine) and 3. his genital arousal and behavior relative to source, direction, aim, and object of gratification (heterosexual, homosexual, or other). A suggested conceptual framework relative to human sexual development is presented. The purpose is to differentiate and clarify existing concepts and terms in the psychosexual area.

This paper is an attempt to clarify the terminology and to present a conceptual schema relative to human sexuality. The term *sexual* has been used so broadly as to include everything from biological differentiation of male and female, to orgasm, masculine or feminine role behavior, parental behavior, and even the pervasive psychic energy implied in the Freudian usage of the term libido. The boundaries of human sexuality are, in short, unclear. The terms and concepts in this area often lack precise meaning and not infrequently lead to conceptual confusion. Examples of this ambiguity may be seen in the fact that the following terms are used more or less synonymously: male and masculine; female and feminine; hermaphroditism, transvestism, transsexualism, homosexuality, and sexual inversion; and sexual drive, libido, and eroticism.

From Daniel G. Brown and David B. Lynn, "Human Sexual Development: An Outline of Components and Concepts," *Journal of Marriage and the Family,* Vol. 28, No. 2 (May 1966), pp. 155–162. Reprinted by permission.

* Daniel G. Brown, Ph.D., is a Consultant in Mental Health, Mental Health Services, U.S. Public Health Service, Region IV, Atlanta, Georgia. David B. Lynn, Ph.D., is in the Department of Psychology, College of San Mateo, San Mateo, California.

In recent years there has been an accumulation of research concerned with human sexuality indicating that the notion of an innate, predetermined psychologic sexuality does not correspond with existing evidence.[1]

Rather, recent investigations suggest that the psychosexual status of the individual is undifferentiated at birth. The individual begins life psychosexually plastic, capable of developing along a variety of lines depending upon the definition of sex roles in his particular culture as well as his unique learning experiences in the first few years of life especially. This psychosexual plasticity has been convincingly demonstrated by research showing that hermaphroditic children, i.e., those with a mixture or inconsistency of male and female components, usually grow up as masculine *or* feminine depending on the sex assigned them and the sex role in which they are reared. Research also suggests, however, that at least as far as sex role identity is concerned, this plasticity does not persist beyond early childhood; once a masculine or feminine sex role is established, it may be extremely difficult for this basic pattern to be changed or reversed later in life.[2]

The research with hermaphrodites blends well with recent research and theoretical developments concerning sex-role identification, indicating that masculinity or femininity does not emerge as an automatic unfolding, but rather results from familial and other influences as the individual develops.[3]

The following outline is an attempt to provide clarity and a basis for integrating recent findings in the field into a systematic framework. Three major independently varying components of human sexual development and behavior will be differentiated. These are 1. *the biological-constitutional* component, i.e., hereditary, congenital, and maturational factors; 2. *sex role,* the individual's identification of himself with one sex or the other; and 3. *genital-sex object preference,* the source, aim, and direction of sexual stimulation, desire, activity, and satisfaction. These major components will be reviewed in terms of hypothesized primary determinants, basic terminology, operational definitions, general manifestations, standard developmental outcome or norm, and nonstandard developmental outcome or deviation.

---

[1] J. Money, "Psychosexual Development in Man," in *The Encyclopedia of Mental Health,* ed. by A. Deutsch, New York: Franklin Watts, 1963, pp. 1678–1709.

[2] J. L. Hampson and J. G. Hampson, "The Ontogenesis of Sexual Behavior in Man," in *Sex and Internal Secretions,* ed. by W. C. Young, Baltimore: Williams & Williams, 1961, pp. 1401–1432; and J. Money, "Sex Hormones and Other Variables in Human Eroticism," in *Sex and Internal Secretions,* ed. by W. C. Young, Baltimore: Williams & Williams, 1961, pp. 1383–1400.

[3] See, for example, D. G. Brown, "Psychosexual Disturbances: Transvestism and Sex-Role Inversion," *Marriage and Family Living,* 22:3 (August 1960), pp. 218–226; R. E. Hartley, "A Developmental View of Female Sex-Role Definition and Identification," *Merrill-Palmer Quarterly,* 10:1 (January 1964), pp. 3–16; and D. B. Lynn, "Sex-Role and Parental Identification," *Child Development* 33:3 (September 1962), pp. 555–564.

BIOLOGICAL CONSTITUTIONAL COMPONENT

Hypothesized Primary Determinants

The hypothesized determinants of the biological-constitutional component are hereditary, congenital, and maturational.

Basic Terms

The basic terms are male-maleness and female-femaleness. These terms should be used to refer only to the biological aspects of sexuality and should be distinguished from masculine-masculinity and feminine-femininity, which refer to the psychological characteristics and behavior patterns typical of one sex in contrast to the other.

Operational Definitions

Here the concern is with the relationship between male and female factors in the physiology of the individual, specifically the degree of male and female factors in the following structures and functions: 1. chromosomal composition (XX or XY); 2. gonadal composition (ovarian or testicular tissue); 3. hormonal composition (estrogen-androgen balance); 4. internal accessory structure (vagina, uterus, and fallopian tubes or seminal vesicles and prostate); and 5. external genitalia (clitoris and labia majora and labia minora or penis and scrotum).

General Manifestations

In addition to the overall anatomical and physiological differences in genitalia between the sexes, there are also differences in general physique, body shape, physical dimensions, and other similar manifestations. Even in preschool years there are marked sex differences in body composition in that girls have more fatty tissue, while boys, although only slightly heavier, have more muscle tissue.[4] In adulthood a layer of subcutaneous fat develops, rounding and softening the contours of the face and body of women. The greater growth of the larynx in males results in a deeper voice than that of women. Females develop enlarged breasts, an enlarged bony pelvic

[4] S. M. Garn, "Roentgenogrammetric Determinations of Body Composition," *Human Biology,* 29 (1957), pp. 337–353; and S. M. Garn, "Fat, Body Size, and Growth in the Newborn," *Human Biology,* 30 (1958), pp. 256–280.

basin, and relatively wide hips; whereas males have a widening of shoulders. In addition to differences in pubic hair distribution, males are characterized by a heavy growth of facial and body hair; whereas females develop a light down on the upper lip, forearms, and lower legs.

Standard Developmental Outcome or Norm

The standard outcome in the biological development of the individual is a predominance of anatomical and physiological structures and functions that are the basis of either maleness or femaleness; that is, the chromosomal, gonadal, internal accessory structures, external genitalia, and general manifestations are consistently male or female at maturity.

Non-Standard Developmental Outcome or Deviation

One of the more significant deviations in the biological sexual composition of the individual is that of hermaphroditism. There are other atypical forms of development, such as precocious puberty in which appropriate sex hormones function prematurely. However, hermaphroditism, sometimes referred to as intersexuality, is a biological anomaly of special interest in the behavioral sciences because it provides a basis for studying the interaction of physiological, social, and psychological variables in the sexual development of the individual. Hermaphroditism is a condition in which there is inconsistency in or among one or more of the following factors in the biological composition of the individual: chromosomal, gonadal, hormonal, internal accessory structures, and external genitalia. Examples include an individual showing ambiguity in external genitalia, a person having ovaries and a penis, or one who is chromosomally male but has a vagina and female accessory organs. Androgyny refers to the condition in which a male has female biological traits; gynandry involves a female with male biological traits.

Money, Hampson, and Hampson list the following six varieties of hermaphrodites: [5]

1. Congenital hyperadrenocortical females—externally hermaphroditic; normal internal reproductive organs and sex chromatin pattern. Without cortisone therapy, growth and development is precocious and virilizing.

2. Hermaphrodites with ambiguous or masculinized external genitals —normal functional female internal reproductive structures and ovaries and female sex chromatin pattern. Unlike females with hyperadrenocorti-

    [5] J. Money, J. G. Hampson, and J. L. Hampson, "Hermaphroditism: Recommendations Concerning Assignment of Sex, Change of Sex, and Psychological Management," *Bulletin of Johns Hopkins Hospital,* 97 (1955), pp. 284–300.

cism, this group does not show progressive virilization; secondary feminiza-
tion at puberty is the rule with reproduction possible.

3. Classical true hermaphroditism—testicular and ovarian tissue both
present; enlarged phallus; variable development of the genital ducts; male
or female sex chromatin pattern.

4. Cryptorchid hermaphrodites with relatively complete Müllerian differentiation—penis, hypospadic or normal; possible virilizing at puberty;
male sex chromatin pattern.

5. Cryptorchid hermaphrodites with relatively incomplete Müllerian
differentiation—hypospadic or clitoral phallus; possible virilizing at puberty;
male sex chromatin pattern.

6. Simulant females with feminizing inguinal testes and vestigial Müllerian differentiation—blind vaginal pouch; male sex chromatin pattern.

SEX-ROLE COMPONENT

Hypothesized Primary Determinants

The determinants hypothesized for the sex-role component are environmental conditioning and the social learning experiences of the individual.

Basic Terms

Masculine-masculinity and feminine-femininity are the basic terms, in
contrast to male-maleness and female-femaleness, which, as previously indicated, refer to the biological composition of the individual.

Operational Definitions

Here the concern is with the extent that a person's behavioral patterns
and psychological traits are typical of one sex in contrast to the other in a
given culture and social environment. In this connection sex-role identification may be distinguished from sex-role preference.[6] Sex-role preference
refers to the desire to adopt the behavior associated with one sex or the perception of such behavior as preferable or more desirable. Identification may
also be contrasted to sex-role adoption, the latter referring to the actual
adoption of behavior characteristic of one sex or the other, not simply the
desire to adopt such behavior.[7] The fact that a woman on appropriate occa-

[6] D. G. Brown, "Sex-Role Preference in Young Children," *Psychological Monographs,* 70:14 (1956), (Whole No. 421).

[7] D. B. Lynn, "A Note of Sex Differences in the Development of Masculine
and Feminine Identification," *Psychological Review,* 66:2 (1959), pp. 126–135.

sions wears trousers or short hair does not necessarily mean that she is identified with the masculine role even though she is adopting certain aspects characteristic of that role. Sex-role identification is reserved for reference to the introjection and incorporation of the role of a given sex and to the basic, underlying reactions characteristic of that role.

Thus, a person may identify with the opposite sex but for expediency adopt much of the behavior characteristic of his own sex. In some respects he may prefer the role of his own sex, although there is considerable identification with the opposite-sex role. One would expect such a person, having identified substantially with the opposite sex, to have a number of underlying reactions characteristic of the opposite-sex role despite his adopting much of the behavior characteristic of the same-sex role. On the other hand, the woman who on appropriate occasions adopts aspects characteristic of the opposite-sex role, such as wearing trousers or wearing short hair, is certainly not necessarily identified with the masculine role. Thus, sex-role adoption refers to overt behavior characteristic of a given sex, while sex-role identification refers to a more basic, internalized process in which behavioral characteristics of one sex role or the other are incorporated.

General Manifestations

Certain attitudes, preferences, social motives, fantasies, dreams, and feelings; gestures, gait, and other expressive movements and postures; general demeanor; communicative qualities such as spontaneous topic of conversation and casual commitment, enunciation, word associations, and word choices; some patterns associated with paternal or maternal behavior; and various everyday habits and mannerisms typical of the masculine or feminine role constitute the general manifestations.

Standard Developmental Outcome or Norm

The standard outcome is identification with, preference for, and adoption of the sex role that is consistent with a person's biological constitutional composition, i.e., the acquisition of a masculine role in males and a feminine role in females.

There has been an increasing amount of research and theoretical formulations in recent years concerning sex-role behavior.[8] In general,

---

[8] See, for example, A. Bandura and A. C. Huston, "Identification as a Process of Incidental Learning," *Journal of Abnormal and Social Psychology,* 63:2 (September 1961), pp. 311–318; U. Bronfenbrenner, "Freudian Theories of Identification and Their Derivatives," *Child Development,* 31:1 (March 1960), pp. 15–40; Brown, "Psychosexual Disturbances: Transvestism and Sex-Role Inversion," *op. cit.;* Hartley, *op. cit.;* J. Kagan, "The Concept of Identification," *Psychological Review,* 65 (1958), pp. 296–305; R. R. Sears, "Identification as a Form of Behavior Develop-

there is considerable agreement as to the importance of learning in the individual's attaining the role appropriate to his or her sex, i.e., there is a consensus that the individual learns to identify with a given sex role, to prefer one role or the other, and to adopt aspects of one role or the other. Emphasis on the learned aspect of sex or gender role acquisition has been given much support by recent research on hermaphroditism. As previously indicated, individuals of comparable anatomical and physiological deviation in composition have been reared successfully as either boys or girls. These studies show that chromosomal sex and gonadal sex can be overridden by learning experiences. That hormonal sex can also be overridden is demonstrated by female hermaphrodites with an androgenital syndrome, but who are raised and living as women. Before the recent advent of cortisone therapy to suppress adrenal androgens, these women were heavily virilized and totally lacking in female secondary sexual characteristics; they sometimes had a very enlarged clitoris, and sometimes a fused, empty scrotal sac. Nevertheless, their assigned sex as women generally dominated their hormonal sex. In reference to the singular importance of sex-role assignment and rearing, Money points out that it is possible for psychosexual differentiation in a person to be contradictory of chromosomal, gonadal, hormonal, or external genital and internal genital sex and to agree instead with assigned sex.[9] The crucial significance of learning in the acquisition of gender role is clearly indicated.

Workers concerned with hermaphroditism have suggested a parallel between the acquisition of sex or gender role in humans and imprinting in lower animals. Thus, there may be a critical period within which the gender role of an individual is established.[10] In a review of the factor of age in psychosexual development in children, Brown suggests that sex-role differentiation is a gradual process beginning between the first and second year of life and becoming definitely established by or during the fifth year.[11] On the basis of hermaphroditic cases of sex reassignment, Money concludes that the critical period for "gender imprinting" is between eighteen months and

---

ment," in *The Concept of Development,* ed. by D. B. Harris, Minneapolis: University of Minnesota Press, 1957, pp. 149–161; B. Sutton-Smith, J. M. Roberts, and B. G. Rosenberg, "Sibling Associations and Role Involvement," *Merrill-Palmer Quarterly,* 10:1 (January 1964), pp. 25–38; and R. F. Winch, *Identification and Its Familial Determinants,* Indianapolis: Bobbs-Merrill, 1962.

[9] J. Money, "Developmental Differentiation of Femininity and Masculinity Compared," in *Man and Civilization: The Potential of Women,"* ed. by S. M. Farber and R. H. L. Wilson, New York: McGraw-Hill, 1963, p. 56.

[10] See, for example, Brown, "Psychosexual Disturbances: Transvestism and Sex-Role Inversion," *op. cit.;* D. G. Brown, "Homosexuality and Family Dynamics," *Bulletin of the Menninger Clinic,* 27:5 (September 1963), pp. 227–232; Hampson and Hampson, *op. cit.;* and Money, "Sex Hormones and Other Variables in Human Eroticism," *op. cit.*

[11] D. G. Brown, "Sex-Role Development in a Changing Culture," *Psychological Bulletin,* 54 (1958), pp. 232–242.

three years of age, beginning with the onset of mastery of language.[12] He considers the die to be well cast by the age of six with major realignment of gender role and sexual identity rare after that.

Non-Standard Developmental Outcome or Deviation

The non-standard outcome is the acquisition of a sex role or certain aspects of a sex role not consistent with a person's biological composition.[13] Several examples are discussed below.

1. *Transvestism* involves the desire for, act of, and emotional satisfactions connected with wearing the apparel of the opposite sex. Apart from their cross-sex dress, transvestites may otherwise establish a heterosexual adjustment. This points up the necessity of clearly distinguishing between transvestism and other concepts, such as homosexuality and sex-role inversion.[14] One factor often found in the life histories of transvestites is that during the first two or three years of life, the child intentionally or otherwise often wears and fondles clothes of the opposite sex and in some instances is praised for his appearance in the clothes of the opposite sex. In childhood some male transvestites have long hair that is curled as a girl's; in the background of still others is a mother who wanted a girl rather than a boy.

2. *Sex-role inversion* is the phenomenon in which a person of one biological sex learns to think, feel, and act like the opposite sex. This involves the acceptance and adoption of the sex role of the other sex. Although transvestism is a component of inversion, it is *not* unique to inverts. Transvestism will almost always be found in cases of inversion since desiring and wearing the clothes of the other sex is one of many aspects of adopting the role of that sex; however, the converse is not true—inversion is *not* necessarily found in transvestites. Thus, a transvestite may be atypical in his sex-role functioning *only* with respect to this lifelong but relatively isolated, compulsive behavioral pattern.

Various incongruous combinations of sex-role behavior may occur in a given person. For instance, a boy may dislike playing with girls, but show an interest in domestic activities, such as cooking, sewing, housekeeping, and using make-up, as well as a liking for mechanical toys, tools, and building materials.[15]

[12] Money, "Sex Hormones and Other Variables in Human Eroticism," *op. cit.*

[13] Actually, the hermaphrodite who has a consistent sex role is, by definition, non-standard in that his role must be at variance with some aspect of his ambiguous biological composition.

[14] D. G. Brown, "Inversion and Homosexuality," *American Journal of Orthopsychiatry,* 28 (1958), 424–429.

[15] Brown, "Psychosexual Disturbances: Transvestism and Sex-Role Inversion," *op. cit.*

Instances in which a male child has a relatively positive attachment to the father, or at least a relationship which is free of basic rejection or hostility, and at the same time has a mother who allows, encourages, or forces him to wear feminine dress and to develop other feminine patterns are likely to result in some degree of confusion or duality in sex-role development. The person may show some uncertainty as to his sex role, or he may actually develop *two relatively dichotomous selves,* one of which is masculine and one feminine. An individual may describe himself as "ruggedly masculine and aggressive" when dressed in masculine clothes but "passive, gentle and submissive" when attired in feminine clothes. It is evident in such a case that two sex roles coexist in the same personality. A variation of this pattern is seen in the case of a person who reported that he often felt "like two people in one, male and female" and "never completely male and never completely female." [16] This individual during his childhood showed a mixture of feminine interests—dolls, cooking, sewing—as well as masculine pursuits—mechanical tasks, tools, playing cowboys. As an adult he alternated between muscle-building exercises and efforts to be "more of a man" and wearing feminine clothing, using cosmetics, and trying to appear more like a woman. Still another person reported that when he was in his feminine phase he tried to approximate the ideal-image of women whom he admired when he was in his masculine role. He attempted to become the kind of woman that his masculine self found most attractive. While in his masculine role his whole personality would change, and he would become thoroughly masculine in interests, dress, and behavior.[17]

It is interesting to note that cases such as those described above bear some resemblance to instances of dual or multiple personality in that there is an alternation between different roles of sex, rather than between roles of "good" and "bad." Part of the time the person is masculine in appearance and behavior; at other times the same person is feminine. Instead of a Dr. Jekyll and Mr. Hyde or an Eve White and Eve Black, there is a "Mr." Doe and a "Miss" Doe. However, there is an important difference between individuals with dual sex roles and those with dual personalities. In contrast to cases of dual personality, in which one of the two selves is amnesic for the other, individuals who develop two sex roles are aware of the existence of both roles. Thus, when such a person is in the feminine role, he will dress, talk, and act like a woman; although he is quite aware of his other self in which he dresses, talks, and acts like a man.

In addition to transvestism, homosexuality should be differentiated from sex-role inversion. While homosexuality typically occurs in individuals who show sex-role inversion, there is considerable evidence that a number of other factors may predispose the individual to the development of homo-

[16] B. Karpman, "Dream Life in a Case of Transvestism," *Journal of Nervous and Mental Disease,* 106 (1947), pp. 292–337.

[17] C. V. Prince, "Homosexuality, transvestism and transsexualism," *American Journal of Psychotherapy,* 11 (1957), pp. 80–85.

sexuality as well. The homosexual is an individual who desires and/or obtains predominant or exclusive sexual satisfaction with members of his own sex; the invert is one whose thoughts, perceptions, attitudes, fantasies, feelings, preferences, interests, and behavioral tendencies are typical of the opposite sex.[18]

With reference to the determinants of sex-role identification, it might be predicted that a male displaying gender role inversion would have a father who, during the individual's early childhood, had been physically absent most of the time, psychologically ineffective and socially distant, or chronically abusive and cruel to the boy and, in addition, a mother who is "idolized" by the boy, emotionally "smothers" him, or to whom the boy is excessively close and attached. For girls inversion would be expected to develop only in cases in which there is a serious disruption in the mother-daughter relationship and early abnormal attachment to the father that prevents the little girl from identifying with the mother or where the mother herself denies or despises her own femininity and thus exposes the daughter to a distorted feminine model. Another predisposing family pattern, which might function in isolation or in conjunction with those already mentioned, is one in which the parent or parents actually encourage and rear a child of one sex to feel, think, and behave like that of the other.

3. *Transsexualism* involves sex-role inversion and also the desire for surgical sexual transformation, such as the case of George (Christine) Jorgensen. As in most other psychosexual disturbances, transsexualism is primarily associated with men rather than women. For example, following the publicity concerning the "change of sex" case of Jorgensen in Denmark, the endocrinologist who supervised the changeover received three times as many letters from men as from women expressing a desire for medical change of sexual identity.[19] This differential might partially be explained by the fact that the particular operation given the publicity was one involving a change from male to female. Perhaps the apparently greater feasibility of surgical procedures involved in amputating the penis than in constructing male genitalia may also have been a factor. However, it is probable that the suggested predominance of transsexualism among men has more deeply rooted origins than the above explanations. Among the factors which predispose males more readily than females to sex-role inversion may be the fact that, since all infants are attached to the mother or mother-substitute in earliest life, it is the boy, not the girl, who must shift from an initial identification with the feminine model to masculine role identification with the father or father-substitute. In addition, because fathers in this culture are usually away from home much of the time, the girl typically has her model for identification, the mother, with her more often than the boy has his model, the father, with him.

[18] D. G. Brown, "The Development of Sex-Role Inversion and Homosexuality," *Journal of Pediatrics,* 50:5 (May 1957), p. 614.
[19] D. G. Brown, "Inversion and Homosexuality," *op. cit.*

GENITAL-SEX OBJECT PREFERENCE

Hypothesized Primary Determinants

Environmental conditioning and social learning experiences are hypothesized as the primary determinants for the third component of sexual development, genital-sex object preference.

Basic Terms

Genital sex desire, drive, and gratification are the basic terms. The Freudian term *libido,* although defined variously during the many years of Freud's writing, always encompassed more than genital sex desire, drive, and gratification.

Operational Definitions

Genital-sex object preference is defined as the source of genital sex arousal, the aim and direction of genital sex drive, and the nature of the object and situation with which genital gratification or orgasm occur.

General Manifestations

This component is manifested in genital sex arousal, excitement, and behavior either directly observable or covertly present at the level of fantasy, dreams, and imagination.

The male orgasm is a relatively simple and easily observable reaction. However, the orgasm in women has been less well understood until the recent highly significant research of Masters and Johnson.[20] These investigators furnish evidence that the muscular spasms of ejaculation in the male have their counterpart in the female. Photographic documentation indicates the tumescence of a cylindrical orgasmic platform immediately inside the vagina and extending along the vaginal barrel for about one third of its length. The orgasmic platform and adjacent tissues outside the vaginal

[20] W. H. Masters and V. C. Johnson, "The Physiology of the Vaginal Reproductive Function," *Western Journal of Surgery, Obstetrics and Gynecology,* 69 (1961), pp. 105–120; and W. H. Masters and V. C. Johnson, "The Sexual Response Cycle of the Human Female. III. The Clitoris: Anatomic and Clinical Considerations," *Western Journal of Surgery, Obstetrics and Gynecology,* 70 (1962), pp. 248–257. All of the major research and significant findings of Masters and Johnson will be published in a book now in press.

orifice throb and contract spasmodically during the time orgasm is reported. Meanwhile, the innermost end of the vagina has ballooned out and the cervix has somewhat retracted. The manifestations of orgasm are identical whether stimulation is masturbatory and clitoral or produced by artificial coitus with a hollow, clear-plastic object simulating the phallus.

Although the focus of this section is on genital sexual arousal, extremely intense sexual experience is possible independent of genitopelvic happenings. The paraplegic has no neural connections between the upper and lower parts of the nervous system. Nevertheless, some paraplegic patients describe vivid orgastic experiences in erotic dreams which simulate true genital orgasm. These "orgastic" dreams, of course, lack erection or ejaculation, because no neural connections exist between the brain and the genital region.[21]

Standard Developmental Outcome or Norm

The standard outcome is heterosexuality. More specifically, the prescribed outcome in our society is monogamous heterosexuality. Heterosexuality has been so taken for granted that until recently it was assumed to be completely biologically determined and any deviation therefrom, the result of some biological defect. The previously mentioned studies, showing that hermaphroditic children with the same anomaly grow up as masculine or feminine in agreement with the assigned sex and acquire the genital-sex object preference appropriate to that sex, make it evident that environmental conditioning and social learning experiences are of crucial importance. In addition, since the male hormone androgen apparently functions as the erotic hormone for women as well as men, an increase in the androgen level may very well increase the erotic drive of a woman yet not result in a shift of her sex object preference nor motivate her to take a masculine role in erotic activity. In other words, a heterosexual woman given androgen may become more strongly erotically motivated, but she does not become homosexual in her desires.

Those investigators who have studied hermaphroditism conclude that genital-sex object choice may be the result of appropriate imprinting at the critical period in the child's development. In this regard Money suggests that a person may engage in a homosexual act when past the critical period without becoming a chronic homosexual. Money reports that, in general, imprinted eroticism appears to be permanent and ineradicable.[22]

---

[21] J. Money, "Phantom Orgasm in the Dreams of Paraplegic Men and Women," *Archives of General Psychiatry,* 3 (1960), 373–382.

[22] Money, "Sex Hormones and Other Variables in Human Eroticism," *op. cit.*

Non-Standard Developmental Outcome
or Deviation

The following are examples of deviations in the genital component:

1. *Autosexuality* (masturbation) is the genital stimulation and gratification of a person by himself. This sexual outlet is statistically so common, occurring in practically all males and the majority of females, it is considered non-standard only when it is the exclusive or nearly exclusive erotic preference of an individual. It is also recognized that when masturbation occurs it is often in connection with fantasied heterosexual or homosexual situations.

2. *Homosexuality* refers to the phenomenon in which an individual predominantly or exclusively desires and/or obtains genital sexual stimulation and gratification with a person of the same biological sex.[23] In a previous section of this paper, sex-role or sexual inversion was differentiated from homosexuality. Almost invariably the individual with inverted gender identification desires sexual activity with a person of the same anatomic sex, and when this is the case can be regarded as homosexual. However, there are many homosexuals who are not inverted in their sex or gender role. Homosexuals have in common only their preference for sexual partners of the same biological sex. Often the inverted male homosexual corresponds to what has traditionally been called the passive male homosexual, who takes the role of the opposite sex in homosexual activity. The non-inverted homosexual corresponds to the active male homosexual, the one taking the role appropriate to his own biological sex. Similarly, the inverted female homosexual often corresponds to what has been called the active female homosexual, the one taking the masculine role in homosexual activity; and the noninverted female homosexual, the passive female homosexual, often corresponds to the one taking the feminine role in homosexual activity. However, homosexuals sometimes "switch roles" in their sexual activity; the one who is the passive partner on one occasion acts as the active partner on the next occasion. It is very unlikely that they switch sex-role identification in the sense of their basic personality structure, showing role inversion one day and normal role behavior the next, unless there is involved also the dual sex-role phenomenon mentioned previously. Inversion, therefore, should refer to the individual's total personality structure. The invert may be described as a psychosomatic misfit with the physical characteristics of one sex, such as being anatomically male, but the personality characteristic of the other sex, being psychologically feminine.

[23] This concept of homosexuality becomes extremely blurred when dealing with the erotic life of a hermaphroditic individual since his biological sex is ambiguous.

One would predict that the etiology of homosexuality in cases which are inverted would be quite dissimilar from those which are not inverted. In a previous section the hypothesized determinants of inversion were conditioning experiences. Money considers imprinting an important part in homosexuality, but he does not distinguish between homosexuals who are or are not inverted. "Effectively imprinted at the critical period to respond to homosexual stimuli—a person becomes a chronic homosexual. Effective stimuli may be extremely specific and variable from person to person, which may account for the varieties of homosexual preference." [24] However, Money does not elaborate on the nature of the experiences occurring between the age of eighteen months and three years—the critical period— which may lead to chronic homosexuality.

3. *Other deviations* include bisexuality, zooerasty, pederasty, exhibitionism, fetishism, sadism, and masochism, all of which involve genital desire, stimulation, and gratification that deviate from the normal heterosexual, interpersonal relationship.

[24] Money, "Sex Hormones and Other Variables in Human Eroticism," *op. cit.,* p. 1397.

32

Eleanore B. Luckey *

FAMILY LIFE ED AND/OR SEX ED?

The writer defines distinctions involved in sex education, family life education, interpersonal relations, and human development. The content of sex in family life education can be presented in separate courses integrated with other subjects. The training of the teachers involved is perceived as especially important. To date we have had a hodge-podge of poorly taught material in this area.

The terms "family life education" and "sex education" are equally disadvantageous. The assorted connotations that each has had appended to itself through the years has made each term unacceptable to given segments of our population. Yet for a lack of anything better, we continue to use them, dislike them, puzzle over them, even argue over them and have now begun to think of them as two areas which may polarize the professionals concerned with their content.

Nowhere are there functional definitions of the terms that differentiate or delineate these as *separate* areas. The definitions offered by TEACHER EXCHANGE as a basis to this article demonstrate how inseparable the two are. At a time when we as educators are hoping to bring about an integration of personality and cognition, of learning and behavior, of emotion and reason, and of the understanding of man both as an individual and as a social being, it is a sad commentary that we are discussing "family life education and/or sex education" as if they were separate entities—or perhaps even as if they were entities at all.

The two terms, as they are defined, cannot be used as global concepts; at best they indicate only specific areas of *emphasis.* "Family life" is used when we speak of the interaction of personalities and roles within the setting

From Eleanore B. Luckey, "Family Life Ed and/or Sex Ed?" *Journal of Marriage and the Family,* Vol. 29, No. 2 (May 1967), pp. 377–380. Reprinted by permission.

* Eleanore B. Luckey, Ph.D., is Professor and Head, Department of Child Development and Family Relations at the University of Connecticut School of Home Economics, Storrs, Connecticut, and Consultant on Family Life Education, Youth Services Unit, Welfare Administration, Department of Health, Education, and Welfare, Washington, D.C.

of family; however, a great deal more is involved in family living than personality and role interaction. "Sex education" is thought of as primarily being concerned with the physiology of reproduction and sexual functioning. Neither of these areas stands well without the other.

The "parcelling out" would never have come about had we not been so desperately afraid of sex. Long before we could say s-e-x aloud, we were able to talk about educating for marriage and family living. It was not that we did not know that marriage and sex went together; we just did not want to talk about it. The result was that family living courses generally tended to emphasize the budget and avoid coitus.

If one studies the curriculum guides, course outlines, and materials that have been the basis for family life education in the schools for the last ten or 15 years, one begins to see quite clearly why "sex education" came into being. It is an attempt to put some sex into family life! And most of us agree it ought to be there.

It would be unfair, however, to let family life education bear the total responsibility for the forced birth of sex education. Biology classes often left the study of the reproductive system until the end of the semester when there would be less time for questions! Diagrams of the genitalia were omitted from the text as if they did not exist. Social science classes discussed modern problems with no reference to sex. Courses that dealt with human growth and development covered personality development and interpersonal relations, ignoring sexual factors. Health courses talked about care of the teeth, hair, and nostrils but did little about menstruation, venereal disease, and conception.

At present there is an odd reversal that still gives evidence of our continuing fear of sex; instead of family life courses that omit mention of sex, there are courses being given which are called "family living" and which deal with little more than menstruation and reproduction education. These are indeed classes in *sex education,* but they are euphemistically calling themselves by what is considered a more socially acceptable name!

So the dichotomy is perpetuated on a completely fallacious assumption that sex is not an integral part of family living or that family life has less than a central role in the way one uses himself sexually. No one actually believes this nor verbalizes it. No educator on either side of the fence—if unfortunately there be a fence—defends this kind of cleavage nor wants it. No one contends that sex can be dealt with except that it be set into *some* context. As a matter of fact it is best presented when it is seen in a variety of settings—physiological, psychological, social, moral, artistic, and so on.

There are positive aspects of the terms as well as the negative, however. Many of us in the field have not shied from the term "sex education" and like it because it is a label that is honestly and openly descriptive. "Family living" has that same virtue, especially when it fully encompasses the many aspects of life that goes on in the family. "Family life education" denotes a broader area than "sex education." Even more encompassing are the terms "interpersonal relations," "human relations," or "human growth and development." One of these, in fact, may serve our purpose better.

In the last analysis the adequacy of the course itself will establish its reputation regardless of what it is called. However, as a step toward integrating and expanding the subject matter area, perhaps old terms should be avoided and a new one—more comprehensive and with less negative history—should be substituted.

FAMILY LIFE EDUCATION, AN ENTITY

It is difficult to predict just how and where family life education including sex will eventually develop. It is clear that it will not be left to any one social institution, the home, the school, or the church, but that it will become the concern of many social institutions, including government agencies and big business concerns. Each agency will pursue its own best interests, and a multitude of approaches will develop.

Currently family life education including sex is most frequently considered a part of the school curriculum, possibly a subject-matter course in itself like mathematics, language, or health or, at least, a systematized unit of study within some other subject-matter course such as home economics, biology, or sociology. Establishing a separate subject-matter course may perpetuate what seems to be a gulf between family life and sex education (as well as between other areas such as nutrition, home management, design, and clothing) because it attempts such broad and varied coverage and yet confines these in a packaged one- or two-semester unit.

Finding an adequately prepared teacher for such complex and conglomerate areas is nearly, if not entirely, impossible. The psychologist and sociologist may not be able to discuss the physiology of conception and pregnancy and areas of nutrition, clothing, and housing. The doctor, the biology teacher, and the physiologist in their turns may be incompetent to discuss social sexual roles, the transition of social values, the subtleties of dynamic psychological interaction between persons, and the problems of management and economics. The home economist (in whose department the most classes in family life exist, at least at the secondary school level) may be deficient in both biological and social sciences but well prepared in management and design of the home, in nutrition of the family, and in clothing. Each teacher is likely to emphasize the areas in which he is more competent and to neglect the areas about which he knows little. The results are not likely to be very satisfactory for any point of view.

TEACHER PREPARATION, A NECESSITY

The principal factor in developing school courses that will be well rounded and inclusive is the preparation of those who will teach family life and/or sex education. Is it possible to prepare one individual broadly enough in all interdisciplinary fields involved? Certainly our teachers are not now being so trained.

It is unfortunate that states have not set up standards of certification for family life teachers based upon the broad interdisciplinary needs of the field. It is even more unfortunate that some educators believe that no special preparation is necessary for teachers in this field. All that is necessary, it is said, is a well-intentioned teacher who relates warmly to students and who has the time in his schedule. Nothing could be farther from reality. The family life teacher, more than any other in the school system, needs special and comprehensive preparation.

Such breadth is not easy to develop, especially if it is to be more than superficial. Most university and college programs would not attempt to prepare a teacher in any depth in psychology, sociology, physiology, nutrition, family economics, design, clothing, and education in less than six to eight years of full-time course work. And even this preparation would be highly compartmentalized and lack any centralization in terms of *the family*. Some kind of integration—which does not now exist in most colleges—is necessary.

Some kinds of courses which consolidate these disciplines around the family are necessary. In some departments of child development and family relations such work is now being offered, but, even with these kinds of courses, a five-year preparation program for the family life teacher is a likely minimum.

Short of such broad and intensive training, the answer may lie in the emergence of team teaching or shared teaching in which we rely on the specialists. In our day of expanding knowledge, this is perhaps the more logical approach. A number of specialists, of which the "sex educator" may be one, would be required. Equally important is the child developmentalist, the psychologist, the sociologist, the home economist, the health educator, the teacher of literature, and the counselor. These specialists could be "tied together" or integrated by a single teacher who would be a generalist. The specialists would probably be affiliated with their original field of study and "borrowed" for the family life course. For example, the physiological aspects of the course would be taught by the biology teacher, the nutritional aspects by the home economist, and so on.

Mastering the content is not the only ability that is a necessary part of the equipment of one who would teach in this field. Competency in teaching skills and in counseling both with individuals and with groups is necessary. Conveying information is only a part of the educational job to be done. Probably more important is helping students develop values that are appropriate and that contribute to society's functioning and helping them work through their own individual problems and grow toward a sense of integrity. The development of these skills requires additional university study as well as considerable natural ability.

Whether courses are given by one teacher or by teams, the training of teachers is a crucial concern. It will require a *new* approach by institutions of higher learning. It will require careful prescription by boards of certification and standards.

INTEGRATION WITHIN ALL SUBJECTS, AN ALTERNATIVE

The ideal would be to have teachers of *every* field so well prepared in the field of human relations that there would be no necessity of singling out any one area that could be called either family life or sex education. The materials usually dealt with in family life and sex could be integrated into a variety of subject-matter fields which already exist: natural science, behavioral sciences, social studies, literature, art, and home economics.

The grade placement of material would be determined by the child's own curiosity, his ability, and his exposure in his society. The pace for his learning about interpersonal relationships, sex, home, and family would be set appropriately by his own rate of development. There would be no units, no courses; there would be no problems of segregating the sexes for lectures, no enormous trifles about *what* to teach *when*. The process would be continuous and ongoing; the subject matter would be found in literature, science, the arts, and *life*.

The preparation of teachers dealing with the material in this way would have to be different from that for those who would be offering family life as a single subject-matter course. All teachers, no matter what their field of specialization, would have to be broadly trained in human growth and development, interpersonal and sexual relationships, and family relations. Again, the implication is that institutions involved in teacher training would have to create, revise, and implement present course offerings in such a way that these objectives could be met. However, the prospect of completing such preparation in the usual four-year period is somewhat greater.

Much of what is now considered family life or sex education material falls very naturally into other subject-matter courses and is appropriately emphasized in courses already in established departments. The teacher who has majored in sociology and teaches high school social science should be expected to deal with the family as a social institution and to design units of study appropriate to a sociology course. Individual growth and development, personality needs and expressions, and interpersonal relationships (*including sex* as an interpersonal relationship!) falls within the social science or psychology sequence of study and in literature and the arts. Care of the body, health, and disease are a part of health study. Reproductive systems and functions are a part of natural science.

Teachers of all of these subjects would need to be capable of dealing with the formation of social attitudes and values. They would need to be confident of their ability to deal in the field of human relationships and to communicate effectively. They would need to be sensitively alert to the opportunities to emphasize or clarify human relations materials.

To the usual courses required in the major field might be added courses that would help teachers-in-training deal effectively with themselves, their feelings, and attitudes; courses in ethics, values, and morals; and a course that would synthesize and reemphasize the kinds of family and sex problems that might appropriately be considered in the area of the specific major discipline.

SUMMARY

"Sex education" has been considered a part of "family life education" which in turn may be subsumed under "interpersonal relations" or "human development." Two ways of presenting its content have been considered: (1) as a subject-matter course in itself, handled either by a single teacher or by a team composed of a generalist and a variety of specialists, or (2) as an integrated part of subjects already taught in the elementary and secondary schools. In either case, it was pointed out that the preparation of the teacher would be crucial and would determine the format of the material as well as the quality of the teaching.

Decisions regarding teacher preparation will determine in large measure which method of presentation will develop as the mainstream. The challenge to make meaningful *any* term used to designate what is currently being called "family life and/or sex education" faces the teacher training institutions. Without more inclusive and specialized preparation, we will continue to have a hodgepodge of poorly taught material that will soon earn discredit for itself no matter what it is called.

ADDITIONAL READINGS

Bell, Robert R. *Premarital sex in a changing society.* Englewood Cliffs, N.J.: Prentice-Hall, 1966. Bell reviews the research literature on premarital sex and also cites spokesmen for the conservative points of view. He himself adopts the "permissiveness-with-responsibility" position which is popular now.

Broderick, Carlfred B., & Rowe, George P. A scale of preadolescent heterosexual development. *Journal of Marriage and the Family,* February 1968, **30** (1), 97–101. An analysis is provided supporting the idea that most pre-adolescent boys and girls undergo an orderly pattern of progression in heterosexual development. The specific stages in such development are tentatively described.

Chamove, A., Harlow, H. F., & Mitchell, G. Sex differences in the infant-directed behavior of preadolescent rhesus monkeys. *Child Development,* June 1967, **38** (2), 329–335. Fifteen pairs of pre-adolescent rhesus monkeys matched for rearing experience were tested with a 1-month-old infant. Pre-adolescent females directed significantly more positive social behavior and less hostility toward the infant than did males. The results were taken as evidence that hormonal changes at puberty are not the only variables producing sex differences in infant-directed behavior.

Children, March–April 1963, **10** (2), 43–75. These pages comprise six articles relating to problems of illegitimacy and unwed mothers and fathers.

Couch, Gertrude B. Youth looks at sex. *Adolescence,* Summer 1967, 2 (6), 255–266. A one-day conference with a group of young people was held in 1966, sponsored by the Detroit Commission on Children and Youth, to consider social problems related to sexual behavior. What these youth seemed to be asking for ranged from approval of free sex relations, information on how to avoid the social consequences of the sex act, without moralizing and criticism on the one hand, to attitudes of faith, trust, understanding, and more adequate instruction about sex on the other.

Ford, Clellan S. & Beach, Frank A. *Patterns of sexual behavior.* New York: Harper & Row, 1951. Pp. 178–192. This selection from a book, which surveys sex practices around the world, helps lend perspective to sexual values and practices in this country. The writers conclude that the American sexual code relating to children and adolescents is a restrictive one.

Freedman, Mervin B. The sexual behavior of American college women: An empirical study and an historical survey. *Merrill-Palmer Quarterly,* January 1965, **II** (1), 33–48. This paper reports the results of a study of the sexual behavior of a sample recent graduates of an Eastern women's college. The test data were based on whole classes of students.

Kuhlen, Raymond G., & Houlihan, Nancy Bryant. Adolescent heterosexual interest in 1942 and 1963. Child Development, December 1965, **36** (4), 1049–1052. A sociometric questionnaire identical to that administered in 1942 to boys and girls in grades 6, 9, and 12, was given in 1963 to pupils in grades 6 through 12. More cross-sex choices were made in the later study.

LaBarre, Maurine. Pregnancy experiences among married adolescents. *American Journal of Orthopsychiatry,* 1968, **38** (1), 47–55. This paper discusses the experiences and problems of pregnant married teen-agers and calls attention to the need for studies of the life-situational and dynamic factors involved in such cases.

Lessler, K. Sexual symbols, structured and unstructured. *Journal of Consulting Psychology,* 1962, **26,** 44–49. Lessler's data indicate that sex awareness arises rapidly at adolescence. All ages (4th grade, 9th grade, and college) identified sex symbols successfully, with great accuracy, with the accuracy improving after the 4th grade.

Malfetti, James L., & Rubin, Arline M. Sex education: Who is teaching the teachers? *Teachers College Record,* December 1967, **69** (3), 213–222. The writers assert that most members of present teaching staffs are not prepared to teach sex education and propose beginning steps to help resolve the dilemma. They further add that the schools will apparently have to provide sex education whether they are ready to do so or not.

Pope, Hallowell & Knudsen, Dean D. Premarital sexual norms, the family, and social change. *Journal of Marriage and the Family,* August 1965, **27** (3), 314–323. Data suggest that changes in premarital sex norms since the 1930's have been limited. The present code of "permissiveness with affection" may give way to one of "permissiveness with contraception" when complete confidence in contraceptive technology is established.

Reiss, I. L. *Premarital sexual standards in America.* New York: Free Press, 1960. Reiss analyzed standards and attitudes undergirding sexual practices as well as the behaviors themselves, and concluded that new standards have developed over the last half century or so. Although the direction is away from a double to a single standard, he asserts that strong traditional forces prevent rapid change.

Rubin, Isadore. Transition in sex values—implications for the education of adolescents. *Journal of Marriage and the Family,* May 1965, **27** (2), 185–189. Six contending value systems are examined along a repressive-permissive continuum. An "open forum" is deemed necessary if teachers are to engage in a meaningful dialogue with youth. The basic values of sex education must be sought from the core values of our democratic society.

Shipman, Gordon. The psychodynamics of sex education. *The Family Co-ordinator* (Journal of Education, Counseling and Services), January 1968, **17** (1), 3–12. An exploratory study of 400 university students confirmed the absence of sex training of children by their parents. An analysis is presented of factors associated with this role of parents, including the incest taboo, the need for privacy, and mutual denial of personal sexuality of both parents and children.

Wright, Mattie K. Comprehensive services for adolescent unwed mothers. *Children,* September–October 1966, **13** (5), 171–176. The article describes a pilot demonstration project designed to meet the comprehensive needs of a selected number of unwed pregnant adolescent girls.

XVI. Social-Sex Role

Only in recent years have psychologists accorded much attention to social-sex role, that is, to the part an individual plays as girl or boy, w(man or man. In earlier textbooks the growing individual was generally treated as a child or an adolescent, with little differentiation by sex. However, studies of human development have indicated sharp distinctions between boys and girls, especially in cultures where sex roles are highly polarized or strongly distinctive for the sexes. In time, therefore, writers and researchers have come to treat sex role as a significant factor in human development.

People generally raise few questions about sex roles because they believe them rooted in biology. Boys are believed innately to make better leaders, and girls better baby-sitters. Boys are deemed naturally more logical, and girls more intuitive. Such ideas receive some support from research. Among monkeys, male youngsters engage in rougher play and make more threats than their sisters.[1] Biological correlates of characteristic sex behaviors also exist among humans. Periods of the ovarian cycle have been found to correspond to irritability, flightiness and introversion-extroversion.[2] Castrated males report reduced aggressiveness and lowered energy level.

Nevertheless, it is improbable that psychosexual differentiation, at least for humans, is genetically determined. In cases of hermaphroditism, where the individual has external primary sex characteristics of both sexes, a child may simply be designated as a boy or as a girl.[3] Even if the sex assigned him be directly contrary to his true gender, his psychosexual identity becomes that of the assigned sex. The critical period in the acquisition of psychosexual role, believes Money, is about the same time as the establishment of native language.[4]

Apparently, the processes of identification, canalization, and reinforcement all are involved in the acquisition of sex role. A child may identify

[1] H. F. Harlow, "The Heterosexual Affectional System in Monkeys," *American Psychologist,* Vol. 17 (1962), pp. 1–9.

[2] T. Benedek and B. B. Rubenstein, "Correlations Between Ovarian Activity and Psychodynamic Processes: The Ovarian Phase," *Psychosomatic Medicine,* Vol. 1 (1939), pp. 245–270.

[3] J. Money, "Developmental Differentiation of Femininity and Masculinity Compared," in Seymour M. Farber and Roger H. L. Wilson (Eds.), *Potential of Women* (McGraw-Hill, New York: 1963), pp. 52–56.

[4] J. Money, "Psychosexual Differentiation," in J. Money (Ed.), *Sex Research: New Developments,* (New York: Holt, Rinehart and Winston, 1965), p. 12.

with his like-sex parent. Also, the stage is set (canalization) so that it comes easier to behave as one sex or the other. Meantime, society rewards children for following the prescribed sex role (positive reinforcement) and punishes those who do not (negative reinforcement). Girls are granted greater latitude than boys, the reasons not being entirely unclear, but may not themselves exceed certain limits. However, the girl's freedom to depart from the norms shrinks somewhat in the teens.

The current status of the sex roles is unclear. It has been suggested that the roles are gradually becoming less differentiated, or depolarized. For one thing, parents themselves treat boys and girls more alike than formerly. However, this trend is more prominent among the well-educated and upper classes than their opposites.[5] Consider, too, the figures which indicate increasing employment of women outside the home, often cited to prove that women are tending to reject their traditional sex role. However, sheer numbers constitute a shaky basis for formulating hypotheses. Actually, most women still view homemaking and child-rearing as their primary role. Women generally seek employment to provide a better life for the children rather than to establish a career.[6] That is, changes appear to be in peripheral rather than basic areas of behavior. What the roles ideally should be, or how active a role society should take in altering them, is debatable. For the most part, changes in sex role simply evolve with little conscious planning by society.

Several factors operate to obstruct change, one being the fact that males hold various sex advantages and also the power to preserve their preferred status. Females are taught from birth to be passive, hence, are unlikely to protest the secondary role assigned them. Both sexes ordinarily believe the differences in their role natural, and therefore unsusceptible to fundamental change.

Teen-agers face various problems related to sex role, partly because adolescence high-lights differences between boys and girls. Teen activities are polarized—in dancing the boy leads, the girl follows. Such polarization may arouse jealousies and hostility, often unconscious. Moreover, when an individual matures sexually, he is expected simultaneously to adopt mature behaviors appropriate to his sex. Since these behaviors vary widely from those of childhood, considerable adaptation may be required. An individual who adjusted very well to the more neutral sex role of childhood, may have a greater problem in adolescence. The homely looking girl who never has dates, feels lonely among peers who boast of their conquests. The boy from a lower-class home may lack the graces required at mixed social functions at school.

[5] U. Bronfenbrenner, "The Changing American Child—A Speculative Analysis," *Journal of Social Issues,* Vol. 17 (1961), p. 1.

[6] Ruth E. Hartley, "Current Changes in Sex Role Patterns," *Merrill-Palmer Quarterly,* Vol. 6 (1960), pp. 153–164.

Adaptations to each sex role pose certain problems. The boy's role is more discontinuous than the girl's—that is, his role as a child makes less provision than hers for what the corresponding adult role will be. The girl's assistance of her mother and play with her dolls are directly related to the domestically oriented role of the woman. However, the boy's pursuits may vary widely from his later roles as worker and father. Also, the boy, more so than the girl, is driven to achieve and to prove himself sexually.

The girl has her special problems, too. Often, she is uncertain about what her own role should be. Perhaps the difficulty is in integrating the complex factors involved in determining the modern girl's self image. To a considerable extent, it involves harmonizing the contradictory roles of being both feminine and modern. Each role, says Komarovsky, is mutually exclusive, carrying with it contrasting sets of personality traits. Each role involves certain attitudes toward work, men, love, and self.[7] Moreover, society ordinarily fails to discriminate between active and aggressive women. Many active women are quite feminine, and care nothing for wearing the pants. Nevertheless, they wish to strive for some purpose, not in competition with men, but in pursuit of worthwhile goals. Nevertheless, such a girl, the more so because she is feminine, may feel anxious whenever she departs from the traditionally passive female role.[8]

In general, boys accept the roles assigned them more easily than do girls. For one thing, they are pressured by parents and peers to do so.[9] Males are also accorded higher status, especially as they grow older. In consequence, notes Ausubel, "the male counterpart of a 'tomboy' who relishes sewing and reads girls' books is indeed a rarity." [10] By contrast, girls may be discontent, at least with certain aspects of their role. Our age does not value the role of housewife, states Korner, in education or in school. Instead, there is a "thorough indoctrination that being a housewife is a fate not a call." [11] In like vein, Steinemann says that the traditional role of the woman is other-oriented in the sense that she achieves fulfillment by proxy.[12]

Actually, adaptation to sex role is a highly personal matter, dependent on a particular individual's traits and experience. The 12-year-old tomboy may have trouble evolving into a demure young lady. A shy insecure boy

[7] Mirra Komarovsky, "Cultural Contradictions and Sex Roles," *American Journal of Sociology,* Vol. 52 (November 1946), pp. 184–189.

[8] Bruno Bettelheim, "The Problem of Generations," *Daedalus,* Vol. 91 (Winter 1962), p. 95.

[9] Ruth E. Hartley, "Sex-Role Pressure and the Socialization of the Male Child," *Psychological Reports,* Vol. 5 (1959), pp. 457–468.

[10] D. P. Ausubel, "Ego Development Among Segregated Negro Children," *Mental Hygiene,* Vol. 42 (1958), pp. 362–369.

[11] I. N. Korner, "Of Values, Value Lag, and Mental Health," *American Psychologist,* Vol. 11 (1956), pp. 543–546.

[12] A. Steinemann, "A Study of the Concept of the Feminine Role of 51 Middle-class American Families," *Genetic Psychology Monographs,* Vol. 67 (1963), pp. 275–352.

may find that the adolescent male role requires a degree of dominance he does not possess. Another boy may enjoy adolescence but dread the responsibilities associated with full manhood. A girl who has achieved prominence in high-school activities may resist succumbing to a secondary role in marriage.

Implicit in the foregoing discussion are the many and complex issues relating to sex role. Should teachers and parents attempt to make less masculine boys more so, and masculine girls less so? Should society undertake deliberate attempts to modify less desirable features of sex role? To what extent, if any, might adaptation to sex role be facilitated by hormonal injection, perhaps during the prenatal period? What sorts of sex roles are needed for modern society? Are less differentiated roles actually more functional nowadays? Certainly, many assumptions relating to sex role warrant re-examination. Traditionally, departures from sex-typical behaviors are assumed to be abnormal and undesirable; however, a broader interpretation of sex role is more congruent with full personal development.[13]

The following two articles provide a helpful background for considering such matters. The first, by Lynn, provides a comprehensive theory concerning sex-role identification. Lynn has written widely on the subject and has suggested various provocative hypotheses. Douvan indicates how sex-role factors serve to differentiate the development of boys' and girls' character formation. In every area of personality development investigated, sex role is proving a significant factor. However, questions remain as to what extent such factors are socioculturally determined and subject to change, to what degree they are inherent in genetic factors, and what amount of change in sex roles is needed.

---

[13] Patricia Minuchin, "Sex-Role Concepts and Sex Typing in Childhood as a Function of School and Home Environments," *Child Development,* Vol. 36, No. 4 (December 1965), pp. 1032–1048.

33

David B. Lynn *

THE PROCESS OF LEARNING PARENTAL
AND SEX-ROLE IDENTIFICATION †

This paper summarizes Lynn's theoretical formulations concerning sex-role identification, and attempts a more comprehensive, coherent clarification of concepts. Research is quoted in support of the newer hypotheses.

The purpose of this paper is to summarize the writer's theoretical formulation concerning identification, much of which has been published piecemeal in various journals. Research relevant to new hypotheses is cited, and references are given to previous publications of this writer in which the reader can find evidence concerning the earlier hypotheses. Some of the previously published hypotheses are considerably revised in this paper and, it is hoped, placed in a more comprehensive and coherent framework.

THEORETICAL FORMULATION

Before developing specific hypotheses, one must briefly define identification as it is used here. *Parental identification* refers to the internalization of personality characteristics of one's own parent and to unconscious reactions similar to that parent. This is to be contrasted with *sex-role identification,* which refers to the internalization of the role typical of a given sex in a particular culture and to the unconscious reactions characteristic of that role. Thus, theoretically, an individual might be thoroughly identified with the role typical of his own sex generally and yet poorly identified with his same-sex parent specifically. This differentiation also allows for the converse circumstances wherein a person is well identified with his same-sex

From David B. Lynn, "The Process of Learning Parental and Sex-Role Identification," *Journal of Marriage and the Family,* Vol. 28, No. 4 (November 1966), pp. 466–470. Reprinted by permission.

* David B. Lynn, Ph.D., is in the Department of Psychology, College of San Mateo, San Mateo, California.

† Presented at the Annual Meeting of the American Orthopsychiatric Association, 1966.

parent specifically and yet poorly identified with the typical same-sex role generally. In such an instance the parent with whom the individual is well identified is himself poorly identified with the typical sex role. An example might be a girl who is closely identified with her mother, who herself is more strongly identified with the masculine than with the feminine role. Therefore, such a girl, through her identification with her mother, is poorly identified with the feminine role.[1]

Formulation of Hypotheses

It is postulated that the initial parental identification of both male and female infants is with the mother. Boys, but not girls, must shift from this initial mother identification and establish masculine-role identification. Typically in this culture the girl has the same-sex parental model for identification (the mother) with her more hours per day than the boy has his same-sex model (the father) with him. Moreover, even when home, the father does not usually participate in as many intimate activities with the child as does the mother, e.g., preparation for bed, toileting. The time spent with the child and the intimacy and intensity of the contact are thought to be pertinent to the process of learning parental identification.[2] The boy is seldom if ever with the father as he engages in his daily vocational activities, although both boy and girl are often with the mother as she goes through her household activities. Consequently, the father, as a model for the boy, is analogous to a map showing the major outline but lacking most details, whereas the mother, as a model for the girl, might be thought of as a detailed map.

However, despite the shortage of male models, a somewhat stereotyped and conventional masculine role is nonetheless spelled out for the boy, often by his mother and women teachers in the absence of his father and male models. Through the reinforcement of the culture's highly developed system of rewards for typical masculine-role behavior and punishment for signs of femininity, the boy's early learned identification with the mother weakens. Upon this weakened mother identification is welded the later learned identification with a culturally defined, stereotyped masculine role.

1.* *Consequently, males tend to identify with a culturally defined masculine role, whereas females tend to identify with their mothers.*[3]

---

[1] D. B. Lynn, "Sex-Role and Parental Identification," *Child Development,* 33:3 (1962), pp. 555–564.

[2] B. A. Goodfield, "A Preliminary Paper on the Development of the Time Intensity Compensation Hypothesis in Masculine Identification," paper read at the San Francisco State Psychological Convention, April, 1965.

[3] D. B. Lynn, "A Note on Sex Differences in the Development of Masculine and Feminine Identification," *Psychological Review,* 66:2 (1959), pp. 126–135.

* Specific hypotheses are numbered and in italics.

Although one must recognize the contribution of the father in the identification of males and the general cultural influences in the identification of females, it nevertheless seems meaningful, for simplicity in developing this formulation, to refer frequently to *masculine-role identification* in males as distinguished from *mother identification* in females.

Some evidence is accumulating suggesting that 2. *both males and females identify more closely with the mother than with the father.* Evidence is found in support of this hypothesis in a study by Lazowick [4] in which the subjects were 30 college students. These subjects and their mothers and fathers were required to rate concepts, e.g., "myself," "father," "mother," etc. The degree of semantic similarity as rated by the subjects and their parents was determined. The degree of similarity between fathers and their own children was not significantly greater than that found between fathers and children randomly matched. However, children did share a greater semantic similarity with their own mothers than they did when matched at random with other maternal figures. Mothers and daughters did not share a significantly greater semantic similarity than did mothers and sons.

Evidence is also found in support of Hypothesis 2 in a study by Adams and Sarason [5] using anxiety scales with male and female high school students and their mothers and fathers. They found that anxiety scores of both boys and girls were much more related to mothers' than to fathers' anxiety scores.

Support for this hypothesis comes from a study in which Aldous and Kell [6] interviewed 50 middle-class college students and their mothers concerning childrearing values. They found, contrary to their expectation, that a slightly higher proportion of boys than girls shared their mothers' childrearing values.

Partial support for Hypothesis 2 is provided in a study by Gray and Klaus [7] using the Allport-Vernon-Lindzey Study of Values completed by 34 female and 28 male college students and by their parents. They found that the men were not significantly closer to their fathers than to their mothers and also that the men were not significantly closer to their fathers than were the women. However, the women were closer to their mothers than were the men and closer to their mothers than to their fathers.

Note that, in reporting research revelant to Hypothesis 2, only studies of *tested similarity,* not *perceived similarity,* were reviewed. To test this hypothesis, one must measure tested similarity, i.e., measure both the child

[4] L. M. Lazowick, "On the Nature of Identification," *Journal of Abnormal and Social Psychology,* 51 (1955), pp. 175–183.

[5] E. B. Adams and I. G. Sarason, "Relation Between Anxiety in Children and Their Parents," *Child Development,* 34:1 (1963), pp. 237–246.

[6] J. Aldous and L. Kell, "A Partial Test of Some Theories of Identification," *Marriage and Family Living,* 23:1 (1961), pp. 15–19.

[7] S. W. Gray and R. Klaus, "The Assessment of Parental Identification," *Genetic Psychology Monographs,* 54 (1956), pp. 87–114.

and the parent on the same variable and compare the similarity between these two measures. This paper is not concerned with perceived similarity, i.e., testing the child on a given variable and then comparing that finding with a measure taken as to how the child thinks his parent would respond. It is this writer's opinion that much confusion has arisen by considering perceived similarity as a measure of parental identification. It seems obvious that, especially for the male, perceived similarity between father and son would usually be closer than tested similarity, in that it is socially desirable for a man to be similar to his father, especially as contrasted to his similarity to his mother. Indeed, Gray and Klaus [8] found the males' perceived similarity with the father to be closer than tested similarity.

It is hypothesized that the closer identification of males with the mother than with the father will be revealed more clearly on some measures than on others. 3. *The closer identification of males with their mothers than with their fathers will be revealed most frequently in personality variables which are not clearly sex-typed.* In other words, males are more likely to be more similar to their mothers than to their fathers in variables in which masculine and feminine role behavior is not especially relevant in the culture.

There has been too little research on tested similarity between males and their parents to presume an adequate test of Hypothesis 3. In order to test it, one would first have to judge personality variables as to how typically masculine or feminine they seem. One could then test to determine whether a higher proportion of males are more similar to their mothers than to their fathers on those variables which are not clearly sex-typed, rather than on those which are judged clearly to be either masculine or feminine. To this writer's knowledge, this has not been done.

It is postulated that the task of achieving these separate kinds of identification (masculine role for males and mother identification for females) requires separate methods of learning for each sex. These separate methods of learning to identify seem to be problem-solving for boys and lesson-learning for girls. Woodworth and Schlosberg differentiate between the task of solving problems and that of learning lessons in the following way:

> With a problem to master the learner must explore the situation and find the goal before his task is fully presented. In the case of a lesson, the problem-solving phase is omitted or at least minimized, as we see when the human subject is instructed to memorize this poem or that list of nonsense syllables, to examine these pictures with a view to recognizing them later.[9]

Since the girl is not required to shift from the mother in learning her identification, she is expected mainly to learn the mother-identification lesson as it is presented to her, partly through imitation and through the

[8] *Ibid.*
[9] R. S. Woodworth and H. Schlosberg, *Experimental Psychology,* New York: Holt, 1954, p. 529.

mother's selective reinforcement of mother-similar behavior. She need not abstract principles defining the feminine role to the extent that the boy must in defining the masculine role. Any bit of behavior on the mother's part may be modeled by the girl in learning the mother-identification lesson.

However, finding the appropriate identification goal does constitute a major problem for the boy in solving the masculine-role identification problem. When the boy discovers that he does not belong in the same sex category as the mother, he must then find the proper sex-role identification goal. Masculine-role behavior is defined for him through admonishments, often negatively given, e.g., the mother's and teachers' telling him that he should not be a sissy without precisely indicating what he *should* be. Moreover, these negative admonishments are made in the early grades in the absence of male teachers to serve as models and with the father himself often unavailable as a model. The boy must restructure these admonishments in order to abstract principles defining the masculine role. It is this process of defining the masculine-role goal which is involved in solving the masculine-role identification problem.

One of the basic steps in this formulation can now be taken. 4. *In learning the sex-typical identification, each sex is thereby acquiring separate methods of learning which are subsequently applied to learning tasks generally.*[10]

The little girl acquires a learning method which primarily involves (a) a personal relationship and (b) imitation rather than restructuring the field and abstracting principles. On the other hand, the little boy acquires a different learning method which primarily involves (a) defining the goal (b) restructuring the field, and (c) abstracting principles. There are a number of findings which are consistent with Hypothesis 4, such as the frequently reported greater problem-solving skill of males and the greater field dependence of females.[11]

The shift of the little boy from mother identification to masculine-role identification is assumed to be frequently a crisis. It has been observed that demands for typical sex-role behavior come at an earlier age for boys than for girls. These demands are made at an age when boys are least able to understand them. As was pointed out above, demands for masculine sex-role behavior are often made by women in the absence of readily available male models to demonstrate typical sex-role behavior. Such demands are often presented in the form of punishing, *negative* admonishments, i.e., telling the boy what not to do rather than what to do and backing up the demands with punishment. These are thought to be very different conditions from those in which the girl learns her mother-identification lesson. Such methods of demanding typical sex-role behavior of boys are very poor methods for inducing learning.

[10] D. B. Lynn, "Sex-Role and Parental Identification," *op. cit.*
[11] *Ibid.*

5. *Therefore, males tend to have greater difficulty in achieving same-sex identification than females.*[12]

6. *Furthermore, more males than females fail more or less completely in achieving same-sex identification, but they rather make an opposite-sex identification.*[13]

Negative admonishments given at an age when the child is least able to understand them and supported by punishment are thought to produce anxiety concerning sex-role behavior. In Hartley's words:

This situation gives us practically a perfect combination for inducing anxiety—the demand that the child do something which is not clearly defined to him, based on reasons he cannot possibly appreciate, and enforced with threats, punishments and anger by those who are close to him.[14]

7. *Consequently, males are more anxious regarding sex-role identification than females.*[15] It is postulated that punishment often leads to dislike of the activity that led to punishment.[16] Since it is "girl-like" activities that provoked the punishment administered in an effort to induce sex-typical behavior in boys, then, in developing dislike for the activity which led to such punishment, boys should develop hostility toward "girl-like" activities. Also, boys should be expected to generalize and consequently develop hostility toward all females as representatives of this disliked role. There is not thought to be as much pressure on girls as on boys to avoid opposite-sex activities. It is assumed that girls are punished neither so early nor so severely for adopting masculine sex-role behavior.

8. *Therefore, males tend to hold stronger feelings of hostility toward females than females toward males.*[17] The young boy's same-sex identification is at first not very firm because of the shift from mother to masculine identification. On the other hand, the young girl, because she need make no shift in identification, remains relatively firm in her mother identification. However, the culture, which is male-dominant in orientation, reinforces the boy's developing masculine-role identification much more thoroughly than it does the girl's developing feminine identification. He is rewarded simply for having been born masculine through countless privileges accorded males but not females. As Brown pointed out:

[12] D. B. Lynn, "Divergent Feedback and Sex-Role Identification in Boys and Men," *Merrill-Palmer Quarterly,* 10:1 (1964), pp. 17–23.
[13] D. B. Lynn, "Sex Differences in Identification Development," *Sociometry,* 24:4 (1961), pp. 372–383.
[14] R. E. Hartley, "Sex-Role Pressures and the Socialization of the Male Child," *Psychological Reports,* 5 (1959), p. 458.
[15] D. B. Lynn, "Divergent Feedback and Sex-Role Identification in Boys and Men," *op. cit.*
[16] E. R. Hilgard, *Introduction to Psychology,* New York: Harcourt, Brace, and World, 1962.
[17] D. B. Lynn, "Divergent Feedback and Sex-Role Identification in Boys and Men," *op. cit.*

The superior position and privileged status of the male permeates nearly every aspect, minor and major, of our social life. The gadgets and prizes in boxes of breakfast cereal, for example, commonly have a strong masculine rather than feminine appeal. And the most basic social institutions perpetuate this pattern of masculine aggrandizement. Thus, the Judeo-Christian faiths involve worshipping God, a "Father," rather than a "Mother," and Christ, a "Son," rather than a "Daughter." [18]

9. Consequently, with increasing age, males become relatively more firmly identified with the masculine role.[19]

Since psychological disturbances should, theoretically, be associated with inadequate same-sex identification and since males are postulated to be gaining in masculine identification, the following is predicted: 10. *With increasing age males develop psychological disturbances at a more slowly accelerating rate than females.*[20]

It is postulated that as girls grow older, they become increasingly disenchanted with the feminine role because of the prejudices against their sex and the privileges and prestige offered the male rather than the female. Even the women with whom they come in contact are likely to share the prejudices prevailing in this culture against their own sex.[21] Smith [22] found that with increasing age girls have a progressively better opinion of boys and a progressively poorer opinion of themselves. 11. *Consequently, a larger proportion of females than males show preference for the role of the opposite sex.*[23]

Note that in hypothesis 11 the term "preference" rather than "identification" was used. It is *not* hypothesized that a larger proportion of females than males *identify* with the opposite sex (Hypothesis 6 predicted the reverse) but rather that they will show *preference* for the role of the opposite sex. *Sex-role preference* refers to the desire to adopt the behavior associated with one sex or the other or the perception of such behavior as preferable or more desirable. *Sex-role preference* should be contrasted with *sex-role identification*, which, as stated previously, refers to the actual incorporation of the role of a given sex and to the unconscious reactions characteristic of that role.

Punishment may suppress behavior without causing its unlearning.[24]

[18] D. G. Brown, "Sex-Role Development in a Changing Culture," *Psychological Bulletin*, 55 (1958), p. 235.

[19] D. B. Lynn, "A Note on Sex Differences in the Development of Masculine and Feminine Identification," *op. cit.*

[20] D. B. Lynn, "Sex Differences in Identification Development," *op. cit.*

[21] P. M. Kitay, "A Comparison of the Sexes in Their Attitudes and Beliefs About Women: A Study of Prestige Groups," *Sociometry*, 3 (1940), pp. 399–407.

[22] S. Smith, "Age and Sex Differences in Children's Opinion Concerning Sex Differences," *Journal of Genetic Psychology*, 54 (1939), pp. 17–25.

[23] D. B. Lynn, "A Note on Sex Differences in the Development of Masculine and Feminine Identification," *op. cit.*

[24] Hilgard, *op. cit.*

Because of the postulated punishment administered to males for adopting opposite-sex role behavior, it is predicted that males will repress atypical sex-role behavior rather than unlearn it. One might predict, then, a discrepancy between the underlying sex-role identification and the overt sex-role behavior of males. For females, on the other hand, no comparable punishment for adopting many aspects of the opposite-sex role is postulated. 12. *Consequently, where a discrepancy exists between sex-role preference and identification, it will tend to be as follows: Males will tend to show same-sex role preference with underlying opposite-sex identification. Females will tend to show opposite-sex role preference with underlying same-sex identification.*[25] Stated in another way, where a discrepancy occurs both males and females will tend to show masculine-role preference with underlying feminine identification.

Not only is the masculine role accorded more prestige than the feminine role, but males are more likely than females to be ridiculed or punished for adopting aspects of the opposite-sex role. For a girl to be a tomboy does not involve the censure that results when a boy is a sissy. Girls may wear masculine clothing (shirts and trousers), but boys may not wear feminine clothing (skirts and dresses). Girls may play with toys typically associated with boys (cars, trucks, erector sets, and guns), but boys are discouraged from playing with feminine toys (dolls and tea sets). 13. *Therefore, a higher proportion of females than males adopt aspects of the role of the opposite sex.*[26]

Note that Hypothesis 13 refers to *sex-role adoption* rather than *sex-role identification* or *preference. Sex-role adoption* refers to the overt behavior characteristic of a given sex. An example contrasting sex-role adoption with preference and identification is an individual who *adopts* behavior characteristic of his own sex because it is expedient, not because he *prefers* it nor because he is so *identified.*

SUMMARY

The purpose of this paper has been to summarize the writer's theoretical formulation and to place it in a more comprehensive and coherent framework. The following hypotheses were presented and discussed:

1. Males tend to identify with a culturally defined masculine role, whereas females tend to identify with their mothers.

[25] D. B. Lynn, "Divergent Feedback and Sex-Role Identification in Boys and Men," *op. cit.*

[26] D. B. Lynn, "A Note on Sex Differences in the Development of Masculine and Feminine Identification," *op. cit.*

2. Both males and females identify more closely with the mother than with the father.

3. The closer identification of males with their mothers than with their fathers will be revealed most frequently in personality variables which are not clearly sex-typed.

4. In learning the sex-typical identification, each sex is thereby acquiring separate methods of learning which are subsequently applied to learning tasks generally.

5. Males tend to have greater difficulty in achieving same-sex identification than females.

6. More males than females fail more or less completely in achieving same-sex identification but rather make an opposite-sex identification.

7. Males are more anxious regarding sex-role identification than females.

8. Males tend to hold stronger feelings of hostility toward females than females toward males.

9. With increasing age, males become relatively more firmly identified with the masculine role.

10. With increasing age, males develop psychological disturbances at a more slowly accelerating rate than females.

11. A larger proportion of females than males show preference for the role of the opposite sex.

12. Where a discrepancy exists between sex-role preference and identification, it will tend to be as follows: Males will tend to show same-sex role preference with underlying opposite-sex identification. Females will tend to show opposite-sex role preference with underlying same-sex identification.

13. A higher proportion of females than males adopt aspects of the role of the opposite sex.

34

Elizabeth Douvan

SEX DIFFERENCES IN ADOLESCENT CHARACTER PROCESSES [1]

The development of boys and girls is seen as distinctly different. The boy is supported by a strong superego while the girl relies on externally imposed standards. Differential character development, in turn, modifies the respective identities of the sexes. For the boy, character development is part of the broader crisis of defining personal identity. By contrast, there is pressure on the girl not to define her identity during the adolescent years. To do so would be maladaptive and make it hard to adjust to her future husband.

According to psychoanalytic theory, adolescence represents a recapitulation of the Oedipus conflict. The relative calm and control achieved during latency suffer a disruption at this point because of the re-emergence of intense sexual impulses, and the child is plunged once more into Oedipal conflict.

Several new critical features mark this re-enactment of the Oedipal drama, however, and distinguish it from its earlier counterpart. The ego of the puberal child, enriched and articulated during latency, is in a more advantageous position in relation to the impulses than it was in the Oedipal phase. For during its struggle with impulses the ego has gained an ally in the agency of the super-ego. And the fact of genital capability opens for the child new possibilities for resolving conflict. The male child need not simply repress his love for the mother and gain mastery of his ambivalence and fears through identification. He may now seek substitutes for the mother, substitutes who are suitable love objects. Though he may identify with the father in a more or less differentiated fashion, he need not use identification as a global defense against overpowering fear of the rival father, since the father is no longer his rival in the same crucial way.

Part of the outcome of the adolescent struggle is the renegotiation of the ego—super-ego compact: that is, a change in character. As part of the process of remodeling his original identifications, the child establishes a set

From Elizabeth Douvan, "Sex Differences in Adolescent Character Processes," *Merrill-Palmer Quarterly,* Vol. 6 (1960), pp. 203–211. Reprinted by permission.

[1] This article is based on a paper read at the American Psychological Association meetings, September, 1957.

of values and controls which are more internal and personal than earlier ones and which reflect his new reality situation as an adult.

This is the developmental task and context facing the adolescent boy. But what of the task confronting the girl at this period? With what resources and what history does she enter adolescence? Analytic theory, though wanting in specificity, gives us some broad clues about this development, its unique characteristics, and the ways in which it differs from development in the male child.

First, we expect that super-ego is less developed in women (and in adolescent girls). Since the little girl has no decisive motive force comparable to the boy's castration anxiety, she does not turn peremptorily against her own instinctual wishes nor form the same critical and definite identification with the like-sexed parent. Her motives for internalizing the wishes of important adults are fear of loss of love and a sense of shame. According to Deutsch (1), an important step in the socialization of girls occurs when the father enters an agreement with the little girl whereby he exchanges a promise of love for her forfeiture of any direct expression of aggressive impulses.

A significant difference may be noted at this point: the boy who has accomplished the Oedipal resolution now has an *internal* representative of the parents which he must placate and which serves as a source of reinforcement for his acts. The little girl, on the other hand, continues to look to the parents as the source of reward and punishment since her identifications are only partial and primitive.

At adolescence this difference has a critical significance: the boy enters the adolescent contest with an ego that is reinforced by a strong ally, a vigorous super-ego. And in reworking the relation between the ego and the impulses, there is an internal criterion by which the boy judges the new arrangement. His new values and controls are an individual accomplishment and are judged, at least in part, by individual standards. The girl meets the rearoused instincts of adolescence with an ego only poorly supported by partial identifications and introjections. She still needs to rely heavily on externally imposed standards to help in her struggle with impulses.

With this formulation as a starting point, we made a number of predictions about sex differences in character development and looked at data from two national sample surveys of boys and girls in the 14 to 16 year age group for tests of our predictions.[2] Specifically, we explored the following conceptions:

1. Adolescent girls will show less concern with values and with developing behavior controls than will boys; that is, character will show

[2] The studies were conducted at the Survey Research Center of the University of Michigan. Respondents were selected in a multistage probability sampling design, and represent youngsters of the appropriate age in school. Each subject was interviewed at school by a member of the Center's Field Staff; interviews followed a fixed schedule and lasted from one to four hours. For details about the studies, and copies of the complete questionnaire, readers may refer to the basic reports (2, 3).

rapid development in boys during adolescence, while girls will be less pre-occupied with establishing personal, individual standards and values.

2. Personal integration around moral values, though crucial in the adjustment of adolescent boys, will not predict adjustment in girls. Rather, sensitivity and skill in interpersonal relationships will be critical integrative variables in adolescent girls and will predict their personal adjustment.

Our studies yield substantial support for the first speculation. Girls are consciously less concerned about developing independent controls than boys are. They are more likely to show an unquestioned identification with, and acceptance of, parental regulation. They less often distinguish parents' standards from their own, and they do not view the parents' rules as external or inhibiting as often as boys do. Boys more often tell us they worry about controls—particularly controls on aggression; when we ask them what they would like to change about themselves, the issue of controls again emerges as an important source of concern. More important, per-haps, as evidence of their greater involvement in building controls, we find that boys tend to conceive parental rules as distinctly external, and, to some extent, opposed to their own interests. So when we ask why parents make rules, boys underscore the need to control children (e.g., to keep them out of trouble). Girls reveal an identification with the parents when they say that parents make rules to teach their children how to behave, to give them standards to live by, to let children know what is expected of them. Boys think of rules as a means of restricting areas of negative behavior, while girls more often see them as a means of directing and channeling energy.

In answer to all of our questions about parental rules, boys repeatedly reveal greater differentiation between their own and their parents' stand-ards.[3]

One of the most impressive indications of the difference between boys and girls in their stance toward authority comes from a series of projective picture-story questions. At one point in this series a boy or girl is shown with his parents, and the parents are setting a limit for the child. We asked respondents to tell what the child would say. A quarter of the boys questioned the parental reaction—not with hostility or any sign of real conflict, but with a freedom that implies a right to question—while only 4 per cent of the girls in the same age group responded in this way. On the other hand, a third of the girls reassured the parents with phrases like "don't worry," or "you know I'll behave, I'll act like a lady"; the boys almost never gave answers comparable to these.

Both of these response types reveal a respect for one's own opinions.

[3] In the full series, we asked respondents why parents make rules, what would happen if they didn't, when a boy might break a rule, whether the respondent himself had ever broken a rule, and what kind of rule he would never break. For exact phrasing and order of questions, the reader may refer to the basic study reports (2, 3).

They both indicate autonomy, but very different attitudes toward parental rules: the boy openly opposes; the girl not only acquiesces to, but reinforces the parents' regulation.

Girls are more authority reliant than boys in their attitudes toward adults other than their parents. And we find lower correlations among internalization items for girls, indicating less coherence in internalization for them than for boys.

Table 34–1   Extreme Groups on an Internalization Index Compared on
Measures of Other Ego Variables (Boy Sample)

Selected Measures of Ego Variables	Internalization Index		Chi Square	P Level
	High	Low		
I. Achievement				
a. prefer success to security	.64	.47	8.140	< .01
b. choose job aspiration on achievement criteria	.78	.62	9.331	< .01
c. choose job aspiration because of ease of acquiring job, minimum demands	.01	.13	13.758	< .001
d. upward mobile aspirations	.70	.53	7.158	< .01
II. Energy level				
a. high on index of leisure engagements	.49	.40	2.729	< .10 > .05
b. belong to some organized group	.77	.65	5.50	< .05
c. hold jobs	.63	.42	12.576	< .01
d. date	.66	.52	6.007	< .05
III. Autonomy				
a. rely on own judgment in issues of taste and behavior	.40	.20	12.786	< .01
b. have some disagreements with parents	.67	.49	12.804	< .01
c. choose adult ideal outside family	.23	.14	4.547	< .05
d. have no adult ideal	.07	.16	8.621	< .01
e. authority reliant in relation to adult leaders	.23	.54	28.544	< .001
IV. Self-confidence				
a. high on interviewer rating of confidence	.43	.22	11.213	< .01
b. low on interviewer rating of confidence	.16	.35	14.205	< .001
c. high on rating for organization of ideas	.65	.43	9.861	< .01
d. low on rating for organization of ideas	.08	.28	19.006	< .001

Table 34-1 *(Continued)*

V. Self-criticism
 a. wish for changes that can
    be effected by individual
    effort   .36   .12   16.22   < .001
 b. wish for changes that can-
    not be effected by individ-
    ual effort   .14   .30   12.613   < .01
 c. no self-change desired   .27   .42   7.498   < .05

VI. Time perspective
 a. extended   .44   .28   7.604   < .05
 b. restricted   .14   .33   15.721   < .01

Note.—The Internalization Index is based on responses to three questions: (a) What would happen if parents didn't make rules? (b) When might a boy (girl) break a rule? (c) one of the picture-story items: What does the boy (girl) do (when pressed by peers to ignore a promise to parents)? External responses are those which see children obeying only out of fear, breaking rules when they think they will not be caught, relying exclusively on externally imposed guides. Internal responses, in contrast, reveal a sense of obligation or trust about promises given, consider rules unbreakable except in emergencies or when they are for some other reason less critical than other circumstances, and think that children would rely on their own judgment were parental authority no longer available. Subjects who gave internal responses to two or three questions are included in the High category; those who gave two or more external responses are grouped in the Low Internalization category.

These are examples of differences that support the claim that boys are actively struggling with the issue of controls, that they are moving in a process of thrust and counterthrust toward the construction of personal, individuated control systems more conscious and rational than previous global identifications; and that girls, on the other hand, are relatively uninvolved in this struggle and maintain a compliant-dependent relationship with their parents.

The second hypothesis suggested at the beginning of this paper deals with the significance of progress in internalization for the personal integration and adjustment of boys and girls. Having found that girls are less urgently struggling for independent character, we wonder what this means about their general ego development and integration. Are girls relatively undeveloped in these areas as well as in independence of character?

The analysis we have done to date indicates that the second alternative is at least a viable hypothesis. In an analysis of extreme groups, we find that the well-internalized boy is characterized by active achievement strivings, independence of judgment, a high level of energy for use in work and play, and self-confidence combined with realistic self-criticism. He is well developed in the more subtle ego qualities of organization of thought and time-binding. The boy who has not achieved internal, personal controls and who responds only to external authority is poorly integrated, demoralized, and deficient in all areas of advanced ego functioning (Table 34-1).

Again, we ask, what does girls' relatively common reliance on external controls mean about their ego integration? We find when we analyze extreme groups of girls that internalization of individual controls is no guarantee of ego development, and that girls who are dependent on external controls do not show the disintegration and demoralization that mark the noninternalized boy. In short, internalization of independent standards is not an efficient predictor of ego organization or ego strength in girls.

There are several possible explanations for this absence of significant association in girls. High internalization in girls may not reflect independence of standards. Deutsch (1) has observed girls' greater capacity for intense identification, compared to boys; and we may have in the girls' apparently well-internalized controls a product of fusion with parental standards rather than a differentiated and independent character. Moreover, dependence on external standards is the norm for girls in adolescence. Parents are permitted and encouraged to maintain close supervision of the growing girl's actions. Under these circumstances, compliance with external authority is less likely to reflect personal pathology or a pathological family structure.

To this point, then, we have seen that girls are less absorbed with the issue of controls, and that the successful internalization of controls is less crucial for their integration at this age than it is for boys.

We speculated that the critical integrating variable for the girl is her progress in developing interpersonal skill and sensitivity. A striking continuity in feminine psychology lies in the means of meeting developmental crises. In childhood, adolescence, and adulthood, the female's central motive is a desire for love, and her means of handling crises is to appeal for support and love from important persons in her environment. This contrasts with the greater variety of methods—of mastery and withdrawal—that the male uses in meeting developmental stresses. The girl's skill in pleading her cause with others, in attracting and holding affection, is more critical to her successful adaptation.

We designed a test of the importance of interpersonal development in boys and girls. Again, taking extreme groups, those who reveal relatively mature attitudes and skills in the area of friendship and those who are impressively immature, we compared performance in other areas of ego development. With girls we found clear relationships between interpersonal development and the following ego variables: energy level, self-confidence, time-perspective and organization of ideas, and positive feminine identification (Table 34–2).

Interpersonal skill in boys is not significantly related to activity level, time-binding, self-confidence, or self-acceptance. In short, it does not assert the same key influence in the ego integration of boys that it does in feminine development.

What significance do these findings have? What are the sources of the differences we have observed, and what do they mean about the later settlement of character issues in the two sexes in adulthood?

Table 34-2 Extreme Groups on an Interpersonal Development Index
Compared on Measures of Other Ego Variables (Girl Sample)

Selected Measures of Ego Variables	Interpersonal Development Index		Chi Square	P Level
	High	Low		
I. Energy level				
a. high on index of leisure engagements	.41	.27	9.335	< .01
b. belong to some organized group	.97	.75	37.012	< .001
c. hold jobs	.60	.51	2.444	< .10 > .05
d. date	.81	.66	10.98	< .01
II. Self-confidence				
a. high on interviewer rating of confidence	.47	.32	9.071	< .01
b. low on interviewer rating of confidence	.17	.30	11.522	< .01
c. high on interviewer rating for poise	.38	.14	29.613	< .001
d. low on interviewer rating for poise	.14	.29	15.072	< .001
III. Time perspective				
a. extended	.50	.37	8.621	< .01
b. restricted	.04	.13	12.714	< .01
IV. Organization of ideas				
a. high on interviewer rating	.51	.34	12.401	< .01
b. low on interviewer rating	.14	.28	13.168	< .001
V. Feminine identification				
a. high on index of traditional feminine orientation	.37	.11	37.93	< .001
b. choose own mother as an ideal	.48	.30	14.14	< .001

Note.—The Interpersonal Development Index is based on responses to three questions: (a) Can a friend ever be as close as a family member? (b) What should a friend be or be like? (c) What makes a girl (boy) popular with other girls (boys)? Answers counted highly developed are those that stress intimacy, mutuality, and appreciation of individuality and individual differences. Our High category consists of subjects who gave such answers to all three questions. The Low group comprises youngsters who gave no such answers to any of the three critical items.

Differences in character processes in boys and girls probably reflect both basic constitutional and developmental differences between the sexes and also variation in the culture's statement of character crises for boys and girls.

Perhaps the most crucial factor leading to boys' precocity in moral development is the more intense and imperious nature of the impulses they must handle. The sexual impulses aroused in the boy at puberty are specific and demanding and push to the forefront the need for personal controls which accommodate his sexual needs. Acceptance of parental standards or maintenance of the early identification-based control would require denial of sexual impulses, and this is simply not possible for the boy after puberty.

The girl's impulses, on the other hand, are both more ambiguous and more subject to primitive repressive defenses. She has abandoned aggressive impulses at an earlier phase of development and may continue to deny them. Her sexual impulses are more diffuse than the boy's and can also more readily submit to the control of parents and to the denial this submission may imply.

The ambiguity of female sexual impulses permits adherence to earlier forms of control and also makes this a comfortable course since their diffusion and mystery implies a greater danger of overwhelming the incompletely formed ego at adolescence. Freud noted the wave of repression that occurs in females at puberty and contrasted it to the psychic situation of the boy (5).

Additional factors leading to postponement of character issues in girls are their greater general passivity and their more common tendency toward intensive identifications in adolescence and toward fantasy gratification of impulses.

I would like to mention one final point which, I think, has critical implications for character development in girls. Building independent standards and controls (i.e., settling an independent character) is part of the broader crisis of defining personal identity. In our culture there is not nearly as much pressure on girls as on boys to meet the identity challenge during the adolescent years. In fact, there is real pressure on the girl *not* to make any clear settlement in her identity until considerably later. We are all familiar with the neurotic woman who, even in adulthood, staunchly resists any commitment that might lead to self-definition and investment in a personal identity, for fear of restricting the range of men for whom she is a potential marriage choice. This pattern, it seems, reflects forces that are felt more or less by most girls in our culture. They are to remain fluid and malleable in personal identity in order to adapt to the needs of the men they marry. Too clear a self-definition during adolescence may be maladaptive. But when broader identity issues are postponed, the issues that might lead to differentiation of standards and values are also postponed. I do not, then, feel with Pope that most women have no character at all. I do think that in all likelihood feminine character develops later than masculine character, and that adolescence—the period we ordinarily consider *par excellence* the time for consolidation of character—is a more dramatic time for boys than for girls.

REFERENCES

1. Deutsch, Helene. *The psychology of women.* New York: Grune & Stratton, 1944. 2 vols.
2. Douvan, Elizabeth, & Kaye, Carol. *Adolescent girls.* Ann Arbor, Mich.: Survey Research Center, University of Michigan, 1956.
3. Douvan, Elizabeth, & Withey, S. B. *A study of adolescent boys.* Ann Arbor, Mich.: Survey Research Center, University of Michigan, 1955.
4. Fenichel, O. The pregenital antecedents of the Oedipus complex. *Int. J. Psychoanal.,* 1931, **12**, 141–166.
5. Freud, S. Female sexuality. *Int. J. Psychoanal.,* 1932, **13**, 281–297.

ADDITIONAL READINGS

Cohen, Mabel Blake. Personal identity and sexual identity. *Psychiatry,* 1966, **29**, 1–14. Cohen objects to the narrow concepts of masculinity and femininity, and suggests that they be modified in accord with individual needs as they are actually found in males and females. Data obtained in a study of pregnancy underscored the importance of men and women feeling a sense of security and worth as sexual beings.

Degler, Carl N. Revolution without ideology: The changing place of women in America. *Daedalus,* Spring 1964, **93** (2), 653–670. Degler traces the story of feminism in America, and concludes that the American woman still views her role as primarily within the home.

Douvan, Elizabeth & Adelson, Joseph. *The adolescent experience.* New York: Wiley, 1966. In Chapter 7, the authors consider how today's adolescent girl resolves her feminine role. Most girls hold an image of adult femininity corresponding to that portrayed in mass media. The individual girl's pattern of femininity depends on whether she is unambivalently feminine, ambivalently feminine, nonfeminine, achievement-oriented, boyish, antifeminine, or sexually neutral.

Heilbrun, Alfred B., Jr. Sex role instrumental-expressive behavior, and psychopathology in females. *Journal of Abnormal Psychology,* April 1968, **73** (2), 131–136. An investigation into the relationship between sex-role identity (masculinity-femininity) in late adolescent females and their adjustment. Comparison of the personality attributes of these masculine

and feminine girls with their maladjusted counterparts found little difference between the feminine groups.

Iscoe, I. & Carden, J. A. Field dependence, manifest anxiety, and sociometric status in children. *Journal of Consulting Psychology,* 1961, **25,**
184. Using experimental measures of field dependency which had previously revealed stable sex differences in early adulthood, but not at
younger ages, these researchers disclosed that popular boys tend to be
field independent and popular girls field dependent. Moreover, the most
popular boys and girls conformed rather closely to the prescribed sex
roles.

Kammeyer, Kenneth. Sibling position and the feminine role. *Journal of
Marriage and the Family,* August, 1967, **29** (3), 494–499. College
girls' sibling positions are related to appropriate feminine role behavior
and beliefs about female personality.

Minuchin, Patricia. Sex-role concepts and sex typing in childhood as a
function of school and home environments. *Child Development,* December 1965, **36** (4), 1033–1048. This study compares sex-role attitudes
and sex-typed reactions of children from "traditional" middle-class
schools and homes with those of children from "modern" middle-class
schools and homes.

Podell, Lawrence. Sex and role conflict. *Journal of Marriage and the Family,* May 1966, **28** (2), 163–165. Female role conflict, within the context of the predominant American value system, may be less than
sometimes suggested. Certain adaptations of females to the value system suggest interesting alternative marital patterns.

Steinmann, Anne & Fox, David J. Male-female perceptions of the female
role in the United States. *The Journal of Psychology,* 1966, **64,** 265–276.
The data presented are designed to answer two questions: first, how do
women view themselves, considering themselves as they are, as they would
like to be, and as they think men would like them to be; and second, how
do men see their ideal women?

Sutton-Smith, B. & Rosenberg, B. G. Age changes on the effects of ordinal
position on sex-role identification. *Journal of Genetic Psychology,* 1965,
107, 61–73. The writers report that the development of sex-role identification is influenced by the presence of siblings of the same sex. At all
ages (six, ten, and college), boys with brothers had higher masculinity
scores than did boys with sisters, and girls with sisters had higher ratings
on femininity.

Webb, A. P. Sex-role preferences and adjustment in early adolescents.
Child Development, 1963, **34,** 609–618. In a study of sex-role preferences and adjustments, boy's adjustment was improved through making a masculine sex-role preference, the girl's through effecting a flexible
sex-role preference.

Five

Issues in Developing Values
and Social Consciousness

XVII. Youth's Values

Throughout the ages, writers have taken it upon themselves to define youth's values, with controversy focused on three issues. What are youth's values? How good are they? What sort of values does youth need? Some critics assume the role of youth's defenders, others that of youth's detractors. A well-known developmental psychologist, Elizabeth Hurlock, deplores youth's shoddy values. They care little for being groomed, she says, and dismiss decent appearance as non-essential. They live by the motto, "Eat, drink, and be merry," and take no thought for the future. Uncle Sam will take care of you. Virginity is rejected as mid-Victorian. She feels that this deplorable result comes from mass media that glamorize extravagance, and from the peer group itself.[1]

Allport (see reading that follows), like Hurlock, sees youth as somehow missing the mark. He blames educators for having failed to help youth find their way, and challenges them to rectify this deficiency.

Other writers come out squarely on the side of youth. Young people face a difficult task, says Parsons, in preparing themselves for a nuclear age. Society is changing so rapidly that the older generation cannot supply adequate role models—they are already out of date. Hence, the young person gropes his way, and charts his own course as best he can. Nor have youth failed to meet the challenge this dilemma imposes. They recognize the need for good school work and its importance for the future. Indeed, concludes Parsons, the most significant fact about current youth culture is its concern for meaningfulness. The exception is in the lowest sector, where truancy and delinquency are common. Such a result is understandable, because heightened expectancies have placed lower-class youth at a correspondingly greater disadvantage.[2]

Who is to judge the judges, and determine whose views are right? And on what will such judgments be based? What kinds of questions can we pose to get at values? Can we trust youth's verbalizations of their beliefs? Coles and Prentice comment on a summary-critique, by Jacob, of studies of youth's values. In his critique (quoted in the first selected reading) Jacob reports students to be self-centered. What would he have them be, asks

[1] Elizabeth Hurlock, "American Adolescence Today—A New Species," *Adolescence,* Vol. 1, No. 4 (Spring 1966), pp. 7–21.
[2] Talcott Parsons, "Youth in the Context of American Society," *Daedalus,* Vol. 91 (1962), pp. 97–123.

450 Developing Values and Social Consciousness

Prentice. Church-centered? Government-centered? They are said to accept the business culture of society. Should they reject it? What alternatives to youth's current values exist, given the constraints of present-day society? Youth are also labelled conformist. How may conformity be differentiated from convergent values accruing to common experience?

Coles also questions Jacobs' conclusions, but on less theoretical grounds. The studies from which Jacobs' conclusions are drawn, he points out, date back two decades. Besides, they involve data-collecting procedures, such as objective type or multiple-choice instruments, of questionable validity. Coles also notes Jacobs' report that students failed to name religion as one of three life activities affording greatest satisfaction. On this basis, he asks, may it be assumed that religion plays but a small place in students' lives? Possibly some students define "satisfaction" in hedonistic terms, and if so, would hardly report religion as "satisfying." [3]

Anyhow, most individuals may have no need for values in a complex, science-oriented, big-system kind of society. Such a system will require a highly educated elite to engineer society, while other individuals may simply "go along," with their role defined by computers. That is, the masses will be measured and conditioned to fit into the slot considered best for them.

On the other hand, if it be decided that youth do need values, what form should they take? Wirth detects in youth themselves a yearning for real-life substance. Youth resent the isolation of education from life which Dewey warned against. They are hungry for genuine participant roles in the off-campus community. Therefore, we should help youth relate meaningfully to the out-of-school world. They could help reclaim projects in mountain areas, clean up urban slums or, taking a note from the Russians, work in industrial labs or experimental gardens, without being forced to wait until they get their Ph.D.'s. [4]

Some writers simply describe youth's values, without passing value judgments or prescribing what they should be. Teen magazines, says Bernard, portray faithfully what youth care about. Beauty, fun, and popularity are the values most frequently encountered there. [5] Scholarship is more valued than formerly, but still less than athletics. However, athletic prowess is growing less important, at least on the college level.

Parsons discerns certain changes, among them a decreased respect for sheer male physical prowess, especially in athletics, except among de-

[3] W. C. H. Prentice, Irwin Abrams, and James S. Coles, "Does Higher Education Influence Student Values?" [accompanied by] "Some Reactions," *National Education Association Journal,* Vol. 47 (1958), pp. 35–38.

[4] Arthur G. Wirth, "The Deweyan Tradition Revisited: Any Relevance for Our Time?" *Teachers College Record,* Vol. 69, No. 3 (December 1967), p. 68.

[5] Jessie Bernard, "Teen-Age Culture: An Overview," in Jessie Bernard (Ed.), *Teen-Age Culture,* Philadelphia: The American Academy of Political and Social Science, Vol. 338 (November 1961), p. 5.

linquent groups. Youth's attitudes toward alcohol and sex are changing, too. Formerly, youth often expressed rebellion through these media. Nowadays youth continue to indulge as much as formerly, but for different reasons. Indeed, drinking is more widespread, but generally moderate; and sex relations are taken seriously. Youth have simply become more integrated into the adult culture, and reflect society's growing acceptance of sex activity and alcohol.[6]

In sum, the picture of youth's values is confusing, with little agreement as to what they are like or how worthwhile they are. Of the numerous writers who have commented on the subject, two of the more frequently quoted, Jacobs and Allport, have contributed the selections that follow.

[6] Talcott Parsons, *op. cit.*, pp. 115–116.

35

Philip E. Jacob

A PROFILE OF THE VALUES OF
AMERICAN COLLEGE STUDENTS

This selection reports on a study designed to determine changes which occur in students' patterns of value during college. Specific topics include contemporary patterns of value among American students, overall effect of college experience on students' values, influence of instruction and curriculum, especially social science, on values, and the relationship of student personality to the effect of college on values. The excerpt given here summarizes tentative conclusions of the study.

The values of American college students are remarkably homogeneous, considering the variety of their social, economic, ethnic, racial, and religious backgrounds, and the relatively unrestricted opportunities they have had for freedom of thought and personal development.

A dominant characteristic of students in the current generation is that they are *gloriously contented* both in regard to their present day-to-day activity and their outlook for the future. Few of them are worried—about their health, their prospective careers, their family relations, the state of national or international society or the likelihood of enjoying secure and happy lives. They are supremely confident that their destinies lie within their own control rather than in the grip of external circumstances.

The great majority of students appear unabashedly *self-centered.* They aspire for material gratifications for themselves and their families. They intend to look out for themselves first and expect others to do likewise.

But this is not the individualistic self-centeredness of the pioneer. American students fully accept the conventions of the contemporary business society as the context within which they will realize their personal desires. They cheerfully expect to conform to the economic status quo and to receive ample rewards for dutiful and productive effort. They anticipate no die-hard struggle for survival of the fittest as each seeks to gratify his own desires, but rather an abundance for all as each one teams up with his fellow self-seekers in appointed places on the American assembly-line.

Social harmony with an *easy tolerance of diversity* pervades the student environment. Conformists themselves, the American students see little need to insist that each and every person be and behave just like themselves. They are for the most part (with some allowance for sectional difference) ready to live in a mobile society, without racial, ethnic or income barriers. But they do not intend to crusade for non-discrimination, merely to accept it as it comes, a necessary convention in a homogenized culture.

The traditional *moral virtues are valued* by almost all students. They respect sincerity, honesty, loyalty, as proper standards of conduct for decent people. But they are not inclined to censor those who choose to depart from these canons. Indeed they consider laxity a prevalent phenomenon, even more prevalent than the facts seem to warrant. Nor do they feel personally bound to unbending consistency in observing the code, especially when a lapse is socially sanctioned. For instance, standards are generally low in regard to academic honesty, systematic cheating being a common practice rather than the exception at many major institutions.

Students normally express a *need for religion* as a part of their lives and make time on most weekends for an hour in church. But there is a "ghostly quality" about the beliefs and practices of many of them, to quote a sensitive observer. Their religion does not carry over to guide and govern important decisions in the secular world. Students expect these to be socially determined. God has little to do with the behavior of men in society, if widespread student judgment be accepted. His place is in church and perhaps in the home, not in business or club or community. He is worshipped, dutifully and with propriety, but the campus is not permeated by a live sense of His presence.

American students are likewise *dutifully responsive towards government*. They expect to obey its laws, pay its taxes, serve in its armed forces —without complaint but without enthusiasm. They will discharge the obligations demanded of them though they will not voluntarily contribute to the public welfare. Nor do they particularly desire an influential voice in public policy. Except for the ritual of voting, they are content to abdicate the citizen's role in the political process and to leave to others the effective power of governmental decision. They are politically irresponsible, and often politically illiterate as well.

This disposition is reflected in *strangely contradictory attitudes towards international affairs*. Students predict another major war within a dozen years yet international problems are the least of the concerns to which they expect to give much personal attention during the immediate future. The optimism with which they view their prospects for a good long life belies the seriousness of their gloomy prophecy. They readily propose some form of supra-national government as a means of preventing war, but a very large number display only a limited knowledge of and confidence in the United Nations as an instrument of cooperative international action.

Turning to their immediate preoccupation, the pursuit of an education, students by and large *set great stock by college* in general and their own college in particular. The intensity of their devotion varies quite a bit with the institution and sometimes with the nature of the students' educational goals. And the real point of the devotion is not the same for all. Only a minority seem to value their college education primarily in terms of its intellectual contribution, or its nurturing of personal character and the capacity for responsible human relationships. Vocational preparation, and skill and experience in social "adjustment" head the rewards which students crave from their higher education.

These values are not the unanimous choice of American college students. The available data indicate that the profile just given may apply to 75 per cent or 80 per cent of them. In the remaining minority are individuals who forcefully refute some or all of the generalizations. Furthermore, on some issues students have no common mind—for instance, on how much discipline children should have, how much government the country needs, how far power should be relied on in international affairs and to what extent political dissidence should be repressed for the sake of national security. But for the most part, a campus "norm" of values prevails in the 1950's, coast to coast, at state university or denominational college, for the Ivy Leaguer or the city college commuter.

Against the background of earlier generations, these values of today's students look different. The undergirding of the Puritan heritage on which the major value assumptions of American society have rested is inconspicuous, if it is present at all. Perhaps these students are the forerunners of a major cultural and ethical revolution, the unconscious ushers of an essentially secular (though nominally religious), self-oriented (though group-conforming) society.

VALUE-OUTCOMES OF A COLLEGE EDUCATION

The main overall effect of higher education upon student values is to bring about general acceptance of a body of standards and attitudes characteristic of college-bred men and women in the American community.

There is more homogeneity and greater consistency of values among students at the end of their four years than when they begin. Fewer seniors espouse beliefs which deviate from the going standards than do freshmen. The student has ironed out serious conflicts of values or at least achieved a workable compromise. Throughout, no sharp break seems to occur in the continuity of the main patterns of value which the students bring with them to college. Changes are rarely drastic or sudden, and they tend to emerge on the periphery of the student's character, affecting his application of values, rather than the core of values themselves.

To call this process a *liberalization* of student values is a misnomer. The impact of the college experience is rather to *socialize* the individual, to refine, polish, or "shape up" his values so that he can fit comfortably into the ranks of American college alumni.

The values of the college graduate do differ in some respects from the rest of the society. He is more concerned with status, achievement and prestige. Proportionately more college graduates distrust "welfare economics" and "strong" government than in the country at large. Paradoxically they tend to be somewhat more tolerant and less repressive of "radical" ideas and unconventional people, also less prejudiced towards minority groups and alien cultures. They share few of the cold-war suspicions of the subversiveness of college faculties, nor do they support the popular stereotype of the colleges' godlessness. Religiously, they may be less superstitious or other-worldly than their fellow countrymen. The college man or woman thus tends to be more self-important—more conservative—more tolerant—and less fearful of evil forces in this world and outside than those who have not been "higher-educated."

It seems reasonable to credit these differences in value to the college experience, partly to its positive influence in bringing students' outlook into line with a college "standard," partly to an even more subtle selective process which ferrets out those students who are not sufficiently adaptive to acquire the distinctive value-patterns of the college graduate. Many whose values are too rigidly set in a mold at odds with the prevailing college standard apparently never consider going to college in the first place. Many of those who do enter (perhaps 50 per cent) drop out, the greater proportion probably because they have not found their experience or associations really congenial. The great majority who are left find little difficulty in making the rather modest jump which is required from the values they held in high school to college sophistication. The transition is especially easy for those with parents who went to college and are engaged in professional occupations.

THE INFLUENCE OF THE CURRICULUM

This study has not discerned significant changes in student values which can be attributed directly either to the character of the curriculum or to the basic courses in social science which students take as part of their general education.

For the most part, the values and outlook of students do not vary greatly whether they have pursued a conventional liberal arts program, an integrated general education curriculum or one of the strictly professional-vocational options. The more liberally educated student may take a somewhat more active interest in community responsibilities, and keep better informed about public affairs. But the distinction is not striking and by no means does it occur consistently among students at all colleges. It does *not* justify the conclusion that a student acquires a greater maturity of judgment on issues of social policy or a more sensitive regard for the humane values because he had a larger dose of liberal or general education.

Even fundamental revisions of the formal content of the curriculum designed to confront students more forcefully with problems of personal and social conduct and to involve them in a searching examination of value-issues rarely appear to have brought about a marked difference in students' beliefs and judgments, let alone their actual patterns of conduct. Nor is there solid evidence of a delayed reaction or "sleeper effect." The alumnus of several years exhibits no unusual trademarks identifying the character of his undergraduate curriculum.

The same negative conclusion applies to the general effect of social science courses. The values expressed by those who are most interested in social sciences are little different from those of other students. This is true not only of personal moral and religious values, but also of attitudes towards social and political issues regarding which the social science students are presumably more concerned and better informed. Neither the students' interest nor their instruction in social science seems to exert a broad influence on their beliefs, or their judgments of conduct and policy.

This finding from a synoptic perspective is reinforced by the results of most attempts to measure objectively the impact of particular courses. Few social science courses have demonstrated a capacity to alter attitudes or beliefs to a much greater degree or in a different direction than in the student body as a whole at the same institution (or among "control" groups of students who were not enrolled in the particular course).

What does happen frequently as a consequence or at least a corollary of a basic introduction to one or more of the social sciences is a redirection of the academic and vocational interests of some students. They are captivated by the subject and decide to change their majors and perhaps later their careers. It is clear too that students interested in social science tend to have more appreciation for general education than for vocational preparation as an educational goal. Large numbers of students also testify that their social science courses have increased their understanding of world affairs, and interest in politics. How much weight should be given to such subjective and indefinite evaluation is questionable, however, especially when there is little evidence that actual participation in public life has been increased. A distinction in *interest,* but not in *value,* may come from basic education in the social sciences, but, contrary to some expectations, mere interest in social science does not appear to generate corresponding value judgments.

IMPACT OF THE INSTRUCTOR

Equally disturbing is evidence that the quality of teaching has relatively little effect upon the value-outcomes of general education—in the social sciences or in other fields—so far as the great mass of students is concerned.

The personality, skill and devotion of teachers to their students and their subject varies tremendously within and among institutions. So do their personal and educational philosophies, the intensity of their value-commitments, and the degree to which they deliberately pursue value-goals in class and outside.

Students, for their part, have demonstrated a capacity for shrewdly evaluating the performance of instructors. They particularly value the teacher who couples high respect for students as persons, with a capacity to arouse interest in his subject.

Yet by and large the impact of the good teacher is indistinguishable from that of the poor one, at least in terms of his influence upon the values held and cherished by his students. Students like the good teacher better, and enjoy his classes more. But their fundamental response is little different than to anyone else teaching the course. With important individual exceptions, instructors seem equally *in*effective in tingling the nerve centers of students' values.

In the process of mass education, many students appear to take the instructor for granted, as he comes, good or bad, a necessary appliance in Operation College. His personal influence washes out in such an atmosphere, especially in regard to the deeper issues of life-direction, and the recognition and resolution of basic value-conflicts. A teacher can be recognized as a *good* teacher by his students, but with increasing rarity is he an *effective* teacher in the communication and maturing of values. Something in the contemporary social or educational climate curtains him off from the inner recesses of his students' character and freezes their motivational responses.

Student testimony and perceptive observation by educators and counsellors indicates, however, that *some* teachers do exert a profound influence on *some* students, even to the point of causing particular individuals to reorient their philosophy of life and adopt new and usually more socially responsible vocational goals. What it is that ignites such influence can hardly be defined, so personal, varied, and unconscious are the factors at work. It is perhaps significant, however, that faculty identified as having this power with students are likely to be persons whose own value-commitments are firm and openly expressed, and who are out-going and warm in their personal relations with students. Furthermore, faculty influence appears more pronounced at institutions where association between faculty and students is normal and frequent, and students find teachers receptive to unhurried and relaxed conversations out of class.

EFFECTS OF TEACHING METHODS

The method of instruction seems to have only a minor influence on students' value judgments.

"Student-centered" techniques of teaching and a stress on discussion in contrast to lecture or recitation have been strongly advocated as effective means of engaging the student's personal participation in the learning process, and encouraging him to reach valid judgments of his own on important issues. Studies of the comparative effectiveness of such methods do *not* generally support such a conviction.

Under certain circumstances, notably a favorable institutional environment, student-centered teaching has apparently resulted in a somewhat more satisfactory emotional and social adjustment by the students, and a more congenial learning situation. But there is little indication of a significantly greater alteration in the beliefs or behavioral standards of students taught by one method or another.

The response of a student to a given type of instruction often reflects his personality or disposition *previous* to entering upon the course. Some students react very negatively to a more permissive teaching technique. They feel frustrated and uneasy without more direction and authority exercised by the teacher. Consequently, they may actually learn less, and be less profoundly affected by a course taught in this manner, than by a more formal, definitely structured approach. In any case, the evidence is not conclusive that the potency of general education in influencing student values may be consistently strengthened by using a particular method of teaching.

However, students are often deeply affected by participation in experiences which vividly confront them with value issues, and possibly demand decisions on their part whose consequences they can witness. As a rule, the more directly that general education in social science hooks into students' own immediate problems and links the broader value questions with which it is concerned to personal student experiences, the more significant is its impact.

THE PECULIAR POTENCY OF
SOME COLLEGES

Similar as the patterns of student values appear on a mass view, the intellectual, cultural or moral "climate" of some institutions stands out from the crowd. The response of students to education within the atmosphere of these institutions is strikingly different from the national pattern.

The very individuality of these places makes comparisons unreal, but they do seem to have in common a high level of expectancy of their students. *What* is expected is *not* the same. It may be outstanding intellectual initiative and drive, profound respect for the dignity and worth of work, world-mindedness or just open-mindedness, a sense of community responsibility or of social justice, a dedication to humanitarian service, or religious faithfulness. Everyone, however, is conscious of the mission to which the institution stands dedicated, though this is not necessarily loudly trumpeted at every convocation, nor elaborated in fulsome paragraphs of aims and purposes in the college bulletin.

Where there is such unity and vigor of expectation, students seem drawn to live up to the college standard, even if it means quite a wrench from their previous ways of thought, or a break with the prevailing values of students elsewhere. The college serves as a cocoon in which a new value-orientation can mature and solidify until it is strong enough to survive as a maverick in the conventional world.

A climate favorable to a redirection of values appears more frequently at private colleges of modest enrollment. In a few instances, something of the sort has also emerged within a particular school or division of a larger public institution.

With a distinctive quality of this kind, an institution acquires a "personality" in the eyes of its students, alumni and staff. The deep loyalty which it earns reflects something more than pride, sentiment or prestige. A community of values has been created. Not that every student sees the whole world alike, but most have come to a similar concern for the values held important in their college. The hold of these institutional values evidently persists long after graduation and often influences the choice of college by the next generation.

STUDENT PERSONALITY AND
EDUCATIONAL INFLUENCE

Recent research has identified certain personality characteristics of students which "filter" their educational experience.

Some students have a set of mind so rigid, an outlook on human relations so stereotyped and a reliance on authority so compulsive that they are intellectually and emotionally incapable of understanding new ideas, and seeing, much less accepting, educational implications which run counter to their pre-conceptions. This particularly limits their responsiveness in the social sciences and the humanities whenever controversial issues arise. Such students quail in the presence of conflict and uncertainty. They crave "right answers." They distrust speculative thought, their own or their fellow students'. They recoil from "creative discussion."

Under most conditions of general education, where content and teaching method have been more or less standardized to suit what faculties consider the needs of the "average" student, the personalities just described become deadwood. As an out-of-step minority, they appear impervious to a real educational experience, even though the brainier ones may survive academically by parrotting texts and instructors on examinations. Many educators have concluded that such students do not belong in college; others insist that at least some liberalizing influence may rub off on them if they are obliged to run a lengthy gauntlet of general courses in social science and humanities, distasteful as the student may find them. A few institutions, however, are exploring special approaches to general education for this type of student, with promising results.

On the basis of the limited experimentation to date, such a "remedial" approach to social education for the "stereotype-personality" appears to require: 1. a careful and impersonal technique of identifying the students in need of special attention, 2. considerable homogeneity of personality in the classroom, 3. a well-ordered syllabus with rather definite assignments and clearly stated, frequently repeated, guiding principles (at least in the earlier part of the course), 4. an instructor who has great patience, and great belief in the potentialities of *these* students, and who can sensibly combine a fair amount of personal direction with persistent and imaginative efforts to engage the students' own intellectual powers in the learning process. The instructor needs to lead these students—but not dictate to them. He needs to wean them gradually from their excessive dependence on authority, slowly increase their sense of security in the face of the new, the unexplored and the different, and nurture self-confidence and respect for their own capacities to judge and to reason independently.

Not enough is yet known to insure the general success of such teaching, and few of these students will achieve the autonomy of those whose personality was freer to start with. But they have shown striking gains in critical thinking and developed more responsible and sensitive social values when their general education in social science has been so tailored to their particular needs. Because the number of students with such personality characteristics is large and growing, this type of experimentation seems unusually important.

SUMMARY

This study has discovered no specific curricular pattern of general education, no model syllabus for a basic social science course, no pedigree of instructor and no wizardry of instructional method which should be patented for its impact on the values of students. Student values do change to some extent in college. With some students, the change is substantial. But the impetus to change does not come primarily from the formal educational process. Potency to affect student values is found in the distinctive climate of a few institutions, the individual and personal magnetism of a sensitive teacher with strong value-commitments of his own, or value-laden personal experiences of students imaginatively integrated with their intellectual development.

36

Gordon W. Allport

VALUES AND OUR YOUTH

Dr. Allport first reviews the somewhat disturbing research relating to youth's values, and then calls on the schools to do a more adequate job in this area. He feels that the teacher should pay special attention to the incidental learnings that pupils acquire along with prescribed curricula. Also, experiences should be arranged so that questions of value relate to the child's own needs and become functional in his own life. Values to be encouraged include not only those embraced in the Judeo-Christian ethic but others, often neglected, such as intellectual curiosity and human brotherhood.

One aim of education is to make available the wisdom of the past and present so that youth may be equipped to solve the problems of the future. If this is so, then we have good grounds for a feeling of consternation concerning the adequacy of our present educational procedures. The reason is that in the immediate future, the youth of today will have to live in a world very unlike the world of the past from which our store of wisdom has been drawn.

SOME PROSPECTS

Think of the vastly changed nature of life in the future, for which we have little relevant wisdom from the past to call upon:

1. The new generation of students will have to face an ever increasing domination of life by science, by technology, and by automation. (One thinks of the story of two cows grazing along the roadside. An immense milk truck passes with the painted legend: Pasteurized, Homogenized, Vitamin B Added. One cow turns to the other and says, "Makes you feel inadequate, doesn't it?")
2. The new generation will have to recognize the impossibility of living any

From Gordon W. Allport, "Values and Our Youth," *Teachers College Record,* Vol. 63 (1961), pp. 211–219. Reprinted by permission.

Adapted from an address delivered during the 1961 Summer Lecture Series at the Western Washington College of Education, Bellingham, Washington.

longer in a state of condescension toward the colored peoples of the world (about three-quarters of the world's population). Centuries of comfortable caste discrimination and segregation are from here on impossible to maintain.
3. The coming generation will have to deal with a population explosion whose predicted magnitude staggers our imagination.
4. It will need a completer understanding of world societies and their marked differences in values. In the past, we could be politely ignorant of such places as Africa, Latin America, and Asia in a way that is no longer possible.
5. It will have to create a world government or, at least, an effective confederation to forestall the threat of thermonuclear war.
6. As if a planetary world view were not difficult enough to achieve, the coming generation may have to develop an interplanetary point of view. (I find this prospect especially alarming because we seem to be solving the problems of outer space before those of the inner space of mind, character, and values.)

It is no wonder that this preview of problems confronting our youth throws us educators into a state of self-scrutiny bordering sometimes on panic. Where can youth find the needed equipment? Are they sound enough in mind and morale?

Sometimes our dismay finds an outlet in gallows humor. They tell of the benevolent lady who saw a depressing specimen of the very young generation sprawled on the curb of a city street, swilling down cans of beer. Greatly shocked, she asked, "Little boy, why aren't you in school?" "Cripes, lady," he replied, "I'm only four years old."

And they tell the story of the London bobby. London police, we know, are well trained for social work, even for psychotherapy. This bobby's beat was Waterloo Bridge. He spotted a man about to jump over and intercepted him. "Come now," he said. "Tell me what is the matter. It is money?" The man shook his head. "Your wife perhaps?" Another shake of the head. "Well, what is it then?" The would-be suicide replied, "I'm worried about the state of the world." "Oh, come now," said the bobby. "It can't be so bad. Let's walk up and down the bridge here and talk it over." Whereupon they strolled for about an hour discussing the state of the world, and then they *both* jumped over.

Humor helps us put our dilemma into sane perspective, but it does not solve the problem. The vague apprehension we feel has led to certain empirical studies of the values of today's youth, with results, alas, that are not reassuring.

ASSESSING VALUES

Not long ago, Professor Phillip Jacob undertook to survey (5) all available studies concerning the values held by college students. He found a marked uniformity among them. Fully three-quarters of the students were "gloriously contented, both in regard to their present day-to-day activity and their outlook for the future." Their aspirations were primarily for material gratifications for themselves and their families. They "fully accepted the conventions of the contemporary business society as the context within which they will realize their personal desires." While they will not crusade against segregation and racial injustice, they will accept non-discrimination when it comes as a "necessary convention in a homogenized culture." They subscribe to the traditional virtues of sincerity, honesty, and loyalty, but are indulgent concerning laxity in moral standards. They normally express a need for religion, but there is a hollow quality in their beliefs. They do not desire to have an influential voice in public policy or government. Their sense of civic duty stops at the elementary obligation of voting. They predict another major war within a dozen years, but they say that international problems give them little concern and that they spend no time on them. Only a minority value their college education primarily in terms of its intellectual gains. They regard it as good because it gives them vocational preparation, social status, and a good time. Such is the flabby value-fibre that Jacob discovers among college students of today.

The picture becomes more vivid when viewed in cross-national perspective. James Gillespie and I, in a comparative study (3) of the values of college youth in 10 nations, asked students to write their autobiographies of the future ("My life from now until the year 2000") and also gave them an extensive questionnaire. The instrument was translated into nine different languages.

In comparison with youth of other nations, young Americans are delightfully frank and open, unsuspicious and cooperative. Their documents had no literary affectation (and, I may add, little literary quality). But the most important finding was that within these 10 nations, American students were the most self-centered, the most "privatistic" in values. They desired above all else a rich, full life for themselves, and showed little concern for national welfare or for the fate of mankind at large. The context of their outlook was private rather than public, passive rather than pioneer. The essential point is made clear by two excerpts, the first drawn from the autobiography of a Mexican girl, 18 years of age, and the second from a Radcliffe student of the same age:

Since I like psychology very much, I wish, on leaving this school, to study it, specializing in it and exercising it as a profession. I shouldn't like to get married right away, although like any woman I am desirous of getting married before realizing all my aspirations. In addition, I should like to do something for my country—as a teacher, as a psychologist, or as a mother. As a teacher, to guide my pupils in the best path, for at the present time they need solid bases in childhood in order in their future lives not to have so many frustrations as the youth of the present. As a psychologist, to make studies which in some way will serve humanity and my beloved country. As a mother, to make my children creatures who are useful to both their country and all humanity.

Now follows the Radcliffe document. Its flavor of privatism is unmistakable:

> Our summers will be spent lobster fishing on the Cape. Later we'll take a look at the rest of the country—California, the Southwest, and the Chicago Stockyards. I want the children, when they get past the age of ten, to spend part of the summer away from home, either at camp or as apprentices to whatever profession they may show an interest in. Finally, I hope we will all be able to take a trip to Europe, especially to Russia, to see what can be done about Communism.

Many critics have called attention to the same American value predicament. Our current social pattern, they say, is almost completely geared to one objective alone, namely a profitable, expanding production. To insure expanding production, there must be more and more consumption. Hence comes the expensive glamor of our advertising and its control of our mass media. The sole objective seems to be to stimulate the accretion of goods. Self-respect and status, as well as comfort, are acquired in this way. Someone has called our national disease "galloping consumption." Half a century ago, William James saw the peril and was much worried by what he called "the American terror of poverty." He saw there was truth in the jibes that other countries direct at our "materialism."

HOPE IN UNEASINESS

Now in a high standard of living is not in itself an evil thing. All the world wants what we already have. But the single-minded pursuit of production and consumption has brought a dulling of other values. One consequence is symbolized by the scandal of rigged quiz programs. These were in the service of advertising, which in turn was in the service of a profitable expanding economy. Another consequence is the accumulated froth of our TV, radio, and movies. Another is the widely discussed conformity of the organization man, as well as the futile rebellion of the beats. An especially peppery critic, Paul Goodman (4), has shown that the starved lives of juvenile delinquents and of young people caught in the organizational grind are at bottom much alike. Both are attracted to the cult of easiness and aspire to nothing more than amiable mediocrity. Both styles of living fail to prepare youth for the problems that lie ahead for themselves and for the nation.

A somewhat vulgar story seems to me to summarize all this mordant criticism. Moses, a stalwart leader of the old school, said to the Israelites in

Egypt, "Load up your camels, bring along your asses, and I'll lead you to the promised land." By contrast, the modern American prophet seems to urge, "Light up your Camels, sit on your asses, and I'll bring you the promised land."

All this familiar criticism is irritating; yet the fact that it flourishes is a hopeful sign. We suspect it may be too harsh. I am inclined to think so. It is rash indeed to indict a whole generation. At worst, Jacob's gloomy picture held for three-quarters of the college students studied, but not at all for a vital and far from negligible minority. And even though the gloomy generalizations have some truth in them, are the assets given fair attention? I myself have some favorable impressions, although one man's view is not reliable. But youth today appears to enjoy a certain freedom and flexibility that was not common in the more rigid days of our parents and grandparents. I even have the impression that there is less neuroticism among students now than among those of a generation ago. What is more, young people, I find, are not blind to the world changes that are occurring. Their apparent repression of the challenge is due largely to their bewilderment concerning proper paths to take. (And one has the feeling that our own statesmen in Washington are no less bewildered.) All in all, these are hopeful signs that should not be overlooked.

VALUES AND THE SCHOOL

Another hopeful sign is the fact that many teachers are asking, "What can we do to be helpful?" They know, and we all know, that the ability of the school to give training in values is limited. For one thing, the home is vastly more important. A home that infects the child with galloping consumption, that encourages only canned recreation and has no creative outlets, can only with difficulty be offset by the school. Another limitation lies in the fact that the school is ordinarily expected to mirror current social values and to prepare the child to live within the existing frame. It is an unusual school system and an unusual teacher who even *wish* to transcend the current fashions of value.

But assuming that we have an unusual school system and an unusual teacher, what values shall they elect to teach? If they do not choose to follow the prevailing fashions, what standards shall they follow? The ancient Romans were fond of asking, "Who will judge the judges?" and "Who will guard the guardians?" Can the guardians turn perhaps to standard discussions of "the aims of education"? Such discussions are numerous, abstract, and often dull. Their weakness, I feel, is their effort to formulate absolute goals, vistas of abstract perfection. The result is often a series of platitudes or generalizations so broad as to be unhelpful. Of course we want to develop "good citizenship"; we certainly want to "free the child's intellect." These and all other absolutes need to be reduced to concrete, stepwise processes before they can guide us in the strategy of teaching values.

The teacher must start with the situations as he or she finds it and in concrete instances sharpen the value-attributes of the lesson being taught. To a considerable extent, these value-attributes can be drawn from the codified wisdom of our nation. We cannot neglect the value of profitable production and high living standards, for all our vocational and professional education contribute to this end. But the codified wisdom of our unique society extends far beyond the obsession of today. Our values include also such matters as respect for civil liberties. Does the school accent this value? They include approval for individual initiative, for philanthropy, for compassion. And they imply much concerning civic duties that are the reciprocal of civic rights. What must we do to deserve our precious cornucopia of freedom? Vote? Yes. But voting does no good unless the voter is informed above the stereotyped level of the mass media. He must also pay taxes willingly. Do schools and colleges teach the young to pay a glad tax? I wonder. To me the most disturbing finding in *Youth's Outlook on the Future* lay in the elaborate talk about one's right to a rich, full life and in the almost total silence regarding one's duties.

I am saying that in the first instance teachers should choose the values they teach from the whole (not from a part) of our American ethos. Deep in our hearts we know, and most of the world knows, that our national values, derived, of course, from Judeo-Christian ethics, are about the finest mankind has yet formulated. In no sense are these values out of date, nor will they go out of date in the world of tomorrow. Yet many of them are badly rusted. Unless they are revitalized, however, our youth may not have the personal fortitude and moral implements that the future will require.

THE LARGER ANCHOR

Excellent as the American Creed is as a fountainhead of values, it does not contain them all. It says nothing explicitly, for example, about intellectual curiosity. And yet surely schools exist to augment this value. The most severe indictment of our educational procedures I have ever encountered is the discovery that a sizeable percentage of graduates of our colleges after completing their formal education never afterward read a single book.

There are other important values that are not spelled out in our American Creed. I am thinking of those details of human relationships that make all the difference between boorishness and brotherhood in the human family. As our population increases, it becomes more and more important to teach the elements of the new science of human relations which go far toward smoothing the roughness of common life by leading us to respect effectively the integrity of the other fellow. I recall a teacher of English whose class was studying *The Merchant of Venice*. She turned a wave of incipient anti-Semitism in her class to a sound lesson in values. Shylock, she explained, was like the resentful, self-seeking portion of every person's nature. We are all potential Shylocks. But while self-love is prominent in all of us, we are so constructed that it need not be sovereign in our natures.

To return for a moment to the relation between home and school—the former, as I have said, is far more important. Recognizing this fact, some people say, "Well, let's leave the teaching of values to the home and to the church. Schools can't do much of anything about the matter."

This position is untenable. If the school does not teach values, it will have the effect of denying them. If the child at school never hears a mention of honesty, modesty, charity, or reverence, he will be persuaded that, like many of his parents' ideas, they are simply old hat. As they grow toward adolescence, children become critical of the teaching of both parents and the church. They are in a questioning stage. If the school, which to the child represents the larger outside world, is silent on values, the child will repudiate more quickly the lessons learned at home. He will also be thrown onto peer values more completely, with their emphasis on the hedonism of teen-age parties or on the destructiveness of gangs. He will also be more at the mercy of the sensate values peddled by movies, TV, and disk jockeys. What is more, some homes, as we have said, give no fundamental value training. In such a case, it is *only* in the school that the child has any chance at all of finding ethical anchorage.

This brings us to the hardest question: How does the teacher, the instructor, the professor, handle his assignment in the classroom? How is it possible to teach values, including the value of intellectual curiosity?

THE MEANING OF VALUE

Before tackling this question, we must pause to define what we mean by value. You will recognize that I am using the term psychologically, not in its objective philosophical sense. Values, as I use the term, are simply *meanings perceived as related to self*. The child experiences values whenever he knows that a meaning is warm and central to himself. Values, to borrow Whitehead's term, are "matters of importance" as distinct from mere matters of fact.

So much for definition. Now the hard-pressed teacher is given a solid substantive curriculum to teach. The curriculum in its original state consists of mere matters of fact. And on the number of facts absorbed the pupil's standing depends. It takes virtually all of a teacher's time to convey factual information and grade the pupil on his achievement. There is little time left to transmute these matters of fact into matters of importance, let alone teach all of the moral and social values we have thus far been discussing.

The curriculum itself is not, and should not be, a direct aid. Prescribed instruction in values would be laughed out of court. We have recently been bumped by Sputnik headforemost into core subjects. Get on with science, mathematics, language! Away with courses in folk-dancing, personal adjustment, and fudge-making! I agree that value-study has no place in curriculum planning, but not because it is a frivolous subject—rather, because it is a subject too hard and too subtle for curriculum makers.

Education for values occurs only when teachers teach what they themselves stand for, no matter what their subject is. If I were to write a treatise on the teaching of values, I would give most of my emphasis to the moral pedagogy that lies in a teacher's incidental comments, to the *obiter dicta*. The hard core is central, but the hard core has a penumbra of moral significance. I mentioned the teacher of English who made a value-lesson out of Shylock. I recall also my college professor of geology who paused in his lecture on diatom ooze to say to us, "Others would not agree with me, but I confess that whenever I study diatoms, I don't see how anyone can doubt the existence of God because the design and behavior of these protozoa are so marvelous." Is it not interesting how we all recall the *obiter dicta* of our teachers, the penumbra of value they point out to us, surrounding the hard-core data? We remember them better than the subject matter itself.

Why does the student remember them so well? No current theory of learning seems able to tell us. I suspect it is because values, being matters of importance to the self, are always warm and central and ego-involved and therefore claim priority on our attention. The child, being value-ripe, cannot help being impressed when the teacher betrays excitement and enthusiasm for a mode of thought or for the content of the subject being studied. True, the youngster does not, and should not, adopt the teacher's values ready-made; but the teacher's self-disclosure leads the student to self-discovery.

What wouldn't we give if we could develop intellectual ardor in every child for hard core subjects? Why is it that for most pupils arithmetic, spelling, physics, remain forever dull matters of fact and never become a meaning perceived as related to the self? One reason, I think, is that the weary teacher fails to convey his own sense of the importance of the subject to the student. If he did so, he would, as I have said, at least fix attention upon the value-potentiality of the subject.

Another reason perhaps is that not all of a teacher's *obiter dicta* are wholesome. Some, indeed, may be deeply damaging, though the teacher may be innocent of any such intent. Sometimes we hear incidental (but still attitude-forming) remarks like this one: "All right now, children. You have had a good time playing at recess; now settle down to your English lesson." Play is recognized as a matter of joyful importance. English, the teacher is saying in effect, is a mere routine matter of fact.

VALUES AND LEARNING

I think our educational psychology has been mostly wrong about the process of learning—or perhaps not so much wrong as woefully incomplete. At the beginning of his learning career, a young child cannot, of course, be expected to feel adult enthusiasm for the intellectual content of his studies. He does his work in the first instance to avoid a scolding or because he has a habit of obeying instructions. Soon he finds added incentive. The teacher—really in the role of mother—gives praise and love ("Susan, I am proud of you"). There is a great deal of such dependency in the learning situation. Love and social reward (as well as some fear of punishment) sustain the processes of attention and retention. When the child puts forth intellectual effort, he does so in order to obtain a gold star, commendation, or other symbols of love.

All these incentives are extraneous to the subject matter. The youngster does not learn it because it is a matter of importance. When he leaves school or college, he loses these extraneous supports. He finds his love relations directly; they are no longer a reward for intellectual effort. Hence, intellectual apathy sets in, and, distressing to say, no further books are read.

In such a case as this, intellectual curiosity was never tied to independence, only to extraneous supports. At some point in the schooling—and the earlier the better—intellectual activity should become not a second-hand but a first-hand fitting to the sense of self. At the beginning, all learning must be tied, perhaps, to specific reinforcements; but if the dependency is long continued, authentic curiosity fails to develop.

It would be going too far to put the blame for intellectual apathy onto our current teaching of educational psychology. Yet I am inclined to feel somewhat punitive about this matter. Psychology has not yet settled down to the problem of transforming matters of fact—whose acquisition current learning theories explain fairly well—into autonomous matters of importance—which they do not explain at all.

Our emphasis has been on learning by drill and reinforcement. Such "habit acquisition" receives all the emphasis. But the learning theory involved postulates a continuing dependency relation (extraneous reinforcement). When the relation terminates, the habits of study simply extinguish themselves. I am surprised, therefore, that stimulus-response psychologists do not see this consequence of their own theory. Insofar as teachers employ an educational psychology of this order, they are not likely to break the dependency relation, which belongs properly only to the earlier stages of schooling.

Matters of importance, I strongly believe, are not acquired by drill or by reinforcement. They are transformations of habits and skills from the "opportunistic" layer of personality into the ego-system itself (1). Once inside the ego-system, these habits and skills turn into true interests and utilize the basic energy, the basic spontaneity, that the organism itself possesses. They are no longer sustained as "operant conditionings" by outside rewards. The interest, now being the very stuff of life itself, needs no outer supports.

FUNCTIONAL AUTONOMY

I have called this process of transforming means into ends, of changing extrinsic values into intrinsic values, *functional autonomy*. Concerning this concept, I am often asked two questions: How do you define "functional autonomy, and how does functional autonomy come about"?

For a definition, I offer the following: Functional autonomy refers to any acquired system of motivation in which the tensions involved are no longer of the same kind as the antecedent tensions from which the acquired system developed.[1] To answer the question of how functional autonomy comes about requires a more extended and technical discussion. I can only hint at the direction of my answer. Neurologists are gradually discovering a basis for what I would call "perseverative functional autonomy." I refer to the "self-sustaining circuits," "feedback mechanisms," and "central motive states" that are now commonly recognized to exist in the nervous system. This line of discovery, I find, provides a partial answer to the question. But I believe we have to go further and call on the concept of self. Values, we have said, are meanings perceived as related to the self. Functional autonomy is not a mere perseverative phenomenon; it is, above all, an ego-involved phenomenon. Besides admitting an opportunistic layer to personality, which is the exclusive concern of most current theories of learning, we have no choice but to admit also a "propriate" layer. It is in this layer that all matters of importance reside.

The goal of the educator, then is to shift the content of the subject he teaches from the opportunistic (matter of fact) layer to the propriate. But there is no sure-fire, mechanical strategy to use. The best general rule, one that John Dewey saw clearly, is to strive ceaselessly to integrate routine matters of fact into the growing experience system of the child himself. It would take a long treatise to specify various detailed strategies of teaching that would help achieve this goal.

Let me focus on only one aspect of this topic, upon a common mistake that teachers make. I myself am a continual offender. It is to present students with our own carefully thought out conclusions when they themselves lack the raw experience from which these conclusions are fashioned.

This particular error is inherent, for example, in the lecture system. Instead of lecturing on comparative religion, for instance, it would be much

---

[1] If this definition seems too technical to be immediately helpful, see Ch. 10 of *Pattern and Growth in Personality* (2) for a more extended treatment of functional autonomy.

better to require all students to attend services of worship that are unfamiliar to them. If raw experience is present, then perhaps a lecture may be effective. Much of the intellectual apathy we complain about is due to our fault of presenting conclusions in lieu of first-hand experience. To us, our well-chiseled conclusion, summing up a long intellectual struggle with a problem of knowledge or of value, seems like a beautiful sonnet. To the student, it may be gibberish.

The fallacy of giving conclusions holds both for subject matter and for values. A lad of 15 cannot profit from the fully fashioned philosophy of life of a man of 50. To register at all, a statement about values must fall precisely on his present growing edge.

Teaching, then, is not the art of offering conclusions, however hard won and valid they may be. No teacher can forcibly enter the students' proprium and plant a functionally autonomous motive. He can at best open channels of experience and, by his *orbiter dicta,* sometimes lead the student to see the value-potential in the experience.

The theory of personality that we need to guide a more fully developed educational psychology will teach us something important about our basic verb "to educate." It will show us that only at the outset of learning is it a transitive verb. By drill, by reward, by reinforcement, the teacher does indeed educate the child—in matters of fact. But true maturity comes only when the verb is reflexive. For in matters of importance, where values lie, the growing individual alone can educate himself.

REFERENCES

1. Allport, G. *Becoming.* New Haven: Yale Univer. Press, 1955.
2. Allport, G. *Pattern and growth in personality.* New York: Holt, Rinehart, and Winston, 1961,
3. Gillespie, J. & Allport, G. *Youth's outlook on the future.* New York: Random House, 1955.
4. Goodman, P. *Growing up absurd.* New York: Random House, 1960.
5. Jacob, P. *Changing values in college.* New York: Harper, 1957.

ADDITIONAL READINGS

Blousteen, Edward. The value vacuum on college campuses. *Teachers College Record,* December 1966, **68** (3), 261. Blousteen asserts that colleges should be centers of moral dialogue but are not. They should devote themselves as earnestly to a critical discussion of moral problems as they do to the resolution of problems of science and nature.

Denney, Reuel. American youth today: A bigger cost, a wider screen. *Daedalus,* 1962, **91** (1), 124–144. Denney describes the character structure of today's youth and portrays new dilemmas posed by social change.

Douvan, Elizabeth & Adelson, Joseph. *The adolescent experience.* New York: Wiley, 1966. In Chapter 4, "Values and Controls," adolescent moral controls are related to ego processes and ideals. The moral development of males and females is portrayed as distinctly different. The chapter provides a useful frame of reference for understanding adolescent values.

Gray, J. Glenn. Salvation on the campus: Why existentialism is capturing the students. *Harpers,* May 1965, **223,** 53–59. Gray portrays college students as rejecting the moral values of their parents and "painfully searching" for a different kind of authority which will make their new freedom meaningful. He asserts that students badly need their professors' guidance.

Keniston, Kenneth. Social change and youth in America. In Erik H. Erikson, (Ed.), *Youth: Change and challenge.* New York: Basic Books, 1963. Pp. 161–187. The writer discusses youth's outlook and sees a lack of deep commitment to adult values and roles. He sees a lack of rebelliousness against the older generation, and a feeling of powerlessness in youth themselves. In consequence, youth have retreated into the private sphere, looking out only for themselves.

Porter, Blaine R. American teen-agers of the 1960's—our despair or hope? *Journal of Marriage and the Family,* May 1965, **27** (2), 139–147. Today's teen-agers are growing up in the period of the greatest scientific breakthroughs in history, and face problems of an unprecedented nature. To solve the problems of power, money, sex, and prejudice which confront them they need parents, adults, and local and national leaders who can serve as models of fairness, morality, and leadership.

Williamson, E. G. Youth's dilemma: To be or to become. *Personnel and Guidance Journal,* October 1967, **46** (2), 1731–77. This paper portrays youth as engaged in three basic moral or intellectual activities: selecting life purposes, limiting their concern for immediate satisfaction, and striving to become their highest and best potentiality. Educators and counselors are challenged to assist youth to grow through successfully resolving the dilemmas inherent in these problems.

XVIII. Conflict Between Generations

Writers have, for many years, commented on the conflict of genera-tions, the causes of which have been variously defined. Much of the con-flict apparently derives from the process of cultural change, which may even overshadow cross-cultural differences. That is, the gap between age-groups is often greater than that existing between cultures; for example, among Americans, Japanese-Americans, and Japanese.[1]

Friedenberg sees the conflict as originating with adults. Their hostility, he asserts, derives from their anxiety about adolescents. Many of them are frightened or enraged by teen-agers' spontaneity. They also fear aging, and find youth's youthfulness an affront. They fail to realize that those who love youth stay young the longest.[2] Another cause of conflict is prolonged edu-cation which often creates an equally long dependency in youth. Parents project onto the youth they support their dreams, expectations, and rules. Some parents pressure their children to enter a prestigious college, and to choose high-status occupations. Another aspect of the conflict is the parent who sees his child's main task as performing his will.[3] If the youth fights back, a psychological impasse is reached. At other times, a gap exists be-cause adults simply fail to fulfill their role as exemplars and counselors of youth. Having lost their social and ethical bearings, they provide nothing the youth can cling to. Hence, the youth suffers a confusion of goals, and lacks a clear program for reaching them.

The generations conflict has assumed special modifications in recent times. For one thing, schooling has become prolonged, and parents find themselves confronted, not with a set of individuals to be trained for adult-hood, but with small social systems. These teen groups present a united front to the overtures made by the adult society.[4] Moreover, the massing together of large numbers in high schools and colleges has produced an atmosphere in which the legitimacy of adult authority has been called into question. In the nineteenth century youth rarely challenged their elders' basic right to authority. Even the riots which marked nineteenth-century

---

[1] F. K. Berrien, Abe Arkoff, and Shinkuro Iwahara, "Generation Difference in Values: Americans, Japanese-Americans and Japanese," *Journal of Social Psychology,* Vol. 71 (1967), pp. 169–175.

[2] Edgar Z. Friedenberg, *The Vanishing Adolescent* (Boston, Beacon Press, 1959), p. 117.

[3] Bruno Bettelheim, "The Problem of Generations," *Daedalus,* Vol. 91 (1962), pp. 68–96.

[4] J. S. Coleman, *The Adolescent Society* (New York, Free Press, 1961).

college life were more like peasant revolts against tyranny than like revolutionary movements. Today, generational revolt often brings apparent victory, but the young cannot afford to go their own way. They continue to depend on adults, and must accept the fact that adults control assignment of status within the society.[5]

In any case, the generations conflict is subsiding. Adult permissiveness and the understanding of youth culture have become increasingly institutionalized. Yesterday's parents, lacking clear-cut guidelines, often set up arbitrary rules governing their own youngsters' participation in youth culture. Moreover, taking a pot-shot at youth was an accepted, even approved, adult practice. However, expectations have gradually changed, so that adults find themselves expected to be accepting.[6] Also, rebellion assumes that the target of one's hostility is an active threat. But, when the adult's world seems terribly remote, the youth is not threatened by it. Besides, the youth feels so distant from his parents, in generational if not affectional terms, he can afford to understand them, and "even to show a touching sympathy for their hesitant efforts to guide and advise him." [7] On their part, parents realize they are dated and hesitate to impose their values and preferences on their children. The result is a sort of gentleman's agreement between the generations that neither will interfere with the other. Meantime, this attitude creates certain problems. Young people feel cheated if denied models; and often they feel they have never really had parents.

Some writers deplore the narrowing of the gap between generations. Adult-adolescent conflict, says Friedenberg, is inherent in the personality development of Western man. In certain primitive societies, such as Somoa, the young "pass delicately as Ariel through puberty into adulthood." But these people, though charming, seem insufficiently characterized, hardly like adults. In complex societies like ours, conflict is the instrument by which an individual learns "the complex, subtle differences between himself and his environment." In this sense, conflict is not war—it is dialectical and leads as a higher synthesis, to the youth's critical participation in adult society. Nor is the conflict to be considered as identical with the pretense of toughening up the adolescent. Conflict does mean resisting authority, when such authority makes no sense. Its polar opposite is the fawning acceptance of authority. Nor is this sort of conflict expressed in delinquency, which essentially is conflict-gone-wrong.

In short, a youngster who has abandoned the task of defining himself in dialectical combat with society becomes its captive.[8] Bettleheim agrees

---

[5] Christopher Jencks, "The War Between the Generations," *Teachers College Record*, Vol. 69, No. 1 (October 1967), pp. 1–21.

[6] Talcott Parsons, "Youth in the Context of American Society," *Daedalus*, Vol. 91 (1962), pp. 115–116.

[7] Kenneth Keniston, "Social Change and Youth in America," *Daedalus*, Vol. 91 (1962), p. 156.

[8] Edgar Z. Friedenberg, *op. cit.*, pp. 14–15.

with Friedenberg that something is irreparably lost in the diminution of adult-youth conflict. How can youth test his worth, he asks, or his own strength and vitality—the things he feels most dubious about—if he finds himself pushing against a vacuum? Youth benefits from testing himself against an established order, because nothing else is so safe a testing ground.[9]

Most discussions of the generations conflict has applied, at least implicitly, to males; and certainly the matter affects the sexes differently. For boys, says Bettelheim, conflict is more crucial. Young men expect to displace their elders and to take their place in running their country's affairs. In days when vigor and strength were essential in a head of household, it was accepted as natural that a young man, at his physical peak, should take over. Nowadays when experience counts more than brute strength, the young man can no longer count on his elders to move over, and sometimes must challenge them with force.

The girl's situation is somewhat different, since biology brings an end to the mother's role of childbearing and, as a consequence, child rearing. If the daughter's perception of her own role is the same there is no essential conflict. Her mother has been prepared by nature to move over.

In the first selection, Ernest Smith examines the nature and causes of the conflict between generations as related to American youth culture. Specifically, he attributes the conflict to such factors as questions of authority, problems of status role, and cultural discontinuity. Smith simply assumes that a generations conflict exists, and constitutes an important aspect of adolescence. The selection by Bealer, Willits, and Maida suggests that the generations conflict has been grossly exaggerated. Actually, youth reflect, rather than contradict, the standards of the larger society. In sum, the issue is not yet resolved. Does a generations conflict, of any consequence, exist; and if so, what are its causes and significance?

[9] Bettelheim, *op. cit.,* pp. 81–82.

37

Ernest A. Smith

YOUTH-ADULT CONFLICT IN AMERICAN SOCIETY

Smith considers the nature and sources of the very considerable amount of youth-adult conflict. He considers youth's conflicts with their parents and with other adults in the society.

PARENT-YOUTH CONFLICT

The effective and continuous point of contact between youth culture and adult culture is found in the relations of youth and their parents in the context of the family. Although the immediate items on which this facet of youth and adult cultures come into conflict are petty details, the over-all effect is so impressive that many analysts assert that parent-youth conflict in America is typical and even structurally necessary in consequence of the existence of youth culture (see, for example, Davis, 1944, p. 526; Truxal and Merrill, 1947, p. 457; Nye, 1951, p. 349). Bernard sees parent-youth conflict as normal and that parents should see in such conflict healthy progress toward the independence of maturity (Bernard, 1957, p. 183).

Specific disputes in parent-youth conflict are the end-product of a process of opposition beginning in early family relations and developing in the youth culture period. A poll of a freshman high-school class revealed that 45 per cent of the boys and 31 per cent of the girls objected to parents' interference in their affairs ("What Teen-Agers Prefer," 1951, p. 104). One study of college women revealed that the major area of disagreement with parents was over dating (Connor, Johannis, and Walters, 1954, p. 185). Another study showed that father-daughter conflict increased through the teen years, while conflict with the mother decreased (Liccione, 1955, p. 424).

The family may act as a safety valve for the release of tensions accumulated from other institutions, but a dysfunction appears when this release enforces constant conflict and instability (Merrill, 1948, p. 27).

Frequently the specific issues seem trivial, revolving about such tension points as use of the car, diet, school grades, money, and personal habits. Less emphasized ones are sibling rivalry, vocations, and late hours (Landis, 1945, p. 236). However, the underlying conflict of the two cultures— youth versus adult—is fundamental and may develop into crises as both parental exasperation and youth resentment accumulate. This conflict is intensified by the difference in generation that exists between parents and youth.

CONFLICT BETWEEN GENERATIONS

In modern urban society there is a serious cultural discontinuity between generations. Because of the biological birth cycle, vertical mobility, and rapid social change, adults are out of touch with youth. This discontinuity in structure and in the transmission of culture is illustrated to some extent by a comparison of the different transitional phases of the process of socialization. With the gradual maturation of youth, a radical reversal of roles takes place between adults and youth. As youth mature and assume adult roles, they are passing through a major period of movement into full adult status-roles; whereas parents, as they grow older and relinquish responsibilities, are gradually moving out of the dominant adult structure. Thus rapid social change, in addition to the time interval between generations, creates the discontinuity between youth and adults (Davis, 1944, pp. 523–524). Parent-youth life cycles in America are at different levels of development and, except at the infant level, are potentially subject to conflict. Even without rapid social change, the differences between youth and adult cultures might perpetuate the discontinuity. Pearson points out that the conflict of generations begins with the latency period when children turn from parents to peer groups and no longer trust their parents, but feel hostile to them (Pearson, 1958, p. 90).

American parents condition their children for discontinuity between generations by encouraging horizontal and vertical mobility through shifts in occupation and class level. Since, however, youth are largely identified with the family class-status, open competition arises between parents and children (Davis, 1944, p. 533). As upward mobility may involve the rejection of lower-class affiliations, and as youth groups mute class differences, young people may conceal or withdraw from lower-class associations. Widespread higher education of children leads to vertical mobility as well as to different norms, both of which intensify conflict.

Another important conflict point between generations centers on the exaggerated sex taboos pressed on youth by parents. The greatest exaggeration is found among middle-class families, where extreme morality is emphasized and deviations are labeled as wicked and sinful (Frank, 1936, p. 337). The earliest child-training taboos are compounded during adolescence, when youth are at the peak of sexual capacity and, at the same time, are prohibited any release. This discontinuity between biological and sociological maturity inevitably leads to parent-youth conflict, as most youth must deviate or withdraw (Davis, 1944, pp. 533–534).

Conflict between foreign-born parents and native-born children is a special aspect of parent-youth conflict in America. The importance of this factor is revealed in the large immigrant population. It was estimated that in 1950, about 23 per cent of the American population were either foreign-born or had foreign-born parents. (United States Bureau of the Census, 1956,, Table 27, p. 33; Table 30, p. 35.) This culture conflict is largely a lower-class problem, because the American school system sets up middle-class values for all students regardless of class, and teachers intensify parent-youth conflict by encouraging youth to reject the different culture values of the parents (Bossard, 1948, pp. 487–488).

In lower-class immigrant communities, youth withdraw into a predatory gang culture which relatively isolates them from American middle-class norms. Gang norms may conflict with parental norms, and parental coercive discipline only serves to drive youth into the gang culture and its resulting delinquency (Shaw, 1938, pp. 102, 135–136). The American legal norm, indeed, opposes coercive punishment and enables such youth to turn the courts against their parents for using physical violence.* In these cases, youth are in conflict with the foreign parental norms as well as American adult-culture mores.

CONFLICT OF STATUS-ROLES

The absence of transitional rituals and the prolongation of dependence of American youth lead to parent-youth conflict. In Elmtown, for example, higher-class youth are dependent on their families up to twenty years of age or more (Hollingshead, 1949, p. 365). By this age, youth are supposed to be independent, but there are no objective criteria for the achievement of independence. The American parental system (because of extended education and continuing economic dependence) discourages independence, yet youth are reproached for lacking maturity and responsibility. The fact that adults often insist on adolescent dependence, and youth insist on independence, leads to the greatest contradiction in status-role expectation in our society.

* The Russian Molokan community in Los Angeles well illustrates this breakdown of norms and the emergence of a dominant predatory gang culture (Young, 1932, p. 138).

A further note of uncertainty arises from the asynchrony of physical development and the wide variations in the growth of youth of the same age. Boys face further confusion in that girls mature earlier and faster, and this fact virtually reverses male-female status-roles for a period of about five years. Middle-class boys have little observation of or training in adult economic roles, while the mother sets feminine standards for good behavior. The result is that the male is confused, recalcitrant, and often deviant, and this behavior contributes to parent-youth conflict. It must be born in mind, however, that the parent-youth conflict is but one facet of conflict between adult culture and youth culture, this conflict is intensified by the lack of integration of the adult culture itself.

COMPETITION AND CONFLICT
OF AUTHORITIES

The competition and conflict of authorities both between adult culture and youth culture and within them is so widespread that some view it as predominant and inevitable. Such conflict, however, is not culturally universal; it occurs both where there is distinctive organization of youth culture and where there are discontinuities and dysfunction in formal socializing institutions.

The United States is marked by inconsistency of norms in adult institutions as well as by inconsistency between professed and actual behavior. For example, a study of Prairie City youth revealed marked inconsistencies between moral beliefs and behavior (Havighurst and Taba, 1949, pp. 88–89).

The initial competition and conflict of authorities may arise from differing parental standards in the same family and may be reinforced by experience with other families. This is complicated by the clash of norms between immigrant parents and their American-born children. Special consideration of parent-youth conflict is given in Chapter 3 ("The Family of Orientation"). The broader conflicts between formal and informal institutions, which often operate independently and at cross-purposes, include those among the family, church, school, economic system, and political system, as well as ethnic, racial, class, and regional factors. Similar dissention is found between the segments of youth culture, as in cliques, gangs, dating and courtship relations, and other peer groups.

Not only are adult and youth norms variously interpreted, but there is a strong contrast between adult and youth institutions and behavior. Because youth norms have no formal recognition or approval, adults ignore or reject them. In turn, youth reject an adult system that makes little allowance for youth norms.

CONFLICT OF COMPETING AUTHORITIES

Parent-youth conflict is inherent in the American socialization process, since youth must break away from parental authority in order to become adults. The first break in this authority arises from the child's manipulation of its parents in their quarrels (Zachary, 1940, pp. 314–315). The parents themselves may be the product of different class or culture backgrounds. The child may be able to exploit the observed differences in parental attitudes, values, and behavior.

The first significant competition with outside authorities occurs when the child enters school. The school creates culture conflicts not only by challenging parental norms and offering substitutes, but also by educating youth in the conflicting norms of adult culture (Mead , 1948, p. 459). For example, the school reinforces the American norms of competitive achievement in both academic and athletic spheres and thereby projects the anxiety complex from home to school. Lower-class families face greater difficulties, for the school teaches middle-class norms, which such families may reject. Furthermore, as the school takes over more of the child-care functions of the family, youth lose confidence in their parental standards (Riesman, 1950, pp. 48–50).

With the entrance of youth into high school, numerous nonfamilial institutions appeal for youth allegiance and often attack each other in their attempts to attract youth. A few of these institutions are the school itself (with its manifold activities), community organizations, the church, and commercial establishments. Young people learn about economic, political, and religious differences in their own neighborhoods, consider their parents as extremely fallible, and turn to peer groups for standards (Pearson, 1958, p. 85). An example of institutional conflict is found in Elmtown, where the leaders of school and church openly attack each other, while the theaters run unusually attractive programs to entice youth from school and church affairs (Hollingshead, 1949, pp. 152–153).

None of these adult institutions has as much influence in providing competing norms as youth culture itself. Stouffer states: "Every adolescent is certain to experience situations in which his family and his peer group are in conflict, such that conformity to the norms of one is incompatible with conformity to the norms of the other" (Stouffer, 1949, p. 708).

American middle-class parents define the status-role of youth as one of irresponsibility, good times, athletics, and dating activities. These parents encourage their children's contacts in the neighborhood and school. The school system itself sets up the age-graded culture, which ultimately advances norms that violate school as well as parental norms. In turn, these adult institutions attack youth culture, and this has the effect of unifying it so that it operates to deceive and outwit adults (Partridge, 1943, p. 260).

IDEOLOGICAL CONFLICT

Parents try to protect youths from the "realities of life," thus creating a serious crisis in the lives of young people. Youth soon learn and observe the inconsistencies between what the parents say and what they do. The authority of the father as the judge of good and evil is contradicted by the experience of youth. One solution is to replace the father's judgments with an ideological faith directed toward a better life, but this solution may lead to deviation and conflict with the parents (Mead, 1942, pp. 133–135).

An ultimate contradiction is faced when youth are viewed as disloyal or even punished for trying to carry out the ideal norms of family and religion in adult society. Also, some young people may make a cult of direct disobedience, by consciously adopting ideological standards that conflict with parental patterns. This open antagonism probably initiates the deepest conflicts between parents and youth (Frank, 1944, b, p. 249). These typical conflicts between parents and youth lay the basis for the withdrawal of youth from adult supervision and control in order to avoid judgment and sanctions.

REFERENCES

Harold W. Bernard, *Adolescent Development in American Culture* (New York: World Book Company, 1957), p. 183.

James H. S. Bossard, *The Sociology of Child Development* (New York: Harper & Row, 1948) pp. 487–488.

Ruth Connor, Theodore B. Johannes, Jr., and James Walters, "Parent-Adolescent Relationships," *Journal of Home Economics,* Vol. 46 (March 1954), p. 185.

Lawrence K. Frank, "Society as the Patient," *American Journal of Sociology,* Vol. 42 (November 1936), p. 337.

Lawrence K. Frank, "The Adolescent and the Family," *Adolescence,* The Forty-Third Yearbook of the National Society for the Study of Education, Part I. Edited by Nelson B. Henry (Chicago: The Department of Education, The University of Chicago, 1944, b), p. 249.

Robert J. Havighurst and Hilda Taba, *Adolescent Character and Personality* (New York: John Wiley and Sons, Inc., 1949), pp. 88–89.

August B. Hollingshead, *Elmtown's Youth* (New York: John Wiley and Sons, 1949), p. 365.

August B. Hollingshead, *op. cit.,* pp. 151–153.

Paul H. Landis, *Adolescence and Youth* (New York: McGraw-Hill, 1945), p. 236.

John V. Liccione, "The Changing Relationships of Adolescent Girls," *Journal of Abnormal and Social Psychology,* Vol. 51 (November 1955), p. 424.

Margaret Mead, *And Keep Your Powder Dry: An Anthropologist Looks at America* (New York: William Morrow and Company, 1942), pp. 131–135.

Margaret Mead, "The Contemporary American Family as an Anthropologist Sees It," *American Journal of Sociology,* Vol. 53 (May 1948), p. 459.

Francis E. Merrill, *Social Problems on the Home Front* (New York: Harper & Row, 1948), p. 27.

Ivan Nye, "Adolescent-Parent Adjustment—Socio-Economic Level as a Variable," *American Sociological Review,* Vol. 16 (June 1951), p. 349.

E. Dalton Partridge, "The Sociometric Approach to Adolescent Groupings," *Sociometry* (August 1943), p. 260.

Gerald H. J. Pearson, *Adolescence and the Conflict of Generations* (New York: W. W. Norton and Company, 1958), p. 90

Gerald H. J. Pearson, *op. cit.,* p. 85.

David Riesman, *The Lonely Crowd: A Study of the Changing American Character* (New Haven: Yale University Press, 1950), pp. 48–50.

Clifford R. Shaw, *Brothers in Crime* (Chicago: The University of Chicago Press, 1938), pp. 102, 135–136.

Samuel A. Stouffer, "An Analysis of Conflicting Social Norms," *American Sociological Review,* Vol. 14 (December 1949), p. 708.

Andrew G. Truxal and Francis E. Merrill, *The Family in American Culture* (Englewood Cliffs, N.J.: Prentice-Hall, 1947), p. 457.

United States Bureau of the Census, *Statistical Abstract of the United States,* 77th Ed. (1956) Washington: The U.S. Government Printing Office, pp. 33 and 35.

"What Teen-Agers Prefer," *McCall's Magazine,* Vol. 78 (February 1951), p. 104.

Caroline G. Zachry, *Emotion and Conduct in Adolescence* (New York: Appleton-Century-Crofts, 1940), pp. 314–315.

38

Robert C. Bealer
Fern K. Willits
Peter R. Maida

THE REBELLIOUS YOUTH SUBCULTURE—
A MYTH*

The writers review research relating to adolescent rebellion against parental norms and youth's perception of parents. They fail to find evidence of parent-youth conflict regarding what constitutes proper behaviors, and attempt to account for the myth of parent-youth conflict.

Adolescence in American society is often described as a period of rebellion against parental norms and rejection of traditional attitudes and values. A social counterpart to individual discontent is said to be represented by a distinctive youth subculture which channels and reinforces the rebellion of the individual. However, there is a large body of research findings which does not support the rebellion image as the characteristic or most widespread pattern of adolescent behavior. It is the task of this article to present a small part of the relevant research and to then discuss first, why the rebellion image exists, and second, some detrimental consequences resulting from the persistence of the myth.

RESEARCH EVIDENCE

The degree to which adolescents see parents as significant in their lives can be a convenient starting point for examining the empirical findings against a rebellious youth subculture. In a study of 4 Minnesota rural high schools, 506 students were asked who was the most important reference point in their lives—family, school chums, or someone else. Somewhat over

From Robert C. Bealer, Fern K. Willits, and Peter R. Maida, "The Rebellious Youth Subculture—A Myth," *Children,* Vol. 11, No. 2 (April 1965), pp. 43–48. Reprinted by permission of the authors and CHILDREN, U.S. Department of Health, Education, and Welfare, Welfare Administration, Children's Bureau.

* Based on a paper prepared for the National Conference on Problems of Rural Youth in a Changing Environment, sponsored by the National Committee for Children and Youth.

three-fourths indicated parents; school chums accounted for less than 10 per cent of the answers. (1) The same high incidence of perceived importance of the family on personality development was reported by Oklahoma freshmen. (2)

These studies are in accord with what has been found by outside observers who have noted the correlation of beliefs, attitudes, and practices between generations. For example, it has been found that nationally the political attitudes of lower income and upper income family teenagers closely follow the voting patterns of counterpart adults. (3, 4) Congruity also appears in more rigorous data comparing children and parents directly. In this regard, a study of 1,088 students in 13 different colleges found that most of these young people, particularly the females, conformed to the religious ideologies of their parents. (5) Investigations of participation in formal organizations by approximately 2,000 New York families found that if parents are active in organizations, their children will also tend to be participators. Where parents are nonparticipators, their children usually show the same pattern. (6)

The particular family situation can even override otherwise strong predisposing factors. In orientation to education, persons of lower socioeconomic status usually are unsympathetic to the school. But, in a study of high school dropouts in a midwestern city it was found that while only 13 per cent of the lower class parents whose children dropped out of school opposed the adolescent's leaving, a group of students matched for social class and IQ who stayed in school showed 68 per cent of the parents strongly insisting on attendance. (7)

PERCEPTION OF PARENTS

While parents may be vitally important in determining their children's behavior, it could be that this influence is coercive. The perceived importance of parents could indicate that rebellion, although tried, is unsuccessful. To examine this possibility, data are required which bear on the "favorableness" of the adolescent's perception of his parents, and by inference his felt need to rebel.

A study of 3,000 Minnesota adolescents and pre-adolescents centering on the descriptive terms supplied by them to a sentence completion test of the order, "My father is _ _ _ _ _ _," found that both boys and girls expressed overwhelmingly more favorable than unfavorable attitudes toward their parents. (8) Another study revealed that youth were willing to ascribe even more favorable traits to adults than were their parents. (9)

Studies of rural Pennsylvania high school sophomores in 1947 and 1960 assessed the acceptability of such behaviors as drinking, smoking, school failure, use of makeup, card playing, divorce, dancing, dating, use of money, and church attendance. In both time periods it was found that the youth were most likely to evaluate their parents' point of view toward these actions as "sensible" rather than as "too critical" or "not critical enough." This appraisal of the family's orientation was by far the mode. (10, 11) Thus it would seem that the value positions of youth and adults are not in serious conflict. Indeed, the data imply value congruence between generations.

The similarity in points of view between peers and parents is particularly vital when interpreting the research which shows the characteristic "withdrawal" of adolescents from family-centered activities. Participation in academic and extracurricular school activities usually means physical withdrawal from the family and high exposure to peer influence. However, this need not mean rejection of parental norms. The test of the importance of norms lies in the ability to direct behavior without the literal presence of others for enforcement; in other words, when they have been internalized by the individual. In the Pennsylvania study cited previously (11) as youths increased their involvement in school functions, the proportion of "sensible" answers for the family's attitudes went up, not down, as would be expected if physical withdrawal decreased the saliency of parental norms.

The similarity in values between adults and youth should not imply that disagreements are lacking. On the contrary, in specific decision-making situations what an adolescent's parents believe he "ought" to do and what his peer group thinks would be appropriate behavior may differ. When this happens the question can be raised: Which group does the individual follow? Students in 10 midwestern high schools were asked which would be the hardest result "to take" if, in joining a school club, parents disapproved of it, the teachers were negative, or it required breaking with one's closest friend. Even though the nature of the question seems to carry a bias toward obtaining the last alternative, parents still receive a majority vote. About 53 per cent of the boys and girls said parental disapproval would be the hardest to take while 43 per cent said breaking the friendship would "count" most. (12)

Another study conducted among girls in 7 Georgia and Alabama high schools inquired into 12 specific situations, such as which of 2 dresses to buy and whether or not to report a boy whom one saw damaging school property. The stories which conveyed the situation also indicated what alternative the parents urged and what behavior the peer group desired. The students were then asked what they would do. The tests were readministered after 2 weeks and the peer group and parent expectations were switched. Fifty-seven per cent of the students' responses did not change between the first and second testing. Of the 43 per cent which changed, a majority altered "what they would do" to the parental urging in 9 of the 12 situations. Two of the three situations where the shifts in answer went toward the peer group more often than parents involved matters of dress. (13)

This pattern of relative importance of peers and parents is certainly not always true. Perhaps the best generalization is that there is a flux in reference points depending on the situation. (14) However, the setting would seem rare where the parental wishes are totally ignored. Indeed, if there is to be continuity between generations, there must be some sharing of basic values between adults and youth. That such continuity exists is shown by the simple fact that American society has survived over time. Moreover, "there is remarkable agreement as to what American values are or have been and agreement upon their stability through more than 150 years." (15) Such stability could hardly be evidenced if adolescents rebelled and rejected the basic value tenets of the preceding generation.

In summary we can profitably recall a conclusion given elsewhere:

> The failure to find evidence of parent-youth conflict regarding what constitutes proper patterns of behavior does not necessarily mean that parents and their offspring do not disagree in regard to some—and perhaps many—questions. The adolescent seeking to establish his identity in adult society may disagree with his parents regarding when recognition of his maturity should occur. He may wish to engage in activities which symbolize his adulthood while his parents feel that he is still too young. This type of "rebellion" is as temporary as is the period of adolescence itself, and, rather than rejection of parental norms, it is perhaps better characterized as acceptance of and eagerness to participate in the larger society. Once the youth is accepted as a member of the adult society, this type of conflict ceases. It is this disagreement with parents concerning the adulthood of the adolescent which is probably responsible for the popular image of rebellious youth. However, this cannot accurately be described as a group rejection of societal norms. It constitutes an individual resistance to specific authority patterns.

> Of course, this kind of "rebellion" is important. It is often painfully experienced by both parent and child. It can lead to tragic results in some cases—neurosis, delinquency, even suicide or murder. It helps bring teenagers together in their cliques, friendship groups, and wider modes of affiliation and helps to hold them together as a unit. But, such conflict occurs *within a value framework* and not characteristically *over values*.

WHY THE MYTH?

In light of the foregoing review, the question arises: Why does the myth of a rebellious youth subculture exist? It may be that at least part of the explanation lies in the conceptual framework implicitly or explicitly used to understand "culture."

The meaning of culture, and in turn subculture, is not standardized in the social sciences. Among many professionals interested in the study of human behavior, culture is equated with *all* aspects of man's social actions.

Wearing blue jeans and black leather jackets, listening to Elvis Presley or Pat Boone, drinking beer or chocolate milk shakes—all are taken as equally indicative of, and caused by, one's culture. It is implied that men, through their group affiliations, have defined for themselves correct or appropriate behavior for every phase of life and for all situations. Thus, whatever the individual does is due to his meanings, motives, and definitions of the situation—jointly summed as "his culture." If two persons in a similar setting behave differently, it is because "they have different cultures" stemming from different group affiliations.

This understanding of "culture" is one of preference in emphasis and it has considerable validity. Among other things, it underscores the idea that human behavior is socially conditioned. But, it comes close to substituting social determinism for other forms of single factor explanations. More specifically, we would suggest that this understanding of "culture" helps to explain the presence of the myth. To indicate the way this can occur requires setting out a contrasting conception of culture.

Instead of emphasizing all aspects of human behavior as "manifesting culture," the second understanding of the term is less inclusive. Thus, it is taken that: 1. culture is widely shared or held in common by the members of a society but, 2. those things which are shared are the ideals for behavior, the values or criteria by which both the ends and the means to them ought to be selected. Whether in fact actual behavior conforms to cultural standards or values is problematic. Characteristically, the ideal pattern is only approximated by actual behavior. This is so if for no other reason than that the values are *general* and action situations are *specific*.

While one can take honesty as a value, just what acts fulfill honesty are not always clear. Culture here is taken as a recipe calling for a dash of ground garlic (not $\frac{1}{4}$ teaspoon), a medium wedge of cheddar (not 8 ounces), salt to taste, and so on. The results of persons following such a recipe are variable, although the outcome is still identifiable as cheese sauce and not bouillon. This conception of culture assumes that expressed behavior is not a simple and direct reflection of cultural standards. Rather, it makes room for genetic and physiological differences in personality; allows that physical conditions influence behavior; and recognizes that factors such as the size of groups, their number, and heterogeneity all help to determine human action.

The distinction between these two conceptions and their outcomes can be clarified by taking science as an illustration of a culture. Under the first usage a cultural description of "science" would emphasize, for example, the total array of the physicist's behavior—his use of electron microscopes, his precise measurement techniques, rigorous experimental setups, and so on. Turning to sociology, the "culture" of science shows a vastly different set of behaviors and characteristics. For the sociologist there are no machines comparable to electron microscopes; he utilizes relatively imprecise measurement, and he has few laboratory experiment set-ups. Therefore, one is tempted to see two different and, indeed, even conflicting cultures.

CULTURE AS VALUES

In particular actions, the physicist and the sociologist are widely separated. Yet it can be shown that in basic principles they are in agreement. Both sociology and physics subscribe to the same canons for ascertaining truth, particularly the acceptance of the validity of sense data. The second conception of culture emphasizes the essential unity by seeing science *not in terms of particulars and specifics*—which can vary widely—but in terms of the basic values it adheres to in arriving at truth. These values clearly distinguish science from other types of "culture;" for instance, religion with its characteristic emphasis on revelation. The point is that people can vary in the details and particulars of their behavior without that difference necessarily signifying conflict over, or rejection of, underlying principles or values.

Similarly, the behavior of adolescents in American society differs from that of adults. Teenagers' mode of dress and grooming is sometimes radical and given to fads. They have their own magazines which cater to adolescent tastes and reflect their concerns. Among these are such problems as acne, incompetence in interpersonal relations, and knowledge of the opposite sex. Movies, popular music, and radio seem to be their virtual monopoly. The automobile has a crucial and, all too often, a deadly role to play in their lives. Dating provides a mechanism for heterosexual play and experimentation in erotic styles and is a dominant focus of attention and of time consumption. Their vocabulary is sometimes strange to adult ears.

However, the differences in adolescent behavior, while real, are differences in degree rather than in kind. And the degree of dissimilarity has often been overstressed. Adult garb shows yearly change. Dale Carnegie has made a fortune through correcting adults' "shyness," and cosmetics have a tradition of hiding nature's "flaws." The fanfare given Detroit's latest models, the 5 or 6 million new cars sold annually, and the father's usual pride in showing off his new purchase to the neighbors are commonplace. Kinsey's reports, divorce court scandals, and the ever-present aura of sexuality in advertising aimed at adults suggest that cross-sex interest and variety in erotic play does not wither with youth. Adults, too, have their specialized "languages" stemming from their work.

If one ignores the basic similarities between adolescents and adults and emphasizes culture as the "particulars" of behavior, then disagreements and differences at the level of specific action may be misinterpreted and assumed to apply to the general value framework as well. As has been mentioned, however, research has pointed to the fact of congruity between generations. In stressing the similarity in values, in the second sense of culture, one does not say that knowing whether singer X or singer Y is currently in favor at a particular school or in a given town is unimportant. It may be crucial knowledge in gaining and keeping rapport with teenagers. By concentrating on the idiosyncratic aspects of adolescent behavior, however, one can miss the similarity in values between adults and youth. Failure on the part of many writers to distinguish between the two understandings of culture and the resulting tendency to see conflict between youth and their parents in *all* areas of behavior because differences exist in some activities may at least partially explain the presence of the rebellious adolescent subculture myth.

Moreover, viewing the period of adolescence primarily in terms of a distinctive, rebellious subculture can hinder understanding of many aspects of youth behavior. We shall take, as one example, the problem of school dropouts.

SCHOOL DROPOUTS

Focusing on the "rebellion" of the adolescent and implying as this does the discontinuity of values between generations tend to underestimate the difficulty of changing the potential dropout's orientation so as to keep him in school. By viewing the individual as "in rebellion" the image is cast that such a person is adrift. If the teenager has "rejected" his parents, then he will be looking for new anchorages. Thus, the task of keeping the potential dropout in school appears to be a matter of merely presenting and "selling" the values that will make him see the advantages of this course of action. But the notice of youth adrift through rebellion ignores the possibility that there may be stringent competition with the proposed values. By ignoring the fact of continuity in culture, one can be led to miss the simple fact that there is often parental support for the dropout adolescent's decision—support which may be tacit but nonetheless present. That is, some parents tend to see little utility in a secondary education and may openly encourage, or at least reinforce, the youth's choice to leave school. As a result, any attempt to change values must take into account the possible familial buttressing of teenage decisions.

We need to recognize that the adolescent who drops out of school may not be adrift in a rebellious youth subculture. He can, in fact, be closely tied to the relatively stable cultural background of his parents and may leave school prior to graduation because of this very fact. The problem of changing values and influencing these young people to stay in school is not, therefore, a short run task, or is it an easy one. The matter is not as simple as throwing a life preserver to a drowning sailor, for the persistent fact remains that persons often reject such "help" when it is not supported by their social and cultural environment. The limited success of slum clearance projects, educational retraining programs, and efforts to rehabilitate criminals are cases in point. The problems of high school dropouts would seem to be similar. Any remedial program hoping for dramatic gains must be total, involving not just the individual, but his family and perhaps the general community as well. The rebellious youth myth can cause us to overlook this simple but vital fact.

The conception of a rebellious youth subculture emphasizes the generational split as the most important and, hence, directs attention primarily to the age-youth cleavage. It implies that all teenagers can be considered as members of a homogeneous unit standing in opposition to parents. Such a position tends to ignore the variability *among* people—variability which is crucially important in understanding school dropouts.

SOCIAL CLASS DIFFERENCES

One line of important differentiation is a distinction based on social class or socioeconomic status. Research has shown that there are many things involved in a student's leaving school prior to graduation, but the single factor most persistent and widespread in its relationship to early withdrawal is social class position or socioeconomic status. (16) These studies indicate that lower socioeconomic class adults generally place less value on formal education than do middle and upper class persons. This devaluation of school attendance on the part of the adult population is often, in turn, reflected in the adolescent's own decision to withdraw prior to graduation. Such a person manifests a decision which is frequently anchored in the value system of his originating culture. Rather than some sort of rejection of the parentally sponsored norms, the act of dropping from school may represent an affirmation of them.

At the same time one ought to be aware that:

. . . action oriented to the achievement and maintenance of the lower class system may violate norms of middle class culture and be perceived as deliberately nonconforming or malicious by an observer strongly cathected to middle class norms. This does not mean, however, that violation of the middle class norm is the dominant component of motivation; it is a by-product of action primarily oriented to the lower class system. . . . a distinctive tradition many centuries old with an integrity for its own.[17]

Such an idea, of course, runs counter to many persons' conception of lower class culture. Indeed, until quite recently it was fashionable to picture lower class society as unstable, disorganized, and hence exhibiting little continuity from generation to generation. To support this notion writers pointed to, among other things, the high incidence of "broken" homes composed of only mother and children. This is at variance with a normal middle class family in which a father is present. It does not mean necessarily that the mother-child family lacks viability. The contrary is true. For example, the lower class family form in which the father is absent has shown amazing persistence through time. One need not condone this type of family unit nor ignore the possible behavioral outcomes for the children involved, to see its vitality. The person who wishes to change social structure or the values substrating it must start with a recognition of reality and not from his own wishes about it or conclusions drawn from a middle class sense of "correctness." In terms of the values of the potential dropout, the first step in this process is to appreciate the wide variation existing within the grouping, "adolescents."

While social class differences represent perhaps the most striking case of important variability, others also occur and need emphasis. We have stressed class because it is a vital element. However, our discussion should not be taken to mean that no lower class youths finished high school. They do. "There is a sizeable proportion of the lower class group who do not incorporate this [a lower class] value system." (18) We know that parents serve as mediators to the larger cultural milieu and thus particular familial considerations, such as parental encouragement to finish school or to aspire to high status positions, may overcome the effect of typical lower class devaluations of education. (19) We do not know enough, however. What creates the situation for general parental support for high aspirations? The fact that there are some lower class persons who highly value education represents a challenging problem. If the factors causing these persons to reject devaluation of education can be identified, we may be able better to direct other lower class adolescents toward similar goals. In this cause a flexible conception is required which can not only allow for the variation that is lower class culture, but which can see variability within the lower (or other) class itself. Unfortunately, the rebellious structure idea does not foster recognition of any such differentiation.

The idea of varying and possibly competing values needs emphasis not only because of the stress which can result for the target of the change program, but also because it presents certain personal conflicts for the individual who is interested in bringing about change. Most change agents, reflecting the dominant middle class values of American society, tend to see no problems as unyielding in the face of simple educational effort. But values represent basic criteria of worth, and, hence, are not easily changed nor readily amenable to compromise. Therefore, any action program designed to keep teenagers in school is potentially fraught with conflict, for it requires altering the potential dropout's values. Furthermore, this goal transgresses one of the basic value premises of the change agent's own cultural background—the belief that one ought to "live and let live." Since he may be unable or unwilling to accept the possibility of open conflict, it gives him some reassurance to believe that the dropout adolescent is adrift and desires his help. This is often not the case, but the idea of rebellious youth salves one's conscience, eases anxiety, and makes a difficult job appear easier than it is. Perhaps these functions of the myth also help to preserve its existence.

REFERENCES

1. Rose, Arnold M.: Reference groups of rural high school youth. *Child Development,* September 1956.
2. Ostlund, Leonard A.: Environment-personality relationships. *Rural Sociology,* March 1957.
3. Remmers, H. H.; Radler, D. H.: The American teenager. Bobbs-Merrill, Indianapolis, Ind. 1957.
4. Lipset, Seymour M.: Political man. Doubleday & Co., Garden City, N.Y. 1960.
5. Putney, Snell; Middleton, Russell: Rebellion, conformity, and parental religious ideologies. *Sociometry,* June 1961.
6. Anderson, W. A.: Types of participating families. *Rural Sociology,* December 1946.
7. Havighurst, Robert J.; Bowman, P. H.; Matthews, Gordon B.; Pierce, James V.: Growing up in River City. John Wiley & Sons, N.Y. 1962.
8. Harris, Dale B.; Tseng, Sing Chu: Children's attitudes toward peers and parents as revealed by sentence completions. *Child Development,* December 1957.
9. Hess, Robert D.; Goldblatt, Irene: The status of adolescents in American society: a problem in social identity. *Child Development,* December 1957.
10. Bealer, Robert C.; Willits, Fern K.: Rural youth: a case study in the rebelliousness of adolescents. *The Annals of the American Academy of Political and Social Science,* November 1961.
11. Wilson, Paul B.; Buck, Roy C.: Pennsylvania's rural youth express their opinions. Pennsylvania Agricultural Experiment Station Progress Report No. 134. 1955.
12. Coleman, James S.: The adolescent society. The Free Press of Glencoe, New York. 1961.
13. Brittain, Clay V.: Adolescent choices and parent-peer cross-pressures. *American Sociological Review,* June 1963.
14. Solomon, Daniel: Adolescents' decisions: a comparison of influence from parents with that from other sources. *Marriage and Family Living.* November 1961.
15. Kluckhohn, Clyde: Have there been discernible shifts in American values during the past generation? *In* The American style. (Elting E. Morison, ed.) Harper & Bros., New York. 1958.

16. Blough, Telford B.: A critical analysis of selected research literature on the problem of school dropouts. Unpublished dissertation. University of Pittsburgh, Pennsylvania. 1956.
17. Miller, Walter B.: Lower class culture as a generating milieu of gang delinquency. *Journal of Social Issues,* Vol. XIV, No. 3, 1958.
18. Hyman, Herbert H.: The value systems of different classes: a social psychological contribution to the analysis of stratification. *In* Class status and power. (Reinhard Bendix and Seymour M. Lipset, eds.) The Free Press, Glencoe, Ill. 1958.
19. Simpson, Richard L.: Parental influence, anticipatory socialization and social mobility. *American Sociological Review,* August 1962.

ADDITIONAL READINGS

Bettelheim, Bruno. The problem of generations. *Daedalus,* 1962, **91** (1), 68–96. Bettelheim considers youth's problems in relating to the older generation, and distinguishes between the problems of the adolescent male and female. He also indicates special problems of the young in preparing for their role as adults.

Brittain, Clay V. An exploration of the bases of peer compliance and parent-compliance in adolescence. *Adolescence,* No. 8 Winter 1967–68, **2** (8), 445–458. Brittain notes that adolescents are often involved in conflicting parent-peer expectations. He concludes, on the basis of his studies, that adolescents are influenced more strongly by parents in certain types of situations, and by peers in others. They rely on adults in more important, crucial decision.

Count, Jerome. The conflict factor in adolescent growth. *Adolescence,* Summer 1967, **2** (6), 167–180. The writer sees conflict as a built-in critical factor which may either further, retard, or frustrate a youth's full personality development. His elders are also in a state of conflict over their role as a receding generation. The writer suggests that a more intelligent management of adult-adolescent conflict would make for fewer cases of young adults who suffer from delayed adolescence.

Dialogue between the generations, *Harper's,* October 1967, **235**, 45–64. A group of college editors and writers look at the differences in the way the generations perceive each other and the major issues in American society today.

Douvan, Elizabeth & Adelson, Joseph. *The adolescent experience.* New York: Wiley, 1966. Chapter 5 concentrates on the family's role in preparing the adolescent for leaving home and leading his own life. Major topics treated are autonomy, family conflict, parental authority, and discipline.

Elder, G. H., Jr. Adolescent variations in the child-rearing relationship. *Sociometry,* 1962, **25,** 241–262. Elder concludes that by adolescence the child is permitted some freedom to govern his own affairs but is guided in the use of this power by warm, permissive parents.

Fyvel, T. R. *Youth in an affluent society.* New York: Schocken Books, 1962. On the basis of interviews with, and observations of, young people, Fyvel concludes that youth in contemporary industrial societies are more rebellious than youth of previous generations. He is neither sociologist nor psychologist, but makes many astute observations and raises significant questions.

Gottlieb, David & Ramsey, Charles. *The American adolescent.* Homewood, Ill.: Dorsey Press, 1964. The second half of this book portrays adolescence as a period of transition. The problems involved in choosing roles and goals are treated in terms of conflicts generated by the ambiguities implicit in relations between adolescents and adults.

Jennings, Frank G. Adolescents, aspirations, and the older generation. *Teachers College Record,* January 1964, **65** (4), 335–341. Conflicts between the generations are viewed as probably inescapable. They must, therefore, be confronted instead of avoided or glossed over.

Meissner, W. W. Parental interaction of the adolescent boy. *Journal of Genetic Psychology,* 1965, **107,** 225–233. A total of 1,278 boys were asked questions relative to their interaction with their parents. Reactions fell into typical categories but were distinct for mother and father. Shifts in reaction from early to later adolescence were in the direction of parental alienation and increased teen-age rebelliousness.

Raywid, Mary Anne. The great haircut crisis of our time. *Phi Delta Kappan,* 1966, **48** (4), 150–155. The mid-1960's were characterized by considerable conflict between adults and teenagers over the rights of the latter to wear extreme hair styles. Professor Raywid probes questions of the school's authority and teen-agers' rights in the growing up process.

Riesman, David. Two generations. *Daedalus,* Spring 1964, **93** (2), 711–735. Riesman compares many of the values and activities of his own and his daughter's generation. His statements are based on his own observations, and strongly colored by his own value-judgments, but are quite thought-providing.

XIX. Youth as Political Activists

Most writers consider it desirable that youth concern themselves with politics. "Immense and far-reaching changes in men's hopes and desires," says Riesman, "are necessary to create a better world." However, youth need a vision of a "viable and conceivable society," which should not become "fanaticism in pursuit of Utopian goals" nor "an Intellectual swindle for True Believers." [1] Keniston agrees with Riesman: "Society needs youthful activists. Each generation builds on relevant aspects of the past, yet creates new images of life which will provide points of constancy in a time of rapid change." [2] Thus, the gap between generations is bridged. Moreover, asserts Parsons, youthful indictments of our society may be interpreted as a kind of campaign position, which prepares them for their future role when they must take over main responsibilities.[3]

Note, too, the argument by Stone and Church. Youth cannot live comfortably with a set of ideas, they claim, without having tried out a variety, no matter how irrational they may be. Dissatisfaction, unaccompanied by alternative ideas, may produce destruction. Children who are merely against something are, to use Lindner's term, rebels without a cause. Rebellion is good when it is harnessed to idealistic goals no matter how unworkable, but if blind and formless, it sours into cynicism or violence.[4] Finally, Lifton notes that youth, with their fresher view of things, open up new possibilities in the universal task of "coming to grips with the ever accelerating, ever more threatening movement of history." [5]

Traditionally, we have pictured the adolescent as consciously planning for a better world. He dreams dreams, and asks "Why not?," and acts upon those dreams. This image has been true, except in the political sense. At least until the Vietnam situation and the civil rights movement became critical, politics has not been a feature of the American teen culture. Even

[1] David Riesman, "The Search for Challenge," *Merrill-Palmer Quarterly*, Vol. 6, No. 4 (July 1960), pp. 218–234.

[2] Kenneth Keniston, "Social Change and Youth in America," *Daedalus*, Vol. 91 (1962), p. 170.

[3] Talcott Parsons, "Youth in the Context of American Society," *Daedalus*, Vol. 91 (1962), pp. 97–123.

[4] L. Joseph Stone and Joseph Church, *Childhood and Adolescence* (New York, Random House, 1957), pp. 318–319.

[5] Robert Jay Lifton, "Youth and History: Individual Change in Postwar Japan," *Daedalus*, Vol. 91 (1962), p. 195.

now, exchange students from other lands often comment on the relative apathy they find among American youth.

What then accounts for youth's sometimes apathetic, even negative, attitude toward politics? One factor is the insulation of the teen culture from the strains of the larger culture that surrounds it. Another is the relative stability of the American government. Still another is the example adults set for them. Instead of arguing ideologies, say Stone and Church, most adults jostle each other to get into the middle of the road. Consequently, youth have been deprived of things to rebel for as well as against. The youth is even exposed to religions which are merely "well-adjusted working arrangements with reality." [6]

Parsons notes that American youth's susceptibility to political ideologies varies with the times. During the 1930's and 1940's, a limited number of youth were attracted to Communism; and in the late 1960's a resurgence in politics took place. However, this interest focused on specific issues— notably race relations, nuclear war, and the draft, rather than on broader ideologies. Intellectuals deplore this indifference to basic philosophies, but youth simply reflect the larger society. Such activity is most prominent in developing societies where intellectuals play a large role, or where major political transitions and instabilities are in process. [7]

Keniston describes youth's lack of concern for politics as the result of a retreat into the private sphere. He contrasts youth's general apathy toward political activity with the burgeoning of the arts on college campuses. This commitment to the aesthetic instead of the political he ascribes to youth's feeling of helplessness in the face of powerful social and historical forces. Their vision and consciousness are split, one eye on their own welfare, the other on some private utopia. They will be good organizational workers but without the intensity of involvement which will upset "bureaucratic applecarts." The majority will be chiefly concerned with the private sphere, which permits the greatest personal control. Commitment and fidelity will be transferred to the aesthetic, the sensual, and the experiential.

Youth's split consciousness bodes ill both for the individual and for society. Few can comfortably maintain so ambiguous an outlook without psychological strain. Privatism also makes for greater short-run stability of society at the price of long-run stagnation. By exaggerating their own powerlessness, young people see "the system" as more unmalleable than it really is. Given such assumptions, social changes will continue to occur haphazardly, ignoring the needs of the public. We cannot afford such apathy, concludes Keniston. World problems are so acute that for the ablest college students to assume such an indifferent stance seems almost suicidal. [8]

[6] Stone and Church, *op. cit.,* p. 318.
[7] Parsons, *op. cit.,* pp. 117–120.
[8] Keniston, *op. cit.,* p. 167.

Brighter youth, writes Lifton, are perhaps less apathetic than simply ambivalent in their attitude toward vanguard influences. They are attracted toward liberating elements yet fearful of cultural confusion. Therefore, they waver between near total commitment and near total phobic avoidance. Youth's intense reaction to the historical process, concludes Lifton, is most likely when they feel hopelessly dislocated in the face of rapid and undigested historical change.[9]

Denney believes it is fortunate that most young people are *not* running pell-mell to redeem the social order. They seem aware of the tenor of their time and are neither frightened by dreadful freedoms nor oppressed by social tyrannies. They have a talent for the "delayed reflex," which may prove an important resource in the politics of a nuclear age.[10]

In our first selection, Dr. Susanne Shafer pleads for curricula which capitalize on youth's need, and desire, for active involvement in politics. She holds adults, especially teachers, responsible for nourishing in children healthy attitudes and skills in the political area. The second selection, by Fishman and Solomon, endorses by implication Shafer's thesis and expands on her theme. They call for conscious and intelligent attention to the forces that motivate participants in youth movements. They analyze the roots of such behaviors in terms of youth's own special needs for identity, autonomy, and commitment and indicate how activism provides an apprenticeship for later adult roles. Finally, they suggest the need to identify those factors which do, or do not, lead to interest in political activism.

[9] Lifton, *op. cit.*, pp. 194–195.
[10] Reuel Denney, "American Youth Today: A Bigger Coast, a Wider Screen," *Daedalus,* Vol. 91 (1962), pp. 142–143.

39

Susanne M. Shafer

POLITICAL PASSIONS AND RATIONAL ACTIONS

The author urges social studies teachers to educate young people in such manner that they can assume an intelligent role in political action. If these students are to be politically effective as adults they must develop awareness, social trust, enthusiasm, and a feeling of self-regard. Shafer also asserts that many young people today demonstrate as much political commitment and expertise as any in history.

My concern is with the responsibility of social studies teachers for producing young people sensitive to American governmental traditions and both capable and desirous of participating knowledgeably in public affairs. I interpret such participation—or, if you like, political action—as ranging from an informal discussion of current issues to a campaign for public office, seeking support for a petition, or providing organizational leadership within a political party directly engaging in public affairs. As I perceive democracy, a person may freely select the degree and type of political participation, but virtually no segment of the adult population is to be excluded from a share in political life. I accept the importance of political socialization as the process ". . . by which the political norms and behaviors acceptable to an ongoing political system are transmitted from generation to generation."[1] Roberta Sigel points out: "The stability of a political system depends in no small measure on the political socialization of its members."[2] It follows, as I see it, that the social studies teacher ought to contribute to the definition of the process of socialization and to its implementation.

Inferences may be drawn from our knowledge of the behavior of adults and young people in the political arena. It may be that these inferences may help us construct a suitable program of social studies education.

From Susanne M. Shafer, "Political Passions and Rational Actions," *Teachers College Record,* Vol. 48, No. 6 (March 1967), pp. 471–479. Reprinted by permission.

[1] Sigel, Roberta. "Assumptions About the Learning of Political Values." *The Annals,* Vol. 361, Sept. 1965, p. 1.

[2] *Ibid.,* p. 1.

ADULT POLITICAL BEHAVIOR

Recent studies point out the continuing persistence of ethnic voting in our day, although this may be a declining phenomenon.[3] Aging, we learn, "results in greater consistency in political attitudes." [4] Younger voters seem to be more strongly identified with their current party choices than older voters; [5] although, in the '50s, the proportion of older people going to the polls tended to increase.[6]

Where actual participation is concerned, we learn that local party leaders tend to be people who have been "long-term residents" in the locality.[7] Moreover, as Leiserson points out, locally oriented political workers seldom "aspire to a role in state or national politics," and that the highest level they normally reach is that of the state legislature.[8] County chairmen, however, often become delegates to state and national nominating conventions and have an opportunity to wield considerable influence in the selection of candidates and the definition of policies. All county chairmen confront major difficulties when they have to decide how to maintain a viable party organization and, at the same time, wage and win political campaigns.[9]

POLITICAL LEADERS

The nature of political leadership has been frequently and specifically explored. When Matthews [10] posed the question as to whether there exists a ruling class in the United States, he found much evidence in support of an affirmative answer. Although the officials who make the important political decisions "are a fairly heterogeneous lot," he wrote, they differ in origins and experiences. The roads to political power are not wholly closed even to "relatively low-status groups"; but opportunities are best "for those in positions near the top of the American class system and worst for those near the bottom." Political decision-makers, therefore, tend not to be a cross-section. He concluded that "incumbents in the top offices are mostly upper-

[3] Wolfinger, Raymond E., "The Development and Persistence of Ethnic Voting." *The American Political Science Review*, LIX, December, 1965, p. 906.

[4] Campbell, Angus, *et al*, *The American Voter*. New York: Wiley, 1960.

[5] Crittenden, John. "Aging and Political Participation." *Western Political Quarterly*, XVI, June, 1963, p. 325.

[6] *Ibid.*, p. 329.

[7] Patterson, Samuel C., "Characteristics of Party Leaders." *Western Political Quarterly*, XV, June, 1963, p. 342.

[8] Leiserson, Avery. *Parties and Politics*. New York: Alfred A. Knopf, 1958.

[9] Patterson, *op. cit.*, p. 344.

[10] Matthews, Donald R., *The Social Background of Political Decision-Makers*. Garden City, New York: Doubleday & Co., Inc., 1954.

and upper-middle-class people." [11] In his subsequent analysis, he added that lower-status groups nevertheless exert political power "far in excess of their number" in the decision-making positions.

Prewitt extends Matthews' observations when he says that, despite the "tendency to defer to influential persons," not all high-status people go into politics while many individuals do so successfully in spite of severe social handicaps. In our country, an individual apparently needs more than a simple desire for power to enter politics, because of what Prewitt describes as the "premium" put on "cooperative, compromising activity, on subtle rules of the game, and give-and-take negotiation." [12] The democratic selection process, he writes, weeds out the rigid, unadaptable individual and tends to favor the one who can make flexible adjustments.

When one looks more closely at the political socialization experienced by American political leaders, one finds that many were exposed to politics early in life: the Adamses, the Roosevelts, the Kennedys, and such less conspicuous examples as the sons of Harry Byrd and the sons of Wendell Willkie. Even where individuals are the first in their families to seek office, they may have grown up in a setting where politics was a subject of frequent discussion, or where parents had an involvement with politics through such positions as leadership of a trade union, volunteer work, or civic organization leadership. It seems clear that political interest is very often passed on by authority figures who have been politically involved.

Lawyers, of course, turn to politics more frequently than any other group. Some have deliberately chosen the law as a means to political office; others are drawn into public affairs by their legal experience. Epstein's study of Wisconsin politics found an increase in the number of lawyers who became state legislators and the obvious "mobility from farm and manual-worker backgrounds." [13] He also found that the lawyer-legislators were "relatively young and urban, and especially likely, after membership of short duration, to move up or out in the interest of careers which appear to be more political or entrepreneurial in character than legal in a technical or scholarly sense."

THE POOR

Since we have paid so much attention to the struggle of the Negro to achieve equality, we have become sensitized to what Oscar Lewis describes as "the culture of the poor." [14] Many minority group members can be

[11] *Ibid.*

[12] Prewitt, Kenneth. "Political Socialization and Leadership Selection," *The Annals,* Vol. 361, Sept., 1965, p. 99.

[13] Epstein, Leon D., *Politics in Wisconsin.* Madison: University of Wisconsin Press, 1958.

[14] See, *e.g.,* Lewis, Oscar, *La Vida.* New York: Random House, Inc., 1966.

placed among the poor and identified by a particular life-style transcending even regional and urban differences. Lewis characterizes the culture of poverty by its lack of involvement with most major social institutions, its production and receipt of little wealth, unemployment, consensual marriages, etc. He ascribes feelings of helplessness and inferiority to those who participate in such a culture; and he finds a low level of social organization beyond the immediate family among them.

To draw the 20 per cent of the poor who live in such a culture into involvement requires new avenues of economic, political, and social participation. Here and there certain anti-poverty measures have created such avenues; community action groups have sought out indigenous leaders, often from the culture of poverty itself.

YOUTH AND POLITICS

It is evident that the family is of great influence in a child's political socialization, particularly when he identifies with a status person in the family and proceeds to assign similar status to traditional political heroes or to contemporary leaders. Since he absorbs his norms and values from the family at an early age, he is likely to accept the family's party affiliation as well. And, indeed, as Miller demonstrates,[15] identification with a party does begin early and grow stronger with the years. Easton and Dennis [16] indicate that the child tends to move from recognition of authority figures like the police and the President to gradual comprehension of the role played by the Congress in government, and to an ability "to identify government as something that is different from the private sector of life. . . ."

For the child who leaves elementary school with fairly accurate notions about the American government, the secondary school social studies program presumably signifies refinement of ideas. Also, there may be a correlation between his political socialization and his participation in extracurricular activities.

High school extracurricular activities are a source of the informal status network in American secondary schools. The status network and the norms upon which they are based do not inculcate values which stress the intrinsic worth of education. Extracurricular activities are also supposed to teach the attributes of good citizenship. Ziblatt's study found no direct relationship between participation in high school extracurricular activities and attitude toward politics. The teen-ager who participates feels more ingrated into the informal high school status system. This feeling of integration is associated with social trust. The more socially trusting teen-agers

[15] Miller, Warren E., "Party Identification and Partisan Attitudes," *Readings in American Political Behavior,* Raymond E. Wolfinger, Ed. Englewood Cliffs, New Jersey: Prentice-Hall, Inc., 1966, p. 249.

[16] Easton, David and Dennis, Jack. "The Child's Image of Government," *The Annals,* Vol. 361, Sept., 1965, p. 51.

have a more positive attitude toward politics. Teen-agers from working-class backgrounds participate least, but are most likely to see the informal status system as open. It was inferred that these students were insulated by a belief in equality of opportunity from a direct awareness of how the status system actually operates.[17]

The study in question also showed that "teen-agers on the outside of the status system showed more mistrust than those on the inside."

COLLEGE-AGE YOUTH

No group in our society at present indicates greater evidence of political concern than our teen-agers and young adults. That concern is expressed by some through volunteering for the Peace Corps. Others have taken an active part in the integration movement. They have sat down at lunch counters, marched in Alabama, rebuilt burned-down churches in Mississippi, and tutored innumerable of our Negro and other minority children in reading and other basic skills. A number have joined the bitter protests against American policy in Viet Nam. Some agitated for improvement in undergraduate instruction at Berkeley and elsewhere. "Students for a Democratic Society" and the Student Non-Violent Coordinating Committee (SNCC) have drawn into their ranks those who ". . . search for a politic rooted in ethics, for a 'moral equivalent of war,' for a society actually rather than rhetorically dedicated to the greatest good for the greatest number." [18] The New Left's call for a "participatory democracy" may be overly romantic, unrealistic, and somewhat transcendental but it has caught the imagination of some segments of the college-age population. How far members of SDS and SNCC will now be willing to follow Stokely Carmichael's and others' call for "Black power," that is a militant form of political action, remains to be seen. In the meantime there continue to be those who choose to press their political concern through joining the Young Democrats or the Young Republicans, a type of trial run for eventual political leadership within our regular parties.

One cannot turn away from these diverse expressions of political concern without consideration of the models American youth have selected for themselves. Clearly President John F. Kennedy captured the imagination of many of them. Today his brother Robert receives the acclaim of young people at many a political gathering. A number of the leaders of the civil rights movement also have support. Again, social studies teachers will want to watch the emergence of any other individuals who may sway our young adults in their political decisions.

[17] Ziblatt, David. "High School Extracurricular Activities and Political Socialization," *The Annals,* Vol. 361, Sept. 1965, p. 20.

[18] Duberman, Martin. "Geography of the New Left," *New York Times Book Review,* October 23, 1966, p. 7.

THE YOUNG NEGRO

We are aware that Negroes in particular constitute a special case in regard to political socialization. Boxed in by cumulative social constraints, the Negro is learning "norms and roles for political performance . . . in a special Negro subculture, which is at present undergoing basic changes, creating for the next Negro generation new prototypes for political action, and creating also new tensions and frustrations for the individual." [19] In looking at the changing patterns of Negro role-playing and Negro skill-acquisition, it "is still difficult to gauge the changes in Negro attitudes and motivations. It is necessary to remember the backlog of frustration, self-doubt, and anger which the neophyte must somehow control if he is to learn anything effectively."

Attitude studies of how the Negro views the government or how he views the police used to show differences among Northern and Southern Negroes as well as a differentiation from his white fellow-townsmen. None of these are likely to be accurate any longer in view of the rapidly spreading attitudinal changes in our Negro population both North and South. While once most Negroes were taught how to get along in a superior-subordinate relationship, new Negro leaders have emerged who can match white politicians any time in the organizing, campaigning and political bargaining skills that they possess. The growth of Negro militance is a phenomenon being watched all across the country.

Since all youth pass through our schools and our programs of social studies education, it becomes evident that the total spectrum of youth's experiences must be considered by us in drafting an adequate program of political socialization. Present-day aspirations of Negro youth as well as ideals held by youth more generally should provide guidelines for us in this process. My earlier description of adult political behavior patterns needs also to be taken into consideration. As we then develop our program of political socialization, we must add our own knowledge of the relevant disciplines, of social studies methodology, and of learning theories.

ESSENTIALS FOR A PROGRAM OF POLITICAL SOCIALIZATION

In any program of political socialization much will be retained that has traditionally constituted the core of the social studies program. I would

[19] Marvick, Dwaine. "The Political Socialization of the American Negro," *The Annals,* Vol. 361, Sept. 1965, p. 113.

suggest that what we shall conclude is that a shift of emphasis and some revision of methodology is to be recommended.

A careful study of the American Constitution must continue to be included in the social studies program, just as we shall want to continue to teach about the nature of our government and how it evolved in the course of American history. In view of the apparent early decision on the part of the American voter as to which party he claims to belong to, schools surely will need to detail the history and present composition of our two major political parties and to elaborate carefully on the meaning of the concepts of liberal and conservative. With groups like the John Birch Society and also SNCC, as active as they are today, pupils will need to be able to identify the distinguishing ideology of both the "radical" right and the "New Left."

Since a good deal of political influence is expressed through the many special interest groups active on the American scene, students deserve a thorough orientation to them. Labor unions, business organizations such as the Chamber of Commerce or more specialized groups like the Retail Hardware organization, civic groups like the Rotarians or the League of Women Voters, professional organizations for doctors, lawyers, teachers, etc., patriotic groups such as the American Legion, civil rights organizations, groups devoted to humanitarian causes such as the Planned Parenthood organization, religious groups and even the neighborhood associations and local political parties—for all of these their respective goals, organization, and methods of operation need to be explained. That nearly everyone of them maintains lobbyists in Washington should be explained on the basis of the necessity to communicate clearly the wants and needs of each group to those in government who formulate policies directly affecting that segment of the public.

Not only, then, should the outlines of government be described, but the processes by which that government operates must be exposed. Surely the case study approach which we shall hear about shortly serves this purpose. Government will become a dynamic entity to the pupil as he contrasts the American presidency under John F. Kennedy and Lyndon B. Johnson, as he observes a consumer boycott and the response of the Federal Trade Commission, as he watches the agonies of a strike by public employees—subway workers or his teachers, as he studies the Republican Party's organizational maneuvers which resulted in the nomination of Barry Goldwater for President in 1964, as he identifies cause and effect of the eruption in Hough, or as he follows a political campaign on the local level.

Finally, we must add to his growing storehouse of knowledge a grasp of basic principles of economics and of our economic system, of the nature of American society and of other, different societies and groups around the world, of human geography, of related material from the sciences, of the nature of language, particularly as used in the political dialogue, and of the role and influence of the mass media of communication.

SKILLS FOR POLITICS

If we wish our students to have the capability to follow thought by action, we shall want to equip them with a number of rather diverse skills. Through experience in student government and in their ordinary classrooms they have the opportunity to learn to make decisions and to organize themselves into groups for particular purposes. Since the ability to cooperate constitutes an apparent characteristic of political leaders, youth should have a chance to practice it somewhere in school. Extracurricular activities appear to suit that purpose. Also, through a debate club, a speech class, or discussion in the social studies classroom, pupils can learn to express their political ideas persuasively and also soundly. Through problem-solving tasks, or the inquiry approach, in social studies they gain experience in critical thinking and in formulating opinions which they stand ready to defend with logic and facts. Here, too, we allow for divergent thinking, a dire necessity for adulthood if our youth is to aid us in the solution of our varied social and political problems. Through the climate we encourage in our social studies classroom we can try to sensitize pupils to their relations with their peers and others more generally. We can also attempt perhaps through simulated games to develop their skills in reaching compromise or attaining consensus, two essentials in a democracy. Through constant utilization of our mass media, we can help pupils plow their way through propaganda, a skill many of us have had to use extensively during the recent election campaign. We must create in pupils an awareness of the sampling they engage in when reading a political pronouncement in the press or when hearing one on radio or television. According to Berelson, *et al.,* one's political perception leads one to reinterpret what one hears (or reads) in such a way as to make the pronouncement conform with one's existing point of view.[20] Classroom debate of political issues should make students conscious of the innate dangers of distortion and misinterpretation in this connection.

In the course of a sound social studies program pupils should have ample opportunity to foster their skills of identifying values inherent in different political positions and to clarify their own value orientation. The social studies classroom must still allow for a theoretical study of public affairs while at the same time providing pupils with skill and information that are the prerequisites to effective participation in the political dialogue, whether through informal discussion or direct political action. The ambiguity of our values, that is the frequent clashing of avowed moral precepts with observable norms and customs, will have to be aired. But so will the means which men in politics use to formulate policies, reach workable agreements

[20] Berelson, Bernard R., Lazarsfeld, Paul F., and McPhee, William. "Political Perception," *Readings in American Political Behavior,* R. E. Wolfinger, Ed. Englewood Cliffs, New Jersey: Prentice-Hall, Inc., 1966.

on laws, and to place individuals into various political offices. And exposure to Oppenheimer and Lackey's *A Manual for Direct Action: Strategy and Tactics for Civil Rights and All Other Nonviolent Protest Movements* (Chicago: Quadrangle Books, Inc., 1964) might prove to be an important supplement to any genuine study of how a citizen can express his values in the political arena.

ATTITUDES AND POLITICAL ACTIONS

At the heart of the political socialization process lie the attitudes instilled in the youth of the society. Many are transmitted to the young in their early years, as I pointed out earlier. Where then does the school have a role to play? What function ought the social studies program perform in the realm of attitude formation or change?

Inasmuch as attitudes are acquired subconsciously by the child, at some point in the maturing process he must begin to take stock of his personal norms and values. He must be aided to do so against a backdrop of factual information about political matters and the American experience. As he comprehends the political process and a citizen's part in it, he may alter certain views he once held. The social studies teacher has the difficult task of conducting a dispassionate analysis of public affairs while at the same time pressing the pupil's search for values that are in accord with American traditions. As long as our society has substantial areas of disagreement over values and norms, the teacher will have little difficulty in demonstrating the means utilized in a democracy to reach temporary agreements on social, economic, and political change deemed desirable. One attitude which the social studies teacher will therefore instill in the pupils is an acceptance of change as a normal phenomenon and one that man usually controls. He does so often in cooperation with his fellowman and largely in the interest of those affected. Compromises are required but are subject to later revisions. Many avenues exist whereby an individual can try to be heard as change is contemplated.

A second attitude that seems essential if the notion of man-made change is to have meaning concerns the attitude the pupil has of himself. A self-image firmly rooted in the acceptance of the equal importance of each individual would appear to be fundamental if the pupil is to have the self-confidence to seek participation somewhere in the political process. The social studies classroom surely can be utilized in the building of such a self-image by each pupil.

A third attitude that should increase the likelihood of a pupil ultimately engaging in some type of political action is the development within him of what has been termed social trust. Faith in human nature, willingness to cooperate with others, acceptance of one's political opponents, and confidence that citizens can maintain a just government are some basic components of an attitude of social trust.[21] As I mentioned earlier, social trust is an attitude associated with a favorable view of politics and one found lacking in the "culture of poverty," as defined by Oscar Lewis.

A final attitude which I shall recommend is enthusiasm for politics. We have learned that political leaders may emerge from families that have a deep involvement in political affairs. Can we not reproduce a similar atmosphere in the classroom. Let us immerse our pupils in the politics of our nation. Let us devote time to debating current economic, political, and social issues whether of local, national, or international importance. By doing so we shall provide the informational background, the skills, and many times the attitudes which will later encourage youth to become politically active regardless of family background, socio-economic status, occupation, or race.

[21] Almond, Gabriel A. and Verba, Sidney. *The Civic Culture*. Princeton, New Jersey: Princeton University Press, 1963.

40

Jacob R. Fishman *
Fredric Solomon †

YOUTH AND SOCIAL ACTION ‡

This is the report of a study of the psychodynamics of adolescent participation in antisegregation activities. The authors consider participation in such activities as it affects the development of ideology and the identity of a new concept, which the authors call prosocial acting out.

This is the initial report of a study of the psychodynamics of adolescent and student participation in public, risk-taking activities for racial desegregation. The major participants in this movement have been Negro and white college students in the Southern United States. Their most dramatic and perhaps most effective weapon has been a form of public passive resistance known as the sit-in demonstration. Indeed, the whole movement has come to be known as the student sit-in movement, and the term has quickly become part of our contemporary culture.‖

The original targets of these demonstrations were variety stores, which customarily welcome Negro patrons in most departments but exclude them from service at lunch counters. The first student sit-in took place on February 1, 1960, when four freshmen at an all-Negro college in Greensboro, North Carolina, deliberately decided to request service at such a segregated lunch counter. When service was denied them because of their color, they refused to leave; instead they remained seated, reading schoolbooks and Bibles. Since that time demonstrations have spread through many parts of

From Jacob R. Fishman and Fredric Solomon, "Youth and Social Action," *American Journal of Orthopsychiatry*, Vol. 33 (1963) pp. 872–882. Copyright, the American Orthopsychiatric Association, Inc. Reproduced by permission.

* Assistant Professor of Psychiatry and Director, Center for Youth and Community Studies, Howard University.

† NIMH Career Teacher in Psychiatry, Howard University. Formerly, Fellow in Child Psychiatry, Johns Hopkins University School of Medicine, Baltimore, Mary-

‡ Accepted for publication, May 3, 1963.

An earlier version of this paper was presented at the Third World Congress of Psychiatry, Montreal, Canada, June 1961.

land.

‖ Merriam-Webster Dictionary (unabridged), 1962.

the country where such policies are in effect and have been aimed at all kinds of segregated public facilities.

There are several possible results from a sit-in. At one extreme, the segregation policy may be promptly ended and the students served. At the other, the demonstrators may be heckled and assaulted, or arrested, jailed and charged with trespassing or disorderly conduct. Whatever the outcome, the pattern of social crisis is always the same: The students aggressively cross the color line, and then passively allow the consequences to rest on the co-operation of other like-minded people and on the decisions of civic authorities and businessmen in the dominant white majority. In the space of three years the South has witnessed thousands of demonstrations, which have also included boycotts, picketing, mass marches, hunger strikes of jailed students and the "freedom rides" on interstate buses. As of April, 1961 (before the freedom rides), demonstrators had numbered in the tens of thousands and had been active in some 75 Southern towns and cities. Three thousand five hundred demonstrators had been arrested; of these, an estimated 95 per cent were young people of both sexes in their teens or early twenties, both Negro and white.*

These demonstrations have resulted in the desegregation of more than 5,000 eating facilities, as well as hundreds of libraries, places of recreation and churches. The local, national and international news media have provided wide coverage, and the impact has been felt on campuses all over the country. For the Southern United States, this has represented a rate of social change far more rapid than any it has known since the Negro people were emancipated from slavery nearly 100 years ago. (6, 17, 21) In view of the social significance of this student movement, an understanding of the psychodynamic background and motivation of these young people should illuminate some of the relationships among personality, society and social change.

During the past two years we have studied the development of this movement, particularly in the Washington, D.C., area. The present paper represents our tentative psychosocial formulations of some motivational and personality factors in these students. Further data collection and analysis is under way. (5, 18–20) This report focuses mainly on young Negroes, whereas future papers will deal more extensively with the white student demonstrators, as well as with opponents and supporters in surrounding communities. Reports have already been presented on the very first of the organized sit-in demonstrations (18) and on the dynamics of nonviolent action. (20)

Picketing demonstrations in the Washington area have on occasion attracted as many as 200 participants, including, at one point in the summer of 1960, five United States Congressmen. However, the decision-making core of regular demonstrators consisted of about 40 students, calling them-

* Statistics provided by the Congress on Racial Equality, New York, N.Y.

selves "NAG," "Nonviolent Action Group." They felt this name exemplified the group's determination to "nag the conscience of the community." (It also symbolizes the recurrent theme of a passive-aggressive, persevering style of action.) White and Negro students, both male and female, were about evenly represented in the group. The average age was 18 years and six months, most members having completed one year in college, with little or no comparable prior experience with interracial organizations. In its first year of activity, the group succeeded in desegregating about 25 facilities, including restaurants, lunch counters, a movie theatre and the area's only amusement park. In addition, they were an important factor in stimulating the development of a council on human relations in suburban Montgomery County. During the course of these activities, about 100 arrests of demonstrators were made by local authorities. Several members of the original group later went on to become involved in freedom rides and other risk-taking actions for desegregation in the Deep South. (20)

Seventeen students (7 Negroes and 10 whites) in the Washington group were interviewed both individually and in groups. Three others (2 young Negro men who were major leaders, and one young white woman) were interviewed individually in some depth over a period of six months. Of primary interest in the interviews were those factors leading up to a student's decision to involve himself in a public, risk-taking activity for desegregation; a second focus was on family background and parental reactions to the student's participation. The demonstrators readily volunteered to discuss these and related matters, and two of the young Negro leaders have continued to maintain close contact with us. In addition to interviews, direct observations were made of demonstrations and other group activities, and public reaction was followed through the extensive coverage of the local news media.

EMERGENCE OF A NEW
SOCIAL CHARACTER

One of the 19-year-old Negro students recalled his reaction, which was typical, when he read the newspaper report of the very first organized sit-in in Greensboro, North Carolina. He and his friends at Howard University "all rejoiced, and we all felt the opportunity was here; and the fact that college students were doing it is one of the powerful reasons for participating ourselves . . . but more than anything . . . we all realized we had been *wanting to do something* and now was the time." Many of these students remembered that they first began "wanting to do something" in 1954 when they first heard about the Supreme Court decision for school desegregation; the student quoted above was 13 years old at that time, as were most of the young demonstrators in this study.

Thus it was at the threshold of their adolescence that the United States Supreme Court ruled unanimously that the segregated schools these youngsters had been attending were illegal. The Court had decided that systems of separate schools for Negroes and whites were inherently unequal because they generated in Negro students "a feeling of inferiority as to their status in the community that may affect their hearts and minds in a way unlikely ever to be undone." A unique and significant precedent was set in the use of statements of psychologists and social scientists to support this ruling.

This Supreme Court decision immediately received widespread publicity, discussion, denunciation and praise. It was apparent from talking to all of our Negro subjects that its message had been deeply imprinted on their minds and outlook. This public and legal recognition of the desirability of desegregation and its possible achievement in the near future was an experience in the adolescent development of these young people quite different from that of their parents and older siblings. They felt that the older generation had come to accept segregation and social inferiority as the natural order of things. They were aware of the Southern tradition that, when dealing with white people, one should present the appearance of a contented subordinate. However, feeling that desegregation was now their right, these students experienced increasing frustration with its painfully slow implementation and with the seeming hypocrisy of adults who paid lip service to principles but took no risks for implementation. Such feelings were intensified by the contrast of their own situation with that of many African people who were aggressively achieving independence and total public recognition as adults in the family of nations.

Many observers have pointed out that the psychosocial history of the Southern Negro has been largely characterized by his need to suppress and displace elsewhere his feelings of hostility toward the dominant whites. (1, 15, 16) Similarly he has had to suppress and displace any motivation to compete in economic and social spheres. He has been forced to assume a manifest role of passivity and submission, a role which has its social roots in economic and legal dependency on the white majority as well as in fear of punitive retaliation for overstepping color boundaries. These characteristics are expressed and further reinforced through the incorporation by the Negro of certain aspects of Christianity—especially the child-like trust in God, acceptance of one's lot in life, turning the other cheek and a belief in a happy afterlife coming to those good Christians who suffer and endure.(15)

Outbreaks of this bottled-up aggression in the South through crimes directed against whites have been dealt with traditionally in an extraordinarily harsh manner, for example, lynchings. Crimes within the Negro community, however, have received greater toleration from the white authorities, who viewed them as the behavior of irresponsible children who could be taught no better. The inhibited anger against the whites commonly has been turned on the self and displaced into the greatly disguised, stereotyped patterns of laziness, apathy, passivity and unreliability. The hostile roots of such behavior have been so well masked and denied by the defensive operations of both racial groups that, until very recently, the prevalent Southern white's view of the Negro was that of a rather irresponsible but essentially contented child. The Negro's needs were thought to be amply taken care of by a paternal system of social relationship modeled on the traditions of slavery. It comes as a real shock to many Southerners to see a discontented Negro forcefully displaying his discontent in a public, vocal manner. This confrontation is very threatening to some white Southerners, as shown in some of their violent reactions to sit-ins.

The Negro student in the sit-in movement proves he is neither child-like nor contented. The protests are neither indirect nor patient, as tends to be the behavior of the older generation. At the same time they express publically the frustration and resentment that has been so long hidden. Through the force of the moral and democratic principles they invoke to justify their action, they channel aggression into a positive identification with the traditional ego-ideal of the white majority, as well as with that of the world community. Using the terms of Erich Fromm, we may describe this as the emergence of a new social character for the Southern Negro. (8) One prominent white Southern politician has remarked, "These kids seem to be completely new Negroes, the likes of which we've never seen before." This new social character has emerged from the psychological reaction of adolescent members of a social group to changed external realities. It is built upon certain long-standing personality and cultural traits shared by the group's members, as well as the changing events, ideas and circumstances around them.

IDENTITY FORMATION AND "PROSOCIAL ACTING OUT"

Along with these factors of changing social history and new social character, an additional perspective is necessary to understand the student sit-in movement. One must take into account certain features of the developmental and group psychology of late adolescence—with special emphasis on interrelationships between action and identity formation. As Erik Erikson has intimated, the unique needs and strengths of late adolescence frequently focus on the social and intellectual crises of the era, translating issues into the ideology and action of the youth movement. Thus ideology and social action may have a fundamental role in the development of identity in adolescents.

We have already remarked the child-like nature of the Negro stereotype in the eyes of the white Southerners (vividly symbolized in the custom of hailing any adult Negro male as "Boy," instead of "Mister" or "Sir"). Until recently the Negro could either accept that role, or move to the North. In the South he has been largely denied the opportunity to express normal aggressive and masculine strivings through dignified and respected occupations in the general society and in competition with the white male. Under these conditions the Negro male is degraded and depreciated and cannot serve as an adequate ego ideal or model for identification for his children. (12)

The young Negro demonstrators are acutely aware of the lack of adult identity that has characterized their fathers in the South. Both the conscious and unconscious strivings for potent male identification become very apparent in talking to them. In 1955, Rev. Martin Luther King led the entire Negro community of Montgomery, Alabama, in a boycott of the city's transit buses; after one year's struggle, the buses were desegregated. (13) This occurred when many of the students were only 15, two years after the Supreme Court had told them that their anger against segregation was justified and sanctioned. Young people all over the South were vastly impressed with the Montgomery boycott. They felt it was a lesson in the practical and emotional "advantages of direct action" in expressing legitimate Negro discontent.* King became the image of an assertive Negro male assuming freedom of action with dignity, and achieving respectful recognition through successful struggle with the white community (that is, male community). In a sense he became the figure the Negro adolescent wished his father might have been, and as such he was incorporated as part of the ego-ideal. Three years later, soon after leaving home for college, Negroes were acting on the dictates of this identification model through the sit-in. Thus, for the late adolescent in the vanguard of the sit-in movement, the search for recognition as an adult that so characterizes his age group has been intimately interwoven with the struggle of Southern Negroes as a social group for recognition as mature human beings. For the 19-year-old student, then, the creation of a new social character for his people has become identical with the development of his own personality as a young adult.

As part of their struggles to achieve emancipation and identity, many of the Negro students seem to display significant ego-syntonic processes that suggest an acting out through the sit-ins of early childhood frustrations and parental conflicts and wishes. Although the concept of acting out has been used primarily in connection with certain forms of anti-social behavior (10) and problems of psychotherapy, (9) data in the current study suggest a more general role for acting out in character and identity formation. (5, 18) This is illustrated in the following description of B., a seemingly

* It is interesting to note reports that indicate a sharp decline in the incidence of crime among the Negro population of Montgomery, Alabama, during the year of the boycott. (11)

typical, poor, ambitious 19-year-old male Negro college freshman from the Deep South who became a leader of the Washington group of demonstrators. The data and formulations are based on a six-month series of research interviews and subsequent follow-up.

B. was brought up in a matriarchal family in which his step-father was absent most of the time, or jobless and degraded when home. His real father had left when he was still an infant. He is the oldest of eight brothers and sisters. His mother worked as a domestic for a white Southern family. He grew up feeling contemptuous and resentful of his father, but guilty about this resentment and perhaps responsible for the father's failures and absences. B. has ambivalent feelings toward his mother whom he fantasies really loved him most, but was forced to give prime attention to his younger siblings as well as the white family that employed her. He wore the white family's cast-off clothing. His mother was quite harsh with him if ever he expressed resentment about their status or about white people. She told him that they must know their place, and it would do no good to antagonize the whites. She feared losing the meager job which was their only source of income. He associates the lives of his parents with submission to the white community, and displaces onto this social submission much of the resentment, frustration and deprivation he experienced within his family. At the same time he recognizes his parent's passive-aggressive ambivalence to the whites and the different levels of meaning in his mother's prohibitions against open hostility. This perception helps him develop an idealized image of his parents in which they are really eager for and capable of self-assertion (which would mean more love, attention and recognition for him); but their self-assertion is blocked by circumstance or fear.

B.'s decision to participate in a sit-in demonstration was at first quite impulsive, with a great deal of subsequent rationalization. His personal involvement and dedication have been intense, and actions result in much discharge of affect, as anger and depression are transformed into elation. This discharge of affect is related not only to the stimuli of immediate circumstances but also to symbolic mastery of childhood frustrations. Thus, on the one hand, he acts out his long-standing resentment of his parents derived from his repeated experiences of deprivation and displacement as a youngster, which he now sees as a consequence of his parents' social role. On the other hand, when he takes risks and tests the retaliatory dangers of which he has been warned by his family, he may threaten his mother, but he also wins her secret approval. He thereby enhances his self-esteem as an autonomous, masculine adult. He has acted out his family's suppressed resentment of the social system in a dignified and passive-aggressive manner and has responded to his mother's fantasied need for a socially potent male. (It is of interest that, in follow-up interviews two years later, he reports that his whole family has "come around" to open support of his activities.) It can be inferred that for some adolescents acting out has an important role in identity formation and progressive development of ego functions.

In an historical context, B. feels "caught between Uncle Tom and Jim Crow." Uncle Tom represents the internalized ambivalence of his parents in telling him he must be passive. Jim Crow represents the traditional pattern of segregation and sanctions applied by the whites, which also thwarts his aggressive strivings. He is able successfully to act out unconscious parental hostility to the whites that they themselves have been unable to express overtly. Consciously he has an idealized image of what his parents "really" feel or ought to feel about what is right. He also perceives that he is acting according to the dictates of the conscience of the total community and that he is doing what others fear, hesitate or are "too hypocritical" to do.* This perception of the super-ego or conscience of the community and of his parents allows him to rationalize his rebellion against his own family thereby decreasing guilt and anxiety. He feels he is doing what his parents (and the nation) really want him to do but they are afraid to say so openly. We have found similar dynamics in all but two of the young white demonstrators as well. One after another they reported that their parents were both definitely against racial segregation and definitely against doing anything about it. Some were consciously aware of the mixture of anxiety and pride their parents felt about their activities. As it were, they are acting out the conscience of the community.

The acting out of suppressed parental wishes and problems of deprivation, frustration and moral ambiguity has been frequently reported in the psychodynamics underlying adolescent delinquency and antisocial behavior. (10) However, the acting out we have observed here is consciously based on moral imperatives, that is, on the perceived super-ego or conscience of the community, which becomes incorporated into the individual and group functional self-image. Since this perception began in childhood and, as we have shown, was dramatically reinforced during early adolescence, it becomes part of the ego-ideal; action based on its dictates becomes an important source of self-esteem. Therefore, we suggest the term "prosocial" acting out to describe this behavior. (5) This distinction is important. Delinquent acting out is described as antisocial precisely because of its opposition to the morality of the community. Acting out occurs through the delinquent's rebellion against severe super-ego dictates or in the framework of defective super-ego development (for example, "lacunae"). (10) In prosocial acting out, however, the ego-ideal and resultant functional self-image are much more in accord with the dictates of the community morality and conscience. Those involved in the latter require some level of social or moral approval, and their goals are rationalized in the direction of social welfare. This allows a gratifying and self-enhancing resolution of emotional conflict and social identity formation. They feel they are "doing society's work for

* An interesting parallel may exist between the messianiclike feelings and identification of this young Negro leader and those formulated about Moses by S. Freud. (7)

it." The answers to the typical adolescent questions of autonomy, time perspective, work and ideals (2) are vastly different in these two forms of behavior. However, the dynamics seem to have many similarities. It may be that a more detailed understanding of the differing determinants of these two adolescent pathways would have significant implications for the social health of a community, as well as for a new approach to the prevention and treatment of delinquency.

One aspect of the group dynamics of acting out is worthy of note here. Through the conversion of their own anger into a seemingly passive and pious stance these students threaten the bigoted and volatile defenses of the white extremists. In so doing, the demonstrators accomplish a remarkable psychosocial feat, much to their advantage. The white extremists are provoked by the young Negroes to act out for them the very anger and resentment that they (the Negroes) have themselves felt. However, the anger and violence have now been externalized and projected onto the "aggressor," so that the students feel guiltless and even exhilarated in their justifiable indignation. It also helps win the sympathy of the observing public and reduces the fears of whites that Negroes intend to retaliate violently for past suppression. (13) This is probably a prominent feature of the dynamics of nonviolent action as a political weapon.

It is extremely important for these young students to be able to express publicly and directly their discontent and indignation against restriction, dependency and inequity. It allows them to identify their aggressive strivings for independence and recognition, which are intrinsic to the adolescent phase of development, with their desperate need for social emancipation and equality. These demonstrations are certainly aggressive. However, the dignified, well-disciplined, nonviolent style of the student action is calculated to be an effective propaganda weapon that will encourage the more moderate white Southerners to accept some measure of desegregation, as well as win the sympathy and support of news media and public in other parts of the country. The students are also keenly aware of the attention they receive in news media in other parts of the world; they are surprisingly sophisticated in their political and social awareness. Although they are preoccupied with the task at hand, they readily identify with students and movements for recognition and emancipation in other parts of a total world community.

IDEOLOGY AND IDENTITY

The use of nonviolent resistance means that the students will picket, sit-in, ride buses and use facilities that are segregated, but they will not resist when heckled, attacked or arrested. It is consciously conceived of by many as a pragmatic political weapon applicable to the problem of segregation, and is consistent with Christian religious training. Although Biblical and Christian teachings and the traditions of Ghandi and civil disobedience are incorporated into their ideology as formulated by Martin Luther King, (13) these students are generally not pacifists. This is exemplified in the remarks of B., who was very much committed and dedicated to the principles of nonviolence in the sit-in. Soon after quoting from the Scriptures and Ghandi in support of nonviolence, he went on to talk with pride of his own personal ambitions to be a jet pilot in the U.S. Air Force.

At the same time, the philosophy of nonviolence is consistent with the long tradition of minimizing offense to the white community. It is a natural out-growth of the traditional passive and submissive role in the face of white domination and potential retaliation. The internal prohibition against hostility to the whites is deep-seated; this hostility is more readily expressed by first being transformed into love for those who hate you. This process reduces guilt and anxiety and makes easier the students' departure from parental stereotypes; yet at the same time it allows them to identify with the parental religious ego-ideal. The ideology helps the adolescent maintain super-ego control over angry impulses while simultaneously internalizing an ego-ideal of love and respect for all human beings including the enemy, which in turn enhances the sense of identity and self-esteem. This illustrates the connection of ideology and identity formation for many adolescents. (3)

In one sense, then, the sit-in can be described as a passive-aggressive act. For a few it provides the arena for masochism and martyrdom. For all it is a demand to be seen, heard and recognized. As is usual with adolescent movements, it is never anonymous. Names are freely given and no one hides his face when pictures are taken. However, one should not underestimate the intensity of the aggression and hostility being channeled here, especially in the Negro students. We did not need to probe very deeply to find resentment and hostility built on layers of social and personal frustration in the demonstrators we interviewed. The aggression is manifest in the very circumstance that they are coercing people to accept or react to the accomplished fact of sitting-in at a segregated establishment, as well as in the evident satisfaction at stirring social turmoil by what seems to be such a small, quiet initial action; moreover, this is done frequently in areas where the violent and explosive potential of white segregationists is well known.

In our interviews with them, all these students, both Negro and white, saw its high moral purpose as a major feature of their activity. Desegregation and the philosophy of nonviolent resistance are seen primarily as moral rather than political principles. (20) As Erikson has pointed out in describing the process of ideology formation in adolescents, (3) these students take literally the moral commitment of the community and, denouncing what are perceived to be the hypocrisies of the current social and political situation, demand a substantial change. Here the goals of conscience of the students represent not only the traditional Christian morality of the nation but also the well-known and basic American social and political principles of equal rights of freedom of choice. Thus the Negro sit-in youth thinks of himself as more Christian than the white community in the South. He also thinks of himself as more in accord with the highest principles of American democracy than the white hecklers on the sidelines. He derives considerable ego support from thus identifying with the ideals of the right majority and a great feeling of compensatory gratification from the experience of superior moral dedication. This helps him offset traditional feelings of racial inferiority that have been so long a part of the Southern milieu.

Although the ideology is highly moral, this is by no means an intellectual movement. There is a heavy orientation to action and work, even to the point of impatience with prolonged intellectual discussion. During the organization of the first sit-in in the Washington area, the original students, in recruiting others in their dormitory to join them, used as their rallying cry, "There's work to be done." Again and again there was an emphasis on getting down to the work at hand, the picketing or sitting-in, with a minimum of fuss or preliminary discussion. A great deal of gratification was derived from their sense of dedicated work, and it undoubtedly has an important function in the formation of individual and group identity.(2) However, it also illustrates the impulsive urge to immediate action so characteristic of adolescent time perspective and so different from that of the older generation. This sense of immediacy is exemplified in the students' frustration with "plenty of ideals but no action." Such an action orientation leads to considerable risk taking. Since deciding to take a risk is done by an individual student quite on his own (albeit with group support), such a decision helps to develop a feeling of autonomy, as well as proving bravery and the willingness to endure suffering on behalf of one's principles. (4) The mutual experience of action, risk taking and injury does a great deal to solidify the feelings of unity and identity of the group and to insure individual loyalties. Thus the sit-in groups derive great strength from their experiences in jail or in the midst of hostile crowds.

The assertion of freedom of choice in one's own behavior is interestingly parallel to the emphasis on freedom of choice in the principle of desegregation. For example, an 18-year-old white girl with a mixed group being arrested at a suburban bowling alley asked simply, "If these are my friends and I want to bowl with them, why should we be arrested?" For this girl, the need for freedom of choice and action so typical of the adolescent has become identical with the strivings of Negroes in the community at large.

It seems that an element of renunciation of former dependency gratifications is almost always present in the process of growing up. As they approach maturity, social groups as well as individuals must lose some of the security of their former social and economic relationships. A young person feels most free or independent only after having done something active and aggressive to win that independence. In this context, perhaps an "independent" identity can never be freely given—it must be at least partially *taken* by adolescents and, possibly, by young nations as well.

In summary, we would emphasize that one can find in the student sit-in movement patterns of adolescent identity strivings similar to those in many other adolescent groups. These young people, however, are caught on a wave of psychological transition and upheaval. For the Negroes, inferiority, submission and deprivation are their childhood experience; passive-aggressive resolutions their heritage; Christianity their moral background; the Supreme Court decision and the coming of age of new African nations part of the tempo of change. Through these influences are filtered the typical internal pressures and new ego capacities of early and late adolescence. Public action for social goals is their way of at least temporarily resolving issues of identity formation, conscience and aggression. They see themselves as prodders of the national conscience, and derive satisfaction and self-esteem from this role. As a result, they have been forced into synthesizing a new social character with its new problems and anxieties, with its risks and violence, but also with a vitality and optimism for a future that they feel they have had a hand in shaping.

Recent student activities in this and other countries suggest that the motivation and psychodynamics of student involvement in political and social action represents an important area of study. (14, 19, 22) Such studies may help in understanding the effects of social change and crises on personality and identity formation, as well as the converse effects of adolescent striving for recognition and identity on social and political change.

REFERENCES

1. Dollard, J. 1939. Caste and Class in a Southern Town. Harper & Row, New York, N.Y.
2. Erikson, E. 1956. The problem of ego identity. J. Amer. Psychoanal. Assn. 4(1): 56–121.
3. Erikson, E. 1958. Young Man Luther. W. W. Norton & Co., Inc. New York, N.Y.
4. Erikson, E. 1962. Youth; fidelity and diversity. Daedalus 91(1): 5.
5. Fishman, J. R. and F. Solomon. Pro-social Acting out. In preparation.
6. Fleming, H. 1960. The new South and the sit-ins. J. Intergroup Relations 2(1): 56–60.
7. Freud, S. 1934. Moses and Monotheism. Hogarth Press. London, Eng.
8. Fromm, E. 1941. Appendix: Social character and social process. *In* Escape from Freedom. Farrar. New York, N.Y.
9. Greenacre, P. 1950. General problems of acting-out. Psychoanal. Quart. 19: 455–467.
10. Johnson, A. M. and S. A. Szurek. 1952. The genesis of antisocial acting-out in children and adults. Psychoanal. Quart. 21(3): 323–343.

11. Kahn, T. **1960**. Unfinished Revolution (Pamphlet). Igal Rodenko, Printer. New York, N.Y.: 28.

12. Kardiner, A. and L. Ovesey. **1951**. The Mark of Oppression: A Psychosocial Study of the American Negro. W. W. Norton & Co., Inc. New York, N.Y.

13. King, M. L. **1958**. Stride Toward Freedom: The Montgomery Story. Harper & Row. New York, N.Y.

14. Laquer, W. Z. **1962**. History of the German Youth Movement. Basic Books, Inc. New York, N.Y.

15. Myrdal, G. **1944**. An American Dilemma. Harper & Row. New York, N.Y.

16. Powdermaker, H. **1943**. The channeling of Negro aggression by the cultural process. Amer. J. Sociol. **48**: 750–758.

17. Rexroth, K. **1960**. The students take over. The Nation. **191**(1): 4–9.

18. Solomon, F. and Fishman, J. R. Identity formation and crisis in student demonstrators against racial segregation. Presented at the Annual Meeting of the American Psychiatric Association, Toronto, Canada. May 7, 1962.

19. Solomon, F. Youth and social action: students participating in a large "peace" demonstration. Presented at the Annual Meeting of the American Orthopsychiatric Association, Washington, D.C. March, 1963.

20. Solomon, F. Non-violence in the South: a psychosocial study. Presented at the Annual Meeting of the American Psychiatric Association, St. Louis, Mo. May 6, 1963.

21. Wilson, J. Q. **1961**. The strategy of Negro protest. J. Conflict Resolution **5**(3): 291–303.

22. Youth: change and challenge (a symposium). **1962**. Daedalus **91**(1).

ADDITIONAL READINGS

Adelson, Joseph & O'Neil, Robert P. Growth of political ideas of adolescents: The sense of community. *Journal of Personality and Social Psychology,* 1966, **4**, 295–306. Depth interviews conducted with 30 subjects each at ages of 11, 12, 15, and 18, indicated that before the age of thirteen children find it hard to imagine the social consequences of political action. Children younger than fifteen think of government in terms of tangible services, and only later perceive long-range consequences of political action. Finally, in later adolescence, teenagers shift from authoritarian solutions to philosophical principles.

The art of rebellion. *Teachers College Record,* March 1967, **48** (6), 499–502. This article provides commentary about Albert Camus', *The Rebel*

(New York: Alfred A. Knopf, 1954), and the reviewer's reaction to methods of expressions of rebellion. Perhaps the best sort of rebellion is rational, not an all-or-none affair. Instead of suppressing dissent the schools would free young people to define meaning and principle, and to move, as Camus expresses it, "beyond nihilism" to moderation.

Greenstein, F. I. *Children and politics.* New Haven: Yale University Press, 1965. Greenstein's comprehensive study indicates children's knowledge about current affairs and government. Among children in New Haven, 8th graders proved more knowledgeable than 4th graders. Greenstein analyzes in detail the extent of children's political knowledge and the nature of their party loyalties. He also reviews the literature on political socialization.

Middleton, Russell & Putney, Snell. Political expression of adolescent rebellion. *American Journal of Sociology,* March 1963, **68,** 527–535. In a nationwide study, in a sampling of students from 16 colleges and universities across the country, the relationship between parental political viewpoint and parent-child relations was studied. Males proved more likely than females to deviate from parents' views. The relationship between political rebellion and defiance was not significant. Political rebellion seemed most likely to occur when child and parent were emotionally estranged, when the child believed parental discipline to be nontypical, and when the parent was interested in politics.

Shafer, Susanne M. Political passions and rational actions. *Teachers College Record,* March 1967, **48** (6), 471–479. After considering adult political behavior, the writer describes contemporary concerns of young people, many of whom manifest more political commitment than any young generation in history. Through activating youth's awareness, enthusiasm, social trust, and a feeling of high self-regard in individuals, asserts Professor Shafer, teachers can increase the numbers of youth who are politically intelligent and capable of intelligent political activity.

Sigel, Roberta S. Essay review: 'Children and politics'. *The School Review,* Summer 1967, **75** (2), 228–236. This book systematically asks the question: what type of children know and feel what about politics at what age, and constitutes a pioneer work in the fast growing literature of political socialization.

Solomon, Frederic & Fishman, Jacob R. Youth and social action: II. Action and identity formation in the first student sit-in demonstration. *Journal of Social Issues,* 1964, **20** (2), 36–45. This is a report on the student protest movement against racial segregation—the "sit-in" and "freedom-ride" movement. The case history of one demonstrator is given to show how his participation affected the establishment of his own personal identity.

Sorenson, Roy. Youth's needs for challenge and place in society. *Children,* July–August 1962, **9** (4), 131–138. Sorenson discusses youth's place in present-day American society and its implications for adults and social institutions. Suggestions are offered for helping youth to cope more adequately with the problems of a complex society.

Williamson, E. G. & Cowan, John L. *The American student's freedom of expression: A research appraisal.* Minneapolis, Minn.: University of Minnesota Press, 1966. This study, undertaken in 1961 by the National Association of Student Personnel Administrators (the professional organization of American college deans), reports restraints made by colleges on students' active participation in society's problems. The study reveals a wide variation in the degree to which freedom of expression is treated in institutions of higher learning.

Six

Cultural Variants in
Adolescent Problems

Cultural Contexts in
Adolescent Traditions

XX. Adolescents in American Subcultures

Each modern society has not only a culture, but a subculture. Its culture represents those customs, habits, attitudes, knowledges, and mores that distinguish it from other societies and which are shared by the individuals who compose it. Within the larger society are sub-groups, which not only possess the earmarks of the major culture, but characteristic features of their own. We have already commented on the American youth culture, which actually is an American subculture, derived from the age-grading of society. One variant of the youth subculture is the college-student subculture, which may also have variants of its own. Thus, the college is viewed as a distinctive sociocultural system, with a value orientation that contains a variety of goals for the student.[1]

Youth are also members of the subculture of their own social class. Low-income youth, as contrasted with their more well-off counterparts, normally have a greater sense of powerlessness, a more fatalistic attitude toward life, a lack of future orientation, and a greater impulse for "acting out." Most studies also show lower-class youth to be relatively non-verbal, anti-intellectual, and poor in conceptual abilities.[2] What lower-class youth need, says Pearl, is "to be provided an opportunity to form groups which have a link with the future; which permit them to develop marketable competence; and in which they have the right to be wrong, the right to correct wrongs, and mostly, the right to belong."[3]

On the other hand, the lower-class youth has traditionally been spared some of the strains of adolescence. His parents have more willingly accepted him as an adult. He has also felt free to quit school and get a job. Consequently, he has had more spending money, and the opportunity to marry early, thus relieving sexual tensions. Even while lower-class youth have, in some respects, envied upper-class youth, the reverse has also been true. Note that middle-class youth often adopt clothes, expressions, and

---

[1] D. Gottlieb and B. Hodgkins, "College Student Subcultures: Their Structure and Characteristics in Relation to Student Attitude Change," *The School Review,* Vol. 71 (1963).

[2] Arthur Pearl, "Youth in Lower Class Settings," in Muzafer Sherif and Carolyn W. Sherif (Eds.), *Problems of Youth: Transition to Adulthood in a Changing World* (Chicago: Adline Publishing Company, 1965) p. 89.

[3] *Ibid.* p. 108.

music of the lower classes. Therefore, even as upper-class ways seep downward, so do lower-class ways filter upward.[4]

Until recently, Negro youth were almost wholly lower class; and like other members of their class, they had no youth culture. More recently, a Negro middle class has developed, whose children finish school, and often college. However, perhaps even more than before, the Negro teen-ager finds himself trapped between two cultures. When he had no hope to achieve the rewards of the larger culture, he often resigned himself to the way of life of his subculture. But now he has hope, and resists the discriminations placed upon him. He wants the best of both worlds, his own and the white man's.[5] In our first selection, Dr. Joseph Himes, Professor of Sociology at North Carolina College, in Durham, describes the Negro subculture as a "melange of general adolescent patterns and unique ethnic practices."

Regardless of race or social class, youth also dwell in the subculture of their particular locale, whether rural, small town, or urban. In certain respects, rural farm, rural non-farm, and urban youth are alike in experiencing parent-youth conflict; however, both rural youth and their parents are more traditional than their urban counterparts.[6] Farm youth are also closer to their parents, and the traditionally close-knit farm family persists. The characterization of adolescence as a period of rebellion against parental norms and rejection of traditional values is questionable, especially among rural youth. The more remote the area, the less the youth rejects societal norms.[7]

City-dwelling youth may be further subdivided according to sections of the city, which are so different as almost to constitute different worlds. However, all are alike in having access to certain cultural advantages, in living in an environment adapted largely to adults, and in experiencing, at close range, the tempo of change. These distinctions, between youth's life in city, farm area, small town, or suburb, are the subject of our second selection, by Elizabeth Douvan and Joseph Adelson. Students may be interested in comparing, in class discussion, youth patterns in their own home environments with those described here. The Douvan-Adelson selection is based on a national study; and observations by the class will reveal variations on the national theme.

---

[4] L. Joseph Stone and Joseph Church, *Childhood and Adolescence* (New York: Random House, 1957), p. 293.

[5] Jessie Bernard, "Teen-Age Culture: An Overview," in Jessie Bernard (Ed.), *Teen-Age Culture*. Philadelphia: The American Academy of Political and Social Science, Vol. 338 (November 1961), pp. 11–12.

[6] Robert C. Bealer and Fern K. Willets, "Rural Youth: A Case Study in the Rebelliousness of Adolescents in Teen-Age Culture," in Jessie Bernard (Ed.), *Teen-Age Culture*. Philadelphia: The American Academy of Political and Social Science, Vol. 338 (November 1961), pp. 63–69.

[7] S. R. Hathaway, E. D. Monachesi and L. A. Young, "Rural-Urban Adolescent Personality," *Rural Sociology,* Vol. 24 (December 1959), pp. 331–346.

The third selection, by Coles and Brenner, describes the characteristics of adolescents in the mountains of Appalachia. This article highlights the problems of the young people who live in an area radically different from the major culture.

Cultural differences also extend to the times. The America of 1900 is certainly more different from the America of 1969, than the America of 1969 from the Japan of 1969. Changes that would have once taken a century now occur in less than a generation. As a result, the present is soon remote and outdated. In effect, as an individual moves through life-stages, he experiences a succession of cultures. In the same country, these shifting cultures maintain, for varying lengths of time, certain core values; nevertheless, they also display distinctive differences. Since it is totally unpredictable what tomorrow will be like, sons can no longer depend on answers handed down by their fathers. Their education must be such that they will know how to devise new solutions for new-type problems.

On the topic of subculture versus adolescents, various issues suggest themselves. How fundamental are the variations in adolescents by subculture? How specifically may such variations be defined? There is much speculation and theorizing on the subject, but much of it lacks an adequate empirical base. For instance, are the "disadvantaged" youth of lower social classes as unfortunate as they seem from the perspective of middle-class observers? Perhaps they share values within their own milieu—for example, relative freedom from competitive pressures—of which the outsider is only dimly aware. Also, what sort of adaptations should the larger culture, and its agents, the school, make for teen-agers of different subcultures? Should schools be racially integrated? Would it be better to accept the doctrine of pluralism, and to encourage youth of specific subcultures to maintain the values and ways of life characteristic of their families of origin; or should all young people be blended in the same sociocultural melting pot?

41

Joseph S. Himes

NEGRO TEEN-AGE CULTURE

The Negro teen-ager's status in the American Negro teen-age culture is a "melange of general practices." Two modes of aggression are apparent: personal aggression among lower-class youth and the racial protest movement among college youth. This protest, says the writer, is one of the most positive elements in current American teen culture.

SOCIAL SITUATION

The quality of Negro teen-age culture is conditioned by four decisive factors: race, inferiority, deprivation, and youthfulness. Virtually every experience of the Negro teen-ager is filtered through this complex qualifying medium; every act is a response to a distorted perception of the world. His world is a kind of nightmare, the creation of a carnival reflection chamber. The Negro teen-ager's culture, his customary modes of behavior, constitute his response to the distorted, frightening, and cruel world that he perceives with the guileless realism of youth.[1]

A knowledgeable worker in Baltimore reported the life perceptions of poor Negro boys in the following manner.[2] "They feel rejected . . . say they cannot achieve but so much because they are Negroes. Say they have . . . less money . . . worse housing . . . and worse section of town."

Race, inferiority, deprivation, and youthfulness tend to trap Negro teen-agers by forces beyond their comprehension and control. School, the church, the mass media, city streets, and the other institutions of the pageant of American life serve to sharpen the sense of entrapment and deprivation. Oscar Handlin shows with clarity how the New York schools produce these results with Negro and Puerto Rican children.[3]

From Joseph S. Himes, "Negro Teen-Age Culture," in *Teen-Age Culture,* Jessie Bernard (Ed.), Philadelphia, The American Academy of Political and Social Sciences, Vol. 338 (November 1961), pp. 92–101. Reprinted by permission.

[1] See Warren Miller, *This Cool World* (Boston: Little, Brown, 1959).

[2] Field document.

[3] Oscar Handlin, *The Newcomers* (Cambridge: Harvard University Press, 1959), p. 78.

. . . A variety of factors prevent many of them from concentrating on their studies—the inability to use correct English, their own poverty and sometimes the necessity for part-time work, the lack of privacy at home, and the remoteness of the goals toward which education leads. The result is often a high rate of truancy. All too often, also, even those students who attend docilely merely sit out their lessons, without the incentive to pay attention to what transpires in the classroom.

Negro children learn early that only a part of the bright hope and glittering affluence of America is for them. A middle-class teen-ager from St. Paul put it this way: [4] "I have found . . . that as much as I wish to be completely equal, there is still a barrier which I have given up hope to break." Warren Miller notes that the sense of drab deprivation comes as early as the tenth or eleventh year to big-city children.[5]

TWIN CULTURAL HERITAGE

In American society, a real void separates the better educated, the better off, the better situated Negro people from the great mass of poor, ill-educated, slum-dwelling individuals.[6] These two categories of individuals are the carriers of twin cultural heritages. The less numerous high-prestige category stresses moral conformity, good manners and taste, subordination of present gratifications to future achievements, and striving for social recognition and status. The heritage of the low-prestige masses emphasizes immediate material and creature gratifications, the tyranny of in-group standards, personal recognition, and insecurity and "egotouchiness."

Children enter teenhood from the two cultural streams. High-prestige and upwardly mobile low-prestige teen-agers pass into high-prestige adult roles through the college culture. Most low-prestige teen-agers, however, pass directly into the adult job and marriage roles of their original cultural rank. For both groups, the teen-age culture marks an interlude, a sort of cultural *rite de passage*.

WHAT THE TEEN-AGERS DO

Teen-age culture is a variegated complex of behavior patterns. The teen-ager's speech is liberally sprinkled, often monopolized by slang expres-

[4] Personal document.
[5] Warren Miller, *op. cit.*
[6] In *Blackways of Kent* (Chapel Hill: University of North Carolina Press. 1955), pp. 233–256, Hylan G. Lewis differentiates the two traditions as "respectable" and "nonrespectable."
See also Leonard H. Robinson, "Negro Street Society: A Study of Racial Adjustment in Two Southern Urban Communities" (unpublished doctoral dissertation, Ohio State University, 1950).

sions.[7] All reports indicate that profanity and obscenity are commonplace with low-prestige youths, especially boys,[8] although not around adults— parents, teachers, recreation leaders, and persons in similar capacities. With only minor local variations, the vogue is early and almost universal steady dating, a practice that leads to early marriage, sexual laxities, venereal infections, and unplanned pregnancies.[9] Eighty-four per cent of 295 students in a southern urban high school said they thought it was all right for teen-agers to go steady.[10] Some observers report intensive and random dating instead, while others mention steady dating among the younger teen-agers and random dating among the older ones.

The craving for things is intense—cars, clothes, stereo, records, transistors, cameras, and the like. It is widely reported that the teen-agers work, save, and even—especially among the low-prestige category—steal for them. The teen-agers favor such activities as car riding, vigorous dancing, competitive sports, animated "yackity-yacking," transistor toting, record listening, and the like. For example, current dance vogues in Durham, North Carolina, include the "pony," the "continental," the "twist," the "rocking Charlie," the "shimmy," the "watusi," the "booty green," the "jack-the-ripper," the "stran," and the "stupidity."

Field reports from all regions indicate that dress, grooming, and ornamentation are extreme and faddish. High-prestige boys and girls tend to follow the current national teen-age styles. Low-prestige teen-agers, however, are often slightly behind current vogues or distinguished by unique styles. Though there is much variety, some girls seem to favor colored sneakers, socks, flaring skirts, with crinoline petticoats, and sloppy Joe sweaters; others go for short tight skirts, burlap cloth being one current vogue, bulky sweaters with the ubiquitous sneakers and socks, and sometimes stockings. Older low-prestige boys feature caps or derbies, buttondown collars, "continental" jackets, short tight-legged pants, and hard-heeled shoes. "Processed" (straightened and styled) or close-cropped hair for these boys and "shades" (sun glasses) for both sexes are popular. Girls feature heavy eye make-up, light matching shades of lipstick and nail polish, usually chosen to match some color of the outfit, which may include bright unharmonious colors.

The reports show a universal interest in music, which seems to work like a narcotic. The Negro musical heritage is a folk tradition compounded

[7] Theodore M. Bernstein examines some of the functions of slang in "Now It's Watch Your Slanguage," *New York Times Magazine,* February 28, 1960, pp. 31 and 94 ff.

[8] Field documents from Syracuse, Buffalo, Baltimore, Washington, Durham, N.C., Columbus, Ohio, St. Paul, Detroit, St. Louis, and Houston.

[9] James F. Donohue and Others, "Venereal Diseases Among Teen-Agers," *Public Health Reports,* Vol. 70 (May 1955), p. 454 ff.

Emily H. Mudd and Richard N. Hey, "When the Young Marry Too Young," *National Parent-Teacher,* Vol. 55 (September 1960), pp. 24–26.

[10] Teen-Age Survey, Durham, North Carolina, April 1961.

of spirituals, gospel hymns, blues, and jazz. The difference between high- and low-prestige teen-agers is less evident in musical taste than in most other areas. . . .

THE STREET

One unique feature of Negro teen-age behavior results from the relative lack of private facilities—bowling alleys, skating rinks, tennis courts, swimming pools—which forces Negro teen-agers into public recreational agencies, commercial hangouts, beer joints, and city streets.

The street as a social institution is an important factor in Negro culture, as it is in many European cultures. It is frequented by teen-agers as well as by adults and the following analysis is as accurate for them as for older persons.[11]

Whatever may be said in the way of explanation of the special significance that the street has for its habitues, the conclusion is unavoidable that it envelops a way of life defined not so much by those who participate in and share it, as by those who do not. The tendency on the part of the law enforcement agencies to permit a wide range of "shady" and illegal social and economic activity, the leniency on the part of the courts in disposing of many petty criminal cases involving Negroes only, and the more or less apathetic and indifferent attitudes of the larger [public] as well as a part of the Negro community help determine and define it. These factors designate the street area as one of special permission. Within this environment—relatively free from restrictions and taboos of the dominant moral order—the habitue receives a sense of belonging and a greater feeling of personal worth. This is evident in the self-assertiveness that characterizes much of his behavior. On the street, he is ready to laugh, play, and have fun. He is equally prepared to feud, fuss, and fight. This tendency to run the emotional gamut from sociability to aggression is definitive of many interpersonal relationships.

The function performed by the street for the total culture is, according to this reporter, to serve as a sluice for the aggressions resulting from frustration; without the permitted aggression, race relations would deteriorate. Thus: [12]

Within the public world of the street, as much the creation of the majority which lives outside it as the minority which shares it, the nature of the adjustment that the Negro makes depends very largely on the extent, at any particular time, that the larger controls are applied. To the degree that there are no controls, the Negro "problem" turns inward and "race relations" are accord-

[11] Leonard Harrison Robinson, "Southern Urban Communities," *Journal of Human Relations,* Vol. 3 (Summer 1955), pp. 82–83.
[12] *Ibid.,* p. 83.

ingly "good." The street in this sense exhibits a sort of "organized disorganization" in which various elements of the Negro population find expression and
adjustment and onto which the majority group "unloads" a potential "problem." "No control" for the one group becomes a form of social control for
the other.

It is suggested that were the larger community to invoke the full weight
of the legal and moral codes by which it governs its own conduct, without at
the same time permitting the Negro a wider range and greater intensity of participation in the social and economic life, the "problem" would accordingly
turn outward and "race relations" would in proportion become "bad."

Since the above analysis was made, the aggressions of high-prestige
teen-agers have, in fact, been aimed outward rather than exclusively toward
the in-group, and, as predicted, race relations have become—at least tran-
sitionally—bad. We shall have more to say about the outward-aimed aggressions presently, but, at this point, it is interesting to note that, despite
the large part that the street plays in the culture of the Negro teen-ager
and despite—perhaps because of—the large amount of interpersonal aggression, fighting gangs are not characteristic of Negro teen-age culture.

NO GANGS

Thus, the field reports indicate that organized gang behavior is not a
feature of general Negro teen-age culture. In Durham, North Carolina, only
11 out of 334 students who replied to the questionnaire admitted that they
belonged to gangs.[13] Rather, the low-prestige youths tend to participate
habitually in loose, fluid, shifting bands. Such bands appear to lack regular
leaders, well-defined membership, and clear-cut organization. The comment of an observer in Syracuse is typical. "Leisure time activities seem to
include . . . hanging around in large groups. I would not consider this
a gang since the composition of the group is constantly changing though
some few individuals are always the same."

A knowledgeable boys-worker in Baltimore wrote as follows about the
situation in that city. "Have no gangs. Found clusters of individuals in and
out of school. They just hang around. They are not fighting gangs." The
observer in Buffalo stated: "Organized boys' gangs occasionally have fights.
There are no girl gangs or auxiliaries. Gang activities are mild—usually
consist of threatening clubs and groups from other parts of the city."

These bands hang out on street corners, soda shops, beer joints,
dance halls, and frequently at recreational centers and playgrounds.

Sometimes they just wander about aimlessly, "looking for something
to do." Idle, bored, and unsupervised, they are inclined to be touchy and

[13] Teen-Age Survey, Durham, North Carolina, April 1961.

resentful of such authorities as parents, teachers, ministers, recreation leaders, and policemen. At night, they crowd the dance floors of recreation centers, and, by day, they listen to records in the hangouts, play their transistors, and ride about in jalopies. But mostly they just "yackity-yack." The talk, too, is aimless, full of slang, profanity, and obscenity, and about their own doings, song hits, television shows (The Untouchables, Gunsmoke being favorites), clothes styles, Negro athletes, and so on. The talk, as well as the gregariousness, reveals their intense need to be accepted by peers. Almost always, also, a current of aggression runs just below the surface of this stream of talk—teasing, bantering, boasting, disparaging, blustering, threatening, cursing, playing the dozens. Occasionally, the aggression breaks through the veneer of talk into quick savage fights or delinquent acts.

The research suggests that organized gang behavior is part of the teenage tradition only in specific slum areas of the great cities.[14] When Negro or Puerto Rican families invade these areas and succeed the prior populations, they tend to inherit the juvenile gang tradition along with the houses and institutions. Apparently, Negro teen-agers have not yet come into a tradition of organized gang behavior in the other urban centers. Dan Wakefield explains how Puerto Rican youths in New York acquired the pattern of gang behavior.[15]

Successive migrant groups have lived in similar conditions of poor housing and poverty, and followed similar patterns in forming gangs. The Puerto Rican teen-age gangs of today are not descended from any tradition of the streets of San Juan, but the streets of New York.

ASPIRATION LEVELS

Aspiration patterns provide other keys to Negro teen-age culture. Significant models are compounded of traditional deprivations and the exciting new vistas of opportunity. Low-prestige teen-agers who can see no escape from the racial trap of deprivation tend to look forward to adult work and marriage roles of their social rank. But they have caught something of the spirit of the affluent society and so set great store by money and the things and immediate gratifications that money can buy. Moreover, many have sensed the spirit of quick, easy money through the ethical compromise, the confidence trick, the easy job, and "big shot" symbols. For example, when asked "Is it worse to cheat than to get caught cheating?" 122,

[14] Clifford R. Shaw and Henry D. McKay, *Juvenile Delinquency in Urban Areas* (Chicago: University of Chicago Press, 1942). Frederick M. Thrasher, *The Gang* (Chicago: University of Chicago Press, 1936). Albert K. Cohen, *Delinquent Boys* (Glencoe: Free Press, 1955).

[15] Dan Wakefield, "The Other Puerto Ricans," *New York Times Magazine,* October 11, 1959, p. 24.

or 37 per cent, of 328 students in a southern urban school said, "No." [16]

High-prestige teen-agers and, to a lesser degree, the upward mobile low-prestige ones, too, enjoy wider cultural communication, broader actual experiences, a tradition of long-range aspirations, and a less acute sense of racial entrapment. They are stirred by the ferment of social change and racial advancement that is abroad in the land.[17] The visible Negro success figures, the militant Negro press and organizations, expanding career opportunities, the new romance of engineering and science, and the increased affluence of the Negro middle classes all exert a powerful impact upon their levels and goals of aspiration. As will be shown below, one consequence is the Negro college-student protest movement. The romantic lure of Africa, thanks to stirring native nationalism and the strong pitch of the Peace Corps, is now bursting upon these teen-agers. In addition to Negro white-collar careers, today's teen-agers want to be engineers, scientists, aviators, technicians of all kinds, social workers, professional athletes, entertainers, radio and television workers, and so on.

INTERLUDE OF AGGRESSION

American teen-agers express aggression in the revolt against authority, bravado behavior, delinquency, gang activity, vandalism, and the like. Such forms of aggressive behavior are discussed elsewhere in this volume. For most youngsters, teenhood comprises an interlude of aggression between childhood and adulthood. For Negro teen-agers, the interlude has at least two dimensions that merit examination. For them, it is the hiatus between the awareness of entrapment and the onset of compliance. For Negro teen-agers, too, the interlude is uniquely characterized by purposeful struggle.

Ultimately, most Negro teen-agers abandon the uneven struggle. The low-prestige ones tend to accept defeat in some version of the inferiority pattern. The high-prestige and upward mobile low-prestige teen-agers, however, tend to sublimate the struggle by adopting the middle-class pattern of respectability and formal protest.

Two patterns of aggression, namely, personal hostility and racial protest, comprise distinctive elements of the Negro teen-age culture. The former constitutes a carry-over into teenhood of low-prestige cultural patterns. Racial protest, on the other hand, is a cultural invention of Southern Negro teen-agers and represents a fusion of adolescent aggression, middle-class tradition, and college culture.

[16] Teen-Age Survey, Durham, North Carolina, April 1961.
[17] For a provocative comment on changing Negro teen-agers' aspirations, see Ernest Q. Campbell, "On Desegregation and Matters Sociological" (unpublished working paper, Institute for Research in Social Science, University of North Carolina), pp. 9 ff.

PERSONAL HOSTILITY

For many of the big-city teen-agers, the sublimations of school, recreation center, church, job, and the like are both inadequate and inaccessible. Unexpended aggressions are turned inward upon themselves, their parents, their siblings, their friends, their schoolmates, and other teen-agers. The low-prestige tradition of their families and neighborhoods provides ready-to-hand the patterns and rationalizations of personal aggression.[18] The patterns range from use of derogatory words to deadly weapons, from talk to violence. Familiar examples include cursing, playing the dozens, blustering, threatening, fighting, and carrying knives or even pistols.

Personal aggression is reported from all sections of the country. For example, a perceptive Young Men's Christian Association (YMCA) worker in Baltimore reports that loose aggregations of low-prestige boys, sometimes numbering a hundred or more, roam about the city at night, crashing private parties, and making disturbances.[19] Occasionally, they precipitate fights in which knives and other weapons are flashed. An observer in Detroit wrote as follows: [20]

Boys who have been brought up in very scanty environment learn to fight for everything they want or need. Every new person is originally seen as trying to do the boy out of something. . . . They will pick fights with friends occasionally, but with just as much ferocity as if they had been enemies.

As noted above, profane and obscene language is almost universal among low-prestige boys. The observers suggest that this language constitutes a mode of vicarious aggressive behavior. It is authoritatively reported that the carrying of knives is common among low-prestige individuals. Ninety-two, or 28 per cent, of 328 students in a southern urban high school said they thought it was all right to carry a knife.[21] Two-thirds of 318 students in the same school said they would "fight if someone messes with your money or food."

RACIAL PROTEST

In the racial protest movement, southern Negro college-student teen-agers are creating a tradition of rational and disciplined aggression. The genius of this development is the fact that adolescent aggression against

[18] See Lewis, *Blackways of Kent, op. cit.,* pp. 233–256 *passim.*
[19] Field document.
[20] Field document.
[21] Teen-Age Survey, Durham, North Carolina, April 1961.

authority is fused with struggle for a cause.[22] Ruth Searles and J. Allen Williams, Jr., observe in this connection: [23] "The psychological functions of the movement would be to provide a 'legitimate' outlet for aggression and promote the loss of self through social devotion to a cause."

Although the sit-ins are the best known form of racial protest demonstration, there are at least three others:

1. Applications by Negro children and their parents for public school transfers under the so-called "pupil assignment laws"; and applications of Negro college students for admission to southern state universities.[24]

2. Boycott-picket efforts to promote hiring and/or upgrading of Negro workers in retail stores.

3. Pickets, with supporting boycotts, to promote abandonment of racial segregation in motion picture theaters.

CONCLUSION

Bearing the inscription "Made in America," Negro teen-age culture comprises one submotif in the American cultural mosaic. It is compounded of typical adolescent behavior and unique group patterns, of earnest confidence in future promise and sullen resignation to present deprivation. A northern observer complains that the title "Negro Teen-Age Culture" begs the question, since he sees significant behavior differences as class-linked rather than racial. The southern spectator, however, is likely to be impressed by the Negro teen-age protest demonstrations.

Some thoughtful people believe that the teen-age racial protests have made a substantial impact on contemporary American life. They point to the new electric quality of interracial tension, the widespread response of the public opinion media, and recent changes of institutional structure. Yet, white teen-agers remain largely unresponsive to the challenge of organized serious social action. A few, both southern and northern, participated in the

[22] In the United States, general teen-age action appears to be typically nonserious, nonconstructive, noncause-linked, an expression of what Bernard calls "contra-culture." Witness, for example, recent moblike demonstrations in Fort Lauderdale, Florida, Bowling Green State University, Ohio, and Galveston, Texas. Overt, often organized, sometimes violent politicosocial action, however, appears to be relatively characteristic of teen-agers and young adults in many European, Asian, and African countries.

[23] Ruth Searles and J. Allen Williams, Jr., "Determinants of Negro College Students' Participation in Sit-ins" (unpublished working paper, Institute for Research in Social Science, University of North Carolina, April 2, 1961).

[24] There is a voluminous literature on school desegregation. Among the definitive studies of specific situations, see Wilson and Jane Cassels Record, *Little Rock, U. S. A.* (San Francisco: Chandler Publishing Company, 1960); Ernest Q. Campbell *et al.*, *When a City Closes Its Schools* (Chapel Hill: University of North Carolina, Institute for Research in Social Science, 1960).

racial protest demonstrations. The majority, however, continues to be un-involved with the serious issues of our times.

Two years ago almost no one could have predicted the dime-store sit-ins. It is equally difficult to predict today what Negro teen-agers may be doing two years hence. Some people seem to believe that protest activity is merely a teen-age fad. Some others see in it the wave of the future.

However, some of the trends which may condition Negro teen-age culture in the future are already evident. They include the following:

1. Steadily improving levels of education and general cultural exposure.

2. Widespread increase of the economic resources available to Negroes.

3. Continuing expansion of opportunities for social participation and individual expression.

4. Intensification of the stimulations and incentives to participate and achieve.

5. Growing dissatisfaction with existing gulfs between aspirations and achievements.

It seems likely that Negro teen-agers may become more conscious of the squeeze placed on them by traditional institutions and patterns. One can only hope that the resultant aggressions will be imaginatively sublimated through such mechanisms as protest movements and the Peace Corps.

42

Elizabeth Douvan
Joseph Adelson

SUBCULTURES

*In this excerpt from the report on a nation-wide study of early adoles-
cence, the writers report how adolescent experience is affected by selected
demographic factors, including social class, and growing up in city, farm, or
suburb. The suburbs proved to be most favorable as an environment for teen
development, the farm the least favorable. Life in big cities posed special pressures on parent-child relationships.*

In this chapter we shall look closely at the demographic side of our
findings. Throughout this account we have remarked on demographic
factors in their relation to other variables: sometimes offhandedly, as in
reporting that a certain relationship holds up when, say, social class is
controlled; sometimes systematically, when we have explored the interaction between a demographic factor and other variables. We have just seen,
as an example, that the meaning of full-time maternal employment differs
for middle- and lower-class girls; we also saw that ordinal position, size of
family, and social class, when taken together, can illuminate the psychological meaning of demographic "position." Thus, the first-born girl in a large
and low-status family tends to be antifeminine and gives signs of emotional
disturbance; the first-born girl from a large but high-status family shows no
signs of personal difficulties, and a different posture toward femininity.

In some instances we have noted that demographic factors seem to
enlarge or diminish relationships. For example, low-status girls who have
some share in making rules at home are more independent than low-status
girls who do not; yet they are less so than middle-class girls who report
having their say about rules. Similarly, middle-class boys who are physically
punished have a lower energy-level than others of equal social status, yet
are more active than lower-class boys who are so disciplined. In these cases,
the family's specific practices are apparently supported by other elements
in the class culture. When the family deviates from class norms the effect on

From Elizabeth Douvan and Joseph Adelson, *The Adolescent Experience* (New
York, John Wiley, 1966), pp. 310–319. Reprinted by permission.

adolescent development is not as striking as in those cases where the family's ways are in tune with the norms.

Before we get to the substance of this chapter, we would like to say a few words on the strategy which will guide our report on demographic variables. We are wary of the misplaced encyclopedism which can tempt the investigator, particularly now that computer resources are so readily available. Demographic analyses in a study such as ours—with a large sample and a great number of variables—can yield literally tens of thousands of "findings." If sanity is to be preserved, some principle of selection is essential. We shall report relationships when we believe they add to our understanding of the ways in which demographic characteristics are translated into the adolescent's experience. In some cases we are led by—or, as it may turn out, misled by—established findings and theory on the connections between social structure and experience; in other cases, we follow, informally, our sense of relevance.

URBANIZATION

Two geographic variables were analyzed in relation to specific features of adolescent activities, interests and development. One of these, geographic region, proved disappointing. As far as we can determine, clear regional differences exist only in highly specific activities which depend on climate or special geographic features. Adolescents in the South do not know winter sports; those in the urbanized East report active leisure centered on camping or field interests less often than do children in the West. We found other more interesting differences (for example, in some areas of family interaction and independence training) between adolescents in the North and the South, but almost all of these differences fade when social class or urbanization is controlled. Traditional concepts of child raising are not significantly more common in the South, nor are Southern girls oriented toward a traditionally conceived adult feminine role. These and other stereotyped notions of a more stable and tradition-tied Southern culture may have some validity for a very small upper-class segment of the South, but no general validity can be claimed for them. At least in areas covered by our studies, the unique Southern culture, if it exists, does not have a visible effect on adolescent development.

The second geographic variable, urbanization, gives more interesting findings. Here too we find obvious differences in activities—city youngsters do not camp, and those from farms have less access to organized social activities and the arts—but we find other differences too. Two groups stand out in this analysis—adolescents from suburban communities in the major metropolitan areas and youngsters from truly rural areas. These two environments have an impact on adolescent development more comprehensive than any simple density factor can explain. They seem to represent rather separate and coherent cultures with distinctive styles of family life and child raising; other points on the urbanization scale look more like variations on (certain definable and) relatively narrow themes.

Perhaps this is a clue to the most efficient presentation in this section. We shall first consider findings that most clearly tie to the density variable, those that change directly with community size; we shall then describe the special characteristics of suburban and farm children.

Generally, adolescents from smaller communities have more active, diversified, and organized leisure lives. Adolescents in large cities spend less time with their parents and report somewhat less congenial family relationships. They are more often either rebellious or overdependent on adult authority. And they show an eagerness for adult status in several ways. When asked what age group they would choose as companions in a club, big city youngsters are much more likely than those from smaller communities to want to be youngest in a group of older children. When they suggest activities for a club, they give a much narrower range of activities and concentrate specifically on social activities—parties and dances. They rarely suggest outdoor programs, which is to be expected, but neither do they mention any of the arts and crafts, hobbies, or individual sports as often as adolescents from small communities. City youngsters do not hold jobs as often as do boys and girls from smaller cities and towns, but when they do, they work longer hours and in more adult-like positions. City girls have heavier home duties than girls in small communities, and they begin steady dating at an earlier age; although dating in general is more common and begins earlier in the smaller towns. City girls more often do not date at all or date only one boy.

The complexity of life in a major city imposes certain pressures on the family and on parent-child relationships. Parents do not have the closer control of adolescent activity that comes with the parent-involving organized leisure and joint family activities that are common in smaller communities. The city child spends more of his free time beyond the range of control of parents and parent surrogates. The less active, less organized leisure of city children seems to reflect the fact that cities are not designed for children. Perhaps this is why city children seem so eager to arrive at adulthood. The city offers most of its advantage to adults.

SUBURBS

In this respect—in the degree of orientation to child-rearing—the suburbs are polar to the central city. The environment not only relieves the child of having to adapt to a complex adult life pattern, but in fact seems consciously designed for children. Suburban children differ from those who live in urban centers in all the areas we have described above as distinguishing between city children and those from smaller communities. The large cities, smaller cities (50,000 to 300,000), and towns (10,000 to 50,000) consistently arrange themselves in order of size, with leisure activity increasing as community size decreases. The suburbs are out of order in the sense that they are like the small cities, only more so. It is the suburban adolescents who exemplify what is often taken to be the American pattern of active organized leisure. They stand out in the range and diversity of leisure, in dating, group membership, and joint family activity.

Two features of the pattern are noteworthy. One is that, although suburban children are unusually advantaged in their present lives, they also show the heightened interest in adult status we noted among city children. They are precocious in social development, dating earlier and more frequently than the youngsters in any of the other categories (although they do not go steady as often as city children); they mention social activities first in suggesting programs for a club, although they also suggest other kinds of activities; they clearly prefer coed to like-sexed groups, and they show the same preference that city children do for companions older than themselves. Certain other findings, to be presented shortly, lead us to conclude that in suburban children this eagerness for adult activity is part of a general drive toward maturity rather than a desire to be done with the disadvantages of childhood.

A second feature about the activity preferences of suburban children is that when we look at responses to the questions, "What kind of activities do you think a club like this should have?" "What do you think boys (girls) your age like to do best?" we find that suburban children suggest a profile of activities that is not distinguished for the two sexes; in all other urbanization categories activity profiles do differ sharply for boys and girls. The leisure activities suburban boys and girls actually engage in are also more alike than is true in any of the urbanization categories. Girls in the suburbs play games and sports more than do city girls or those from smaller communities, and they do not show the marked preference for traditional feminine activities that we find in girls from smaller towns and cities. Boys in the suburbs both know and suggest hobbies and creative activities more than do boys in any other community setting.

Our interest in this group of findings centers on the lack of sex-specific activity prescriptions. Many observers have suggested that American society is diluting the meaning of the sex roles, and that in part this dilution is produced by a socialization system which does not distinguish between activities appropriate for boys and girls. Our data support this contention to a limited extent, as far as it applies to the suburban milieu. The fact that suburban children are those with whom most social critics live and have contact should caution those who generalize easily about American adolescents as a whole.

Beyond the area of leisure activities, suburban adolescents look different from the general population in several aspects of ego development, and in certain phases of family relations. They stand out, as we hinted earlier, in their orientation toward the future and adulthood. When we ask what they do that makes them feel important and useful, suburban boys and girls more often allude to taking adult responsibilities. They tend to have a more extended time perspective than other adolescents, and to have plans for the future which are both well-formulated and strong in achievement themes. They more often plan to go to college and to enter the professions.

Relationships in suburban families show the influence of liberal modern child-raising ideology. We find here both high parent involvement in the child's life and activities and an apparent encouragement of the child's developing autonomy. Adolescents in this setting are generally less authority-reliant than their age-mates from other kinds of communities, and they more commonly disagree with their parents (particularly about ideas). Suburban boys depend less on parental opinion in deciding issues of personal taste; girls more often have a part in making rules at home. In these respects suburban youngsters seem to have achieved greater autonomy and to have done so with their parents' encouragement. A further sign of a distinctive suburban family culture emerges in the area of discipline. Suburban parents use psychological punishment more and physical punishment less than do parents in large cities or smaller communities.

We wonder, of course, whether these findings may be the result of status or education differences, since the suburbs are in all likelihood heavily advantaged in both regards. We do note a dilution of certain of the relationships when we control father's occupation or education.[1] In the activity areas, suburban youngsters at every status level stand out in contrast to those from other kinds of communities, and the difference is especially large in the lower-class levels. In other areas of ego development and in family relationships, some of the variation we have noted is indeed attributable to status. Although differences do not disappear, they are reduced when status is held constant. Our interpretation of these findings follows: the suburban community is dominated by highly educated adults whose conceptions of family relations and of child raising are infused with values on activity, autonomy, and achievement. These families set the atmosphere in the community, encourage community facilities for young people, and press for certain practices and policies in the educational system. The advantages they seek and develop for their own children (for example, advantages in leisure facilities) become advantages for all the children of the community. Activity differences between suburban children and those from other community settings do not disappear when class is

[1] The relationship between suburban residence and status is not as striking as we might expect.

controlled, and, as we have said, differences are generally larger in the lower class.

When we look at other areas of ego functioning, we are considering aspects of development less effectively touched by the community. To some extent community leaders affect the orientation and philosophy of the schools, and this in turn may have an impact on the development of all children in the community. This may account for the greater autonomy of suburban children vis-à-vis adult authority. Irrespective of social status, the suburban children tend to be more independent in their stance toward unrelated adults. The areas in which suburb-nonsuburb differences depend largely on status differences all involve close family interaction, specific behaviors or patterns of behavior which would presumably be less open to the effects of the educational system or other community agencies.

FARM

By and large we find, as we have reported, that the smaller the community in which an adolescent lives, the greater his advantages in leisure activities, opportunities for independence, and other areas of personal and social development. At the lower end of community size, however, this trend reverses itself; youngsters from rural areas are as deprived as those from the meanest urban environment. They have fewer opportunities in all areas of life—in leisure activities, organizational membership, part-time employment, and friendly interaction with unrelated adults. And they show a pattern of unique characteristics that goes well beyond community factors, a pattern that indicates a distinctive subculture with a family style and ideology of its own. The only group in our studies which shares even part of the pattern is the extreme lower-class urban group, those children who represent unskilled working-class families.

Farm children seem to be less at ease socially than city children. They are less poised in the interview, less confident, and less organized. They embarrass more easily than other adolescents, and they are rated lower in verbal ability both by interviewers and by coders who read their transcribed responses.

In the crucial adolescent areas—autonomy, internalization, and attachment to peers—they also look less advanced than their urban peers. We find among farm families a strong and traditional parental control, slow to give privilege or loosen reins, often enforced by physical punishment (although, peculiarly, farm children often report psychological punishment too). Farm children rely heavily on adult authority and generally on external controls. They are usually dependent on the family—they choose their models within the family; they have few disagreements with their parents. Farm boys look to their parents for advice on issues of taste; farm girls spend their leisure time within the family more commonly than do other girls. On most of the items used to measure independence from the family or internalization, farm boys and girls are significantly less developed than city children. And their parents do not apparently encourage autonomy. Farm girls infrequently have a part in making rules at home, and they do not think of self-reliance or independence as the thing their parents want or expect of them as often as other girls do. Farm children, both boys and girls, are disciplined with physical punishment more commonly than adolescents from any other community background.

Thus, the rural group seems the most distinctive of our geographic categories. Adolescents in this setting present a remarkably uniform picture of traditional conceptions of family life and of their limited effects on adolescent development. The most conspicuous effect of the farm environment and culture seems to be a severe limitation on the adolescent's social growth. Beyond this we find a marked inhibition of fantasy. Farm children, as we have said, have a more difficult time in the interview, and are less verbal than city youngsters. These differences, in combination with their less highly developed fantasy life, might lead us to conclude that American farm families are a low IQ group.[2] Although this may be the case, we doubt it. For one thing we do not find gross differences in educational achievement between farm and nonfarm parents. If we exclude from urban families the professional group of highly educated parents, the distributions of fathers' education for urban and rural samples are indistinguishable. We believe that farm youngsters are less developed both socially and internally because their environment either fails to stimulate (in the case of fantasy) or actively inhibits (in autonomy and internalization) this development.

SOCIAL CLASS

Social status is surely the most thoroughly explored variable in all of the social sciences. Even if we limit ourselves to studies conducted on adolescent samples, the number of references which report class differences is nearly overwhelming. Among the more important reports and analyses are those of Hollingshead (1949), Himmelweit (1955), Centers (1949), Lipset and Bendix (1960), Coleman (1961), to mention but a few.

What can we expect to find? Obviously, the mere fact of privilege, and its effects, should make its way into the findings. Higher-status children will have had greater opportunities for leisure and in groups devoted to it, and this should have some influence on their social relationships both with peers and adults. Socialized to middle-class standards, at home in a world of middle-class premises, we expect them to show greater poise in an inter-

---

[2] Compare this to Terman's norms, which do indicate a relatively lower intelligence among rural populations.

view with an adult middle-class interviewer. Their sense of the future, their sense of themselves in the future, should be firmer, and more articulated. The middle-class is future-oriented, and in any case they can count on parental support to ease and guide their way in the future. The values of achievement and self-determination, although generally felt in American society, are more forcefully implanted in the middle-class family and milieu, and in addition are buttressed by a more favorable material climate, by the fact that opportunities to achieve and to determine one's fate are more likely to be present. Another source of differences between the classes will be found in the ideology and practice of child-rearing. Our findings have led us to expect an authoritarian parental climate in the working class, and an easier (although internally perhaps more rigorous) one in the middle class. This difference may well influence the child's sense of his freedom, the way he views authority, and ultimately the moral style he composes.

On the other hand, we did not expect class differences to be quite as sharp as much of the literature has seemed to suggest. Both life styles and ideological modes overlap strata, and there is, we felt, an American consensus which in many areas overrides the marginal differences associated with social status. There is, of course, a world of difference between a physician's son and an unskilled laborer's son; but perhaps there is not so much difference, if any at all, between the bank teller's boy and the electrician's boy. Furthermore, class differences, we thought, might be stronger when tested in adults than in adolescents. We were impressed by the extremely strong effects associated with mobility aspirations. Many of those in the working class are aimed upward, and have absorbed the attitudes and viewpoints of the middle class; and some middle-class youngsters seem to be drifting downward. The fluidity of status among adolescents, the contamination of position by aspiration would, we suspect, act to weaken class effects in our sample.

These, then, were the expectations with which we initiated the social class analysis. We shall look at the results of the analysis shortly, after one additional comment, about measurement and the relative effectiveness of various class indices.

In our studies we had three potential measures of social class—father's occupation, father's education, and a crude economic index based on the family's possession of certain consumer goods. We did not have information about family income since we found in pretests that adolescents rarely have such information. Of the three available measures, father's occupation is by far the most useful and yields the most significant findings. We cannot place farm families in a social class category on the basis of occupation, but these are virtually the only cases lost. Almost all children know what work their fathers do, while a large (13%) proportion do not know the father's educational background. Even when the adolescent claims to know, we find many cases in which the information he gives seems factually unreliable.

The economic index we used distinguishes very poor families from others, but it is not effective in differentiating middle-class families from the large body of blue-collar working-class families. Owning a home, having a telephone, and owning a car are so common in our society that they no longer provide a meaningful measure of status. We did find the economic index useful in assigning farm families to two rough status categories, and we used it for this purpose.

REFERENCES

R. Centers, *The Psychology of Social Classes: A Study of Class Consciousness* (Princeton: Princeton University Press, 1949).

J. Coleman, *The Adolescent Society* (New York: Free Press, 1961).

Hilde Himmelweit, "Socioeconomic Background and Personality," *International Social Science Bulletin,* Vol. 7 (1955), pp. 29–34.

A. B. Hollingshead, *Elmtown's Youth* (New York: Wiley, 1949).

S. M. Lipset and R. Bendix, *Social Mobility in Industrial Society* (Berkeley and Los Angeles: University of California Press, 1960).

43

Robert Coles
Joseph Brenner

AMERICAN YOUTH IN A SOCIAL STRUGGLE (II): THE APPALACHIAN VOLUNTEERS

College students from across the country spent the summers of 1965 and 1966 helping Appalachian mountain people. This article describes the social order and psychological characteristics of the people of Appalachia. The excerpt given here (pp. 35–44) tells of adolescence in this region.

OBSERVATIONS

In a sense, the students who were Appalachian Volunteers had to come to terms right off with "life" as it is lived in the region—by the individuals who make up its population. Just as no account of what the Volunteers did can ignore the economic, cultural, and historical forces each student—in whatever town or hollow—had to comprehend, it is equally certain that none of the Volunteers could escape the brunt of the region's very particular social and psychological "climate," its set of customs and habits, in the words of W. J. Cash its "mind." (4) There are many ways to be rich or poor; and certainly there are many ways to bring up children and get along with one's neighbors, relatives—or strangers.

In this paper we shall try to describe the Appalachian "life" which the young Volunteers encountered, as well as the actual work they did. We intend at a later time to discuss some of the psychological hazards such youth face; in sum, they are very much the same hazards we have already described for the students who worked in Mississippi. (10)

From Robert Coles and Joseph Brenner, "American Youth in a Social Struggle (II): The Appalachian Volunteers," *American Journal of Orthopsychiatry,* Vol. 38, No. 1 (1968), pp. 31–46. Copyright, the American Orthopsychiatric Association, Inc. Reproduced by permission.

GROWING UP IN APPALACHIA

To begin with, one has to give people—most of them—credit for a rather considerable emotional leeway: in the mind, kindness and spite, generosity and envy, vitality and discouragement may be found—usually—in enough supply to "explain" all sorts of behavior. The important point is that what is in the mind, its fantasies or dreams, cannot fully explain what goes on in the street or the market place. Put differently, we know more about what people *think* than why they *act* as they do. Indeed, when we want to study as psychiatrists the actions of people, the very nature of the research is different—it being one thing to ask a fearful patient in an office what is on his mind, and quite another to learn (by seeking him out in his home) why a Kentucky mountaineer gets upset about a federal program that "outsiders" are gratuitously (so he sees it) forcing on him to no good end that he can discover.

If the Southern white is indiscriminately called racist, the Southern Negro characterized as frightened and unimaginative, the migrant farmer as shiftless and indigent (these are the people whose children one of us has studied over the past years), then the Appalachian, the mountaineer who lives on or near the hills of states like Kentucky and West Virginia, is likely to be quickly labeled sullen, suspicious, backward, and significantly apathetic. The breezy visitor—be he student, tourist, or earnest worker of one sort or another trying to do *his* (well-meaning) best for *those* (poor, "unfortunate") people—looks about him and soon enough draws his conclusions. Often though they are conclusions easily made somehow worthier or more valid by resort to the language of the social sciences: it is a subculture, Appalachia. The people are inordinately "passive-aggressive," prone to fits of alcohol and violence that alternate with longer episodes of inertia, resignation, and depression. The social structure of the region is rural, rigid, closed, excessively traditional. Finally, in the words of the historian Arnold Toynbee, "The 'Mountain People' of Appalachia are ci-devant heirs of Western Civilization who have relapsed into barbarism under the depressing effect of a challenge which has been inordinately severe." (19)

We have no intention of adding yet another conceptual generalization to those already made about Appalachian people. What we would like to do is rather in the opposite direction: offer the direct observations of two psychiatrists in the hope that they may give a view of what it is often like for a child to grow up in the particular kind of country that is the Appalachian mountains—in comparison, say, with Southern children of both races in the Mississippi Delta, or migrant farm children who trek up and down the Atlantic Coast by the season, or children who live in a Northern ghetto or middle-class suburb. That said, we will start at the mountain child's birth and work our way up his or her years.

A baby born to a woman who lives in the region is unlikely to get constant medical scrutiny, with vitamins, fluorides, innoculations, and immediate tests or treatment for metabolic or congenital diseases. He is more than likely a child whose growth and development is not followed closely before birth by an obstetrician, and after birth by a pediatrician. In the past he may well have been delivered at home; in some cases that holds to this day. Nurses and relatives, and even doctors, do for many women in their bedrooms what in urban, middle-class America turns out to be a week-long medical ritual: hospitalization, the doctor's arrival, the labor room, the delivery room, the recovery room, and finally the ward, with its extended isolation of the mother from her newborn child as well as from her other children, her husband, and her neighbors. Again and again we heard mountain women tell us that they wanted to go to a hospital to have their children but leave in a day or two at the most—and they were obliged.

Appalachian mothers to our eyes seem at once close to their children and yet detached from them; close, because they hold them with obvious warmth and delight, and breast-feed them with pleasure whenever they cry for milk; detached, because the baby's presence, his movements and noises, do not command from the mother a continuing attention or at least an obvious concern. In this respect we would contrast mountain women to the well-to-do suburban mother, for whom child-rearing is a *very* serious (and sometimes anxious) business; to the Negro mothers we know, who immediately upon the child's birth establish an almost devotional closeness to him; and finally, to the rural white mothers of the South, who we think are less intimate with their children than their Negro counterparts, and far more casual toward them (if that is the word, and we are not sure it is) than is the case with Appalachian mothers.

In example: a colicky infant recently fed but still crying loud and strong will be held and held by his Negro mother; he will be held then put down by his Southern white mother, who nevertheless will be made fretful and irritable; he will be alternately held and put down by his middle-class suburban mother while, you can be sure, a doctor will be called, a book read, perhaps some medicine or a pacifier given. In the case of the Appalachian mother, the child's cry will be heard but somehow accepted as (so I've heard several women say) "the way it goes for a while." Of course we do not mean to be rigid about these distinctions. They merely represent certain general trends, the product, no doubt, of complicated historical, social, cultural, and psychological influences which in given locations among certain people sort themselves out into particular patterns. Just as it is not at all irrelevant to remember that Negro mothers once (not so long ago) had to surrender their children to the demands of slave markets—and thus

have good historic reason to keep close to their children now—so it may
well be that a mother herself born and reared in a region whose fate seems
unshakable will find the vicissitudes of the growing baby to be yet another
reflection of just that fate.

What can be said about the way Appalachian children are characteristically trained and taught at home—about the way they learn their rights
and wrongs, learn to see the world about them, and get along with their
parents, their brothers and sisters, their neighbors and relatives? We have
again had to take notice of the very real relationship between the region's
past, its physical setting, its social and cultural characteristics, and the
quality of its family life, including child-rearing practices. In the outlying
valleys and hollows, where plumbing may be virtually nonexistent, one can
see an almost uncanny mixture of the tidy, the orderly, the neat and the
messy, the littered, and the unkempt. Among migrants and sharecroppers
we have come to expect a pervasive lack of interest in the home, its appoint-
ments and appearance. (9) "We leave them, one after the other," a migrant
farm worker once told one of us when he was asked whether he ever tried
to give his home the same scrubbing he was then giving his car. Likewise,
among tenant farmers in the rural South we have seen a similar indifference,
with shrugged shoulders the response to a child's unruly assault upon what
meager, already damaged furniture there is.

We need not describe the prevalent American middle-class regard for
antisepsis, lustre, newness, and property that is "kept up." We judge Appalachian mountain parents to be somewhere in between their rural neighbors to the South and their urban neighbors both inside and outside the
region. Children are trained to use the woods or an outhouse at a time many
city doctors would today call rather early—before the third year begins—
and they are trained to do so by mothers who appear anxious and determined. Migrant farm mothers quickly and decisively manage to teach their
children to use as a bathroom whatever field is nearby; but mountain women
stay put, and they want an outhouse used rather than a nearby plot of land
that, of course, will always be the same land. They thus spend more time
getting the child to comply with their wishes. They start earlier than do other
rural women we know, and they themselves become angrier and more upset
while doing the job. Yet, in contrast to many comfortably urban housewives,
they do have an alternative for their children—who are often allowed to be
quite thoughtless and even destructive within the home, crashing about and
creating disorder not in a "play room" but anywhere they please.

In point of fact, the mountain child is allowed a good deal of freedom
with his body, his legs and arms as he learns to explore, climb, run, and
strike out. Brothers and sisters are likely to be much closer to one another;
indeed, they live and play together without evidence of the charged, defiant
"individuality" one finds so often in middle-class city homes. We are not
saying that there is no "sibling rivalry," no tension and envy between the

children of the hollows, but we are asserting a greater sense of family, of shared allegiance to parents and grandparents that somehow makes for relatively more cooperative activity, frolic, and (eventually) work than one sees among many other American children.

Boys and girls are not given individual rooms but sleep together, often as if a community themselves, bed beside bed, not always with one occupant to each mattress. Families tend to be large, and there is just so much time a mother can have for any one child. Beyond that, however, is the more positive value of kith and kin, of doing things together—particularly since there are only a limited number of people around at all. Toys, reading matter, coloring sets, are of course far less in evidence than the child's very real and very actual engagement with indoor and outdoor *tasks*. While migrant children of five or six are often taken to work and left beside the fields to play, and sharecropper children left at home with a grandparent, mountain children are set to work: doing errands, helping about the home or the land, learning what often is far more important to them than school—how to use one's hands in farming, in caring for animals, in fetching water or preparing food. The knife is mastered by boys, and perhaps a guitar. Dogs are companions and helpers in hunting. Girls learn to work the land and look after animals. The mountain child does not spend an extended time with books, in listening to stories, in hearing fantasies of one kind or another, so familiar an experience to some American children. There is adventure enough, there are good times enough, but they usually occur in the midst of doing things, going somewhere, trying to start or finish something. "The kids relax together after they've done their chores, and I tell them they have to, because there are more to come." Those words from a mother in Kentucky reminded us that play can be an interlude, not a goal in itself.

For hollow children school is also an interlude, even for those who want very much to make it a long one, and indeed use the interlude as a launching pad for a better life, a different life, and inevitably, a life far away. The relationship of the rural schools of the region to its family life —not to mention its political life—is no easily discussed matter. The one-room schoolhouse particularly, but also the larger schools, are frequently the single buildings whose activities and functions unite in a personal way people spread over considerable distances. For millions of American children elsewhere, the first day of school marks a decisive break with the past and a nervous entrance into an important unknown. There are tears, from both parents and the young, and enough anxiety in some of them to forbode a variety of future difficulties. Indeed, while there are not more than a few hundred child psychiatrists in this nation, I dare say all of them find that the so-called "learning problems" or "school phobias" make up a very large part of their practice. In contrast, we have seen few of those "neurotic" problems in mountain schools. The teachers report retarded children, or what they call "slow children," but they do not describe (and we have not seen in our classroom or home observations) that particular mixture of ability and nonperformance, of anxious effort and surprising collapse, of earnest desire and almost retaliatory reluctance that characterizes the child with a "learning block."

Appalachian children often play near their schools, and may go visit them with their brothers or sisters before they ever formally (or rather, informally) enroll themselves. The teacher is, of course, a neighbor, and if a person of considerable influence and significance, still a neighbor. We do not mean to belabor the obvious, but one has to think in contrast of migrant children, some lucky to find their way to any school, and others wandering from one strange school to another. Or of the ghetto schools, large and impersonal like many first-rate suburban ones, but also dreary, rat-infested symbols not of an "interlude" but a dead end.

In brief, then, the school emphasizes what the home teaches the mountain child: the definition of the community. If there are any American children who understand the meaning of *territoriality* as it has recently been described by ethologists, they are to be found in the hills of Appalachia. What city folk call a "neighborhood school" is of course no such thing in comparison to the one-room school house—but even the regional schools we have visited are by comparison a no-man's land crowded with strangers. In a sense, then, the mountain school emphasizes the relative isolation or loneliness of the child by bringing together those whose fate is similar. We hear a good deal about the school's role in teaching children to know and feel at home with "others," with the diverse population that makes up this country. A school can also confirm the child's sense of what he *already* knows—by telling him that people are the same as far elsewhere as he is ever apt to go.

It is during the first school years, anyway, that the child begins to learn almost hungrily about the larger world that exists outside his home and backyard. For the majority of American children of five to ten, both people and machines appear as constant sources of confusion, fascination, instruction, and possible danger. The body's natural urge to move and exercise its growing bones and muscles meets up with the limitations of an exceedingly complicated human and technological world. The child learns about streets and traffic, property limits and restrictions, the laws of entry and exit in buildings. If he is a Negro child there is a whole world of special rules and fears to master and have at one's command—yes, fears, because without fear a colored child in the South may eventually lose his life, and in the North run into any number of embarrassing and even dangerous situations.

Even in the countryside around our cities the child has to learn much more than we sometimes realize, much of it information that regulates and controls his life, his actions, his sense of space and time. A white mother we know who recently came North from Kentucky expressed her surprise and dismay as follows: "You get up here, and you can get a job better than back home, but whether it's worth it or not, to tell the truth I'm not sure. The other day I told my husband that I don't think my children ever see the earth anymore. There are the buildings, and the sidewalk, and the roads, then there's some more buildings. Outside in the back, it's all brick and what isn't is covered with garbage and cans and glass and paper; so if there's the ground underneath, no one can see it. I used to hear my daddy tell us one day he'd take us to Cincinnati or Chicago, and then we'd see the big buildings and the airports. But the way I see it, I'm going to be telling my little kids that someday we'll go back home, and they'll see what the earth looks like, and the trees, and then they'll be able to walk as they please, and they won't have to worry about red lights and green lights, and what the signs say and the lines on the road and the clock telling you to go here and there, the way it does for them at school every ten minutes or so my daughter tells me. Now, here in the city they even say the air is bad, and it's hurting your lungs, so I'm waiting for them to tell us how much we should breathe in by the minute."

There it is, put as bluntly as it should be—the meaning of migration to the child. In those words, also, one finds evidence of what children who don't leave our rural country, in this case our rural mountain country, can take for granted—space, time, movement, and a good deal of natural life and animal life that many children see only in those notorious primers.

What one finds then in mountain children is their developing intimacy with the soil, the land's surface and variations, its changing height, its bodies of water, its ability to produce food or supply ore. One also sees children who live closely together, but have wide distances to travel or use for play —distances always defined, it must be added, by hills or mountains that for boys and girls are impassable. If cars come, they do so as an event, and animals are as familiar as the automobile engine. What animals teach children, and how children use animals is itself a subject for an essay—though since psychiatrists seem to live in cities, we doubt it will be written. Sex may be a mystery to large numbers of middle-class children whose parents are "inhibited," whose lives are sheltered and heavily weighted toward "privacy"; but not so for boys and girls who live intimately with horses and dogs, chickens and pigs. Children learn to care for animals, to feed them and clean up after them, to help them in sickness and profit from the various rewards they offer, to have them as company, a kind of uncomplicated, nonhuman company—perhaps more easily loved, or abused.

The drawings one of us asked young Appalachian children to do show how very different their world is to the one usually painted or sketched by middle-class children from either the city or the suburbs. Land, trees, flowers, animals, the sky and the sun appear regularly, and not as some decorative afterthought. Indeed, what we find lacking in the pictures of mountain children are buildings and machines, roads and traffic, even, in a significant number of cases, people. These children after all paint what they see and have come to perceive—though not self-consciously—as their world.

Next, what of adolescence in western North Carolina, or eastern Kentucky? At that time a youth looks both backward and forward with a special intensity and vulnerability, and learns what the society (as well as his or her own body or daydreams and nightmares) has to say. Once again we have to contrast the rural Appalachian youth with his counterparts in other sections of this country. In times of crisis—and adolescence is likely to be such a time—what might otherwise go unnoticed becomes rather apparent. Coming of age in the mountain families we have studied is, literally, growing up in a family—and not leaving it conclusively, rebelling from it dramatically, scorning it eagerly, or doing anything possible to make its life hard and troubled. A nation that knows widespread delinquency—of a kind that is commonly serious crime rather than a variety of petty, frivolous, or "symbolic" misdemeanors—will be interested in looking at the relationship between the nature of the mountain family and the young people who live in those families—very often never to leave them.

Even before adolescence, mountain children learn that a family is no laughing matter—no temporary arrangement, characterized by divorce, constant movement, and a strictly limited membership, lucky to include anyone outside a set of parents and, most likely, a matching set of children. Kin—relatives of one sort or another—have a real and well-known meaning in the region, but we are not so sure the psychiatric implications of that meaning have been spelled out. American child psychiatrists tend to treat children whose loves and hates are narrowly confined to a mother and a father and perhaps one or two brothers or sisters. When one of us left such work, gave up a position in a children's hospital in Boston to work in the South with white and Negro children going through the social crisis of school desegregation, he had to accommodate himself to children who grew up in homes where fathers were often absent, more children were around, and in particular grandmothers were extremely important figures, even among white families in the rural South. Yet, nowhere down there did he meet up with a real *sense* of family, only a change in the nature of the family. It was in western North Carolina that he began to see what a difference uncles and aunts and cousins can make to a growing child—that is, when such relatives are felt to be a real part of the family, not vaguely connected to it.

The intensity between parents and children can be attenuated when there are many children and many "parents"—grandparents, great aunts and uncles, aunts and uncles, older cousins who in fact are parents themselves. Children in the hollows are very conscious of who they are, of what their name means, of who is kin to them, of what blood means. "Who am I," one hears from our middle-class college youth so often. In fact, Erik Erikson's work on identity (12) has achieved prominence in this country for a very good reason: immigrant groups have come here and spread over the land, all too commonly surrendering themselves and their children to the dispersal that our expansive technological society seems to ask of its members. If there were advantages—money, comfort, success, the new roots of California, the eastern suburbs—there was also a price to pay, in feelings of rootlessness and an almost desperate need for attachment to a plot of land, to the house on the land, to those few who live in the house. We are not claiming a social cause for all the mental ills of children; but for the forms some of them take, yes. The rivalries and fears, the "blocks" and terrors in mountain children are of a different order than those treated in middle-class child guidance clinics. And certainly the intense private relationship between the growing mountain child and his parents is far less prevalent than is the case in, say, Boston or perhaps any region of the country outside Appalachia.

For the adolescent, home can and does become a touchy subject. But again we have to comment on the difference between a youth who may have "little" (in the economic sense) ahead of him, but a firm idea of exactly who he is, where he comes from, and even what he would like (if it were possible to have it)—the difference between him and a youth who has a "lot," though he is uneasy about how he will keep it, and about where he will have to go or what he will have to do, almost from year to year. It is absurd to turn the harsh destiny that many Appalachian youth constantly must face into a story of serenity and joy; but it also gets us nowhere to see only the weakness of their position, the gloom and frustration they face because of the scarcity of jobs throughout a region—let us remember—they leave reluctantly, and always with the hope of returning.

They want to return because they have strong ties to cousins, to neighbors, to a host of relatives as well as to parents. (15) They thus stand out as psychological exceptions in a nation that has made almost a virtue of youth's rebellion and fast departure from home—often enough a final departure. We are a country where long-distance calls occasionally remind families that in fact they once existed. We need not remind anyone who knows Kentucky or West Virginia how faithfully their roads receive the return of native youth, gone North to work, but in mind and spirit still home, and ready to prove it come weekend or holiday.

Most of these youths are loyal to old but still persuasive traditions. They want to work, but generally not in order to surpass their brothers or friends. There is a powerful ethic of active sharing and of a shared fate, a shared access to whatever there is. Obviously even in the poorest counties there are a few who have more than the rest, but we suspect those few know they are striking exceptions. Indeed, the open violence endemic to some counties may well come from the conflict between an ideal of relative equality and a reality that is characterized by grave inequalities.

We must ask how mountain youths handle the tensions that go with little or no work and with a family life that is wanted but nevertheless deprives its young members, at a sensitive time, of considerable freedom and independence. For one thing, there are friends, and together people can often manage what alone they cannot. There is an ironic mixture of isolation and intimacy in those lonely hill people—and among the youths in particular one can see how the dangers of individual loneliness or anxiety are countered by the formation of cliques, perhaps ever so small and innocuous in comparison to these seen in the city but nonetheless vital and helpful to the young men involved.

Young women of course tend to stay nearer home and help in the daily chores of rural living. The division of labor between men and women can be dramatically sharp, but also blurred, particularly where farming is done. Certainly a number of young women find their way into teaching or nursing, and often emerge the mainstay of their future family, psychologically as well as economically. On the other hand, the kind of matriarchy that observers describe among lower class Negroes is not the rule in Appalachia.

Passivity, fear, dependency, insularity—they are all words that have their relevance in any description of Appalachian people. Still, there is another way of seeing them and their "character." They are stubborn and proud people, and very much attached to what they know and feel to be both familiar and "right." They may appear isolated to an outsider, but they are members of a community whose solidarity is real, even as its definition is; certainly the credentials required for membership in it are clear-cut and far less confusing (or even sinister) than those imposed on millions of other lonely Americans by many other social "communities."

In fact, for all the isolation one sees in those mountains, homes separated from homes by miles of woods, hollows virtually oblivious to the outside world, mountains sealing off whole towns from all but the most determined technological attack, the youth of Appalachia impress us as far less distrustful than those we have seen in other rural communities, whether white or Negro. By that we mean distrustful *to one another*. In fact, once grown up we think Appalachian people tend to be patient, shrewd, and resigned—but also dependent on one another, if in a characteristically "formal" way. Since families mean a lot, in old age they continue to mean a lot. The elderly are usually spared that final sense of abandonment and uselessness so commonly the fate of the middle-class, suburban aged. Life goes on within the family for young adults and older ones: work or idleness, hunting and fishing, church, sitting, meeting up with neighbors, an unhurried life, both formal and informal in its emotional tone.

Against the background of such a survey of human development as it takes place in a particular region, what can one say in summary about the psychological problems and potentialities in Appalachian people? We have described people hemmed in from the rest of the country. We have emphasized the relatively quiet, unassuming quality to the people, their reserved almost shy appearance often masking a wry acceptance of hardship rather than a devotion to it as a virtue in itself—though we have admittedly met some Calvinist mountaineers. With regard to sex, the region is loyal to its past; the subject is not mentioned, but clearly the practice continues. Families are large, and sex is done, not constantly hinted at or turned to increasingly bizarre humor. In that sense we judge America's upper-middle-class sexual morality far more Victorian (in an inverted fashion) than Appalachia's. Perhaps it is because the region was sheltered from the worst of the nineteenth century; just as much of it is still sheltered from the worst (but the best, too) of the twentieth.

Finally, in an area where there isn't much at all to go around, where land and money are precious even as families are large, where work is by no means to be taken for granted, what there *is* must be regulated, apportioned, and transmitted by firm habit and law, or a struggle may arise. One does not have to spend too much time in a hollow to see and hear the people struggling with one another in those half-concealed ways they do everywhere, but especially so where the stakes are virtually for survival. Jokes and contests, drinking bouts and dances, all provide avenues of "release," especially so in a tight-knit, circumscribed community.

It is there, in those small communities and some larger ones, that the Volunteers stayed. What we have just described, a regional way of life, is what they each encountered—and more, had to confront. . . .

REFERENCES

1. Agee, J. 1959. A Death in the Family. Avon Books, New York.
2. Anderson, S. 1935. Puzzled America. Scribner's, New York.
3. Brooks, M. 1965. The Appalachians. Houghton Mifflin, Cambridge.
4. Cash, W. J. The Mind of the South. Knopf, New York.
5. Caudill, H. M. 1962. Night Comes to the Cumberlands: A Biography of a Depressed Area. Atlantic-Little, Brown, Boston.
6. Coles, R. 1963. Southern children under desegregation. Amer. J. Psychiat. 120(4).
7. Coles, R. 1963. Serpents and doves: nonviolent youth in the south. *In* Youth: Change and Challenge. Erik Erikson, ed. Basic Books, New York.
8. Coles, R. 1964. Social struggle and weariness. Psychiat. 27(4).
9. Coles, R. 1965. The lives of migrant farm workers. Amer. J. Psychiat. 122(3).
10. Coles, R., and J. Brenner, 1965. American youth in a social struggle: the Mississippi summer project. Amer. J. Orthopsychiat. 35(5).
11. Coles, R. 1966. Mountain thinking. Appalachian Review. 1(1).
12. Erikson, E. 1963. Childhood and Society. Norton, New York.
13. Ford, T., ed. 1962. The Southern Appalachian Region. Univ. of Kentucky, Lexington.

14. Kemphart, H. 1913. Our Southern Highlander. Outing Publishing Co., New York.
15. Matthews, E. 1965. Neighbor and Kin. Univ. of Vanderbilt, Nashville.
16. Mental Health in Appalachia. 1965. A report based on a conference sponsored by National Institute of Mental Health, U.S. Dept. of Health, Education & Welfare. Public Health Service Publication No. 1375.
17. Munn, R. 1961. The Southern Appalachians: A Bibliography and Guide to Studies. West Virginia Univ., Morgantown.
18. Sherman, M., and T. Henry, 1933. Hollow Folk. Crowell, New York.
19. Toynbee, A. 1946. A Study of History. Oxford University Press, New York.
20. Weller, J. 1965. Yesterday's People. Univ. of Kentucky, Lexington.

ADDITIONAL READINGS

Burchinal, Lee G. & Cowling, James D. Rural youth in an urban society. *Children,* September–October 1963, **10** (5), 167–174. This article discusses rural youth in terms of background, educational attainments and aspirations, achievements, personal characteristics, and assistance with vocational planning.

Coles, Robert. Northern children under "desegregation." *Psychiatry,* February 1968, **31**, 1–15. The author, a research psychiatrist, studied children in the Boston area who were bussed to predominantly white schools. In general, they seem to adjust very well, but in contrast with their counterparts in the south, evidence more bitterness and anger toward white people. The white children display a wide range of emotions toward the Negroes from scorn and rebuff to curiosity and friendliness.

Douvan, Elizabeth & Adelson, Joseph. *The adolescent experience.* New York: Wiley, 1966. Chapter 9 considers how youth's problems and way of life vary with demographic factors. Subcultural influences treated here include geographic variables (city, suburb, small town, farm), family style, family mobility, and religion. Despite integrating themes which reflect the larger culture, subculture variations are complex and significant.

Eaton, Joseph W. *Adolescence in a communal society. Mental Hygiene,* 1964, **48**, 66–73. This paper describes patterns of growing up among the Hutterites, a sect of Swiss-German origin, who live in eastern South Dakota. In common with many American rural farm people, youth are encouraged to participate meaningfully in the adult community, hence are inducted gradually, and without difficulty into the large adult society.

Gottlieb, David & Ramsey, Charles. *The American adolescent.* Homewood, Illinois: Dorsey Press, 1964. In the first half of this book the writers outline the distinctive patterns of adolescent attitudes and behavior, and describe subcultural variations deriving from class and ethnic values of the adult world. The focus on peer relations raises theoretical issues yet to be resolved. They also review the literature on the changing conditions of adolescence in American society in terms of the content and consequences of youth culture.

Holzman, Mathilda, Luria, Zella, & Sherman, Herbert. Adolescent subculture: Endeavor, New England. *The School Review,* June 1968, **76** (2), 231–245. This study was designed to define the values and occupational goals of high school students in the Endeavor, New England, public schools, and to relate these values and goals to academic capabilities, performance, and home background.

Hsu, Francis L. K., Watrous, Blanche G., & Lord, Edith M. Culture pattern and adolescent behavior. *The International Journal of Social Behavior,* 1961, **7**, 33–53. In the cross-cultural study described here, white American adolescents living in Chicago are compared with Chinese teen-agers living in Hawaii. The Chinese youth appear to be unmoved by issues, while the American boys and girls grow up with an idealistic attitude toward life. The Americans become distressed when they find an imperfect world, but go on to attempt to improve the situation.

Sollenberger, Richard T. Chinese-American child-rearing practices and juvenile delinquency. *The Journal of Social Psychology,* February 1968, **74** (Part I), 13–23. The investigator lived in Chinatown for seven weeks and interviewed 69 Chinese mothers in order to discover those factors which account for the low rate of delinquency. These factors appear to include: abundant nurturance and protection in early childhood; a close-knit, mutually respecting family life; abundance of desirable adult models; and adult intolerance of child aggression.

XXI. Cross-Cultural Variants in Adolescents

Culture may be defined as the way of life of a society, and includes its habits, morals, customs, beliefs, and knowledge. Social scientists widely agree that culture leaves a deep impact, and indelibly stamps individuals who share it. Each culture is considered to have its distinguishing features, both for society at large, and for specific age groups. In general, American culture is distinguished by its emphasis on education, luxury, generosity, surface friendliness, and efficiency.

In all cultures, the way of life differs in varying degrees from one age-stage to another. That is, in a particular culture, child, adolescent, and adult, in effect, live in different worlds, each with its distinguishing features. Some writers identify features within particular cultures, features that distinguish adolescence. For example, in America Bernard notes phenomena having special impact on adolescents. In general, American adolescents are compressed into a prolonged period of dependence—economically, socially, and intellectually. Education is prolonged; work opportunities are delayed; and early marriage frowned upon. Another force affecting adolescents is the rapid pace of societal change. As a result, the gap between generations widens, and communication grows more difficult. Also, adults are uncertain about morals and ethics, and communicate their confusion to youth. Adolescents are also confused by the conflict between ideals and reality which they perceive in the "real world." Another problem is the uncertainty of obligatory military service, including whether and when one will be called, and how long one may serve. Meantime, urbanization has placed many adolescents largely under the control of women and thereby deprived them of adequate contact with adult male models. However, the employment of more male teachers and the greater participation of fathers in family life may help create a balance.[1]

Various writers suggest that American youth may actually benefit from the stresses placed upon them. In one study, American adolescents living in Hawaii were compared with white American adolescents living in Chicago. The Chinese youth, reported this study, are inducted into the world of adults at an early age and readily conform to traditional institutions. By

[1] Harold W. Bernard, *Human Development in Western Culture* (Boston: Allyn and Bacon, 1962), pp. 254–259.

contrast, American youth are relatively insulated until adulthood, and permitted to become self-reliant. Also, they grow up with an idealistic attitude toward life. When they finally come face-to-face with an imperfect world, they experience a certain amount of trauma. This condition is not to be deplored, for, by its very impact, the young person is stimulated to improve matters.[2]

Anyhow, the stresses of American culture may have been overemphasized. Conferences, news articles, and writers concentrate on adolescents with problems, creating the impression that well-adjusted teenagers are rare. Actually, only about 5 per cent of adolescents act out their frustrations in a deviant manner.

Often we lump American adolescents with others in the Western world; and teen-agers in Western cultures do possess certain characteristics in common. In general, they have more money, permitting greater independence and more separateness from adults, than young people in have-not countries. Their way of life has more material aspects, including cars or motor scooters, camping gear, and the like. Because their education is extended, school plays a relatively large place in their lives. However, youth vary within the Western culture itself. For example, French children learn very early to respect man-made limits of their society; while American youth absorb the idea that they should discover such rules for themselves.[3]

The question inevitably arises: what sort of culture is best for individuals involved? It has often been claimed that civilization places undue burdens on adolescents. By contrast, in primitive societies progress toward adult status proceeds smoothly and without interruption. Strains inherent in ambiguity are absent because the child's life is patterned, and choices are not to be made. In Samoa, writes Margaret Mead, growing up proceeds smoothly. The easy tempo, the close ties, the single moral standard, and the relaxed attitude toward sexual expression all constitute positive features. Since little privacy exists, facts of physical development are learned naturally. Life, including adolescence, says Mead, is easier in Samoa.

Primitive cultures do have their disadvantages. Civilization is static and individual potential unrealized. Besides, the features of primitive life, which serve to reduce strain, could hardly be superimposed onto Western culture.

The first selection, by S. N. Eisenstadt, defines youth as a universal phenomenon. The basic elements of primitive and traditional societies are identified, and found to have much in common. In the last portion of his article, omitted because of space considerations, Eisenstadt suggests that

[2] Francis L. K. Hsu, Blanche G. Watrous, and Edith M. Lord, "Culture Pattern and Adolescent Behavior," *The International Journal of Social Psychiatry,* VII (1961), pp. 33–53.

[3] Laurence Wylie, "Youth in France and the United States," *Daedalus,* Vol. 91 (1962), pp. 198–215.

the framework is changing. For example, he perceives a "flattening of po-
litical-ideological motives and a growing apathy to them," and a meaning-
lessness of social relations, resulting from an age of consumption and mass
society.

The second selection, by Sherman, describes Soviet youth, about
whom Americans typically have hazy and confused notions. Especially,
since democracy and communism represent the two dominant ideologies
in the world today, it behooves American youth to understand their counterparts in the most powerful of Communist countries. Youth in Russia,
says Sherman, are no one thing. Their situation is not static, but undergoing
steady change. Sherman describes typical youth patterns in Russia and
analyzes forces of change.

The third article by Rabin compares adolescents who were reared in
the Israeli kibbutz with others reared in a conventional family setting.
Because of the unusual nature of the kibbutz experiment-in-living there has
been considerable concern whether children reared there would be as well-
adjusted as others.

44

S. N. Eisenstadt

ARCHETYPAL PATTERNS OF YOUTH

*Eisenstadt considers youth as a universal phenomenon, with parallels
between primitive and historical and modern societies. However, he also analyzes
current social processes and indicates how they affect the basic archetypal elements of youth. A new configuration of youth is emerging with new possibilities
and problems.*

Youth constitutes a universal phenomenon. It is first of all a biological
phenomenon, but one always defined in cultural terms. In this sense it
constitutes a part of a wider cultural phenomenon, the varying definitions of
age and of the differences between one and another.[1] Age and age differences are among the basic aspects of life and the determinants of human
destiny. Every human being passes through various ages, and at each one
he attains and uses different biological and intellectual capacities. At each
stage he performs different tasks and roles in relation to the other members
of his society: from a child, he becomes a father; from a pupil, a teacher;
from a vigorous youth, a mature adult, and then an aging and "old" man.

This gradual unfolding of power and capacity is not merely a universal,
biologically conditioned, and inescapable fact. Although the basic biological
process of maturation (within the limits set by such factors as relative
longevity) are probably more or less similar in all human societies, their cultural definition varies from society to society, at least in details. In all societies, age serves as a basis for defining the cultural and social characteristic
of human beings, for the formation of some of their mutual relations and
common activities, and for the differential allocation of social roles.

The cultural definitions of age and age differences contain several different yet complementary elements. First, these definitions often refer to the

From YOUTH: CHANGE AND CHALLENGE, edited by Erik H. Erikson, ©
1961 by the American Academy of Arts and Sciences and © 1963 by Basic Books,
Inc., Publishers, New York.

[1] A general sociological analysis of the place of age in social structure has been
attempted in S. N. Eisenstadt, *From Generation to Generation* (Chicago: The Free
Press of Glencoe, Illinois, 1956).

social division of labor in a society, to the criteria according to which people occupy various social positions and roles within any society. For instance, in many societies certain roles—especially those of married men, full citizens, independent earners—are barred to young people, while others —as certain military roles—are specifically allocated to them. Second, the cultural definition of age is one important constituent of a person's self-identity, his self-perception in terms of his own psychological needs and aspirations, his place in society, and the ultimate meaning of his life.

Within any such definition, the qualities of each age are evaluated according to their relation to some basic, primordial qualities, such as vigor, physical and sexual prowess, the ability to cope with material, social, and supernatural environment, wisdom, experience, or divine inspiration. Different ages are seen in different societies as the embodiments of such qualities. These various qualities seem to unfold from one age to another, each age emphasizing some out of the whole panorama of such possible qualities. The cultural definition of an age span is always a broad definition of human potentialities, limitations, and obligations at a given stage of life. In terms of these definitions, people map out the broad contours of life, their own expectations and possibilities, and place themselves and their fellow men in social and cultural positions, ascribing to each a given place within these contours.

The various qualities attributed to different ages do not constitute an unconnected series. They are usually interconnected in many ways. The subtle dialectics between the unfolding of some qualities and the waning of others in a person is not a mere registration of his psychological or biological traits; rather, it constitutes the broad framework of his potentialities and their limits throughout his life span. The characteristics of any one "age," therefore, cannot be fully understood except in relation to those of other ages. Whether seen as a gradually unfolding continuum or as a series of sharp contrasts and opposed characteristics, they are fully explicable and understandable only in terms of one another. The boy bears within himself the seeds of the adult man; else, he must as an adult acquire new patterns of behavior, sharply and intentionally opposed to those of his boyhood. The adult either develops naturally into an old man—or decays into one. Only when taken together do these different "ages" constitute the entire map of human possibilities and limitations; and, as every individual usually must pass through them all, their complementariness and continuity (even if defined in discontinuous and contrasting terms) become strongly emphasized and articulated.

The same holds true for the age definitions of the two sexes, although perhaps with a somewhat different meaning. Each age span is defined differently for either sex, and these definitions are usually related and complementary, as the "sexual image" and identity always constitute basic elements of man's image in every society. This close connection between different ages necessarily stresses the problem of transition from one point in a person's life to another as a basic constituent of any cultural definition of an "age." Hence, each definition of age must necessarily cope with the perception of time, and changes in time, of one's own progress in time, one's transition from one period of life to another.

This personal transition, or temporal progress, or change, may become closely linked with what may be called cosmic and societal time.[2] The attempt to find some meaning in personal temporal transition may often lead to identification with the rhythms of nature or history, with the cycles of the seasons, with the unfolding of some cosmic plan (whether cyclical, seasonal, or apocalyptic), or with the destiny and development of society. The nature of this linkage often constitutes the focus round which an individual's personal identity becomes defined in cultural terms and through which personal experience, with its anguish, may be given some meaning in terms of cultural symbols and values.

The whole problem of age definition and the linkage of personal time and transition with cosmic time become especially accentuated in that age span usually designated as youth. However great the differences among various societies, there is one focal point within the life span of an individual which in most known societies is to some extent emphasized: the period of youth, of transition from childhood to full adult status, or full membership in the society. In this period the individual is no longer a child (especially from the physical and sexual point of view) but is ready to undertake many attributes of an adult and to fulfill adult roles. But he is not yet fully acknowledged as an adult, a full member of the society. Rather, he is being "prepared," or is preparing himself for such adulthood.

This image of youth—the cultural definition of youth—contains all the crucial elements of any definition of age, usually in an especially articulated way. This is the stage at which the individual's personality acquires the basic psychological mechanism of self-regulation and self-control, when his self-identity becomes crystallized. It is also the stage at which the young are confronted with some models of the major roles they are supposed to emulate in adult life and with the major symbols and values of their culture and community. Moreover, in this phase the problem of the linkage of the personal temporal transition with cosmic or societal time becomes extremely acute. Any cultural definition of youth describes it as a transitory phase,

---

[2] The analysis of personal, cosmic, and societal time (or temporal progression) has constituted a fascinating but not easily dealt with focus of analysis. For some approaches to these problems, see *Man and Time* (papers from the Eranos Yearbooks, edited by Joseph Campbell; London: Routledge & Kegan Paul, 1958), especially the article by Gerardus van der Leeuw. See also Mircea Eliade, *The Myth of the Eternal Return.* Translated by W. R. Trask. New York: Pantheon Books, 1954 (Bollingen Series).

couched in terms of transition toward something new, something basically different from the past. Hence the acuteness of the problem of linkage.

The very emphasis on the transitory nature of this stage and of its essentially preparatory character, however, may easily create a somewhat paradoxical situation. It may evolve an image of youth as the purest manifestation and repository of ultimate cultural and societal values. Such an image is rooted first in the fact that to some extent youth is always defined as a period of "role moratorium," that is, as a period in which one may play with various roles without definitely choosing any. It does not yet require the various compromises inherent in daily participation in adult life. At the same time, however, since it is also the period when the maximum identification with the values of society is stressed, under certain conditions it may be viewed as the repository of all the major human virtues and primordial qualities. It may then be regarded as the only age in which full identification with the ultimate values and symbols of the society is attained—facilitated by the flowering of physical vigor, a vigor which may easily become identified with a more general flowering of the cosmos or the society.

The fullest, the most articulate and definitive expression of these archetypal elements of youth is best exemplified in the ritual dramatization of the transition from adolescence to adulthood, such as the various *rites de passage* and ceremonies of initiation in primitive tribes and in ancient civilizations.[3] In these rites the pre-adult youth are transformed into full members of the tribe. This transformation is effected through:

1. a series of rites in which the adolescents are symbolically divested of the characteristics of youth and invested with those of adulthood, from a sexual and social point of view; this investment, which has deep emotional significance, may have various concrete manifestations: bodily mutilation, circumcision, the taking on of a new game or symbolic rebirth;

2. the complete symbolic separation of the male adolescents from the world of their youth, especially from their close attachment to their mothers; in other words, their complete "male" independence and image are fully articulated (the opposite usually holds true of girls' initiations);

3. the dramatization of the encounter between the several generations, a dramatization that may take the form of a fight or a competition, in which the basic complementariness of various age grades—whether of a continuous or discontinuous type—is stressed; quite often the discontinuity between adolescence and adulthood is symbolically expressed, as in the symbolic death of the adolescents as children and their rebirth as adults.

4. the transmission of the tribal lore with its instructions about proper

―――――――――

[3] For a fuller exposition of the sociological significance of initiation rites, see Mircea Eliade, *Birth and Rebirth* (New York: Harper & Brothers, 1958) and *From Generation to Generation* (ref. 1).

behavior, both through formalized teaching and through various ritual activities; this transmission is combined with:

5. a relaxation of the concrete control of the adults over the erstwhile adolescents and its substitution by self-control and adult responsibility.

Most of these dramatic elements can also be found, although in somewhat more diluted forms, in various traditional folk festivals in peasant communities, especially those such as rural carnivals in which youth and marriage are emphasized. In an even more diluted form, these elements may be found in various spontaneous initiation ceremonies of the fraternities and youth groups in modern societies.[4] Here, however, the full dramatic articulation of these elements is lacking, and their configuration and organization assume different forms.

The transition from childhood and adolescence to adulthood, the development of personal identity, psychological autonomy and self-regulation, the attempt to link personal temporal transition to general cultural images and to cosmic rhythms, and to link psychological maturity to the emulation of definite role models—these constitute the basic elements of any archetypal image of youth. However, the ways in which these various elements become crystallized in concrete configurations differ greatly from society to society and within sectors of the same society. The full dramatic articulation of these elements in the *rites de passage* of primitive societies constitutes only one—perhaps the most extreme and articulate but certainly not the only—configuration of these archetypal elements of youth.

In order to understand other types of such configurations, it is necessary to analyze some conditions that influence their development. Perhaps the best starting point is the nature of the social organization of the period of adolescence: the process of transition from childhood to adulthood, the social context in which the process of growing up is shaped and structured. There are two major criteria that shape the social organization of the period of youth. One is the extent to which age in general and youth in particular form a criterion for the allocation of roles in a society, whether in politics, in economic or cultural activity—aside from the family, of course, in which they always serve as such a criterion. The second is the extent to which any society develops specific age groups, specific corporate organizations, composed of members of the same "age," such as youth movements or old men's clubs. If roles are allocated in a society according to age, this greatly influences the extent to which age constitutes a component of a person's identity. In such cases, youth becomes a definite and meaningful phase of transition in an individual's progress through life, and his budding self-identity acquires content and a relation to role models and cultural values. No less important to the concrete development of identity is the ex-

[4] See Bruno Bettelheim, *Symbolic Wounds, Puberty Rites and the Envious Circle* (Chicago: The Free Press of Glencoe, Illinois, 1954).

tent to which it is influenced, either by the common participation of different generations in the same group as in the family, or conversely by the organization of members of the same age groups into specific, distinct groups.

The importance of age as a criterion for allocating roles in a society is closely related to several major aspects of social organization and cultural orientation. The first aspect is the relative complexity of the division of labor. In general, the simpler the organization of the society, the more influential age will be as a criterion for allocating roles. Therefore, in primitive or traditional societies (or in the more primitive and traditional sectors of developed societies) age and seniority constitute basic criteria for allocating social, economic, and political roles.

The second aspect consists of the major value orientations and symbols of a society, especially the extent to which they emphasize certain general orientations, qualities, or types of activity (such as physical vigor, the maintenance of cultural tradition, the achievement and maintenance of supernatural prowess) which can be defined in terms of broad human qualities and which become expressed and symbolized in specific ages.

The emphasis on any particular age as a criterion for the allocation of roles is largely related to the concrete application of the major value orientations in a society. For instance, we find that those primitive societies in which military values and orientations prevail emphasize young adulthood as the most important age, while those in which sedentary activities prevail emphasize older age. Similarly, within some traditional societies, a particular period such as old age may be emphasized if it is seen as the most appropriate one for expressing major cultural values and symbols—for instance, the upholding of a given cultural tradition.

The social and cultural conditions that determine the extent to which specific age groups and youth groups develop differ from the conditions that determine the extent to which age serves as a criterion for the allocation of roles. At the same time, the two kinds of conditions may be closely related, as we shall see. Age groups in general and youth groups in particular tend to arise in those societies in which the family or kinship unit cannot ensure (it may even impede) the attainment of full social status on the part of its members. These conditions appear especially (although not uniquely [5]) in societies in which family or kinship groups do not constitute the basic unit of the social division of labor. Several features characterize such societies. First, the membership in the total society (citizenship) is not defined in terms of belonging to any such family, kinship group, or estate, nor is it mediated by such a group.

[5] A special type of age groups may also develop in familistic societies. See *From Generation to Generation* (ref. 1), ch. 5.

Second, in these societies the major political, economic, social, and religious functions are performed not by family or kinship units but rather by various specialized groups (political parties, occupational associations, etc.), which individuals may join irrespective of their family, kinship, or caste. In these societies, therefore, the major roles that adults are expected to perform in the wider society differ in orientation from those of the family or kinship group. The children's identification and close interaction with family members of other ages does not assure the attainment of full self-identity and social maturity on the part of the children. In these cases, there arises a tendency for peer groups to form, especially youth groups; these can serve as a transitory phase between the world of childhood and the adult world.

This type of the social division of labor is found in varying degrees in different societies, primitive, historical, or modern. In several primitive tribes such a division of labor has existed,[6] for example, in Africa, among the chiefless (segmentary) tribes of Nandi, Masai, or Kipigis, in the village communities of Yako and Ibo, or in more centralized kingdoms of the Zulu and Swazi, and among some of the Indian tribes of the Plains, as well as among some South American and Indian tribes.

Such a division of labor likewise existed to some extent in several historical societies (especially in city states such as Athens or Rome), although most great historical civilizations were characterized mainly by a more hierarchical and ascriptive system of the division of labor, in which there were greater continuity and harmony between the family and kinship groups and the broader institutional contexts. The fullest development of this type of the social division of labor, however, is to be found in modern industrial societies. Their inclusive membership is usually based on the universal criterion of citizenship and is not conditioned by membership in any kinship group. In these societies the family does not constitute a basic unit of the division of labor, especially not in production and distribution, and even in the sphere of consumption its functions become more limited. Occupations are not transmitted through heredity. Similarly, the family or kinship group does not constitute a basic unit of political or ritual activities. Moreover, the general scope of the activities of the family has been continuously diminishing, while various specialized agencies tend to take over its functions in the fields of education and recreation.

To be sure, the extent to which the family is diminishing in modern societies is often exaggerated. In many social spheres (neighborhood, friendship, informal association, some class relations, community relations), family, kinship, and status are still very influential. But the scope of these relations is more limited in modern societies than in many others, even if the prevalent myth of the disappearance of the family has long since been

[6] For fuller details, see *From Generation to Generation*, especially chs. 3 and 4.

exploded. The major social developments of the nineteenth century (the establishment of national states, the progress of the industrial revolution, the great waves of intercontinental migrations) have greatly contributed to this diminution of scope, and especially in the first phase of modernization there has been a growing discontinuity between the life of the children, whether in the family or the traditional school and in the social world with its new and enlarged perspectives.

Youth groups tend to develop in all societies in which such a division of labor exists. Youth's tendency to coalesce in such groups is rooted in the fact that participation in the family became insufficient for developing full identity or full social maturity, and that the roles learned in the family did not constitute an adequate basis for developing such identity and participation. In the youth groups the adolescent seeks some framework for the development and crystallization of his identity, for the attainment of personal autonomy, and for his effective transition into the adult world.

Various types of youth organizations always tend to appear with the transition from traditional or feudal societies to modern societies, along with the intensified processes of change, especially in periods of rapid mobility, migration, urbanization, and industrialization. This is true of all European societies, and also of non-Western societies. The impact of Western civilization on primitive and historical-traditional peoples is usually connected with the disruption of family life, but beyond this it also involves a change in the mutual evaluation of the different generations. The younger generation usually begin to seek a new self-identification, and one phase or another of this search is expressed in ideological conflict with the older.

Most of the nationalistic movements in the Middle East, Asia, and Africa have consisted of young people, students, or officers who rebelled against their elders and the traditional familistic setting with its stress on the latters' authority. At the same time there usually has developed a specific youth consciousness and ideology that intensifies the nationalistic movement to "rejuvenate" the country.

The emergence of the peer group among immigrant children is a well-known phenomenon that usually appears in the second generation. It occurs mainly because of the relative breakdown of immigrant family life in the new country. The more highly industrialized and urbanized that country (or the sector absorbing the immigrants) is, the sharper the breakdown. Hence, the family of the immigrant or second-generation child has often been an inadequate guide to the new society. The immigrant child's attainment of full identity in the new land is usually related to how much he has been able to detach himself from his older, family setting. Some of these children, therefore, have developed a strong predisposition to join various peer groups. Such an affiliation has sometimes facilitated their transition to the absorbing society by stressing the values and patterns of behavior in that society—or, on the contrary, it may express their rebellion against this society, or against their older setting.

All these modern social developments and movements have given rise to a great variety of youth groups, peer groups, youth movements, and what has been called youth culture. The types and concrete forms of such groups varies widely: spontaneous youth groups, student movements, ideological and semipolitical movements, and youth rebellions connected with the Romantic movement in Europe, and, later, with the German youth movements. The various social and national trends of the nineteenth and twentieth centuries have also given impetus to such organizations. At the same time there have appeared many adult-sponsored youth organizations and other agencies springing out of the great extension of educational institutions. In addition to providing recreative facilities, these agencies have also aimed at character molding and the instilling of civic virtues, so as to deepen social consciousness and widen the social and cultural horizon. The chief examples are the YMCA, the Youth Brigades organized in England by William Smith, the Boy Scouts, the Jousters in France, and the many kinds of community organizations, hostels, summer camps, or vocational guidance centers.

Thus we see that there are many parallels between primitive and historical societies and modern societies with regard to the conditions under which the various constellations of youth groups, youth activities, and youth images have developed. But these parallels are only partial. Despite certain similarities, the specific configurations of the basic archetypal elements of the youth image in modern societies differ greatly from those of primitive and traditional societies. The most important differences are rooted in the fact that in the modern, the development of specific youth organizations is paradoxically connected with the weakening of the importance of age in general and youth in particular as definite criteria for the allocation of roles in society.

As we have already said, the extent to which major occupational, cultural, or political roles are allocated today according to the explicit criterion of age is very small. Most such roles are achieved according to wealth, acquired skills, specialization, and knowledge. Family background may be of great importance for the acquisition of these attributes, but very few positions are directly given people by virtue of their family standing. Yet this very weakening of the importance of age is always connected with intensive developments of youth groups and movements. This fact has several interesting repercussions on the organization and structure of such groups. In primitive and traditional societies, youth groups are usually part of a wider organization of age groups that covers a very long period of life, from childhood to late adulthood and even old age. To be sure, it is during youth that most of the dramatic elements of the transition from one age to another are manifest, but this stage constitutes only part of a longer series of continuous, well-defined stages.

From this point of view, primitive or traditional societies do not differ greatly from those in which the transition from youth to adulthood is not organized in specific age groups but is largely effected within the fold of the family and kinship groups. In both primitive and traditional societies we observe a close and comprehensive linkage between personal temporal transition and societal or cosmic time, a linkage most fully expressed in the *rites de passage*. Consequently, the transition from childhood to adulthood in all such societies is given full meaning in terms of ultimate cultural values and symbols borne or symbolized by various adult role models.

In modern societies the above picture greatly changes. The youth group, whatever its composition or organization, usually stands alone. It does not constitute a part of a fully institutionalized and organized series of age groups. It is true that in many of the more traditional sectors of modern societies the more primitive or traditional archetypes of youth still prevail. Moreover, in many modern societies elements of the primitive archetypes of youth still exist. But the full articulation of these elements is lacking, and the social organization and self-expression of youth are not given full legitimation or meaning in terms of cultural values and rituals.

The close linkage between the growth of personality, psychological maturation, and definite role models derived from the adult world has become greatly weakened. Hence the very coalescence of youth into special groups only tends to emphasize their problematic, uncertain standing from the point of view of cultural values and symbols. This has created a new constellation of the basic archetypal elements of youth. This new constellation can most clearly be seen in what has been called the emergence of the problems and stresses of adolescence in modern societies. While some of these stresses are necessarily common to adolescence in all societies, they become especially acute in modern societies.

Among these stresses the most important are the following: first, the bodily development of the adolescent constitutes a constant problem to him (or her). Since social maturity usually lags behind biological maturity, the bodily changes of puberty are not usually given a full cultural, normative meaning, and their evaluation is one of the adolescent's main concerns. The difficulty inherent in attaining legitimate sexual outlets and relations at this period of growth makes these problems even more acute. Second, the adolescent's orientation toward the main values of his society is also beset with difficulties. Owing to the long period of preparation and the relative segregation of the children's world from that of the adults, the main values of the society are necessarily presented to the child and adolescent in a highly selective way, with a strong idealistic emphasis. The relative un-reality of these values as presented to the children—which at the same time are not given full ritual and symbolic expression—creates among the adolescents a great potential uncertainty and ambivalence toward the adult world.

This ambivalence is manifest, on the one hand, in a striving to com-municate with the adult world and receive its recognition; on the other hand, it appears in certain dispositions to accentuate the differences between them and the adults and to oppose the various roles allocated to them by the adults. While they orient themselves to full participation in the adult world and its values, they usually attempt also to communicate with this world in a distinct, special way.

Parallel developments are to be found in the ideologies of modern youth groups. Most of these tend to create an ideology that emphasizes the discontinuity between youth and adulthood and the uniqueness of the youth period as the purest embodiment of ultimate social and cultural val-ues. Although the explicitness of this ideology varies in extent from one sector of modern society to another, its basic elements are prevalent in almost all modern youth groups. . . .

45

George Sherman

SOVIET YOUTH: MYTH AND REALITY

The author describes types of Soviet young people and their problems in the post-Stalin environment. The focus is on youth in the large industrialized cities.

My purpose is not to analyze how far this virus of experimentation has spread among Soviet citizens, or to estimate its ultimate impact on the society. Soviet society is still a very closed one, despite increased contacts with the outside world. The old myths are still religiously (although more gently) fostered from the top down. Numerous insights are now possible into underlying reality, but they are still only isolated fragments of unverified truth.

My purpose is rather to describe types of Soviet young people and their problems in the post-Stalin environment. Some have adjusted to that environment, some have not. My observations are based primarily on intermittent experiences with such people as Yuri over a five-year period (1955–1959). Wherever possible, they are supplemented by increasingly frank revelations on the part of the Soviet press and Mr. Khrushchev himself.[1] My main focus is on the large industrialized cities, whose better standard of living, cultural life, educational institutions, and factories·attract congregations of young men and women. In these centers the persistent tussle between old myths and new realities is more readily observable.

The young people who have attracted most public attention at home and abroad are the *stilyagi,* the "style-chasers," the rough Soviet equivalent of the British "teddy boys" or the American "drug-store cowboys." In the beginning the *stilyagi* were not necessarily juvenile delinquents. They were boys and girls who appeared in public in "Tarzan" haircuts, bright American-style shirts and too narrow trousers or skirts—teenagers and beyond who called each other by American nicknames, illicitly recorded American

From YOUTH: CHANGE AND CHALLENGE, edited by Erik H. Erikson, © 1961 by the American Academy of Arts and Sciences and © 1963 by Basic Books, Inc., Publishers, New York.

[1] For instance, Mr. Khrushchev has given the best exposé of the snobbishness of the elite system in Soviet higher education: "Memorandum on School Reorganization," *Pravda,* 21 September 1958, pp. 2–3.

jazz, and made primitive attempts at rock n' roll. In the end, however, the *stilyagi* have become a catch-all label in popular parlance for "anti-social" conduct—the "hooligans" who create drunken brawls, the black marketeers or "center boys" who trade counterfeit ikons for foreign tourists' clothes around the central hotels, the "gilded youth" who use their parents' influence to evade social duties and responsibilities.

A delving press has uncovered the spread of special slang among youth —labeled a "stilyaga-ism of speech." Young band musicians have begun to refer to their engagements as "playing at a funeral." One writer overheard the following conversation between students: "Well, let's fade. I still have to hit the hay; there's going to be a big shindig at a pal's shack."

The writer was even more dismayed at finding the "linguistic nihilism" spreading from students to workers. Instead of "Let's eat!" they are beginning to say, "Let's feed," or "Let's chop." Instead of buying something, the young workers now "grab" or "tear it off." The word "mug" is now used instead of "face," and the television set (*televizor*) has become the "telik." [2]

The line between innocent innovation and criminal delinquency is hard to draw in the Soviet Union. Any action not officially inspired and controlled is potentially dangerous to the regimented society. A kind of Victorian puritanism, inflexible and humorless, dominates the scene. Established authority makes full use of it to stamp hard on all overt signs of nonconformity. A vicious campaign in the press has sent the most extreme fads underground. Informal "comrades' courts" have been set up in factory and office to criticize and ostracize minor offenders—the girl who wears too much lipstick or the worker who arrives at work with vodka on his breath.

In Ivanovo, a textile town 300 miles northeast of Moscow, the sprawling Park of Culture features a row of life-sized posters ridiculing young culprits most recently apprehended by the People's Militia. These public caricatures change every two weeks. A girl worker, with vodka bottle at her lips, lounges lazily on the sunny beach; Marina has spent two weeks in jail, the doggerel underneath explains, "because the sun made her insides too warm." Another caricature shows feline Alexandra, a "beautiful cat," preening herself before the mirror, "because she would rather have a man than work." [3]

The protection of standard culture for the masses has collided head-on with the drive for sophistication among educated and quite respectable young people. On the one hand, they are exposed to an increasing number of fashion shows, articles, and books on refined manners, and to more limited numbers of foreign cultural imports such as British and French film

---

[2] "On Slang and Fashionable Catchwords," *Neva*, Leningrad, September 1960, 9: 200–203, as translated in *Current Digest of the Soviet Press*, 1960, *XII, 46:* 15–16.

[3] I saw these posters during a visit to Ivanovo at the end of July 1959.

festivals, a Polish exhibition of modern art, a Czechoslovak glass exhibit, and several American exhibitions. On the other hand, the new fashions which spread from the capital to the provinces fall victim to organized Komsomol scorn.

Letters and articles in the Moscow press complain that roving bands of "Komsomol police" have hunted down and molested vacationing young men in bright shirts and young women in slacks on the streets of fashionable Sochi.[4] Stylish girls have had their hair chopped off with "sheer violence." Two young girls from the distant province of Amur in Siberia complain that they were treated "like *stilyagi*" in their village because they wore one-piece fitted dresses. Their Komsomol Committee told them: "Dress so that you will not be different from others!"[5] *Komsomolskaya Pravda*, the chief youth paper in the Soviet Union, has had to reassure Kiev residents that the "music patrols" set up by the Kiev Komsomol do not have the power to prohibit the playing of "good jazz."[6]

The effect of the excesses has been a slow swing of the social pendulum toward some kind of compromise over developing tastes. Official attacks on intolerance bring with them demands for an "ethic of mutual respect."[7] In practice, that seems to mean greater individual freedom in private or semi-private, while paying lip-service in public to slowly changing social conventions. Public dance halls in Moscow, Stalingrad, and Sochi all still look much the same: young people in open-necked shirts and shapeless dresses move around crowded floors to conventional waltzes, some folk-dance music, and nondescript foxtrots for the "masses." Komsomol police see that no one steps out of line. In the expensive restaurants and hotels, however, an air of relaxed sophistication is becoming more noticeable. In the National Hotel dining room in Moscow or the Gorka Restaurant in Sochi, popping champagne corks punctuate the occasional cha cha cha, rock n' roll, and other improvisations the dance bands have learned from the Voice of America. Toward the end of the evening several well-dressed couples may prove that the ban on "unorthodox dancing" is not uniformly enforced.

Changes are also going on just beneath the surface in the field of art. Although "abstractionism," or "formalism," or "subjectless art" (in fact most experimentation) is officially condemned, some of the younger intelligentsia are tasting the forbidden fruit. A network of "private" Soviet art is spreading in the cities, aided by Mr. Khrushchev's drive for socialist legality. A friend in Leningrad who collects and disperses "modern art" for artist friends said he now had little fear that the police would invade his rooms simply to remove paintings from the wall. Officials of the Artists Union had threatened to inspect the studio of one of his clients, a well-

[4] "Patrol in Knee Pants," *Komsomolskaya Pravda*, 13 December 1960, p. 2.
[5] *Ibid.*
[6] "Soviet Jazz Awaits Its Composers," *Komsomolskaya Pravda*, 25 December 1960, p. 4.
[7] "Patrol in Knee Pants," *op. cit.*

known artist. They suspected he was dabbling in unorthodox art—as indeed he was. The artist (who is also well-known for his war record) bluntly replied he would throw out anyone who entered without permission or a search warrant. He would publicly display what pictures he chose. Any others were his own affair. The artist evidently carried the day, for the threat was dropped, and he is still painting.

The drive against the *stilyagi* has hampered but not destroyed the development of (Soviet-style) "beatniki" among the younger artistic and literary intelligentsia. Criticism has made them more discreet, less flamboyant. Neither by past training nor present desire do they reject society. Not even the most radical would follow American beatniks in debunking the central tenet of Soviet life: the sacredness of work. As a young Soviet writer put it to me, anyone who does not at least pretend to work is soon investigated and chastised by his local "block committee."

The tendency of Soviet "beatniki" is to emulate what they consider the Left-Bank bohemianism of Paris. It is a faint whisper of a similar movement among young East European intellectuals, particularly in Poland, to make ultrasophistication their mark of separateness from "proletarian" society. In the semiprivacy of their artists and writers clubs, or in their homes, they may don the long cigaret holder, dark glasses, bright orange lipstick, or tight skirt. Perhaps the closest thing to public spontaneity comes in the groups of young people who gather on summer evenings in Moscow to read their poems before the statue of the Soviet poet-hero, Mayakovsky. The stereotyped imagery of socialist realism still predominates, but innovation is more evident. University newspapers and their literary supplements also begin to allow more scope for individual creativity. . . .

The controversy over modes of dress and social behavior is much more than the Soviet version of a universal problem with youth. It reflects a much deeper social conflict in the Soviet Union: the conflict between stifling paternalism and rebellious youth, characterized in less regimented societies as the "conflict between generations." According to Communist mythology, this conflict cannot exist in socialist society. All generations are supposed to be helpmates along the predetermined road to a new heaven on earth. In fact, however, Soviet society today is grappling with a central paradox. Old controls imposed in the name of that heaven are increasingly questioned by the young reapers of half-way prosperity.[8]

The problem can be sensed in the perplexed words of a middle-aged engineer, speaking about his son: "Sometimes I do not understand him," he told me, "he wants everything in the world right away. He thinks too much about 'me,' and not enough about 'us.' For this man and his genera-

[8] See *Komsomolskaya Pravda,* 28 February 1957, p. 1, for a decree of the Central Committee of the Komsomol which comes close to admitting this conflict of generations. The younger generation has not been through "the severe school of revolutionary struggle," it says, and therefore takes the "great achievements of the Soviet people" for granted or does not appreciate them at all.

tion, serving the "collective" was an imperative of survival. Stalin had been their idol; the suffering and sacrifices of the 1930's and 1940's, their religion.

For the young, this past lives only in stories or dim childhood memories. Their Soviet society is no longer revolutionary, it is established. Relaxation is as evident as is the increase in consumer goods that heralded it. For forty-odd years the Russians have been loudly beating their collective chest about the glories of building socialism. Now it is built. Many doting parents encourage their children to enjoy the youth they lost. People can afford to be less vocal and more confident. They begin to worry less about the socialist image and more about the substance of their own lives.

The virus of easy wealth is most deadly among the *lumpen-proletariat*. Many of the real delinquents covered by "stilyaga-ism" are recruited from their ranks. They become the professional speculators who make their living on foreign goods, currency, and innumerable domestic rackets. Their inner bearings differentiate them from the *nouveaux-riches* and even more elite "gilded youth" who lavishly spend their own and their parents' money on scarce luxuries they consider stylish.

By comparison, the young speculators have been raised in working-class slums. They have seen their parents (many of whom were peasants new to city factories) work long years for a single room in a prerevolutionary apartment shared with four other families. One younger worker I visited had obtained his privacy by a pasteboard partition around one corner of the room. The whole family had to cook over one gas jet on the communal stove in the communal kitchen of the apartment. Given such cramped quarters and full working hours for each adult—raising children is more a responsibility of the "collective"—family life virtually disappears and the harsh life of the street takes over.[9]

The young speculator begins with a yearning to break out of these surroundings. He is impatient for a better lot, without the hard work which has brought parents and friends small reward. He dismisses the modest improvement of living standards since Stalin's death as inadequate. For him the glamor of Western "easy living" is irresistible. The means for making a quick—if illegal—fortune are close at hand. The advent of more foreign tourists, more Soviet trips abroad, and more private wealth combines with inferior consumer goods and a chaotic distribution system to provide a golden opportunity for black marketeers. Despite official strictures, these speculators make a good living while they fulfill a real economic function.

The price they pay is high. They are not only outside the law; they are totally outside the pale of respectability. And respectability counts for

[9] See George Z. F. Bereday, William W. Brickman, Gerald H. Read (editors), *The Changing Soviet School* (Cambridge: Riverside Press, 1960), p. 423, for the impressions of a group of American educators as to the effect of disorganized family life on delinquency in the Soviet Union.

much in Soviet Victorian society. These young people dress well, eat and drink the best food and wines, but they are still *déclassés*. An amateur Soviet sociologist, himself quite respectable, described the type:

> They become empty human beings. They have nothing but their own fine appearance. They set out to push themselves to the top, but they end up belonging nowhere. No good family will have anything to do with these *stilyagi* except for "business."

Superficially, the wayward "gilded youth" have many of these same antisocial habits. They dabble freely in illicit foreign goods, from clothes to books. They are certainly as lawless and immoral. They take out their boredom in wild drinking bouts and parties in their parents' apartments or country *dachas*. They make free use of the family ZIM limousine, which technically belongs to the State ministry or enterprise. In private, however, these reprobates are regarded as the Soviet equivalent of Shakespeare's "Prince Hal." The parents' position in society constantly pulls them toward respectability, while the parents' influence prevents the "adolescent flings" from becoming public scandal. Time and age are supposed to bring the middle- and upper-class delinquents back to the confines of conventional society.

It must be emphasized at this point that the maladjusted young people described above do not mean that the whole rising generation in the Soviet Union are problem children. Quite the contrary. The bulk of Soviet young people emerge as conventionally minded as the Communist apparatus intends. This is particularly true of the young workers. My amateur sociologist friend described them as the "gold of the system." They are hardworking yet submissive. Paternal authority channels their thinking toward ever greater material rewards for increased production. Young "Stakhanovites" and "brigades of Communist labor" are praised at every turn for setting the pace on the production line. Professional Komsomol "students" lead extracurricular political lectures and study groups in the factories after work hours. The factory collective, run by factory committee and trade union, makes sure they are integrated into social clubs and sports programs. Young workers are further encouraged to study in factory trade schools and technicums. The more intelligent and hard-working still have access (although more limited) to the prized professional institutes and even the university.

The result is a political passivity which seems assured so long as the over-all system remains stable. In the words of the sociologist cited above: "These young workers may grumble and protest when they receive 800 roubles bonus at the end of the month instead of the 1000 promised, but they soon tell themselves that 800 is better than the 600 they used to receive. So long as they have enough money and more things to buy, they are happy enough."

The same attitude is roughly true of most institute and university students, although they have scarcely any affinity with the working class. They judge the value of their education according to the status and money it will earn them, not on its intrinsic worth. In this, they are the logical heirs of Stalin's abandonment of egalitarianism in the early 'thirties for more prosaic reward incentives. All the powerful and influential occupations established during that period of the "building of socialism" can now be obtained only through the higher institutes and universities. Furthermore, the number of openings in each category are strictly tied to the needs of the plan. These limitations, plus the social values of a newly industrialized society, have dictated the upgrading of some professions and the downgrading of others. For instance, students specializing in engineering, chemistry, and physics have a higher prestige and will earn higher salaries than those in the humanities (a preparation for teaching), in law or in medicine— careers that are not in such great demand.[10]

The overwhelming emphasis on scientific disciplines is borne out in the educational statistics. In a thorough-going study, Nicholas DeWitt has found that in the sample year 1954, 60 per cent of Soviet classes graduating from higher institutes and universities were majors in engineering, physical, and other natural sciences. This figure excludes graduates of scientific pedagogical institutes which train secondary-school teachers. In the field of higher graduate and research degrees, the figure is even higher: 70 per cent of all advanced degrees in 1954 were in scientific fields.[11]

While the demands of the newly industrialized economy and the built-in bias of the economic plans undoubtedly promote this popularity of applied and theoretical science, powerful psychic and monetary incentives reinforce the appeal of the career for the young. My friend Yuri, vacationing in southern Sochi from the far North, is an example of the salaries and the opportunities open to young engineers. But any young man—or woman —chosen for research in one of the institutes at the top of the scientific hierarchy is also assured of working with the best equipment, of having every possible professional resource available, and of receiving good housing in the attractive (but crowded) urban centers. Success while young also holds out the promise of higher salaries, higher status, and the greater personal freedom given senior scientists.

[10] See George Z. F. Bereday and Jann Pennar, *The Politics of Soviet Education* (New York: Frederick A. Praeger, 1960), ch. 4, "Class Tensions in Soviet Education," pp. 57–88, for a more comprehensive analysis of the conflict between egalitarianism and status in Soviet education.

[11] Nicholas DeWitt, *Soviet Professional Manpower* (Washington: National Science Foundation, 1955), pp. 167–169, 217. Mr. DeWitt also found that, while Soviet higher education graduated 40 per cent less than American colleges and universities, only 25 per cent of American bachelor degrees went to scientific engineering students.

Science offers the greatest possible retreat from politics in a system in which everything is political to a greater or lesser degree. As will be discussed shortly, young scientists, like other young people in institutes and offices, are subject to constant political supervision by Party or Komsomol "activists." If they overtly transgress the bounds of political orthodoxy outside their work, scientists suffer the same Party reprimands, loss of career opportunities, or even imprisonment, in extreme cases.

On the other hand, *inside* their work, research scientists (with notable exceptions such as biologists) do not have to spend their lives dodging Party doctrine. The intellect remains relatively unscarred by the demands of dogmatic truth. Unlike students or young professionals in such politically sensitive disciplines as history, art, and the humanities, scientists have an autonomy free of the day-to-day dictates of shifting ideological interpretation. Of course, this adds to the appeal of scientific studies and detracts from the appeal of the humanities. Any pitfalls which may lie ahead for the young scientist engaged in the most basic research—in the way of potential conflict with Marxist-Leninism—must seem a far-off danger, indeed, compared to immediate advantages.

One observer has characterized the resulting situation in the schools: [12]

Arithmetic, algebra, trigonometry, geometry, the laws of classical physics, chemistry—these remain the same whether politically biased phraseology is used or not. . . . Thus the teaching of these subjects suffers less than those fields where an interpretive bias can be freely applied. These conditions are but the starting point in a race in which the sciences win and the humanities lose in the Soviet educational setting.

This "other-worldliness" of science—particularly research—in which scientists of all ages find intellectual satisfaction by losing themselves completely in their work, tends to give the profession a unity and to diminish that conflict of generations more evident in other fields. Older scientists and professors are genuinely revered for knowledge and talents easily divorced from the particular political and social setting. They are people to be emulated, not displaced. So, in the case of young scientists, the rationalization of their mentors' work under Stalin comes easily with the "proof" that their internationally recognized achievements were not directly tied to the revealed tyranny of the despot.

This is not to say, however, that the experimental faculty of scientific youth is uniformly walled off from Soviet life, or that the regime is content with the political attitudes of the scientific profession. Young scientists appear to be some of the most caustic critics of the over-all system, if not of the place of their own profession has in it. During a visit to Harvard University earlier this year, the young Soviet poet Evtushenko (an aggressive "reform" leader since 1956) said that he preferred to read his poetry

12 *Ibid.,* p. 41.

to young scientists and engineers because of their "fresh minds." He believed his work enjoys its greatest success among this group, who read it in their spare time. And back in the troubled fall of 1956, the questioning of Party truth seems to have been as widespread in the scientific faculties and institutes as in the liberal arts and humanities.

Mr. Khrushchev has thrown some light on this unrest among young scientists. In a recently published speech to "representatives of the Soviet intelligentsia," he singled out three anonymous young scientists to prove that no profession is too valuable to be above or beyond politics. He was discussing the disciplinary steps taken by the regime to still the storm of 1956. Mr. Khrushchev said the three renegades had been thrown out of the Party organization in their institute for "anti-Party" activities. When a "famous academician" had telephoned to plead for the future of these "talented boys," Mr. Khrushchev responded that their actions—unspecified —had not been children's play. He refused to relent, and went on to gloat over the calm such stern action had restored to the Soviet intelligentsia.[13]

Scientists, while perhaps more privileged than others of the intelligentsia, have much in common with certain young elite in other professions. The various frames of mind with which this young intelligentsia has emerged from the psychological upheaval of 1956 will be discussed in a section below.

The system of rewards through education has led to one of the greatest contradictions in Soviet society: although common physical labor is loudly praised, children of the powerful professional groups consider themselves failures if reduced to it. Their world is increasingly separated from that of the working class. Professional military officers vie with one another to get their sons into the elite Suvorov and Nakhimov military academies. The budding civilian aristocracy asserts its exclusiveness through unpublicized special secondary schools, like the one near Sokolniki Park in Moscow, where instruction is carried on exclusively in English, French, or German.[14] The ballet schools in Moscow and Leningrad have become another important status symbol. Generally speaking, the well-equipped ten-year secondary schools in the cities are far surer stepping stones to success than their seven-year counterparts still remaining in the countryside.

These educational gaps have conflicted sharply with the egalitarian features built into the over-all educational system from the revolutionary past. An upward mobility of workers and peasants has been encouraged in the name of that revolution. Everyone, regardless of social position or

[13] Although this speech was actually delivered 17 July 1960, it was not published until May 1961. N. S. Khrushchev, "Toward New Success of Literature and Art," *Kommunist,* May 1961, 7: 6–7.

[14] *Ibid.,* p. 120. David Burg, a student in Moscow until 1956, writes that the children of Mr. Malenkov attended the English-language school near Sokolniki Park while he was premier. This confirms my personal observations during 1959 about the exclusiveness of this school.

sex, has access to a free secondary-school education. Informal relationships between teacher and pupil, an overbearing emphasis in primary and secondary school on collectivism, and the enforcement of a common culture and language through centralized controls also have a leveling effect (although in the latter case poor instruction in Russian in the national republics hampers the advancement of these minorities in All-Union careers). This egalitarianism puts an unbearable strain on the higher educational establishments, which, by design of the economic plan, cannot absorb all secondary-school graduates.

With characteristic directness, Mr. Khrushchev has set out to undo Stalin's legacy through a wholesale shake-up of the educational system. "The chief and fundamental defect of our secondary and higher schools is the fact that they are detached from life," was his way of expressing it in September 1958.[15] He noted that in 1957 some 800,000 of 2,500,000 secondary-school graduates could not go on to higher education, but that they were prepared for nothing else. He discovered that only 30–40 per cent of students in Moscow higher schools came from worker and peasant families. He found that many families had a "haughty and contemptuous" attitude toward physical work and that their children considered factory and farm work "beneath their dignity."

Mr. Khrushchev's proposed solution: "polytechnical" education in secondary schools to "establish ties with life" (work); a requirement that all students entering professional institutes and universities have at least two years' work experience; and a much closer alignment of specialized studies with practical work. Although this radical proposal was somewhat watered down through negotiation with Soviet educators, essential changes were introduced at the opening of the academic year 1959–1960.

There is no space here to analyze all the changes and their myriad exceptions. It is also too soon to judge the final impact of the reforms, for they will not be completed until 1964. It must be stressed, however, that their aim is *not* to reduce the number of students in higher education or to throw a huge supply of unskilled child labor onto the market. That intention might have been read into Mr. Khrushchev's first pronouncements. In practice, however, the reform (at least in the big cities) has added one year onto the old ten-year middle schools and shifted the curriculum for the last three years toward more "knowledge of production." In the school I visited in Moscow, this means that, beginning with the ninth grade, students spend four days a week in the school, and two days in a "patron factory" learning industrial skills. The principal, Maria Skyartsova, said the extra year had also allowed them to broaden the teaching of literature, physics, chemistry, and mathematics, and to add a new course on world history since World War I.[16]

[15] Mr. Khrushchev's "Memorandum on School Reorganization," *op. cit.*
[16] Middle School No. 49, which I visited on 28 September 1959.

The aim is to change the orientation of students, not to reduce their numbers. Secondary-school graduates must be able to go into practical work; some may go on to full-time higher education in two years, others will have to be content with night school or vastly expanded correspondence courses.[17] The privileged ones who do become full-time day students are to be thoroughly reliable. According to new rules published early in 1959, they must have "good" recommendations from the Communist Party group, trade union, and Komsomol in the factory, as well as support from the factory director or collective farm board.[18]

Loopholes in the rules have already appeared. Given the power of the professional groups affected, those holes may be expected to become larger rather than smaller. First, at least 20 per cent of first-year students are still to be chosen directly from secondary middle schools, although the new admission rules are notably ambiguous about students of the humanities.[19] This general 20 per cent is a minimum figure; in fact, in 1959, 45 per cent came directly from secondary schools.[20] This leeway in avoiding the work requirements obviously intensifies, rather than relieves, that cut-throat competition among well-placed parents which Mr. Khrushchev attacked in 1958. They still pull every possible string to get their children into the higher schools. Second, it is doubtful that those children are going to acquire that "worker's mentality" Mr. Khrushchev so admires by serving time in a factory or on a collective farm, or that the manual labor is going to aid their future careers. Sons and daughters of ensconced officialdom are already claiming confidentially that they will find suitable apprenticeships in good laboratories or executive offices. Some I met felt the elite would have no difficulty in getting the necessary recommendations for university entrance well ahead of the end of the two-year period.

The immediate political imperative for these reforms grew out of the unrest in 1956–1957. The debunking of Stalin, a near revolt in Poland, a real revolution in Hungary, armed intervention, and their aftermath produced a crisis of confidence among the young intelligentsia which clearly frightened Mr. Khrushchev and his hierarchy. That latent conflict of attitudes between generations had never before come so close to the surface, nor had it ever borne such ominous political overtones. Here were privileged students—particularly in the elite institutes and universities of Leningrad and Moscow—who reacted to Khrushchev's revelations with a barrage of confused criticism, not with the embarrassed silence of their elders. They

[17] P. I. Polukhin, a spokesman for the All-Union Ministry of Higher Education, told me on 4 December 1959 that one-half of the two million students then enrolled in higher education were in night school or taking correspondence courses.

[18] *Pravda,* 4 April 1959, p. 4.

[19] *Ibid.:* this article seems to suggest that *all* students in these disciplines must have the preliminary work experience.

[20] According to P. I. Polukhin in the interview noted above.

were young enough to question profoundly, old enough to know what to question. Although no one knows how many students displayed "unhealthy attitudes" in 1956–1957, enough existed at the very summit of Soviet education to warrant strong attacks in the press.[21] Soviet intervention in the Hungarian revolution and concomitant police coercion and social pressures at home finally silenced their protests but did not correct the condition underlying them. When Mr. Khrushchev later began demanding the resurrection of ties between the schools and "life," he really meant restoring firm ties between education and the Communist leadership.

Yet the reforms have come too late to affect the rebels of 1956–1957. Today they are no longer students, but they are not yet seasoned members of the "establishment." They are still grappling with the shock from the denunciation of Stalin, the thaw, the new freeze, and then the more careful relaxation since 1959. The result, I believe, is two recognizable strains in this part of the young intelligentsia: the "intellectuals" and the "men of action." Sometimes both strains coexist uneasily in the same person, sometimes not, but both types represent important ingredients in the present Soviet environment.

The "intellectuals" are the ones who have turned their backs on the establishment. They have not stopped questioning; they do not accept the materialistic red herrings Mr. Khrushchev has provided. They have a guilty conscience about the past. As one critic put it: "The intellectuals come straight out of Dostoevski, wailing and worrying about the future of society, about abstract ideas like 'justice,' but they can never take a decision, they can never do anything." In 1956, they were students who turned university seminars into serious political discussion groups and later expressed sympathy with the Hungarian rebels. Some were reprimanded, others were expelled, and still others, imprisoned. Now conditions have returned to "normal"; they are lonely, disillusioned and bitter.

"We have found out that when you beat your head against a stone wall, you break your head, not the wall," a dissident confided in Leningrad, more in sorrow than in anger. "The secret police have changed their tactics, they are more polite. Whether they call it arrest or education, however, their power amounts to the same thing. They are the stick, and the leadership of the Party wields it."

These young men and women in their middle and late twenties provide penetrating (and not always unsympathetic) insight into their more con-

[21] David Burg, "Observations on Soviet University Students," *Daedalus*, Summer 1960, pp. 520–540. This article gives a detailed report on student reactions to the events of 1956. See also S. V. and P. Utechin, "Patterns of Nonconformity," *Problems of Communism*, 1957, *3:* 15–23. *Komsomolskaya Pravda*, 16 December 1956 and 28 December 1956, tells of handwritten magazines in Leningrad bearing such names as *Fresh Voices and Heresy*. See also "Strength and Faith," *Izvestia*, 6 September 1959, p. 4, for an account of the Soviet handling of another student conspiracy.

formist fellows. "The bright young people see that this system has lasted over forty years and is growing steadily stronger," this ex-student said. "They believe the mistakes of the past are being corrected. So they conform. They fulfill all the outward norms, but in reality they are indifferent to politics. Do not think the lie they live is a conscious one. They honestly believe they are doing the right thing. Nagging doubts remain, but they are subconscious. That explains the loud enthusiasm for Khrushchev's great Seven Year Plan. If that succeeds, if the Soviet Union emerges with the highest standard of living in the world, these people feel their last troublesome doubts will die."

Some of the "intellectuals" are prone to analyze the effect of future prosperity. Some believe it will so mellow the "petty bourgeois" mentality of the ruling bureaucracy that nonconformists will be left more to their own devices. The progress of industrialization, the increased infiltration into Party ranks on the part of the rising technical intelligentsia, the slow expansion of "socialist legality" in day-to-day life—all these developments, they believe, may produce an "old-fashioned" dictatorship under which lip-service is still paid to totalitarian doctrine, but substantial areas of personal freedom exist. On the other hand, some of the more extreme believe the spiritual decay beneath the material prosperity will be the downfall of the whole Communist system. . . .

The "man of action" tends to dismiss these malcontents. For him, they are spiritual outcasts, powerless and meaningless. He compares them to Pasternak's Dr. Zhivago and himself to Lopatkin, the inventor-hero who triumphs over bureaucracy in Dudintsev's *Not By Bread Alone*. Zhivago is the man who claims to feel strongly about "right" and "wrong," but he irritates these young people because he can never choose sides. (Most have read only the selected excerpts of the book printed in the *Literaturnaya Gazeta* for 25 October 1958.) Lopatkin, on the other hand, is supposed to be "Soviet" to the core. He works and suffers through the system but comes out on the other side. One acquaintance compared Dudintsev's book to Chernyshevski's *What Is To Be Done?* of the last century. Both books had a "revolutionary" impact at different moments in history.

"Pasternak may write beautifully," he said, "but his ideas are outmoded. Dudintsev writes badly, but what he writes is social dynamite. I stayed up all night reading it."

The ideal young "man of action" claims he has reconciled himself to his system. He may be sensitive in his inner life, but he is utterly realistic about his social environment. Above all, he is diligent and ambitious. He respects power at home and abroad. By devious means he is working his way up in the ministries and industry to wield power. He joins the Communist Party to get ahead but thinks little of ideology. He reveres Lenin but admits that Marx could not foresee twentieth-century development. He (or she) aspires to dress like Americans, but neither envies nor fears the

Americans. He wants to learn their technical—not their political—skill. He wants peace, for the success of his economic gamble depends on it.

The cynicism about world revolution is barely disguised. One evening in late 1959 in the Praga Restaurant in Moscow, I commented on the number of Africans on the dance floor: "They must be among the revolutionaries being trained here."

"Too well dressed," my companion took up the jest.

"Part of the Khrushchev era," I ventured.

"Then they are certainly not for world revolution," he countered.

The Chinese offend this attitude, no matter how prized or necessary an ally they remain. They offend because they remind. There they are, suddenly aping all the early Soviet antics with a vengeance. They blaze with a genuine revolutionary fervor that most thoughtful Russians long ago abandoned to the slogan writers. They sound a clarion call from the past which many would like to ignore but cannot. China has become the revolutionary conscience, irritating because it can neither be stilled nor forgotten. Even those young Soviet zealots who yearn to return to the revolutionary ideals of Lenin are put off by the seemingly inhuman discipline of the Chinese. Their own deeply ingrained chauvinism is offended by the rising national power of 650 million Chinese to the East.

By 1959 at least some Soviet students no longer tried to put the gloss of solidarity over this distaste for the Chinese mentality. "They volunteer for the hardest work during vacations and then refuse payment," one student almost shouted over the clanking of metal in the self-service canteen of Moscow University. "They seem to love political meetings. Nothing official like ours. Someone simply decides a subject, they all excitedly agree, and then spend days priming for it."

A student in Leningrad related what had happened when his dormitory Komsomol organized a "voluntary Sunday." These days used to be popular during the 'twenties and 'thirties, when people donated leisure time to social work and slum clearance. Times have changed, he said.

"This project was rubbish clearance. Twenty out of twenty-two Chinese in the dormitory appeared. The other two were certified as ill. Do you know how many Russians turned up?" he asked rhetorically, and laughed. "Two out of three hundred—the organizer and the secretary of the Komsomol!"

The Komsomol or young Party workers are the basest offshoots of the "man of action" type. Superficially, they are sterling examples of the ideal "Soviet man." They are enrolled in the higher schools, receive diplomas in the various faculties, like all students, and at the same time lead all kinds of required "social work" on the side. They are the guardians of moral and political conformity in the Komsomol, to which more than 90 per cent of students belong. In fact, this minority of activists are unbelievably cynical. One observer has set their number at between ten and fifteen per cent of Soviet students.[22] Quite early in their student life, they sort out the mechanism of political power and fashion their careers accordingly. They learn the prescribed liturgy of Marxism-Leninism by heart and achieve progress through their ability to follow orders in enforcing it. Technically, they are elected to their Komsomol offices, but in fact, they are appointed by the bureaucratic apparatus. They are out of their depth when they have to engage in serious discussion outside the established framework, and they avoid it wherever possible. Mr. Khrushchev's sudden denunciation of Stalin and the moves to "democratize" Komsomol life in 1956 threw their ranks into complete disarray. The chain of command was temporarily broken, their confidence shattered, for no one from the top down knew any longer quite what line to enforce.

Now that the situation has been stabilized, these activists are firmly back in the saddle. They continue to exercise enormous power through the Komsomol role in the administration of the higher schools. The three-year work assignment a student receives on graduation depends as much on his Komsomol recommendation as on his grades. As noted above, the Komsomol also has new power in recommending which students are to be admitted to higher studies after working two years. The nature of these recommendations in turn depends on a student's willingness to serve in numerous "extracurricular" activities such as the voluntary Sundays or summer work on collective farms. This power over a student's future naturally leads to Komsomol meddling in the most intimate human relationships. Activists extract public confessions, enforce punishment, make certain that no one publicly transgresses the bounds of propriety. A rebellious student risks expulsion from the Komsomol, and this is tantamount to social ostracism and expulsion from the university.

Mr. Khrushchev's great problem is how to foster the "spirit of revolution" among the educated young while maintaining this essential Komsomol control. The contradiction between means and ends here sets the dimensions of potential tragedy in the Soviet leader's policy. On the one hand, he has fathered imaginative frontier plans for developing virgin lands in the Far East and South. Through these programs, more than half a million young people have moved out of Western Russia. He has also increased material incentives at all levels of society and has begun to fulfill some of the old promises about consumer prosperity. In the schools—beside polytechnical reforms for secondary day schools—he has instituted since 1956 a network of boarding schools (*internati*) which give increasing numbers of children from the age of seven on a proper "Communist upbringing" outside the family. By 1965 these *internati* are scheduled to have 2,500,000 out of the more than 30 million primary- and secondary-school pupils in the country.

[22] David Burg, *op. cit.,* p. 525.

All these moves are attempts to maintain the momentum of Communist revolution without the excesses of Stalin.

On the other hand—working against those moves—Mr. Khrushchev's revelations about Stalin and the omnipresent hypocrisy of Soviet society today have destroyed much of the idealism necessary to maintain revolutionary momentum. Calculation rather than spontaneity is a young person's guide to success in the Soviet Union. Young people in both factory and university work out elaborate methods for escaping the snooping and the commands of the Komsomol without impairing their future. Among the students especially, service extorted in the name of socialist society is no longer an honor but a duty to be avoided wherever possible. Constant press attacks on the Komsomol's failure to enlist the "best" recruits for the virgin lands, coupled with reports of wild juvenile delinquency on the frontier, bear witness to the success of many evaders.[23] A growing emphasis on more persuasion and less coercion (with concomitant relaxation) only gives more scope for this evasion. The greater material rewards offered young people become incentives for more cynicism, not more idealism, because they can only be had by those who pay the price of enforced conformity.

Mr. Khrushchev's brand of Communism indisputably is opening up new vistas for Soviet youth. At the same time, the measure of those vistas must surely be the types of adults who emerge. The Soviet social scene is changing too rapidly to make any definite predictions. The answers lie well beyond Mr. Khrushchev, in what or who follows him. At this point, however, present signposts indicate, for better or for worse, that the oncoming adult generation little resembles the ideal Soviet Man of Communist mythology.

[23] See *Literatura i Zhizn,* Moscow, 17 February 1961, as reported in *The New York Times,* 18 February 1961, p. 1, for an account of gang warfare and murder among youths in Vladivostok.

46

Albert J. Rabin

KIBBUTZ ADOLESCENTS

Projective techniques were administered to kibbutz-reared adolescents and to adolescents reared in the conventional family and social setting. The kibbutz-reared adolescent appeared at least as well-adjusted as his conventionally reared counterpart. He was less in conflict with his parents but more rigidly concerned with taboos on premarital sexuality.

Two previous reports before the meetings of the American Orthopsychiatric Association were concerned with comparisons, along several psychological dimensions, between different age groups of Kibbutz-reared children and their non-Kibbutz age peers. Our findings were that the infants in the Kibbutz setting lagged in some aspects of their development behind the non-Kibbutz infants (9). However, no residues of this slower start in ego development were noted in the comparative study of Kibbutz ten-year-olds. As a matter of fact, it appeared that these children gave indications of more mature ego development than the ten-year-olds raised outside the Kibbutz structure (8). In a subsequent report (11) we have also pointed out that the Kibbutz educational setting does not affect adversely the children's attitudes to parents and family. On the contrary, the findings were that more Kibbutz children had positive attitudes to the family than did the non-Kibbutz controls.

In the present paper we will follow the pattern or design of the previous studies and report its application to groups of adolescents. We shall attempt a comparison between Kibbutz and non-Kibbutz adolescents with respect to a number of pertinent and relevant psychological variables. More specifically, we shall address ourselves to two broad questions: 1) Are the gains in ego strength observed in Kibbutz preadolescents, as measured by our instruments, also maintained during the adolescent period? 2) What are the qualitative differences in terms of fantasy content and inferred dynamics, in social and family interrelationships, in heterosexual attitudes, and in goals

From Albert J. Rabin, "Kibbutz Adolescents," *American Journal of Orthopsychiatry*, Vol. 31 (1961), pp. 493–504. Copyright, the American Orthopsychiatric Association, Inc. Reproduced by permission.

and future perspectives, between the Kibbutz-reared adolescents and a similar age group reared in the conventional family setting?

PROCEDURE

In order to try to obtain some answers to these questions two groups of 30 Kibbutz and 25 non-Kibbutz 17-year-olds, roughly equally divided between the sexes, were examined by means of several projective methods.[1] The Kibbutz children were drawn from four different Kibbutzim, while the non-Kibbutz adolescents resided in three different villages of the conventional variety. All subjects were at the time pupils of the twelfth grade in their local high schools. Group and individual examinations took place in special rooms designated for the purpose in the school buildings through the cooperation of the local authorities.

The projective techniques employed were: the Rorschach, the Sentence Completion Test, which was an expanded version of the one used with the younger children (11), and the Thematic Apperception Test. The Rorschach was administered individually, while the other two tests were administered in small groups.

Limitations of space would prevent us from reporting the complete rerults obtained with each of these methods. Consequently, only the data which are more or less directly relevant to the questions which we have raised in the introductory section of this paper will be summarized and discussed. Thus, only some of the Rorschach indices will be included; the response patterns to several of the 52 incomplete sentences will be noted; and the analysis of TAT cards 1, 2, and 4 only will be reported.

RESULTS

The Rorschach Test

The first aspect of this test that may be noted is that of productivity, i.e., the number of responses given to the inkblots. The median number of responses for both groups combined is 31, which is consistent with the usual expectancies. However, the Kibbutz group tended to be more productive. Sixty-two per cent of the Kibbutz subjects exceeded the 31 responses, whereas only 36 per cent of the non-Kibbutz group did so. This difference approaches statistical significance ($p = .08$).

Another interesting index is "first reaction time." This refers to the time it takes the subject to give a response after the card is presented. On

[1] The numbers of individual tests vary somewhat owing to absence or incompleteness of record in a few instances.

eight of the ten cards the average first reaction time of the Kibbutz adolescents is shorter than that of the parallel group. In the remaining two (V and VII) the difference is negligible in the opposite direction. Moreover, the differences on the first card are very significant statistically ($p = .02$). Generally, the Kibbutz group reacts more immediately, with less anxiety and inhibition (see Table 46–1).

Table 46–1   Median Reaction Times for the Rorschach Cards
(In Seconds)

	I*	II	III	IV	V	VI	VII	VIII	IX	X
Kibbutz	6.8	12.2	11.0	17.0	8.0	20.0	16.5	11.5	22.5	24.8
Non–Kibbutz	19.0	17.0	11.5	19.5	7.0	37.5	16.0	12.0	32.5	30.0

* Difference significant at the .02 level.

Since Rorschach's movement response is assumed to reflect fantasied behavior, we followed the notion that some need is expressed in its content. As our guide is classifying the movement content, we followed Kaplan (6), who employed Murray's classification of needs. We utilized only 8 of the 17 categories listed by Kaplan, for only a negligible number of responses was classifiable in the omitted categories (see Table 46–2).

Table 46–2   Themes Represented in the Movement (M) Responses
of the Rorschach Records of the Two Groups

	No. of Subjects		Percentages	
Needs	K	NK	K	NK
Play*	18	7	69	32
Achievement	7	7	27	32
Aggression	4	7	15	32
Activity	12	8	46	36
Cognizance	6	5	23	23
Affiliation	5	4	19	18
Orality	5	1	19	4.5
Passivity	17	14	65	63

* Chi^2 = 6.80; $p < .005$.

The most outstanding difference between the groups is with respect to the "play" category. Nearly 70 per cent of the Kibbutz subjects have it in their records as compared with 32 of the non-Kibbutz adolescents. The other differences are less striking. The non-Kibbutz group includes more individuals who utilize the "aggression" category, and the Kibbutz youngsters have more in the "orality" category. However, the differences on these and the remaining categories are not statistically significant.

Lastly, an index of what may be called "general adjustment" was applied to the Rorschach data. Davidson (3) reported a series of "signs of adjustment," based on the Rorschach, which she found useful in her investigations. We employed 15 of the suggested 17 signs; these are least susceptible to subjective judgment. The range of adjustment signs for individuals in both groups is from 4 to 11. The average number of signs for the Kibbutz and non-Kibbutz group is 8.04 and 7.95 respectively. This is obviously a small and insignificant difference. The two groups do not differ on this index of adjustment or lack of emotional disturbance.

If we are to summarize the Rorschach data only provisionally, for we shall return to integrate them with the findings on the other tests, we can state as follows: The Kibbutz adolescents are more productive and less inhibited in responding to the test; they emphasize more play and orality themes and less aggression themes in the content; their over-all adjustment, i.e., freedom from signs of deviation, is similar to that of the control group.

THE SENTENCE COMPLETION TEST

This instrument is an extended version of the test used with the ten-year-olds (11) and was obtained from the same source (13). The 52 sentence roots deal with 13 different areas—four sentences for each area. Consonant with our present limited objectives, we shall deal with 6 of these areas in the present context—Family, Father, Mother, Sexuality, Goals, and Future.

The first three areas were assessed globally, i.e., the four completions in each area were rated as a whole in terms of the positiveness of the attitude which they express. The results are based on a combination of the ratings of two judges working independently. See Table 46–3.

No significant differences between the groups with respect to the incidence of "positiveness" of attitude to Family, Father and Mother were reflected in the findings. Very similar proportions of both groups indicate positive attitudes in these three areas. In terms of relative numbers, more of

Table 46-3   Global Combined Ratings of Family, Father and Mother
Areas Based on Sentence Completion Responses

	Family		Father		Mother	
	Positive	Other	Positive	Other	Positive	Other
Kibbutz	11	17	12	16	14	14
Non–Kibbutz	11	13	9	15	8	17

the Kibbutz adolescents indicate positive attitudes to Father and Mother. This is a mere trend, however, since the differences are not great enough to be statistically significant.

In the area of sexuality one sentence (out of four) yielded significant group differences. The sentence reads: "If I had sexual relations. . . ." The vast majority of the Kibbutz group rejected this idea unequivocally. "I would discontinue" or "Not at my age" were some of the most frequent responses. About one third of the non-Kibbutz adolescents also rejected the idea. However, most of them indicated positive or neutral attitudes to this hypothetical possibility. The differences between the groups were highly significant statistically ($p < .01$).

In the areas of Future and Goals, three of the eight items yielded interesting and significant differences between the two groups (see Table 46–4). On item 16 ("I would be definitely satisfied if . . . ") more of the Kibbutz group are concerned about being "a good pupil" or "if I am permitted to continue to study," whereas the non-Kibbutz subjects stated more specific goals—"if I were able to be a pilot," for example. On item 29 ("My secret ambition in life . . . ") more of the non-Kibbutz group indicate specific personal ambitions ("to be a successful farmer" or "to be a literary man"), while the Kibbutz adolescents are less specific ("continue living in the

Table 46–4   Significant Differences Between the Groups
on Future and Goals Items

Item 16	K	NK	Item 29	K	NK	Item 30	K	NK
School	14	3	Personal ambition	7	14	Long range	12	18
Other	10	12	Other	18	9	Trivial	12	4
Chi^2	5.40			5.42			4.98	
p	< .02			< .02			< .03	

Kibbutz") or deny having such ambitions altogether. In a similar vein, responses to item 30 ("One of these days, I . . . ") show that the non-Kibbutz group have by-and-large long-range goals, being a teacher, building a farm, etc. Half of the Kibbutz group have similar long-range perspectives, but the other half mention short-range or trivial aims, such as going home, climbing a mountain, and so on. Even the greater interest of the Kibbutz group in school (see item 16) is not an expression of any specific long-range goals; there is no implication of preparation for something specific.

A provisional summary of this material would seem to indicate that the Kibbutz adolescents do not differ from the controls with respect to intra-familial attitudes, that they reject sexual relations at an early age, and that their goals and future aspirations are less specific (and probably less mature) than those of their non-Kibbutz peers.

The Thematic Apperception Test

Since we did not have a direct measure of the intellectual level of our subjects, we attempted to use the TAT stories, written by them, as a basis for such an evaluation. A psychologist,[2] a native Israeli, was asked to classify the complete records without knowing to which group they belonged. On the basis of facility in the use of language and style, he placed the subjects in three categories—below average, average and superior. The Kibbutz adolescents were nearly evenly divided between the superior and the other two categories combined. Only 5 of the non-Kibbutz group placed in the superior category, while the remaining 18 subjects were put in the average or below average categories (see Table 46–5).

Table 46–5 Productivity and Estimates of Intelligence Based on TAT Stories

	Productivity (Mdn. No. Words)			Intelligence (Subjects Rated)		
	Card 1	Card 2	Card 4	Low	Average	Superior
Kibbutz	94	. 102	90	2	11	10
Non–Kibbutz	84	60	55	3	15	5

Productivity on the three TAT cards, in terms of word count per story, was also calculated. The Kibbutz group was on the average consistently more productive, on each card, than the control group. These findings are quite consistent with the higher Rorschach productivity referred to above.

In comparing the content of the TAT stories, i.e., the fantasy material of the subjects, we attempted to employ some of the categories reported in normative studies with adults (4, 12). However, with our small samples of adolescents this was only partially applicable. The final classifications that evolved were most meaningful for, and were dictated by, the material itself.

Card 1. Murray (7) describes this picture as that of "a young boy [who] is contemplating a violin which rests on a table in front of him."

The stories in response to this card were analyzed in terms of the dominant characteristics of the hero and in terms of the major themes contained in them. The vast majority of the Kibbutz adolescents describe the hero as "a child who has a violin" or "a pupil." Most of the non-Kibbutz adoles-

---

[2] The author is grateful to Dr. Joshua Levy for his assistance with this aspect of the study.

cents see either a talented child or one who is in the process of obtaining a violin despite economic limitations. Most of the non-Kibbutz themes involve ambition and high motivation for achievement whereas the Kibbutz themes involve more ambivalence about practice and rejection of the musical endeavor altogether. They view playing the violin as not self-motivated, but as a result of pressure exercised by parents and teachers. Examples of the two types of stories are as follows:

Kibbutz—Card 1. Violin pupil—not anxious about playing. His parents are pressing him to do this. He is before some boring exercise. He has no desire to play. He is thinking of his friends' games outside.
At the end the pupil will begin to understand the music and love playing, although it will not become the center of his life.
Non-Kibbutz—Card 1. In this picture I see a lad with ambitions and stirrings to be a great violinist. The lad played and played, then got tired and put the violin on top of the music. He is looking at the music notes and the violin and is thinking that these two things are his entire life. Slowly he sinks into thought and pictures his future for himself.

Card 2. "Country scene: in the foreground is a young woman with books in her hand; in the background a man is working in the fields and an older woman is looking on."
The "latent stimulus demand" of this picture, according to Henry (5), involves the "eliciting feelings toward interpersonal interaction, toward parent-child relations, and toward heterosexual relations"; also "the contrast between the new and the old . . . girl going off for education as opposed to the farm folk." Wittenborn (15) states that it "may reveal yearnings for independence, ambition . . . the conflict of the socially mobile student."
The relationship between the characters portrayed in the stories and the themes involved were of paramount interest in the present context. More than 90 per cent of the non-Kibbutz adolescents see blood relationships between two or all characters; most often they are seen as members of one family. This is in contrast with the Kibbutz group; 64 per cent of this group see such a relationship. The themes are even more revealing of the differences between the groups. (See Table 46–6.)
About two-thirds (68 per cent) of the non-Kibbutz stories on this card have conflict as their major theme—conflict with parents or internal conflict over leaving the farm and going to the city, over changing occupational status, etc. Less than one fifth of the Kibbutz adolescents project this theme in their stories. They merely describe the pastoral scene, but comparatively rarely see conflict between "new and old," farm and city, and so on.
Examples of contrasting stories follow:

Kibbutz—Card 2. Illana loved to go out every evening to the field and landscape to be acquainted with and know and feel the country, the soil, the fatherland. As usual, also, this evening Illana went up among the rocks on the

Table 46-6 Characters and Major Themes in TAT Stories
(Percentages of Groups)

Descriptions of hero and major themes in response to card 1

Hero			Theme		
	K	NK		K	NK
Talented child	4	26	Ambition-motivation	17	65
Tries to obtain violin	17	56	Ambivalence-rejection	61	17
Has violin	78	17	Other (incl. damage to violin)	22	17

Identification of characters and major themes in response to card 2

Characters			Theme		
	K	NK		K	NK
Members of one family	55	68	Conflict over aspirations	18	64
Not related	36	9	Economic frustration	5	9
Two related	9	23	Description	68	18
			Love triangle	9	9

Characters and major themes in response to card 4

Characters			Themes		
	K	NK		K	NK
Husband and wife	35	47	Infidelity	10	52
Two in love	35	47	Aggression	50	11
Fellow and girl	30	5	Rejection of love	30	5
			Miscellaneous	10	32

Action		
	K	NK
Prevent separation	35	74
Prevent aggression	40	21
Embrace	25	5

side of the village, at twilight, looking as she is absorbed in thoughts and ideas. The village is peaceful and quiet; tractors and machines do not disturb the peace and quiet. And the thoughts flow and well up in her—thoughts of love and tenderness—love for the entire world, nature, quiet and peace, for the plowing horse and the man who is walking in his footsteps and for his and everybody's landscape—for all the country folk in the world. How beautiful!

Non-Kibbutz—Card 2. The family is a simple agricultural family and have no connection with education. Agriculture is the magic of the life of the family. But the daughter is dissatisfied with such a narrow outlook. She leaves agriculture and turns to the city. The father terminated his relations with her and does not speak to her. He is tired of all the persuasion which was useless, but mother has not yet given up—looking at father and daughter. She is hoping for an answer from both of them. The daughter does not give in, leaves home and goes away.

Card 4. "A woman is clutching the shoulders of a man whose face and body are averted as if he were trying to pull away from her." There is also a hazy image of another woman in the background, not mentioned in the standard description in the manual.

Henry (5) feels that "attitudes toward heterosexual relationship are . . . of course the central issue of importance in this card." "Refusal to see the sexual implications of this picture," according to Wittenborn (15), "is particularly indicative of a type of immature psychosexual adjustment common in young men."

Some differences in the nature of the main characters portrayed may be noted. Ninety-five per cent of the non-Kibbutz stories specify the relationship of the man and the woman as "married" or "in love." This is true to a lesser degree in the Kibbutz stories, of which 70 per cent delineate this relationship, but 30 per cent mention no close relationship—just "a fellow and a girl." (See Table 46–6—part 3.)

The differences become more salient when we turn our attention to the themes involved. More than half of the non-Kibbutz stories deal with the issue of infidelity. This theme is represented to a negligible extent (10 %) in the Kibbutz stories. Instead, half of the stories have aggression as their major theme, and 30 per cent deal with outright rejection of love and heterosexuality (usually male rejecting female). The "action" involved parallels closely the themes described. The following are two kinds of stories which correspond to the contrasts just discussed:

Kibbutz—Card 4. He is a worker and she is on a farm. They met after a short time that they have not seen each other. They met accidentally at the entrance to one of the movies which described prostitution. They went into the movie with their thoughts. After it is over the woman asks the man to kiss her; she sees it in the film, she sees the couples kissing each other. But, something else entirely different than joy pierces the mind of the worker. He is not joyous, but analyzes and thinks about the problems in the movie—the problem of unemployed workers who find their satisfaction by going to houses of ill fame. Can that go on for long? No—I will change the situation. I will unite the workers around the condition of their brethren. I will bring out workers full of consciousness among them.

Non-Kibbutz—Card 4. In this picture the man is seen between the arms of his wife and the arms of sin. We see him at home.

When he got married he considered himself happy and loved his wife very much; but, accidentally, on one occasion he met a dancer in a cheap club; she attracted him and he fell in love with her. His wife, who felt that something is the matter, tried to stop him and he, still in love with her, did not know what to decide. In the picture we see them together; he wants to go and meet the other one and his wife is holding him back. We see the prostitute in the background, the one he fell in love with, as if she is coming out of his head. It is impossible to know what he will decide.

The major trends elicited from the TAT stories may now be pulled together. The Kibbutz adolescents appear to be less achievement oriented and less motivated. Their stories tend to be less populated with family-related characters. They also see less conflict between the parents and their children. There is also a greater tendency to reject heterosexuality altogether and also not to see infidelity as a possible problem.

Perhaps important sex differences may also be gleaned from these data. However, this will take us too far afield. We shall address ourselves to this issue on another occasion.

COMMENT

We shall attempt to gather the several strands of evidence and try to integrate them, see their dynamic interrelationship and relate the differences that have evolved from the material to known differences in the experiences of the two groups of adolescents.

We may note, especially from the Rorschach data, that there are no marked differences between the groups with respect to over-all "adjustment." There are a few deviant and tense individuals in both groups, but the over-all picture with respect to what we might infer as ego development is essentially the same for the vast majorities of Kibbutz and non-Kibbutz adolescents. The evidence points to a greater degree of spontaneity (productivity on Rorschach and TAT; first reaction times) in the Kibbutz group. Moreover, there is also some justification for rating the Kibbutz adolescents somewhat higher on the continuum of intellectual development. The quality of the Kibbutz *Mosad* (high school) and the relatively sophisticated intellectual atmosphere in most Kibbutzim must be in part responsible for this fact.

Two problems which are part of the *Sturm und Drang* period of adolescence have been stressed by various authors (1, 14)—heterosexuality and independence or emancipation. With respect to the first problem, we note a fairly consistent puritanical trend in the Kibbutz group. Whether it is immaturity or suppression is a question not easily settled. There are three sources of information that may be considered. In the first place there is some evidence of the lesser oedipal intensity in Kibbutz children (10); also, that little emphasis on sexual segregation is placed in Kibbutz rearing— boys and girls sleep in the same rooms, take showers together, etc. Finally, with all that, there are fairly rigid rules involving adult disapproval and group ostracism with respect to sex play and premarital sexual intercourse. Thus, there is relatively little of the sexual curiosity noted in adolescents who are not brought up in the Kibbutz (14); less of it is involved in the fantasy of the Kibbutz adolescents as noted in the TAT. Fewer Kibbutz adolescents deal with love and sex in their stories of card 4. The picture has less potency for them in this respect; thus, they include more themes of aggression and the role of the woman as the peacemaker. In most stories of Kibbutz adolescents in which heterosexuality is the major theme, rejection occurs, probably because of the cultural taboos.

Because of the relative independence of the children from their parents from the very beginning, in the Kibbutz setting, the issue of emancipation is not a crucial one. Thus, very few Kibbutz adolescents see the conflict between the generations, between agriculture and culture and education, which is noted by the majority of the non-Kibbutz respondents to card 2 of the TAT. This fact, perhaps, accounts for the tendency of the Kibbutz group to involve fewer parents and relations in their TAT stories. The parental figures are less fraught with conflict and less represented in fantasy. The relatively conscious attitudes to the parents as expressed in the Sentence Completion Test are, by and large, positive and not different from those of the control group.

In considering the data relative to goals and ambitions, two major differences between the two groups, emanating from differences in the family vis-à-vis the socioeconomic structure of the settlements, should be scrutinized. In the first place, as Eisenstadt (3) has pointed out, there is a discontinuity of roles in the Kibbutz rearing process from childhood to adulthood. By that is meant that until the child becomes eligible for membership in the Kibbutz (following graduation from high school) he virtually has no economic responsibilities. Whatever work he does is primarily educational—not "work" in the economic sense of the adult. Thus, in this respect there is a discontinuity in roles in the Kibbutz as contrasted with the continuity in the role of the village child who begins to participate in the adult economic workaday world at a relatively young age.

Another relevant difference is that Kibbutz education is geared toward perpetuation of the Kibbutz, i.e., membership in it. This means general personality attributes, but no specific occupational specialization or achievement in the broader "outside" world. This is in contrast with the village child who is reared in the tradition of "rugged individualism" and is preparing for a competitive society.

Bearing these points in mind, the contrast between the groups regarding ambitions, goals and future perspective becomes readily understood. The high emphasis on play in the Rorschach movement content, less emphasis on long-range goals and specific occupational aspirations reflected in the sentence completion material, and the low incidence of themes of ambition and motivation in response to TAT card 1, are all characteristics of the Kibbutz sample which converge on the same point. It involves a shortening of the future perspective as a personal outlook, for the longer future perspective is dependent primarily on the social context and structure, on the peer group, on the collectivity as a whole—the Kibbutz.

If we were to attempt the delineation of a composite picture of the Kibbutz adolescent, we would state that he has an adequately developed ego, is probably above average in intelligence, and is on fairly good terms with his parents, who, however, do not figure importantly in his fantasy, and with whom he is in relatively little conflict. He is relatively less concerned with heterosexuality than the non-Kibbutz age peers and consciously accepts the taboos of his society upon premarital or premature sex play and sexual intercourse. He is not very ambitious or achievement oriented in the world of occupations; in this respect his childhood is prolonged. His goals are not very specific, for they do not require precise definition by the society, and for the social structure, which he expects and is expected to perpetuate.

SUMMARY

In an attempt to tease out some of the psychological differences between Kibbutz-reared adolescents and adolescents (controls) reared in the conventional family and social setting, three projective techniques (Rorschach, Sentence Completion and TAT) were administered to two parallel groups of 17-year-olds. From the data presented, it was concluded that the Kibbutz adolescent is at least as well adjusted as his non-Kibbutz counterpart; there is some evidence that he is more spontaneous and at least as intelligent. The Kibbutz adolescent does not seem to differ from the control with respect to positiveness of attitude to parents; also, he tends to be less in conflict with them and to involve them less in his fantasy productions. He is more rigidly concerned with taboos on premarital sexuality, less self-motivated and less "ambitious" in our conventional sense.

The results were discussed and related to differences in life experience, stemming from differences in the social structure, to which the two groups have been exposed.

REFERENCES

1. Ausubel, D. P. *Theory and Problems of Adolescent Development*. New York: Grune & Stratton, 1954.
2. Davidson, Helen H. *A Measure of Adjustment Obtained from the Rorschach Protocol*. J. Proj. Tech., 14: 31–38, 1950.
3. Eisenstadt, S. N. *Studies in Social Structure: I. Age Groups and Social Structure—A Comparison of Some Aspects of Socialization in the Co-operative and Communal Settlements in Israel*. Jerusalem, April 1950.
4. Eron, L. D. *A Normative Study of the Thematic Apperception Test*. Psychol. Monogr., 64: No. 9, 1950.

5. Henry, W. E. *The Analysis of Fantasy*. New York: Wiley, 1956.

6. Kaplan, B. A. *A Study of Rorschach Responses in Four Cultures*. Papers of the Peabody Museum, **42**: 2, 3–44, 1954.

7. Murray, H. A. *Thematic Apperception Test Manual*. Cambridge, Mass.: Harvard Univ. Press, 1943.

8. Rabin, A. I. *Personality Maturity of Kibbutz (Israeli Collective Settlement) and Non-Kibbutz Children as Reflected in Rorschach Findings*. J. Proj. Tech., **21**: 148–153, 1957.

9. Rabin, A. I. *Infants and Children Under Conditions of "Intermittent" Mothering in the Kibbutz*. Am. J. Orthopsychiatry, **28**: 577–586, 1958.

10. Rabin, A. I. *Some Psychosexual Differences between Kibbutz and Non-Kibbutz Israeli Boys*. J. Proj. Tech., **22**: 328–332, 1958.

11. Rabin, A. I. *Attitudes of Kibbutz Children to Family and Parents*. Am. J. Orthopsychiatry, **29**: 172–179, 1959.

12. Rosenzweig, S., and Edith Fleming. *Apperceptive Norms for the Thematic Apperception Test II. An Empirical Investigation*. J. Pers., **17**: 483–503, 1949.

13. Sacks, J. M., and S. Levy. "The Sentence Completion Test," in *Projective Psychology* (L. E. Abt and L. Bellak, Eds.), pp. 357–402. New York: Knopf, 1950.

14. Spiro, M. E. *Children of the Kibbutz*. Cambridge, Mass.: Harvard Univ. Press, 1958.

15. Wittenborn, J. R. *Some Thematic Apperception Test Norms and a Note on the Use of the Test Cards in Guidance of College Students*. J. Clin. Psychol., **5**: 157–161, 1949.

ADDITIONAL READINGS

Ausubel, David P. *Maori youth*. Wellington, N.Z.: Victoria University of Wellington Publications in Psychology, No. 14. In a compact monograph Ausubel compares the vocational and educational aspirations of matched samples of European and Maori secondary-school boys in two communities, one rural and one urban. The study of youth's aspirations indicates the problems posed by acculturation and urbanization.

Betensky, Mala. The role of the adolescent in Israeli collectives. *Adolescence*, Fall 1967, **2** (7). Betensky describes the kibbutz, then tells how growing up in there relates to economic, marital, and moral maturity. She also defines the function of the adolescent in the kibbutz community.

Kassof, Allen. *The Soviet youth program: Regimentation and rebellion*.

Cambridge: Harvard University Press, 1965. (Reviewed by Kent Geiger in *American Sociological Review*, 1965, **30**, 807) The Soviet youth organizations are consciously employed as instruments of the effort to shape human nature under communism. Little has changed since 1936, when youth organizations became a vast school of indoctrination controlled by the Soviet Communist Party. The reactions of young people to the youth program are discussed, revealing considerable resistance. It is interesting to compare the planned social activism of youth in Russia to the more spontaneous participation in the United States.

Kraft, Ivor. Child rearing in the Soviet Union. *Children*, November–December 1965, **12** (6), 235–238. Kraft says that little is positively known about child rearing in the Soviet Union, but reviews what is known. He discusses family life, child-rearing patterns, and educational goals. In a number of cases, points presented differ from general views Americans hold about life in Russia.

Lifton, Robert Jay. Youth and history: Individual change in postwar Japan. *Daedalus*, 1962, **91** (1), 172–197. This article is based on interviews with students in women's colleges in Tokyo and Kyoto. It considers trends in postwar Japan and the psychological directions in which Japanese young people are moving.

Meredith, Gerald M. Amae and acculturation among Japanese-American college students in Hawaii. *Journal of Social Psychology*, 1966, **70** 171–180. The purpose of this study was to determine the differences between sansei college students and a comparable group of Caucasian Americans on a set of basic personality dimensions. The sansei appeared more introverted, more anxious, closer in proximity to clinically-diagnosed neurotics, and lower in leadership potential than Caucasians.

Peterson Donald R. & Migliorino, Giuseppe. Pancultural factors of parental behavior in Sicily and the United States. *Child Development*, December 1967, **38** (4), 966–991. Child-rearing practices of American and Sicilian parents were studied by means of interviews. Few differences emerged in parental affection, but striking differences appeared in parental control, chiefly in the areas of sexual and aggressive behavior.

Stoodley, Bartlett H. Normative family orientations of Chinese-college students in Hong Kong. *Journal of Marriage and the Family*, November 1967, **29** (4), 773–782. A random sampling of Chinese students were interviewed with reference to family norms. While adopting the western norm of individual choice in marriage, these students only partially accepted Western norms of dating and romantic love. The students are in the mainstream of Western influence but observe certain proprieties of Confucian tradition.

Tefft, Stanton K. Anomy, values and culture change among teen-age Indians: an exploratory study. *Sociology of Education*, Spring 1967, **40** (2), 145–157. A study of teen-agers in several Indian tribes revealed that those in certain tribes had definite value systems. However, the Arapaho teen-agers seemed unable to commit themselves to a set of values, a situation which might possibly be ascribed to anomy (a lack of norms) within their tribe.

Wheeler, D. K. Popularity among adolescents in Western Australia and in the United States of America. *School Review*, **69**, 67–81. The author compares traits and trait groups associated with popularity among adolescents in the United States and in Western Australia. In both countries, the same core values were associated with adolescents' popularity.

Wylie, Laurence. Youth in France and the United States. *Daedalus*, 1962, **91** (1), 198–215. This article treats the basic differences between French and American adolescence which transcend subcultural factors and reflect the cultures themselves.

Index